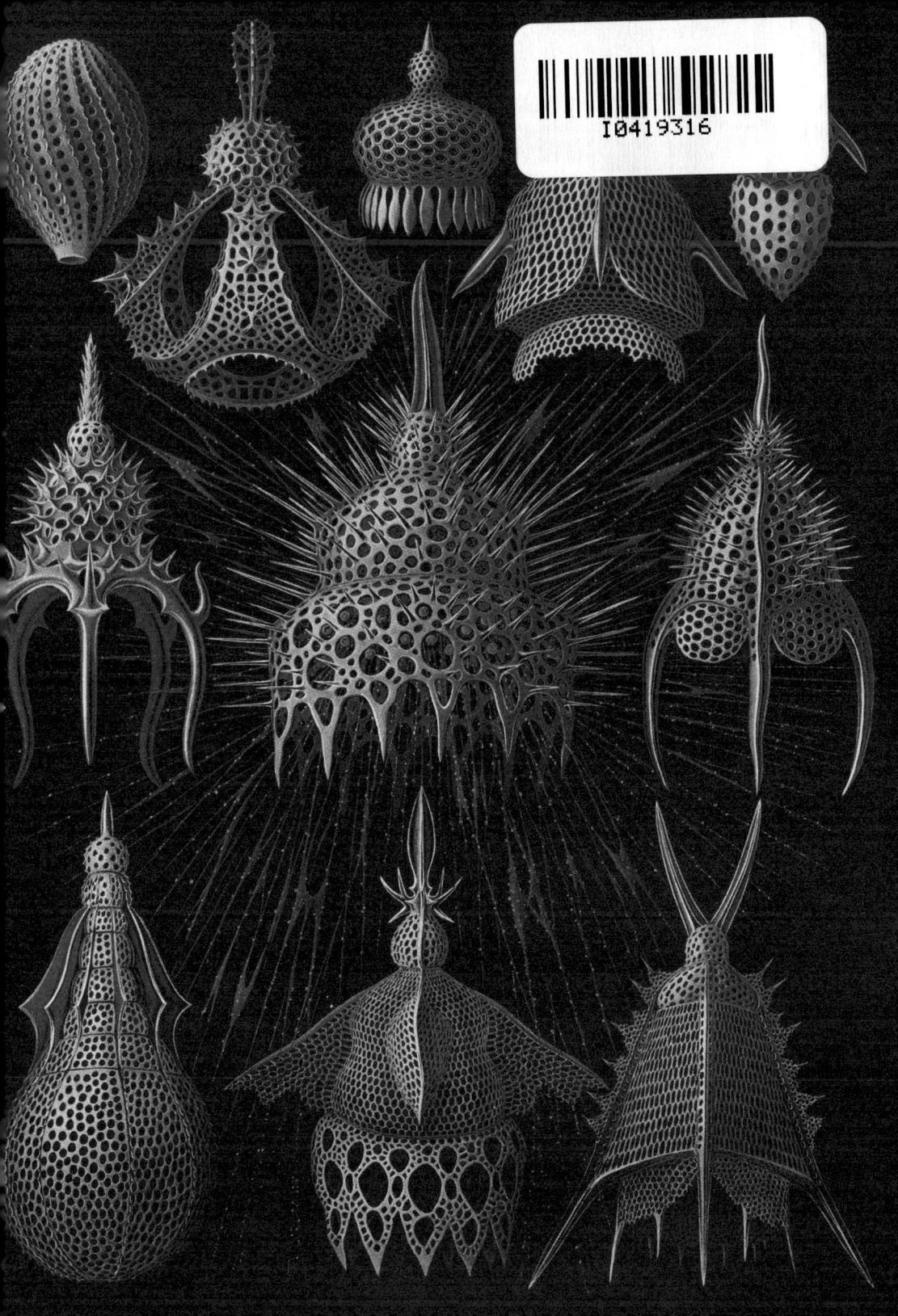

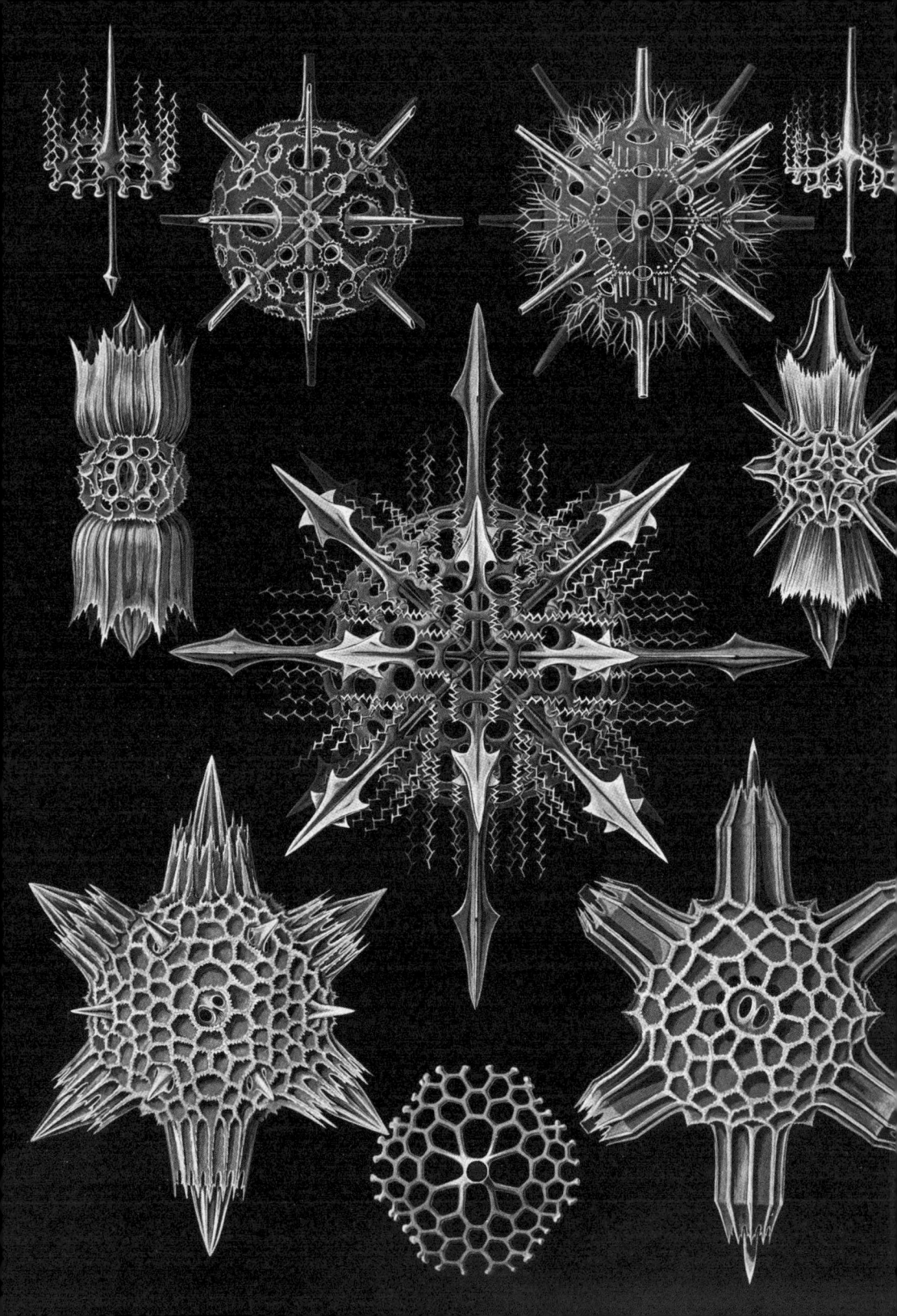

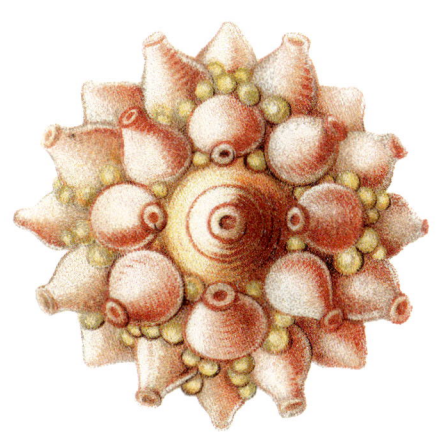

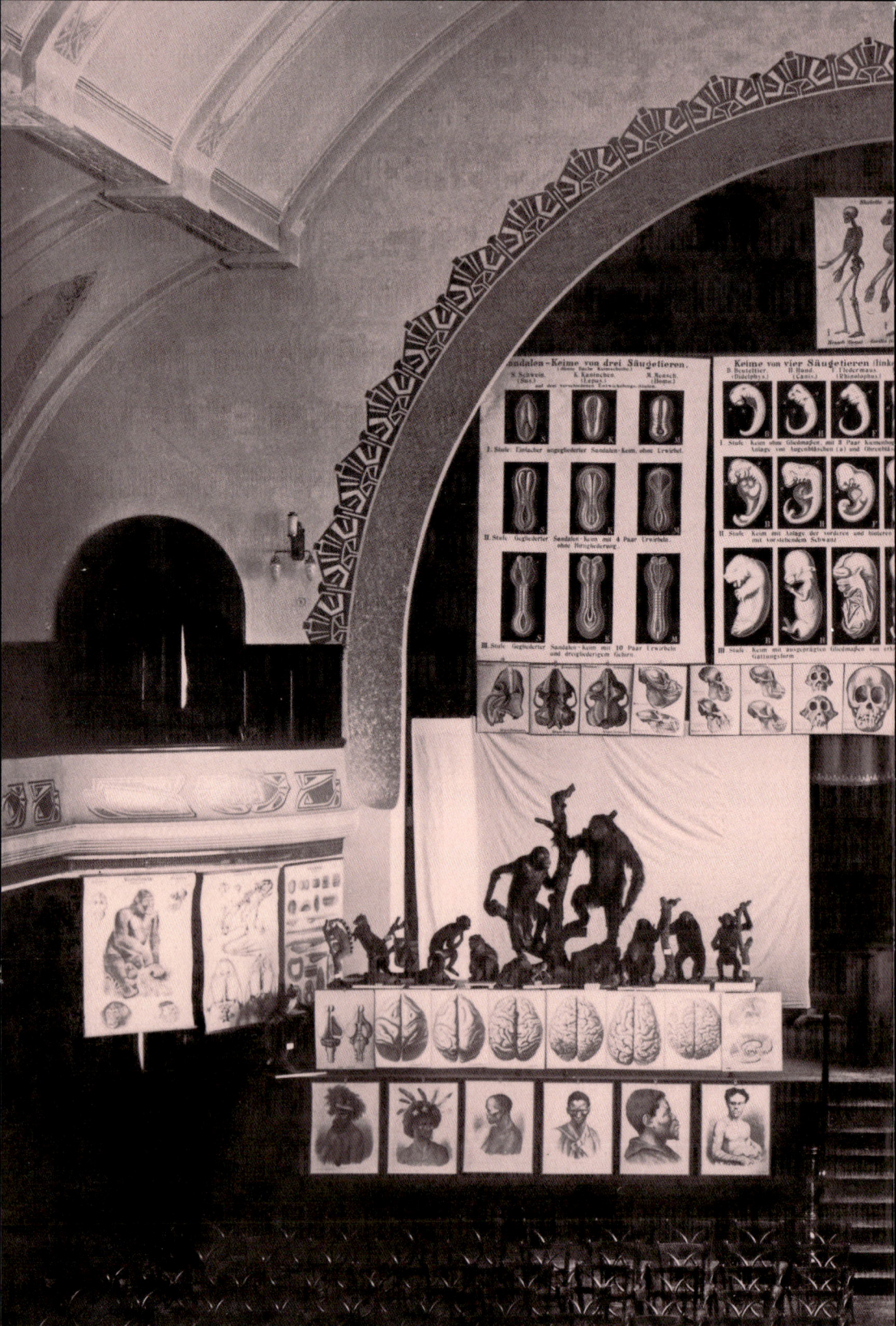

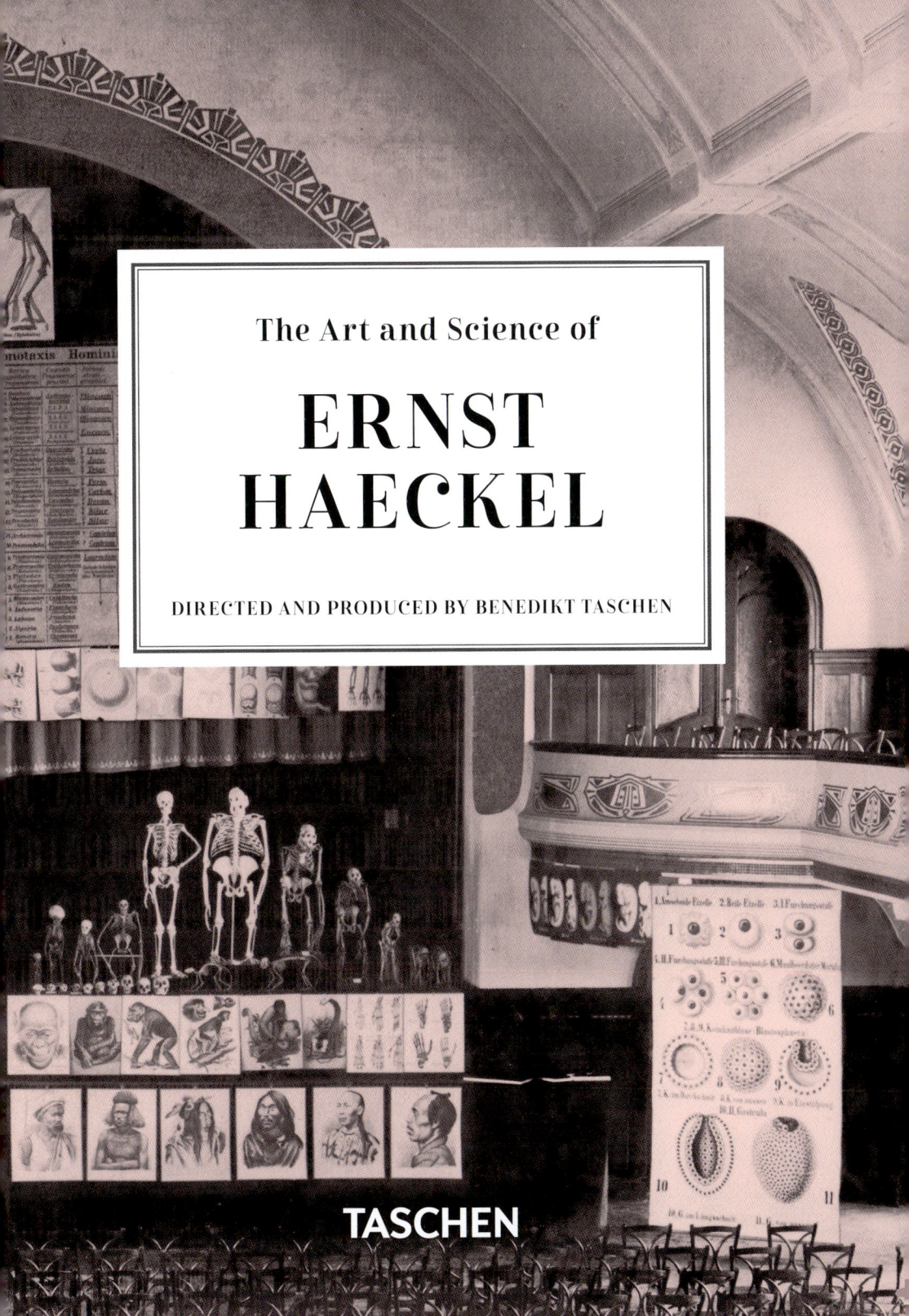

The Art and Science of

ERNST
HAECKEL

DIRECTED AND PRODUCED BY BENEDIKT TASCHEN

TASCHEN

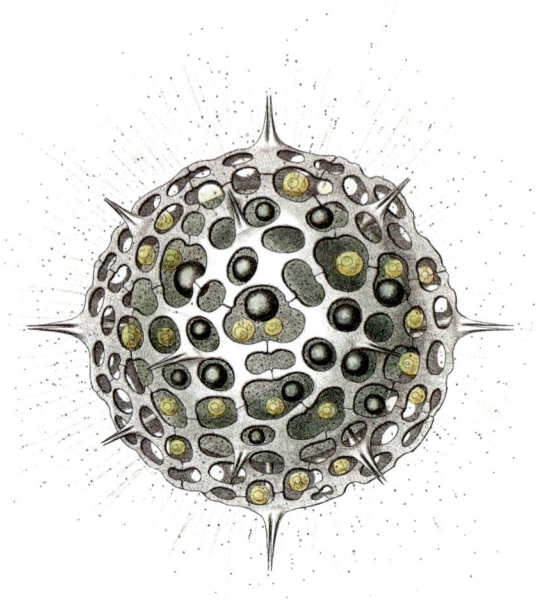

1862–1888

MONOGRAPH
ON THE RADIOLARIA

76

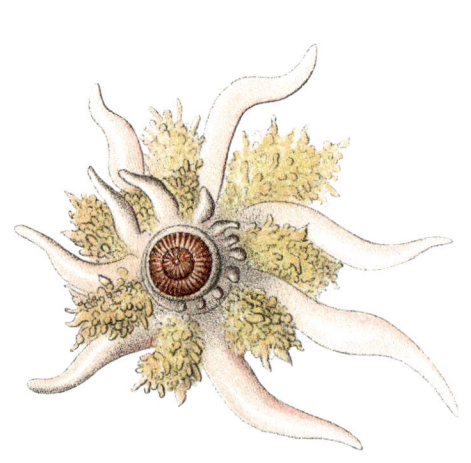

1869–1888

SIPHONOPHORAE

130

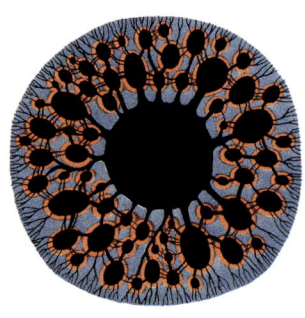

1872

ATLAS OF
CALCAREOUS
SPONGES

190

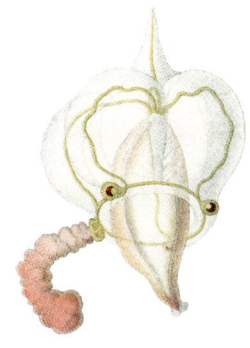

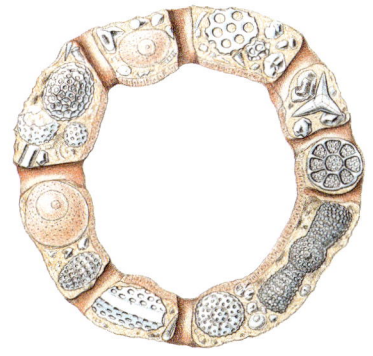

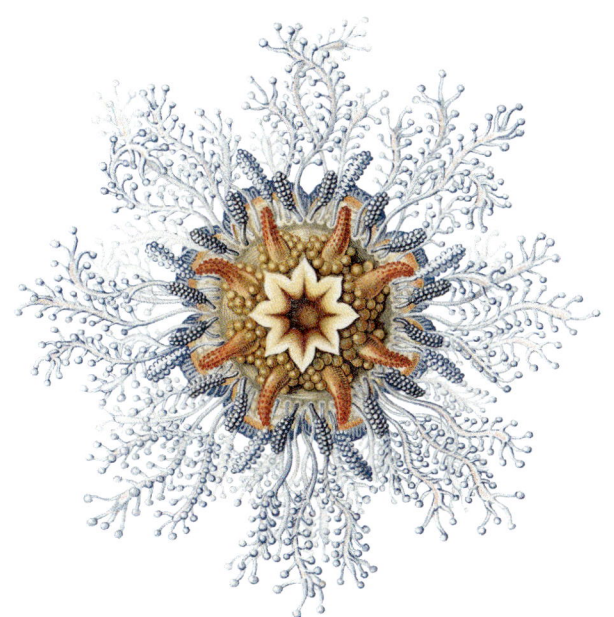

ERNST HAECKEL:
ART FORMS IN LIFE

Rainer Willmann

In May 1860, six months after the first publication of Charles Darwin's *On the Origin of Species*, a young biologist in Berlin by the name of Ernst Haeckel read this work in its German translation. He lost little time in finding himself in agreement with the path-breaking reflections presented in the volume. For these revealed that it was now possible to investigate humanity's ancestors and even – like Darwin himself – establish why there was, in fact, no difference between the two in principle, notwithstanding the differences of degree in the development of the intellectual capacities of humans and animals. Through the dissemination of Darwin's ideas and the popularisation of their implications, Haeckel was himself to become one of the most influential scientists of the 19th century.

Haeckel's own contribution to science and philosophy was to be on a scale all but unequalled. Taking his starting point in Darwin's reflections and drawing also on his own biological research, he would weave his knowledge about the evolution of life into a unified view of the world. In addition, as observed by the geneticist Richard Goldschmidt (1878–1958), Haeckel was in due course to become one of the "most combative individuals ever to emerge in the scientific community in Germany."[1] Haeckel's most widely read work *Die Welträthsel* (*The Riddle of the Universe*), first published in German in 1899, has been translated into about 30 languages, in some cases in editions of hundreds of thousands. Haeckel saw himself as engaged in a world-historical cultural struggle,[2] in as far as knowledge of the evolution of mankind was inextricably linked with fundamental questions of philosophy.[3] And so,

Ernst Haeckel with the skeleton of an ape, 1904
Photograph: Nicola Perscheid, in: *Deutsche Kunst und Dekoration*, vol. xv, October 1904–March 1905

6

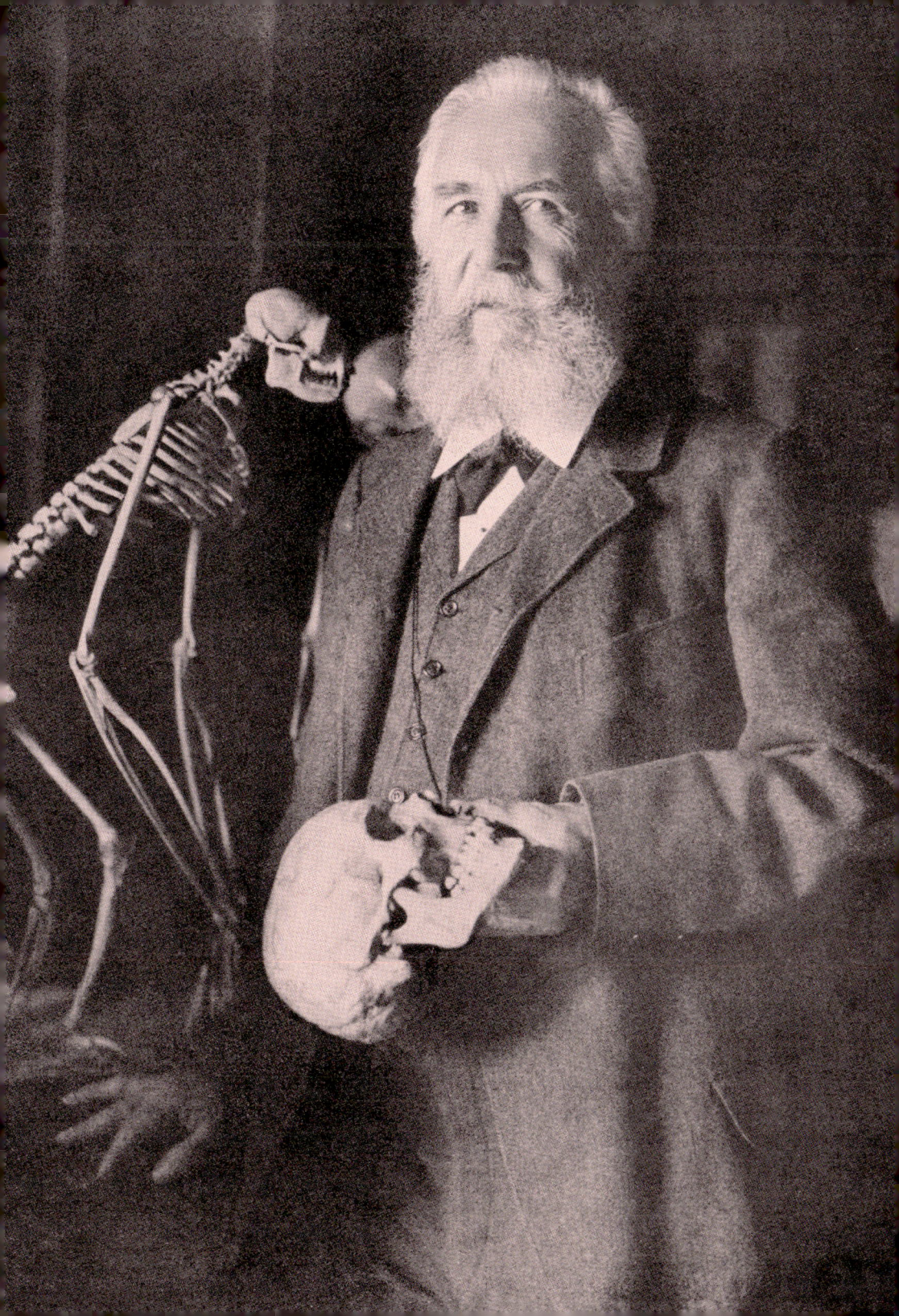

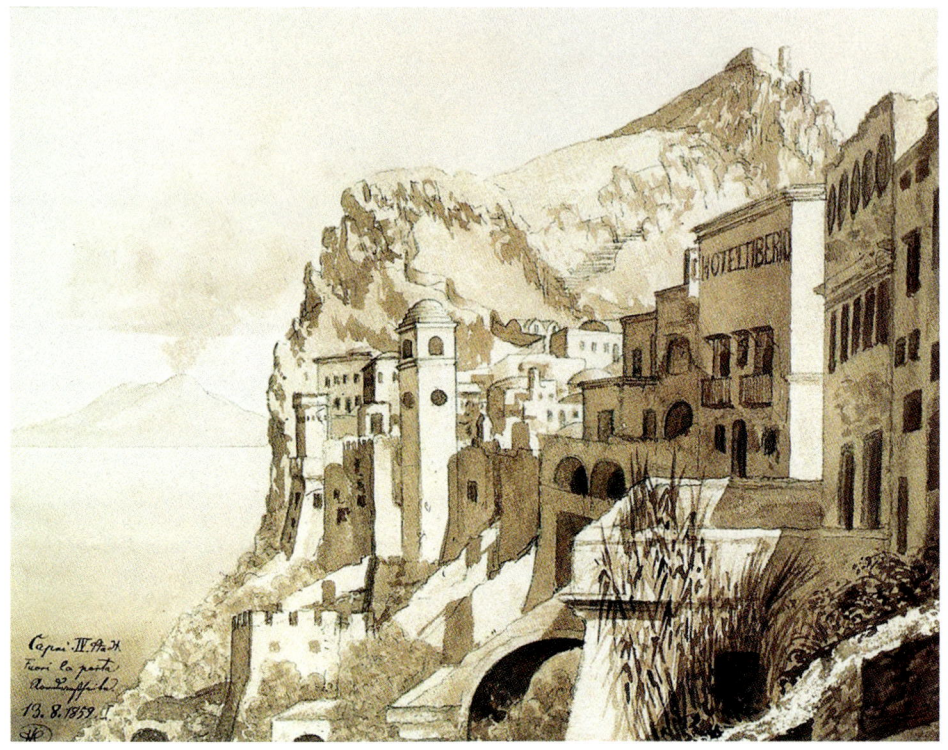

Capri, 1859
Watercolour, 26.2 x 20.7 cm (10¹/₄ x 8¹/₄ in.)
Jena, Ernst-Haeckel-Haus

as Goldschmidt also noted, "Haeckel became both one of the best-loved and one of the most hated men of his age."⁴ As a talented draughtsman, he also put his artistic skills at the service of science. He produced illustrated volumes of enduring value and biological atlases that have remained unparalleled in the appeal and precision of their images. All of these were conceived with the overall aim of demonstrating the connectedness and the boundless diversity of all life forms, both features owed to the process of evolution. Haeckel's illustrated publications repeatedly called forth one re-action above all others: incredulous astonishment at the beauty of objects to be found in nature. These in due course became sources of inspiration for many artists – an out-come that Haeckel had, indeed, intended in continuously reprinting his *Kunstformen der Natur* (*Art Forms in Nature*), originally published between 1899 and 1904 – and they had a particular influence on the stylistic tendency of the years around 1900, that drew a great many of its ornamental motifs from the natural world: Jugendstil or art nouveau. Through his enthusiastic championing of Darwin's ideas, moreover, Haeckel greatly enriched the literature in all those fields touched by his work.

We may see Ernst Haeckel then as located at the heart of cultural creativity in the second half of the 19th century. His splendid drawings and hundreds of watercolours which allow us an insight into worlds that, to some extent, no longer exist in the same form, will surely seem just as valuable to future generations as they appeared to Haeckel's contemporaries.

On account of the sheer range of Haeckel's areas of research and interest, and the complexity of his trains of thought, it is hard to do full justice to him. In many fields his contributions had an influence that endures to this day. It is, above all, to Haeckel that we owe the fact that philosophy has begun to take into account the findings of biology and that contemporary studies in the humanities and the sciences have, in many respects, begun to interact with and to complement each other. And Haeckel, of course, had a significant impact upon the study of biology, also through, in part, his numerous pupils to whom he was able to impart the Goethean tradition of freedom of thought and an interdisciplinary approach to the world. In this respect the landscape of scientific research has continued to profit from Haeckel's influence. Through his lectures and widely accessible publications Haeckel encouraged millions of people to take a lively interest in fundamental questions of life on Earth, and in that way he served as one of the most significant of those engaged in disseminating a true scientific enlightenment.

Paths to Biology

Ernst Heinrich Philipp August Haeckel was born in Potsdam on 16 February 1834. Thanks to the services of a private tutor but, above all, through the support and enthusiasm of his parents, he was introduced at an early age to the study of the natural sciences. The publications of Alexander von Humboldt (1769–1859) and especially Charles Darwin's (1809–1882) *The Voyage of the Beagle* (initially published in 1839 as *Journal of researches into the geology and natural history of the various countries visited by H.M.S. Beagle*), along with further accounts relating to the exploration of nature, aroused in Haeckel a desire to undertake ambitious research trips of his own and, in particular, to study botany. In 1852, he formally embarked on studies of medicine and the natural sciences at the University of Berlin, transferring in the autumn of that year to Würzburg, where he took courses taught by Albert von Kölliker (1817–1905), and Rudolf Virchow (1821–1902; ill. p. 11). Yet even at this early stage, Haeckel had already written to his parents to inform them that he felt he would never become a practising physician.[5] At that time, however, it was the study of medicine that most reliably led on to specialisation in an aspect of the natural sciences; and Haeckel's father encouraged his son to stay the course. After April 1854, now back in Berlin, Haeckel made the acquaintance of Johannes Müller (1801–1858), professor of anatomy and physiology at the University of Berlin, and regarded as "Lord of the Realm of Biology."[6] Among Müller's pupils had been Hermann von Helmholtz (1821–1894), Theodor Schwann (1810–1882), and the aforementioned Rudolf Virchow. Haeckel was to be one of the last to receive from Müller encouragement and inspiration such as would fuel an entire lifetime of scientific research.

In the summer of 1854, Müller invited Haeckel to take part in a research trip to the North Sea island of Heligoland. Haeckel, now 20, wrote to his parents that his ambition was to undertake research, as a zoologist, along the coasts of lands in the Tropics.[7] When, in 1857, he had obtained his doctorate in medicine, with a dissertation based on his research into the river crab, and in March 1858, had received his accreditation to practise as a physician, with a speciality in obstetrics and the treatment of wounds, Haeckel did, in fact, open his own surgery, but took care to ensure that his services would not be greatly in demand: surgery hours were expressly limited to between 5 and 6 a.m. and his advice and assistance as a physician were, predictably, never sought out by more than half a dozen patients overall. For Haeckel it was crucial that his formal accreditation as a "practising" physician now permitted him to devote himself almost exclusively to the study of zoology. Yet he was to find himself isolated as a scientist only a month later when, on 18 April 1858, his revered Johannes Müller was found dead in his apartment. A few weeks after this event, Haeckel became formally engaged to his cousin Anna Sethe (1835–1864). She was to play a significant part in his subsequent research through her deep interest in his endeavours (ill. p. 488).

In early 1859, following a five-week stay in Rome, Haeckel travelled on to Naples. During a trip to Ischia he met the North German painter and poet Hermann Allmers (1821–1902). Together the new friends travelled around southern Italy, an experience that gradually redirected Haeckel's artistic interests to landscape painting (ill. p. 8). In October 1859, however, he embarked on serious research into the marine life to be found in the Gulf of Messina. He evinced a particular fascination for Radiolaria (exceptionally small monocellular marine organisms with an often spiky skeleton) which had been one of Johannes Müller's favoured research subjects. Haeckel now

Written record, with related drawings, of Albert von Kölliker's lecture
on *Comparative Anatomy of the Invertebrate Animals*
Summer semester 1853, 29 x 22.2 cm (11 ½ x 8 ¾ in.), Jena, Ernst-Haeckel-Haus

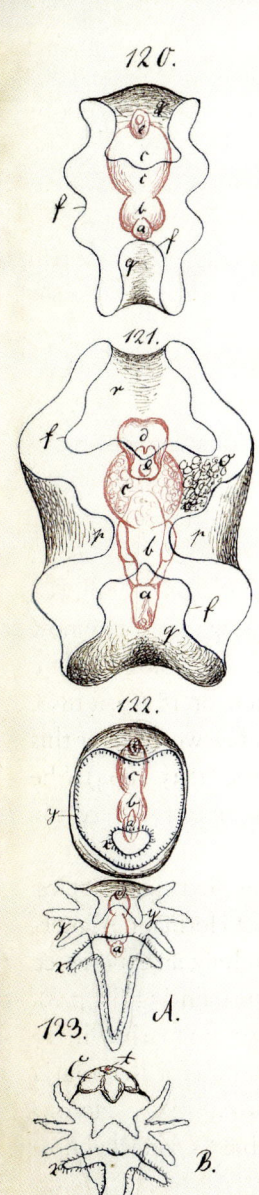

120.

121.

122.

123.   A.

B.

III. Holothuriae.

Die Larven der Seewalzen sehen sich sonderbar, nur die Plaggengestalt der Korrosionsorgane (121) b. Noch sie lassen sich leicht in dem Prototyp (108) ableiten, indem die vorderen seitlichen Längsgürten sich vorwärtswachsend immer nähert (120) Die Seitenrände der Wimperung 5 kronenartig fallen schöner. Die so völlig gebogenen e mit 2 seitlichen (121 p, pe) e 1 vorderen (q) e Spalten (re) Wimpelia nach ihrem vorwärtsgebogenen Rand geht mit einem einzigen Schwingerschein (f) versehene. Indem der innere rasch zusammenweiter, bleibt von der inneren, welchen bandförmig zieht mit nur einer spiralförmigen Fürgleichung ziglerichtig. Die glatte Larve wird so vorläufig werden jünger, entwickelt solche von Magen(A) im Lange e der Seitenteile der jüngeren Holothurie (a) welche die anderen von den anderen Jüngeren abwiescht, daß sie jetzt die ganze Larve, ihren Mund die Magen einnimmt, daß sie später solcher vorrinen werden. Mund e der Magen vorwärtelt, die neugeschlüpfenden Larven der Seewalzen wird die Auricularia genannt.

IIII. Asterida.

Die abenteuerlichen Larven die eigentlichen Seesterne (r der Pflanzensterne, Ophiura) 4—6 lang, weihend der anderen Seewalzen mit 4—1 lang werden; entlehnen nur die Holothurien larven, die d'altfortletts e weifen davon abtrennt von den anderen ab, daß sie nicht nur einzige Schwingerschein (f), sondern 2, nun neueren (ce) e kurz (y) besitzer (123—124). Der Prototyp 108 wendet 5 Dimmung zu ihnen in der Figur 122, welches nur die 2 Schwingerschein gezeichnet ist (Alle Buchstaben haben eine ähnliche Bedeutung) hieraus ist herwärts die Larven der Asterias, *Bipinnaria asterigera* (Figur 123 a, b; 124) abgeleitet, welche einen Schwingerschein am Lauf (y) einen nach vor dem Rücken (x) trägt; Seesterne (y) hat 8, die zweite mit 2—5 Zipfel. Die jüngere Seesterne (123 e 124 C) entwickelt sich von dem Magen von hinten hand, von an e dem Rücken (c), die nur später d' Madreporen glatte selbständig entsteht, weshalb der Mund desselben (t) sieht den Mund der Larven (a) ähnlich zu. Figur 125 ist die Larven der *Brachiolaria*, von sicht sonderbaren Gestalt, e 3 eigenthümliche Fortsätze (u), welchen zwischen Zipfeln, die t der Schwingerschein besitzt sich. Die Echinaster e Aster acaut eben bildets sich in der Leibeswässe der Mutter die jüngere Seesterne e d'ringelsormen Larven t. Ich rasch entwickeln e rasch d'rüheg manichfaltigen Larven der Comatula den speziellen geht d'subeschtung e einer Ophiuren galtung (Ophiolepis) von s, welche lebendigen Jünger gebaut. Die Schwärmen gehen die merkwürdig kurzsichtig spieltiger Symmetrischen e die Echinoderm Larven werden, die sie von sonderbar leibe setzen, sie bilden gestaltlose Schwärmen im Meere.

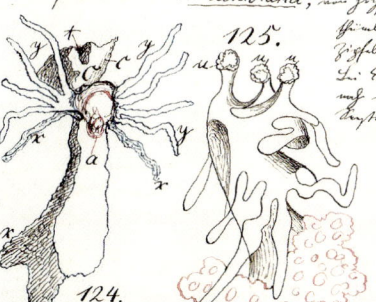

124.

125.

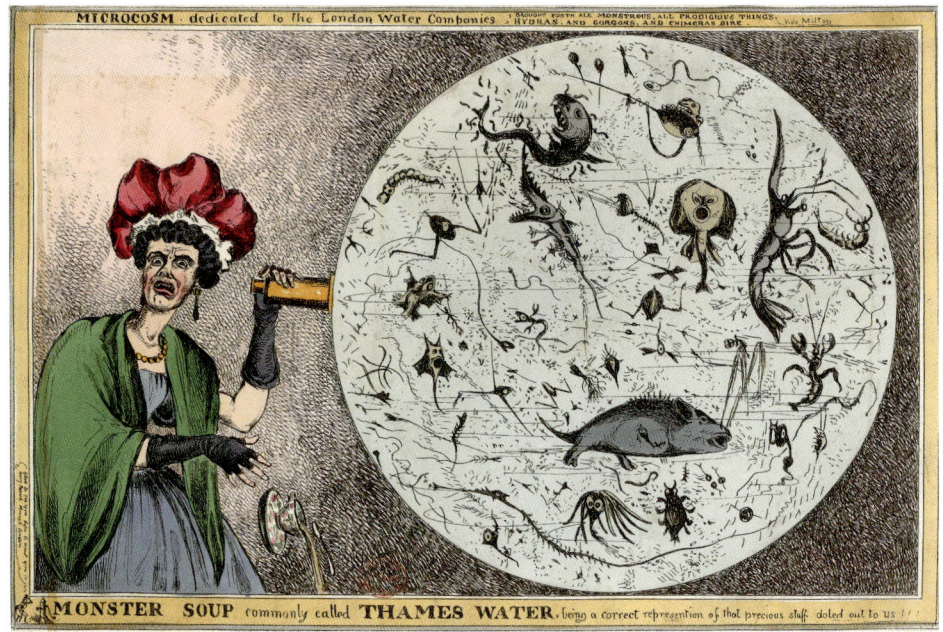

William Heath, **Microcosm, dedicated to the London Water Companies**, 1828
Monster soup commonly called Thames water,
being a correct representation of that precious stuff doled out to us!!!
Etching, 24.4 x 36.1 cm (9 ¹/₂ x 14 ³/₄ in.), London, The British Museum

discovered dozens of new species, immediately recording his spoils in drawings in which he captured the regularly constructed skeletons with a mathematical precision, as he was to report to his fiancée.[8] To assist him in this task he made use of an exceptionally good small microscope which permitted up to a 1,000-fold magnification.[9] Haeckel's record and analysis of his research into Radiolaria was, in March 1861, to serve as the material for his *Habilitation* at the University of Jena, where he then soon embarked on a series of lectures on zoology.

In August 1862, Haeckel married his fiancée Anna Sethe. A few weeks later there followed the publication, complete with 35 splendid plates of illustrations of Haeckel's monograph on the Radiolaria. Such exquisitely detailed renderings of organisms so small in scale had never previously been published. Haeckel had recorded here Radiolaria in all their astonishing diversity: skeletons in the form of interlacing spirals, spherical lattices, and minute pyramids with radiating struts, little stars with branching points and sword-shaped needles as well as remarkable examples combining all these features. This publication immediately attracted the attention of Haeckel's fellow zoologists and marine biologists. This was all the more so as spirited disputes regarding Darwin's ideas had by this time arisen far beyond England, and it was in this work that Haeckel first openly aligned himself with Darwin.[10] Here he acknowledged the variability of species and stated his view that the infinitely varied Radiolaria might even have originated in a single, primal Radiolar, with a skeleton in the shape of a simple spherical lattice. In 1864, Haeckel published an article on small crabs that contained three truly outstanding plates with minutely detailed illustrations of the morphology and anatomy of these creatures (ill. p. 15).

With his publication on Radiolaria Haeckel was assured of his place as a forward-looking biologist. But this on its own would assure him of no more than the respect of his fellow scholars. Rather more than this was suddenly to come his way as a result of the lecture he gave on Darwin's findings at the Reunion of German Natural Scientists and Physicians held in Stettin (now Szczecin, Poland) in 1863,[11] and the subsequent essay elaborating on his topic.

Charles Darwin had discovered that the chief motor for the sequence of gradual changes constituting evolution was a process of selection. In 1859, Darwin described the two distinct mechanisms of the selection process: these he designated "natural selection" and "sexual selection." The biological process of natural selection worked in favour of those individual organisms that proved best fitted to survive within their respective environments. The process of sexual selection (the second mechanism) worked in favour of those individual organisms that proved most likely to be selected as a mate for the purposes of reproduction.

In the absence of knowledge of the processes involved in evolution, numerous biological phenomena could be explained only with difficulty. Likewise, the answers to numerous philosophical questions had heretofore proved unsatisfactory if not impossible. According to Haeckel, "the discovery of natural selection" had thrown such a clarifying light into the "dark chaos" of biological knowledge that no one with an interest in scientific progress would be able in future to ignore the new philosophy of nature thereby emerging.[12] The totality of biological facts and, above all, the parallels between palaeontological, embryological, and systematic development allowed the assured conclusion that all organisms were the descendants of a relatively small number of spontaneously arising primordial forms.[13] And the posited emergence of the simplest organisms out of primordial, anorganic matter was itself a constituent part of the Theory of Evolution.[14]

Clad in this intellectual armour the 29-year-old Haeckel set off in September 1863 for Stettin, on his mission of enlightenment. The lecture he gave there, entitled

"Über die Entwickelungstheorie Darwins" (On Darwin's Theory of Evolution) is regarded as one of the key events in the dissemination and recognition of Darwin's ideas in germanophone Europe. Most of those in Haeckel's audience at Stettin were unaware of what they were about to hear; and neither they nor most of the general public at this time were intellectually prepared to begin thinking in terms of a perpetual process of selection continuously forming and reforming all species of living beings. Haeckel actually went far beyond Darwin in his lecture in that, beginning with the lowliest organisms, he proceeded to sketch out the entire history of the descent of man. He explained that the entirety of the natural system of plants and animals resembled an enormous family or genealogical tree, and that millions of years had been required for the differentiation of the diverse species. Many of Haeckel's older colleagues felt personally threatened by this presentation, for they saw in it an implicit questioning of all that was most fundamental in their own way of thinking, and the influence of which their own ideas had so far been assured. Over and above his own thoughts on evolution in the strict sense, Haeckel also cherished a notion of gradual progress, even of ultimate perfection. To our own way of thinking this notion is surprising. For, since the time of Darwin, evolutionary biologists have viewed evolution as a process of adaptation to diverse environmental factors. While this process implicitly embraces phases of ostensible progress and of ostensible regression, evolution in itself is seen as a sequence of acceptable compromises rather than a means by which there comes about a continuous advance towards perfection.

In 1864, Haeckel was awarded, in recognition of his monograph on Radiolaria, the Cothenius Medal, the highest honour bestowed by the renowned German Academy of Sciences, the Leopoldina. On the very day on which he was due to receive this award, 16 February 1864, which also happened to be his 30th birthday, his wife Anna died at the age of only 29. Until the very end of his life Anna remained for him his unforgettable, truest love. He was repeatedly to name organisms in her memory he had discovered which struck him as exceptionally graceful.

The *General Morphology of Organisms* –
A Guide to the Ordering of all Life Forms

Following the death of Anna, Haeckel was inconsolable; but he sought relief in the distraction and the fascination of his scientific work. Rarely sleeping more than three or four hours a night, he worked at the texts of his lectures as well as on a revised approach to morphology: that branch of biology concerned with the comparative study of organisms. A lecture Haeckel gave in Jena in the winter semester of 1865/66 attracted not only 120 listeners who were students inscribed at the university,

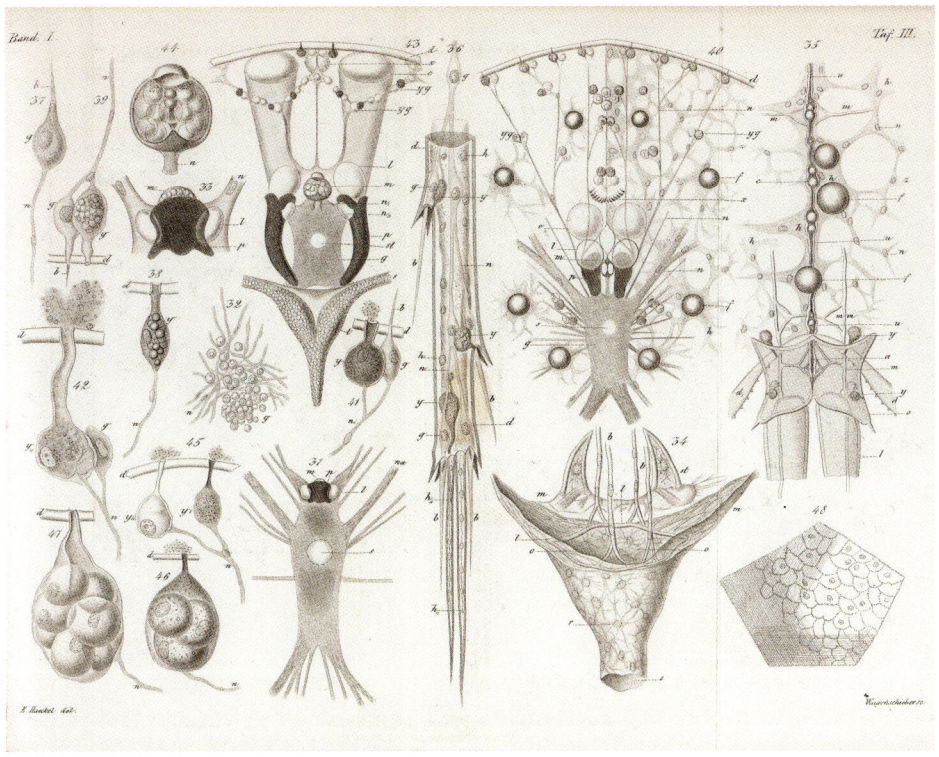

Hyalophyllum and *Sapphirina*, 1864
In: "Beiträge zur Kenntniss der Corycaeiden"
Jenaische Zeitschrift für Medizin und Naturwissenschaft, vol. I, plate III

but also "lay people from every walk of life." For Haeckel had, by now, become, as he explained in a letter of November 1865 to his parents, "[a] subject of general concern in the city and the object of chatter in polite society."[15]

Haeckel's revised approach to morphology appeared in 1866 under the title *Generelle Morphologie der Organismen* (General Morphology of Organisms), as a two-volume publication with a total length of 1,208 pages. At its heart stood knowledge of evolution and, not least, of the origins of humankind. But in this publication Haeckel also touched on advances in the natural sciences in general; he dealt with the mind and its own evolution from the form in which it may have existed in the simplest of organisms to the form it took as consciousness in man; and affirmed the essential unity of nature, knowledge, and belief. In the course of his life Haeckel was repeatedly to return to these topics.

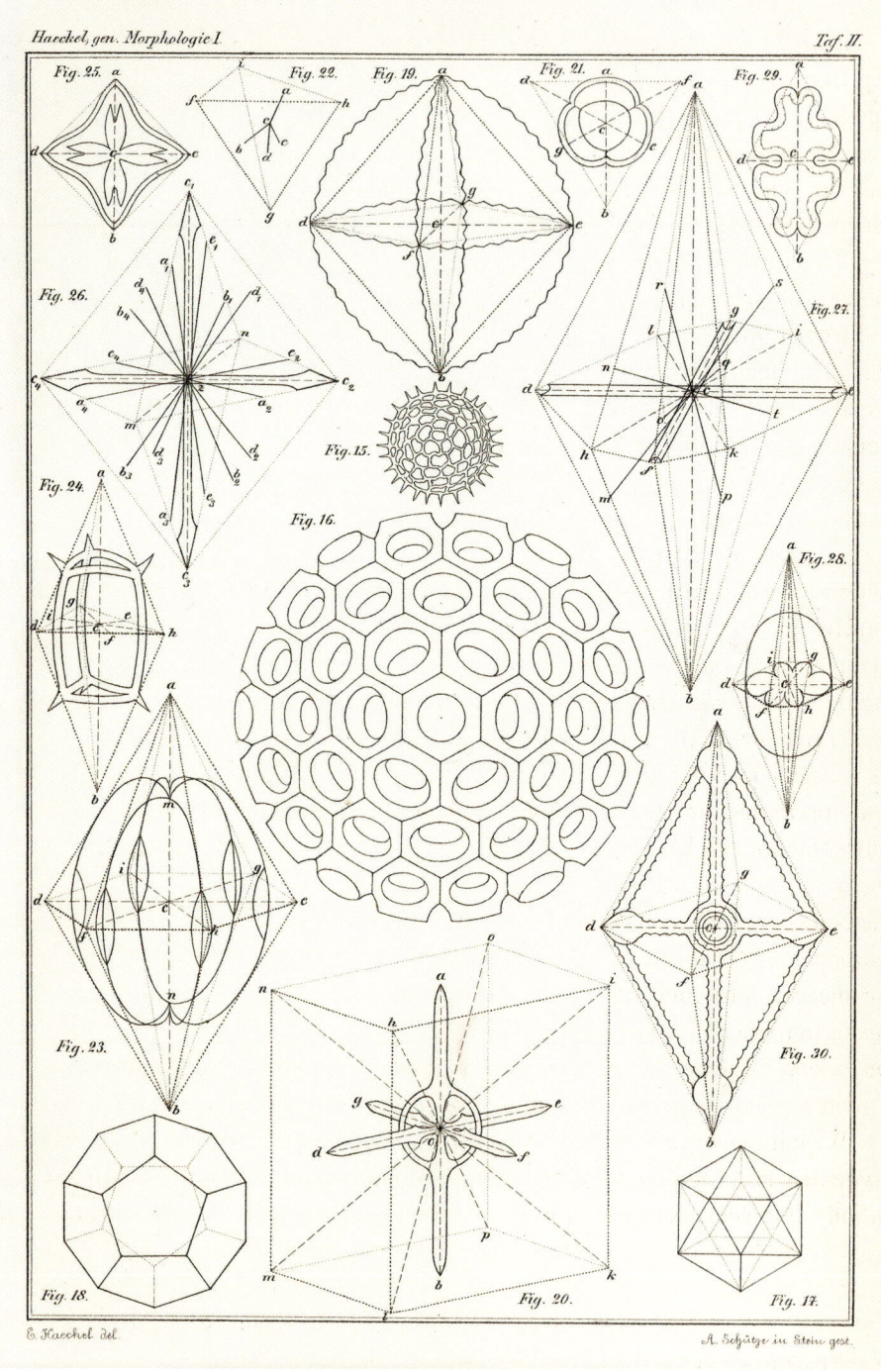

Like Darwin, Haeckel was to be repeatedly accused of an ignorance of philosophy. But in his own view, it was philosophy itself that had now been rendered inadequate. It was philosophy that had originally withdrawn from a study of the natural sciences. And, in philosophy's own later reflections on the origin of organisms, and thus also on the evolution of body and mind and the place of mankind in the overall scheme of nature, philosophy had never taken serious account of the more recent view of the evolution of life. And thus Haeckel was able to find in it no enlightening reference points. Haeckel was well aware, as he explained, that Darwin's findings meant that earlier intellectual support to be found in teleology – that is to say, the notion that all life tended towards a particular goal – was now "shattered." It was in this context that Haeckel felt moved to take issue, in particular, with the late 18th-century German Idealist philosopher Immanuel Kant (1724–1804), who had asserted that the processes of living nature were not accessible to human understanding and could at best be the object of contemplation.[16]

Haeckel, by contrast, wanted to uncover the organisational system underlying living nature and to present to his readers that which went beyond what was already known (ill. p. 16). To this end, in his opinion, several fundamental steps had first to be taken. It would be necessary to restructure the sciences, to introduce new concepts, and to acknowledge the principle of evolution that underlay all phenomena as they appear to man. All this was first encapsulated in his *General Morphology* of 1866. With his veritable flood of new concepts, Haeckel, in fact, overstrained not only his own contemporaries, but also posterity. The biologists of our own day make regular use of only a fraction of Haeckel's terms, but some of them, notably "ontogenesis" and "ontogeny," "phylogenesis," and "phylogeny" have become standard concepts, and it was Haeckel who supplied their definition. Ontogeny (*Ontogenie*) is the history of the development of the individual organism while phylogenesis (*Phylogenese*) is the history of the lineage.[17] The concept of ecology (*Ökologie*) also derives from Haeckel, who used this term to mean "the science of the interaction of organisms with each other,"[18] or the "science of the overall relationships between organisms and their environment."[19] A great many of Haeckel's other neologisms were, however, never adopted.

With his *General Morphology*, Haeckel had created a work that was, at best, benevolently reviewed by commentators but that otherwise found very few readers initially. In Haeckel's own view, this was a fundamental work, for all his subsequent

Ideal basic forms, 1866
In: *Generelle Morphologie der Organismen*, 1866, vol. 1, plate 11
Basic polyaxonic and homopolar forms (Endospherical polyhedra and double pyramids)

publications on the philosophy of nature were to be based upon it or to relate back to it in some way.[20] The *General Morphology* had placed biology on a new footing.

For Haeckel, evolution was the guide for the order of life. With the development of the Theory of Evolution, the question of inheritance attracted considerable interest since evolution signifies the transmission of characteristics to the next generation. Yet a number of questions of central importance were as yet unanswered: How did these characteristics arise? And through what biological process were they inherited? Haeckel adopted the theory put forward by Jean-Baptiste de Lamarck (1744–1829) according to which individuals would be able to pass on to their progeny qualities they had acquired during their own lifetime. As proof of this, Haeckel recounted the story of how once, on a farm near Jena, a stable door had been banged shut thereby inadvertently crushing the tail of a prize bull. The calves subsequently sired by this bull had themselves all been born without tails.[21] Such evolutionary ideas that Haeckel had derived from Lamarck were, in fact, completely flawed.

The Genealogical Tree of Life – A Mirror of Evolution

The evolutionary history of organisms is evident in their relationships, in the history of their lineage. According to Haeckel, if Darwin's Theory of Evolution were true,[22] it would also be possible to construct the lineage for each organism. For such a genealogical tree is none other than a graphic representation of the history of the lineage in question. It was Haeckel's friend August Schleicher (1821–1868) who first gave him the idea of the genealogical tree. This linguist and philosopher had, by way of Haeckel, been alerted to Darwin's work and, in 1863, had sketched out a genealogical tree of the Indo-Germanic languages. Inspired by this example, Haeckel then devised his own series of such trees. To begin with (1866), he devised one out of eight to show the evolutionary relationships between the organisms. The series culminated in 1874 in the image of a gnarled oak (ill. p. 19). But Haeckel soon replaced this type of rendering with schematic drawings, much like those with which we are now familiar (ill. p. 20).

Biosystematic knowledge was, of course, incomplete. As Haeckel learned more, he redrafted his genealogical trees accordingly, always emphasising that these reflected hypotheses must be revised repeatedly in the light of the latest advances in knowledge.

Two propositions play a central role in contemporary biology. One is the frequently cited statement of 1973 by the geneticist Theodosius Dobzhansky (1900–1975):

Stem tree of humankind, 1874
In: *Anthropogenie oder Entwickelungsgeschichte des Menschen*, 1874, plate XII

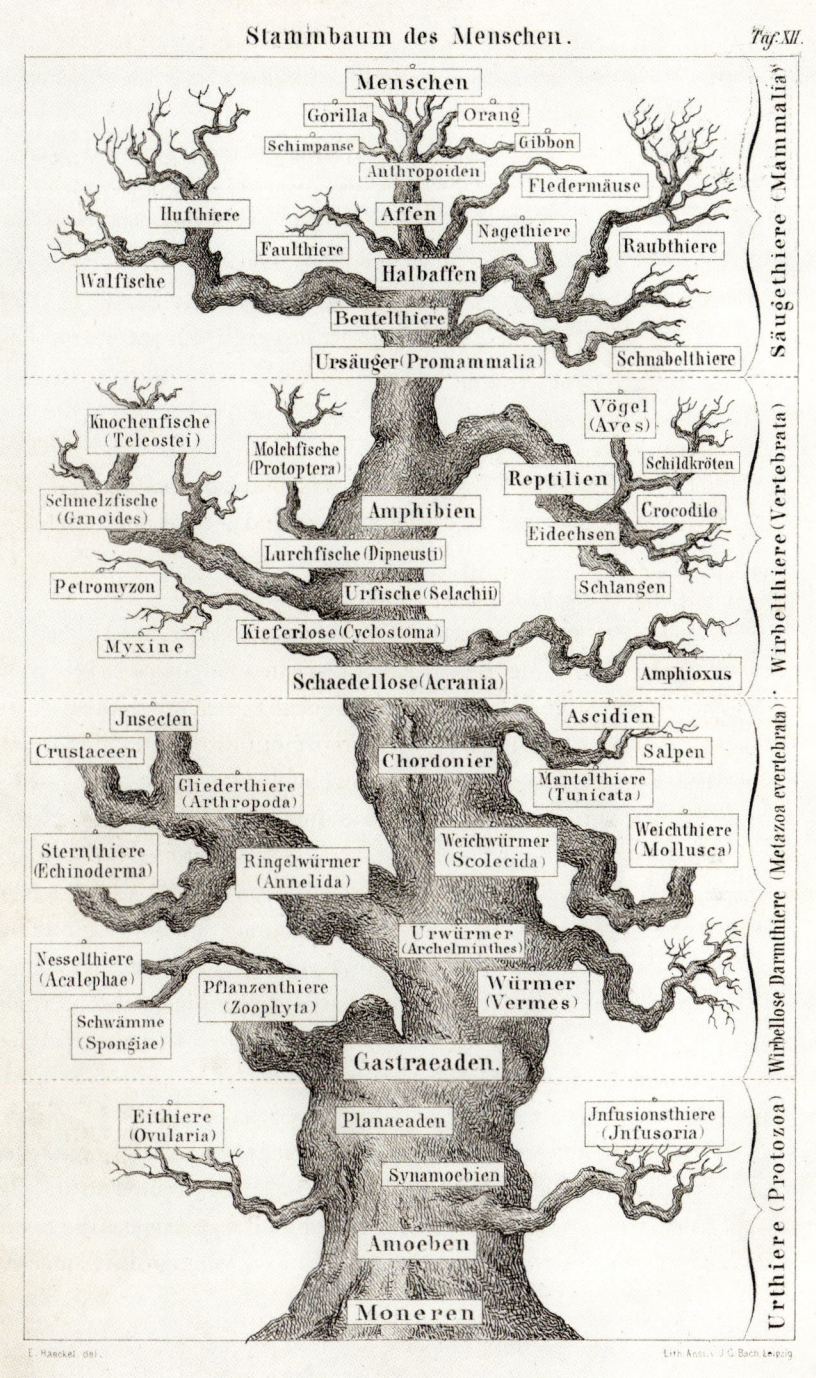

Stammbaum des Menschen.

Taf. XII.

Menschen

Gorilla · Orang
Schimpanse · Gibbon
Anthropoiden
Fledermäuse
Affen · Nagethiere
Hufthiere
Faulthiere · Raubthiere
Walfische · Halbaffen
Beutelthiere
Ursäuger (Promammalia) · Schnabelthiere

Säugethiere (Mammalia)

Knochenfische (Teleostei)
Vögel (Aves)
Molchfische (Protoptera)
Reptilien
Schmelzfische (Ganoides) · Schildkröten
Amphibien · Crocodile
Eidechsen
Lurchfische (Dipneusti)
Petromyzon · Schlangen
Urfische (Selachii)
Myxine · Kieferlose (Cyclostoma)
Schaedellose (Acrania) · Amphioxus

Wirbelthiere (Vertebrata)

Jnsecten · Ascidien
Crustaceen · Salpen
Gliederthiere (Arthropoda)
Chordonier · Mantelthiere (Tunicata)
Weichwürmer (Scolecida) · Weichthiere (Mollusca)
Sternthiere (Echinoderma) · Ringelwürmer (Annelida)
Urwürmer (Archelminthes)
Nesselthiere (Acalephae) · Würmer (Vermes)
Pflanzenthiere (Zoophyta)
Schwämme (Spongiae)
Gastraeaden.

Wirbellose Darmthiere (Metazoa evertebrata)

Eithiere (Ovularia) · Planaeaden · Jnfusionsthiere (Jnfusoria)
Synamoebien
Amoeben
Moneren

Urthiere (Protozoa)

E. Haeckel del.

Lith. Anst. v. J. G. Bach, Leipzig.

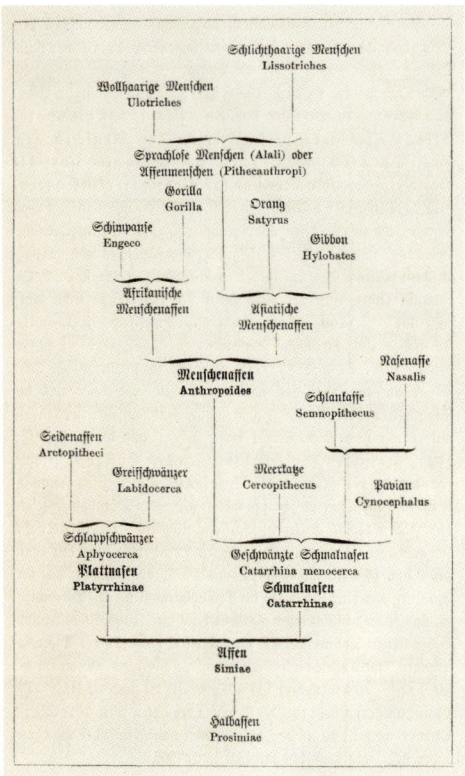

"Nothing in biology makes sense except in the light of evolution."[23] For Haeckel this went without saying. The other statement was formulated in connection with "phylogenetic systematics" developed by the entomologist Willi Hennig (1913–1976): "Nothing in evolution makes sense except in the light of phylogeny."[24] Haeckel would at the least have had an intuitive grasp of this idea. For only when the genealogical relationships are known can one trace the path of evolution. Haeckel did not, however, initially grasp that close relationships could be recognised only in the case of shared derived characteristics (evolutionary innovations). Often enough, he made what we would now recognise as the mistake of deriving, from shared primitive characters, evidence of nearest relationship. Haeckel also distinguished between classification, on the one hand, and relationships, on the other. There were, accordingly, within his own classifications, differences between the relationships and the arrangement of the organisms. An example drawn from Haeckel's last great phylogenetic work elucidates this. Crocodiles, pterosaurs, wingless dinosaurs, and birds all belong to Archosauria. The inherited characteristics they share include both the loss of a bladder and the possession of a heart with four separate chambers. Together with lizards, snakes, varans, tortoises, and other species, Archosauria belong in the Sauropsida. Haeckel was, in principle, aware of this, and of the fact that one could, therefore, as he conceded in 1895, unite crocodiles, pterosaurs, and dinosaurs with birds in a class termed Ornithocrania. This class would also then belong within the Sauropsida. But Haeckel did not take this step within his own system of classification. There crocodiles appear as a group in the Reptilia class[25] while dinosaurs and pterosaurs are in a

Stem tree of the apes with essential characteristics of humankind, 1873
In: *Natürliche Schöpfungsgeschichte*, 1873, p. 571

class of their own (Dracones); birds are in a further class.[26] While correctly discerning the prevailing relationships, Haeckel had nonetheless arbitrarily proposed a classification deviating from these. It was only after Hennig had further developed "biological systematics" into "phylogenetic systematics" that the "classification" of organisms was replaced by their "systematisation," thereby introducing an arrangement of life forms that reflects their natural connections.[27]

Ernst Haeckel was accused on occasion of not proceeding in a sufficiently professional fashion in endeavouring to reconstruct the relationships between the various organisms. It is, nonetheless, astonishing to consider what a fund of knowledge Haeckel brought to his efforts to determine phylogenetic connections.

In 1866, after *General Morphology* had been printed, Haeckel embarked on a trip to the Canary Islands (ill. p. 487). En route to Lisbon he passed through London and from there, on 21 October, he paid a visit to Charles Darwin, who had extended an invitation after receiving from Haeckel proofs of the latter's *General Morphology*. Although Darwin was, in fact, barely able to understand Haeckel's spoken English, he later reported that he had seldom encountered a "more pleasant, cordial, and frank man."[28]

In order to make the essence of his *General Morphology* accessible to a broader readership, Haeckel published his lectures on evolution in 1868 as the volume *Natürliche Schöpfungsgeschichte* (*The History of Creation*). To begin with, this publication was only sparingly illustrated, but with each edition, Haeckel introduced improvements in this respect. The eighth edition, published in 1889, already had numerous illustrations, although these were far below the quality of the elaborate plates adorning his scientific publications. Many were little better than what one might find in a school textbook.

Haeckel was simultaneously working on four volumes on the diversity of species, among them the proboscid jellyfish (1864, 1865) and jellyfish colonies (Siphonophorae, 1869). As in his monograph of 1862 on Radiolaria, Haeckel also set great store in these works by the high quality of the illustrations. In the case of his work on Siphonophorae, by which he was especially fascinated, he showed in numerous images the development from the individual organism to the mature colony. While relatively simple drawings sufficed for the early stages of development, Haeckel provided a particularly impressive image for his colony of *Physophora magnifica* (now *Physophora hydrostatica*, here p. 137).

On the Track of Fundamental Questions of Biology

Johannes Hemleben (1899–1984) opened his own 1964 biography of Haeckel with an affirmation that his achievement was, at the time of publication, regarded as generally outdated. Yet much of Haeckel's work on biology has, in fact, lost none of its significance. The fundamental biogenetic law, then as now, is taught in schools; and much in our current way of thinking would lead us to approve of Haeckel's Gastraea Theory: the notion that all multicellular life forms ultimately derive from a single organism of a particular structure.

The Biogenetic Law

Darwin's own work had suddenly provided an explanation for the fact that the embryos of all animals (including human embryos) often resemble each other in great detail when at an early stage of development. Haeckel interpreted the stages of embryological development largely as illustrations of phylogenetic precursory phases, and he devised the proposition that pupils are still expected to learn by heart: "The theory of evolution [...] shows that ontogeny is nothing more than a rapid recapitulation of phylogeny."[29] This is to say that the development of the individual is a rapid repetition of the development of his or her own ancestors. And this is recognised as one of the most important testaments to the correctness of the Theory of Evolution.[30] In the second edition of *The History of Creation*, published in 1870, Haeckel devised, with reference to this form of parallelism, the concept of a fundamental biogenetic law.

Haeckel took delight in pointing out that individuals of the ruling, privileged classes might well feel "discomfited" upon learning that representatives of the nobility were just as likely to prove indistinguishable – from those of the bourgeoisie during the first two months of their development *in utero*, from the embryo of a dog, complete with tail, or from of one of the other mammals (ill. p. 23).[31]

Yet Haeckel too recognised that the parallels between ontogeny and phylogeny had no general validity. Countless structures cannot be regarded as a reiteration of an earlier primordial form.[32] On this account the fundamental "biogenetic law" could serve only as a general rule. And in some circum-stances, this fundamental biological rule was itself thrown into doubt. On the other hand, with regard to specific structures, it did prove altogether valid.[33] As already observed by Gerhard Heberer (1901–1973), Haeckel had never stated that an individual's forbearers would be reiterated in their entirety, only that "ancestral characteristics" were likely to recur.[34]

The Gastraea Theory

In 1872, following journeys to Norway (1869) and to the Adriatic (1871), Haeckel published a monograph on calcareous sponges. This was yet another series of highly informative plates with reproductions, at diverse degrees of enlargement. Colour illustration was of little advantage here, for these sea creatures exhibited barely any

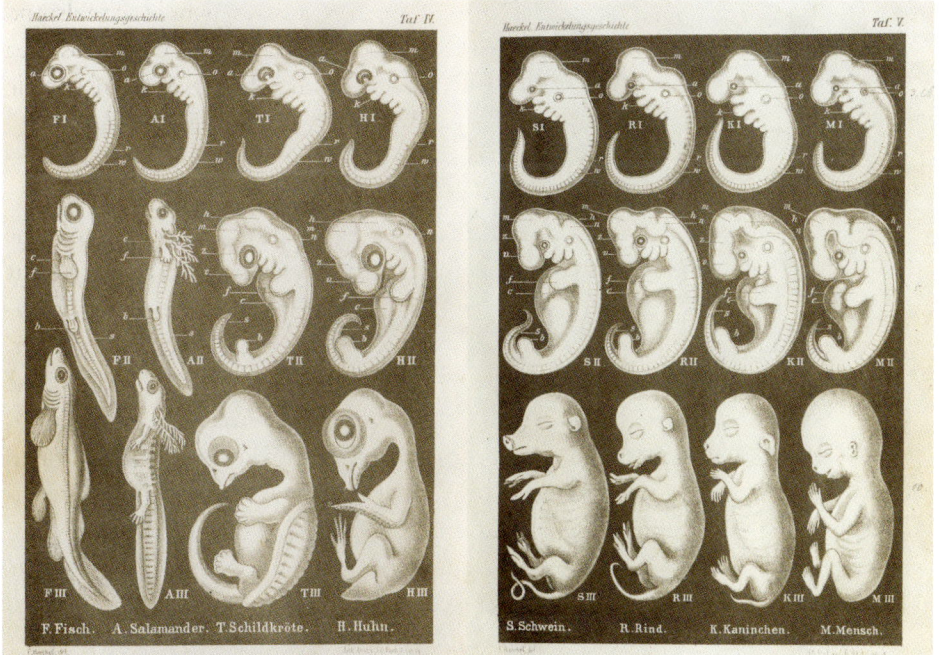

Fish, salamander, tortoise, chicken, pig, cow, rabbit, and human embryos, 1874
In: *Anthropogenie oder Entwickelungsgeschichte des Menschen*, 1874, plates IV, V

colour. In addition, Haeckel often showed mere parts of the whole animal. And yet his schematic drawing of the structure of sponges (plate 40; ill. p. 24) is, in its colouring, among the most striking that Haeckel was to ever reveal to his colleagues. His depiction of many sponges against a deep black background would also have struck them as most unusual (plate 6; ill. p. 27).

Haeckel's monograph on calcareous sponges was to prove a milestone, above all, for another reason. Here Haeckel explained the development of simply constructed sponges from an egg by way of a mass of cells to the form of a hollow sphere. By means of a process of deep indentation (*invagination*), this sphere would receive a hollow, a so-called primordial stomach. The layer of cells remaining on the exterior would then become the outer skin (*ectoderm*), and those lining the indented primordial stomach would become the inner skin (*entoderm*). Haeckel termed this stage of development "Gastrula" (literally: "stomach larva"). As the development of the individual organism had, to judge from its appearance, repeated important stages of the genealogy (fundamental "biogenetic law"), the sponges must have also had, in

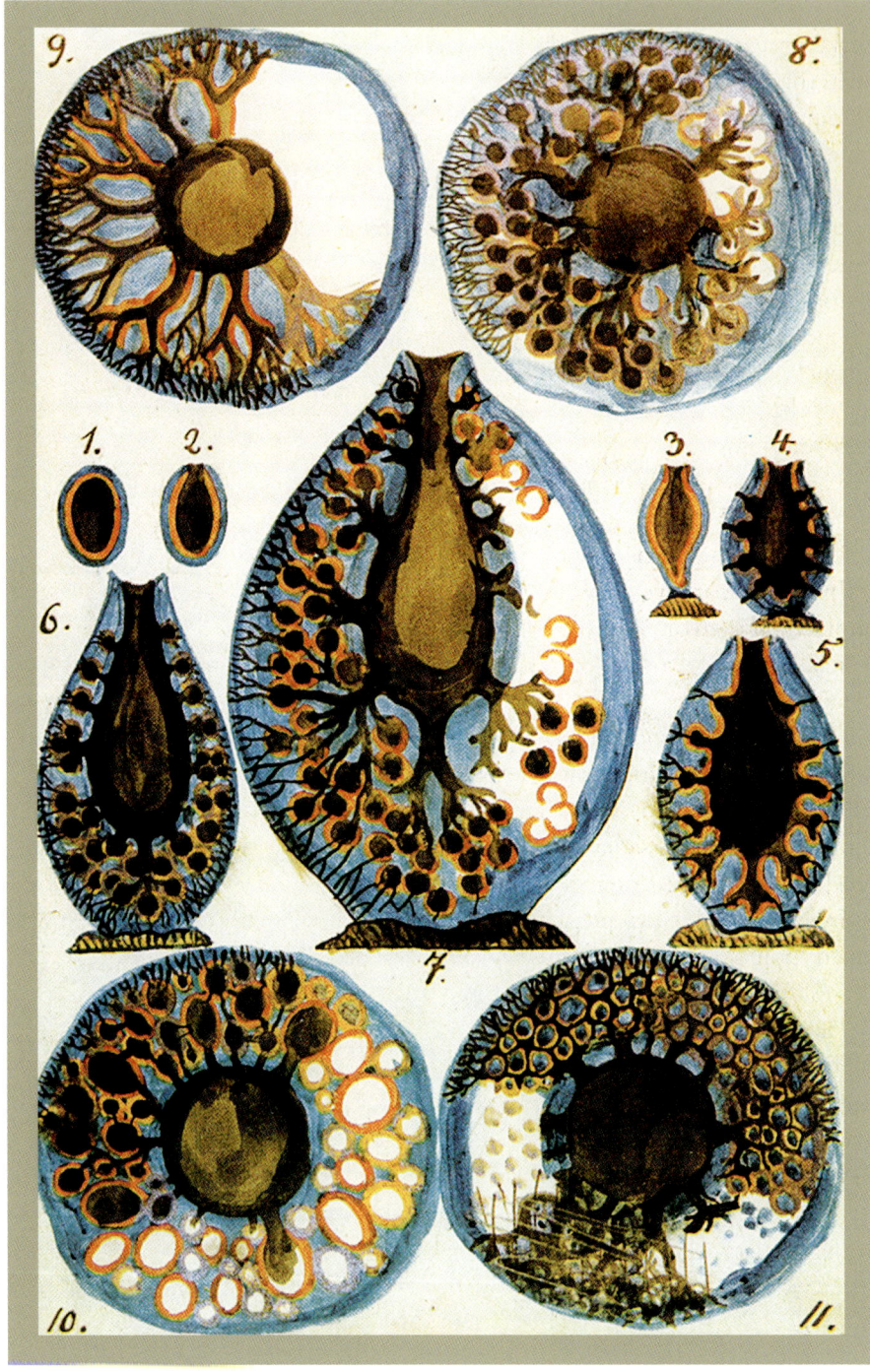

Haeckel's view, an ancestor of this form. In allusion to the term "Gastrula," Haeckel named these hypothetical ancestors "Gastraea."

Haeckel began by assuming that all animals in their development passed through such a stage; that accordingly each was derived from a primordial form of the Gastraea structure. By this means he evolved a compelling theory to account for the appearance of the earliest forms of animal life. Haeckel thus once again attained great fame among biologists. Later research was, however, to reveal that a "stomach larva" can arise in a variety of ways, and not only through the aforementioned process of deep indentation. These observations motivated researchers to a number of different conclusions regarding the earlier development of animal life forms. Nonetheless, most of the evidence reflects favourably on Haeckel's Gastraea Theory as acknowledged, for example, by the important zoologist Adolf Remane (1898–1978).[35] And it is still regarded as the best-supported theory on the origin of the animal body.[36]

Definition of Homology

In the comparative consideration of organisms, a crucial question is whether one is confronted with one and the same organ on any given occasion. In order to reach a conclusion on this point, one must take into account not only the appearance of particular structures, but also the development of each of these and their position within the body as a whole. The term that Haeckel used to refer to the same organ recurring across diverse species was "homologue" (*homolog*). And with his knowledge of evolution he was able to specify that it was necessary in each case to establish whether essentially one and the same organ was acquired by diverse groups on account of their shared ancestry (homologue organs) or, on the other hand, if these organs had been acquired in each case independently of the others (analogue organs).[37] Haeckel thus, defined "homology" as related to genealogy.

Haeckel's Concept of the Species

Today we usually understand the notion of a "species" as naturally occurring groups of populations that are genetically isolated from other such groups. Before Darwin's work, a "species" was defined as a group of individuals that resembled each other. This was a concept of the "species" related to characters. And the choice of characters viewed as significant for species discrimination was in itself arbitrary.

Calcareous sponges, before 1872
Drawings for *Die Kalkschwämme. Eine Monographie in zwei Bänden Text und einem Atlas mit 60 Abbildungen*, 1872, plate 40, 20 x 12 cm (8 x 4 3/4 in.), Jena, Ernst-Haeckel-Haus

Darwin then made it clear that "species" could prove very variable, and that they might, over the course of time, be subject to the processes of natural and sexual selection of particular variants and thus undergo change. Since the time of Darwin, "species" have no longer been understood as arbitrarily delimited groups of individuals, but as entities existing in nature that are engaged in evolution (biological species concept).[38] Haeckel though, did not conceive of "species" as natural entities. It was for this reason that he occasionally used several distinct names to describe forms belonging to one and the same biological "species."

A drastic example of Haeckel's non-biological understanding of the "species" is to be found in his essentially hierarchical arrangement of the evidence of human diversity. In entirely arbitrary fashion, he distinguished between twelve current species of humankind and 36 races.[39] Human beings living in the polar regions, termed by Haeckel *Homo arcticus*, were of such peculiar physical build because they had become adjusted to their environment and the climate that prevailed there, and to such an extent that they might be regarded as representing a separate species.[40] Such a non-biological understanding of the "species" was to have fatal consequences. Long after 1800, for example, it was still argued (by whites) that it was perfectly in order to enslave representatives of races that were non-European or were not closely related to Europeans. For this implied that they belonged to other species – so here the principle of "brotherly love" simply did not apply. In 1854, the palaeontologist Louis Agassiz (1807–1873) even maintained that the diverse sorts of humankind had been created independently of each other.[41] Darwin's champion, Thomas Henry Huxley (1825–1895), by contrast, showed with reference to the flourishing progeny of the mutineers of HMS *Bounty* and their Tahitian wives that all mankind belonged to one and the same reproductive community, and hence to one and the same species – and therefore had to be regarded in an equally humane manner. Haeckel was himself to suffer from the negative consequences of his concept of the "species" – as will be recounted below in the sections "The races of humanity" and "Light and shade."

Bathybius Haeckelii and Other Zoological Discoveries

As early as 1866, Haeckel had formulated an important discovery when he had recognised the cell core as the controller of inheritance.[42] In 1868, Huxley found what he thought might be identified as the simplest form of life in old samples of

Calcareous sponges, before 1872
Drawings for *Die Kalkschwämme. Eine Monographie in zwei Bänden Text und einem Atlas mit 60 Abbildungen*, 1872, plate 6, 20 x 12 cm (8 x 4 3/4 in.), Jena, Ernst-Haeckel-Haus

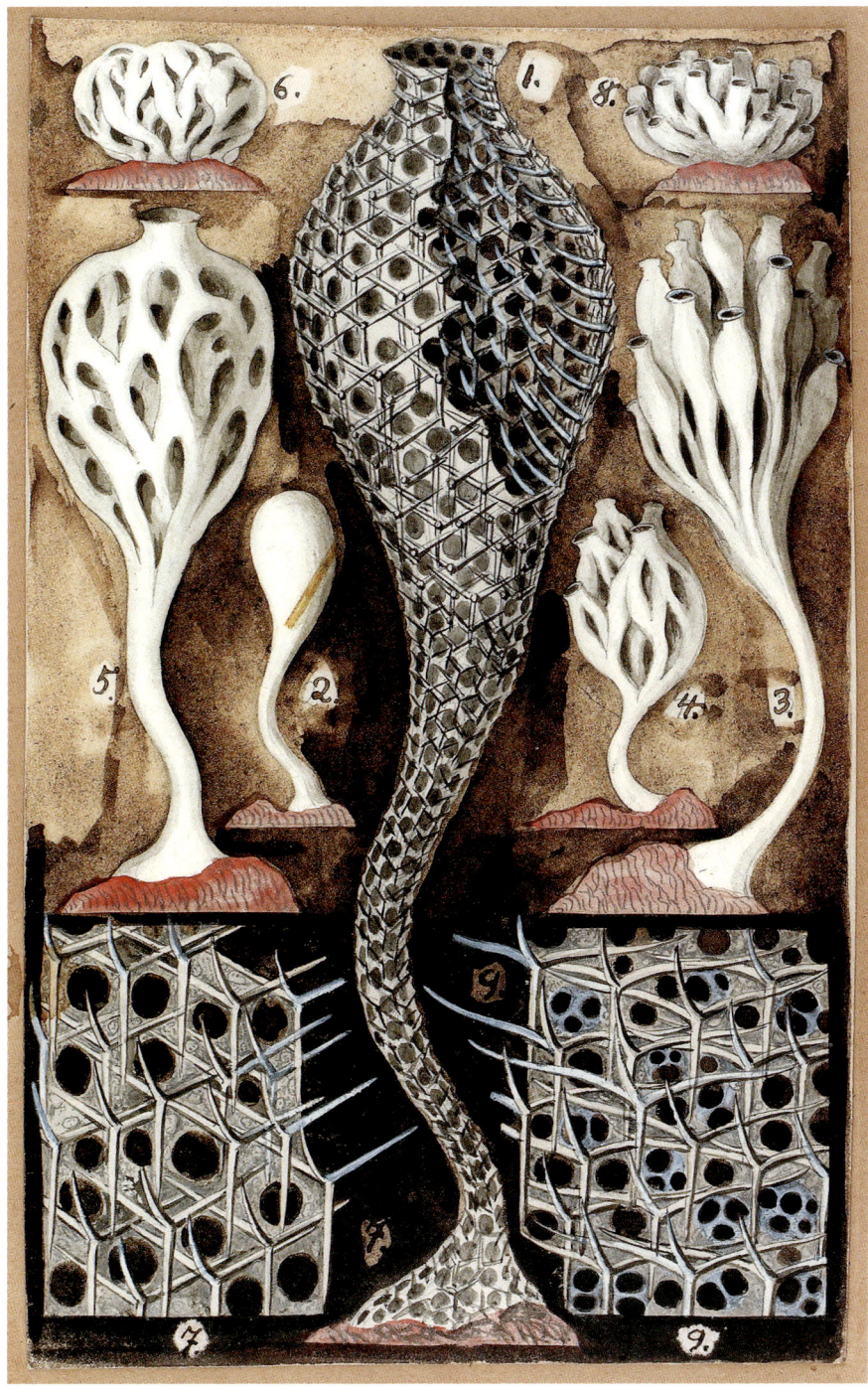

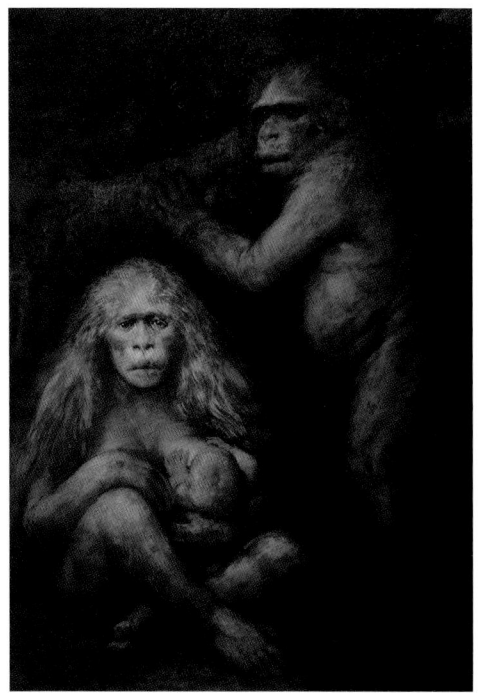

mud from the Atlantic Ocean floor. This he named *Bathybius Haeckelii*. Haeckel immediately integrated it into the second edition of his *History of Creation*, believing that this primordial life form had probably endured.[43] A few years later, however, a number of scientists recognised that *Bathybius Haeckelii* was actually an anorganic sediment, the product of a chemical reaction in the vials in which the samples were kept. Huxley promptly acknowledged his own error, but Haeckel could never entirely break with the notion of *Bathybius Haeckelii* as possibly the simplest form of life.

The Origin of Mankind

In 1863, the biologist Thomas Henry Huxley had introduced a broad readership to the evidence that humankind had descended from the apes. Haeckel went beyond Huxley and, in doing so, proved in most respects to be correct. He emphasised that just as mankind had evolved from apes, so too had these, in turn, evolved from lower mammals, basing that assumption on his belief in a transition from ape to man occurring in the Tertiary Period. That is to say, Haeckel believed mankind to be much older than was then usually assumed. In addition, he postulated a fossil transitional form. For this hypothetical form he had already created a scientific designation: *Pithecanthropus* (ill. p. 28).[44] In 1893, this designation was applied to the primeval man of Java.

It was, above all, in Haeckel's *Anthropogenie* (Anthropogeny) of 1874 that he treated the subject of the evolution of humankind in every possible detail. The last editions of this work were provided with numerous illustrations, many of these

Gabriel von Max, **Pithecanthropus alalus**, 1894
Oil on canvas, 99 x 68.5 cm (39 x 27 in.), Jena, Ernst-Haeckel-Haus
The image is based on a primeval "ape man without the capacity for speech"
hypothesised by Haeckel as a distant ancestor of humankind.

taken from the celebrated *Tierleben* (Life of Animals) by Alfred Edmund Brehm (1829–1884) on account of their impressive verisimilitude. On this occasion Haeckel supplied just a few plates of his own devising (ill. p. 31). Of significance here was his declaration that "[none] of all the apes alive today, and thus none of the so-called anthropoid apes could have been the progenitor of the race of man."[45] Haeckel assumed that mankind had arisen in southern Asia, though he admitted that the place of origin might have been Africa or perhaps a lost continent in what is now the north of the Indian Ocean.[46] Darwin, on the other hand, had determined that humankind first arose elsewhere. As both the gorilla and the chimpanzee were man's closest relatives, our ancestors, he argued, must themselves have lived on the continent of Africa.[47] Darwin was, indeed, to be proven right.

With a sense of certainty that mankind had descended from ancestors who were themselves apes, Haeckel believed that the "key to the solution of all the riddles of the universe" had been found.[48] He argued that those apparently most outraged at the notion of being descended from "real apes" were those who, "apparently on account of their own intellectual education and cerebral distinction, had as yet achieved little distance from our ancestors of the Tertiary Period."[49]

The Dispute over the Embryos

A great many authors had accused Haeckel of having prettified his scientific illustrations. Yet many biologists had and continue to have virtually no experience of their own in pictorial representation, and would be unable to match Haeckel's immense energy or his capacity for detailed observation. As early as 1860, Haeckel had written to his fiancée to describe how meticulously he enquired into his chosen subjects. Haeckel's good relationship with the firm of Carl Zeiss in Jena was a reason for the exactitude found in his later illustrations. This connection assured him of access to the world's best microscopic lenses.[50]

Notwithstanding all his precision, Haeckel, in 1868, proved uncharacteristically careless in a way that was to haunt him ever after. In the first edition of his *History of Creation* he had illustrated the great similarity between the early embryonic stage of the development of dogs, chickens, and tortoises to attest to their evolutionary relationship. To this end he showed three images. However, instead of here reproducing actual embryos of a dog, a chicken, and a tortoise, he simply presented three images all derived from the same printing block. Vehement criticism was immediately forthcoming. In the second edition, which appeared in 1870, Haeckel therefore illustrated only a single embryo and captioned this image accordingly, believing that this would settle the matter. Yet there were many who still wished to brand Haeckel a faker. And thus there arose a dispute that was to drag on for several decades. Haeckel, increasingly at a loss and eventually quite desperate, sought to admit to his own error. In 1899, when his volume *The Riddle of the Universe* had again brought him fame, Haeckel's enemies succeeded once more in digging up the old accusation of fakery. Part of Haeckel's work was termed a "disgrace to German science" ("Schandfleck der Deutschen Wissenschaft"). The new dispute resulted in Haeckel's images of embryos being illustrated in hundreds of newspapers and journals, thereby becoming the most widely discussed reproductions in the history of science.[51] The chief danger now lay in the possibility that, as a result of the accusations of fakery, the entire field of evolutionary biology might be brought into disrepute. In February 1909, 46 highly regarded biologists signed a declaration in which, while they would not approve of a number of Haeckel's schematic drawings, they nonetheless vehemently defended him against the accusation of engaging in an attempt to mislead through fakery. Yet even in 1997, the embryologist Elizabeth Pennisi, in her inexperience, accused Haeckel of deceit – to be followed six years later, and, in this case, quite incomprehensibly, by the Nobel Prize-winning biologist Christiane Nüsslein-Volhard.[52]

Haeckel's Philosophy and the Secularisation of Education

With his discovery of the Principle of Selection, Darwin had written that one could no longer conclude that the joint of a limb had been created in the manner of the hinge of a door by an intelligent being. For Haeckel too, it was clear that in the process of evolution there was no place for a personified notion of a Divinity. He poked fun at the theological-philosophical view as follows: On the one hand, the Creator was envisaged as humanoid, and it was assumed that He was implementing a specific plan. On the other, the Creator was imagined as a gaseous entity, a body devoid of organs, "whereby we attain the paradoxical notion of a gaseous vertebrate, a *contradictio in adjecto*."[53] Soon enough, these observations of Haeckel's, in being reported and re-reported, were distorted into the claim that Haeckel himself envisaged God as a gaseous vertebrate.

Haeckel adopted August Schleicher's concept of monism for a view of the world in which the sheer diversity of phenomena derives from a single principle.[54] For Haeckel, evolution was such a principle: everything evolved, everything could ultimately be related to a single origin, and everything was inextricably interconnected

"Chimpanzee, gorilla, orang-utan, and Negro," 1874
In: *Anthropogenie oder Entwickelungsgeschichte des Menschen*, 1874, plate XI

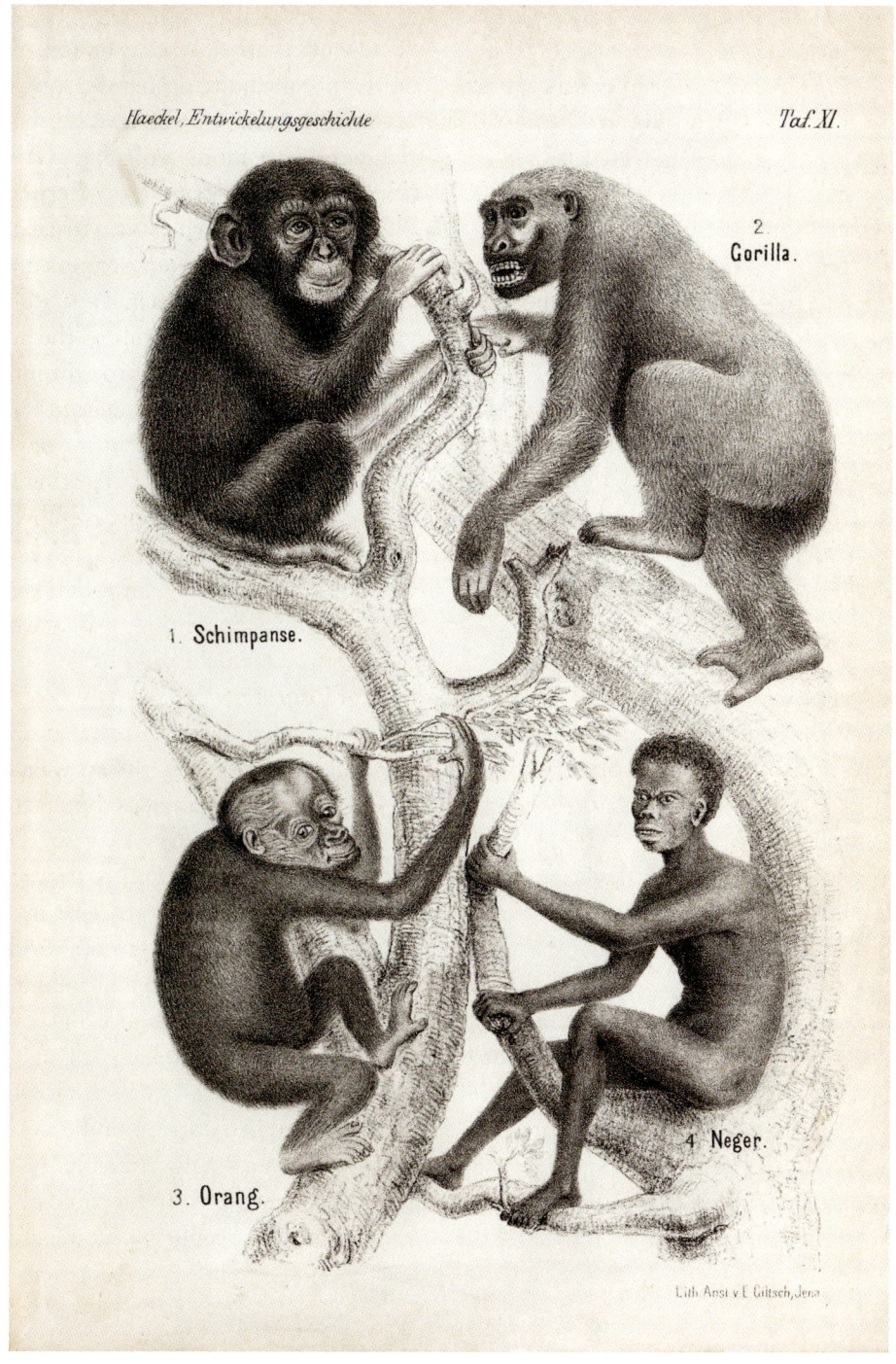

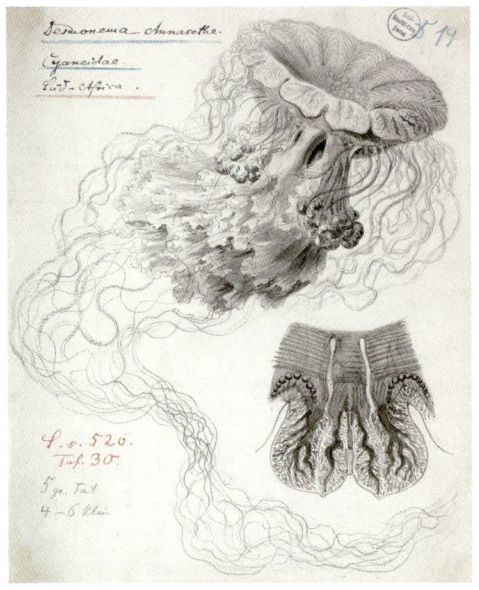

with everything else. Every dualistic world outlook was to be eschewed; matter and spirit were as one, and there also prevailed a unity of the organic and anorganic in nature. And this led Haeckel to his own conclusion: "All true natural science is philosophy and all true philosophy is natural science"[55] – and even that "the entirety of human knowledge" was to be regarded as "a unified knowledge structure," and that "the conventional distinction between the sciences and the humanities [was] to be discarded."[56]

It almost goes without saying that Haeckel would not refrain from bringing up the question of the nature of the soul. Psychic qualities and reactions are to be found in all animals. But not only did the simplest monocellular organisms possess an early form of soul ("cell soul" / "Zellseelen"),[57] one might also regard atoms, on account of their powers of attraction and repulsion, as possessed of a soul.[58] And the same was true of crystals.[59] This point of view was supported in particular by the discovery of liquid crystals, the movement of which Haeckel regarded as evidence of life. In the light of such errors, it has often been overlooked that in Haeckel's day no one presumed to survey the development of life so comprehensively as he did. No philosopher of that period came anywhere close to such a breadth of vision. And very few of Haeckel's contemporaries in any walk of life had understood that it was no longer sufficient for philosophers to proceed in a manner that was merely self-referential, and that they must now attend (as Haeckel, like Darwin, believed) to the knowledge that the natural sciences were continuing to reveal.[60]

Finally, Haeckel supplemented his own adherence to monism through the fundamental "ethical law" of an uncompromising altruism. For Haeckel, there were grave contradictions on this matter in Christianity,[61] and he therefore believed it necessary for State and Church to be divided, for the Church to have no further involvement

Desmonema annasethe
Drawing for *Das System der Medusen. Erster Theil einer Monographie der Medusen. Atlas*, 1879
Plate XXX, 20.9 x 25.9 cm (8 1/4 x 10 1/4 in.), Jena, Ernst-Haeckel-Haus

in education, and for there to be a thorough school reform favouring an educational programme centred on an all-encompassing study of nature. Having made known such proposals, Haeckel soon came to be widely viewed as subversive, and the more so as monism was itself rapidly gaining adherents. The Union of Monists (Monistenbund), founded by Haeckel in 1906, had already acquired 5,000 members by 1911.

For Haeckel as a scientist who knew a great deal about evolution, it was apparent that there was not a trace of evidence to be found for life after death. Accordingly, the duty of mankind was to achieve a life in the here and now that was as ethical and as contented as possible.[62] But Haeckel also drew from this belief certain consequences regarding how one might approach life in the case of individuals whose disabilities left them in perpetual pain. In such circumstances, he believed suicide might well be a form of blessed release. Haeckel went even further, voicing in 1915 his approval for the administration of morphine to the "incurable" so as to free them from their nameless agonies – although naturally only under strict medical supervision and on the advice of specially appointed commissions.[63] Haeckel's thoughts on the matter of human intervention to put an end to life had, by this point, also hardened to the extent that he now openly advocated for the death penalty.[64]

The Races of Mankind

It is astonishing to consider in what detail and how accurately Haeckel was able to reconstruct the history of the distribution across the globe of humankind, notwithstanding an erroneous starting point (ill. p. 19). Haeckel devised genealogical trees for humanity too. While this is not in principle an illegitimate approach, in adopting it he committed an unforgivable error. He presumed to distinguish between distinct categories of humanity in terms of their relative "value." He proceeded on the assumption that of the diverse types of mankind he had identified, "the four lowest species were distinguished by the woolly consistency of the hair on their heads."[65] This demotion ("lowest species") ran, even in this period, counter to every studied instance, and yet Haeckel chose to further emphasise his claim: The "woolly haired" were, he claimed, "incapable of a true inner culture and a higher intellectual development, even in circumstances so favourable to adaptation as are now offered to them in the United States of North America"[66] – and not a word about the fact that they had, until relatively recently, experienced there the most frightful oppression as slaves. Even worse instances of disparagement were to follow.

The Darwins had adopted a quite different approach to this matter. As early as 1787, their family, the Wedgwoods, had been responsible for issuing a medal bearing the rhetorical anti-slavery question (implicitly uttered by an oppressed negro):

"Am I not a Man and a Brother?" And Charles Darwin himself always emphasised humane sympathy as the crucial characteristic of humanity.

Haeckel, however, felt compelled to return again and again to his own perspective on the diversity of humankind, occasionally in what now strikes us as a deeply distasteful manner. While neither an ethnologist nor with any experience in medical research into the human brain, he proceeded to address related matters. It is possible that he drew here on the work of the Jena anatomist and embryologist Emil Huschke (1797–1858), father of his second wife, Agnes. Huschke had distinguished between three fundamentally distinct types of human brain which he believed were possible to categorise in ascending order of cognitive capacity. He had established a typological congruence between the brain of anthropoid apes and that of representatives of one of the "equatorial races" (and also between that of a child and a European woman).[67] Following Huschke's arguments, it was, in fact, assumed by most anatomists in the mid-19th century that higher cognitive and analytical capacity was characteristic of a physically larger brain. In contrast, Thomas Henry Huxley had already sought to persuade his listeners in a lecture of 1867 that there was no secure proof that one race was intrinsically superior to another.[68]

Zoological Research 1875–90 – Haeckel's Great Series of Plates

While Haeckel championed the cause of the Theory of Evolution, made friends among biologists and enemies among philosophers, and trod on many a theological toe in numerous early presentations in his public lectures and in the semi-popular scientific works he published, directly informed by his tireless research he continued to attend to one group of sea creatures after the other in scientific publications. His monograph of 1872 on calcareous sponges was followed by his *Arabische Korallen* (Arabian Corals), albeit with very few plates and of a quality inferior to other earlier examples (here pp. 495, 501). In 1876, Haeckel agreed to the proposal that he study and produce an account of some of the spoils of the legendary marine expedition of the British vessel HMS *Challenger* (here pp. 304–17). For a total of twelve years Haeckel tirelessly researched deep-sea jellyfish, Radiolaria, Siphonophorae, and keratinous sponges, producing scientific volumes with plates of the highest quality which, in turn, were lavishly published.

Floresca Parthenia
Drawing for *Das System der Medusen.*
Erster Theil einer Monographie der Medusen. Atlas, 1879, plate XXXII, fig. 5
20.9 x 25.9 cm (8 1/4 x 10 1/4 in.), Jena, Ernst-Haeckel-Haus

5–8

Floresca Parthenia, E. Hkl.

Z 19 r

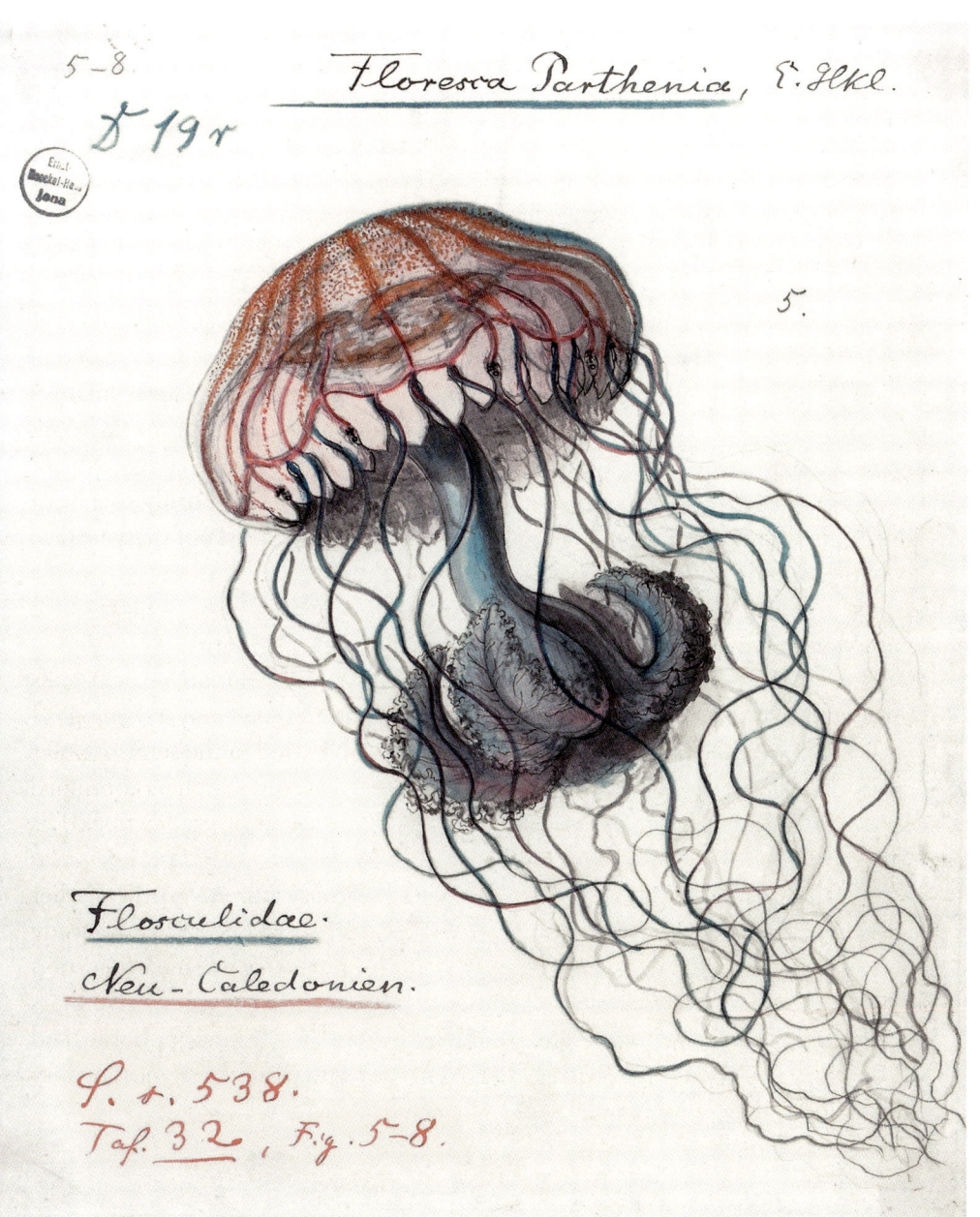

5.

Flosculidae.

Neu – Caledonien.

S. +. 538.
Taf. 32, Fig. 5–8.

The first of these, appearing in 1879, was on the subject of jellyfish, its opening section based on specimens he had assembled himself. In this publication, Haeckel supplied precise descriptions of *Desmonema annasethe* (ills. pp. 32, 270) and of *Mitrocoma annae* (ill. p. 252) which he had named after his beloved first wife Anna. Haeckel illustrated the jellyfish and their respective organs in the liveliest and tenderest colours (ill. p. 35); and in those examples illustrated in black and white, the corresponding drawings were, in accordance with the delicacy of the object, rendered in a restrained monochrome or shown against a tinted background (ill. p. 37). Haeckel's expertise in the depiction of such transient biological structures had first become evident 15 years earlier when he published his work on the proboscid jellyfish in 1864.

Haeckel's images recording the Radiolaria amassed during the HMS *Challenger* Expedition were qualitatively far superior to what he had been able to produce on the occasion of his own publication of 1862 – be it in the refinement of his use of shading or in his skill in representing interlocking skeletal forms (e.g. plates 25, 31, 48; see pp. 113, 117, 118). Colour was occasionally employed to emphasise the contents of a cell. And the plates devoted to the Siphonophorae gathered by the British expedition (those complex organisms that unite to establish extensive colonies) were veritable works of art of a breathtaking beauty. Here we may say that Haeckel was at the peak of his abilities both as a scientist and an artist, in blending precision in his rendering of organic structures with a true aesthetic sensibility. With the last of his work on the material from the HMS *Challenger* expedition and a revision of his own earlier text on spiky skeletal casings – this last included a series of highly ambitious, richly diverse plates – Haeckel brought his biological research to an end.

From *The Riddle of the Universe* to *Art Forms*

In his most widely read book *Die Welträthsel* (*The Riddle of the Universe*) of 1899, Haeckel sought to register the level that human understanding had attained as the 19th century drew to a close. After the uncompromising statements had appeared in Haeckel's earlier publications, it was more or less inevitable that this latest work would give rise to vehement differences of opinion. This time, however, Haeckel had had substantial assistance in the person of a young woman in her early thirties from the Göttingen region: Frida von Uslar-Gleichen who, in early 1898, had embarked on a correspondence with him in the hope of securing his answers on a number of questions that concerned her. It was not long before the continuing correspondence took on a greater frankness and intimacy and, in due course, led each writer to express deep affection for the other, an intensity of emotion only deepened by their relatively few meetings (ill. p. 40). Haeckel believed that he would be able to untangle himself from this emotional preoccupation through embarking on further extensive travels – but to no avail. Selections from this most touching correspondence were to be published in 1927 in the form of the novel *Franziska von Altenhausen* (in which Haeckel is given the pseudonym Paul Kämpfer).[69] It was long believed that the original letters had been destroyed "for all too comprehensible reasons;"[70] but this proved not to be the case. In 2003, these were published in their entirety in a volume of more than 1,200 pages, lovingly edited by Norbert Elsner.[71]

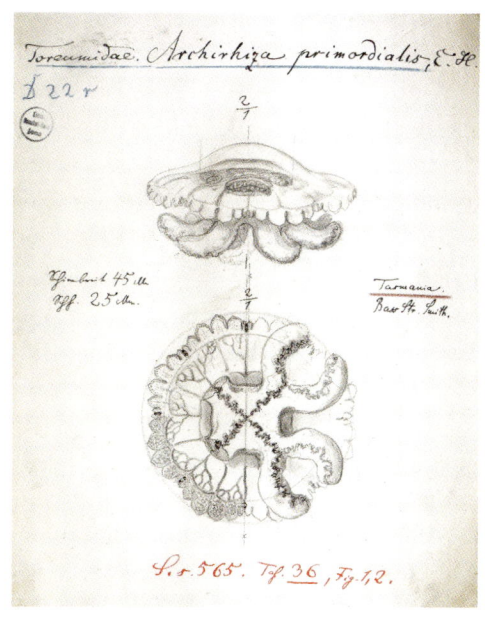

Yet, in spite of the warnings and interventions of Frida von Uslar-Gleichen, Haeckel's *Riddle of the Universe* emerged as a partially polemical presentation of the consequences of recent findings in biology and related scientific disciplines. The thousands of letters received by Haeckel in his capacity as author of this text expressed exuberant agreement and vehement criticism and, above all, posed question after question. Such reactions necessitated further explanations on Haeckel's part. In 1904, during a four-month stay in Rapallo, Haeckel addressed some of these in what became *Die Lebenswunder* (*The Wonders of Life*), intended as a supplement to *The Riddle of the Universe*. The retreat to Rapallo had also been undertaken in order for Haeckel to spend his 70th birthday there without an undue amount of fuss. During his absence from Germany, however, Frida von Uslar-Gleichen died from an overdose of morphine.

Before her untimely death, Frida had also assisted Haeckel as he was contemplating and devising the publication for which he remains best known: *Kunstformen der Natur* (*Art Forms in Nature*), which was to appear in instalments between 1899 and 1904. In his grief Haeckel could only immortalise the memory of his lost love

Toreumidae. Archirhiza primordialis
Drawing for *Das System der Medusen.*
Erster Theil einer Monographie der Medusen. Atlas, 1879, plate XXXVI, fig. 1, 2
20.9 x 25.9 cm (8¼ x 10¼ in.), Jena, Ernst-Haeckel-Haus

in a few plates in this remarkable publication. Almost all of its illustrations were freshly drawn by him, and, of course, informed by his own profound knowledge of biological diversity. His initial plan was for a total of five instalments, each with ten plates. These, however, sold far better than expected and so Haeckel resolved to double the scale of the enterprise, eventually publishing ten instalments, each with ten plates, bringing the total to one hundred. In devising each of these plates, he would sometimes indulge in detail, and at others favour the appeal of simplicity; and a number of them reflect his experience of landscape painting. Indeed, he resorted to every artistic device that he had essayed earlier in his scientific publications. *Art Forms in Nature* was intended for a lay public, but here and there Haeckel described a new species. In this respect the work is also of scientific significance (see pp. 320–23). With *Art Forms* as a highpoint in his artistic-biological output, Haeckel brought to a close his account of the fascinating diversity of life.

Light and Shade

At the end of Haeckel's scientific work there prevailed two distinct and irreconcilable opinions of this celebrated representative of Jena. On the one hand, he was disproportionately admired; on the other, he was often, quite unreasonably deplored. Friedrich Loofs (1858–1928), professor of ecclesiastical history at the University of Halle, composed an explicitly slanderous attack in which he claimed that "[...] all I have said has been 'insulting' to Professor Haeckel [...] and it is meant to be so."[72] He claimed that Haeckel had prostituted himself, that his statements were arrant nonsense or sheer idiocy, and that, in consorting with filthy Jewish blasphemers, he had brought forth something utterly shameful. A compilation of such attacks was edited by Haeckel's assistant Heinrich Schmidt (1874–1935).[73]

Somewhat more objective was the assessment offered by the Berlin pedagogue and philosopher Friedrich Paulsen (1846–1908) who claimed that in *The Riddle of the Universe* one encountered Haeckel in his negative and morose incarnation, his philosophy in reality comprising merely of a series of negations, with no hint of a Divinity dwelling apart from the material world, no soul separate from the human body, and no sense of religious belief existing beyond the realm of knowledge. The fact that Paulsen had, in fact, misunderstood Haeckel is already apparent if we consider just a few statements from the latter's *Wonders of Life*. Here Haeckel claims that if one did not start from the assumption that there was a life after death, and if one understood that no "premonition" pointed to any individual's ultimate destiny, then humankind would gain enormously, for it would strive to organise life in the here and now in the interests of its own happiness and to the greater benefit of society.[74]

It was in these early years of the new century that the increasingly eager military armament of the Great Powers of Europe began to foreshadow the world war. Haeckel himself initially became a convinced pacifist, in 1910 adding his name to a "Declaration of the Formation of a Union for International Understanding." He also championed the work of the pacifist author Bertha von Suttner (1843–1914) who, in 1905, won the Nobel Peace Prize. In 1913, Haeckel joined forces with the French Socialist Henriette Meyer to co-found the pacifist "Institut Franco-Allemand de la Réconciliation," which sought to ensure a lasting peace between Germany and France. Nonetheless, with the first news from the Western Front and the accusations that German troops had committed unspeakable atrocities against the civilian population of Belgium and had been responsible for the destruction of irreplaceable cultural treasures, Haeckel's pacifism gave way to a patriotic nationalism.

Before the end of 1914 Haeckel had readily added his name to a declaration "An die Kulturwelt" (To the World of Culture), signed by a further 92 intellectuals, among them the theatre director Max Reinhardt (1873–1943), the physicists Max Planck (1859–1947) and Wilhelm Conrad Röntgen (1845–1923), the painter Max Liebermann (1847–1935), and the writer Gerhart Hauptmann (1862–1946). The text of this document disputed any kind of German guilt whatsoever in the war, and argued that the international indignation at Germany's conduct was mere calumny. Before the year was out Haeckel also felt moved to publish an entirely unilateral declaration: *Englands Blutschuld am Weltkriege* (*England's Blood-Guilt in the World War*) in which he argued that this antagonist had no other goal in fighting but to further extend its international dominion.

All too soon millions of human lives had been sacrificed to the war. In a publication of 1915, *Ewigkeit* (*Eternity*), Haeckel sought to offer his readers consolation by drawing on his extensive knowledge of the life sciences. In the face of such horror, numerous educated people would assume that this must be in accordance with the will of a Divinity with a conscious plan. But in fact, as he now explained, the question of who lived and who died, even on such a vast scale, was entirely a matter of chance.[75] These observations are then followed by one of Haeckel's crassest racist remarks: "We Germans feel these painful losses especially acutely, for in our case and that of our Austrian confederates, the level of education, and hence the value of each life, is on average much higher than it is in the case of our opponents, who have assembled their vast armies largely from the uneducated masses of the lower classes, from mere mercenaries and from the coloured members of savage or half-savage races from across the globe! The life of a single German warrior [...] has a higher intellectual and moral value than that of hundreds of out-and-out savages."[76]

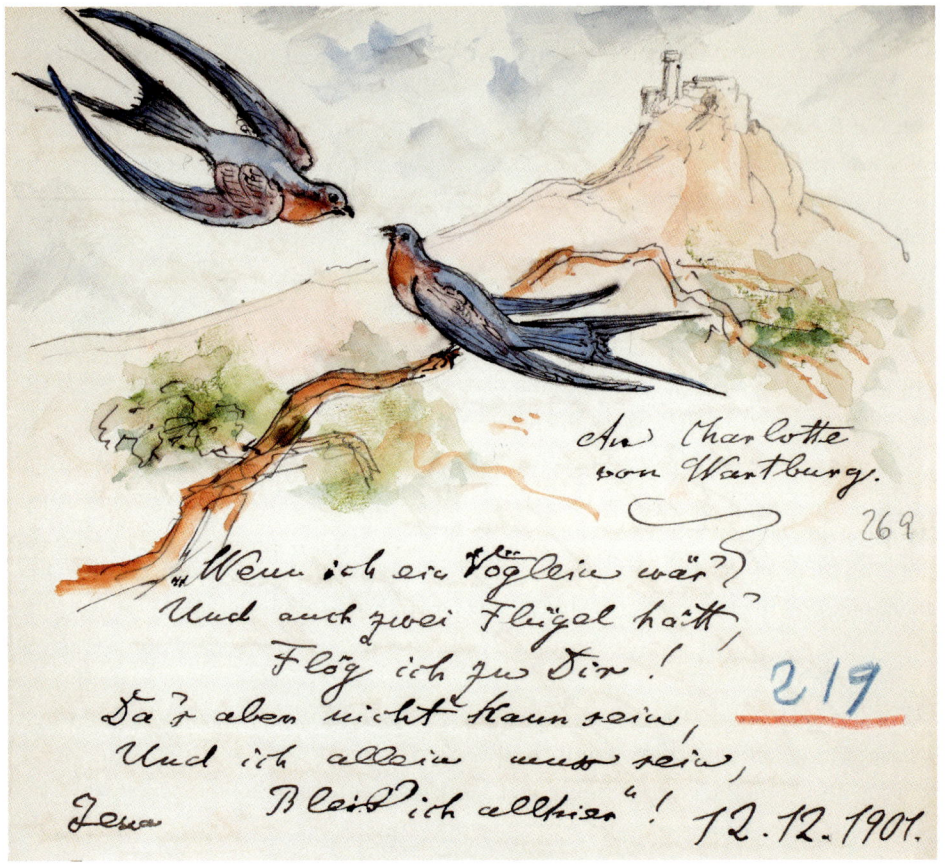

Letter to Charlotte von Wartburg (Frida von Uslar-Gleichen)
Jena, 12 December 1901
Staatsbibliothek zu Berlin – Preußischer Kulturbesitz, Handschriftenabteilung,
Nachlass Ernst Haeckel: Haeckel, Ernst, fol. 269 recto

"If I were a little bird / And thus had two wings, / I would fly to you! /
But that cannot be / and I must be alone / I remain alone!"

On account of their general tendency in this direction, Haeckel's writings were viewed by the American historian Daniel E. Gasman (1933–2012) as an effective prelude to National Socialism.[77] Gasman's view has secured the approval of numerous authors, but this now widely shared assessment of Haeckel overlooks a number of considerations, including the fact that the NSDAP or Nazi Party explicitly refuted monism which it regarded as too much at odds with the *völkisch* and biological preoccupations of the chief ideologues of National Socialism. In 1935, in line with the new "Regulations for the Inspection of the Holdings of the Public Libraries in Saxony," works banned as undesirable included, alongside those by Albert Einstein (1879–1955), by liberal-intellectual Democrats such as Heinrich Mann (1871–1950), and by Jews in general, publications by Ernst Haeckel.[78] In 1998, the Viennese biologist Friedrich Schaller (1920–2018) noted that Haeckel had been judged by many to have unknowingly served as one of the intellectual "grandfathers of Hitler."[79] Gasman and others have additionally accused Haeckel of anti-Semitism. But in this claim too they are demonstrably in the wrong. Haeckel himself had drawn attention to the intellectual contribution to every aspect of German culture that was owed to educated Jewry, which had always courageously championed the causes of enlightenment and freedom. As Robert J. Richards has argued, Gasman irresponsibly ignored the underlying social, political, and economic causes that favoured the rise of Hitler.[80] Haeckel's own racism was, moreover, hardly a rarity during the 19th century, not even among the educated. And merely his unswerving approach to any sort of restriction on the freedom of thought, teaching, and research would surely have made Haeckel a perpetual irritation to the National Socialists.

Finale

Haeckel received numerous high honours during his lifetime – and this has continued in an indirect fashion almost to this day. In 1992, the asteroid 12323, discovered at the observatory in Tautenburg, near Jena, was named after him. Haeckel himself was awarded an honorary doctorate by four universities. On his 80th birthday, in February 1914, commentators throughout the world published admiring surveys of his life and work and this at a point where he had himself ceased to value human company.

At the very end of his career Haeckel returned once again to biology and to monism. With his essay *Fünfzig Jahre Stammesgeschichte* (Fifty Years of Phylogeny) published in 1916, he again emerged as the great phylogeneticist able to unite and reconcile every new finding within his own area of speciality.

In the spring of 1911 Haeckel had broken a thigh bone. From that point on he was cared for by his wife Agnes. When she died in April 1915, the danger of social isolation loomed for Haeckel. He was, however, able to rely upon his granddaughter Else Meyer (1894–1975) who stepped in to keep house for him (ill. p. 490). To his great joy she also took a keen interest in his scientific work. But after Haeckel broke an arm on 5 August 1919 he simply lost the will to continue. He died only a few days later on 9 August.

In the winter semester of the academic year 1919–20, the Berlin zoologist Karl Heider (1856–1935) gave a lecture of his own that had opened with a homage to Ernst

Haeckel: an appreciation of his life and achievement which may serve us here as a conclusion: "Ernst Haeckel has departed from the company of the living. Haeckel was a model for us all; he was the source from which we drew our own efforts to devise new all-embracing points of view, new ways to pose questions; he was our instruction and our inspiration. If we felt ourselves to be close to him, because he was after all our colleague and a leading light in our own field of scholarship, we should not overlook the numerous other fields in which he was also, and just as energetically, active. Haeckel was a philosopher; he posed for us the Riddle of the Universe; he was the founder of monism; he was an artist. Among his contributions to our theoretical concerns, I see as especially valuable his General Morphology. And both his formulation of the Biogenetic Law and his Gastraea Theory have also proved of enormous influence for the development of our science. Nor, finally, must we overlook what a leading role Haeckel played in his own era: a period in which Darwin's teachings were still highly controversial. As an individual, Haeckel was far removed from every form of vanity; he was a man of great warmth and true benevolence; and he was at all times ready to recognise the achievements of others and to encourage the engagement and enthusiasm of the young. The essential simplicity of his character was in his case the sign of true greatness."[81]

Cyanea lamarckii
Blue Jellyfish, before 1879
Drawing, Jena, Ernst-Haeckel-Haus

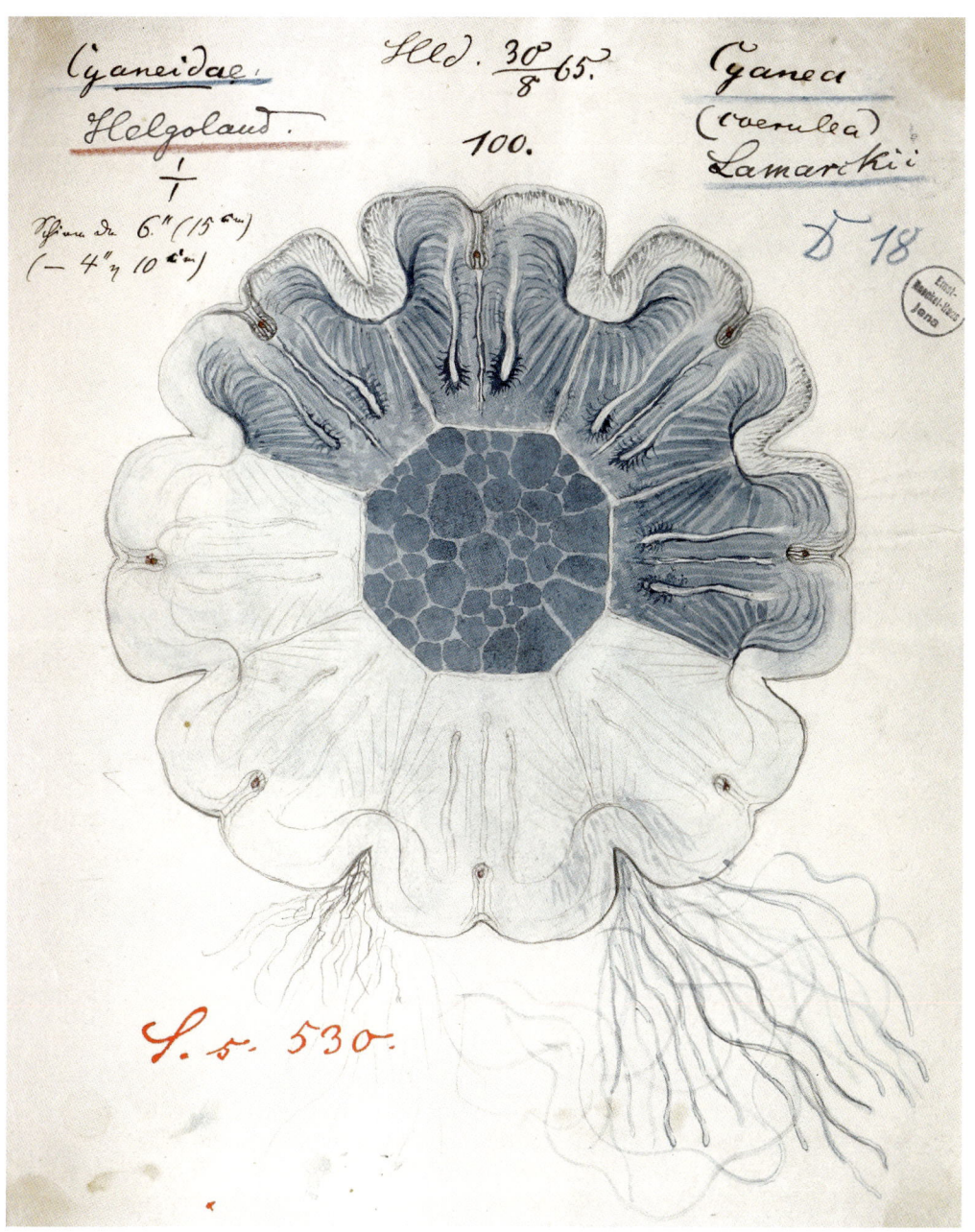

ERNST HAECKEL
AND THE EVOLUTION
OF MODERN ART

Julia Voss

On 30 July 1908, Ernst Haeckel, professor emeritus of zoology at the University of Jena, and by then 74 years old, celebrated the greatest triumph of his career. On that date, this German city Jena acquired its own Museum of Natural History, an institution that Haeckel had himself founded, devised, and designed, and which he termed the "Phyletic Museum" (Museum of the Evolution of Species). At the opening, there were as yet few animals and plants on display; but this paucity was more than compensated for by the care that Haeckel had invested in the artistic decoration of the interior, which was a realisation of his own ideas and sketches. Across the entrance hall ran a banderole bearing a quotation from Haeckel's revered Johann Wolfgang von Goethe (1749–1832): "Whoever is possessed of science and art / Also has religion."[1] And on the ceiling were painted ornaments in the form of medusae, or jellyfish. From 1909 onwards, visitors to the museum were also welcomed by a sculpted female figure, an *Allegory of Truth* by Harro Magnussen (1861–1908). Her right hand held aloft a flaming torch while in her left she clutched the skull of a chimpanzee. Ludwig Plate (1862–1937), the second director of the Phyletic Museum, states: "The truth which separates humanity from its bestial ancestors, will serve as a torch to illuminate the world."[2] Haeckel took very seriously his own acknowledgement of "religion." By this, however, he meant the theory derived from his own view and understanding of the world which he called monism (*Monismus*). In 1904, at the International Congress of Freethinkers in Rome, his followers had acclaimed him an "Anti-Pope."

Leopold and Rudolf Blaschka
Rhegmatodes thalassina, c. 1890
Glass model, London, Natural History Museum

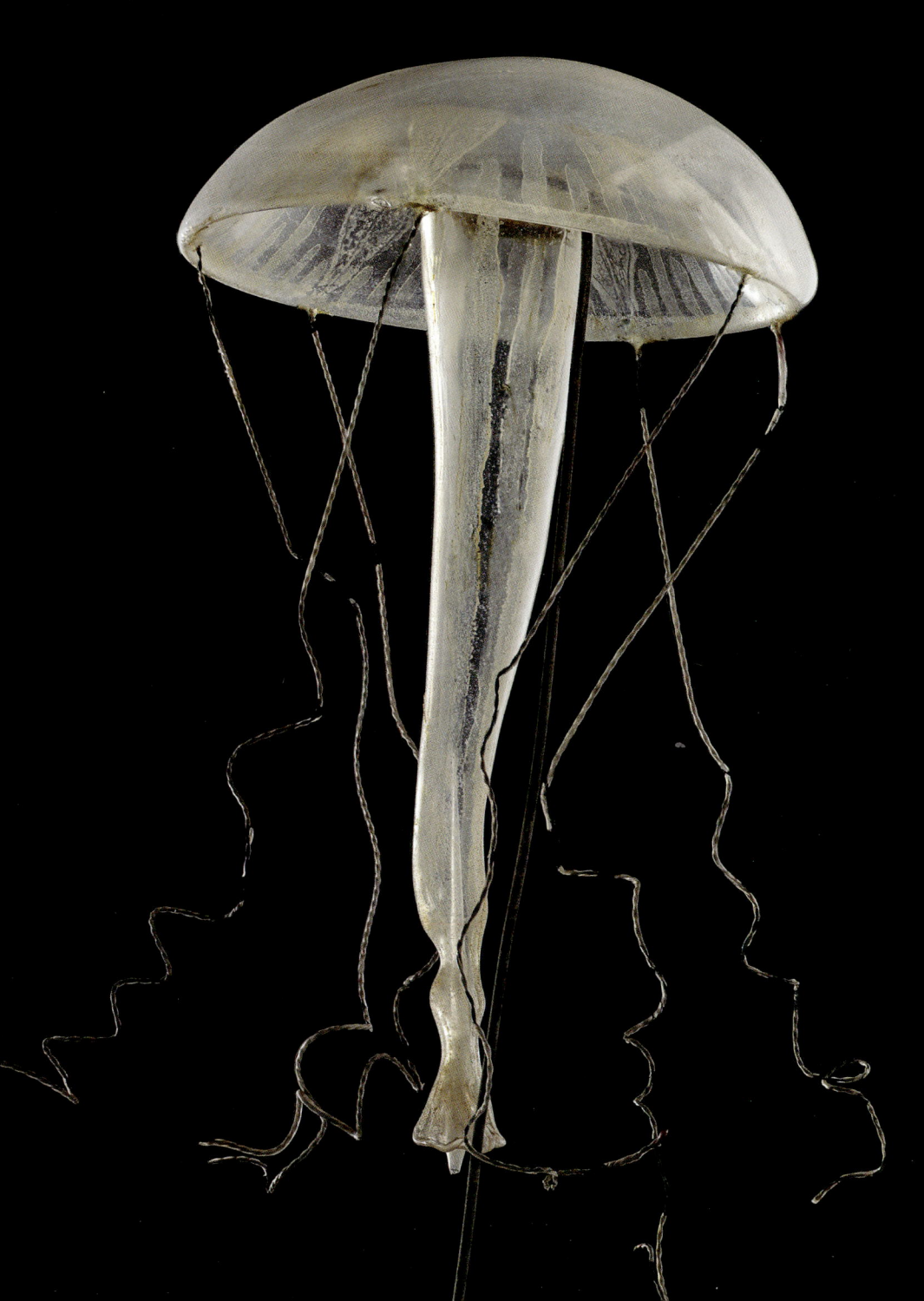

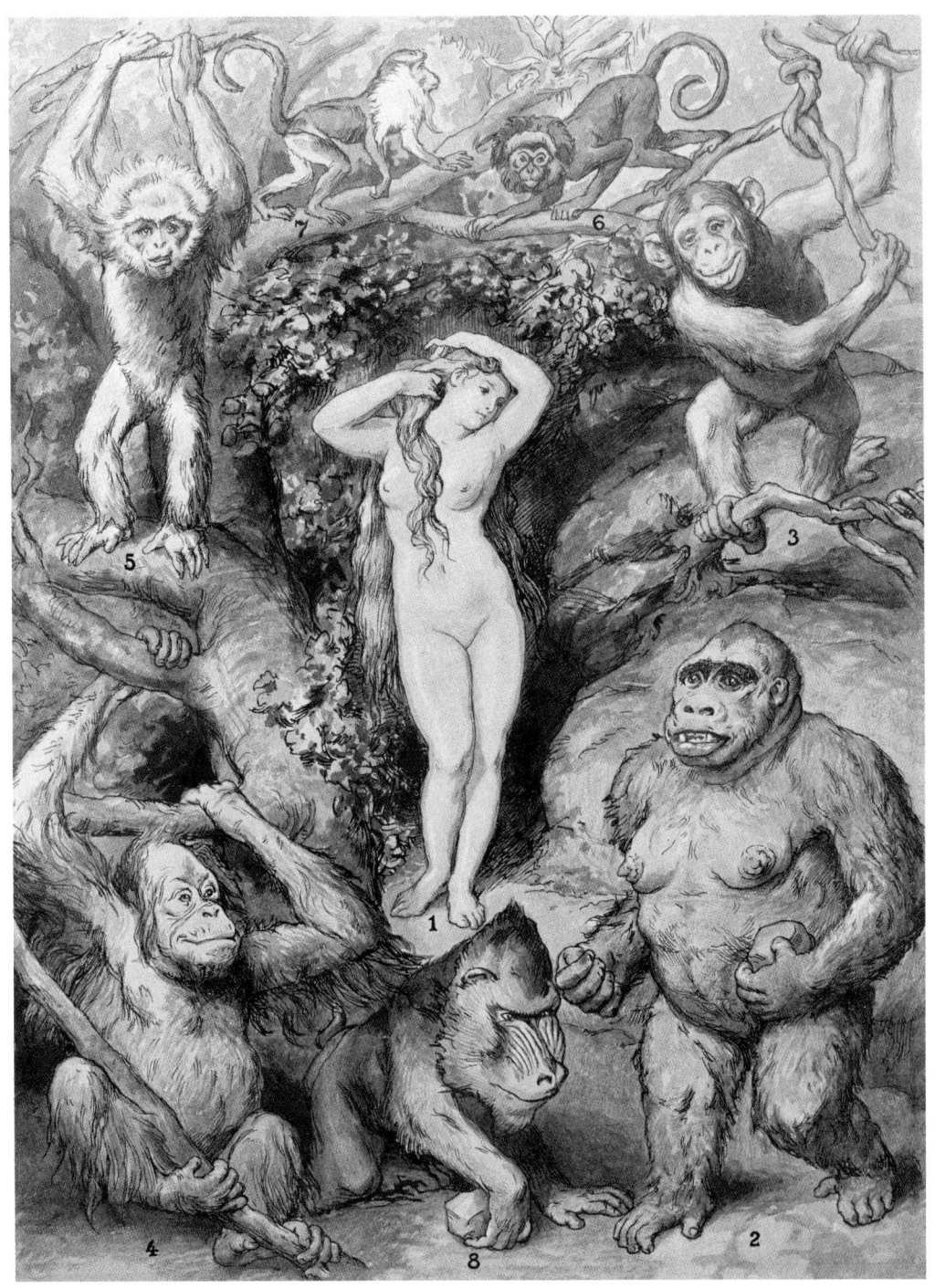

Now, four years later, his religiously reformed reverence for nature had acquired its own "cathedral." For the new museum in Jena was little short of a Basilica of Saint Peter for the Theory of Evolution.

How are we to account for the truly fabulous success enjoyed by Ernst Haeckel within his own lifetime? And for the success of his images which continued to exert their fascination long after his death? In any consideration of the great Western tradition of interaction between science and art, it would be hard to find another scientist whose work had such an impact on areas beyond his own. There have, of course, been physicists, engineers, chemists, physicians, and biologists whose achievements have had a profound influence upon the destiny of humanity – be it through the discovery of penicillin or the invention of the steam engine. The same could not be claimed for Haeckel. And, by comparison with the great minds of the Renaissance such as Leonardo da Vinci (1452–1519), who excelled equally in the realms of technology and art, it is at once apparent that Haeckel's contribution cannot but seem slighter and his influence more superficial. But what other scientist could justifiably claim that his work had an impact on the style of an era, the aesthetic of an age? Not only were Haeckel's images taken seriously by his scientific colleagues, but the deep-sea creatures he drew clambered out from the pages of his *Kunstformen der Natur* (*Art Forms in Nature*, 1899–1904) and into the cities of Europe, their squares and façades onto stage curtains, and into paintings. Artists, architects, designers, and creators of haute couture active around 1900 drew inspiration from Haeckel; and several generations of their successors have continued to do so since. Most of Haeckel's illustrations, or indeed of any era, bear an effective "expiry date," not least in the realm of the natural sciences, where technological innovation relentlessly spurs on image production. But Haeckel's images are still very much with us. Some have, until recently, been used as illustrations in biology textbooks, for example, the fifth edition of Scott Gilbert's *Developmental Biology*, a standard reference book.[3] Haeckel's 1899 volume *Die Welträthsel* (*The Riddle of the Universe*), an exercise in disseminating and popularising scientific knowledge, sold more than 400,000 copies before the First World War[4] and has been translated into about 30 languages. His publications eventually appearing in larger editions in the English-speaking world than in Germany. It has long seemed that no country can withstand the "invasion" of Haeckel's images. And, with the advent of the Internet, this process has greatly accelerated. In our own day they have indeed "gone viral."

Ernst Haeckel and Gabriel von Max
Apotheosis of Evolutionary Thought
First sketch for *Kunstformen der Natur*, plate 100
Published in: *Wanderbilder*, supplementary vol. 1, 1906

A century after Ernst Haeckel's death it is therefore well worth enquiring into the secret of such extraordinary success. In tracing the rise of this Potsdam-born son of a government official to the rank of one of the most outstanding German representatives of the Theory of Evolution and, simultaneously, one of the world's most frequently quoted and copied scientists, we would do well to focus, in turn, on each of his four most celebrated images. The precise total number of images Haeckel produced over the course of his long career would be difficult to ascertain. Some have nonetheless attained iconic status and on account of their sheer recognisability, their emergence and development is easier to follow. Their influence on the visual arts, the applied arts, and architecture will be reflected here through the consideration of specific examples.

The Enigmatic Beauty of Jellyfish

It is to Ernst Haeckel that we owe both the most beautiful and the ugliest views of the Theory of Evolution. Both will concern us here. For the celebrated image of *Desmonema annasethe* (ills. pp. 32, 270, 335) takes us directly to the two hearts that beat in Haeckel's breast from the moment when, as described by his biographer Robert J. Richards, he felt himself splitting in half. Richards specifies the date of 16 February 1864 that became a "radical religious and philosophical turning point in [Haeckel's] life."[5] This was the date on which Haeckel celebrated his 30th birthday and on which he received a medal awarded by the highly regarded German scientific academy, the Leopoldina. But it was also on this date that he lost the love of his life. Anna Sethe (1835–1864), his cousin and first wife, died (in all probability as the result of a ruptured appendix) only 18 months after the couple's wedding. The widowed Haeckel fled to Nice, on the Côte d'Azur. He took long walks on the shore of the Mediterranean in an effort to regain his composure and to find consolation. From Nice he wrote to his parents: "The last eight days have been passed painfully. The Mediterranean, which I so love, has effected at least a part of the healing for which I hoped. I have become much quieter and begin to find myself in an unchanging pain, though I don't know how I shall bear it in the long run."[6]

On one of Haeckel's walks he came upon a jellyfish lying in a pool left behind by the ebbing tide. Its delicate yellow tentacles reminded him of the blond hair of his

Rhopilema Frida
Drawing for *Kunstformen der Natur*, 1899, plate 88, fig. 4
20.9 x 25.9 cm (8 1/4 x 10 1/4 in.)
Jena, Ernst-Haeckel-Haus

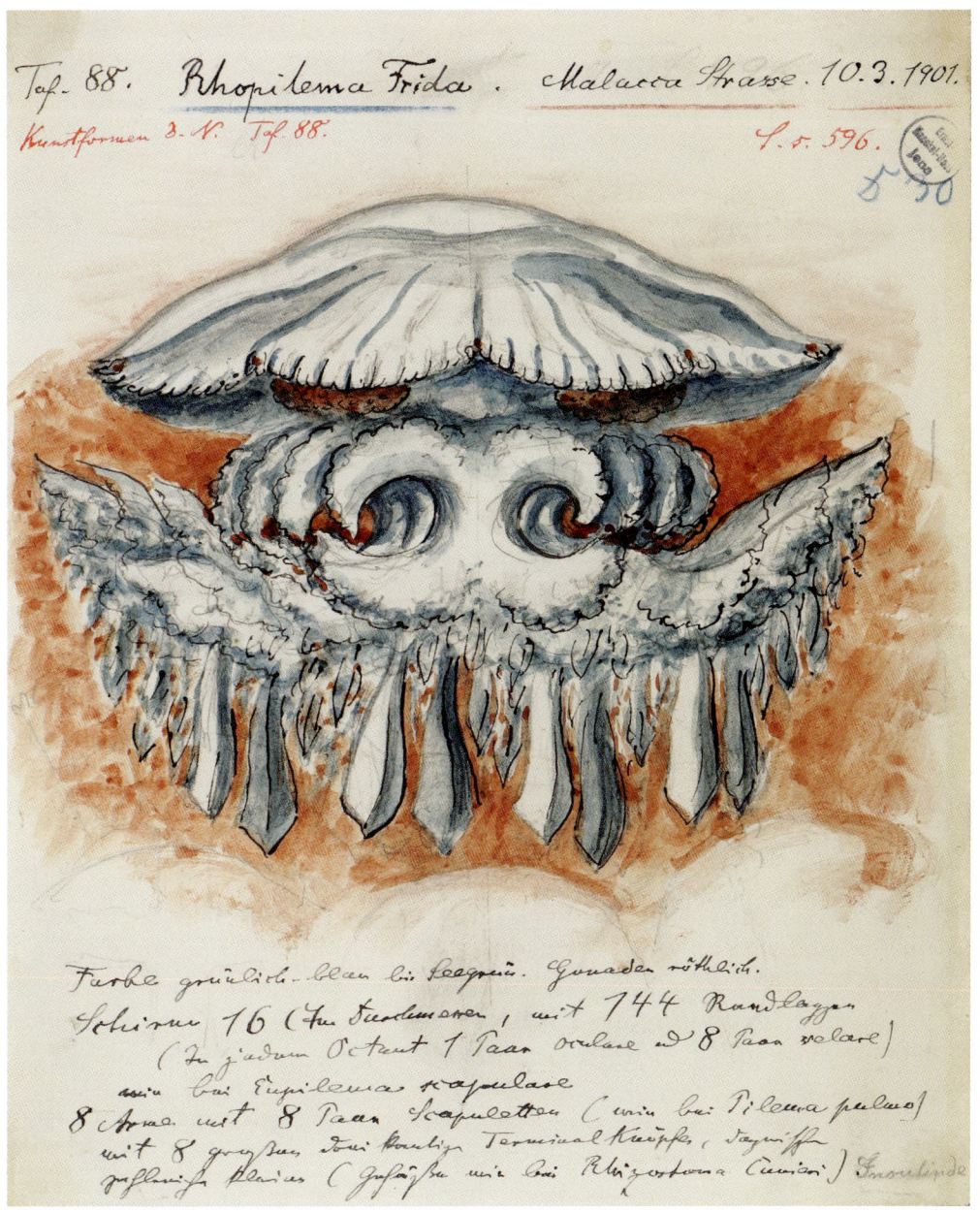

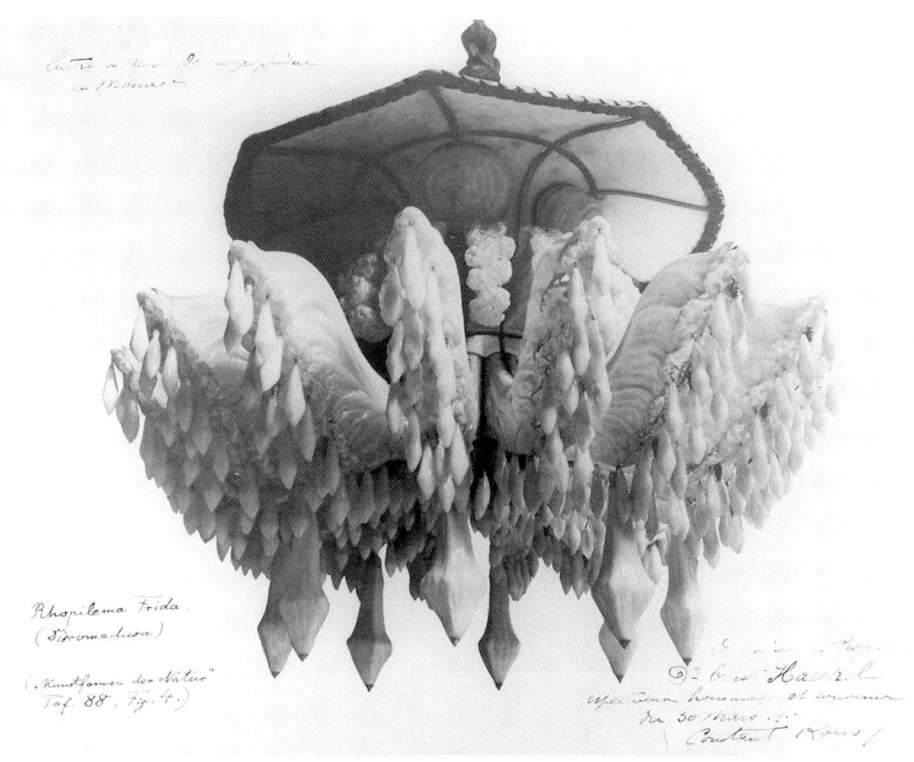

Constant Roux
**Lamp in the form of a medusa for the Oceonographic Museum of Monaco,
modelled after Haeckel's image *Rhopilema Frida***
Photograph with Haeckel's autograph annotations
Jena, Ernst-Haeckel-Haus

beloved Anna Sethe, and he accordingly named this sea creature *Mitrocoma annae* after his deceased wife. Later, on receiving a jellyfish from a colleague that seemed to him even more beautiful, he named this specimen *Desmonema annasethe*. In 1879, he illustrated it for the first time in his monograph *Das System der Medusen* (System of the Medusae; plate 30, p. 270). It was only in 1899, however, and in the aforementioned *Art Forms in Nature*, that *Desmonema annasethe* became a "star player" (plate 8, p. 335). This work originally appeared as a serial publication, in ten instalments (the last published in 1904), each costing only three German imperial marks – a modest price that in itself ensured good sales. In the very first instalment was to be found a plate illustrating three Discomedusae. Haeckel here depicted the appealingly "frilly" *Desmonema annasethe* in blue and gold, its cap resembling a gigantic tropical flower, and its tentacles wafting to and fro across the entire sheet like long strands of hair. By comparison with the overpowering splendour of this rendering, the two other Medusae illustrated in the same plate seemed like ladies-in-waiting attendant upon a princess. The relative scale of these marine creatures, as depicted here, did not, in fact, correspond to reality. Had one discovered them in the depths of the sea, one would note that *Chrysaora mediterranea*, here illustrated at the lower right, was by some measure the largest of the three, while *Floscula prometha*, here shown at the upper left, was a great deal smaller. For Haeckel, however, it was crucial that each creature occupy its allotted place within a symbolic arrangement. His own commentary on *Desmonema annasethe* as shown on this sheet reads: "The species name of this splendid Discomedusa – one of the most beautiful and interesting of all – is intended to honour the memory of Anna Sethe [1835–1864], the highly gifted and sensitive wife, to whom the author of this book of plates owes the happiest years of his life."[7]

By the time *Art Forms in Nature* appeared, Haeckel had, in fact, been married for more than 30 years to his second wife. How unhappy this marriage must have been for her is revealed by these lines.

When Haeckel published *Art Forms in Nature* he was well aware that he was transgressing the nominal boundary between science and art. The success enjoyed by the sciences during the 19th century was owed, above all, to specialisation, to a narrowing of the horizon of enquiry. Haeckel's scientific colleagues published their own findings entirely for the attention of other specialists; and it would not have occurred to most of them to seek to engage the interest of society at large. Haeckel, by contrast, saw in biology a subject that might pioneer the encouragement of a much broader interest in scientific progress while also serving as an overarching context for all other forms of knowledge – philosophical as well as aesthetic. As he observed in his preface: "[...] the visual arts of our own day, as also the now powerfully emerging applied arts, will find a wealth of new and beautiful motifs in these true art forms of nature [...]."[8]

Haeckel was, indeed, to be proven right. In 1910, when the Institut océanographique, founded four years earlier by Prince Albert I of Monaco (1848–1922), opened its own museum, its ceiling featured lamps in the form of Medusae (ill. p. 50). The caps and both the shorter and longer tentacles were here recreated in blown glass. The design was supplied by the French sculptor Constant Roux (1865–1942), who had painstakingly transformed Haeckel's illustrations, noting even to which plate of *Art Forms in Nature* he had referred (ill. p. 458).[9]

The Dutch architect Hendrik Petrus Berlage (1856–1934) similarly drew on Haeckel's treasury of images when he was commissioned to design a new stock exchange for Amsterdam, which opened in 1903. Illuminating its interior was Haeckel's medusa *Rhopilema frida*, recreated in hammered brass and several dozen light bulbs (ills. pp. 49, 53). Berlage had, in fact, used the same image as his model had inspired Roux. The name bestowed by Haeckel in this case recalled a young woman by the name of Frida von Uslar-Gleichen (1864–1903), with whom he had initially entered upon a correspondence in 1898 (ill. p. 40). On their very first meeting he had fallen in love with her, despite the 30-year difference between their respective ages. Like Anna Sethe before her, however, Frida von Uslar-Gleichen died all too young. In December 1903, as her sister was to inform Haeckel, she had overdosed on morphine.

Haeckel's work left its mark not only on the applied arts, but also on painting. We know of many artists active around 1900 who were familiar with Haeckel's books.[10] Not only were they were attracted chiefly by the sheer diversity of forms he had revealed, but also by the distinctive "mood" conveyed by these animal and plant forms. The sort of black background that Haeckel masterfully used to set off a great many of the motifs in his *Art Forms in Nature* recurs, for example, in a gouache of 1906 by Alfred Kubin (1877–1959), *The Deep Sea* (Munich, Städtische Galerie im Lenbachhaus). Here Kubin's medusa, transparent and ghostlike as it wafts along close to the ocean floor, heightens the impression of the uncanny that is already implicit in the restrained beauty of Haeckel's own majestic deep-sea creatures.[11] And no artist was more responsive than Gustav Klimt (1862–1918) to the seemingly erotic allure of Haeckel's literally inhuman underwater world. Just as Haeckel had the tentacles of his Medusae (named after the women he had loved) waft to and fro like hair, so too did Klimt give his own water nymphs hair that resembled tentacles – as in the painting of 1901/02 *Goldfish* (Kunstmuseum Solothurn, Dübi-Müller-Stiftung). The art historian Ursula Harter has observed that many of Klimt's images resemble underwater landscapes (ill. p. 54) and may, on this account, be seen as allegories of evolutionary change: "Gustav Klimt's pictures are infused by a sense of life in perpetual flux."[12] The flux of life – its evolution from primeval sea creatures to mammals roaming the land – was also implicit in Haeckel's *Art Forms in Nature*. The first lithographic plate in the series shows Radiolaria (monocellular marine organisms with an often spiky external skeleton) and the last depicts antelopes, one of the mammals (ill. p. 481). Haeckel originally planned to close the cycle

Hendrik Petrus Berlage
Chandelier at the Stock Exchange in Amsterdam modelled after
Haeckel's image of *Rhopilema Frida*, before 1904
Watercolour and pencil, 34.9 x 24.7 cm (13 3/4 x 9 3/4 in.), Rotterdam, Het Nieuwe Institut

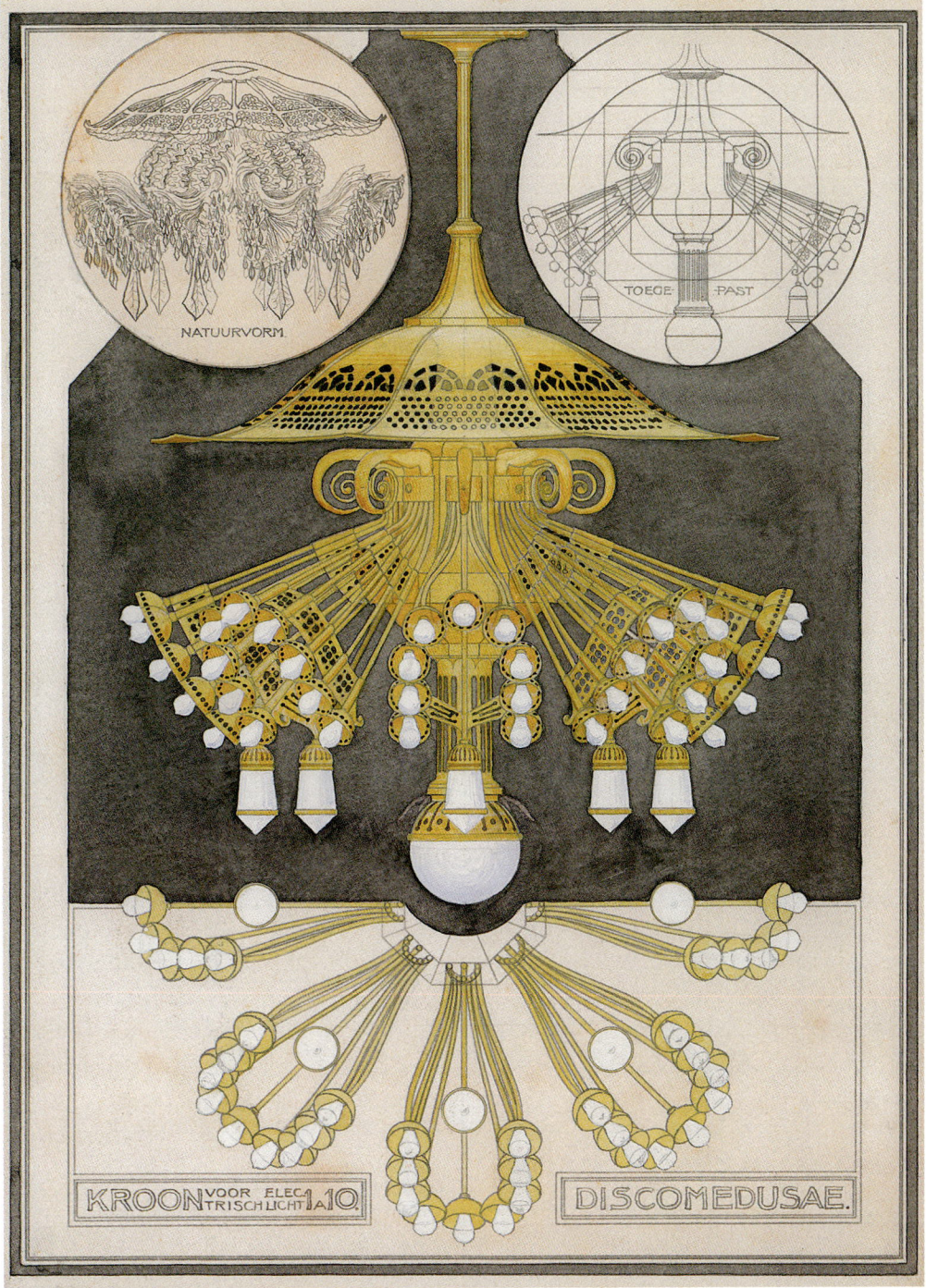

NATUURVORM

TOEGE PAST

KROON voor elec. 1.10 trisch licht 1a. DISCOMEDUSAE.

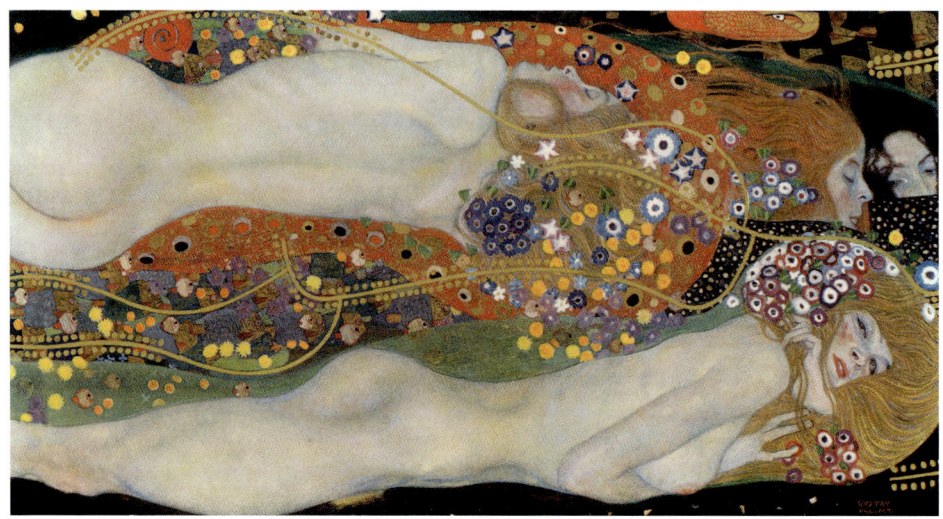

Gustav Klimt
Water Serpents II, 1904 (reworked 1906/07)
Oil on canvas, 57 x 181 cm (22 $^1/_2$ x 71 $^1/_4$ in.)
Private collection

with illustrations of apes and of human beings – a plan eventually left unrealised on account of the objections of the publisher (ill. p. 46).

The glass models made near Dresden by the workshop of the Blaschkas – Leopold (1822–1859) and his son, Rudolf (1857–1939; ill. p. 45) – are still regarded as masterpieces of both art and science. Father and son were in regular communication with Haeckel, who was always ready to advise them on scientific matters.[13] The Blaschkas specialised in recording animals and plants that were difficult to conserve, and which thus rapidly began to decay, for example, mushrooms, sea anemones, and, indeed, jellyfish. In order that such entities might nonetheless be represented in natural history collections, the Blaschkas created breathtakingly precise recreations in their glass-blowing workshop, for which Haeckel's images served as points of reference. Museums of natural history the world over acquired these precious objects; and the largest collection of Blaschka models is now to be found at Harvard University. The quality of the glass models still strikes us as remarkable, even after the passage of more than a century. The Blaschkas' art, informed in turn by Haeckel's expertise, later served as a model for the Danish artist Tue Greenfort (b. 1973) when, in 2007, he made his own glass *Medusa*.

Haeckel, whose own creative energies were not confined to what might be found within the pages of a book, was reluctant to leave the three-dimensional realisation of his images to artists, designers, and architects. He called the house in which he lived in Jena (built in 1892) the "Villa Medusa" after its ceilings, which were decorated to his own design, with motifs reminiscent of jellyfish. While we can hardly be surprised to find that artists such as Henri Matisse (1869–1954) or Sonia Delaunay (1885–1979) invested time and effort in designing the environments in which they lived, among scientists this is rather rare, Haeckel being one of a few exceptions. The fact that the strange beauty of the jellyfish should find its way into Haeckel's domestic surroundings would seem to reflect the way in which these creatures first entered his life. With *Desmonema annasethe* and *Rhopilema frida*, Haeckel created moving images of two women by whom he had been most deeply moved. The sad secret of these images assured them of a particular radiance.

The Magic of Radiolaria

The appeal of Radiolaria is quite different from that of Medusae. While Haeckel's jellyfish are soft and rotund, the radiating forms are angular and sharp. While the former float, seeming to move about autonomously, the latter strike us as static and immobile. From the art-historical point of view, the jellyfish resemble a form that might have originated in the French Rococo. By contrast, the single-cell Radiolaria, whose skeletons have lain for millions of years on the seabed, have always reminded observers of Oriental or Asiatic architectural forms. In reality they are so small as to be undetectable with the unaided human eye. It was only with the application of modern microscopic technology during the 19th century that they came to the attention of scientists (ill. p. 12).

Haeckel, in fact, embarked on his career with research into Radiolaria. In 1862, he published his first book: a monograph entitled *Die Radiolarien*. It was on the strength of this publication that he was appointed, at the age of only 28, to a professorship at the University of Jena. His talent for drawing had been remarked upon by every one of his teachers. It received particular praise from Rudolf Virchow (1821–1902), who had taught Haeckel when he was a student in Würzburg, and who had recognised the young man's gift for recording at astounding speed precisely what he had seen.[14] Another teacher had noted his own surprise on discovering that Haeckel was able to look through a microscope with his left eye while simultaneously attending to the drawing in progress with his right.[15] Haeckel had, in fact, been an autodidact as far as drawing was concerned, having spent two years in his youth colouring in engraved illustrations in the volumes of Eduard Pöppig's (1798–1868) *Illustrirte Naturgeschichte des Thierreichs* (Natural History of the Animal Kingdom). And, in 1850, taking his cue from the first convocation of a German National Assembly at the Paulskirche in Frankfurt am Main in 1848, he gathered images of birds into a "National Collection" of his own, in which each bird family was represented by a "delegate" (ill. p. 57). Haeckel had also been inspired by the approach to nature evinced by the aforementioned Goethe and by Alexander von Humboldt (1769–1859), both of whom upheld a view informed by the totality of experience against the emerging cult of ever more specialised "dissection" derived from experiments in the laboratory. On the numerous journeys and research trips that Haeckel conducted to more than 30 locations across the globe, he always took with him not only pencils and a sketchbook, but also canvas and oil paints. The landscape paintings he produced during his expeditions to Sumatra, Java, and Ceylon (now Sri Lanka) were published in 1905/06 as *Wanderbilder* (A Traveller's Pictures). In Haeckel's manner of arranging animal and plant forms across the page of a book, we can also detect an echo of the tradition of the "ornamental prints" of the Renaissance and the Baroque.[16] But the evidence of such historical antecedents does not alter the fact that Haeckel's capacities as a draughtsman were little short of miraculous. As is almost always the case with great artistic skill, we shall probably never know precisely how Haeckel arrived at such perfection. What we do know is that he had always been interested in painting and that he had a number of friends who were artists. While travelling in Russia in 1897 he visited the collection amassed by Pavel Tretyakov (the future Tretyakov Gallery), first opened to the public four years earlier, enthusing that it offered "1,500 pictures in 22 rooms!" Haeckel stayed to admire the display until the doors were closed for the night, and regretted "not being able to go on revelling in this treasure house of painting."[17] Haeckel did not, however, return the affection for his own "aesthetics of nature" that was avowed by artists of a progressive character. His own artistic taste was for both history painters and landscapists working in a more conservative manner: Ilya Repin (1844–1930), Gabriel von Max (1840–1915), and Otto Knille (1832–1898). The landscapes that Haeckel himself painted were on the whole lacking in the originality that characterises almost every image he prepared for his books.

As we have noted, it was with Radiolaria, which had stood at the start of his scientific career, that Haeckel, in 1899, opened his *Art Forms in Nature*. Only a year later the French architect René Binet (1866–1911) erected a mighty monument to Haeckel in the form of the *Porte Monumentale* (ill. p. 60) which stood on the Place de la Concorde in Paris, where it served as the chief entrance to a prominent section of

Parliament of Birds, 1850
Watercolour, 124 x 64 cm (48 3/4 x 25 1/4 in.)
Jena, Ernst-Haeckel-Haus

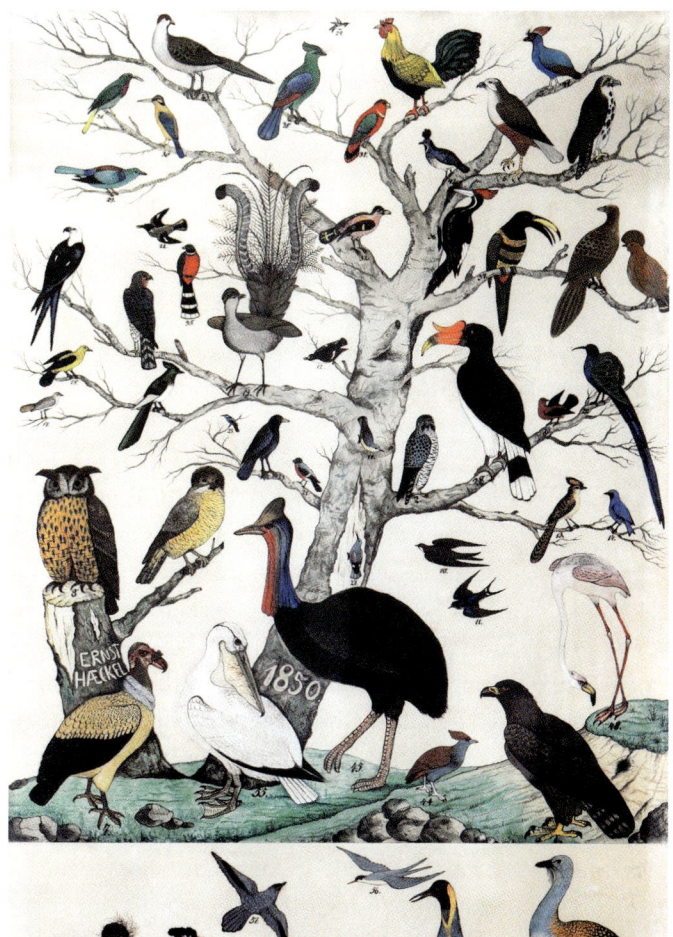

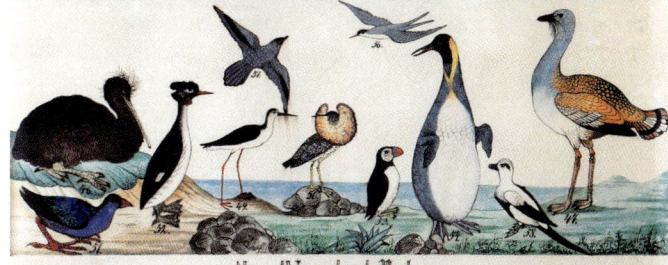

the *Exposition Universelle.* Like Haeckel, who in his own work made use of the latest microscopes produced by the Jena firm of Carl Zeiss, Binet too looked to the cutting edge of technological advances in his own designs. His *Porte Monumentale* was studded from top to bottom with light bulbs and was, in addition, illuminated with light beams of continuously alternating colour, ruby red ceding by way of violet, then blue, to emerald green.[18] The magic of the deep ocean merged here with that of One Thousand and One Nights. By means of this gigantically enlarged representative of the Radiolaria, visitors to the exhibition were symbolically transported back to the beginnings of the history of evolution. Entering through this gate, which alluded to the primeval life forms from which humanity had at length emerged, those alive at the dawn of the 20th century were able to revisit their species' origins in the depths of the ocean. A further context for Binet's design was, however, not recognised by either the architect himself or by visitors to the exhibition. For Binet had taken as the particular model for his gate the *Clathrocanium reginae* from the second part of the monograph on Radiolaria (plate 35, fig. 4; cf. p. 365). Its form recalled the spiked helmet *(Pickelhaube)* worn by Prussian officers, headgear that the German imperial chancellor Otto von Bismarck (1815–1898) himself favoured in his public appearances and in which he is, indeed, recorded in the celebrated 1890 portrait by the Munich artist Franz von Lenbach (1836–1904). Although only evident to those sufficiently well informed, thanks to Binet it was a Prussian Pickelhaube that served as the implicit "crown of creation" throughout the entire duration of the *Exposition Universelle* of 1900.

It was always Haeckel's intention that his images should capture the public imagination in more ways than one. The seductive variety of nature which so entranced artists and architects, but also a broad general public, was only one aspect of its fascination. The other reflected Haeckel's own commitment to a view of nature and of man's place in it that was as sombre as it was misanthropic. Haeckel held his followers' delight in check by offsetting promises of Heaven with the menace of Hell. While inviting his readers into the magic forest of the "art forms," he praised the Spartans of Antiquity for their practice of killing at birth any infants that seemed weak or ill-formed, explaining that "might is right" was a law of nature. In this rhetoric of the superman the history of living beings became an effective gladiatorial arena in which, from the Cambrian (the earliest phase of geological time), by way of the Stone Age, right up to the present day, human beings, animals, and plant forms were engaged in a struggle to bring forth versions of themselves ever better fitted for survival. While the task of the scientist consisted, in reality, in recording and describing the conditions that cause one species to decline and another to flourish – the reasons lying mostly in important changes in the environment and not in the struggle of one species against another – Haeckel seemed to regard war as merely the continuation of biology by other means. When Haeckel writes in this vein, the natural scientist, the observer alert to every detail, and the draughtsman of genius disappear entirely into the background, only to be replaced by an ideologue who resembles a cold-blooded military commander ordering his troops into battle. As early as 1878, Haeckel had written (the emphases are his own): "The cruel and merciless '*struggle for existence*' that rages, as it *must*, throughout the natural world, this unrelenting and inexorable *competition* of everything that is alive, is an undeniable fact [...] One can deeply deplore this tragic *fact*, but one can neither dismiss it nor alter it. The many are called but only the few are chosen!"[19] Statements of this sort were to recur,

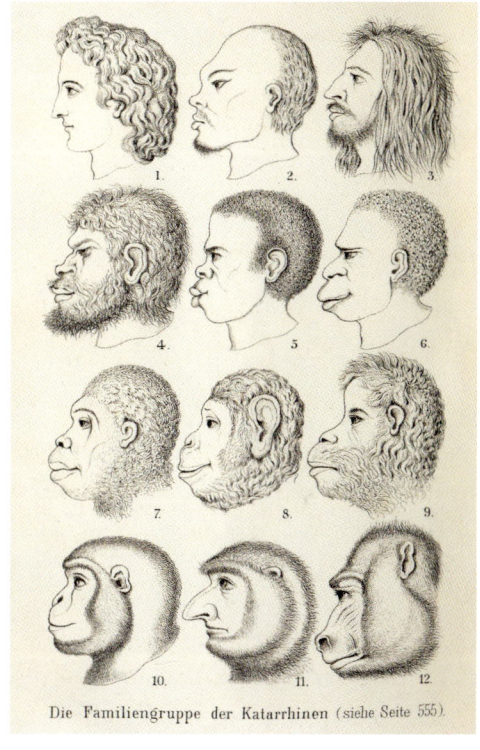

Die Familiengruppe der Katarrhinen (siehe Seite 555).

barely altered, only half a century later in the biology textbooks introduced by the National Socialists into the school curriculum throughout Germany.[20]

Consumed by a ferocious universal loathing, Haeckel gradually gave way to the darkest nihilism, as if determined that the entire natural world should be made to do penance for the void that Anna Sethe's death had left in his life. It was almost in an access of fury that he insisted on the desolation, the meaninglessness, the violence, and the sheer waste and decay to be found in nature. As early as 1868, his lordly disdain for the greater part of humanity had prompted him to open the first edition of his substantial work *Natürliche Schöpfungsgeschichte* (*The History of Creation*) with a plate showing a dozen heads in profile: a set of six belonging to human beings and below this a further set of six belonging to apes (ill. p. 59). The first group was "led" by a representative of what, according to Haeckel, was the highest of the races of humankind:

Species of Catarrhini ("higher" primates):
Heads of six humans and six species of monkeys and apes, 1868
In: *Natürliche Schöpfungsgeschichte*, 1868, frontispiece

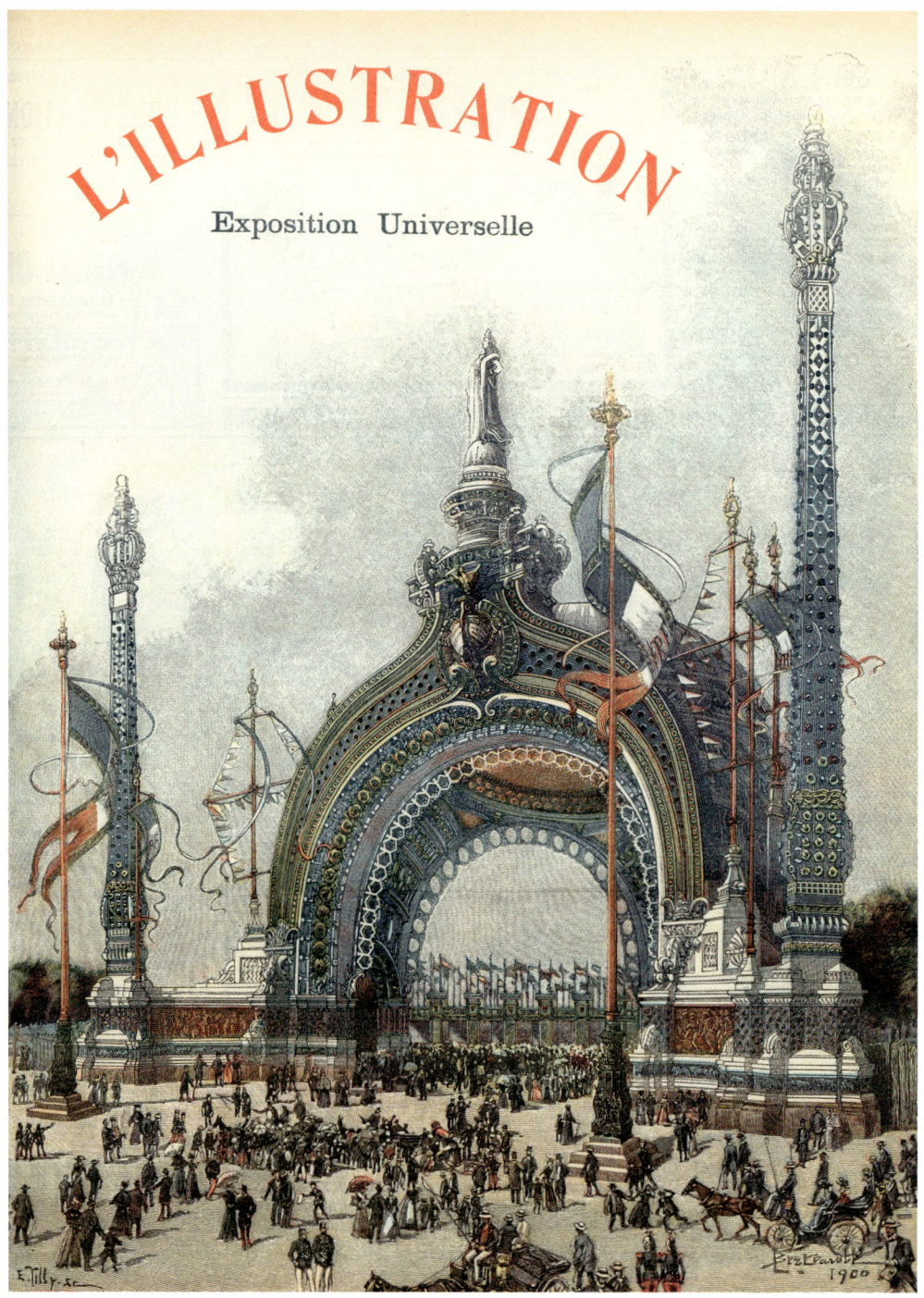

the so-called Indo-Germanic, to which, unsurprisingly, he himself belonged. At the other extreme was positioned what was in Haeckel's view the lowliest of the apes: the baboon. The heads mediating between these two extremes were intended to illustrate a hierarchical regression from the highest type of humanity to the lowest form of ape. "It is clear," observed Haeckel in his commentary on this plate, "that the lowliest forms of humanity (figs. 4, 5, 6) resemble the superior apes (figs. 7, 8, 9) far more closely than they resemble the higher forms of humanity."[21] In Haeckel's opinion, the aboriginal inhabitants of Australia were the closest of all human beings to the apes. By this means Haeckel sought to dress up age-old racist notions in clothing borrowed from the Theory of Evolution. When voices were raised against this particular plate, it was replaced by another. In subsequent editions – by the time of Haeckel's death in 1919 this publication was already in its twelfth – readers on opening the volume would encounter a mysterious, shimmering blue undersea world.[22] It would be hard to envisage a clearer demonstration of the two poles of Haeckel's Theory of Evolution.

The Embryo and the Origins of Life

The astonishing story of Haeckel's celebrated depictions of embryos has been investigated by Nick Hopwood, a historian of science at the University of Cambridge. During the course of his research Hopwood came upon an illuminating contradiction: that it was precisely the severe criticism that these images had provoked that ensured their enduring popularity. The process got underway in 1868 when Haeckel was accused for the first time of having inaccurately rendered the stages of development of mammals, birds, fish, or reptiles in his aforementioned *History of Creation*.[23] As the years passed, criticism of this sort grew louder, until Haeckel was being accused of "deceit" and "forgery" (Arnold Brasz, 1908). More than a century later, creationists in the United States sought to reignite the dispute, in this case so as to bring into disrepute the Theory of Evolution (which they themselves rejected out of hand). The creationists believe that the Bible provides the best explanation as to how life arose and has evolved. In taking issue with Haeckel, however, they, in fact, achieved the opposite of their intended aim. In order to attack Haeckel's images they needed to show them and to ensure that they were sufficiently, widely circulated. According to Hopwood: "In an irony of iconoclasm, Haeckel's figures were never more available, thanks to creationists and the Internet, than when most rejected as fakes."[24] For 150

René Binet
Porte Monumentale at the *Exposition Universelle* in Paris, 1900
In: *L'Illustration*, April 1904, cover

years, in hundreds, perhaps even thousands of articles and books, arguments both for and against Haeckel's embryos have been advanced. Yet each new publication only seems, be it intentionally or otherwise, to increase the familiarity of his illustrations. There is now general agreement among scholars that Haeckel devised a schematic simplification of the developmental stages of various creatures to emphasise the similarities that were important to his own theory. But in doing so, he had not set out to deceive; and for this reason, numerous scholars have at every stage stepped forward to speak in his defence.

Haeckel intended that his illustrations should allow the viewer to observe evolution in a chronologically compressed form – a form later to be associated with time-lapse photography. According to Haeckel, embryos reiterated in their own development, be it in the egg or in the mother's womb, those stages through which the species to which they belonged had already passed in the overall course of evolution: a process that Haeckel encapsulated in the formula "ontogeny recapitulates phylogeny." Haeckel saw in such regularity a fundamental "biogenetic law" (*biogenetisches Grundgesetz*). He was surely not intending to provoke scandal – but neither was he especially inclined to make peace with his enemies.

The scandals that nonetheless repeatedly attached themselves to Haeckel's illustrations certainly do not detract from his retrospective interest for us. It would, moreover, seem that the success he achieved with his work was to some extent the outcome of mechanisms not at all unlike those underpinning the rise of modern art. In both cases, agitation of some kind plays a key role in the story. Like a centrifugal force, this propels an art, initially valued by a select circle, out into the wider society. What would have become of the first Paris exhibition staged by those painters who were later to be termed "Impressionists" if, in 1874, their work had not provoked such heated discussion? What, in 1911, would the Blaue Reiter group have become had it not been for the contempt and ridicule voiced by representatives of the established German art world. What would have been the fate of Gustave Courbet (1819–1877) or of Édouard Manet (1832–1883)? In the case of the Norwegian artist Edvard Munch (1863–1944) it was, incidentally, the adoption of motifs derived from scientific illustrations – in particular that of an embryo – that, in 1894, provoked such a sensation at the artist's exhibition in Stockholm. Among the works shown on that occasion was

Wassily Kandinsky
In Between, 1934
Oil and tempera on canvas, 130 x 97 cm (51 1/4 x 38 1/4 in.)
Hilti Art Foundation, Schaan, Liechtenstein

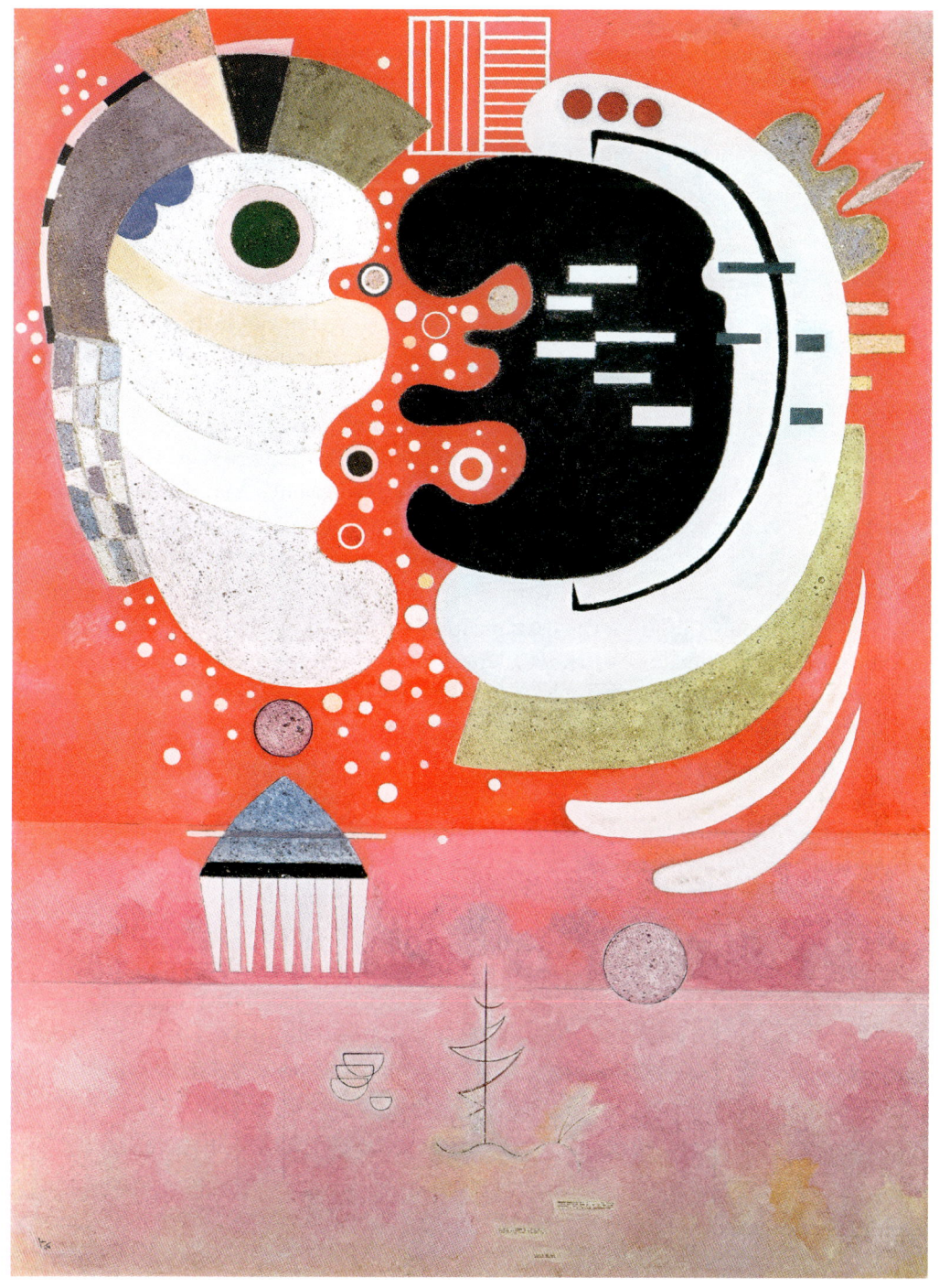

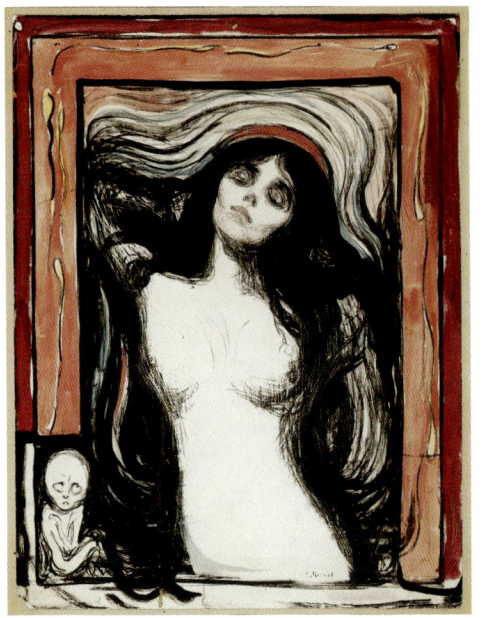

the painting *Madonna*. When first put on display, this is said to have featured borders such as are to be seen in the later lithographic version (ill. p. 64). Munch showed the gleaming white body of his nominal subject surrounded by spermatozoa, these in turn leading the eye to the image of an embryo (or, strictly speaking, a foetus) seemingly immobilised in one of the lower corners. It would appear that, with this painting Munch was affirming the fundamental laws of sexual attraction on a physiological level. The sacred was framed here by the profane, by the forces of nature and the compulsion to reproduce. At the same time, Munch seems to suggest that dying is implicit in every stage of living. His skeletal embryo/foetus recalls the traditional representation of Death as a figure with a scythe: an uncanny and profound parallel that would have delighted Haeckel.

We do not know which image inspired Munch on this occasion. But bearing in mind the depictions of embryos that were widely available in the late 19th century, there is a high likelihood that Munch's work was derived from Haeckel's. This is not because Haeckel was the first to illustrate the evolution of human or animal embryos, but because he was the first to do so not only for other specialists. Haeckel, moreover, supplemented his images with a fascinating narrative, which enabled the reader to travel back to the beginnings of evolution, as if in a time machine. Nor should we underestimate the expressive power of Haeckel's designs in their own right. A number of his human embryos look like babies lying in cradles, while others look painfully cramped and bent as if testifying to some appalling drama. In the German-speaking territories alone, some of these images, incorporated in a number of variants within Haeckel's books, existed in editions of several hundred thousand.[25]

Edvard Munch
Madonna, 1895–1902
Lithograph and woodcut, 60.5 x 44.4 cm (23 3/4 x 17 1/2 in.)
Oslo, Munch-Museet

While Haeckel was convinced that every living thing could only be understood as an outcome of the all-embracing evolutionary process, the Swedish artist Hilma af Klint (1862–1944) was fascinated by the notion that everything might have been quite different. Her own art addresses the futuristic potential for change, and this is especially the case with the abstract pictures that she began to produce in 1906. In *Group IV, No. 9. The Ten Largest, Old Age*, 1907, we observe against a flesh-coloured background a process of genesis that seems to pass through five stages, including growth through cell division and separation, out of which there emerge two figures which appear to turn like huge Ferris Wheels (ill. p. 69).²⁶ More than two decades later Wassily Kandinsky (1866–1944), in a group of works produced just after his move in 1933 from Germany to Paris, also had recourse to Haeckel's embryo images. In a painting of 1934, *In Between* (ill. p. 63), the black-white contrast found in Haeckel's work is reversed.²⁷

The Genealogical Stem Tree and the Evolution of Art

Yet another pictorial invention derived from Ernst Haeckel that was, in more sense than one, to make art history: the diagrammatic tree of evolution (ill. p. 19). Here we are concerned with another sort of image than was the case with the Medusae, the Radiolarian, or the embryos which were eventually to find their way into the fine and applied arts. Haeckel gave his model of evolution the form of an oak; but what he wished to provide was a symbol for ordering information. What we have here then is an image serving as a scientific model. Haeckel was not concerned with illustrating the growth of an oak. Rather, he wished to represent the process of evolution itself: the ramifications and separating of species in the overall history of life. The smaller and larger branches of Haeckel's oak symbolise those subdivisions in the animal kingdom such as class, order, family, genus, and species. Later, Haeckel's model of evolution was transferred from the field of biology to that of art history, serving in both cases to describe a phenomenon these share: alterations in form over the course of time. While the science of biology is concerned with the evolution of species, art history aims at a systematic description of the changes that occur in forms of expression. In terms of the developmental-historical mental model, artists and artistic styles correspond to the species and classes that have, over the centuries, been identified in the natural world. Just as one species may, in due course, give rise to two, and so on, artistic styles may themselves, according to this model, subdivide into distinct tendencies.²⁸

Haeckel could not have possibly guessed that his pictorial invention would find an application even outside the disciplines of the natural sciences. His two-volume work of 1866, in which he had first published his own sketches, initially looked as if it

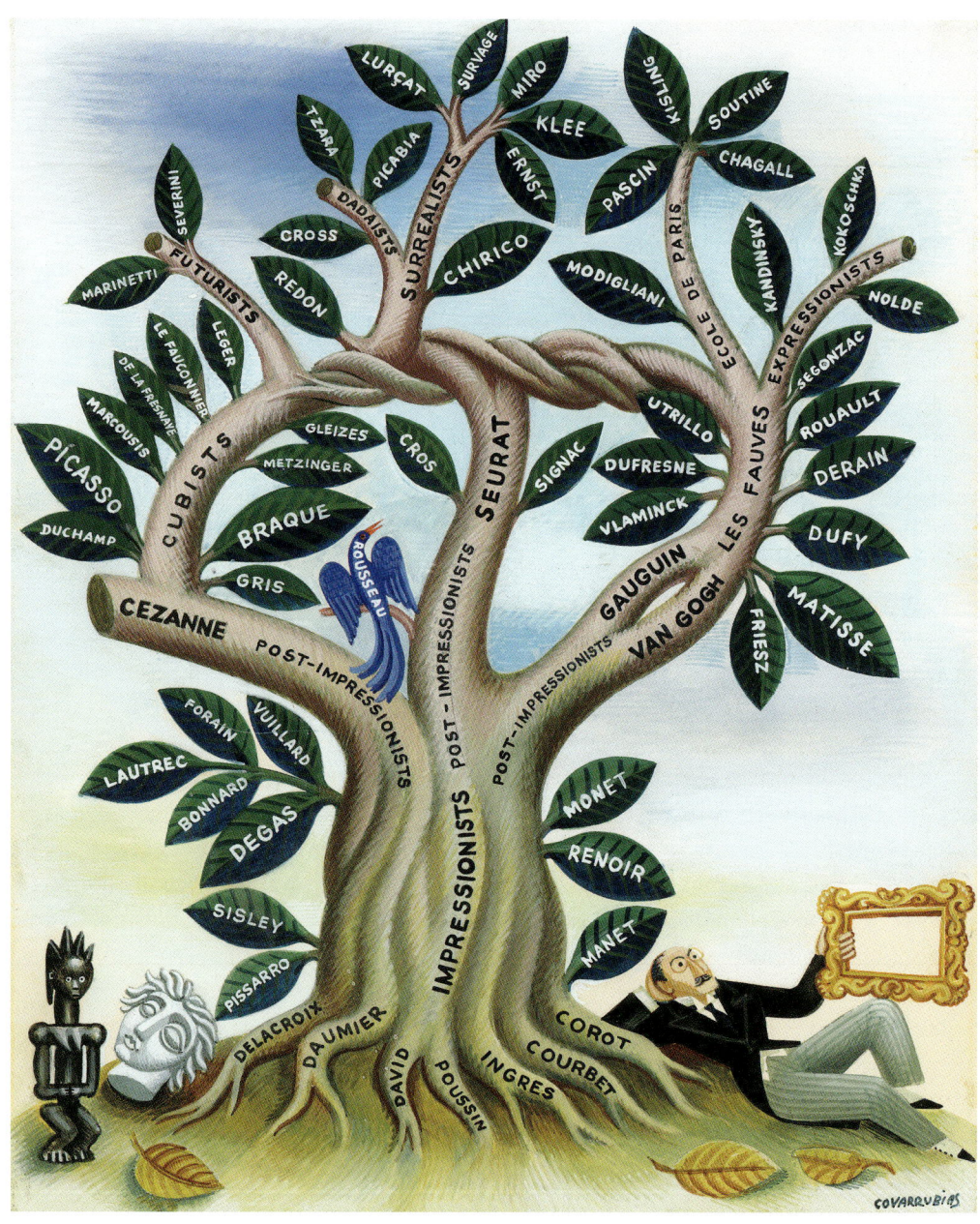

would prove a commercial failure. Two years later, still only a third of the edition of his *Generelle Morphologie der Organismen* (General Morpohology of Organisms) had sold, the sceptical publisher having pragmatically printed only a thousand copies. Yet even though this publication remained a slow seller, it nonetheless brought Haeckel a good deal of praise and recognition from quarters that meant the most to him. Haeckel's pride in having been the first to reconstruct, step by step, the concrete history of animals and plants, was not lost on Charles Darwin (1809–1882). The English scholar had himself not wished to engage in such speculations when, seven years earlier, he had published what would come to be recognised as the founding text of the Theory of Evolution: *On the Origin of Species*. Writing to Haeckel upon receiving a copy of the latter's book, Darwin declared: "My dear Haeckel, / Your boldness sometimes makes me tremble but [...] someone must be bold enough to make a beginning in drawing up tables of descent."[29]

Haeckel dared to go further than Darwin in yet another respect. In 1859, Darwin had expressly treated the human being, indeed the entire evolution of humanity separately from the evolution of other species, not wishing to further enflame debate on the Theory of Evolution. But Haeckel had no such qualms. In his "Stem Tree of the Mammals," he positioned man within the section reserved for anthropomorphic creatures, at the upper right corner of the sheet, side by side with gorillas, and on the same horizontal level as the family of *Felina*, cats (*Generelle Morphologie der Organismen*, Vol. 2, plate 8). Haeckel's first stem tree was, however, rather more of an expansive bush than a tree, with everything at sixes and sevens and a sense of rampant growth in every direction, so that it was only with difficulty, and through resort to a fair amount of compression and compromise that it was possible to contain everything within the confines of the sheet.

Haeckel was to enjoy far greater success when he had finally constrained his original vegetal model into one more resembling a tree and had renarrated human evolution as a history of progress. In the mighty oak that we encounter in his book of 1874, *Anthropogenie oder Entwicklungsgeschichte der Menschen* (Anthropegeny, or the Evolution of Man; ill. p. 19), the human being was no longer a product of chance but now occupied the crown of the oak's foliage. No longer sharing the upper right corner with gorillas and cats, mankind had become both the supreme achievement and the central purpose of evolution. In giving rise to humankind, moreover, evolution had effectively

Miguel Covarrubias
Tree of Modern Art – Planted 60 Years ago, 1933
Gouache, 32.7 x 40.6 cm (12 7/8 x 16 in.), private collection

come to an end. The oak, having attained full growth, with its foliage in full splendour, its massive trunk was now merely housed a stepladder that had served its purpose.

Nearly 80 years later it was to just such a history of progress that Alfred H. Barr (1902–1981), founding director of The Museum of Modern Art (MoMA) in New York looked to when seeking a model through which to encapsulate and communicate the history of art (see the cover of the MoMA exhibition catalogue of 1936, *Cubism and Abstract Art*). The chronological span of millions of years occupied by the history of evolution was now reduced to a mere half century, for Barr's reckoning began in 1890 and ended in 1935. In biological terms there was only one "family" whose genesis Barr was concerned to trace: that of abstract art. The work of the French painter Paul Cézanne (1839–1906) had given rise, in Barr's opinion, to Fauvism and Cubism. Cubism, in its turn, had encouraged the rise of Suprematism and Constructivism. Constructivism had led to the achievements and philosophy of the Bauhaus, and so on. Barr believed that this sequence followed an inner logic, meaning that the emergence of abstraction had been all but inevitable.

Barr had been prompted to devise such a diagram, which he drew himself, for the New York exhibition he organised under the title *Cubism and Abstract Art*. MoMA, founded only seven years earlier, was to become one of the most influential museums in the world. International success was also soon to be achieved by abstraction, and, indeed, by the art-historical model in which Barr had described its own evolution. The "missing link" between Haeckel's own tree of evolution and Barr's later diagram is, incidentally, to be found in the work of Miguel Covarrubias (1904–1957) who, in New York of the 1930s, drew caricatures for a number of American journals (ill. p. 66).[30]

But this was not to be the end of Haeckel's influence within the art world. His own record of calcareous sponges (1872) eventually inspired images devised by the Surrealist Max Ernst (1891–1976). And anyone considering the celebrated 1889 painting *Apes as Art Critics*, in which Gabriel von Max dared to suggest such a comparison, will in due course discover the close connection between Haeckel and this artist.[31] Nor in 2013 did Haeckel seem to be so very far removed from the *55th Venice Biennale*: here, Camille Henrot's (b. 1978) video piece *Grosse Fatigue* (which was awarded a Silver Lion) might equally well have been called *Art Forms in Nature* on account of its celebration of symmetry as a design principle in both nature and art.

Hilma af Klint
Group IV, No. 9. The Ten Largest, Old Age, 1907
Tempera on paper, mounted on canvas, 320 x 238 cm (126 x 93 ¾ in.)
Stockholm, Moderna Museet

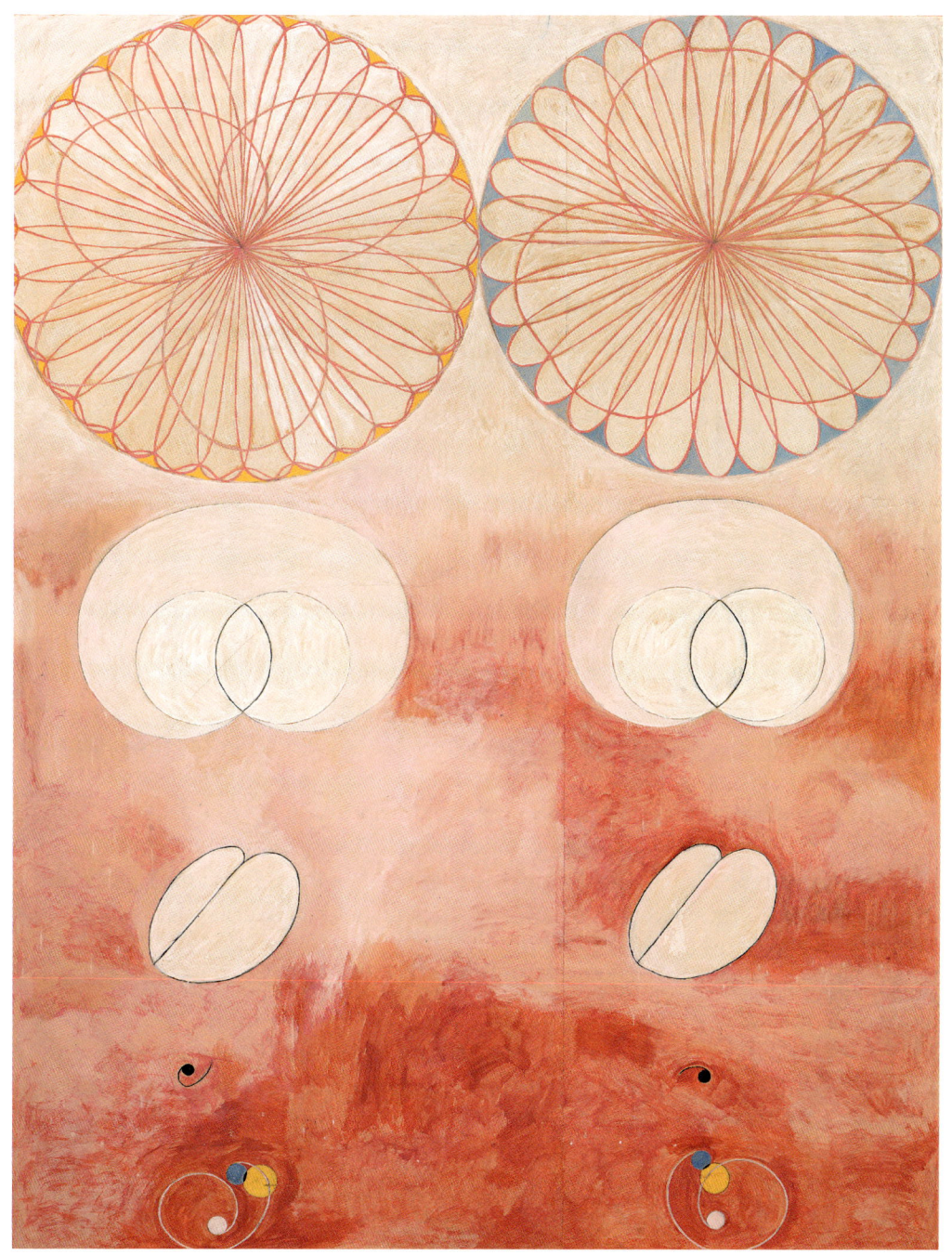

HAECKEL'S VOLUMES OF PLATES

Rainer Willmann, Sophia Willmann,
Julian Leander Willmann

Haeckel's monographs are among the most magnificent scientific publications ever produced; but, for all their high aesthetic quality, it should not be forgotten that they are primarily contributions to the literature of the science of biology, and as such, were addressed to Haeckel's colleagues in this discipline.

The entirety of Haeckel's work came about, and should be understood in the light of ideas about evolution. Unlike Darwin, Haeckel was not chiefly concerned with the factors that occasioned and hastened evolution. His focus was on phylogenetic relationships of which he also sought to convey more vividly an overall understanding to his readers, not least in a series of diagrammatic renderings, of which his *Stammbäume* ("stem trees") are among these. As he expressly observed, each such diagram represented the current state of scientific knowledge and was open to revision as this knowledge progressed.[1] As it was only the recognition of the relationships that allowed the course of evolution to be traced, we may say that Haeckel thereby laid the groundwork for one of the most fundamental areas of biological research. Since Haeckel's time our understanding of the relationships between organisms has in many respects altered. On the other hand, a great many of Haeckel's own assumptions have retained their validity, in itself a testament to how very comprehensive was his own expertise.

Haeckel first made his name as a meticulous biologist who found practical applications for the latest scientific and theoretical developments in his field with his volume on Radiolaria, the monograph on Radiolaria. Published in 1862, it was based on his field research into the fauna of the Gulf of Messina. Seven years later there followed a work in which Haeckel's aims were altogether different. He was now concerned with elucidating the development of a particular type of jellyfish, the Siphonophora, which he had observed off the coast of the island of Lanzarote: his intention here was to provide an account of the development of these animals from their earliest life stages to their full "maturity."

Both in 1869, when in Norway, and in 1871, when in the Adriatic, Haeckel studied the life histories of calcareous sponges; and in 1872, he produced a three-volume work on these containing no fewer than 60 plates. He had discovered that a feature of the early development of these creatures was the formation of a larval form he termed the "gastrula," a life stage that was also to be observed in other organisms. Haeckel's work on this aspect of the calcareous sponges figured in due course in his influential "Gastraea Theory" (see p. 22).

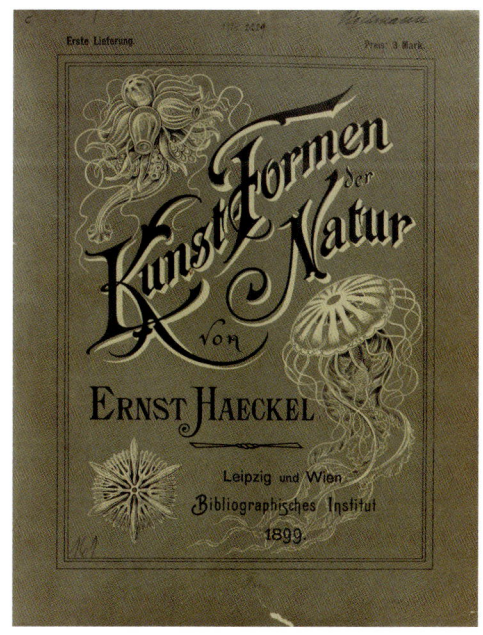

In 1876, with his publication on corals observed in the Red Sea, *Arabische Korallen*, Haeckel ventured beyond a purely "scientific" approach. For this volume is, in essence, the account of a journey. At this time in the early and mid-1870s, the British research vessel HMS *Challenger* was at sea in quite different regions of the globe to accomplish an ambitious mission. Under the overall supervision of Charles Wyville Thomson (1830–1882) and John Murray (1841–1914), a deep-sea research expedition was undertaken, from 1872, on behalf of the Royal Society with the collaboration and support of numerous scientists. This expedition was to continue until 1876 and it was the first on such a scale to be explicitly devoted to pure research. The *Challenger* circumnavigated the globe: Setting out from England, it travelled to the Caribbean, then to South Africa, then on to Australia, New Zealand and Japan, then across the Pacific and to Cape Horn, and in 1876, back to Europe. In addition to physical measurements, chemical analyses of seawater and geological research, a representative sample of marine life was also assembled. One very important discovery was that large expanses of the ocean floor were covered in a mud formed by the accumulated skeletons of Radiolaria. This, in turn, revealed that only a fraction of the true number of existing specimens of this animal group had at that point been discovered and described. Haeckel was one of the many renowned

Kunstformen der Natur (Art Forms in Nature), cover, first installment, 1899

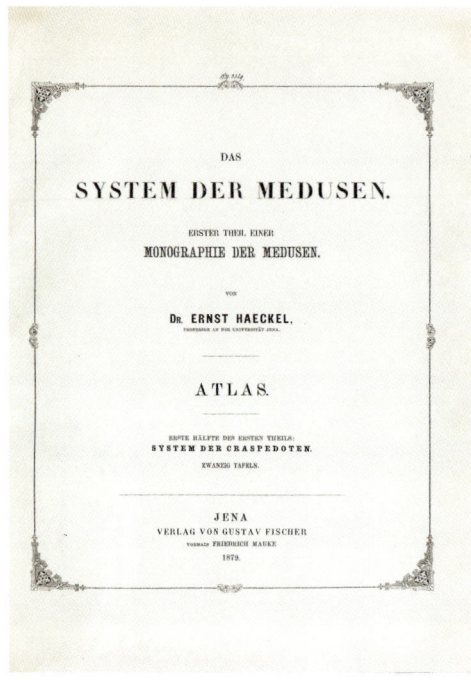

scientists to be invited to analyse the numerous specimens that the *Challenger* had brought back. In 1881, there appeared his volume on deep-sea jellyfish, *Tiefsee-Medusen*, in 1887–88, his study *Die Radiolarien*, in 1888, his *Siphonophorae*, and in 1889, *Die Hornschwämme,* a volume on keratinous sponges. Notwithstanding the enormous effort expended by Haeckel over a total of 12 years, there is no doubt that he was very pleased finding a true intoxication in the formal diversity of the specimens he was able to study. The scale of his output in these years was in itself remarkable, equating a lifetime's work for many of his colleagues in the field of biology: a total of 2,763 pages of text, the description of 739 genera with 4,318 species, not only identified and named, but also illustrated in 230 densely detailed plates.[2] Of Radiolaria alone there were 3,508 species. Especially evident here, in addition, was Haeckel's creative genius in the naming of new species, among them: *Clathrospyris, Clistolynthus, Clistophaena*, and *Coccolarcus*. Nor did Haeckel fail to rise to the challenge of acknowledging the *Challenger* Expedition in this nomenclature, as evinced by *Challengeranium, Challengerantha, Challengerebium, Challengeretta*, and *Challengeron*.

The last of Haeckel's series of plates, his *Art Forms in Nature* is fundamentally distinct from all scientifically oriented atlases he had published earlier. Here Haeckel's aim was to introduce a broad readership to the beauty to be found in nature. In doing so, he drew chiefly on the vast collection of images gathered during his own research. Unlike Haeckel's monographs, each of which was focused on a particular group of animals or unicellular life forms, the *Art Forms* were to embrace examples selected from all the larger groups of organisms. Having completed his work on this project, he offered his readers a supplementary volume of around 50 pages comprising an overview of all the organisms. This aid to orientation was all the more necessary from a scientific point of view in that the sequence of organisms illustrated in the plates did not itself

Das System der Medusen (The System of the Medusae), title page, 1879

correspond with the relationships between the corresponding life forms. Such an arrangement will also be adopted in the present volume: its illustrated section is followed by a summary account of the system of organisms as this is now understood (pp. 492–505). We here depart from the sequence of organisms as it is presented in Haeckel's supplementary volume only where that sequence does not accord with our current knowledge of the relationships concerned. This adaptation is not matched by any proposed alteration in the original sequence of the plates, which we have retained (plates 13, 20, 48, 52, 73, 76 not shown here). This was an arrangement that Haeckel would, in any case, have devised with a degree of spontaneity as he decided upon the groups to be illustrated in the instalments of the *Kunstformen* as these appeared over the course of four years.

Haeckel's Species Groups and Biological Nomenclature

Through the instance of unicellular organisms, we shall here briefly address the issue of the problems facing contemporary biology in the matter of taxonomy. Provisional conclusions, compromised both by the physical inaccessibility of the structures of most unicellular entities and by the relationships between them that Haeckel had himself proposed were revised during the 20th century thanks to the analysis of life cycles and the benefits of electron-microscopy. Yet many questions remained unanswered; and during the 1990s, biological research at the molecular level and comparative DNA-sequencing revealed that relationships between unicellular entities were far more complex than had been previously assumed. It was discovered that many of the groupings proposed by Haeckel could not, in fact, be understood in this way. Yet even some of the first molecular research into the evolution of distinct species was found to have resulted in incorrect conclusions. And so a great many of the names that, as recently as around the year 2000, had been applied to particular groups of unicellular entities had to be abandoned because these entities simply do not exist as natural groups. It is now readily acknowledged that we still possess no reliable image of the phylogenetic relationships between these life forms.

Alterations in the System of Organisms since Haeckel's Time

The "Flagellata" that still feature in *Kunstformen* were a combination of species which were in fact only distantly related; in more recent biology textbooks this group is no longer to be found. Haeckel's "Seaweeds," which he also called "Algae," belong in part to evolutionary branches of their own while others are in part early manifestations of plant life. Fungi, which Haeckel in his volume on general morphology *Generelle Morphologie der Organismen* treated as plants are, in fact, closely related to animals; and the sponges assumed by Haeckel in 1866 to be Protista are themselves actually animals.[3]

And Haeckel's Radiolaria are not, as he had initially assumed, animals but unicellular entities deriving from a separate evolutionary line. Many advances in the knowledge of phylogeny are addressed in our own volume in the section "Relationships Between the Organisms and the Biological System."

Many of Haeckel's scientific names and many of his more vernacular terms have long passed out of use. Haeckel, in addition, greatly enjoyed introducing neologisms, even doing so where there were pre-existing names. Instances of this sort are discussed in the introduction to each of the volumes of plates. At the same time, many of the species described by Haeckel, for example, those of jellyfish, have not been restudied since his times; and Haeckel's designation in these cases may often come to be regarded as a scientifically doubtful name, a *nomen dubium*. This is, in truth, frequently unjustified, for Haeckel's descriptions and illustrations are of such high quality that it should not prove difficult to identify the species concerned on the basis of this evidence. Should doubt, nonetheless, still persist, it might be possible to re-examine those of Haeckel's original specimens that have been preserved in the collections of zoological museums. But this is to assume that specialists sufficiently expert in the species concerned are still available – which is often not the case.

The Naming of Species in this Publication

Each of the plates illustrated in the present volume contains, wherever possible, the names that are now valid alongside Haeckel's original ones (their occasional typographical errors here corrected). In many cases it has not been possible to maintain this method of "updating," especially where this would require a thorough scientific re-examination of the relevant material. Such a process might indeed reveal that far more extensive research was required into the variability of the species. Studies of the range of variability might often prove that many of Haeckel's "species" are merely variations of one and the same biological species (on Haeckel's concept of "species," see pp. 25–26).

In the interests of international comprehensibility, scientific names need to be given in their Latin or Greek forms. Each name of a species comprises a first half (indicating the name of the genus) and a second half the epitheton (which is the true designation of the species within the genus, nowadays always written in lower case). Both halves of this bipartite name should be *in italics*. The name of the species may be followed by the name (often abbreviated) of the individual who happened to be the first to describe and name it; and this may, in turn, be followed by the year in which the new name was first formally published. In the case of plants, fungi, and algae, the name of the individual who first described the species is placed in brackets when the species name has subsequently been combined with another genus name. There then follows the name of

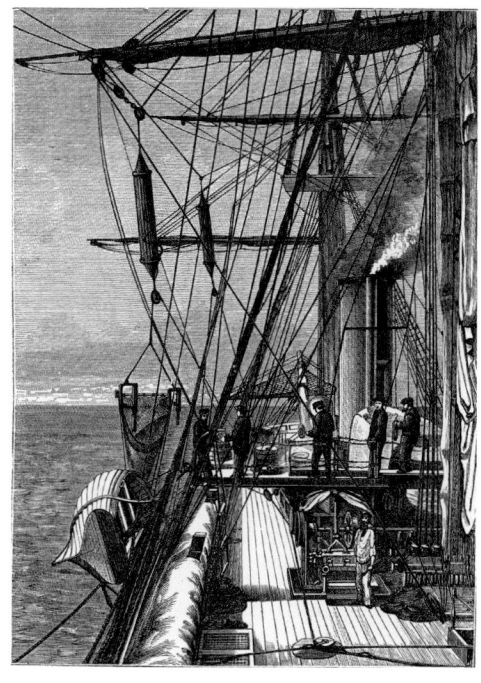

the individual responsible for the new combination, in addition to the year in which this was registered. Similarly, in the case of animals, where a later connection of the name of the species with that of another genus has occurred, the name of the individual who was the first to describe the species is added, in brackets. The name of the individual from whom this rearrangement derives is, however, not cited. Different names and spellings for one and the same species are called synonyms. In principle, only the originally proposed names are valid; but it has often been the case that more recent synonyms have been widely used, and these are then also cited. The names for more comprehensive groups of organisms consist only of a single name (e.g., Plantae for plants, Animalia for animals, although it is often the case that several different names are applied to such groups). The rule for naming species and genera are firmly laid out in the International Codes of Nomenclature.

In the present volume we have departed from the International Codes of Nomenclature in the texts accompanying each plate only to better distinguish the currently favoured names, which are printed *in italics* while Haeckel's original names are not. The expression "current name" often conceals new names for the illustrated species, either because Haeckel himself sometimes erred in identifying species or because new subdivisions within species have, in the meantime, been proposed and generally accepted. Haeckel, in addition, often described a species as "new" (that is to say, "newly discovered") and proposed a name for it, when the species in question had, in fact, already been identified and formally described by other scientists. Here too, not only has Haeckel's naming been updated but the name now viewed as valid is also cited on the basis of the actual affiliation to the species of the illustrated organism.

John James Wild, **Dredging and Sounding Arrangements**
Woodcut from *Report on the Scientific Results of the Voyage of H.M.S. Challenger during the Years 1873–76, Narrative, Vol. 1*, 1885, p. 57

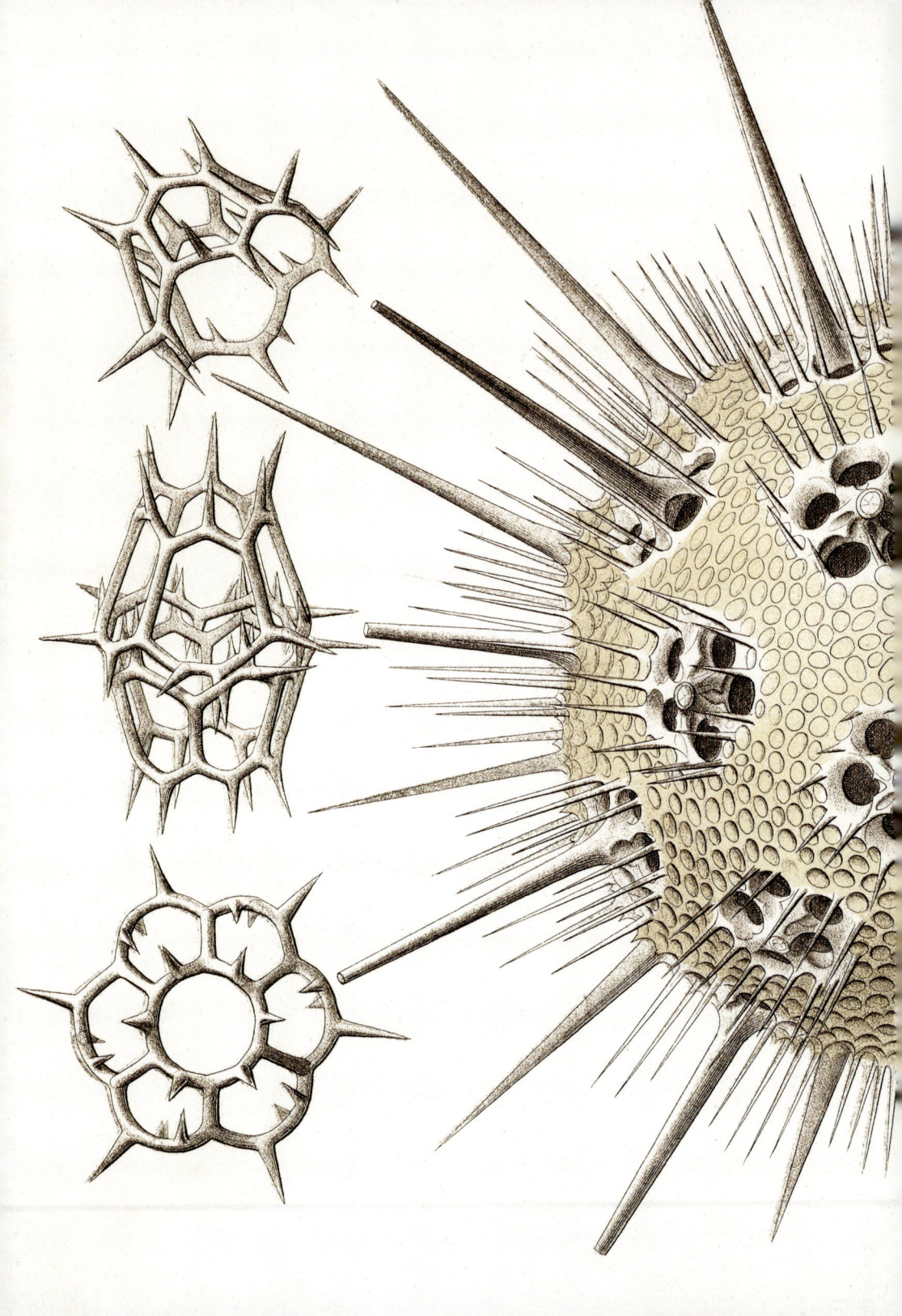

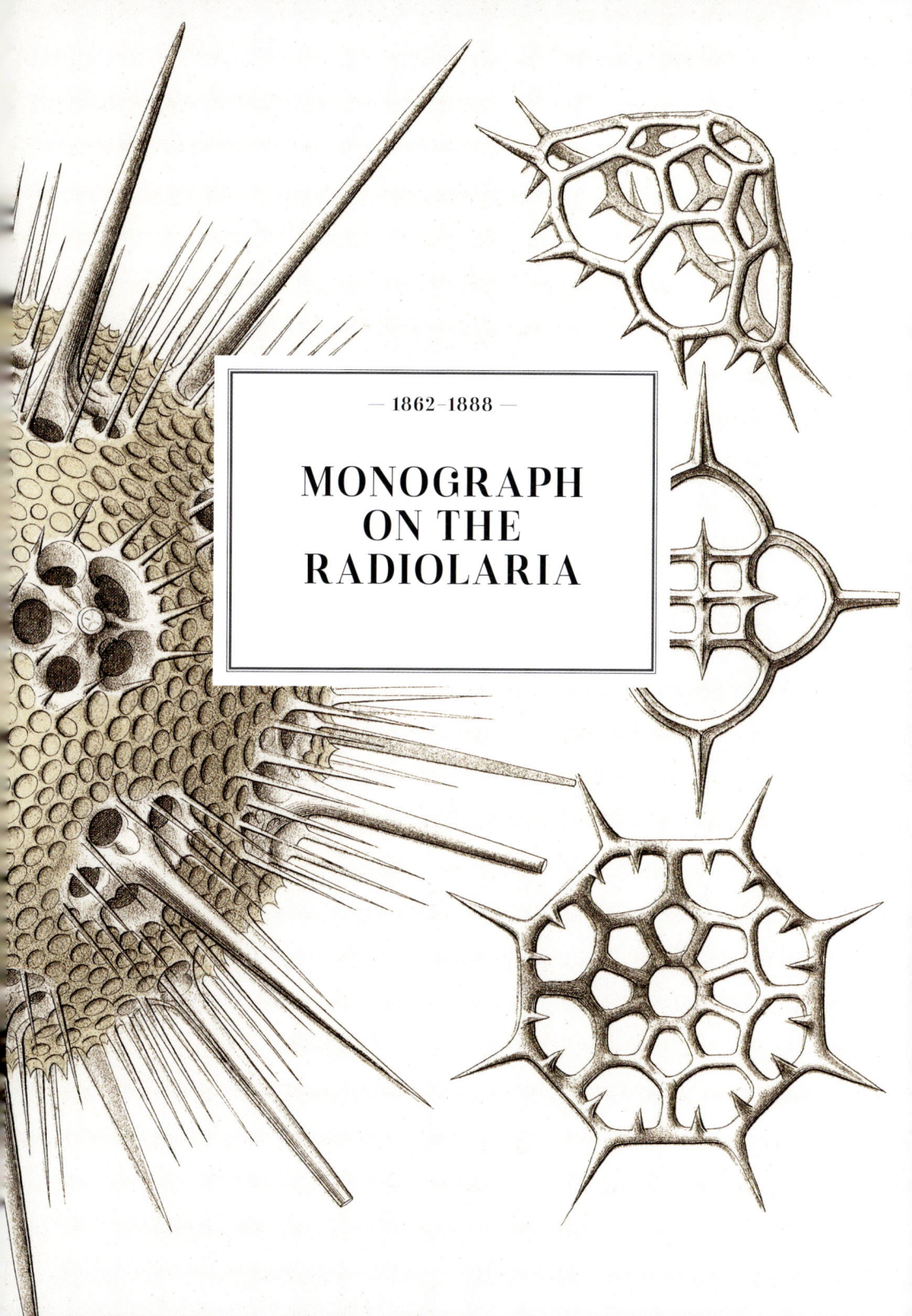

— 1862–1888 —

MONOGRAPH ON THE RADIOLARIA

MONOGRAPH
ON THE RADIOLARIA

From October 1859, Haeckel was engaged in research into marine organisms in the Gulf of Messina. He was interested, above all, in Radiolaria (literally: radials), one of the favoured research subjects of his highly revered teacher Johannes Müller. Before Haeckel had embarked on his own research, 58 species of Radiolaria had been identified and described. But, as early as 1860, he was able to write enthusiastically to his fiancée Anna Sethe that in a single day he had caught no fewer than twelve new species, "[...] among them the most charming little creatures!" And he also spoke of "two new magnificent species, and what's more, one of these also of a new genus, [that] filled me with delight to look upon! [...] So I've now discovered 75 ! new species of Radiolaria, and I have a firm hope that, with just a little more of the same good fortune, I'll soon enough be able to reach a full century."[1] Haeckel was eventually able to register 144 new species and 47 new genera.

At the end of February 1860, Haeckel had reported to Anna on the expeditions during which the Radiolaria were caught: "The little creatures are all (with very few exceptions) microscopically small and thus invisible to the naked eye or, at best, perceptible as the smallest dot. [...] Radiolaria are exclusively pelagic creatures, i. e. they spend their entire lives swimming on the surface of the deep sea, from which they disappear only for short intervals, notably when the turbulent movement of the waves and a storm prompts them to descend to a somewhat greater depth. This makes catching them much easier, indeed, this alone makes capture possible. For one, in fact, scoops them up from the water's surface, where hundreds of them occupy every square foot, using a net with a very fine mesh, a method first employed by Johannes Müller with great success in catching such large quantities of every sort of pelagic creature, that this has opened up the most surprising views into an entirely new world rich with animal life. While the boat proceeds slowly, with only a slight movement of the oars, one holds the net half immersed in the water, and by this means uses it to filter a great deal of it as it passes through. From time to time the net is removed from the sea, tipped upside down and emptied out into a glass or bucket that is itself full of seawater, where these tiniest creatures, which had been caught in the mesh, are then at once again freed and fall to the bottom. The sediment that thus accrues in the base of the containers (when they are brought back home, the clear water they also contain will be discarded) is now a virtually inexhaustible source of the richest and most remarkable delights to be found in nature [...]."[2]

In 1862, Haeckel published his monograph on Radiolaria, *Die Radiolarien (Rhizopoda radiolaria)*, with its 35 splendid plates.[3] In the opinion of the Halle anatomist Max Schultze (1825–1874) in a letter to Haeckel, this was, in artistic terms, "[...] the finest of scientific works on the lesser animals ever to be produced, and I find myself undecided as to whether to feel more astonished by nature itself and its capacity to bring forth such diversity and beauty of forms, or by the hand of the draughtsman in his ability to capture such magnificence on paper."[4]

It was while he was at work on this volume that Haeckel read Charles Darwin's *On the Origin of Species* and in response, began to work in a more consequent fashion, guided by the idea of evolution towards "a natural system of the Radiolaria," a phrase incorporated into one of the chapters of his book. Haeckel envisaged a "primal radiolarian," which he came to associate with representatives of the genus *Heliosphaera*, distinguished by a spherical lattice (plate 9, not depicted). He also acknowledged the variability of the species which appeared to feature numerous transitional forms.

Haeckel's work on Radiolaria ensured that fellow scientists came to respect him as a meticulous, modern-minded biologist. It was only after the book had appeared, however, that it first became evident what further important discoveries it had now made possible. This was shown, for example, in 1876 when Haeckel's pupil Richard von Hertwig (1850–1937) recognised that Radiolaria were unicellular organisms. Haeckel himself had continued to assume that they were multicellular, on account of his erroneous assumption of a proof of this in their apparently strong connection with other organisms (symbionts), in which he had discovered a cell core or nucleus. He had also initially believed Radiolaria to be animals – until he invented the "empire" of the Protista in 1866.

Radiolaria are unicellular organisms which are dispersed as a form of plankton throughout the world's oceans. They are, however, incapable of any form of independent swimming motion. Their delicate skeletons are made of silicic acid or, in the case of the sub-group Acantharia, of strontium sulphate. The skeleton is surrounded by cytoplasm (cellular plasma, the fundamental substance of which a cell is formed); but there are many species that have no skeleton. Most radiolarians measure much less than one millimetre, although a few are as large as two millimetres. Some Radiolaria do, however, form colonies, each comprising many hundreds of cells; these colonies as a whole can be several centimetres long and, in the case of the thread-like colonies, even several metres long. It is possible to find examples of Acantharia in which there may, when they are "in bloom," be up to 500,000 individuals within a square metre of the ocean surface.[5]

The living substance of Radiolaria comprises an internal or central capsule (*intracapsulum*) and an external capsule (*extracapsulum*), the latter forming an outer layer. Both internal and external capsules consist of cytoplasm. The internal capsule is separated from the external capsule by means of a usually perforated wall; and the cytoplasm of the internal capsule is connected with that of the external capsule by means of thin strands, or *fusuli*. These last are a feature unique to radiolarians, including the Acantharia.[6]

The term "Radiolaria" was first introduced by his teacher Johannes Müller (1801–1858) in 1858, four years before the appearance of Haeckel's celebrated monograph. Haeckel partially adopted Müller's division of Radiolaria into five sub-groups: Thalassicollea, Polycystinea, Acanthometrea, Sphaerozoea, and Collosphaerae. We now know that the Thalassicollea (genus *Thalassicolla*), the Sphaerozoea, and the Collosphaerae are in fact among the Polycystinea. And of these we now distinguish between two large sub-groups, the Nasselaria and the Spumellaria, both terms that Haeckel himself was to employ in his later work. There has been some dispute as to the systematic position of the Acantharia, to which Haeckel also devoted a plate in his later *Kunstformen der Natur* (in Müller's own work they were treated as the genus *Acanthometra*). To some extent these were not viewed as one of the Radiolarians. But they do indisputably belong among them, as they are the nearest relatives (i. e. the sister group) of the Polycystinea. From this point of view, Radiolaria include those groups that Müller had also associated with them,[7] albeit sometimes under other names. It was, accordingly, by no means necessary for the Radiolaria, in this original sense, to receive, in 2003, the new name "Radiozoa"[8] – even though this is nowadays often used.

A group that Müller had not known are the Phaeodaria, with which Haeckel chose to open his *Kunstformen der Natur*. Both he and others believed these to be Radiolarians. They belong, however, as revealed by the stem tree (see p. 492) to the group Cercozoa.[9]

With regard to Heliozoa, which had long been associated with Radiolarians, we have now learned, as a result of molecular analyses, that there is no close relation here. Many authors suppressed the term "Heliozoa," introduced by Haeckel in 1866; yet it relates to the genus *Actinophrys* and is in that respect indisputably valid. Nowadays the term "Actinophryida" is often used in place of "Heliozoa" (see stem tree).

Having published his monograph on Radiolaria in 1862, Haeckel later returned to this theme in a series of publications. In 1887 and 1888, he published works that were presented as the second, third and fourth parts of the original monograph respectively so that the publication of 1862 retrospectively became volume 1 of this series.[10]

In volumes 2 to 4 Haeckel published a total of 106 plates selected from the 140 that had appeared in the 1887 English-language report on the radiolarians assembled during the deep-sea expedition of the HMS *Challenger* (we show the most impressive ones in the present publication). Of the 34 plates not featured in the monograph on Radiolaria one is included here (after volume 4 of the series): *Report on the Radiolaria collected by H.M.S. Challenger during the years 1873–76. Report on the Scientific Results of the Voyage of H.M.S. Challenger.*[11] (1,873 text pages, 140 plates, 3,508 new species).

In his preface to the German edition of this volume, Haeckel observed: "After three years of research, I then [in 1862] thought to have acquired a relatively comprehensive understanding of the organisation of these delicate inhabitants of the ocean, on which the fundamental research of my unforgettable teacher Johannes Müller had thrown the first light a few years earlier. I had at that time no idea that the 50 species of radiolarians that Müller had been the first to observe in their natural habitat, and the one hundred and 50 further species that I was able to add to the total, represented only a small fraction of the wonderful world of forms (*Gestalten*) in this most formally rich of zoological classes. Today I am in the fortunate position to be able to introduce over twenty times as many species to those with an interest in the microscopically small life forms."[12] The *Challenger* Expedition had now revealed that Radiolarians lived at very diverse depths of the ocean, and that their siliceous shells were in due course deposited in vast quantities on the ocean floor. The mere tip of a knife's worth of this radiolarian would usually contain thousands of individual Radiolaria, representing hundreds of species, and the mud itself covered thousands of square miles of the ocean floor.

To the memory of his unforgotten first wife Anna, Haeckel dedicated one of the most beautiful species of Radiolarians, which he called *Dictyocodon annasethe*. Her memory is also honoured in the entire fourth volume of the Radiolaria series, it being to her inspiration that Haeckel claimed to owe his work on the original 1862 monograph. Of particular interest too is the Radiolar illustrated as fig. 3 on plate 65 (we see an illustration from *Art Forms in Nature*, plate 31, fig. 6, p. 365). This was named *Alacorys bismarckii* in honour of the first German imperial chancellor Otto von Bismarck (1815–1898). With both a sense of pathos and reflecting the nationalist sentiments of that era, Haeckel later wrote of this species: "This imposing species, resembling a monument atop five columns was named in honour of Prince Otto von Bismarck, the genial founder of the new German Empire and of its future as a colonial power."[13] The lines that follow appear to our eyes almost absurd: "In Jena on 31 July 1892, he [Bismarck], as a practical connoisseur of German phylogeny, was awarded the first Honorary Doctorate in this field."[14] And it had, indeed, been Haeckel who had ensured that the former German chancellor should receive this curious honour on the occasion of his visit to Jena.

Many of the species of Radiolaria that Haeckel was the first to describe were rediscovered during the nine-month deep-sea research carried out by the *Valdivia* Expedition of 1898–99. Their variability was also further explored. This research revealed that several instances of the species *Auloceros* were related by way of transitional forms, meaning that they should henceforth be regarded as a single species. This was also the case with *Aulographis astericus*, with its own transitions to *Aulographis pandora*. As emphasised by the zoologist Valentin Haecker (1864–1927), who was chiefly responsible for the analysis of the findings of the *Valdivia* Expedition, it was even then already a question of showing that many of the diverse developmental stages that Haeckel had himself described as separate species could now, on the evidence of the soft parts of the animal body, be shown to belong to a single species.[15] And Haecker was to be proved right: the thousands of species that Haeckel had described in 1887 were to require further research. Attending to this matter would, however, take us too far beyond our present purpose.

Finally, it is important once again to observe that Haeckel often did not pay sufficient attention to the existing scientific literature. As a result, his own systems and species descriptions have on many occasions been hotly disputed.[16] For the radiolarian genus *Cenosophaera*, which in 1854 had been described by Christian Gottfried Ehrenberg (1795–1876), Haeckel proposed, according to his Heidelberg colleague Otto Bütschli (1845–1920), the further names: "*Heliosphaera*," "*Cyrtidosphaera*," and "*Ceriosphaera*." These names are invalid in so far as they are mere later synonyms of the names first introduced. If, as in the case of the *Challenger* Expedition research plates, in the present volume only the names introduced by Haeckel are employed (most of these still being valid), this is owing to the fact that it was not possible to examine all the subsequently published literature on his "species."

PLATE I
1 5 Thalassicolla pelagica, HKL. – *Thalassicolla pelagica*

84

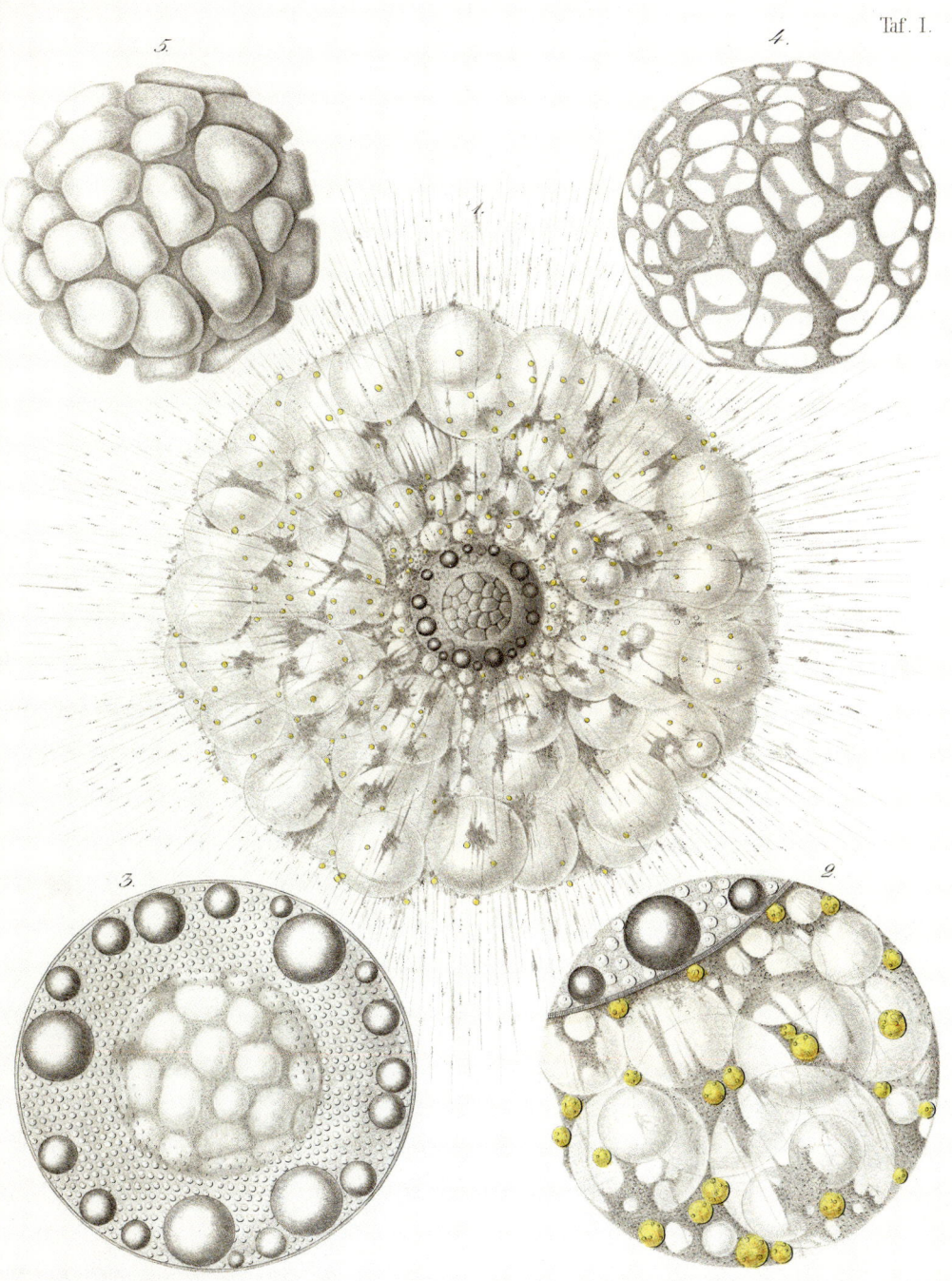

5.

4.

1.

3.

2.

1–5. Thalassicolla pelagica, Hkl.

E. Haeckel del.

Wagenschieber sc.

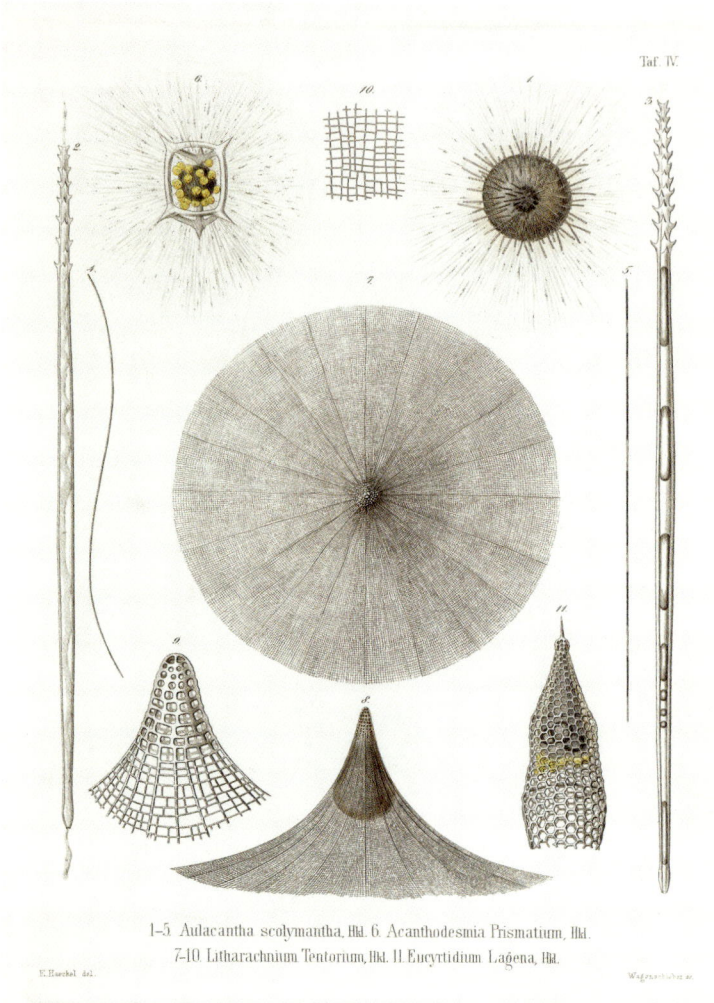

Taf. IV.

1–5 Aulacantha scolymantha, Hkl. 6. Acanthodesmia Prismatium, Hkl.
7–10. Litharachnium Tentorium, Hkl. 11. Eucyrtidium Lagena, Hkl.

E.Haeckel del.   Wagner&Lohn sc.

PLATE 4 *
1–5 Aulacantha scolymantha, HKL. – *Aulacantha scolymantha*
6 Acanthodesmia Prismatium, HKL. | 7–10 Litharachnium Tentorium, HKL. –
Litharachnium tentorium | 11 Eucyrtidium Lagena, HKL. – *Eucyrtidium lagena*
* see page 507

PLATE 5
1 Carpocanium Diadema, HKL. – *Carpocanium diadema*
2 Cyrtocalpis Amphora – *Cyrtocalpis amphora*
3–11 Cyrtocalpis obliqua, HKL. – *Cyrtocalpis obliqua*
12–15 Eucecryphalus Gegenbauri, HKL. – *Eucecryphalus gegenbauri*
16–19 Eucecryphalus Schultzei, HKL. – *Eucecryphalus schultzei*

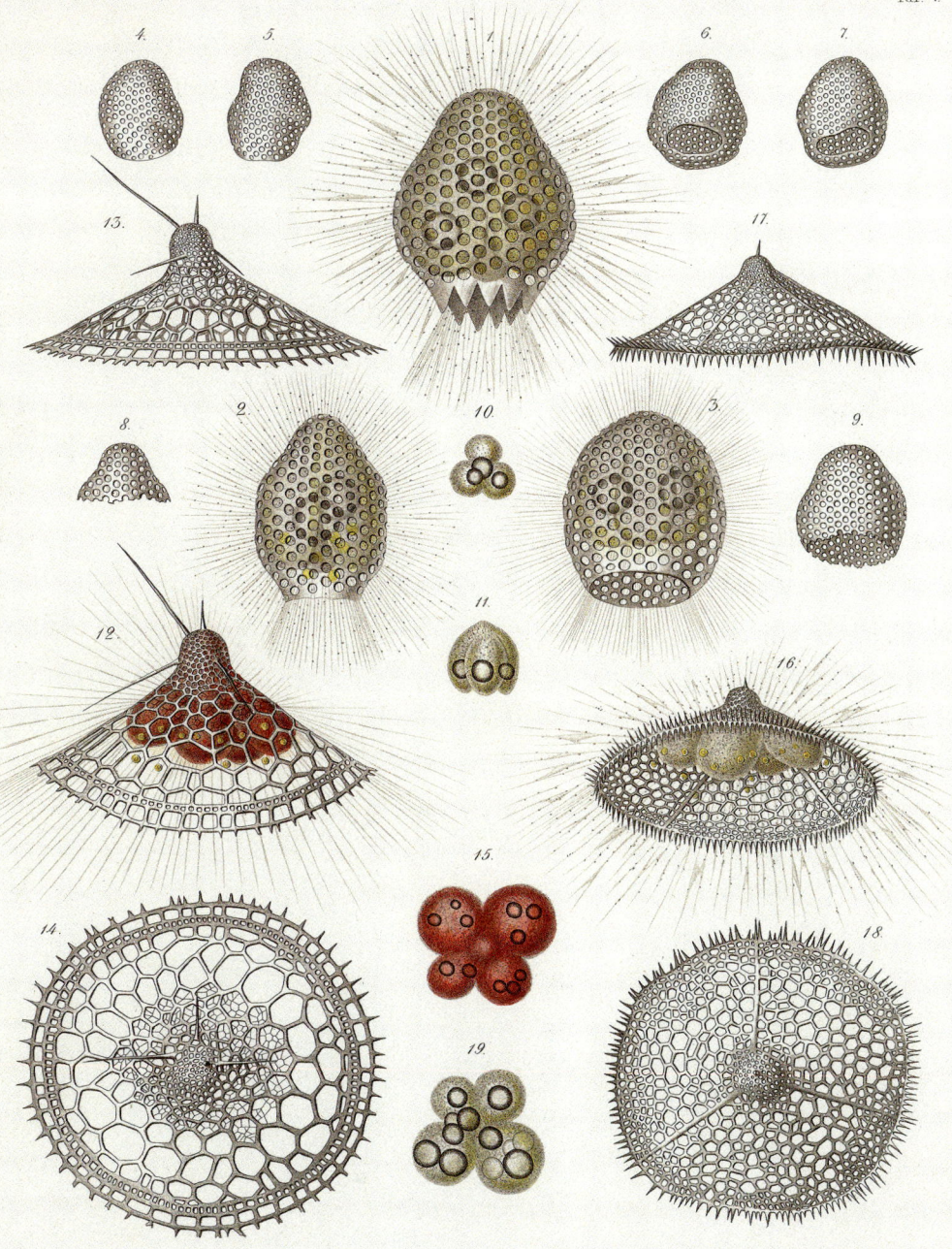

1. Carpocanium Diadema, Hkl. 2–11. Cyrtocalpis. 2. C. Amphora, Hkl. 3–11. C. obliqua, Hkl.
12–19. Eucecryphalus. 12–15. E. Gegenbauri, Hkl. 16–19. E. Schultzei, Hkl.

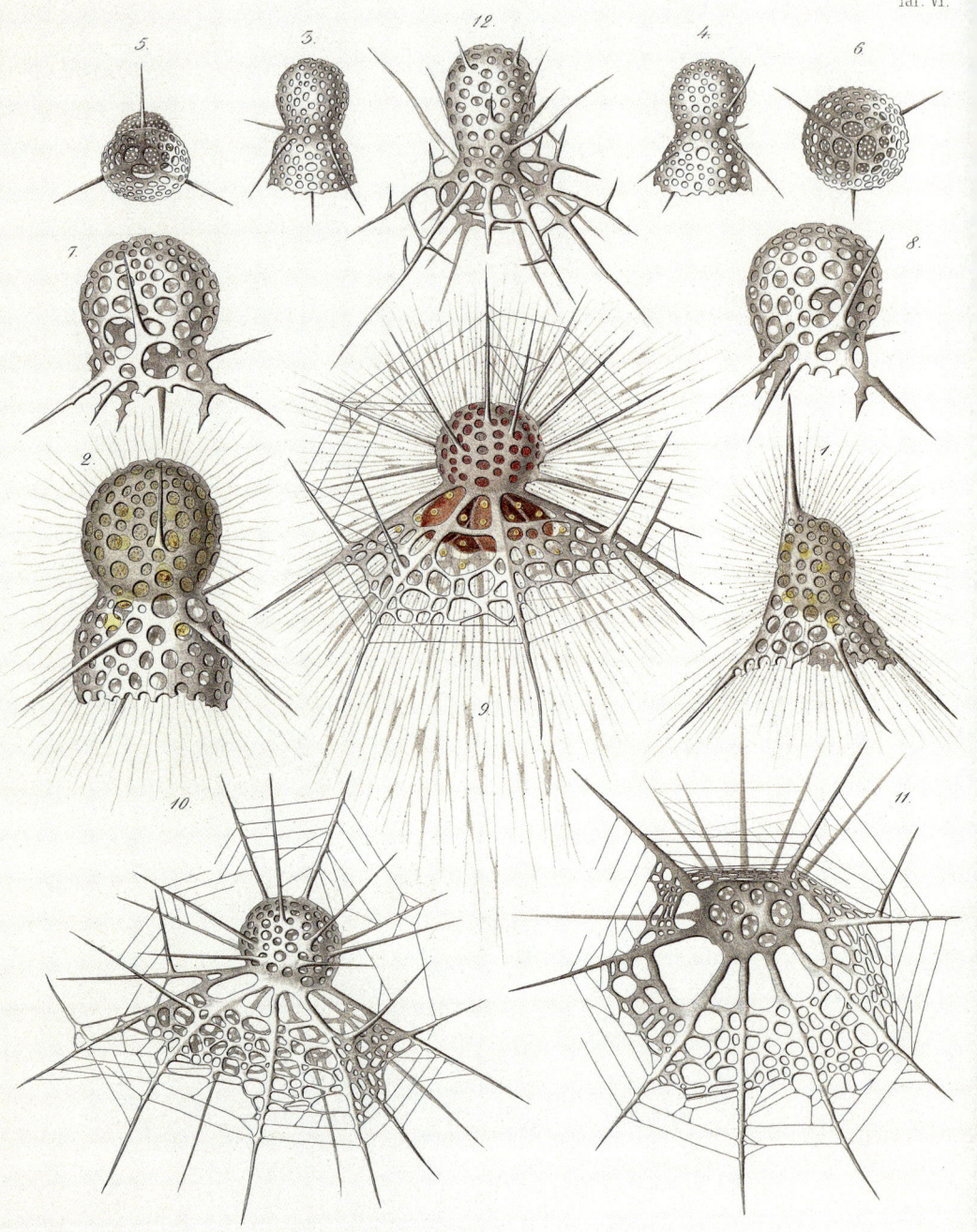

1. Dictyophimus Tripus, Hkl. 2–8. Lithomelissa Thoracites, Hkl.
9–12. Arachnocorys. 9–11. A. circumtexta, Hkl. 12. A. umbellifera, Hkl.

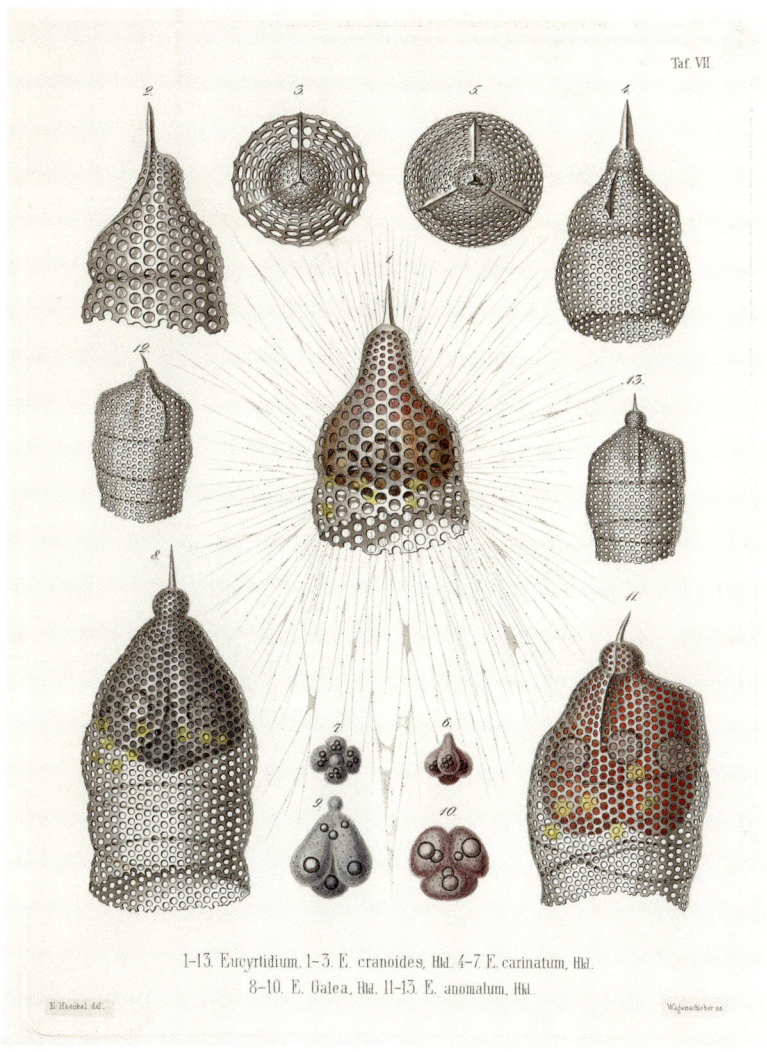

Taf. VII

1-13. Eucyrtidium. 1-3. E. cranoides, Hkl. 4-7. E. carinatum, Hkl.
8-10. E. Galea, Hkl. 11-13. E. anomalum, Hkl.

E. Haeckel del.

Wagenschieber sc.

PLATE 6
1 Dictyophimus Tripus, HKL. – *Dictyophimus tripus*
2-8 Lithomelissa Thoracites, HKL. – *Lithomelissa thoracites*
9-11 Arachnocorys circumtexta, HKL. – *Arachnocorys circumtexta*
12 Arachnocorys umbellifera, HKL. – *Arachnocorys umbellifera*

PLATE 7
1-3 Eucyrtidium cranoides, HKL. – *Eucyrtidium cranoides*
4-7 Eucyrtidium carinatum, HKL. – *Eucyrtidium? carinatum*
8-10 Eucyrtidium Galea, HKL. – *Eucyrtidium galea*
11-13 Eucyrtidium anomalum, HKL. – *Eucyrtidium anomalum*

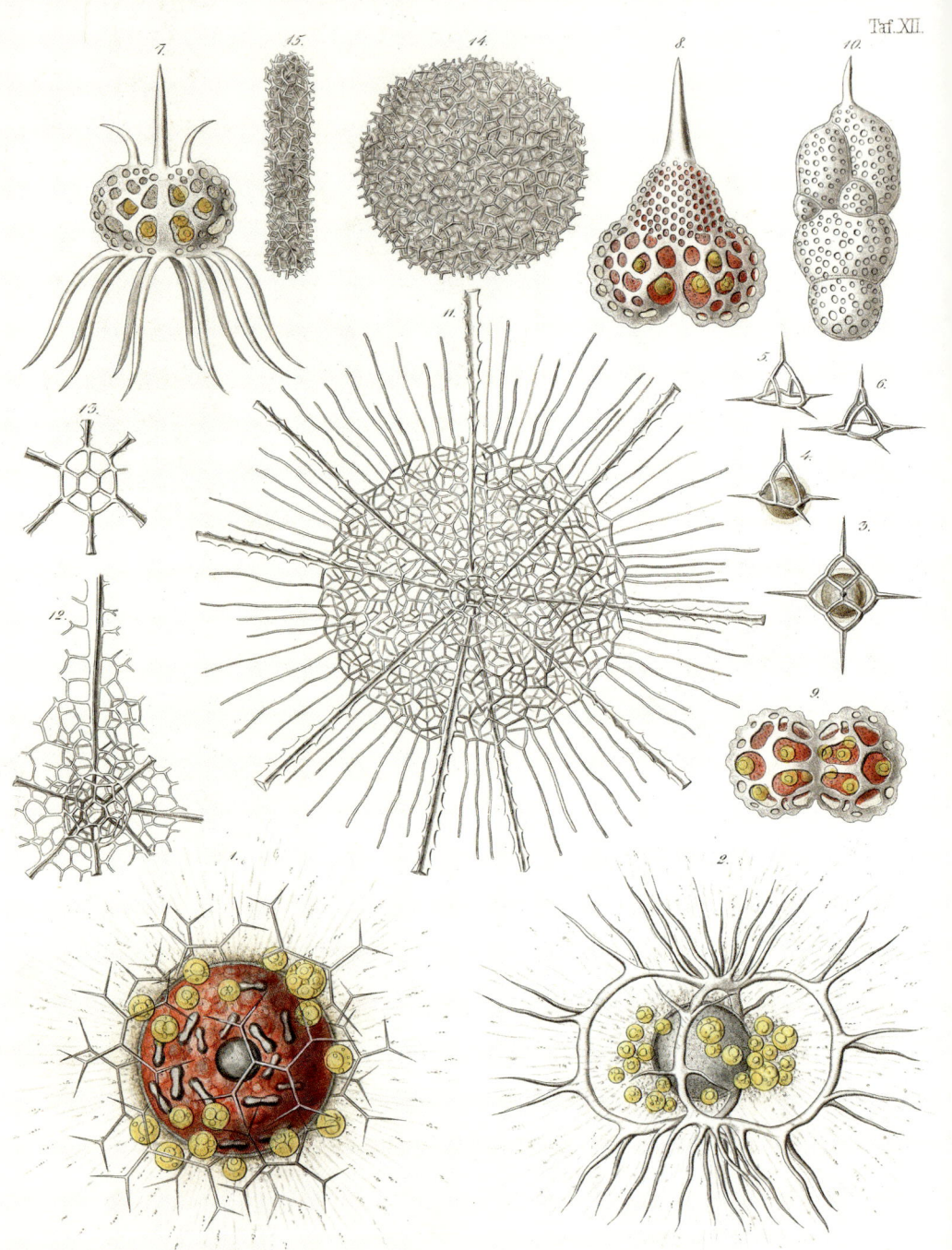

1. Thalassosphaera bifurca, Hkl. 2. Zygostephanus Mülleri, Hkl. 3–6. Dictyocha Messanensis, Hkl. 7. Petalospyris arachnoides, Hkl.
8.9. Spyridobotrys Trinacria, Hkl. 10. Botryocampe hexathalamia, Hkl. 11–13. Spongosphaera helioides. Hkl. 14.15. Spongodiscus Mediterraneus, Hk.

F. Haeckel del.   Wagenschieber se.

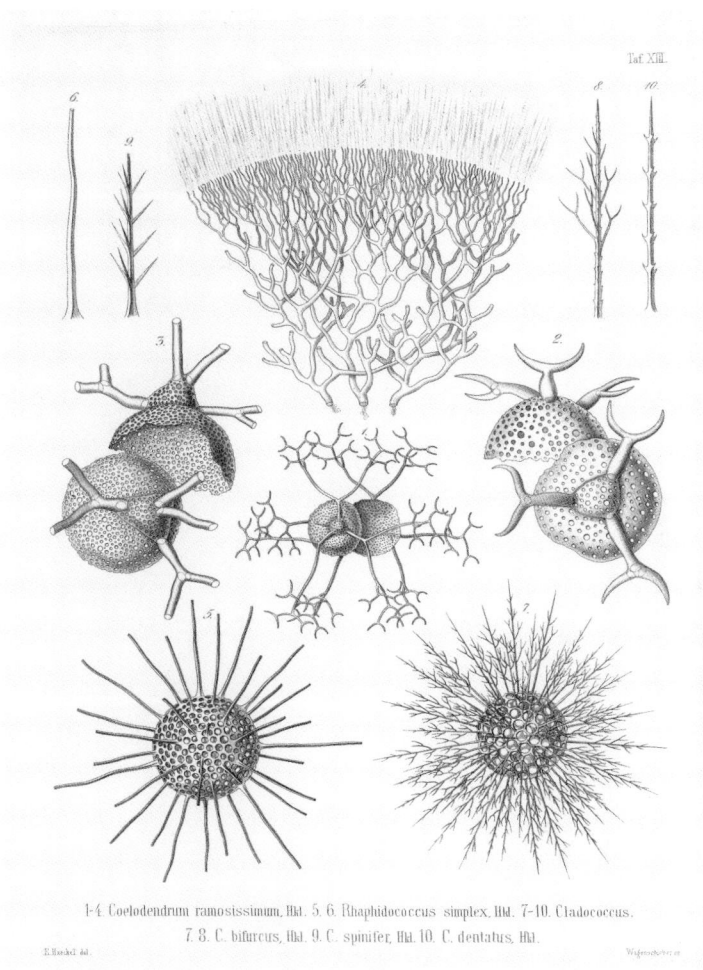

Taf. XIII.

1-4. Coelodendrum ramosissimum, Hkl. 5. 6. Rhaphidococcus simplex, HM. 7-10. Cladococcus.
7. 8. C. bifurcus, Hkl. 9. C. spinifer, Hkl. 10. C. dentatus, Hkl.

E.Haeckel del.

Wagnerschr.vu.w

PLATE 12

1 Thalassosphaera bifurca, HKL. – *Thalassosphaera bifurca* (HAECKEL, 1860) | 2 Zygostephanus Mülleri, HKL. – *Zygostephanus muelleri* HAECKEL, 1862 | 3-6 Dictyocha Messanensis, HKL. – *Dictyocha messanensis* HAECKEL, 1860 | 7 Petalospyris arachnoides, HKL. – *Petalospyris arachnoides* HAECKEL, 1862 | 8–9 Spyridobotrys Trinacria, HKL. – *Spyridobotrys trinacria* HAECKEL, 1862 | 10 Botryocampe hexathalamia, HKL. – *Botryocampe hexathalamia* HAECKEL, 1862 | 11-13 Spongosphaera hehoides, HKL. – *Spongosphaera helioides* HAECKEL, 1862 | 14-15 Spongodiscus Mediterraneus, HKL. – *Spongodiscus mediterraneus* HAECKEL, 1862

PLATE 13

1-4 Coelodendrum ramosissimum, HKL. – *Coelodendrum ramosissimum* HAECKEL, 1860 | 5-6 Rhaphidococcus simplex, HKL. – *Rhaphidococcus simplex* (HAECKEL, 1860) | 7-8 Cladococcus bifurcus, HKL. – *Cladococcus bifurcus* HAECKEL, 1860 | 9 Cladococcus spinifer, HKL. – *Cladococcus spinifer* HAECKEL, 1860 | 10 Cladococcus dentatus, HKL. – *Cladococcus dentifer* HAECKEL, 1860

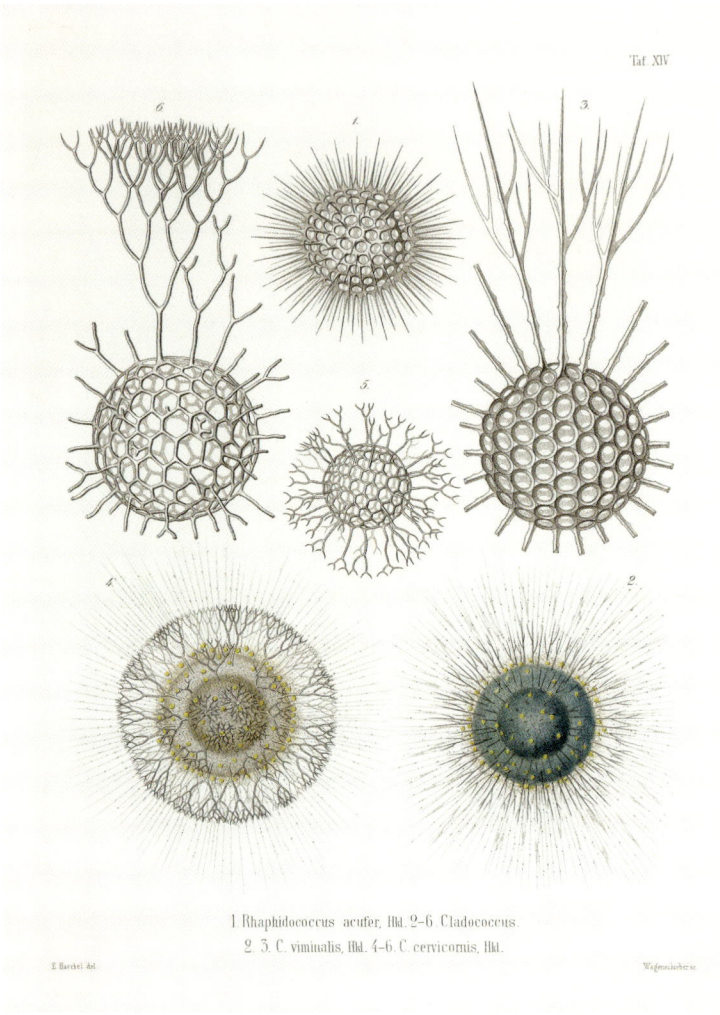

Taf. XIV

1. Rhaphidococcus acufer, Hkl. 2–6 Cladococcus.
2. 3. C. viminalis, Hkl. 4–6. C. cervicornis, Hkl.

E. Haeckel del.   Wagnerscherie.

PLATE 14
1 Rhaphidococcus acufer – *Rhaphidococcus acufer* (HAECKEL, 1860)
2–3 Cladococcus vinimalis, HKL. – *Cladococcus viminalis* HAECKEL, 1860
4–6 Cladococcus cervicornis, HKL. – *Cladococcus cervicornis* HAECKEL, 1860

PLATE 15
1 Acanthometra elastica, HKL. – *Acanthometra elastica*
2 Acanthometra bulbosa, HKL. – *Acanthometra bulbosa*
3 Acanthometra Mülleri, HKL. – *Acanthometra muelleri*
4 Acanthometra fragilis, HKL. – *Acanthometra fragilis*
5 Acanthometra brevispina, HKL. – *Phyllostaurus brevispina*
6–9 Acanthometrae juvenes – *Acanthometra* sp.

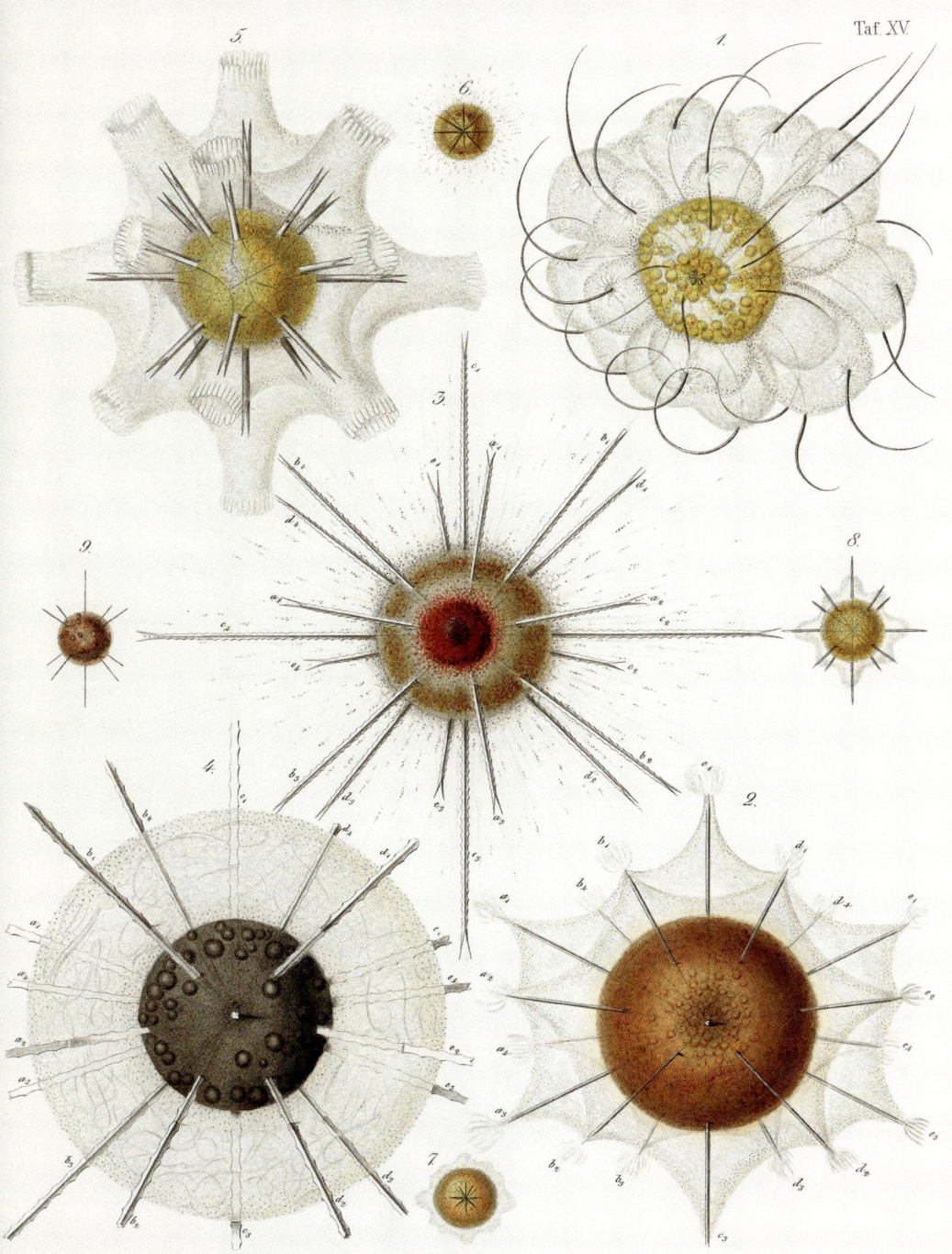

1-9. Acanthometra. 1. A. elastica, Hkl. 2. A. bulbosa, Hkl. 3. A. Mülleri, Hkl.
4. A. fragilis, Hkl. 5. A. brevispina, Hkl. 6-9. Acanthometrae juvenes.

E. Haeckel del.

Wagenschieber sc.

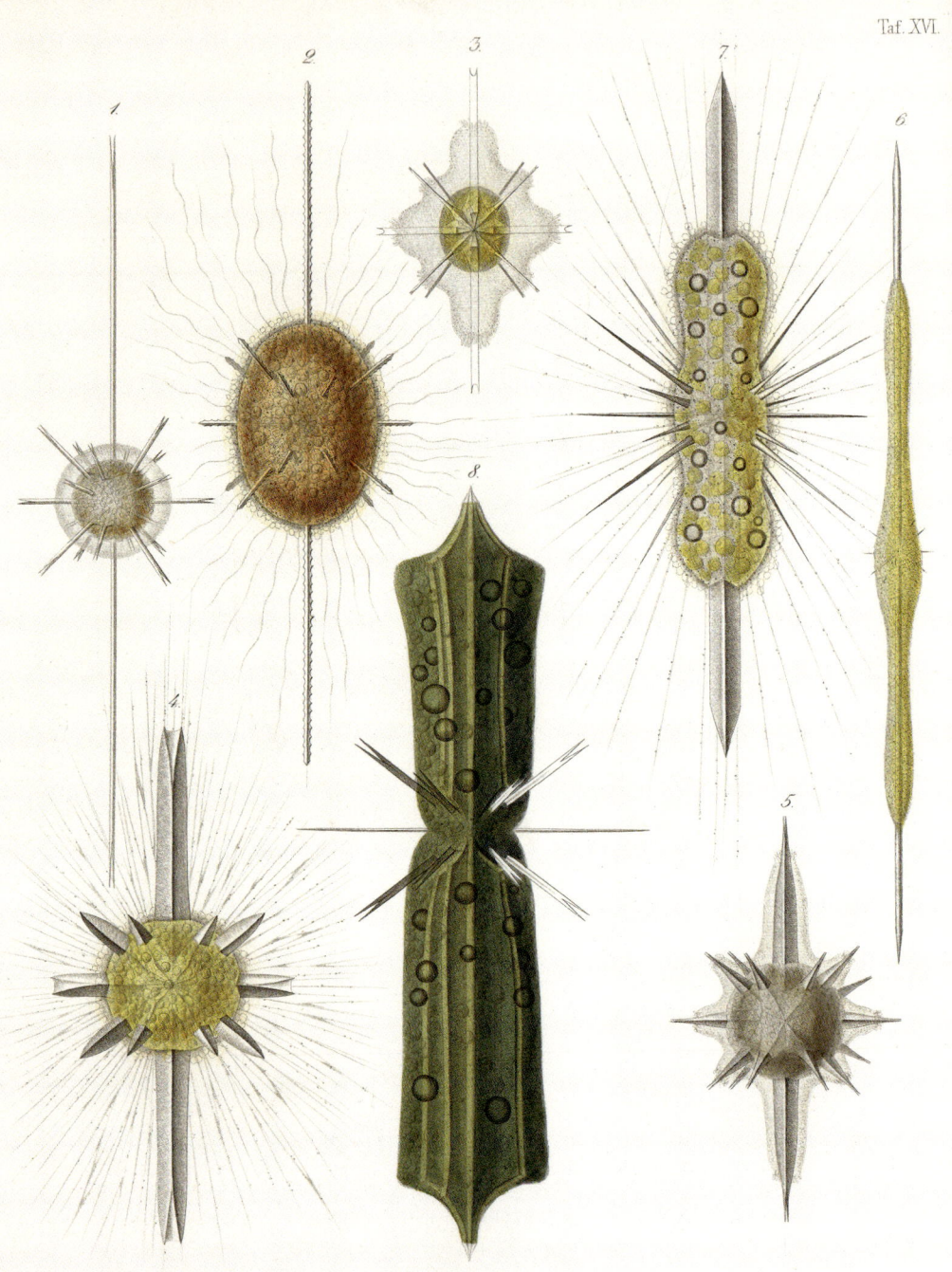

1–8. Amphilonche. 1. A. tenuis, Hkl. 2. A. denticulata, Hkl. 3. A. complanata, Hkl. 4. A. Messanensis, Hkl.
5. A. tetraptera, Hkl. 6. A. belonoides, Hkl. 7. A. heteracantha, Hkl. 8. A. anomala, Hkl.

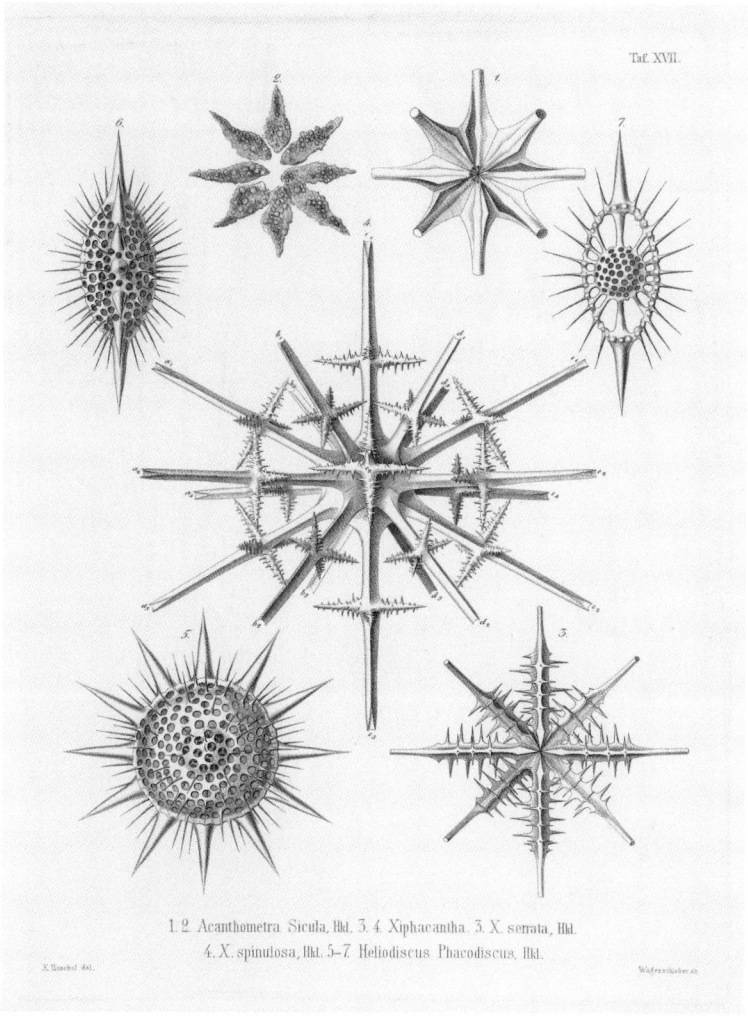

Taf. XVII.

1. 2. Acanthometra Sicula, Hkl. 3. 4. Xiphacantha. 3. X. serrata, Hkl.
4. X. spinulosa, Hkl. 5–7. Heliodiscus Phacodiscus, Hkl.

X. Haeckel del.

Wagenschieber sc.

PLATE 16

1 Amphilonche tenuis, HKL. – *Amphilonche tenuis* HAECKEL, 1860 | 2 Amphilonche denticulata, HKL. – *Amphilonche denticulata* (HAECKEL, 1860) | 3 Amphilonche complanata, HKL. – *Amphilonche complanata* (HAECKEL, 1860) | 4 Amphilonche Messanensis, HKL. – *Amphilonche messanensis* (HAECKEL, 1860) 5 Amphilonche tetraptera, HKL. – *Amphilonche tetraptera* (HAECKEL, 1860) | 6 Amphilonche belonoides, HKL. – *Amphibelone belonoides* (HAECKEL, 1860) | 7 Amphilonche heteracantha, HKL. – *Amphibelone heteracantha* (HAECKEL, 1860) | 8 Amphilonche anomala, HKL. – *Amphibelone anomala* (HAECKEL, 1860)

PLATE 17

1–2 Acanthometra Sicula, HKL. – *Phyllostaurus sicula* (HAECKEL, 1860) | 3 Xiphacantha serrata, HKL. – *Xiphacantha serrrata* HAECKEL, 1860 | 4 Xiphacantha spinulosa, HKL. – *Xiphostaurus spinulosa* (HAECKEL, 1860) 5–7 Heliodiscus Phacodiscus, HKL. – *Heliodiscus phacodiscus* (HAECKEL, 1860)

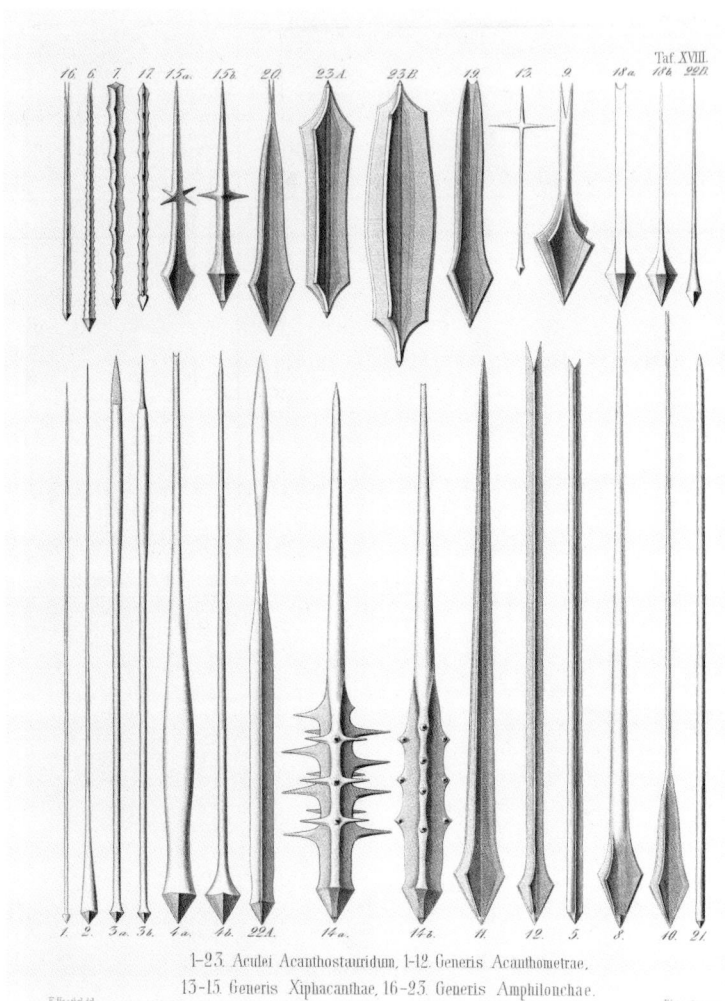

Taf. XVIII.

1–23. Aculei Acanthostauridum, 1–12. Generis Acanthometrae,
13–15. Generis Xiphacanthae, 16–23. Generis Amphilonchae.

E.Haeckel del.

Wagenschieber sc.

PLATE 18
1–23 Aculei Acanthostauridum | 1–12 Generis Acanthometrae
13–15 Generis Xiphacanthae | 16–23 Generis Amphilonchae

PLATE 19
1–2 Acanthostaurus purpurascens, HKL. – *Acanthostaurus purpurascens* (HAECKEL, 1860)
3–4 Acanthostaurus Forceps, HKL. – *Acanthostaurus forceps* (HAECKEL, 1860)
5 Acanthostaurus hastatus – *Lonchostaurus hastatus* (HAECKEL, 1860)
6 Litholophus Rhipidium, HKL. – *Litholophus rhipidium* (HAECKEL, 1860)
7 Acanthochiasma Krohnii, HKL. – *Acanthochiasma krohni* HAECKEL, 1860
8 Acanthochiasma fusiforme, HKL. – *Acanthochiasma fusiforme* HAECKEL, 1860

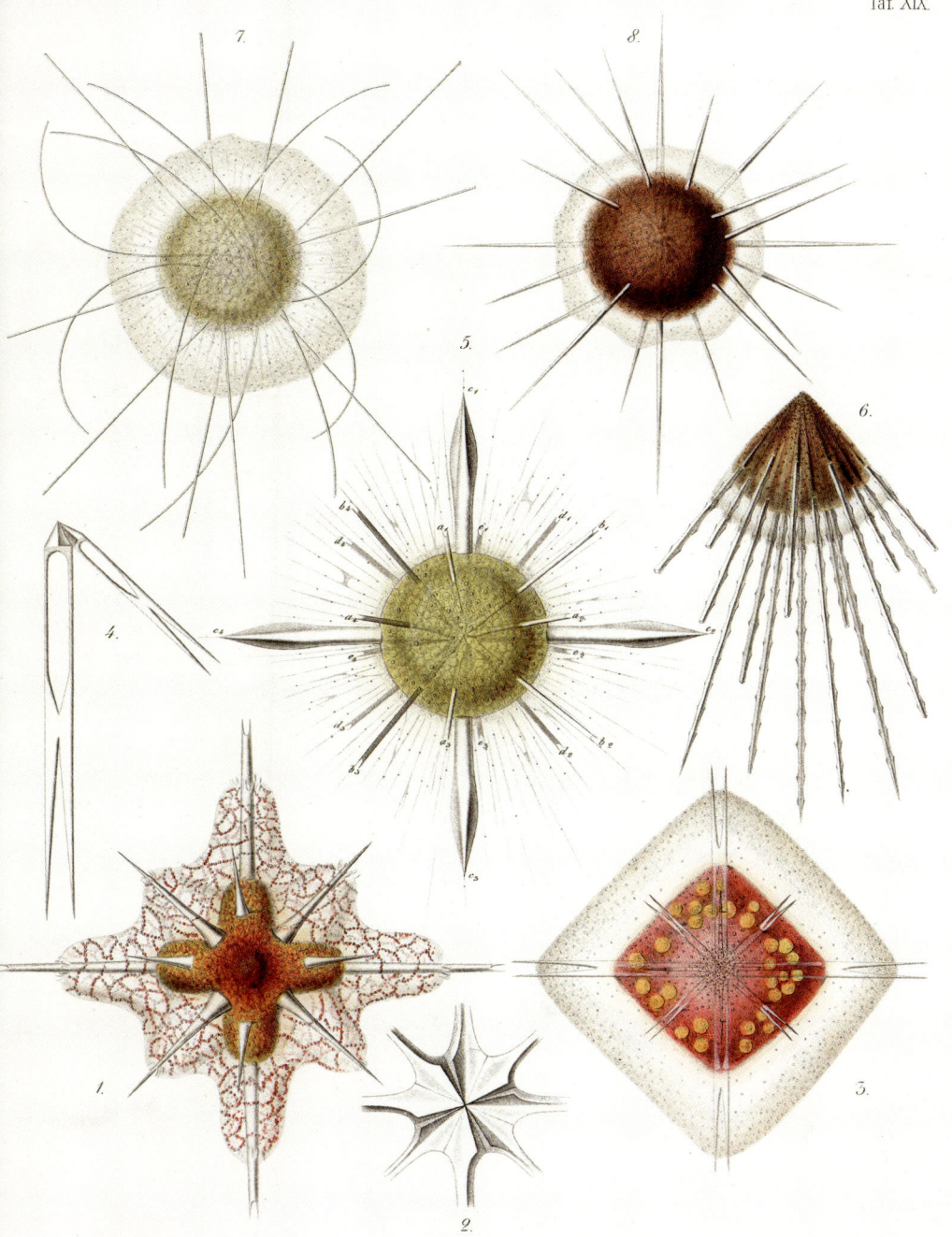

1-5. Acanthostaurus. 1. 2. A. purpurascens, Hkl. 3. 4. A. Forceps, Hkl. 5. A. hastatus, Hkl.
6. Litholophus Rhipidium, Hkl. 7. 8. Acanthochiasma. 7. A. Krohnii, Hkl. 8. A. fusiforme. Hkl.

Haeckel del.

Wagenschieber sc.

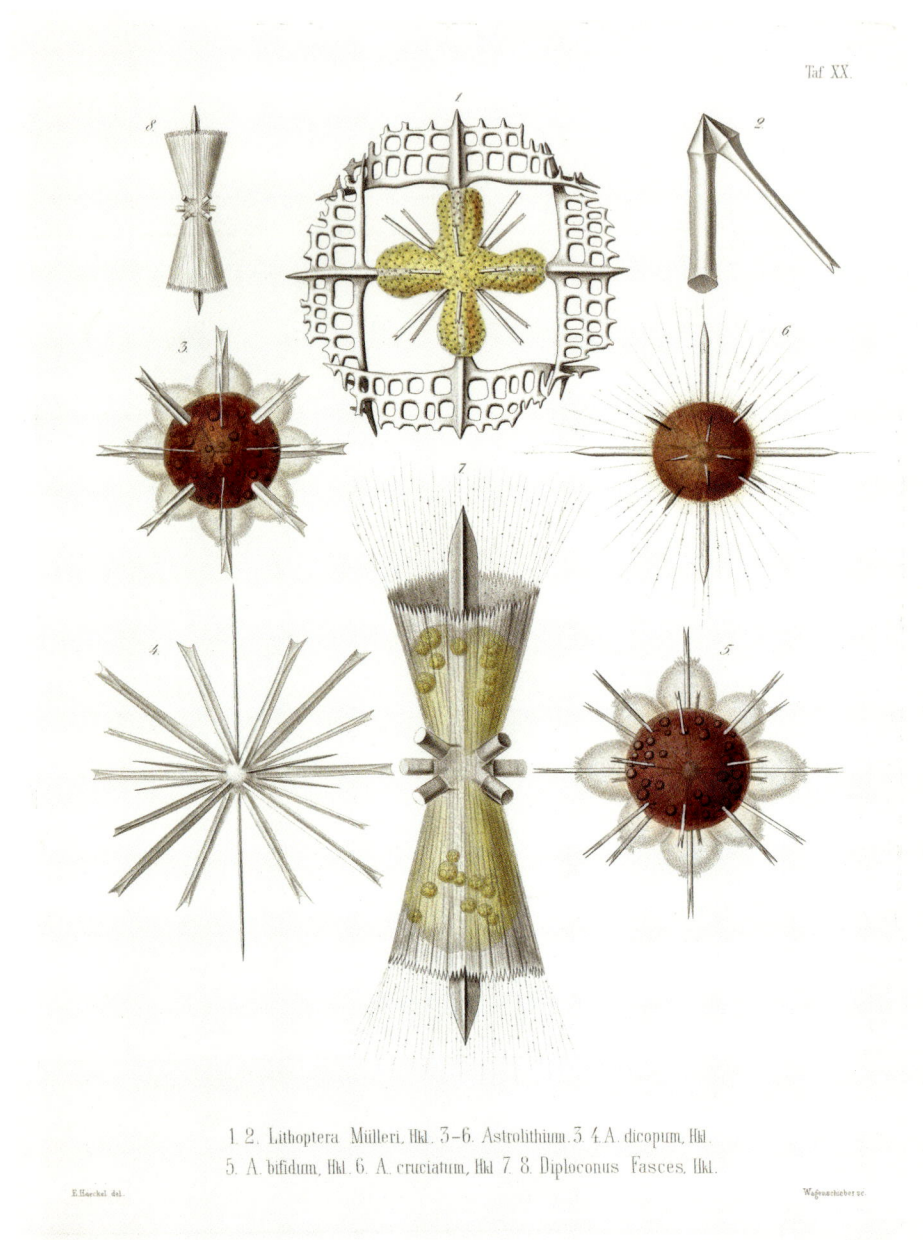

Taf XX.

1. 2. Lithoptera Mülleri, Hkl. 3–6. Astrolithium. 3 4.A. dicopum, Hkl.
5. A. bifidum, Hkl. 6. A. cruciatum, Hkl 7. 8. Diploconus Fasces, Hkl.

E.Haeckel del.   Wafrenschorber sc.

PLATE 20
1–2 Lithoptera Mülleri, HKL. – *Lithoptera muelleri* | 3–4 Astrolithium dicopum, HKL. –
Astrolithium dicopum | 5 Astrolithium bifidum, HKL. – *Atsrolithium bifidum* | 6 Astrolithium cruciatum,
HKL. – *Staurolithium cruciatum* | 7–8 Diploconus Fasces, HKL. – *Diploconus fasces*

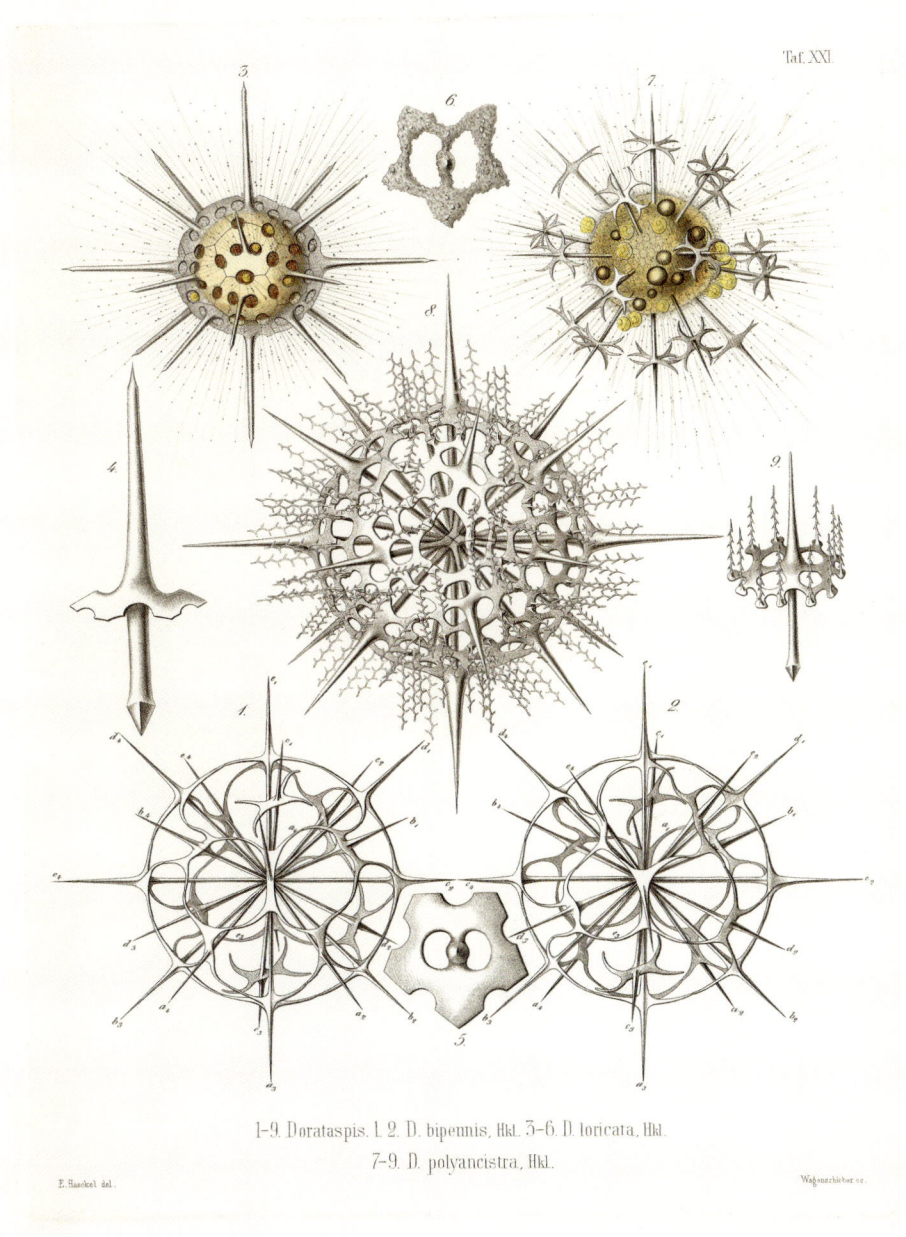

Taf. XXI.

1–9. Dorataspis. 1. 2. D. bipennis, Hkl. 3–6. D. loricata, Hkl.
7–9. D. polyancistra, Hkl.

E. Haeckel del.   Wagenschieber sc.

PLATE 21

1–2 Dorataspis bipennis, HKL. – *Dorataspis bipennis*
3–6 Dorataspis loricata, HKL. – *Dorataspis loricata*
7–9 Dorataspis polyanistra, HKL. – *Dorataspis polyanistra*

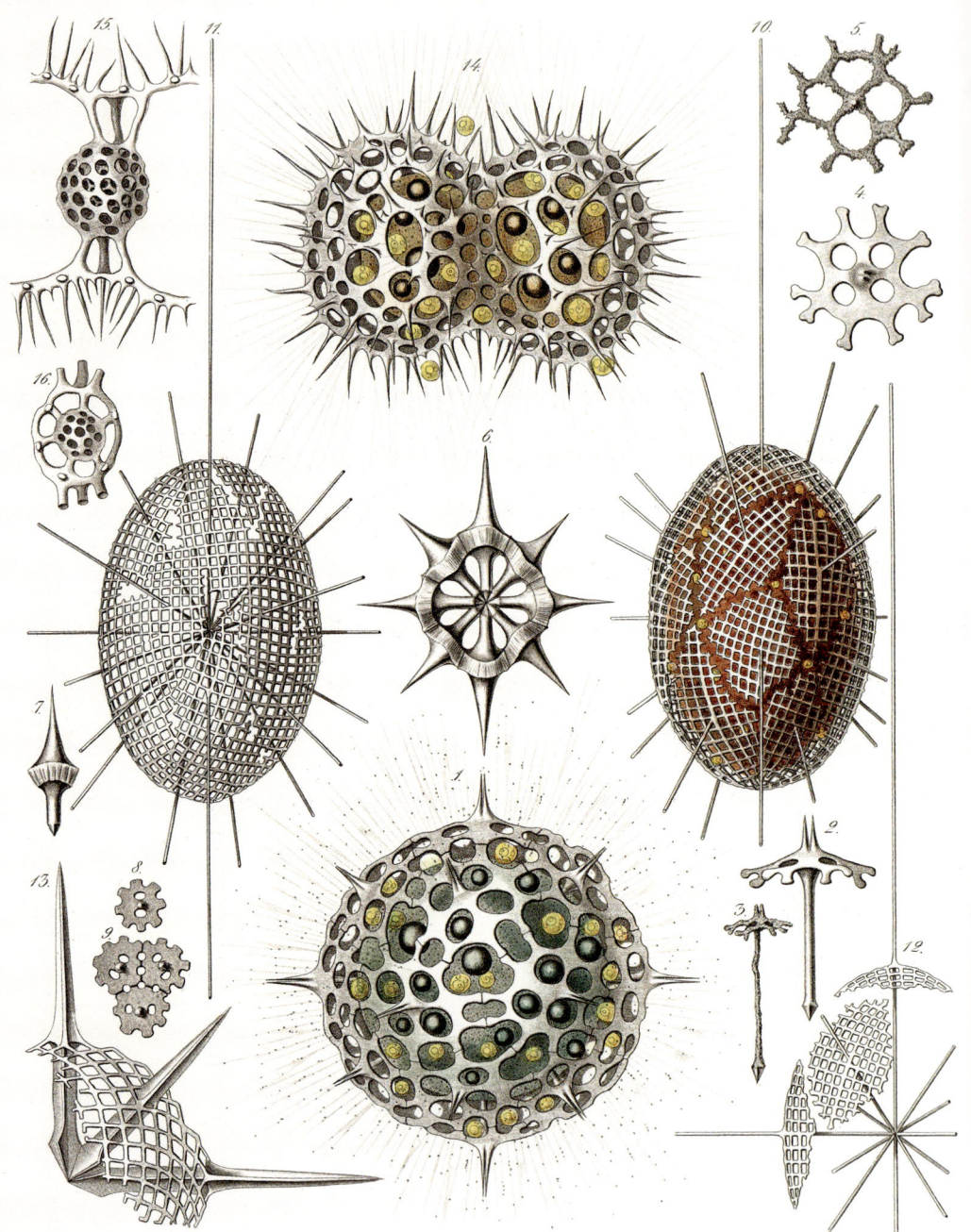

1–9. Dorataspis. 1–5. D. Diodon, Hkl. 6–9. D. solidissima, Hkl. 10–13. Haliommatidium.
10–12. H. Mülleri, Hkl. 13. H. tetragonopum, Hkl. 14–16. Didymocyrtis Ceratospyris.

E. Haeckel del.   Wagenschieber sc.

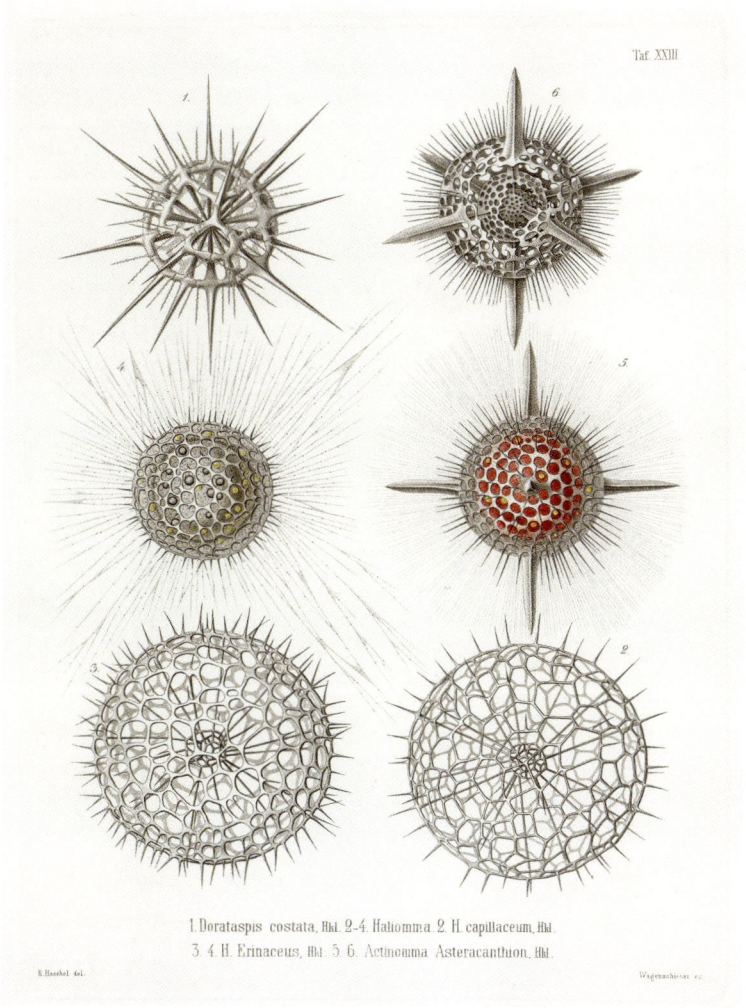

Taf. XXIII

1. Dorataspis costata, Hkl. 2-4. Haliomma. 2. H. capillaceum, Hkl.
3. 4. H. Erinaceus, Hkl. 5. 6. Actinomma Asteracanthion, Hkl.

E. Haeckel del.

Wagenbach sc.

PLATE 22
1–5 Dorataspis Diodon, HKL. – *Dorataspis diodon* HAECKEL, 1860
6–9 Dorataspis solidissima, HKL. – *Dorataspis solidissima* HAECKEL, 1860
10–12 Haliommatidium Mülleri, HKL. – *Haliommatidium muelleri* HAECKEL, 1860
13 Haliommatidium tetragonopum, HKL. – *Haliommatidium tetragonopum* HAECKEL, 1860
14–16 Didymocyrtis Ceratospyris – *Didymocyrtis ceratospyris* (HAECKEL, 1860)

PLATE 23
1 Dorataspis costata, HKL.
2 Haliomma capillaceum, HKL. – *Haliomma capillaceum* HAECKEL, 1860
3–4 Haliomma Erinaceus, HKL. – *Haliomma erinaceus* HAECKEL, 1860
5–6 Actinomma Asteracanthion, HKL. – *Actinomma asteracanthion* (HAECKEL, 1860)

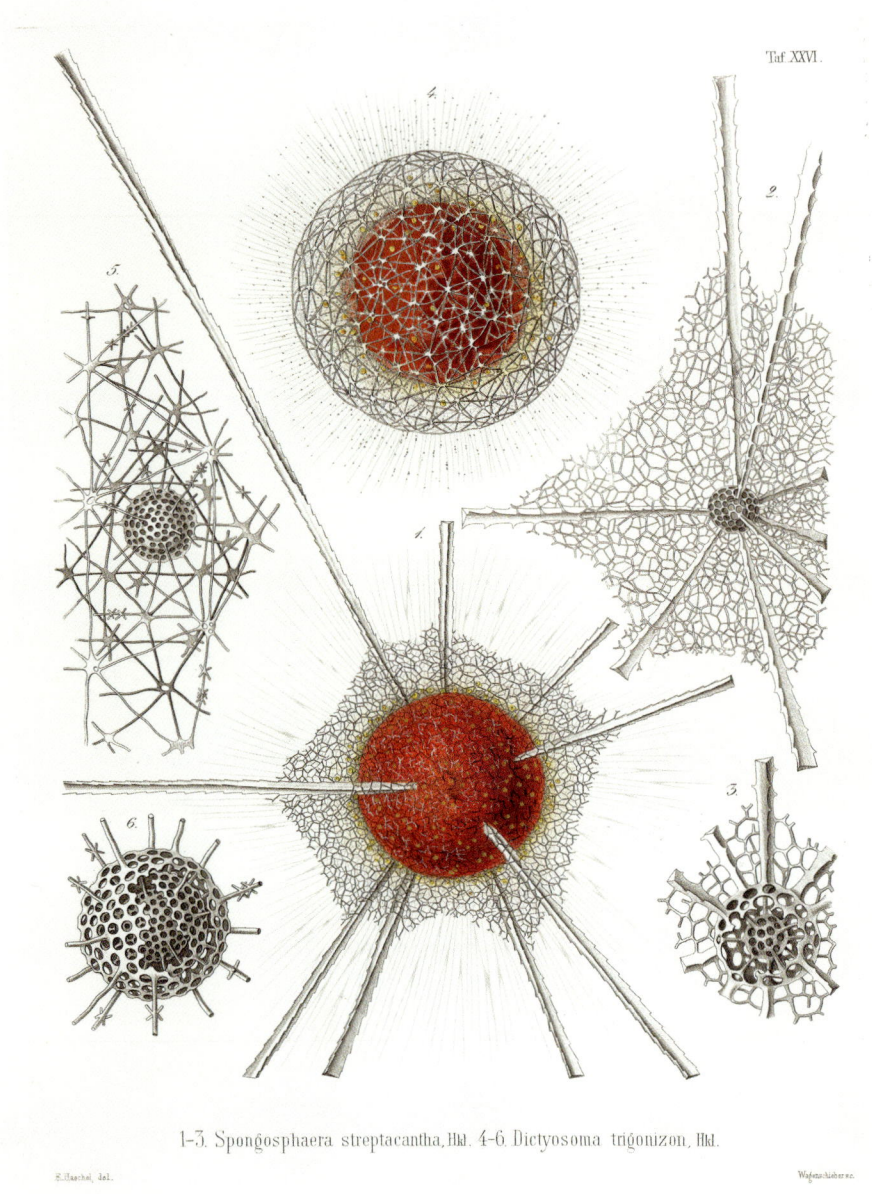

Taf. XXVl.

1-3. Spongosphaera streptacantha, Hkl. 4-6. Dictyosoma trigonizon, Hkl.

E.Haeckel, del.   Wagenschieber sc.

PLATE 26

1-3 Spongosphaera streptacantha, HKL. – *Spongosphaera streptacantha* HAECKEL, 1860
4-6 Dictyosoma trigonizon, HKL.

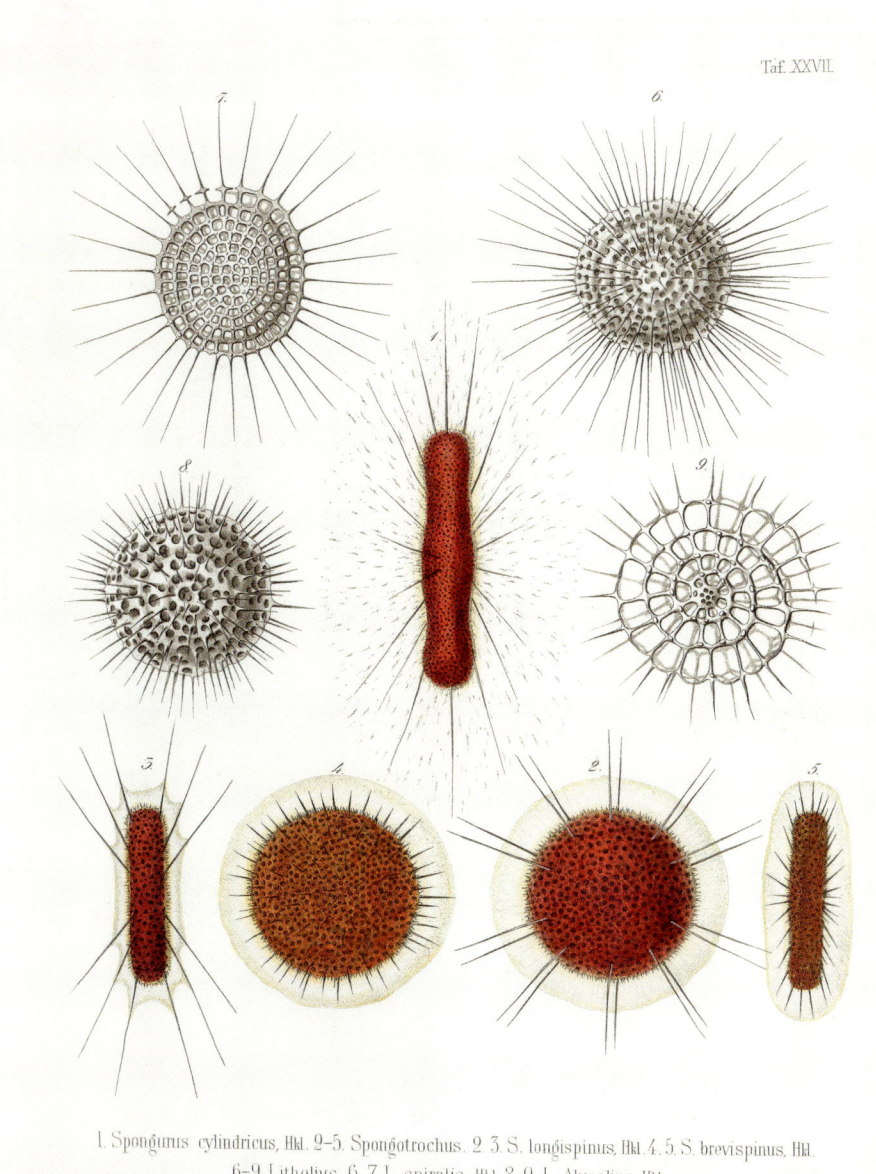

Taf. XXVII.

1. Spongurus cylindricus, Hkl. 2–5. Spongotrochus. 2. 3. S. longispinus, Hkl. 4. 5. S. brevispinus, Hkl. 6–9. Lithelius. 6. 7. L. spiralis, Hkl. 8. 9. L. Alveolina, Hkl.

E.Haeckel del.

Wagenschieber sc.

PLATE 27

1 Spongurus cylindricus, ʜᴋʟ. – *Spongurus cylindricus* ʜᴀᴇᴄᴋᴇʟ, 1860 | 2-3 Spongotrochus longispinus, ʜᴋʟ. – *Spongotrochus longispinus* ʜᴀᴇᴄᴋᴇʟ, 1860 | 4-5 Spongotrochus brevispinus, ʜᴋʟ. – *Spongotrochus brevispinus* ʜᴀᴇᴄᴋᴇʟ, 1860 | 6-7 Lithelius spiralis, ʜᴋʟ. – *Lithelius spiralis* ʜᴀᴇᴄᴋᴇʟ, 1860 | 8-9 Lithelius Alveolina, ʜᴋʟ. – *Lithelius alveolina* ʜᴀᴇᴄᴋᴇʟ, 1862

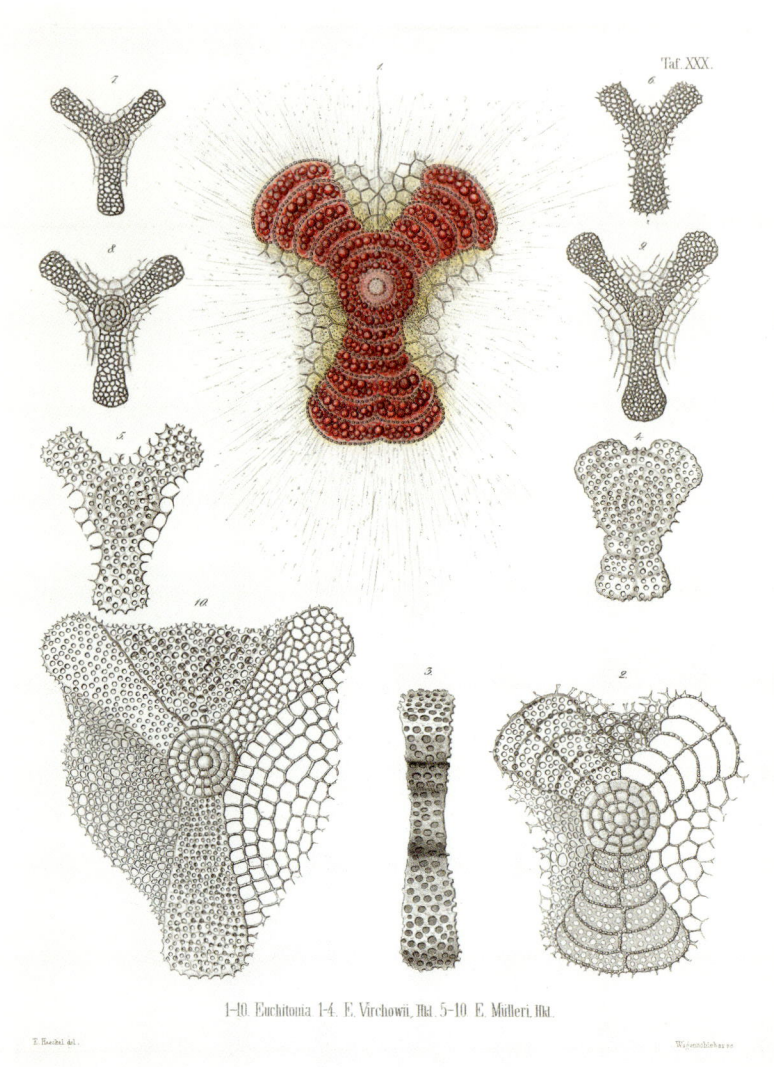

1-10. Euchitonia 1-4. E. Virchowii, Hkl. 5-10. E. Mülleri, Hkl.

E. Haeckel del.

Wissenschieber sc.

PLATE 30
1–4 Euchitonia Virchowii, HKL. – *Euchitonia virchowi*
5–10 Euchitonia Mülleri, HKL. – *Euchitonia muelleri*

PLATE 31
1 Euchitonia Beckmanni, HKL. – *Euchitonia beckmanni*
2–3 Euchitonia Gegenbauri, HKL. – *Euchitonia gegenbauri*
4–5 Euchitonia Leydigii, HKL. – *Euchitonia leydigi*
6–7 Euchitonia Kollikeri, HKL. – *Euchitonia koellikeri*

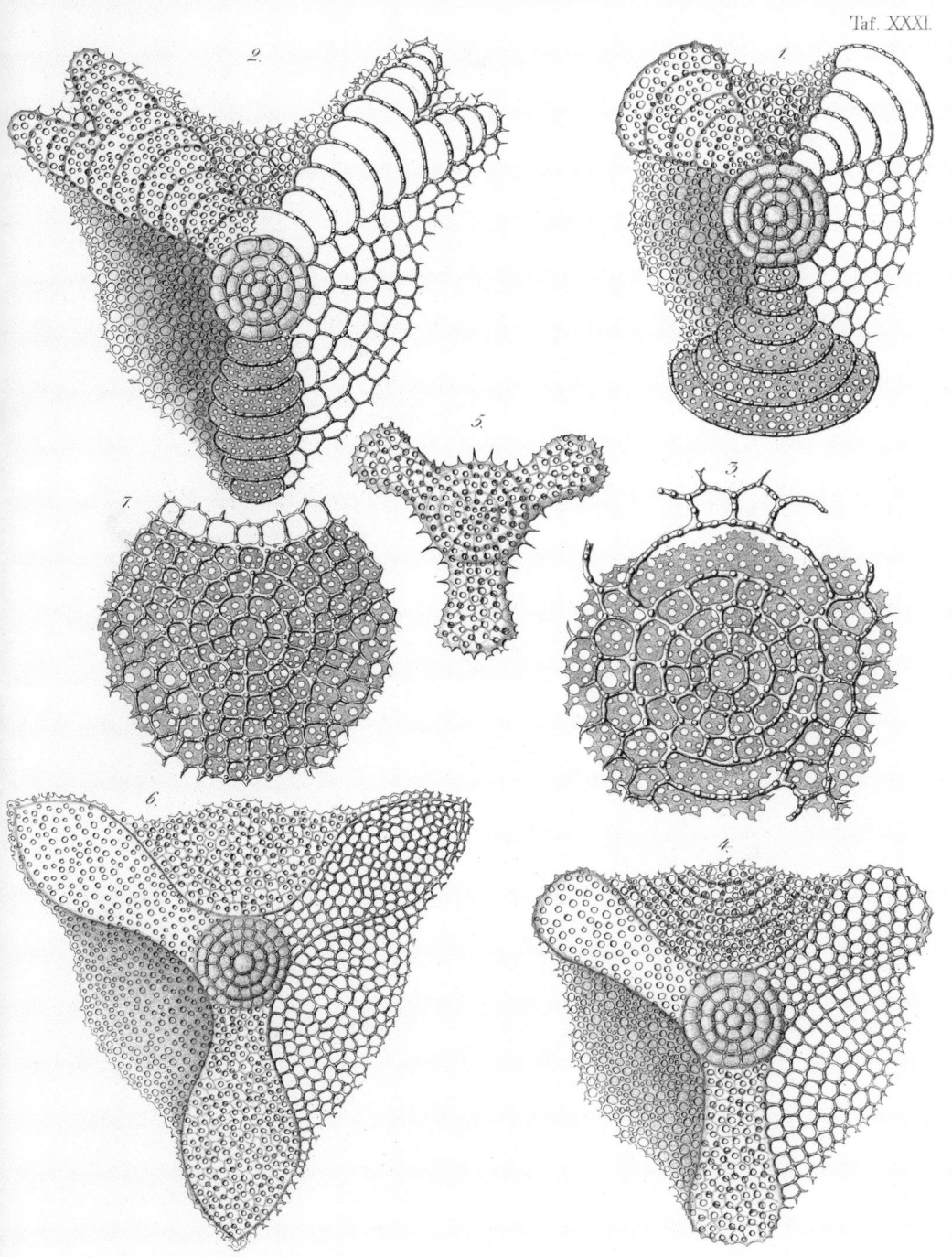

1-7. Euchitonia.1. E. Beckmanni, Hkl. 2. 3. E. Gegenbauri. Hkl.
4. 5. E. Leydigii, Hkl. 6. 7. E. Köllikeri, Hkl.

Haeckel del.

Wagenschieber sc.

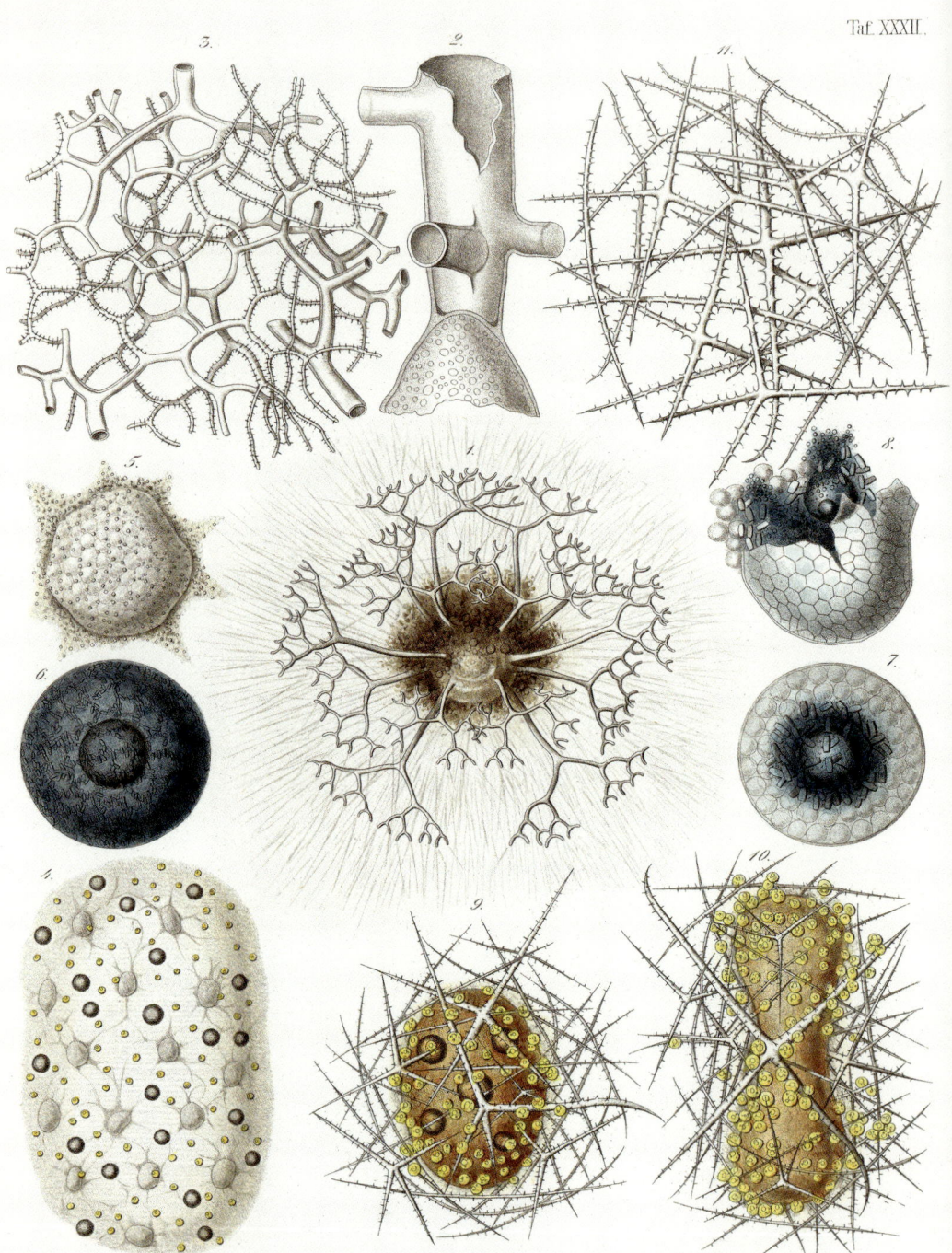

1–3. Coelodendrum gracillimum, Hkl. 4–8. Collozoum. 4 5. C. pelagicum, Hkl.
6–8. C. coeruleum, Hkl. 9–11. Rhaphidozoum acuferum, Hkl.

E. Haeckel del.

Wagenschieber sc

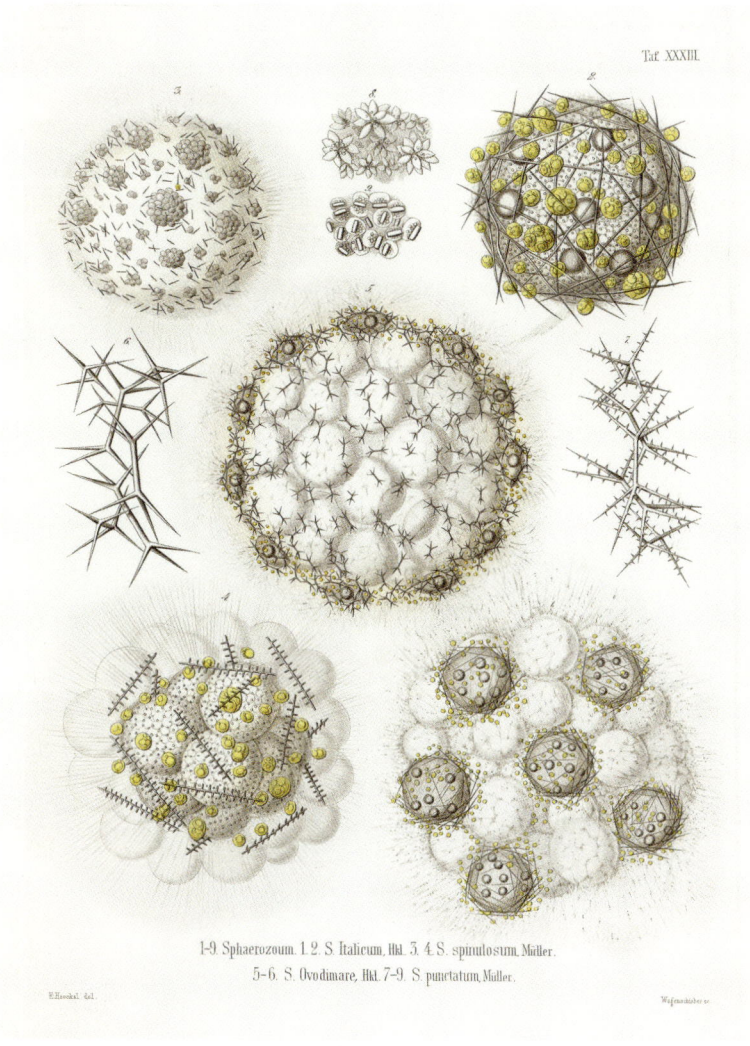

1-9. Sphaerozoum. 1. 2. S. Italicum, Hkl. 3. 4. S. spinulosum, Müller.
5-6. S. Ovodimare, Hkl. 7-9. S. punctatum, Müller.

PLATE 32

1-3 Coelodendrum gracillimum, HKL. – *Coelodendrum gracillimum* HAECKEL, 1862
4-5 Collozoum pelagicum, HKL. – *Collozoum pelagicum* (HAECKEL, 1860)
6-8 Collozoum coeruleum, HKL. – *Collozoum coeruleum* (HAECKEL, 1860)
9-11 Rhaphidozoum acuferum, HKL. – *Rhaphidozoum acuferum* (MÜLLER, 1856)

PLATE 33

1-2 Sphaerozoum Italicum, HKL. – *Sphaerozoum italicum* HAECKEL, 1860
3-4 Sphaerozoum spinolosum, MÜLLER
5-6 Sphaerozoum Ovodimare, HKL. – *Sphaerozoum ovodimare* HAECKEL, 1860
7-9 Sphaerozoum punctatum, MÜLLER – *Sphaerozoum punctatum* (HUXLEY) MUELLER, 1858

PLATE I ❧ — VOL. 2: A NATURAL HISTORY OF RADIOLARIA
1 Actissa princeps | 2 Thalassolampe maxima
3 Thalassopila cladococcus | 4 Thalassicolla maculata
5 Thalassicolla melacapsa

❧ see page 507

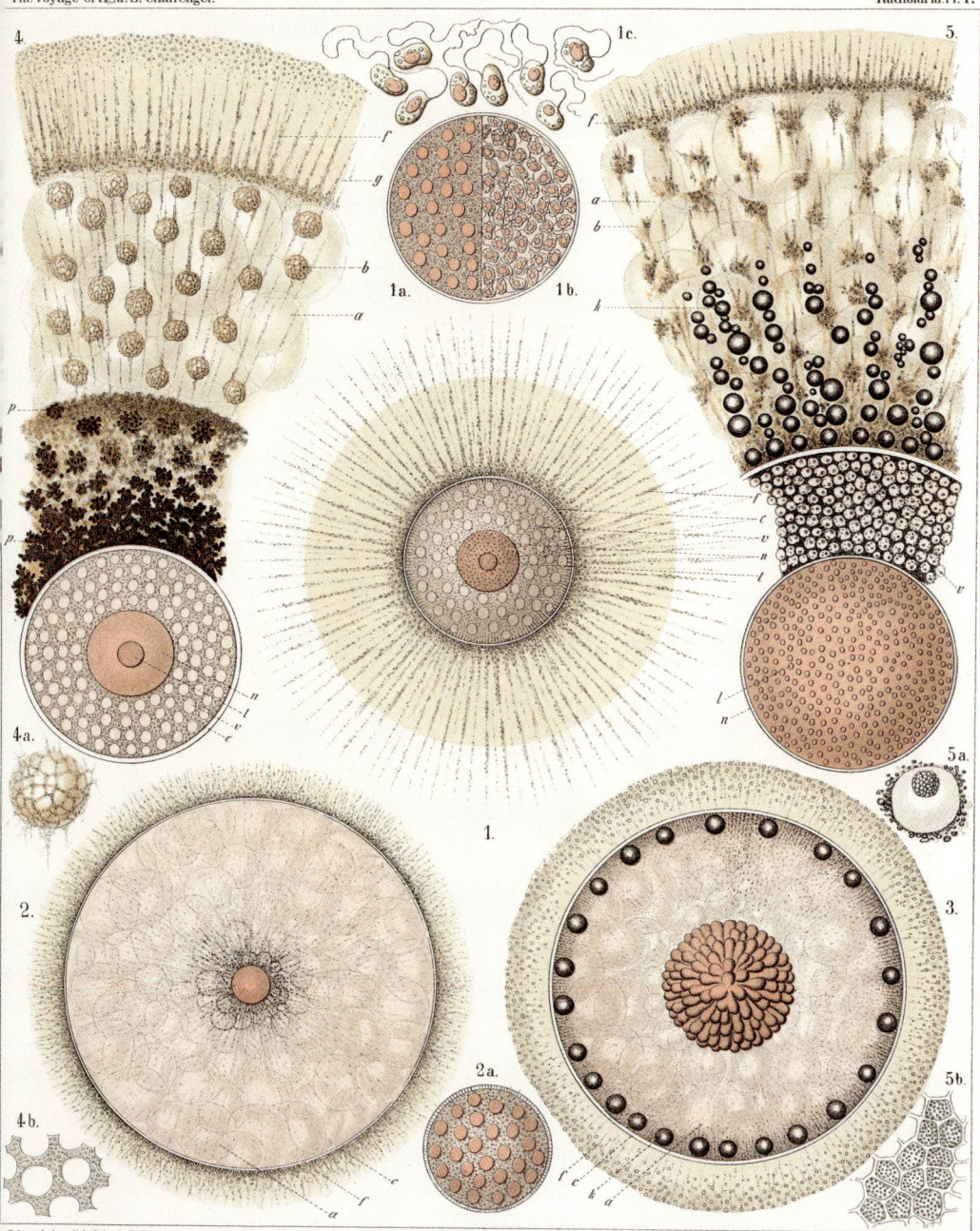

E.Haeckel and A.Giltsch,Del.

E.Giltsch, Jena, Lithogr.

1. ACTISSA, 2. THALASSOLAMPE, 3. THALASSOPILA,
4.5. THALASSOCOLLA.

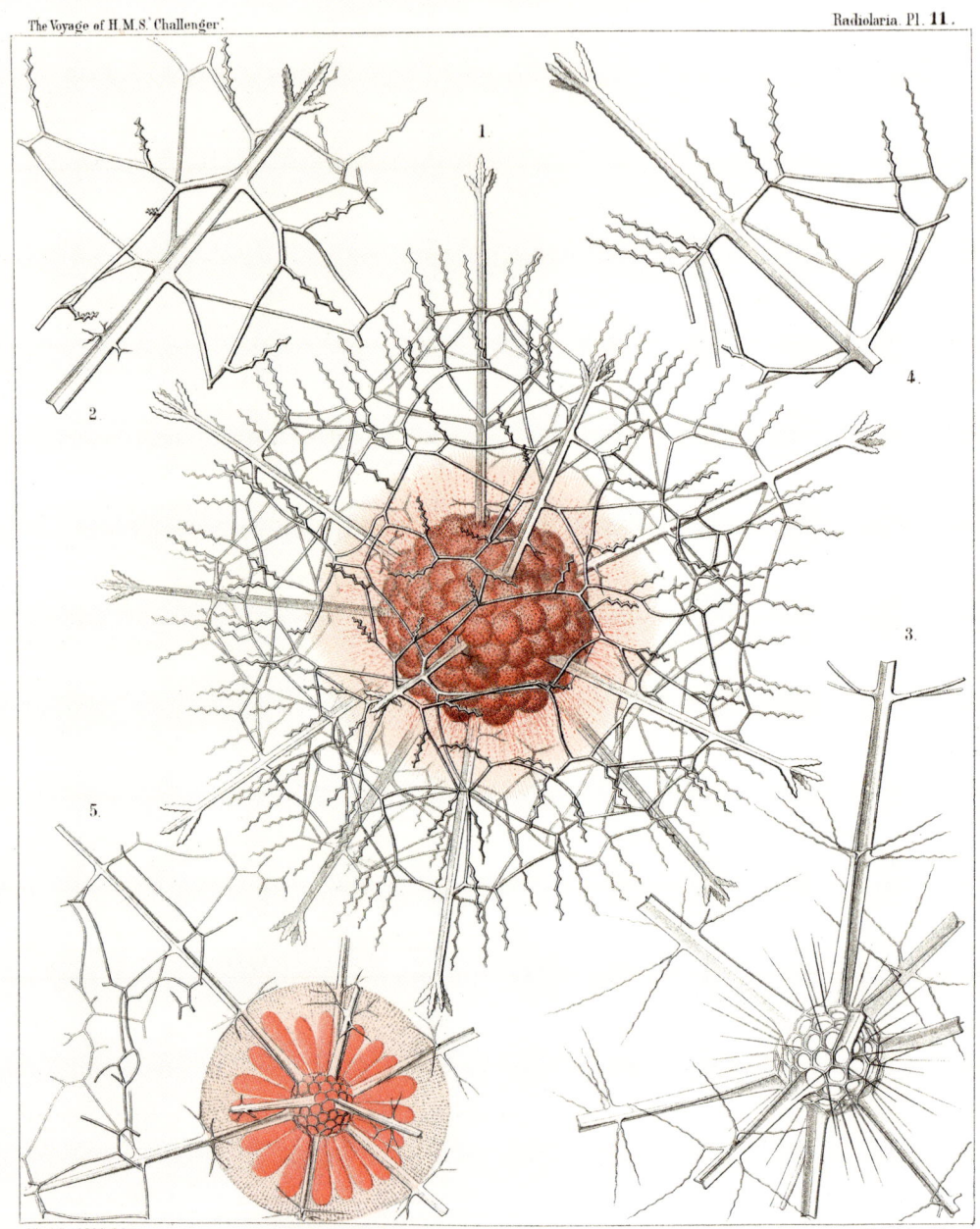

E.Haeckel and A.Giltsch.Del.

F.Giltsch, Jena, Lithogr.

LYCHNOSPHAERA.

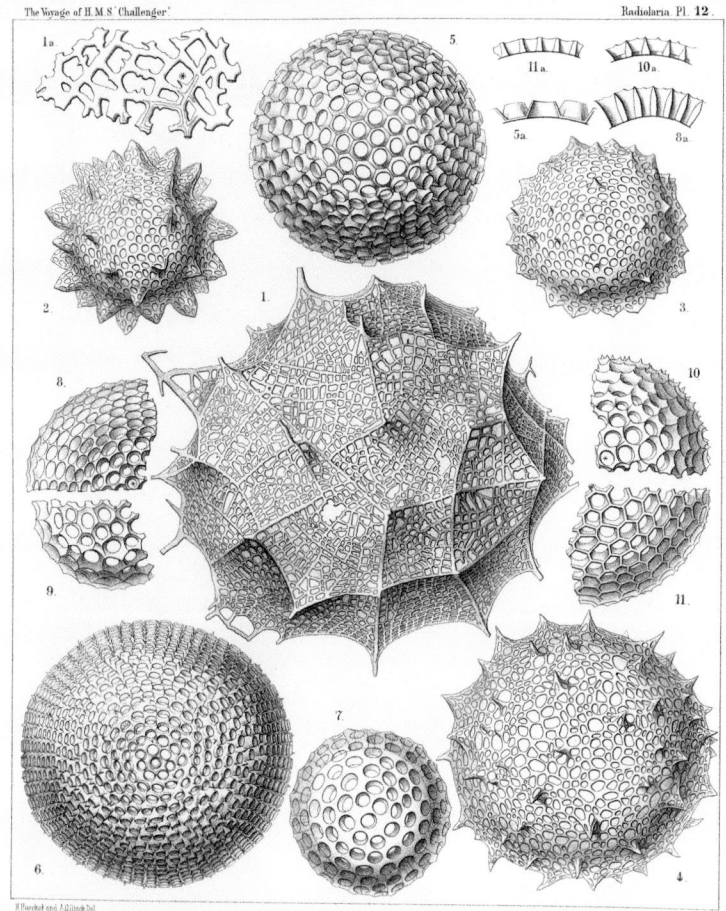

SPUMELLARIA ET NASSELLARIA. TAF. 5.

The Voyage of H.M.S. 'Challenger.'

Radiolaria. Pl. 12.

1. OROSPHAERA. 2-4. CONOSPHAERA. 5.6. ETHMOSPHAERA.
7-11. CERIOSPHAERA.

PLATE 4

1–4 Lychnosphaera regina | 5 Rhizoplegma lychnosphaera

PLATE 5

1 Orosphaera huxleyi | 2 Conosphaera orthoconus
3 Conosphaera platyconus | 4 Conosphaera plagioconus
5 Ethmosphaera conosiphonia | 6 Ethmosphaera polysiphonia
7 Cenosphaera compacta | 8 Cenosphaera elysia
9 Cenosphaera mellifica | 10 Cenosphaera favosa
11 Cenosphaera vesparia

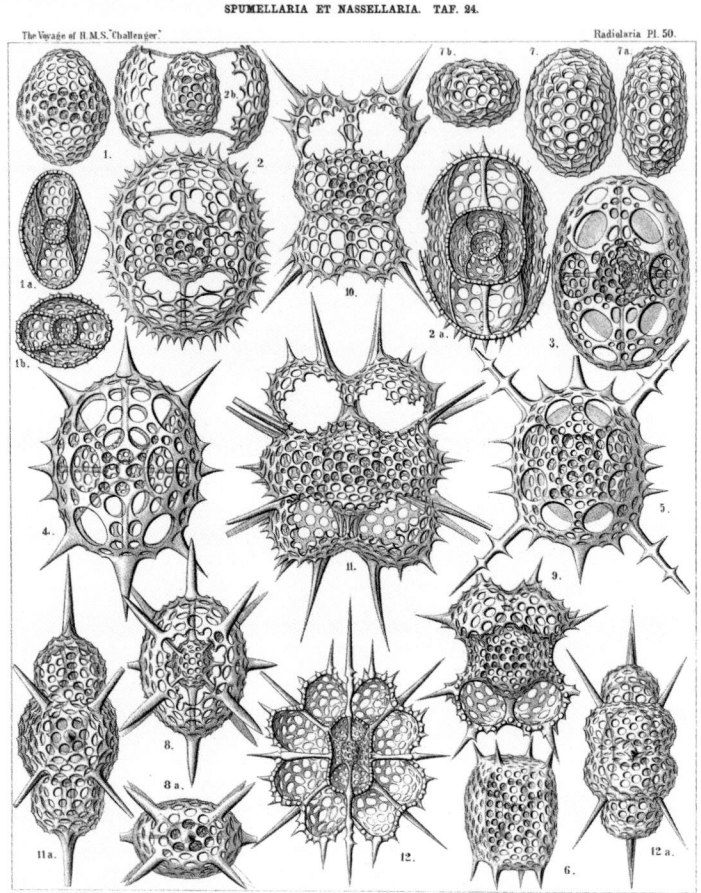

SPUMELLARIA ET NASSELLARIA. TAF. 24.

The Voyage of H.M.S."Challenger."

Radiolaria Pl. 50.

1. LARNACILLA, 2–6. LARNACALPIS, 7. CENOLARCUS,
8. LARCIDIUM, 9–12. ZONARIUM.

PLATE 24

1 Larnacilla typus | 2 Larnacalpis lentellipsis | 3 Larnacalpis triaxonia
4 Larnacantha hexacantha | 5 Larnacantha bicruciata | 6 Larnacantha prismatica
7 Cenolarcus primordialis | 8 Larcidium dodecanthum | 9 Zonarium octangulum
10 Zoniscus tetracanthus | 11 Zoniscus hexatholius | 12 Zonodium octotholium

PLATE 25

1 Tripterocalpis phyllopera | 2 Tripterocalpis conoptera
3–5 Tripterocalpis ogmoptera | 6 Tripterocalpis triserrata | 7 Tridictyopus conicus
8 Tridictyopus vatillum | 9 Cyrtophomis spiralis | 10 Archicorys ovata
11 Cyrtocalpis gromia | 12 Archicorys microstoma | 13 Cyrtocalpis urceolus

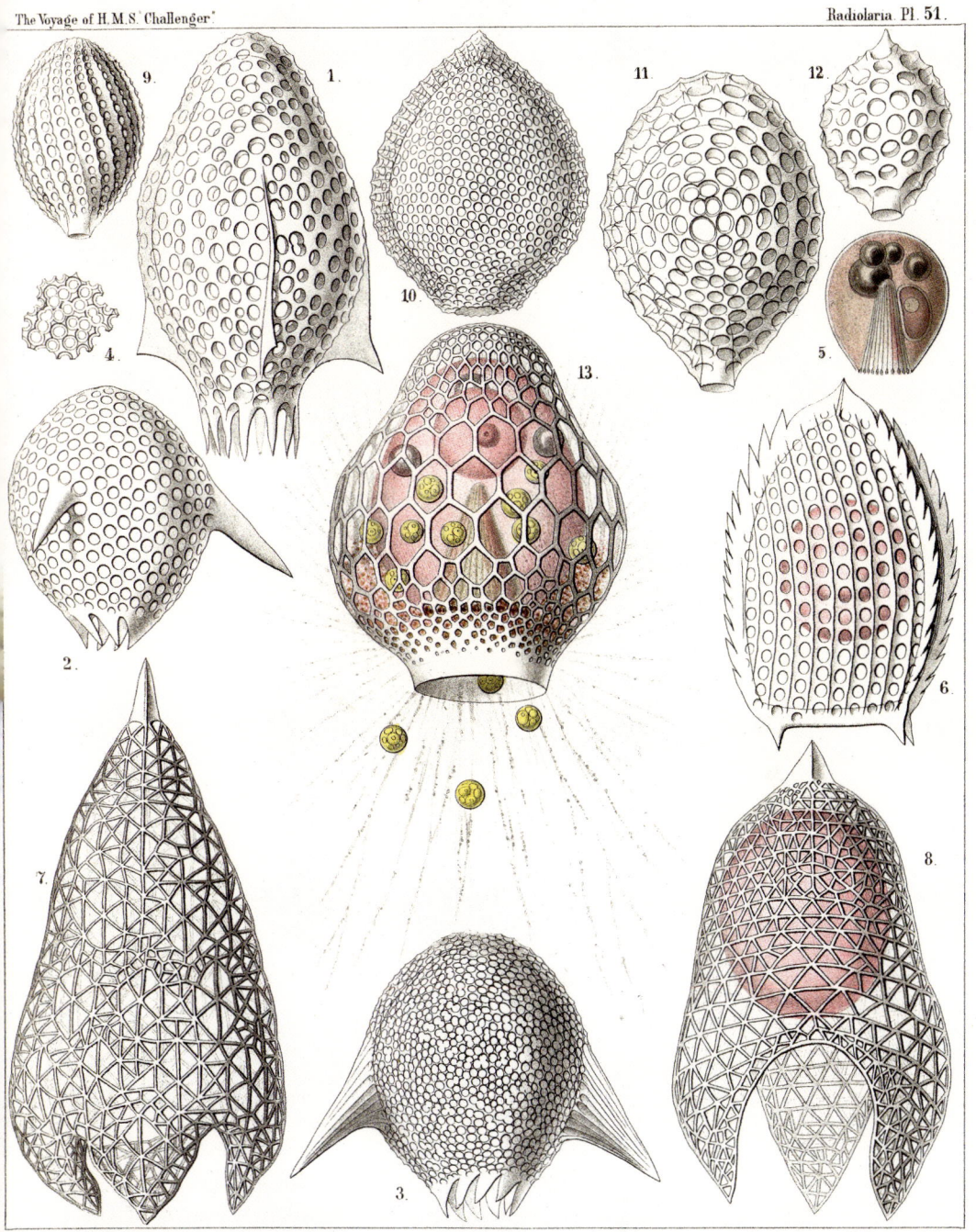

E.Haeckel and A.Giltsch.Del.

E.Giltsch, Jena, Lithogr.

1 – 6. TRIPTEROCALPIS, 7. 8. TRIDICTYOPUS, 9.– 13. CYRTOCALPIS.

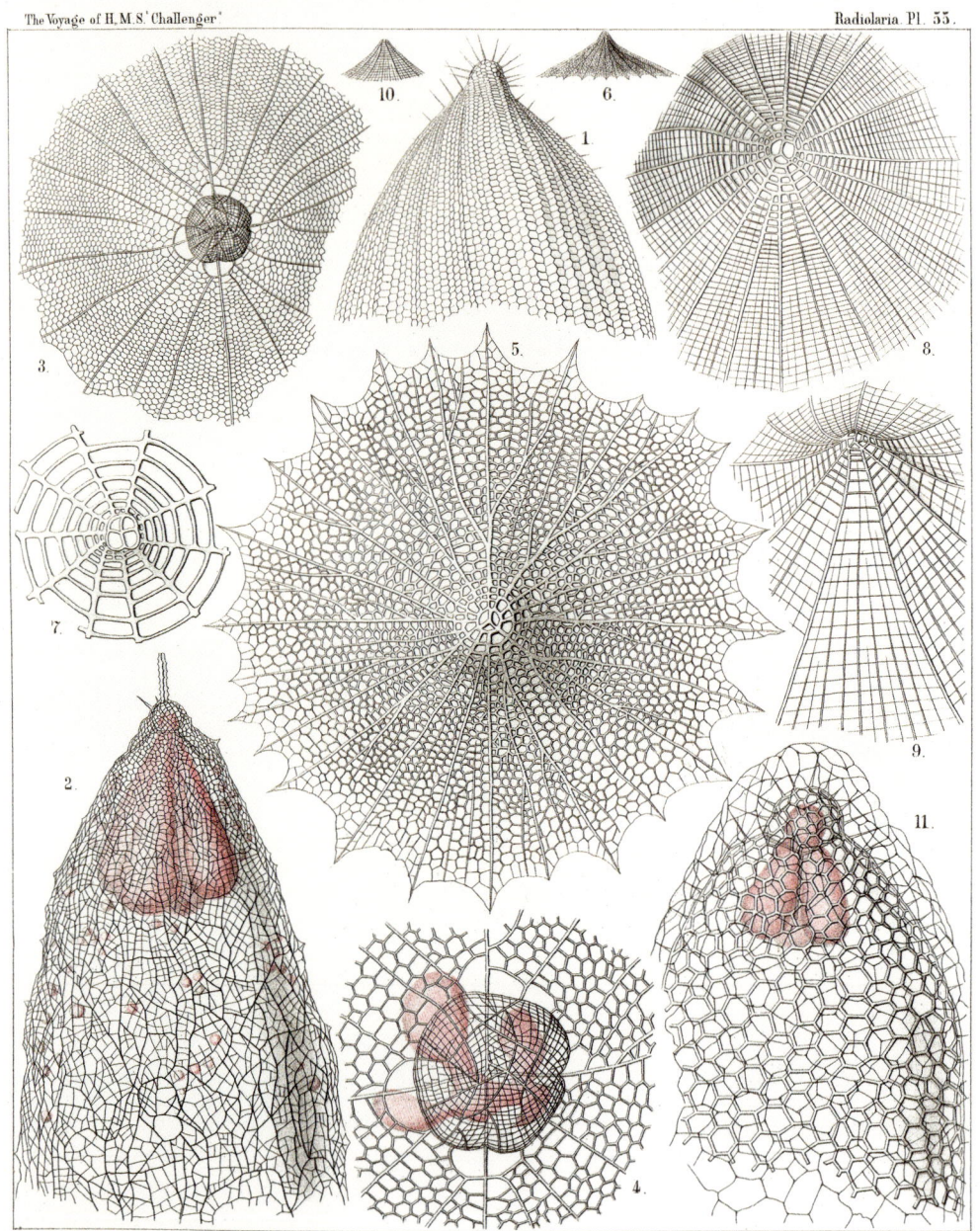

E.Haeckel and A.Giltsch.Del.

E.Giltsch,Jena,Lithogr.

1.2. PHLEBARACHNIUM, 3.4. LEPTARACHNIUM, 5.-10. LITHARACHNIUM.
11. PERIARACHNIUM.

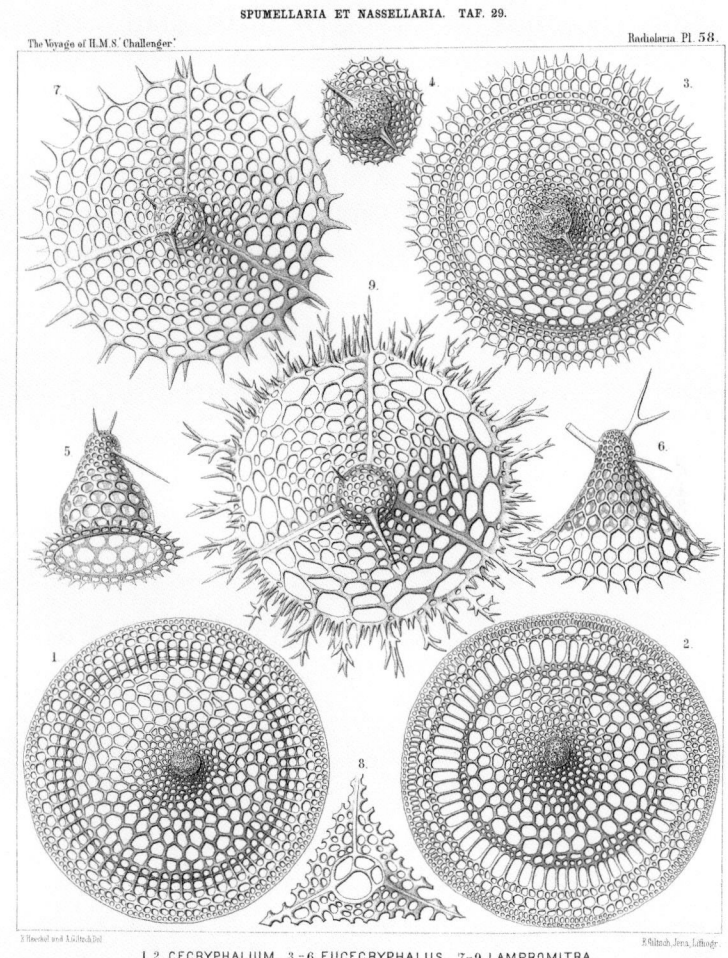

SPUMELLARIA ET NASSELLARIA. TAF. 29.

The Voyage of H.M.S. 'Challenger'.

Radiolaria. Pl. 58.

1. 2. CECRYPHALIUM. 3.–6. EUCECRYPHALUS. 7.–9. LAMPROMITRA.

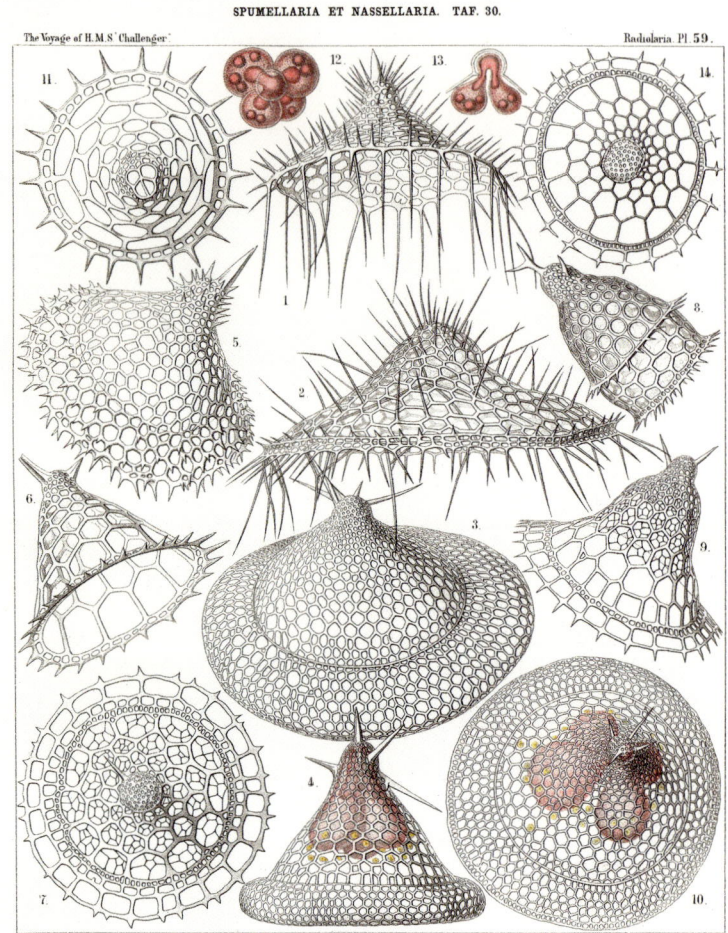

PLATE 30
1 Lampromitra huxleyi | 2 Amphiplecta allistoma | 3 Corocalyptra agnesae
4 Corocalyptra emmae | 5 Clathrocyclas cassiopejae | 6 Clathrocyclas alcmenae
7 Clathrocyclas latonae | 8 Diplocyclas bicorona | 9 Clathrocyclas ionis
10 Corocalyptra elisabethae | 11–12 Clathrocyclas europae | 13–14 Clathrocyclas danaes

PLATE 31
1 Dictyophimus cienkowskii | 2 Dictyophimus bütschlii | 3 Dictyophimus hertwigii
4–5 Dictyophimus platycephalus | 6 Dictyophimus brandtii | 7 Lampromitra coronata
8 Lampromitra arbrescens | 9 Tripcyrtis plagoniscus | 10 Tripcyrtis plectaniscus

H.Haeckel and A.Giltsch,Del.

E.Giltsch,Jena,Lithogr.

1 – 6. LAMPROTRIPUS, 7 – 10. LAMPROMITRA.

SPUMELLARIA ET NASSELLARIA. TAF. 48.

The Voyage of H. M. S. Challenger.

Radiolaria. Pl. 81.

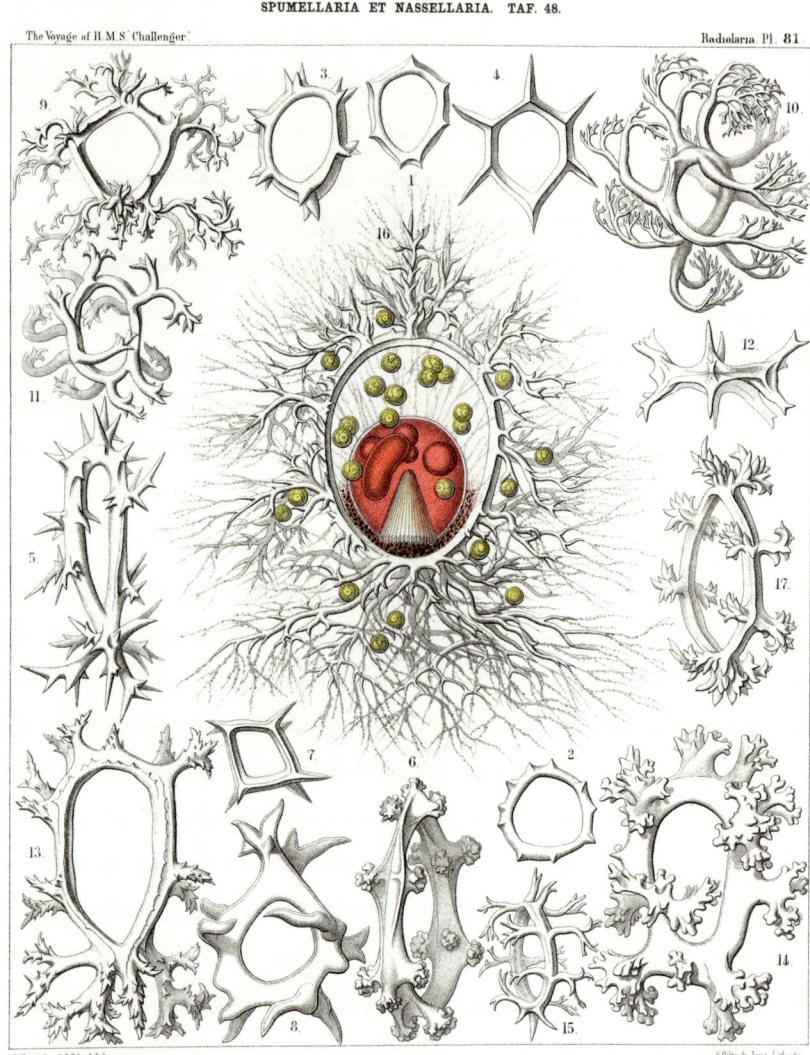

E.Haeckel and A.Giltsch Del.

E.Giltsch, Jena, Lithogr.

1 - 8 LITHOCIRCUS, 9 - 17 DENDROCIRCUS.

PLATE 48

1 Archicircus primordalis | 2 Zygocircus ploygonus | 3 Zygocircus triquetrus | 4 Archicircus hexacanthus
5 Zygocircus acacia | 6 Lithocircus crambessa | 7 Archicircus rhombus | 8 Zygocircus pentogonus
9 Lithocircus quadricornis | 10 Dendrocircus arborescens | 11 Dendrocircus dodecancistra
12 Archicircus sexangularis | 13 Dendrocircus elegans | 14 Dendrocircus stalactites | 15 Lithocircus
decimalis | 16 Lithocircus magnificus | 17 Lithocircus hexablastus

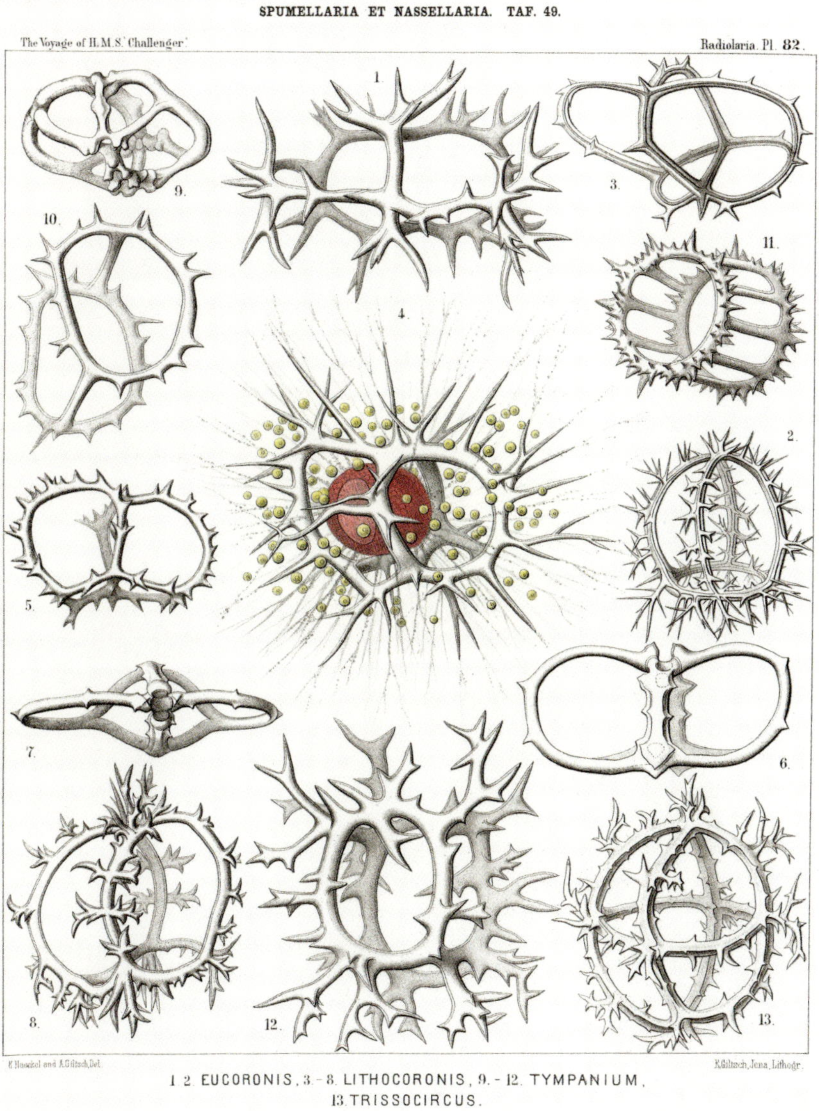

1 2 EUCORONIS, 3.-8. LITHOCORONIS, 9.-12. TYMPANIUM, 13. TRISSOCIRCUS.

PLATE 49

1 Coronidium cervicorne | 2 Coronidium acacia | 3 Eucoronis angulata | 4 Eucoronis challengeri
5 Eucoronis nephrospyris | 6 Eucoronis perspicillum | 7 Coronidium dyostephanus | 8 Coronidium
diadema | 9 Acrocubus octopylus | 10 Parastephanus asymmetricus | 11 Eutympanium militare
12 Lithocubus astragulus | 13 Trissocircus globus

1 Zygostephanus dissocircus | 2 Zygostephanus bicornis | 3 Zygostephanium dizonium
4 Zygostephanium paradictyum | 5 Acanthodesmia corona | 6 Plectocoronis pentacantha
7 Tristephanium quadricorne | 8 Tristephanium octopyle | 9 Tristephanium dimensivum
10 Trissocircus lentellipsis | 11 Trissocircus octostoma | 12 Trissocyclus sphaeridium | 13 Tricyclidium
dictyospyris | 14 Protympanium amphipodium | 15 Acrocubus arcuatus | 16 Acrocubus cortina
17 Acrocubus amphithectus | 18 Toxarium thorax | 19 Toxarium cordatum | 20 Toxarium bifurcum
21 Parastephanus quadrispinus | 22 Prismatium tripodium

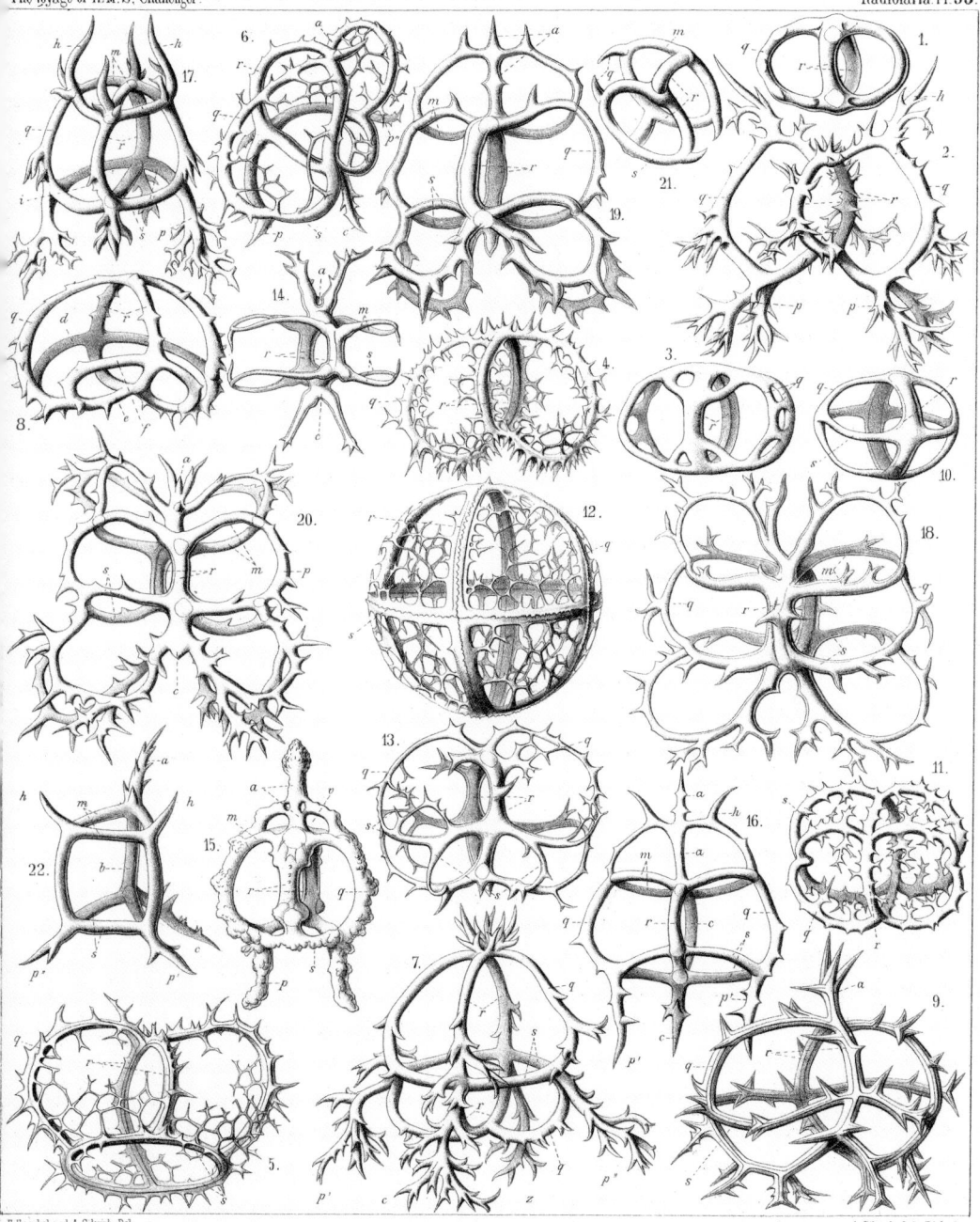

1-4. ZYGOSTEPHANUS, 5-6. ACANTHODESMIA, 7-13. TRISTEPHANIUM,
14-17. ACROCUBUS, 18-20. TOXARIUM, 21.22. PRISMATIUM.

PLATE I — VOL. 3: ACANTHAREA OR ACTIPYLEA
1 Actinelius primordialis | 2 Litholophus decapristis | 3 Chiastolus amphicopium
4-5 Xiphacantha ciliata | 6-8 Acanthometron dolichoscion | 9-11 Acanthonia tetracopa

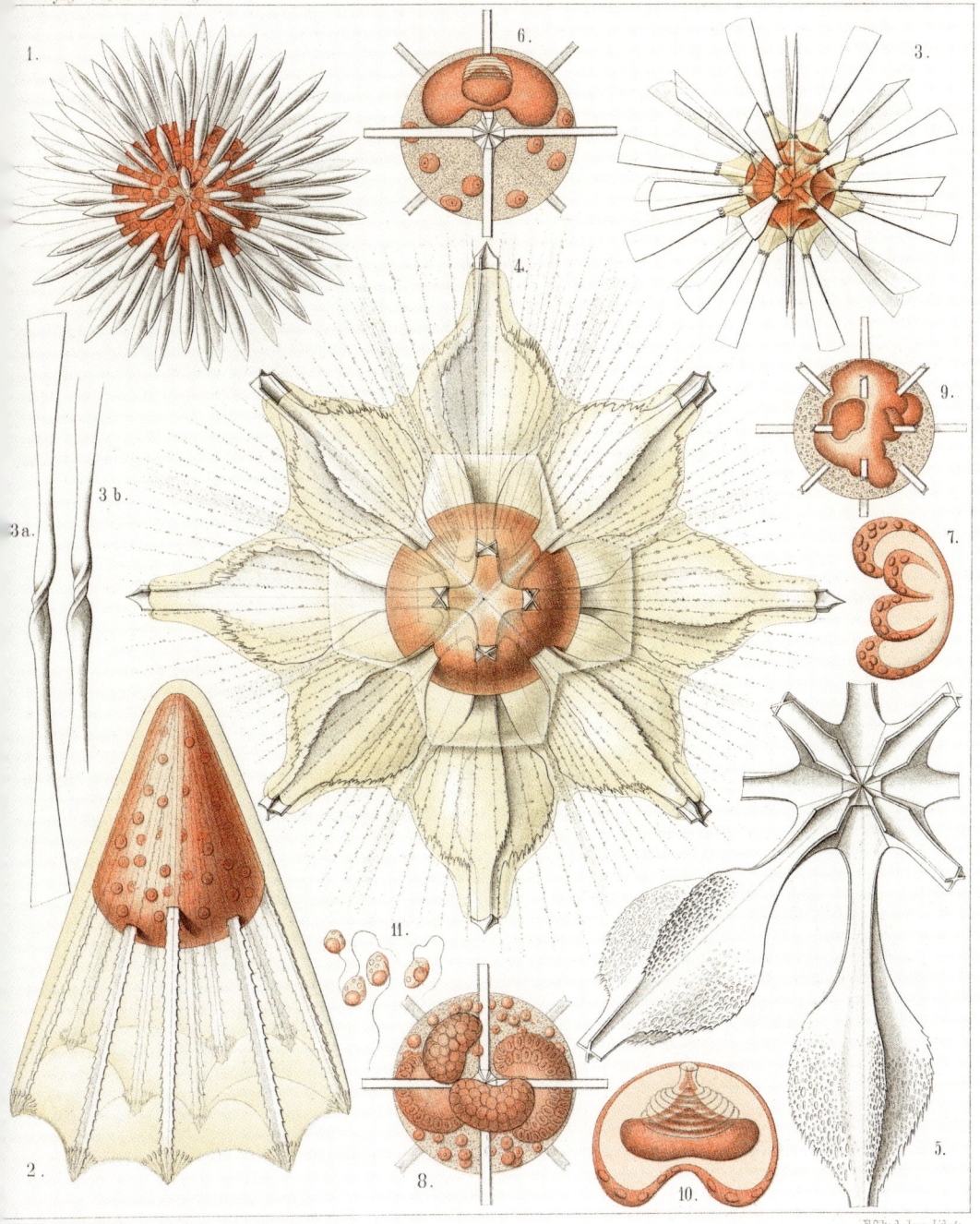

E.Haeckel and A.Giltsch,Del.

E.Giltsch Jena, Lithogr.

1. ACTINELIUS, 2. LITHOLOPHUS, 3. CHIASTOLUS,
4-11.ACANTHONIA.

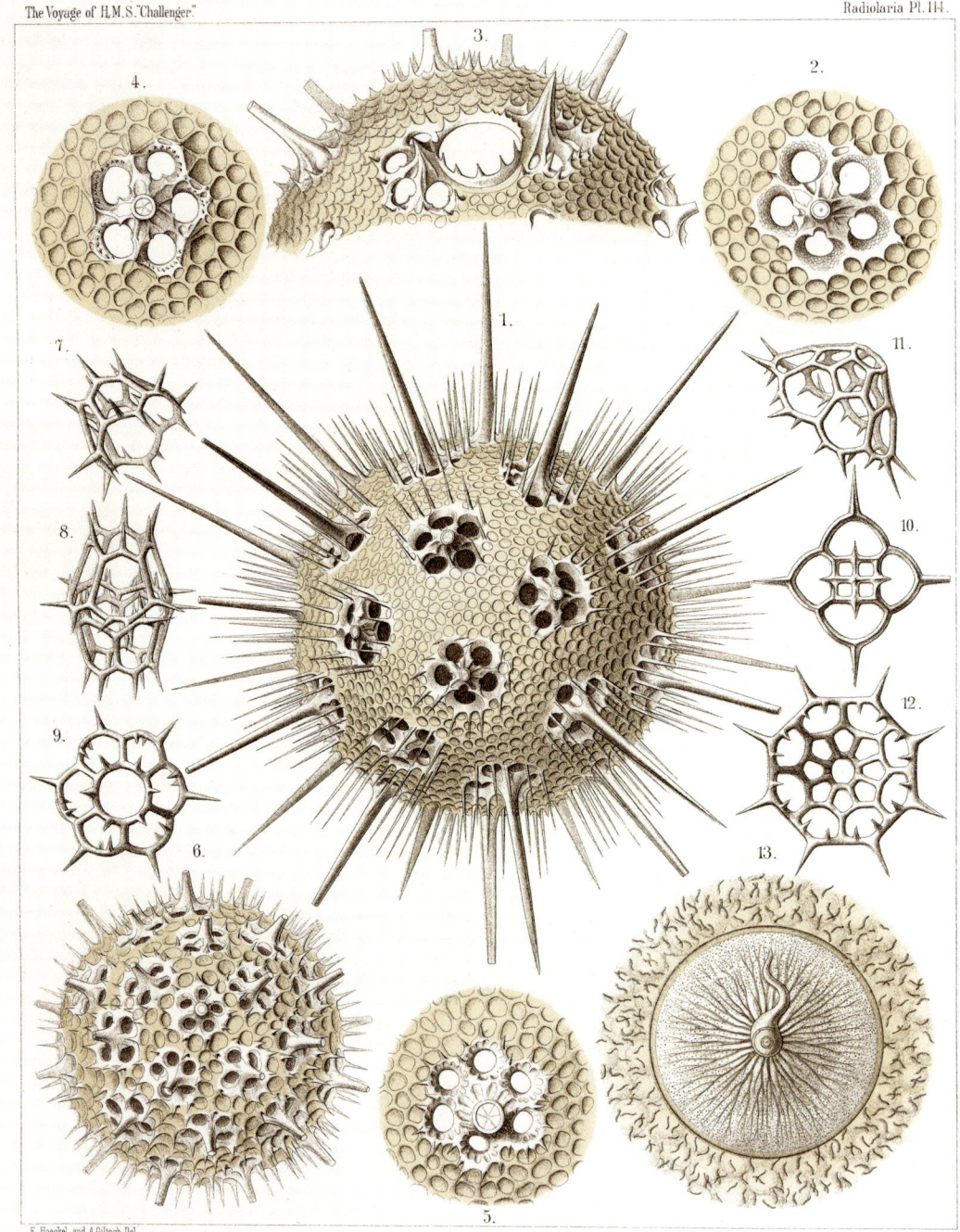

E. Haeckel and A.Giltsch, Del.

A.Giltsch, Jena, Lithogr.

1-6. HAECKELIANA, 7-9. DISTEPHANUS, 10-13. CANNOPILUS.

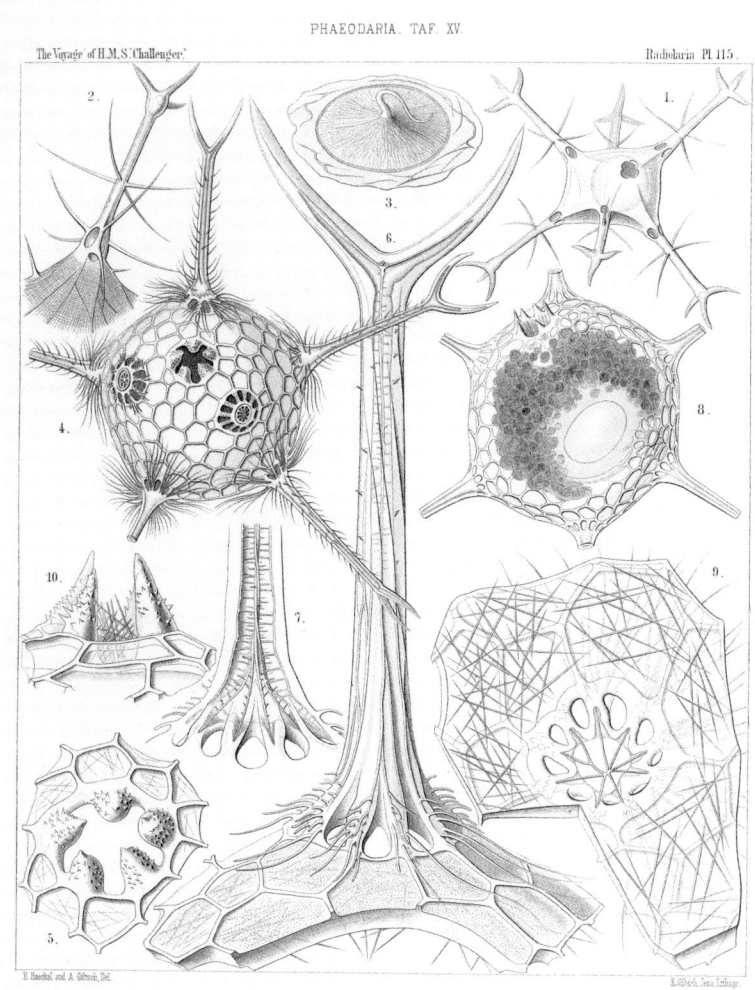

PHAEODARIA. TAF. XV.

The Voyage of H.M.S."Challenger." Radiolaria Pl. 115.

1-3. CIRCOPORUS, 4-10. CIRCOSPATHIS.

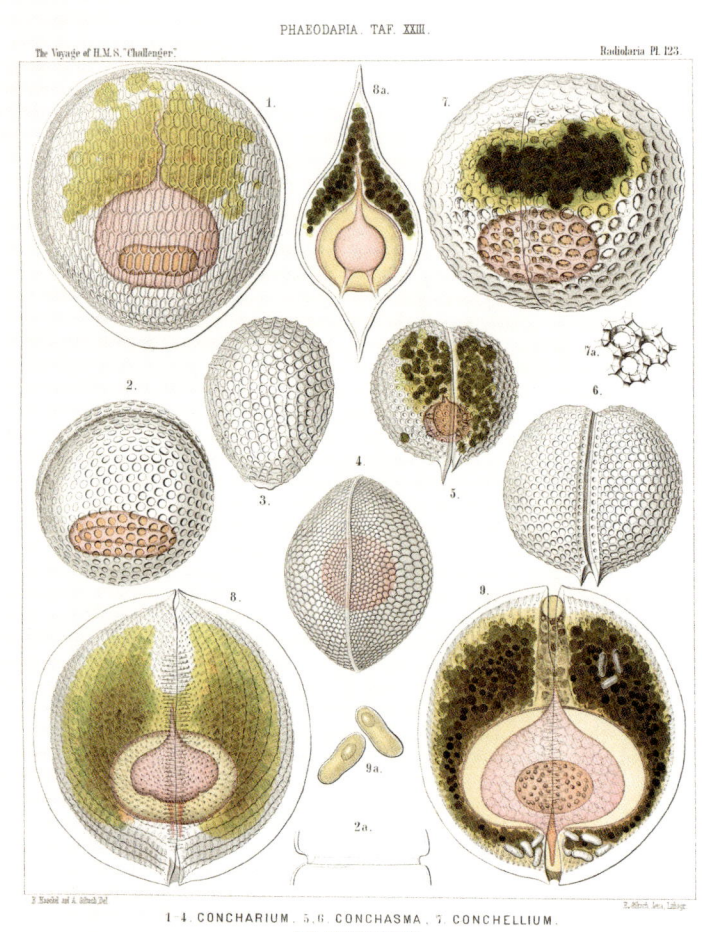

PHAEODARIA. TAF. XXIII.

The Voyage of H.M.S. "Challenger".

Radiolaria Pl. 123.

1-4. CONCHARIUM. 5,6. CONCHASMA. 7. CONCHELLIUM.
8,9. CONCHOPSIS.

PLATE 23

1 Concharium diatomeum | 2 Concharium bivalvum | 3 Concharium nucula
4 Concharium bacillarium | 5 Conchasma radiolites | 6 Conchasma sphaerulites
7 Conchellium tridacna | 8 Conchopsis carinata | 9 Conchopsis lenticula

PLATE 29

1 Challengeria murrayi | 2 Challengeria wildi | 3 Challengeria bromleyi | 4 Challengeria sloggettii
5 Challengeria tritonis | 6 Challengeron diodon | 7 Challengeron pearceyi | 8 Challengeron richardsii
9 Challengeron fergusoni | 10 Challengeron triangulum | 11 Challengeron crosbiei | 12 Challengeron
buchanani | 13 Challengeron willemoesii | 14 Challengeron moseleyi | 15 Challengeron wyvillei
16 Porcupinia cordiformis | 17 Pharyngella gastraea | 18 Pharyngella gastrula | 19 Entocannula
infundibulum | 20 Entocannula hirsuta | 21 Lithogromia diatomacea | 22 Lithogromia silicea

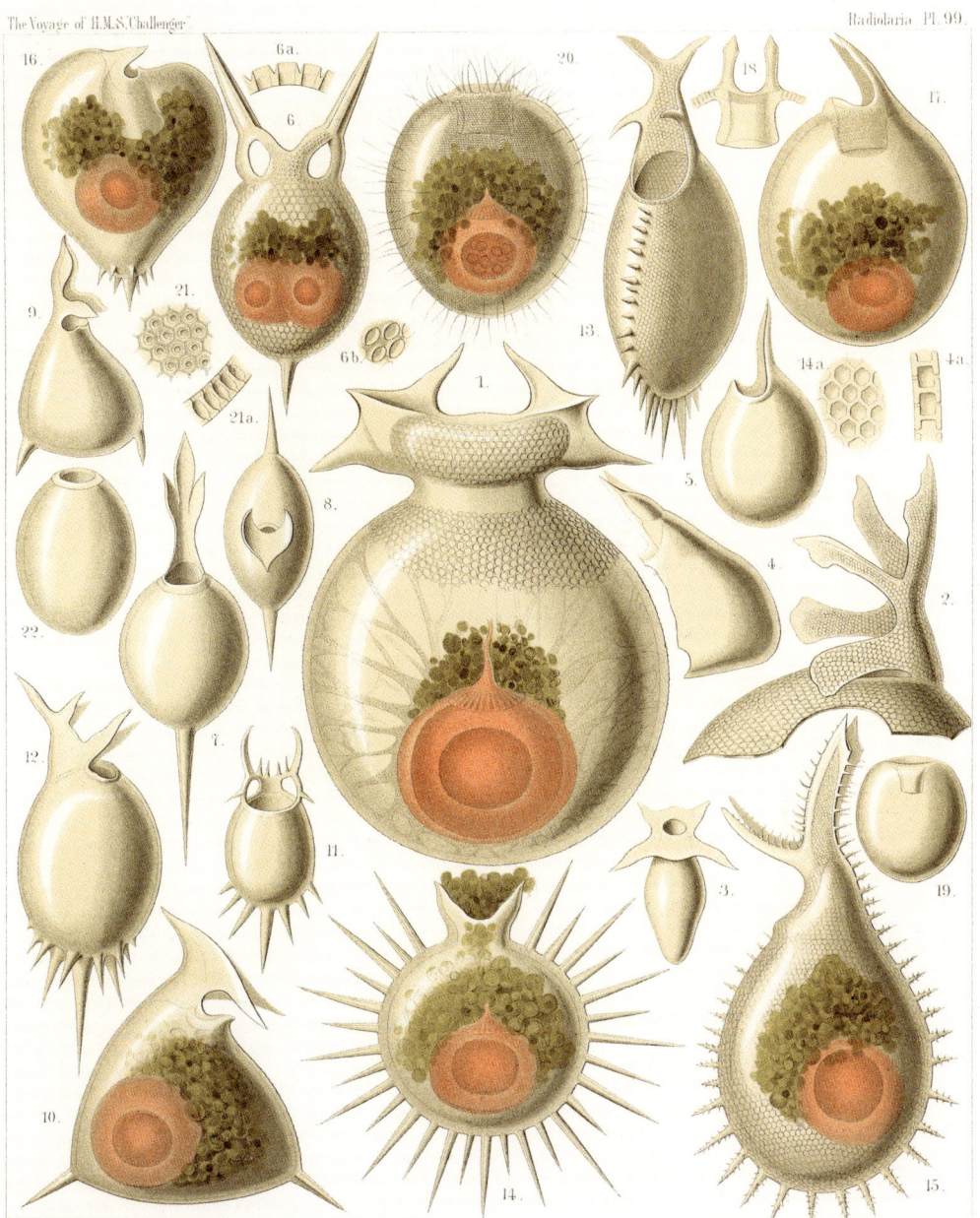

R.Haeckel and A.Giltsch.Del.

E Giltsch Jena, Lith og.

1–15. CHALLENGERIA. 16–18. PHARYNGELLA. 19.20. ENTOCANNULA.
21.22. LITHOGROMIA.

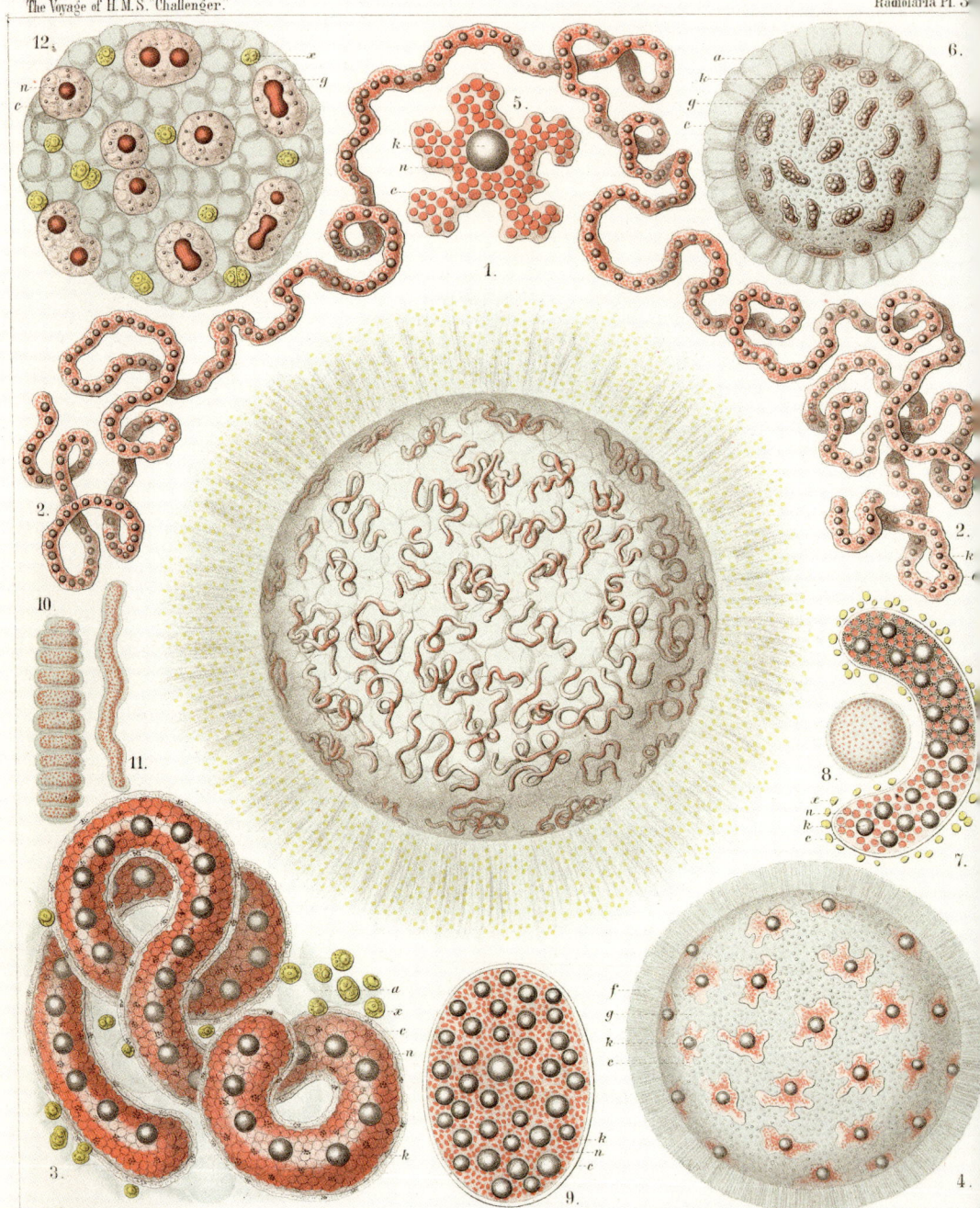

E. Haeckel and A. Giltsch, Del.

E. Giltsch, Jena, lith imp.

COLLOZOUM.

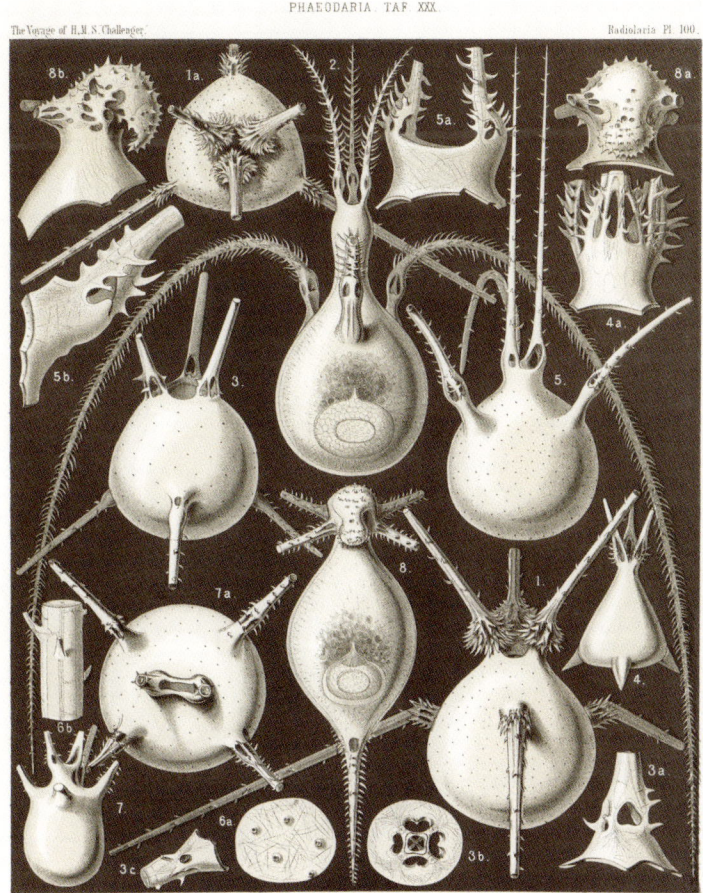

PHAEODARIA. TAF. XXX.

The Voyage of H.M.S. 'Challenger.'

Radiolaria Pl. 100.

TUSCARORA.

PLATE 3 — ADDENDUM: REPORT ON THE RADIOLARIA

1–3 Collozoum serpentinum (*vel* Collophidium serpentinum, HKL.)
4–5 Collozoum amœboides | 6–7 Collozoum vermiforme
8–9 Collozoum ellipsoides | 10–12 Collozoum inerme, HKL.

PLATE 30 — VOL. 4: PHAEODARIA OR CANNOPYLEA

1 Tuscarora bisternaria, JOHN MURRAY | 2 Tuscarora murrayi
3 Tuscarora wyvillei | 4 Tuscarora tetrahedra, JOHN MURRAY
5 Tuscarora tubulosa, JOHN MURRAY | 6 Tuscarora porcellana, JOHN MURRAY
7 Tuscarusa medusa | 8 Tuscaridium lithornithium

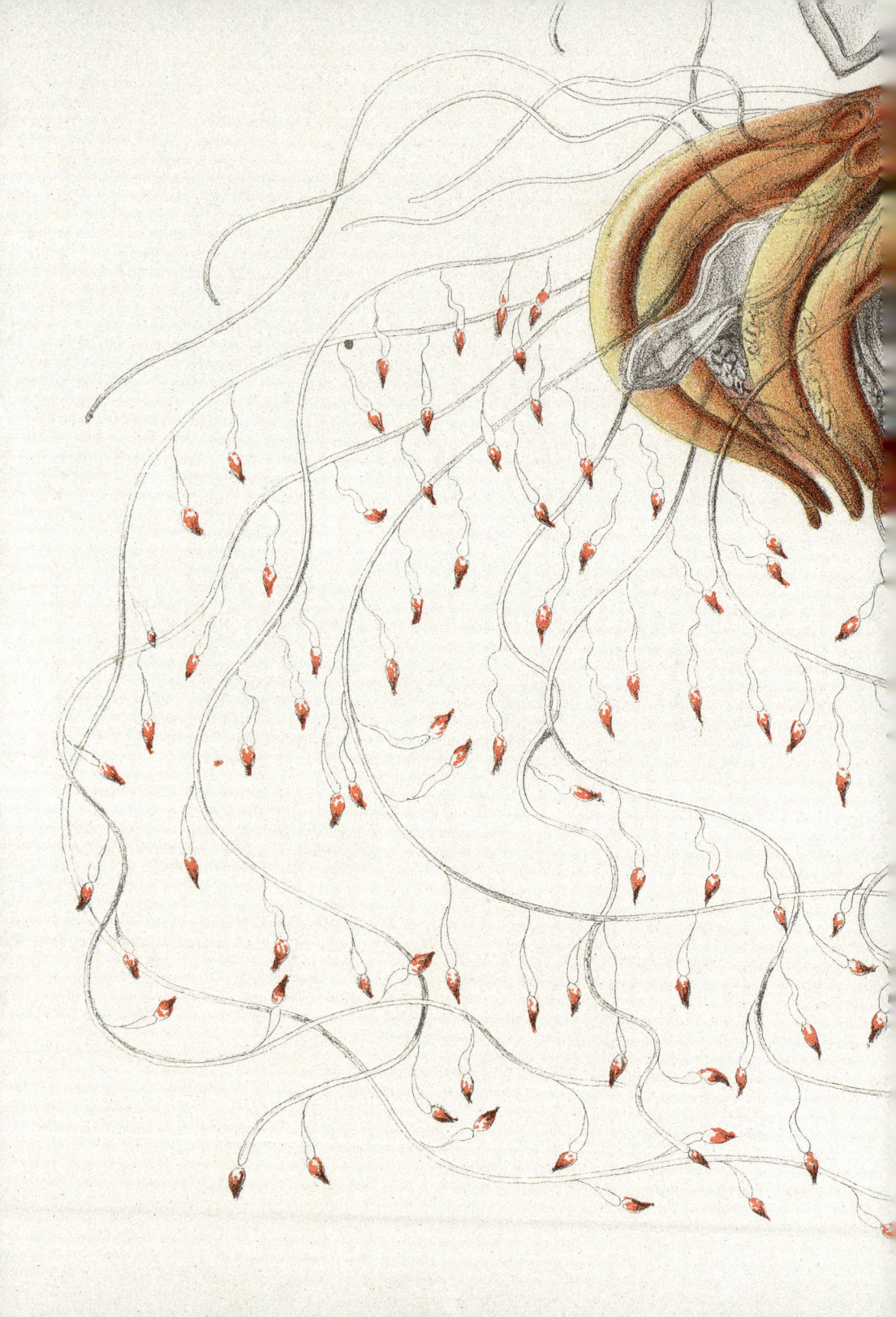

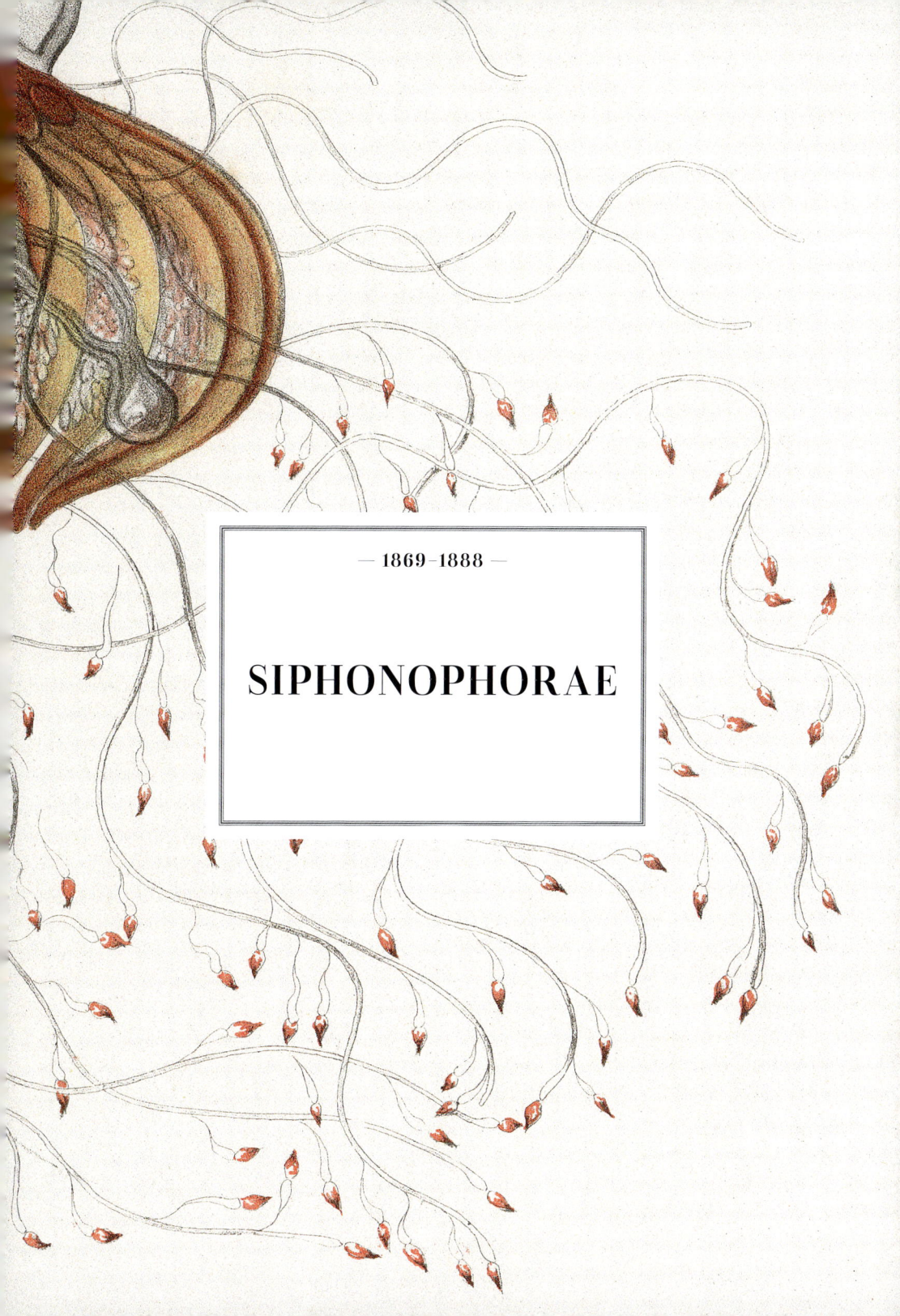

— 1869–1888 —

SIPHONOPHORAE

SIPHONOPHORAE

Haeckel's monograph of 1869 on the development of several species of Siphonophorae preceded his publications on the haul of this animal group from the HMS *Challenger* Expedition. The former had been based on his research into the examples he had caught himself off the coast of the island of Lanzarote and had then observed while they were still alive. In January 1867, he had written to his parents: "All the other animal forms to be found in this ocean are, however, outmatched in terms of great beauty and grace, as also of great scientific interest, by the splendid Siphonophorae, which I have chosen as the particular object of my research. These are swimming colonies of jellyfish, somewhat resembling flowers on tall stalks, their formation of colonies evincing the most interesting instance of a highly advanced distribution of tasks. Try to imagine the graceful, slim stalk of a flower, its leaves and colourful blossoms as transparent as glass, and the whole plant wriggling through the water with the most dainty and lively movements, and then you will have an idea of these wonderful, beautiful and delicate animal colonies. At the upper end of the stalk there usually sits a large air bladder, then comes a double row of distinct swimming creatures, which draw the entire colony through the water. Elsewhere on the long stem are numerous, leaf-like individuals, whose role is to protect the colony, and under whose cloak the devouring and sensory individuals lie concealed. Finally, there sit, in graceful groups distributed around the stem, the reproductive individuals, whose sole role is the production of eggs."[1]

Haeckel initially sent the extensive manu-
script recording his observations to Utrecht to
compete for a prize being offered by the Royal
Academy of Arts and Sciences, the Koninklijke
Akademie van Wetenschappen in Amsterdam.
So that the prize jury should not be influenced
in its deliberations by knowing the name of each
author, all submissions had to be anonymous. The
first prize was awarded to Haeckel's monograph
Zur Entwicklungsgeschichte der Siphonophoren (On the
Development of the Siphonophorae). Haeckel was thereby
yet again honoured as a precise observer and an excellent marine biologist, having
already established his scientific reputation through the 1862 *Atlas der Radiolarien*
(Atlas of the Radiolaria) and his 1865 work on sponges, and subsequently achiev-
ing fame through his *Generelle Morphologie der Organismen* (General Morphology of
Organisms) and his *Natürliche Schöpfungsgeschichte* (*The History of Creation*).

It was Haeckel's celebrity as a specialist in Siphonophorae (now Siphonophora)
that led to his being invited to join the team of scientists who had agreed to study
and report on the material assembled by the HMS *Challenger* deep-sea expedition.
Haeckel used this opportunity to continue his own earlier studies through what might
be learned from the new specimens. After many years of work, Haeckel was able, in
1888, to present his new account of 150 species in a volume of 380 text pages and 50
plates, in the *Report on the Siphonophorae collected by H.M.S. Challenger during the
years 1873–76. Report on the Scientific Results of the Voyage of H.M.S. Challenger.* As
was later to emerge, not all of these 150 are independent species; and a number of the
names introduced by Haeckel are thus no longer viewed as valid.

Of all Cnidaria, the Siphonophora form the most complex colonies. On account of their extraordinary character, we will consider them here in greater detail.
Siphonophora are a subunit of Hydrozoa (one of the four large groups of Cnidaria).
Their name is derived from the swimming, self-propelling colonies that they form,
each colony comprising a large number of interlinked, single "persons," or zooids,
each of these, in turn, being effectively "charged" with a particular task. The colonies embrace up to a thousand such zooids. Most species have a gas-filled swimming
zooid. The stalks (even without their respective catching tentacles) can be up to
three metres in length.

Siphonophora are to be found in all the world's oceans, chiefly occupying the
uppermost 200 metres. Within any period of 24 hours, however, they move up and

down within a range of around 200 to 300 metres. They feed on small animals in a predatory fashion with the help of their tentacles. Their nettle or stinging cells (Cnidocytes) produce a poison that affects the nervous system, in due course paralysing their prey. It is likely that many species, for example, by way of the rhythmic contraction of lateral tentacles, imitate the behaviour of small crabs and other animals so as to lure these creatures' own predators and then prey upon them (aggressive mimicry). The enemies of the Siphonophora include comb jellies (Ctenophora), sea turtles, and fish. The small fish *Nomeus gronovii* is sometimes to be found in the tentacles of the feared Portuguese man-of-war (*Physalia physalis*). Avoiding contact with its host's tentacles, it devours the latter's own prey.

Reproduction occurs by means of distinct male and female cells (sperm and eggs) that are released into the open water. Following their fusion, a larva arises. Germination subsequently issues in a so-called primary zooid (initially in the form of a jellyfish, which is able to swim and has a thread-like beginning of tentacles). Finally, there evolves a primary polyp with a mouth and a stomach cavity. The larvae often live at greater depths for they have no zooid specialised in regulating their buoyancy.

In view of the aforementioned, extensive task differentiation within the colony, the diverse zooids are readily distinguished, often in terms that Haeckel had already used himself. The stem is the bearer of the zooids and has budding zones for the individual "persons." Gonozooids, with no tentacles and no musculature, emit the reproductive cells. Gastrozooids accomplish the absorption and digestion of nutrients. Nectophorae ("swimming bells"), devoid of mouth, tentacles, or sensory organs, execute swimming motions by way of muscular contraction. A pneumatophor – in essence, a form of buoy – is a polyp with a gas-filled gland by means of which Siphonophora can maintain the position of the colony at a particular depth.

One distinguishes two large sub-groups: the Cystonectida and Codonophora.

1. Cystonectida

The best-known form is the aforementioned *Physalia physalis*. This has a large gas bladder (up to 30 centimetres) with a crest that can be lifted by a breeze at the ocean's surface, thus facilitating forward motion. Its catching threads can be as long as 50 metres. *Physalia* lives in swarms and is to be found throughout the world. It is able to cause an extremely corrosive sting, the neurotoxin employed potentially triggering heart cramps in human beings and, on rare occasions, a fatal allergic reaction.

2. Codonophora

2.1.Physophorida: Of this group, only a few species are known. Its colonies are distinguished by the relatively small pneumatophor at their head. With a length of up to 20 metres, many species are among the largest non-vertebrate animals in existence.

2.2. Calycophorida: The representatives of this group (termed Calyconectae by Haeckel), of which there are numerous species, form defensive assemblies of zooids that free themselves from the mother colony and then live independently from this as a so-called Eudoxia, a new generation with its own reproductive cells. The existence of two consecutive generations of Calycophorida – the colony and the Eudoxia – encouraged, during the 19th century, too short-sighted a rush to name species, it being not initially possible to ascertain which freely swimming Eudoxia had derived from which original colony. As a result, diverse genus names tended to be used for both generations. Haeckel himself still followed this principle, for example, when describing *Abyla carina* as a new species. Of this he explained: "[...] after being detached, they swim freely about as Eudoxiae, which assume the characteristic form of *Amphiroa carina.*"[2] In another case Haeckel wrote that the Eudoxia described by him as *Diplophysa köllikeri* had been found in the same glass container as *Sphaeronectes köllikeri*, and might therefore have derived from it.[3] On this account he assumed that here was a case of two generations of one and the same species. That is to say that even when it seemed more or less certain that he was confronted with a case of distinct generations of a single species, Haeckel nonetheless proposed two genus names. On the other hand, apparently, so as to make clear cases of probable affiliation, he would refrain from using distinct species names, in this case employing the names *carina* or *koellikeri* twice. As we have previously observed, only the name first introduced is regarded as valid – in this case *Abiya carina* and *Sphaeronectes koellikeri*.

Notwithstanding intense work on the Siphonophorae even during the 19th century, not least on Haeckel's own part, these creatures are still regarded as little researched.

PLATE 3
Physophora magnifica HAECKEL, 1869 –
Physophora hydrostatica FORSSKÅL, 1775

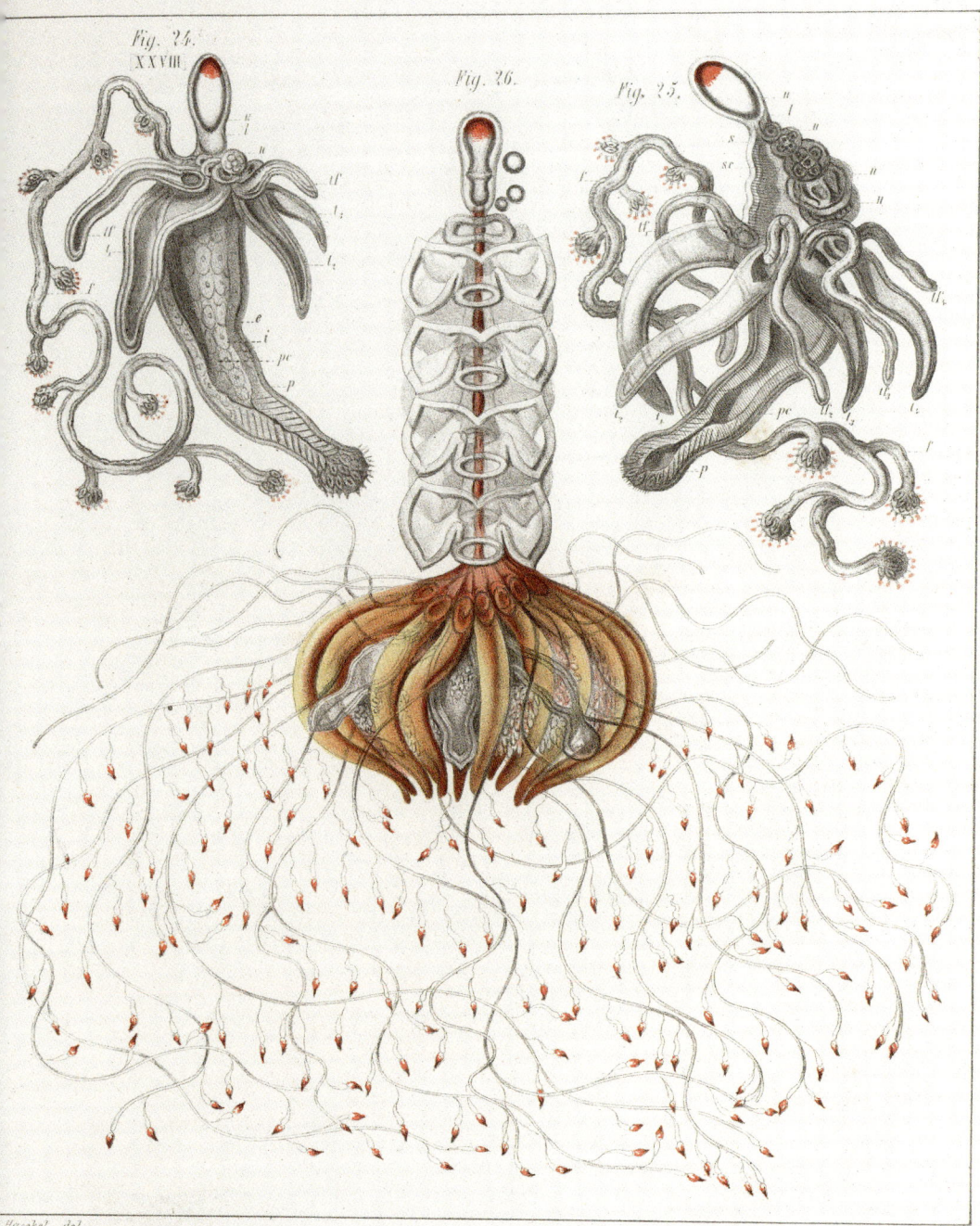

Pl. III.

Fig. 24.
XXVIII

Fig. 26.

Fig. 25.

E Haeckel del.

Lith. P. W. u. d. Heyer. Gotha.

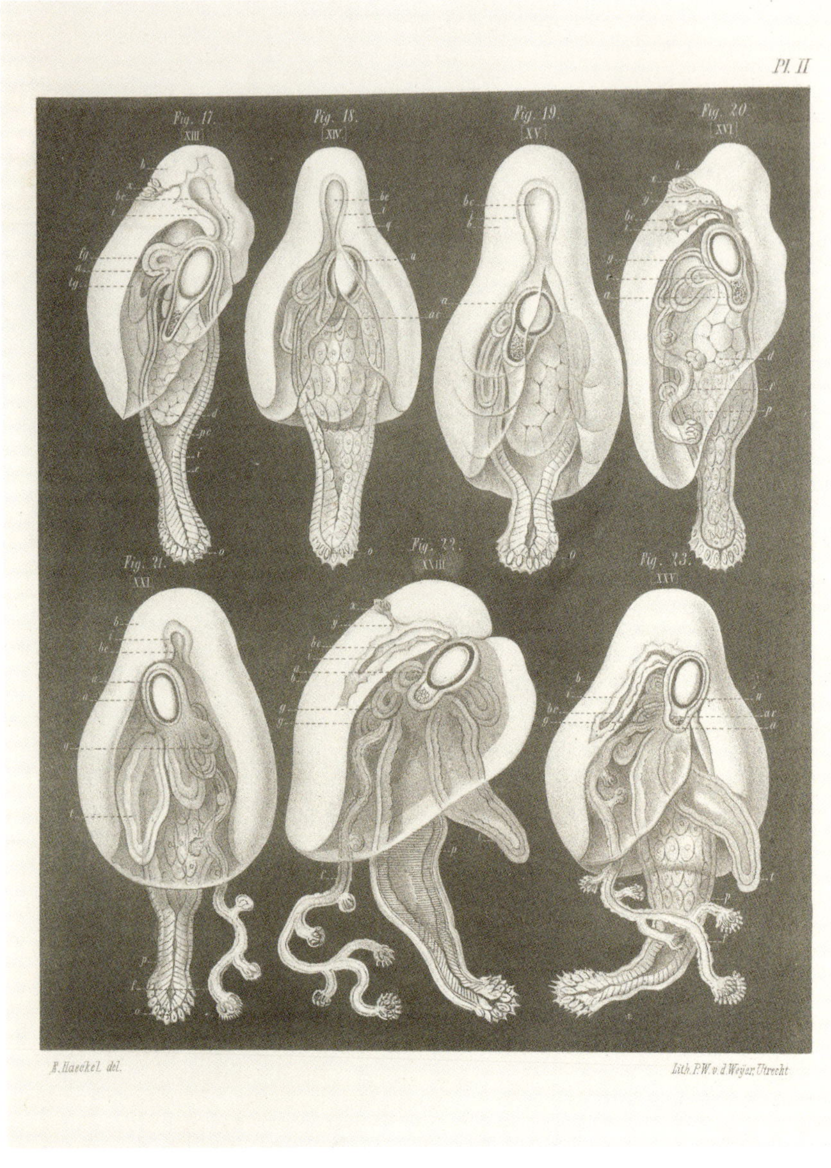

Physophora magnifica HAECKEL, 1869 –
Physophora hydrostatica FORSSKÅL, 1775

Physophora magnifica HAECKEL, 1869 –
Physophora hydrostatica FORSSKÅL, 1775

138

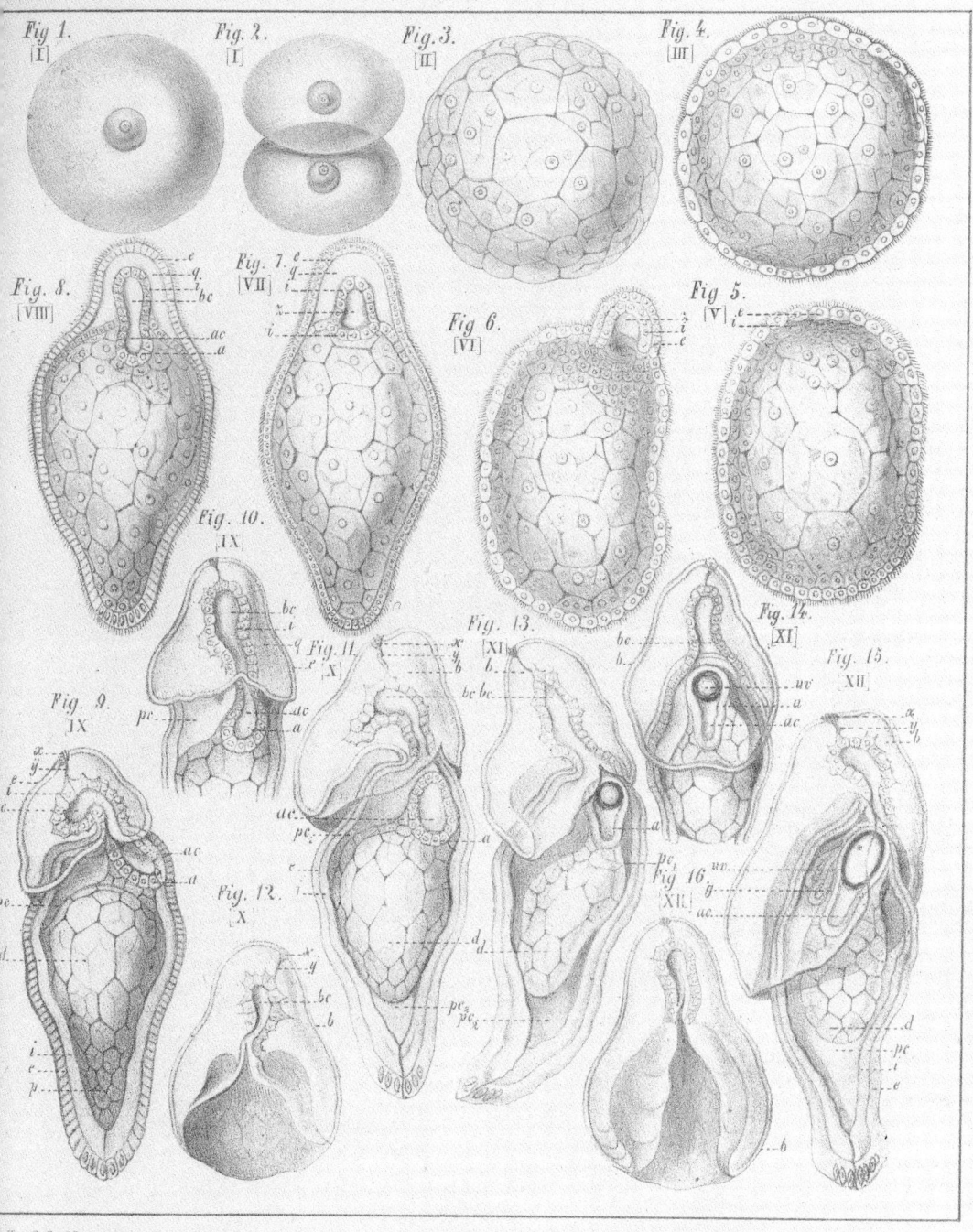

Pl. I.

Fig. 1.
[I]

Fig. 2.
[I]

Fig. 3.
[II]

Fig. 4.
[III]

Fig. 8.
[VIII]

Fig. 7.
[VII]

Fig. 6.
[VI]

Fig 5.
[V]

Fig. 10.
[IX]

Fig. 9.
[IX]

Fig. 11.
[X]

Fig. 13.
[XI]

Fig. 14.
[XI]

Fig. 15.
[XII]

Fig. 12.
[X]

Fig 16.
[XII]

E. Haeckel. del.

Lith F.W. v. Wegar Utrecht.

Pl. IV.

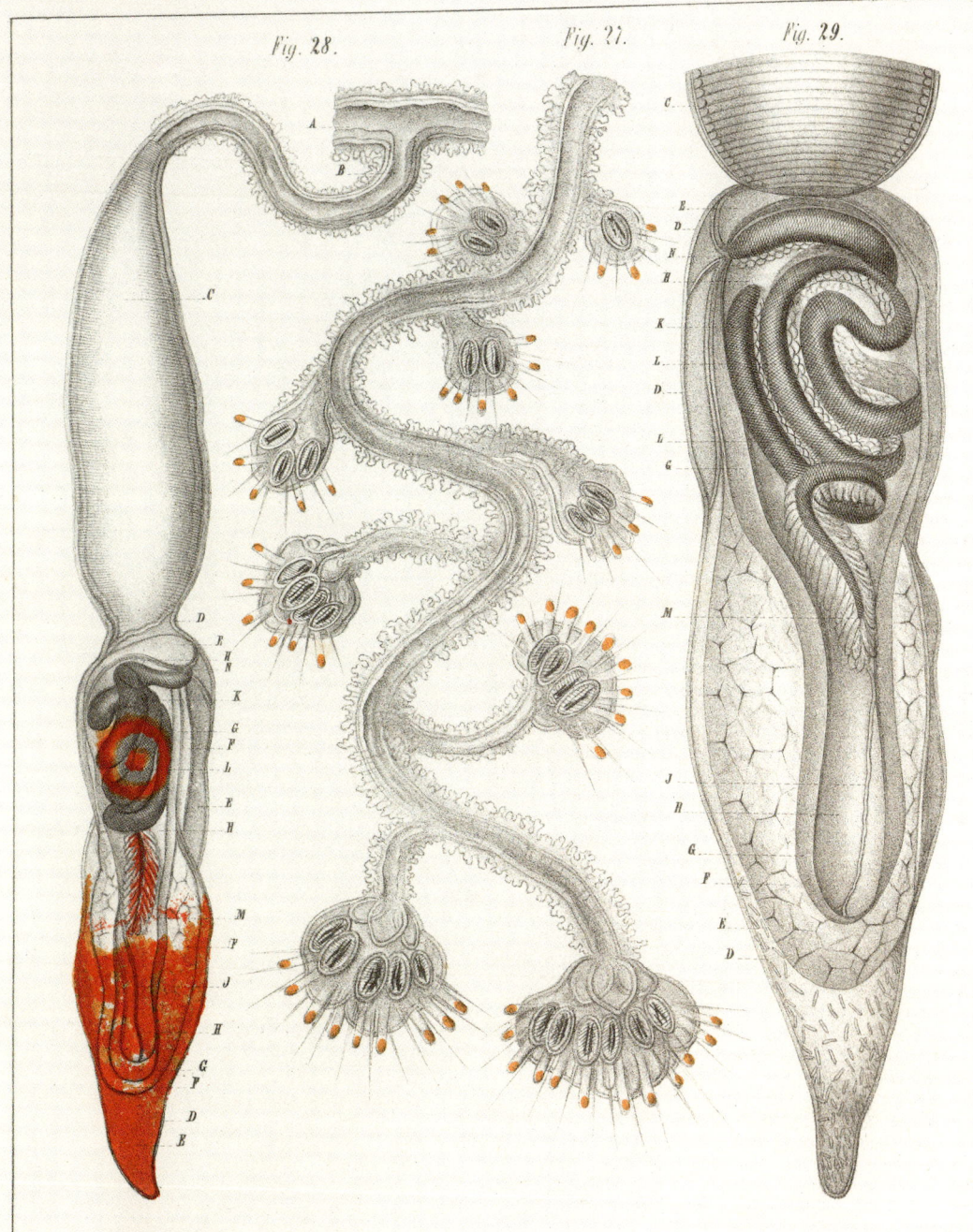

Fig. 28.   Fig. 27.   Fig. 29.

E. Haeckel, del.   Lit. P. W. v. d. Weyer, Utrecht.

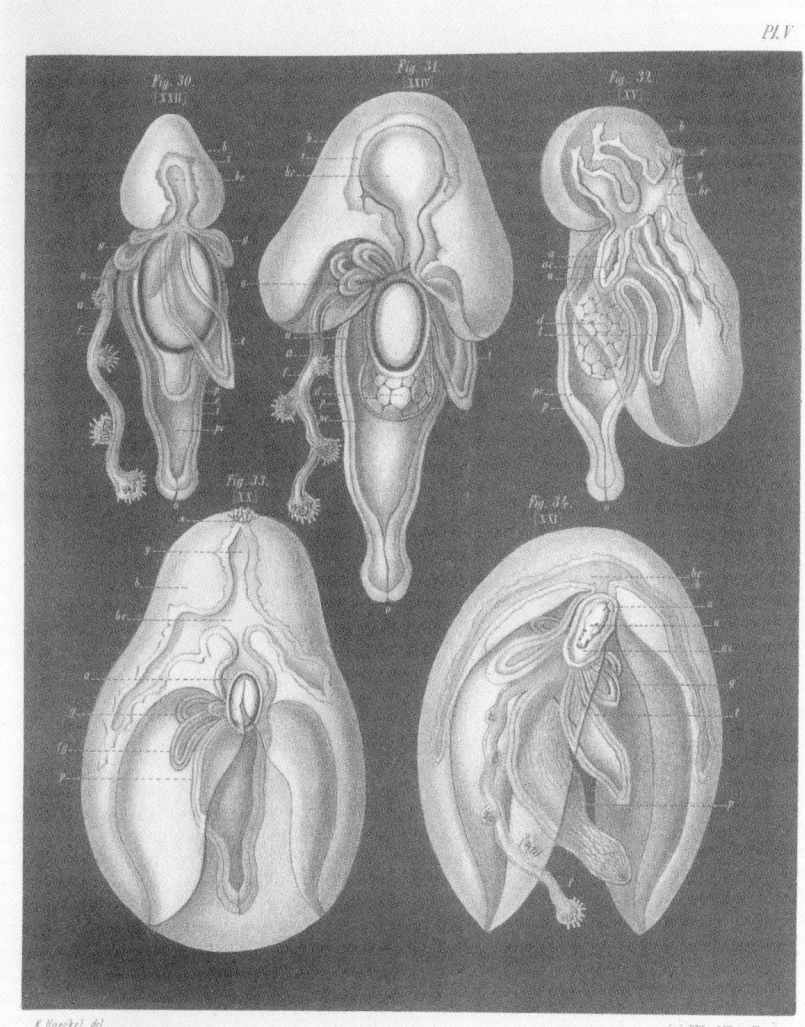

PLATE 4
Physophora magnifica HAECKEL, 1869 –
Physophora hydrostatica FORSSKÅL, 1775

PLATE 5
Physophora magnifica HAECKEL, 1869 –
Physophora hydrostatica FORSSKÅL, 1775

141

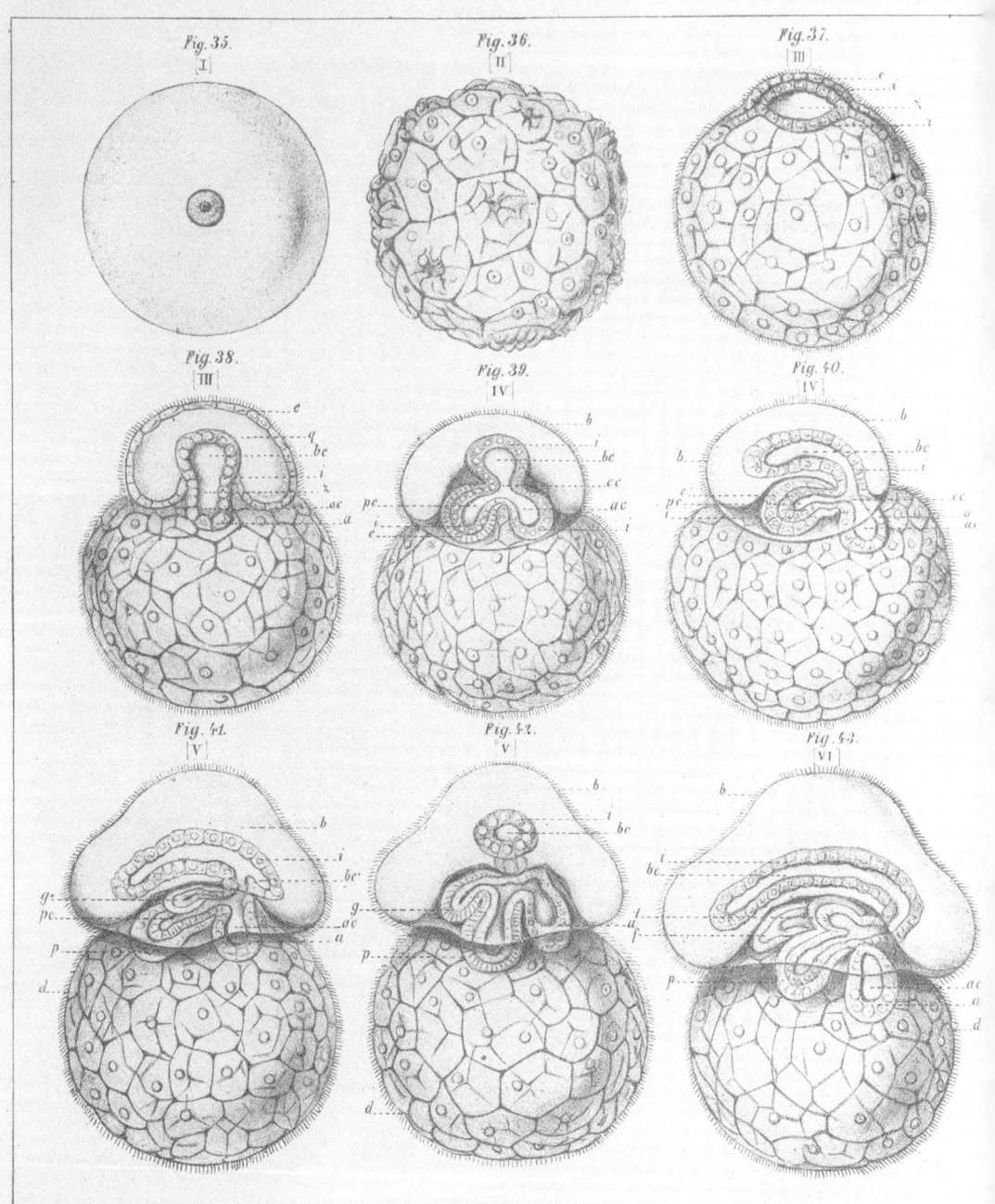

Pl. V

Fig. 35.
[I]

Fig. 36.
[II]

Fig. 37.
[III]

Fig. 38.
[III]

Fig. 39.
[IV]

Fig. 40.
[IV]

Fig. 41.
[V]

Fig. 42.
[V]

Fig. 43.
[VI]

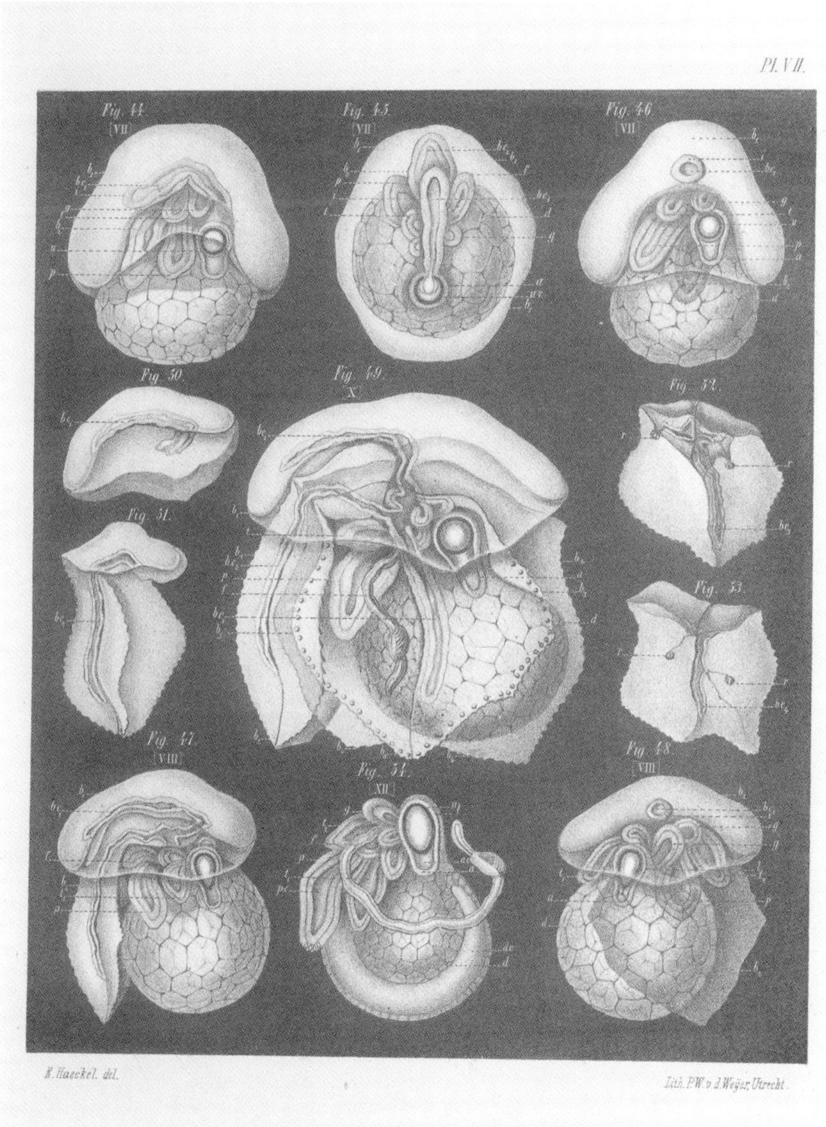

PLATE 6
Crystallodes rigidum HAECKEL, 1869 –
Agalma okeni ESCHSCHOLTZ, 1825

PLATE 7
Crystallodes rigidum HAECKEL, 1869 –
Agalma okeni ESCHSCHOLTZ, 1825

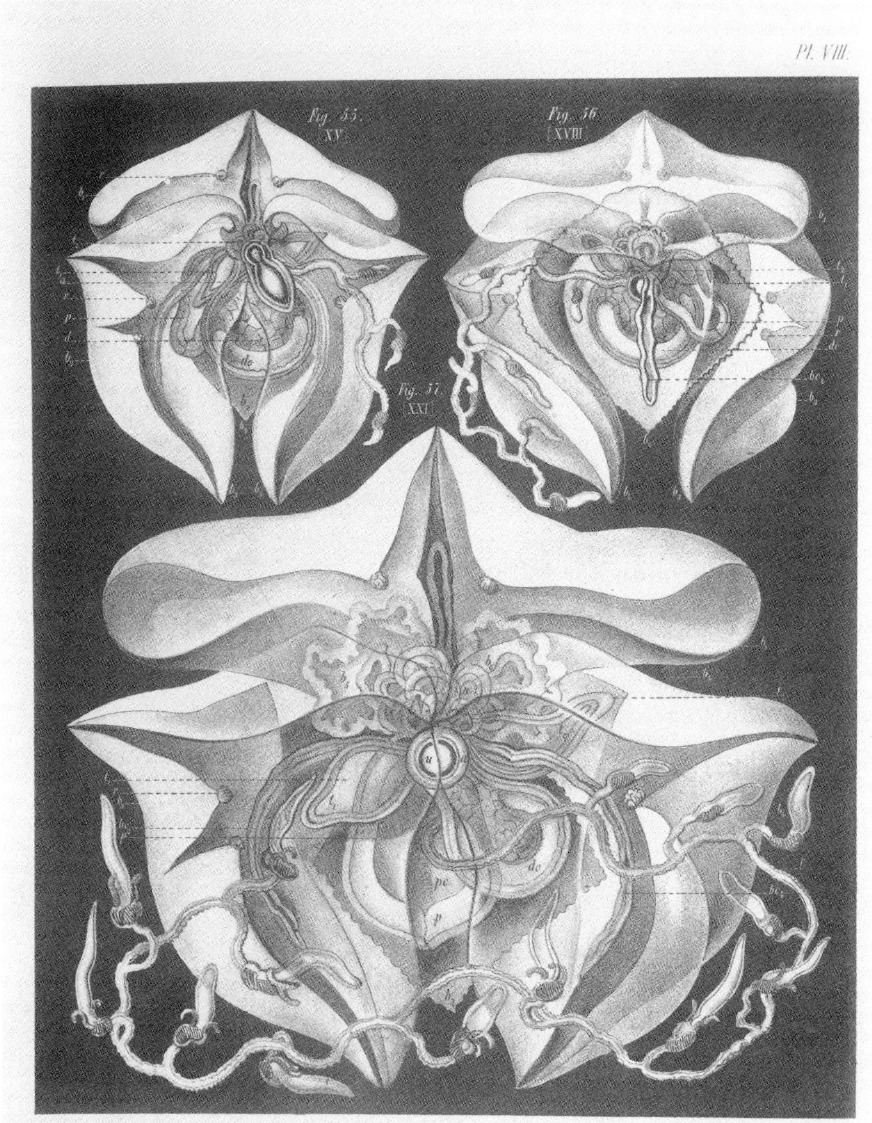

PLATE 8
Crystallodes rigidum HAECKEL, 1869 –
Agalma okeni ESCHSCHOLTZ, 1825

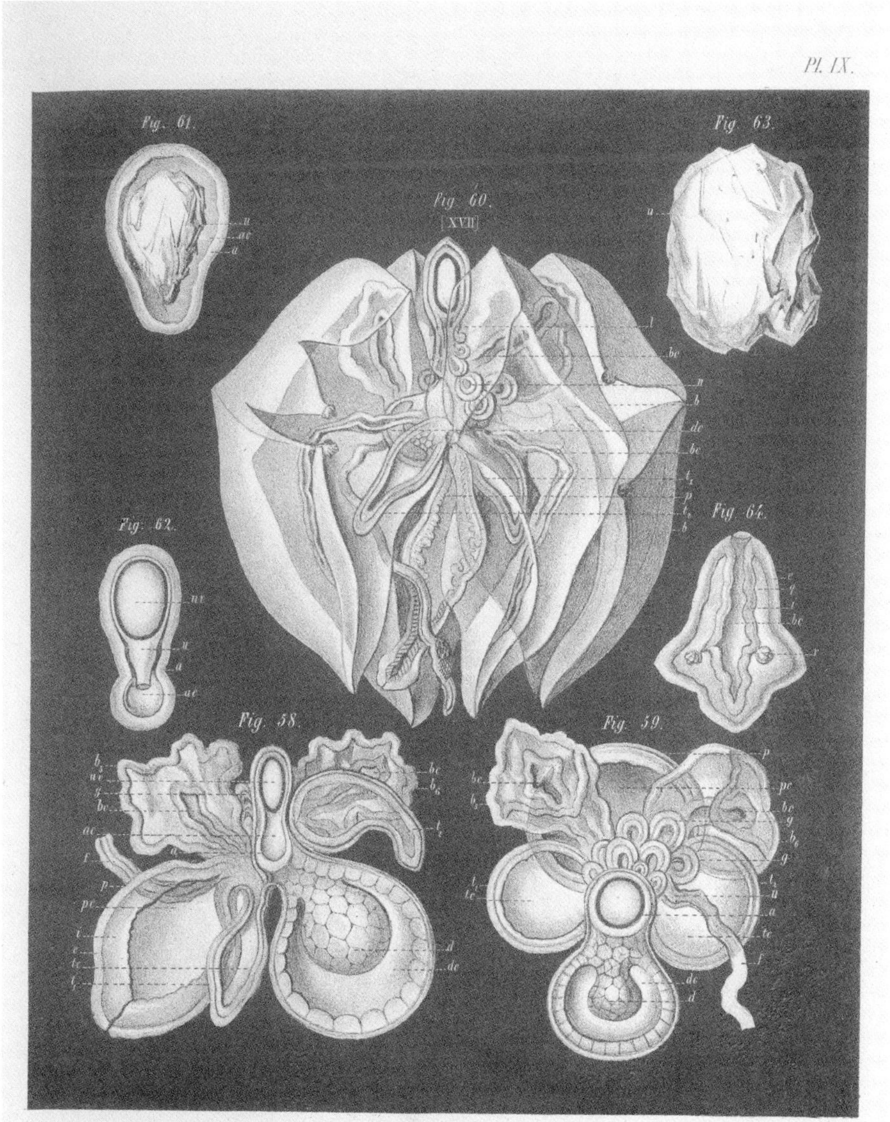

PLATE 9
Crystallodes rigidum HAECKEL, 1869 –
Agalma okeni ESCHSCHOLTZ, 1825

PLATE 10
Crystallodes rigidum HAECKEL, 1869 –
Agalma okeni ESCHSCHOLTZ, 1825

Pl. X.

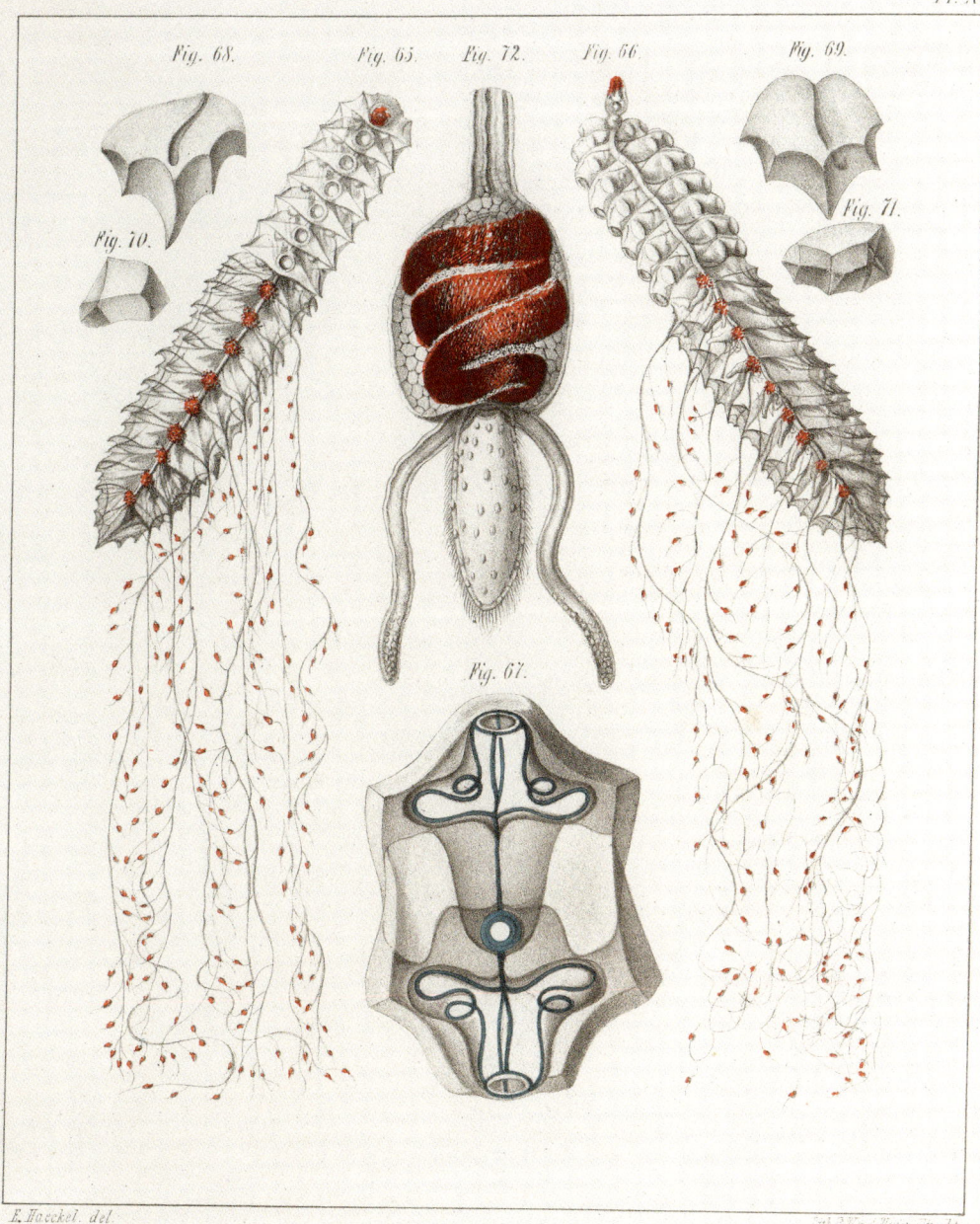

Fig. 68. Fig. 65. Fig. 72. Fig. 66. Fig. 69.

Fig. 70.

Fig. 71.

Fig. 67.

E. Haeckel. del.

Lith.P. W. v. d. Weijer. Utrecht.

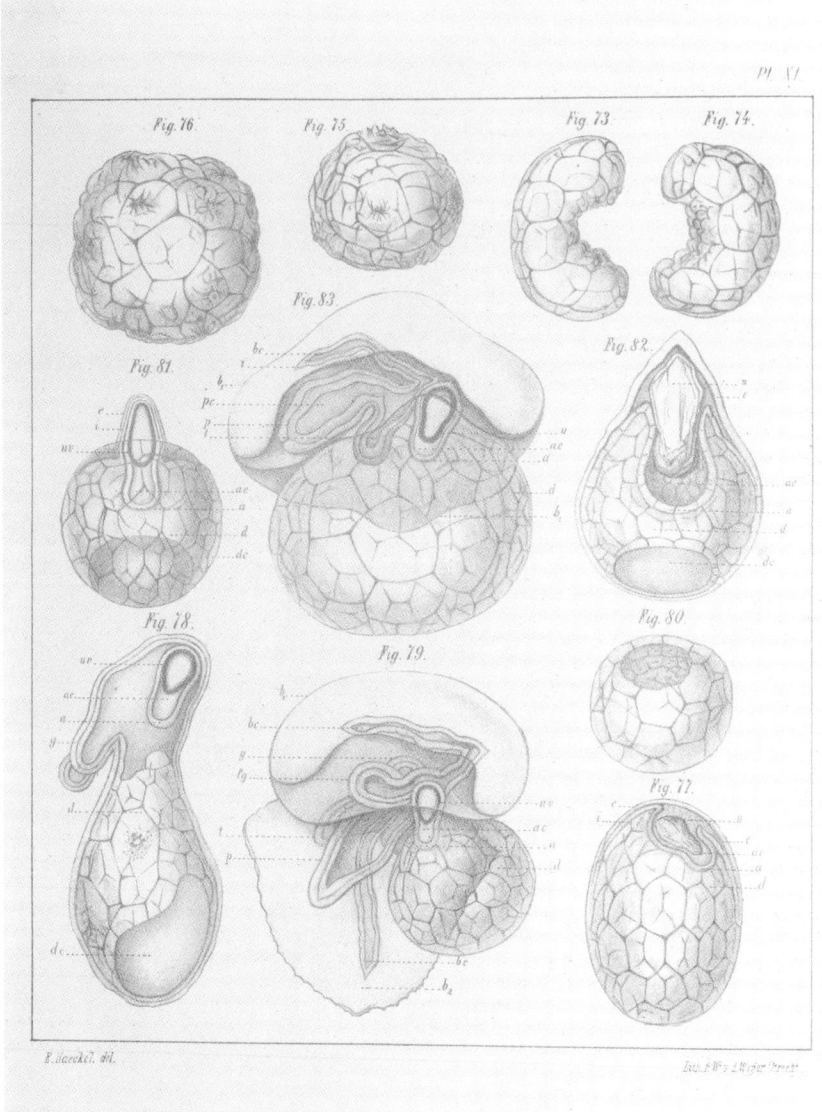

Crystallodes rigidum HAECKEL, 1869 –
Agalma okeni ESCHSCHOLTZ, 1825

1–5 Rhodalia miranda n. sp. –
Rhodalia miranda HAECKEL, 1888

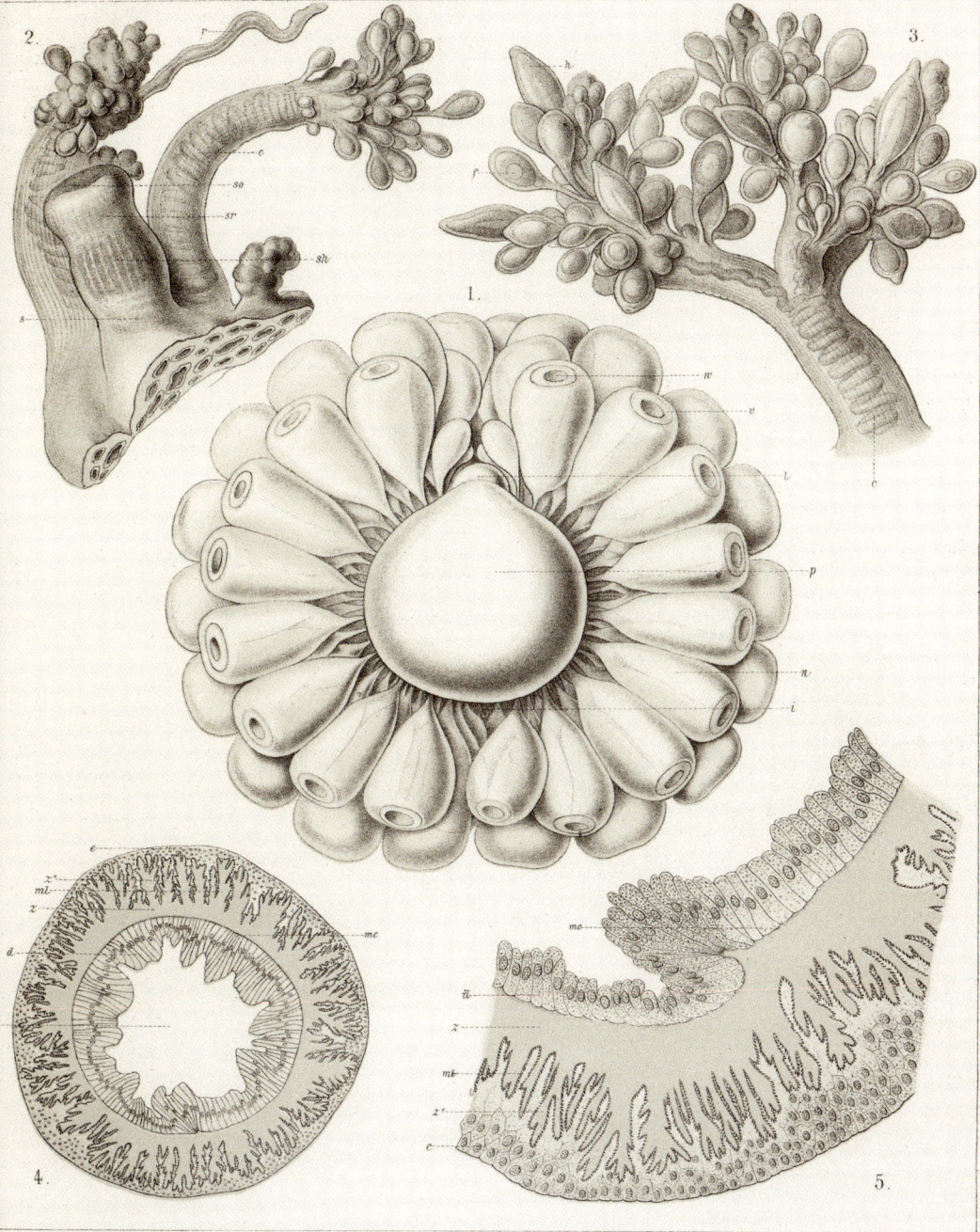

RHODALIA MIRANDA.

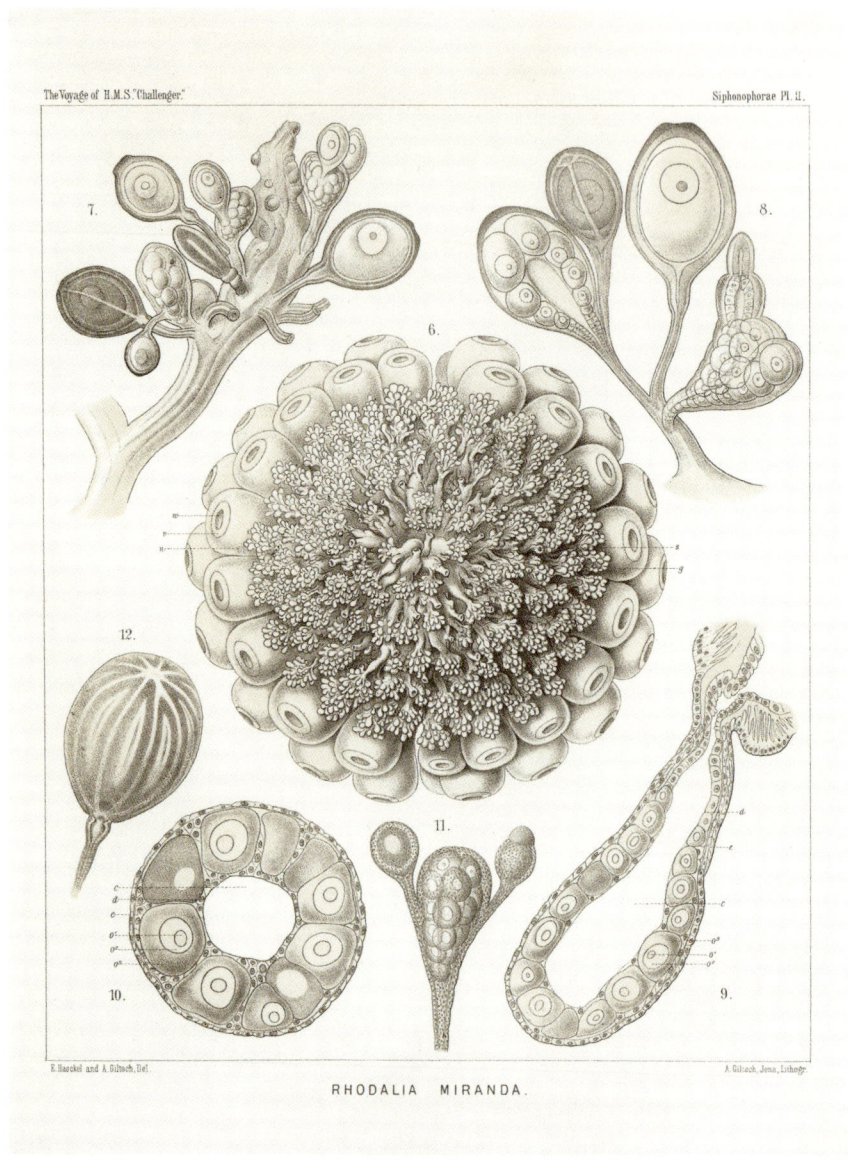

RHODALIA MIRANDA.

PLATE 2

6–12 Rhodalia miranda n. sp. –
Rhodalia miranda HAECKEL, 1888

PLATE 3

13–14 Rhodalia miranda n. sp. –
Rhodalia miranda HAECKEL, 1888

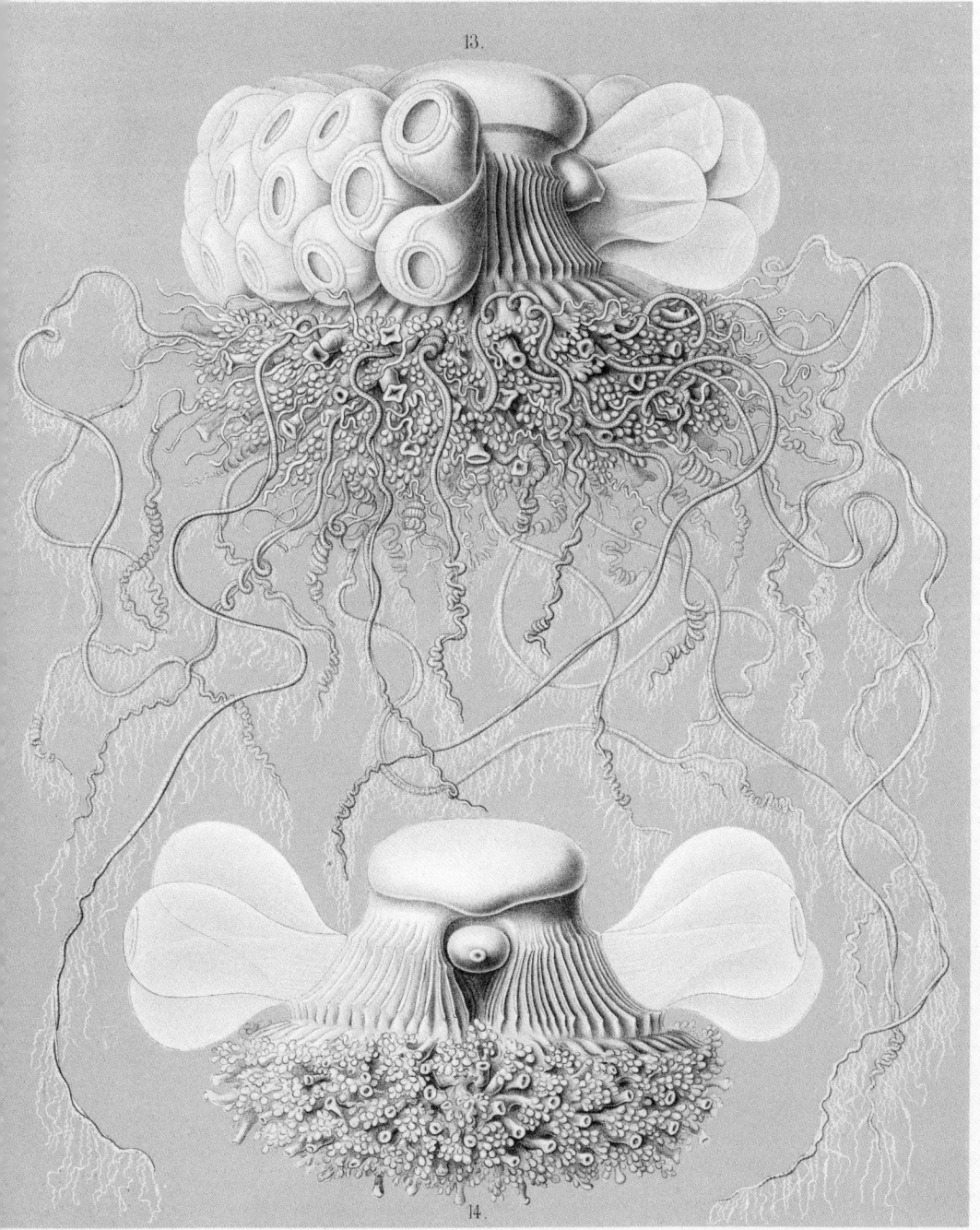

RHODALIA MIRANDA.

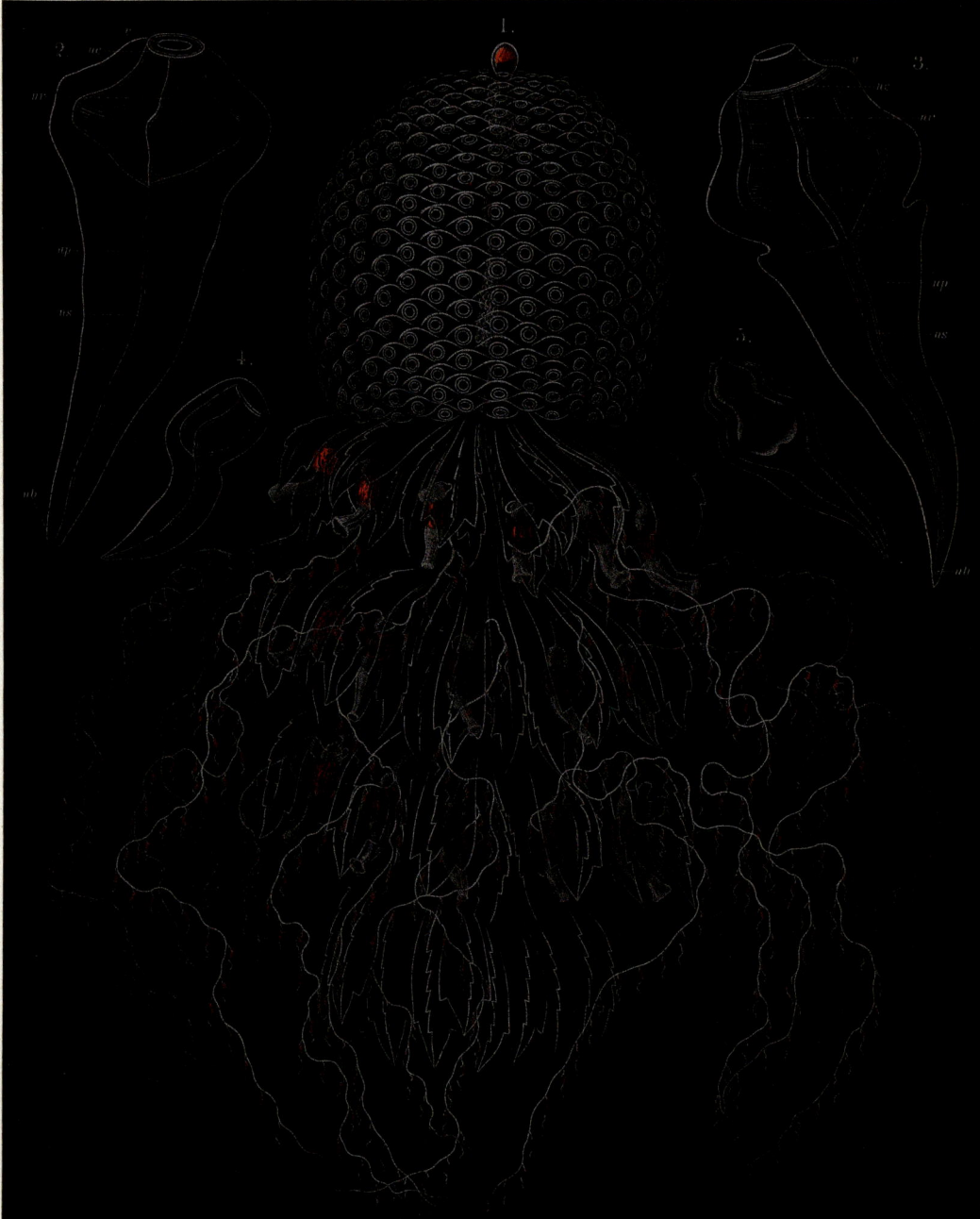

E.Haeckel and A.Giltsch, Del

A.Giltsch, Jena, Lithogr.

FORSKALIA THOLOIDES.

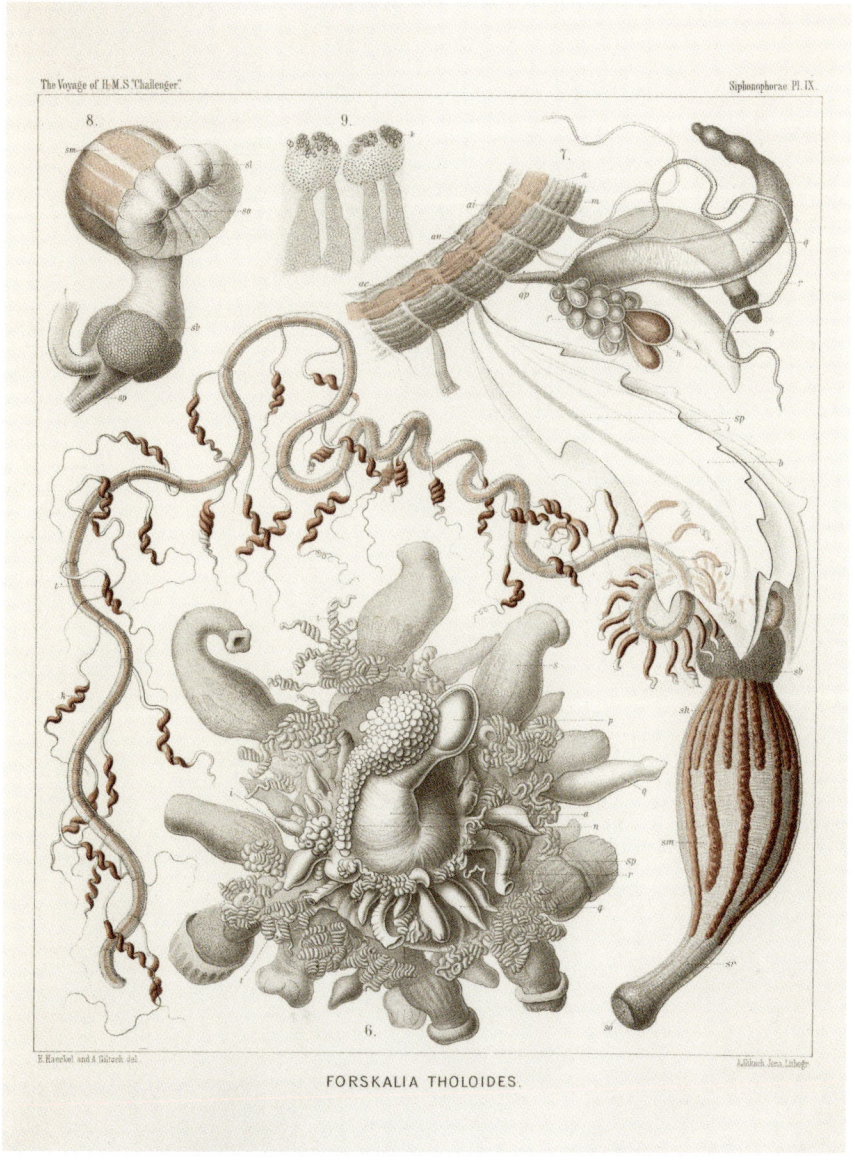

The Voyage of H.M.S "Challenger".

Siphonophorae Pl. IX.

E. Haeckel and A. Giltsch del.

A.Giltsch. Jena. Lith.

FORSKALIA THOLOIDES.

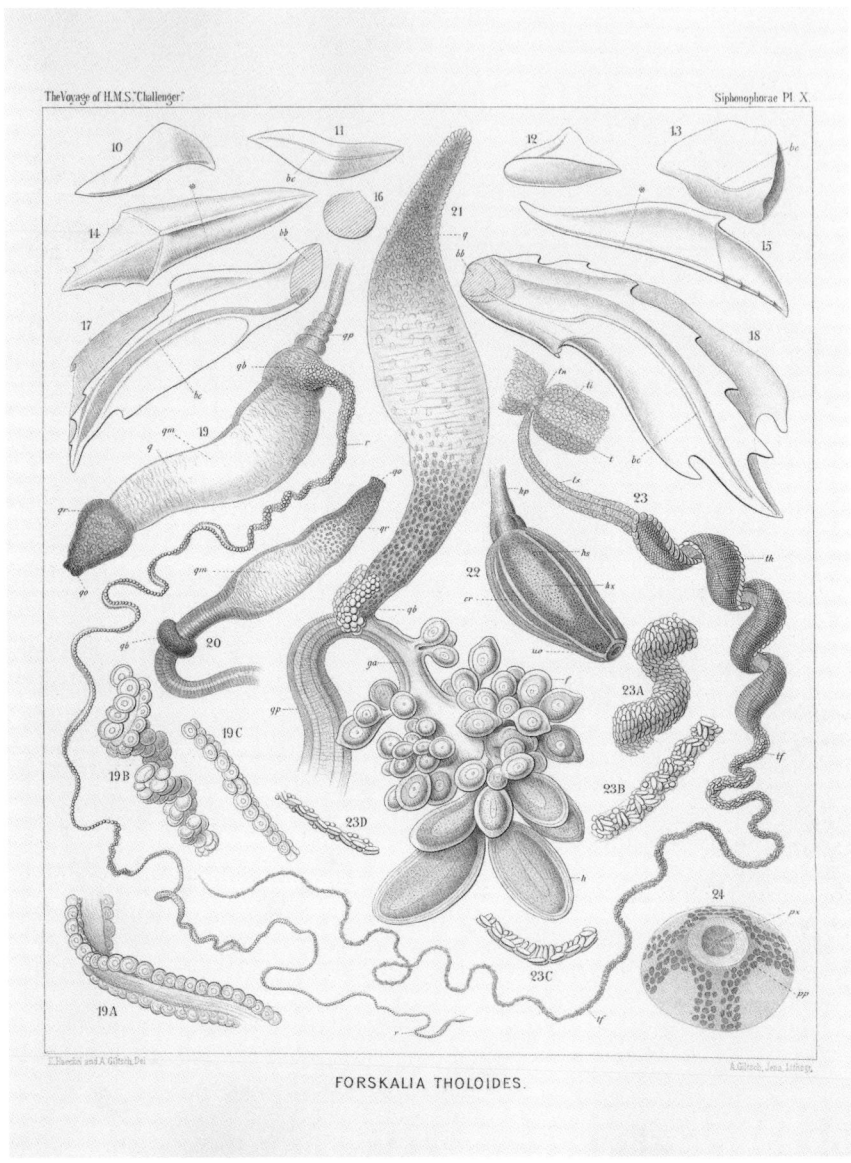

FORSKALIA THOLOIDES.

PLATE 10

10–24 Forskalia tholoides n. sp. –
Forskalia tholoides HAECKEL, 1888

PLATE 11

1–6 Athorybia ocellata n. sp. –
Athorybia ocellata HAECKEL, 1888

154

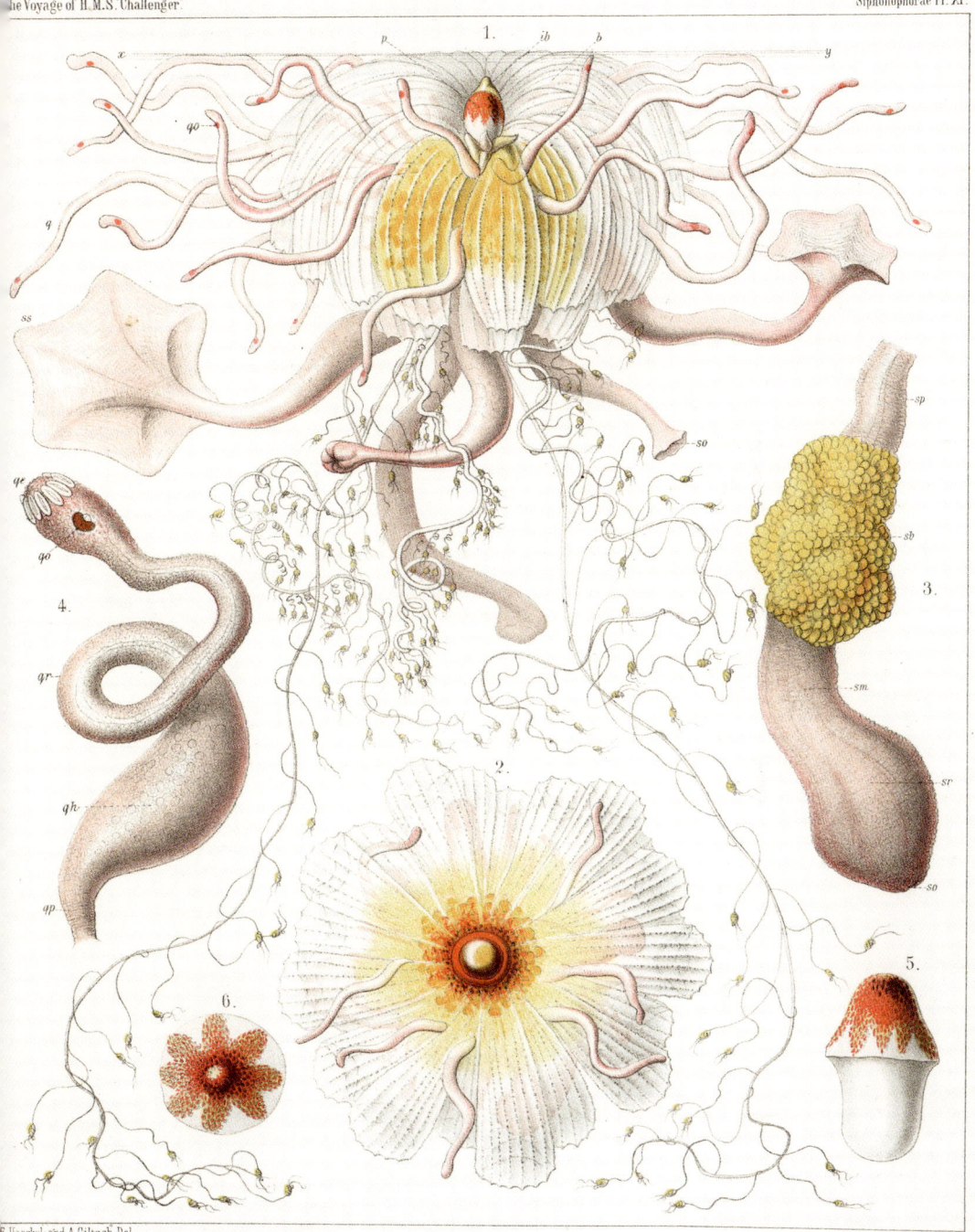

E. Haeckel and A.Giltsch, Del.   A.Giltsch, Jena. Lithogr.

ATHORYBIA OCELLATA

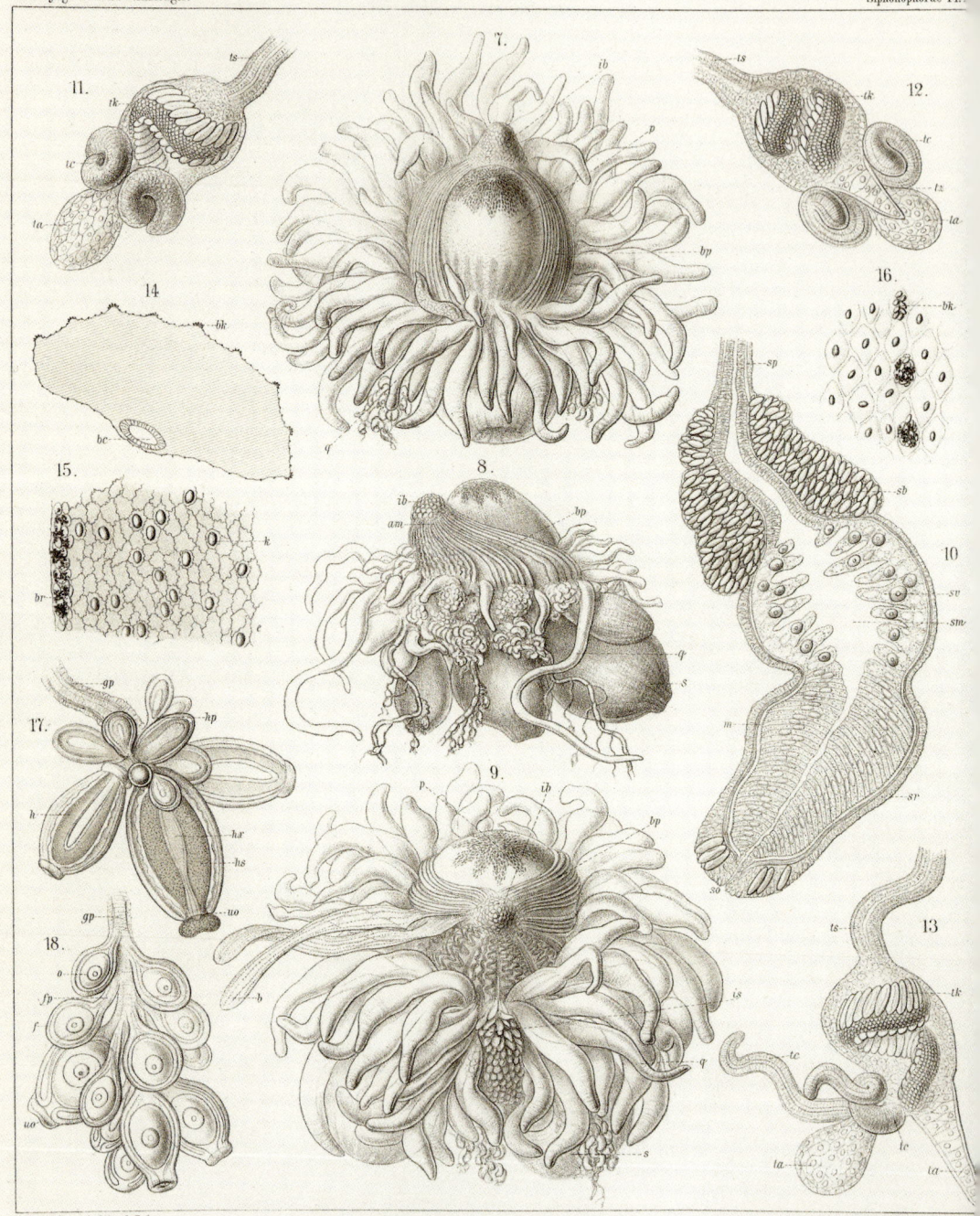

E. Haeckel and A. Giltsch Del.

A.Giltsch, Jena, Litho.

ATHORYBIA OCELLATA

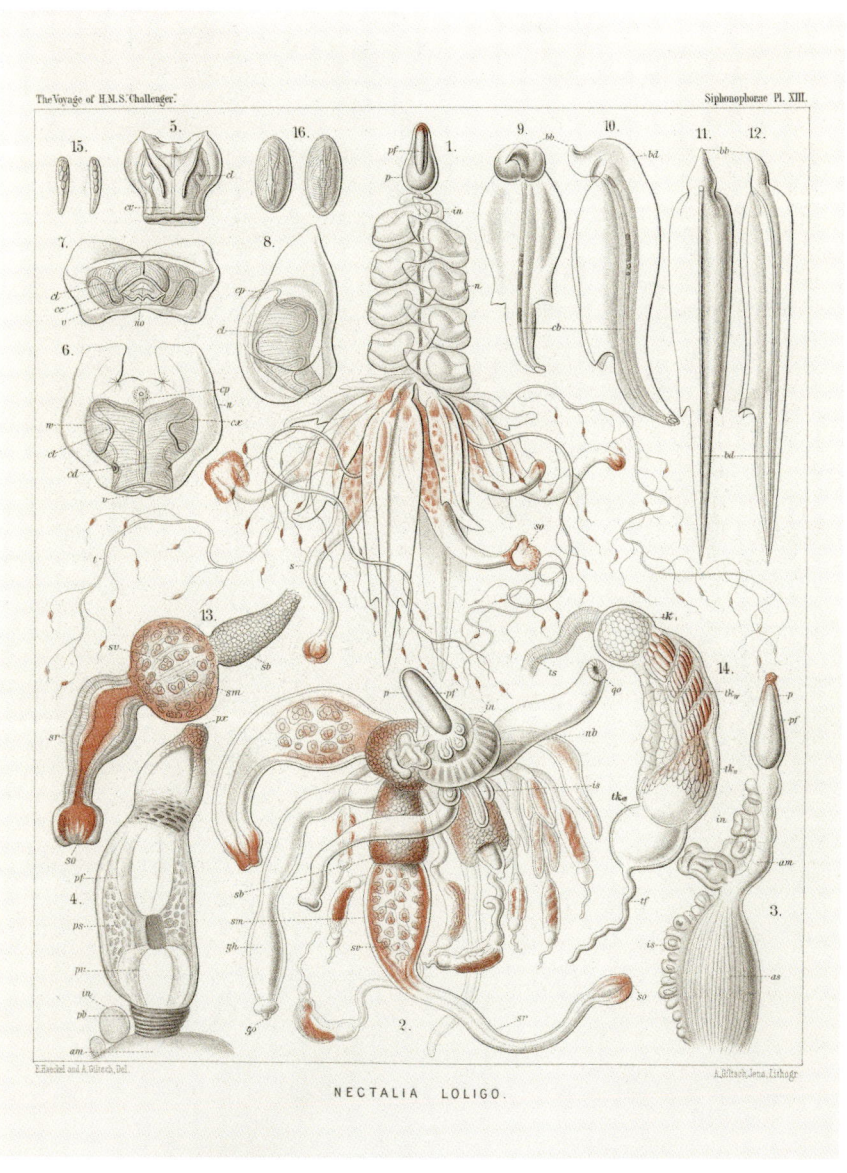

NECTALIA LOLIGO.

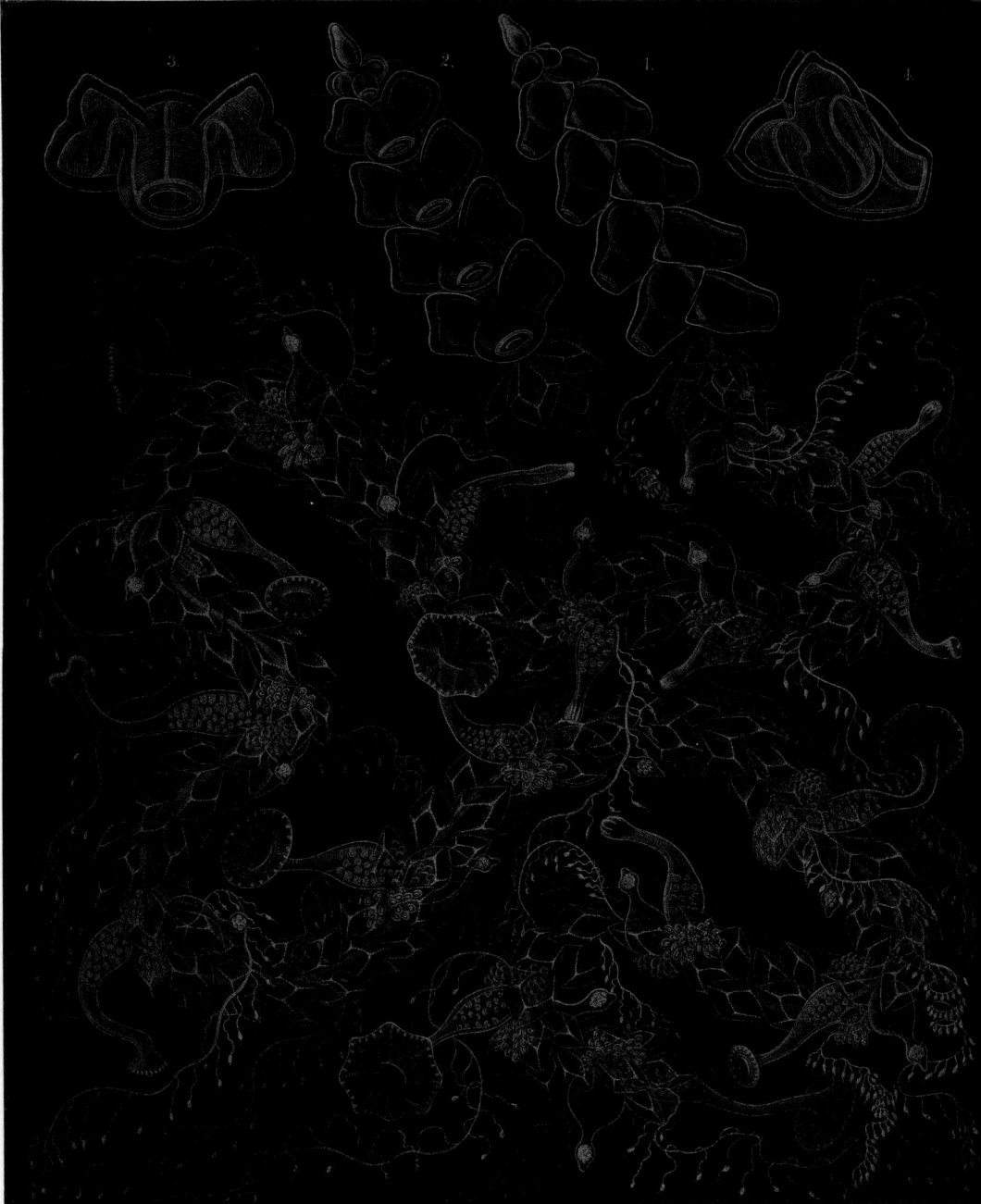

E.Haeckel and A.Giltsch, Del.

A.Giltsch, Jena, Lithogr

ANTHEMODES ORDINATA.

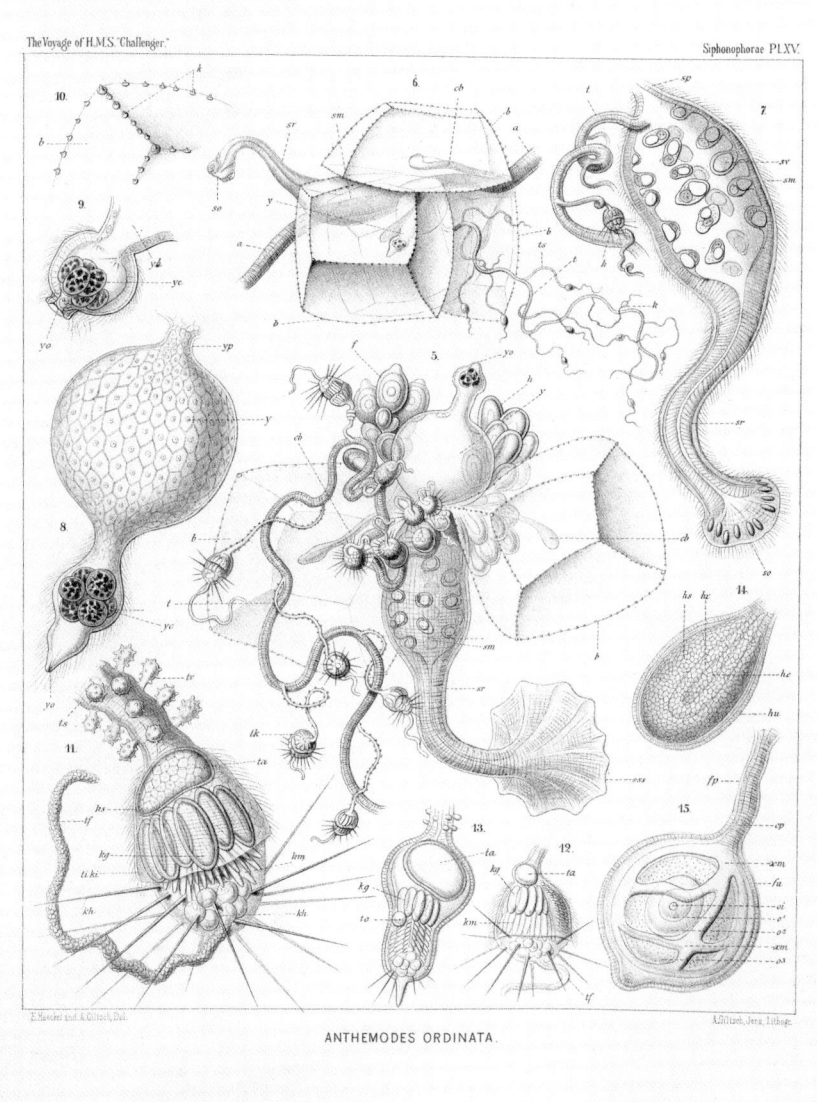

The Voyage of H.M.S. "Challenger."

Siphonophorae Pl.XV.

E.Haeckel and A.Giltsch, Del.

A.Giltsch, Jena, Lithog.

ANTHEMODES ORDINATA.

PLATE 14
1–4 Anthemodes ordinata n. sp. –
Cordagalma ordinatum (HAECKEL, 1888)

PLATE 15
5–15 Anthemodes ordinata n. sp. –
Cordagalma ordinatum (HAECKEL, 1888)

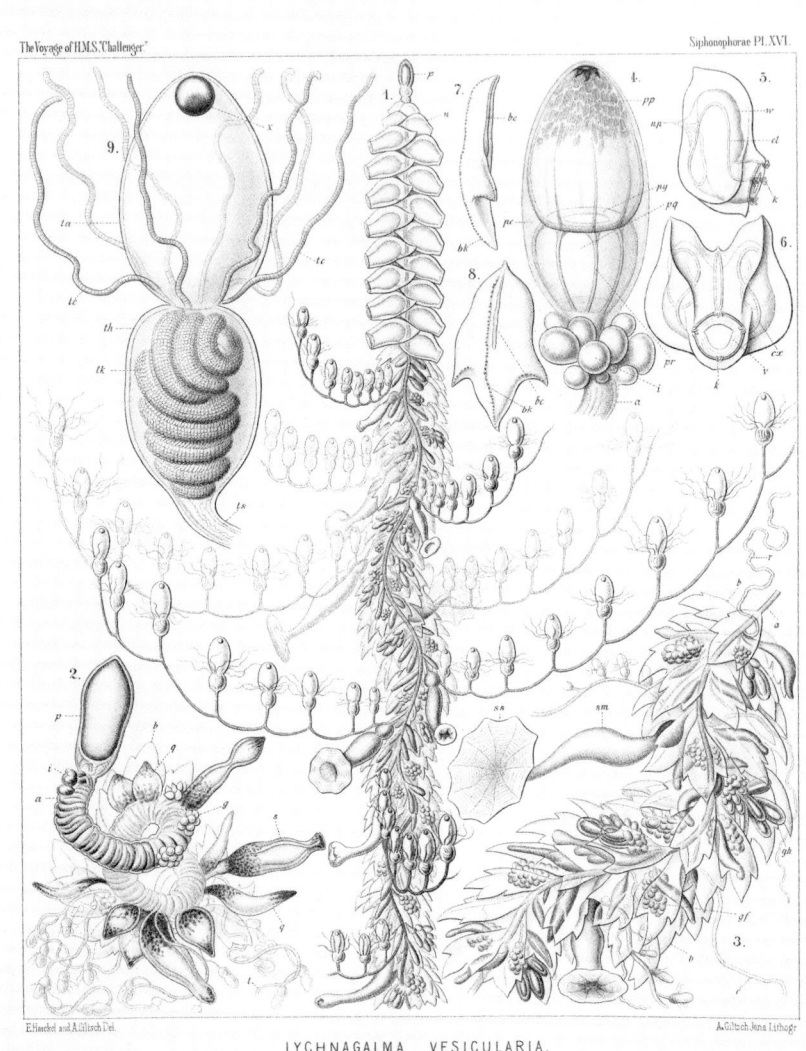

The Voyage of H.M.S. "Challenger"

Siphonophorae Pl. XVI.

LYCHNAGALMA VESICULARIA.

E. Haeckel and A. Giltsch Del.

A. Giltsch Jena Lithogr.

1–9 Lychnagalma vesicularia n. sp. –
Lychnagalma utricularia (CLAUS, 1879)

1–16 Crystallodes vitrea n. sp. –
Agalma okeni ESCHSCHOLTZ, 1825

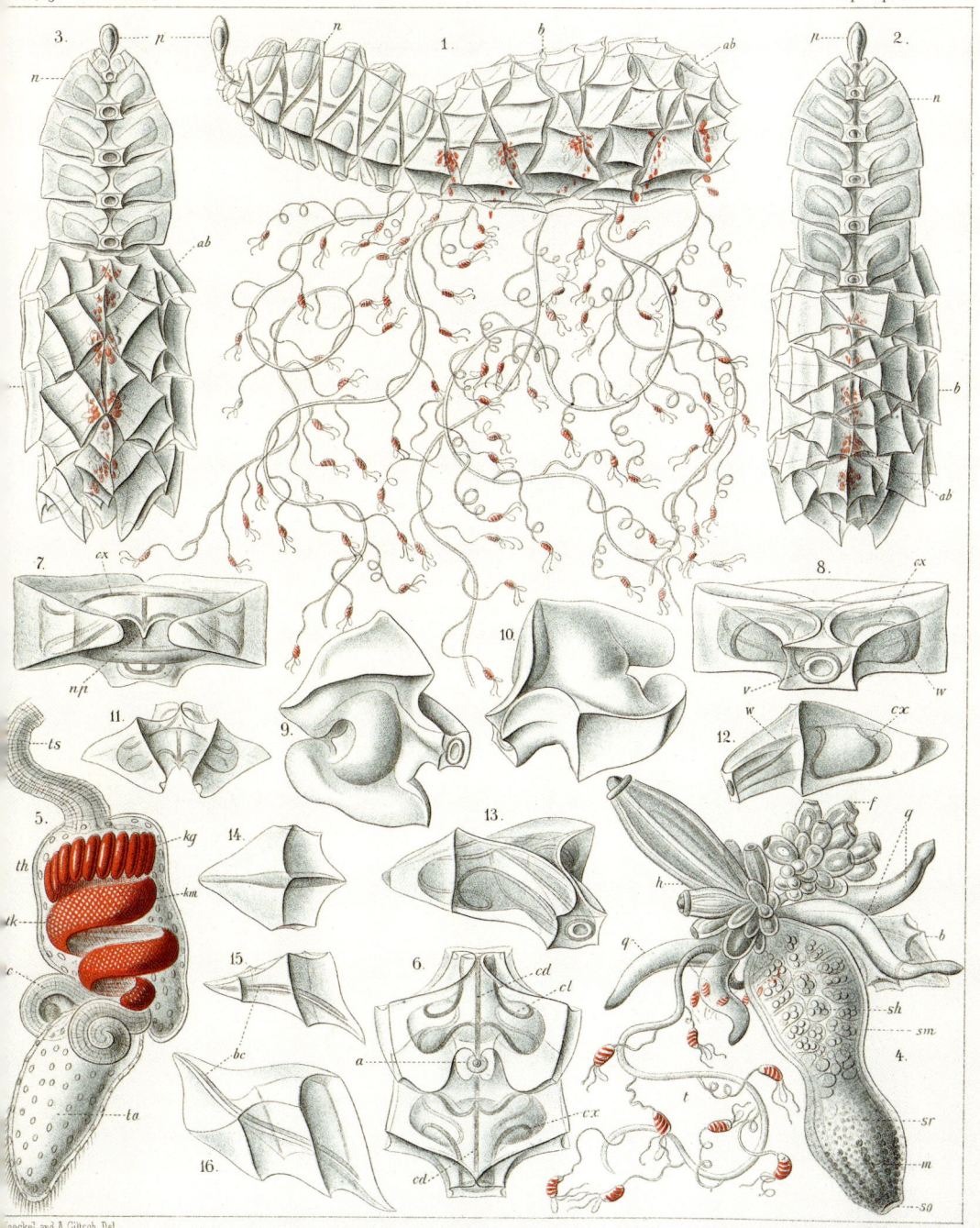

CRYSTALLODES VITREA.

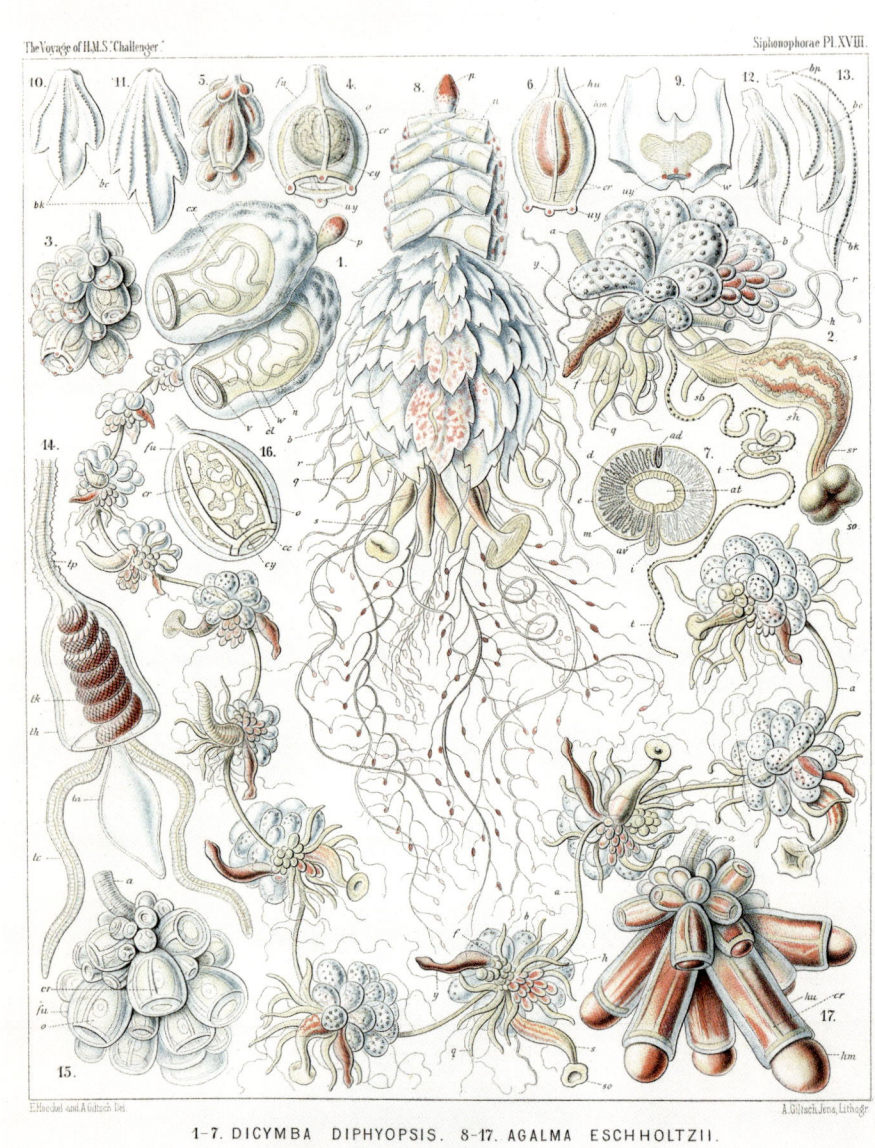

1–7. DICYMBA DIPHYOPSIS. 8–17. AGALMA ESCHHOLTZII.

PLATE 18
1–7 Dicymba diphyopsis – *Apolemia uvaria* (LESUEUR, 1815)
8–17 Agalma eschholtzii n. sp. (sic!) – *Agalma eschscholtzi* HAECKEL, 1888

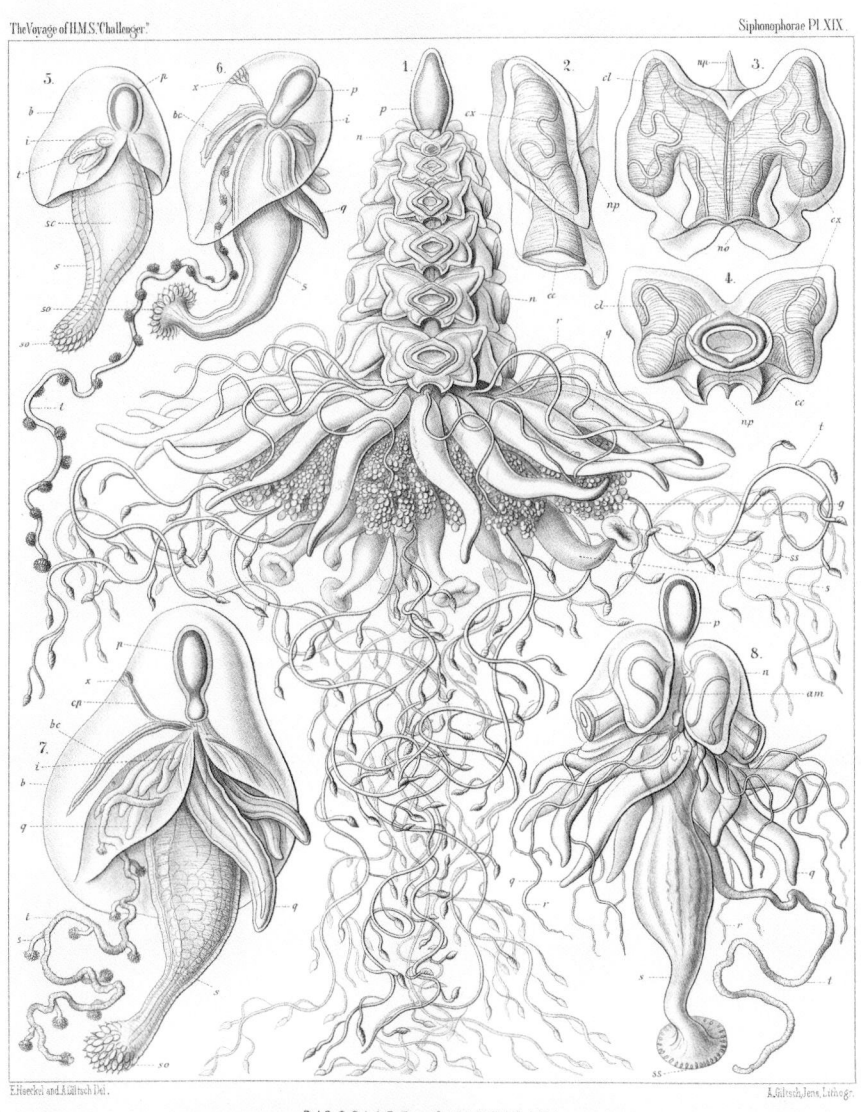

The Voyage of H.M.S. "Challenger."

Siphonophorae Pl. XIX.

DISCOLABE QUADRIGATA.

E.Haeckel and A.Giltsch Del.

A.Giltsch,Jena, Lithogr.

PLATE 19

1–8 Discolabe quadrigata n. sp. – *Physophora hydrostatica* FORSSKÅL, 1775

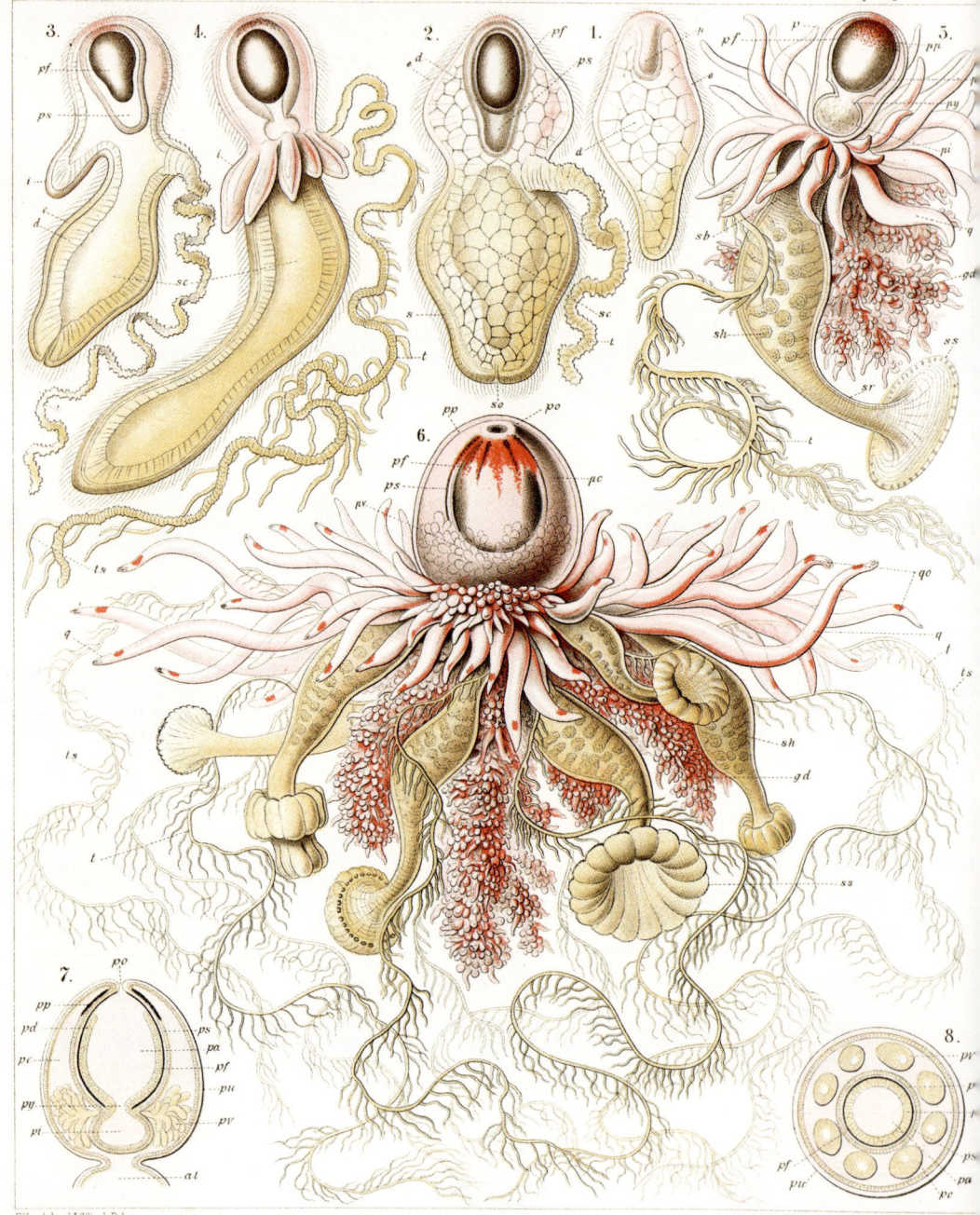

1-5. CYSTALIA MONOGASTRICA. 6-8. EPIBULIA RITTERIANA.

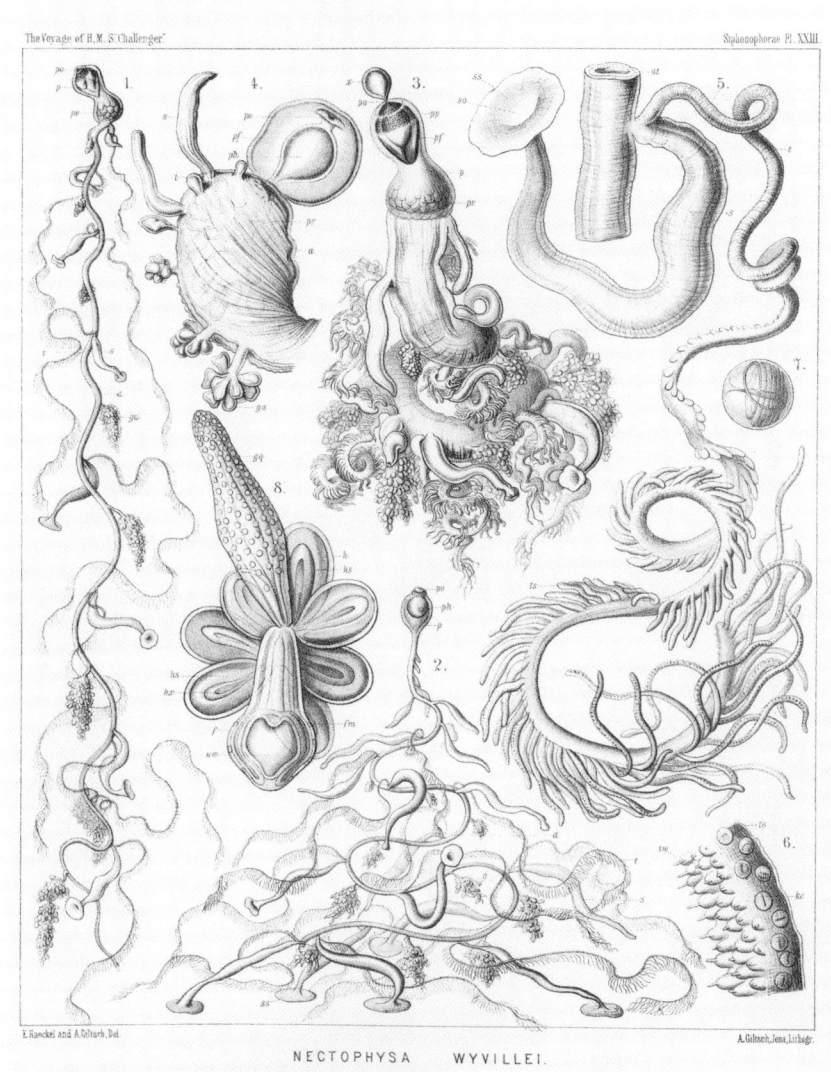

The Voyage of H.M.S."Challenger"

Siphonophorae Pl. XXIII

E.Haeckel and A.Giltsch. Del.

A.Giltsch, Jena, Lithogr.

NECTOPHYSA WYVILLEI.

PLATE 22
1-5 Cystalia monogastrica n. sp. – *Cystalia monogastrica*
6-8 Epibulia ritteriana n. sp. – *Epibulia ritteriana*

PLATE 23
1-8 Nectophysa wyvillei n. sp. – *Nectophysa wyvillei* HAECKEL, 1888

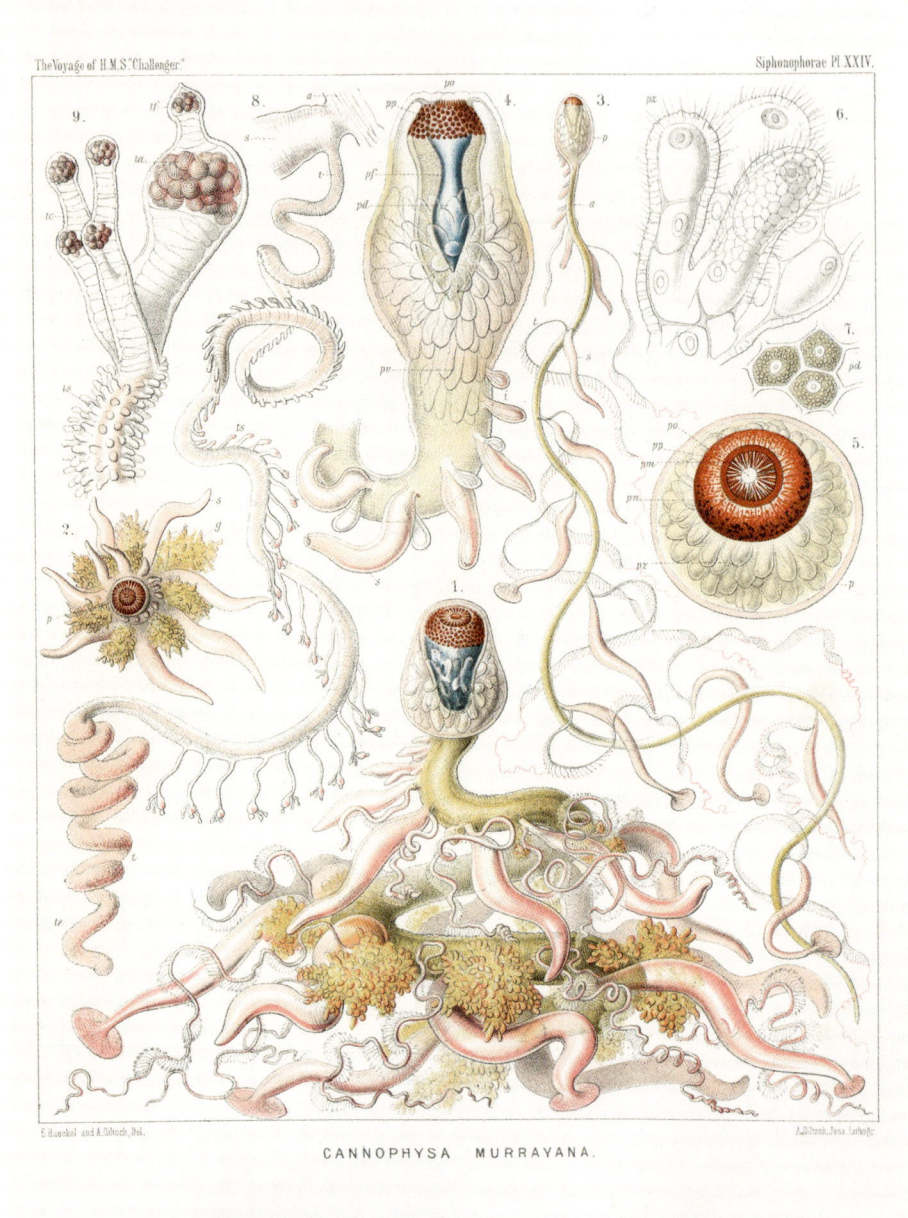

CANNOPHYSA MURRAYANA.

PLATE 24
1–9 Cannophysa murrayana n. sp. – *Rhizophysa murrayana* (HAECKEL, 1888)
(*? = Rhizophysa eysenhardti* GEGENBAUR, 1859)

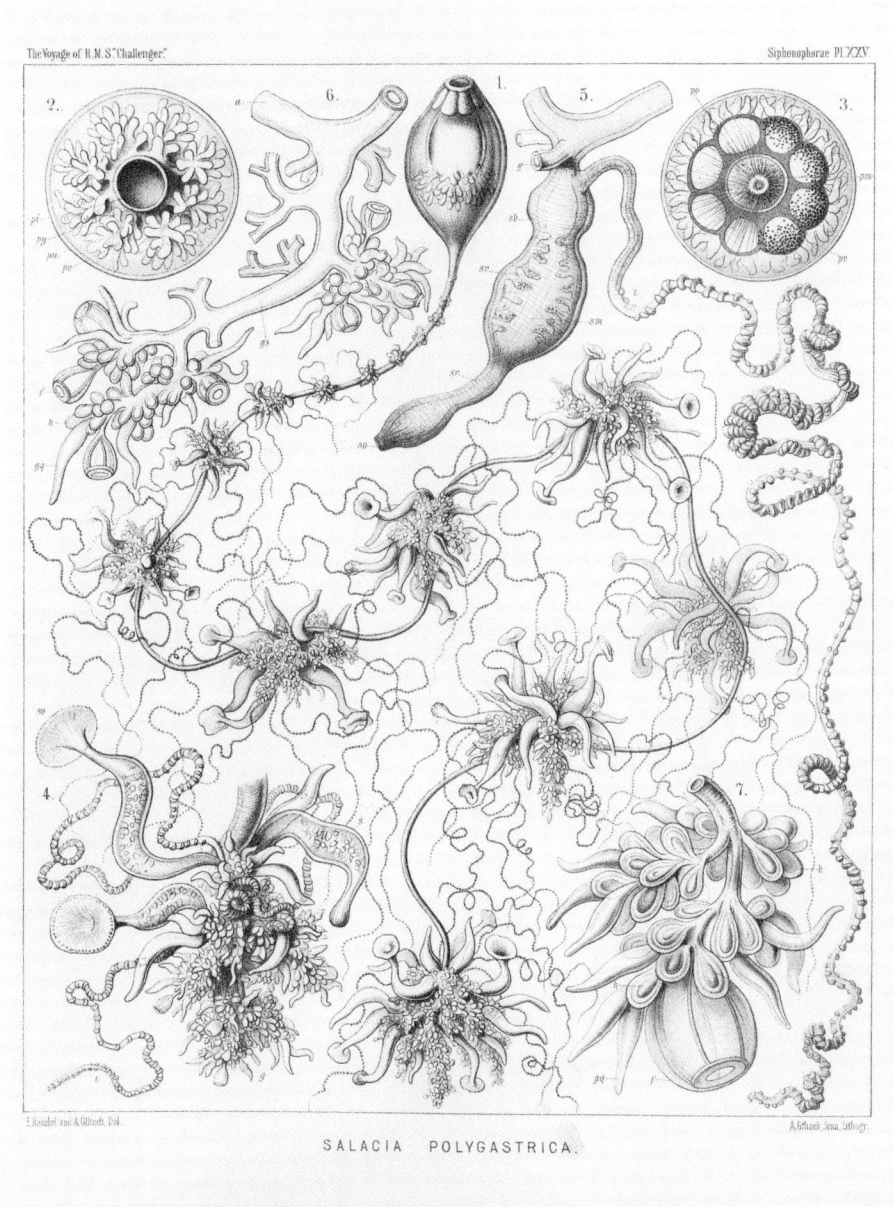

The Voyage of "H.M.S. Challenger." Siphonophorae Pl.XXV.

SALACIA POLYGASTRICA.

E.Haeckel and A.Giltsch, Del.

PLATE 25

1-7 Salacia polygastrica n. sp. – *Salacia polygastrica* HAECKEL, 1888

(? = *Salacella uvaria* FEWKES, 1886)

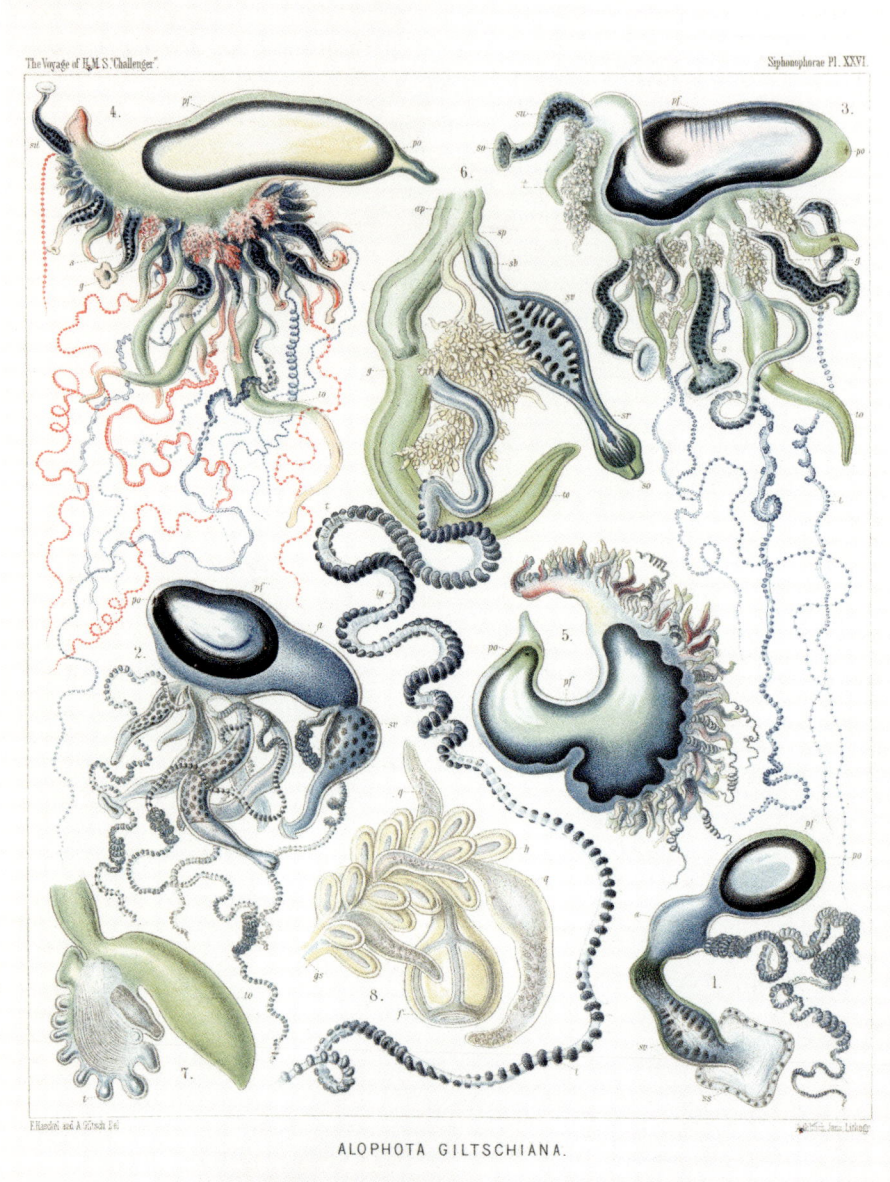

ALOPHOTA GILTSCHIANA.

1–3 **Alophota giltschiana** n. sp. – *Physalia physalis* (LINNAEUS, 1758) ?
4–8 **Arethusa challengeri** n. sp. – *Physalia physalis* (LINNAEUS, 1758)

Portuguese man-of-war, Bluebottle

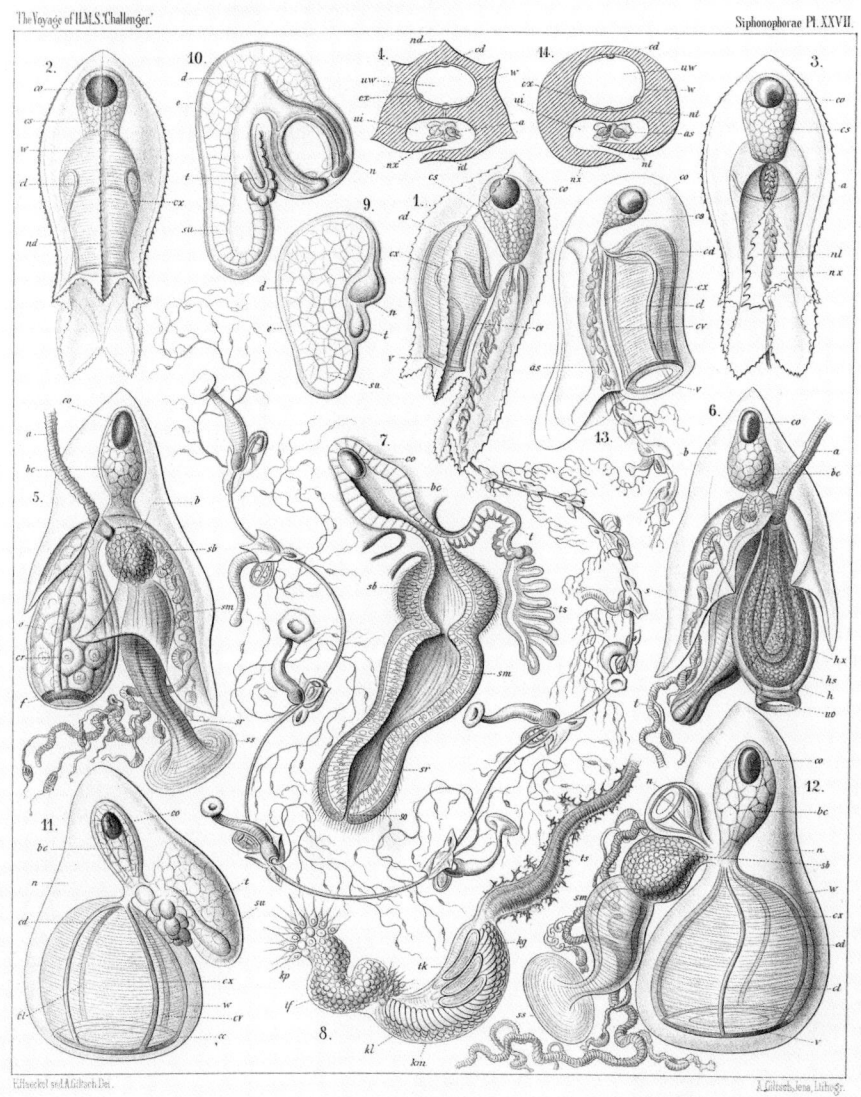

The Voyage of H.M.S. Challenger.

Siphonophorae Pl. XXVII.

1-12, CYMBONECTES HUXLEYI. 13-14, MONOPHYES PRINCEPS.

PLATE 27

1-12 Cymbonectes huxleyi n. sp. – *Muggiaea huxleyi* (HAECKEL, 1888)

13-14 Monophyes princeps n. sp. – *Sphaeronectes princeps* (HAECKEL, 1888)

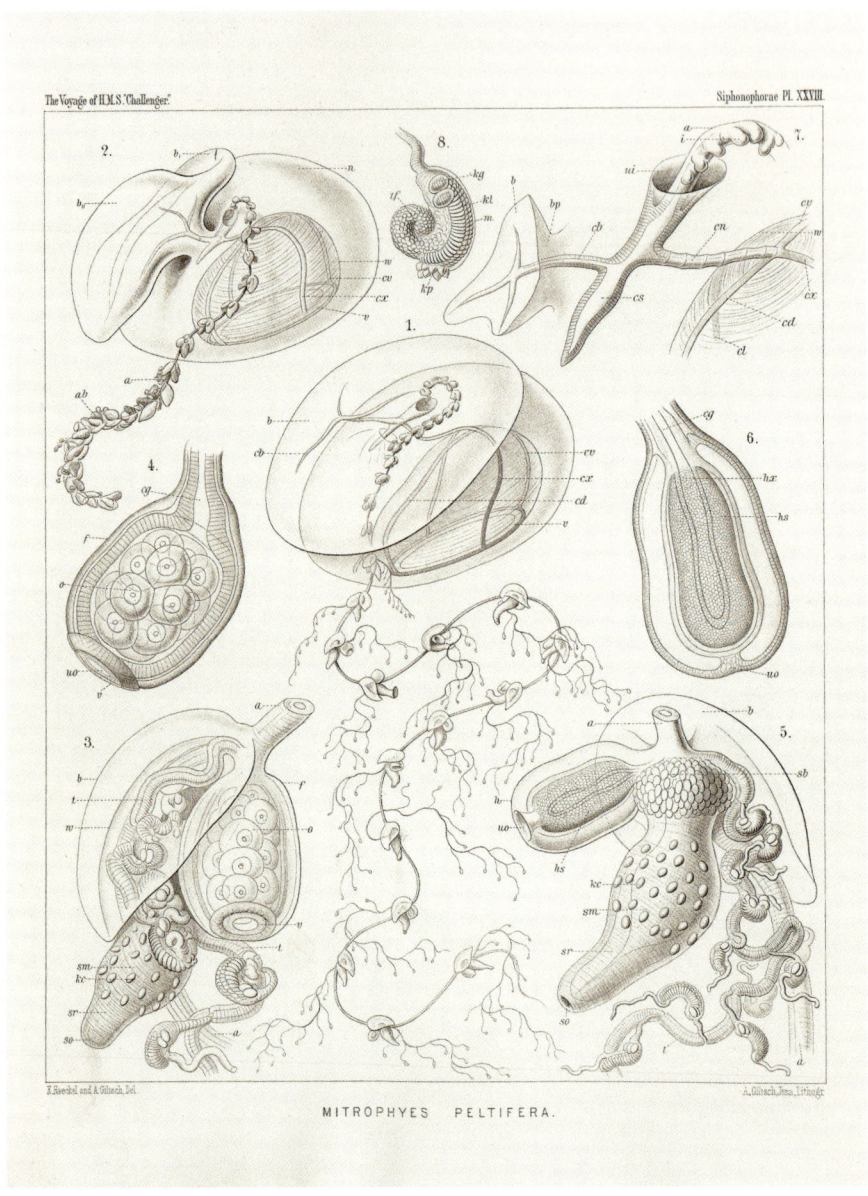

MITROPHYES PELTIFERA.

PLATE 28
1–8 Mitrophyes peltifera n. sp. – *Amphicaryon peltifera* (HAECKEL, 1888)

PLATE 29
1–8 Polyphyes ungulata n. sp. – *Hippopodius hippopus* (FORSSKÅL, 1776)
9–14 Vogtia köllikeri n. sp. – *Vogtia spinosa* KEFERSTEIN & EHLERS, 1861

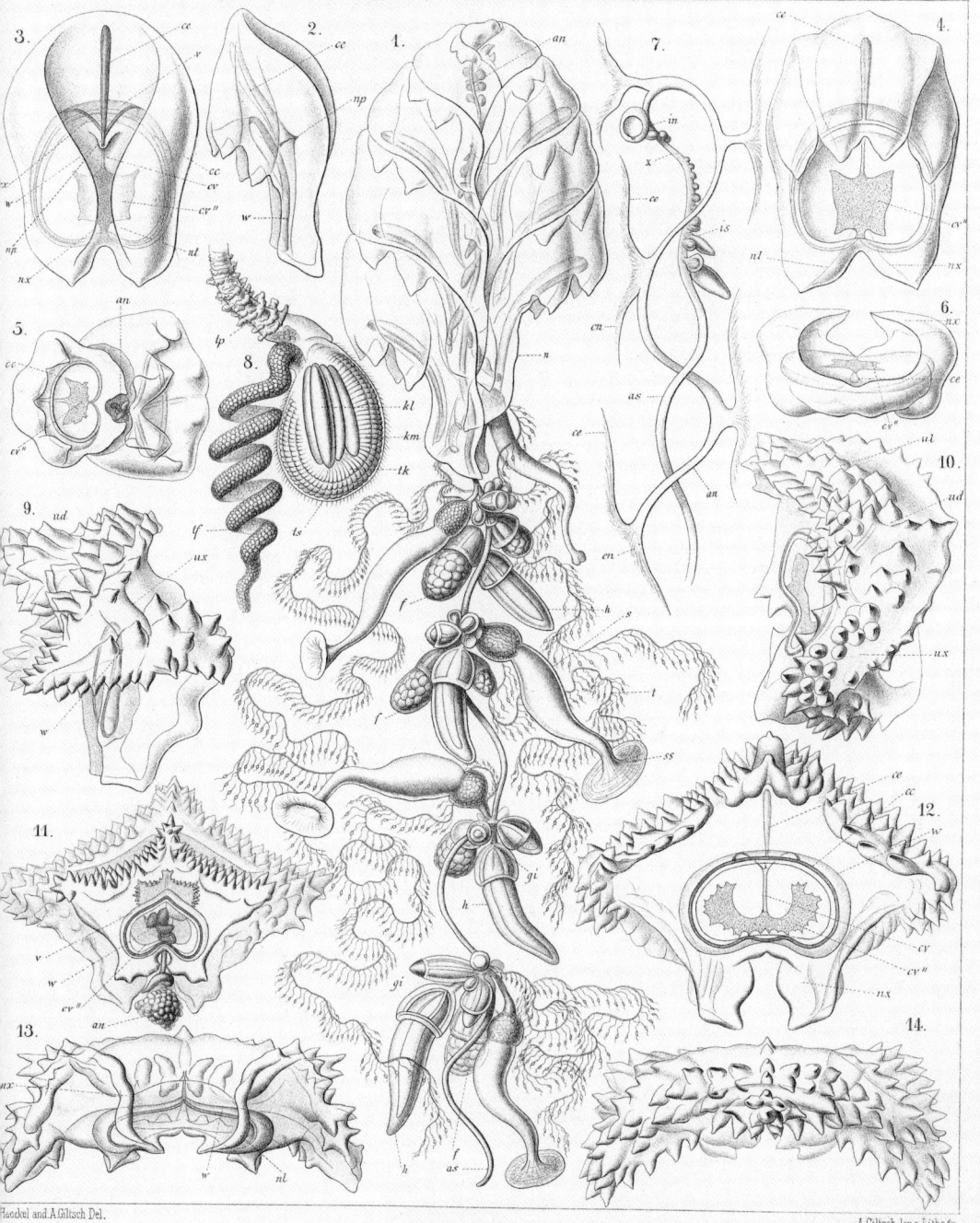

Haeckel and A.Giltsch Del. A.Giltsch Jena.Lithogr.

1–8, POLYPHYES UNGULATA. 9–14, VOGTIA KÖLLIKERI.

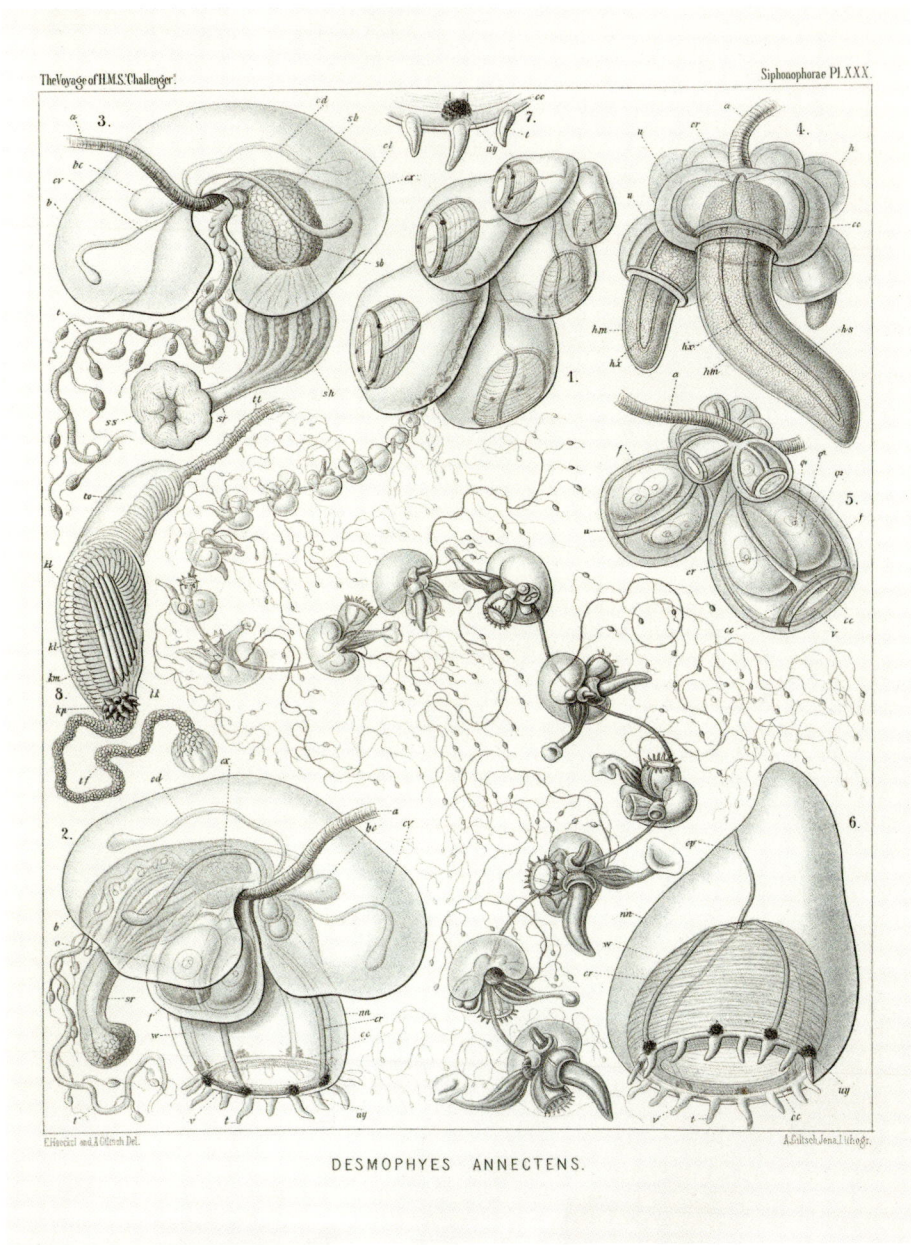

PLATE 30

1–8 Desmophyes annectens n. sp. –
Desmophyes annectens HAECKEL, 1888

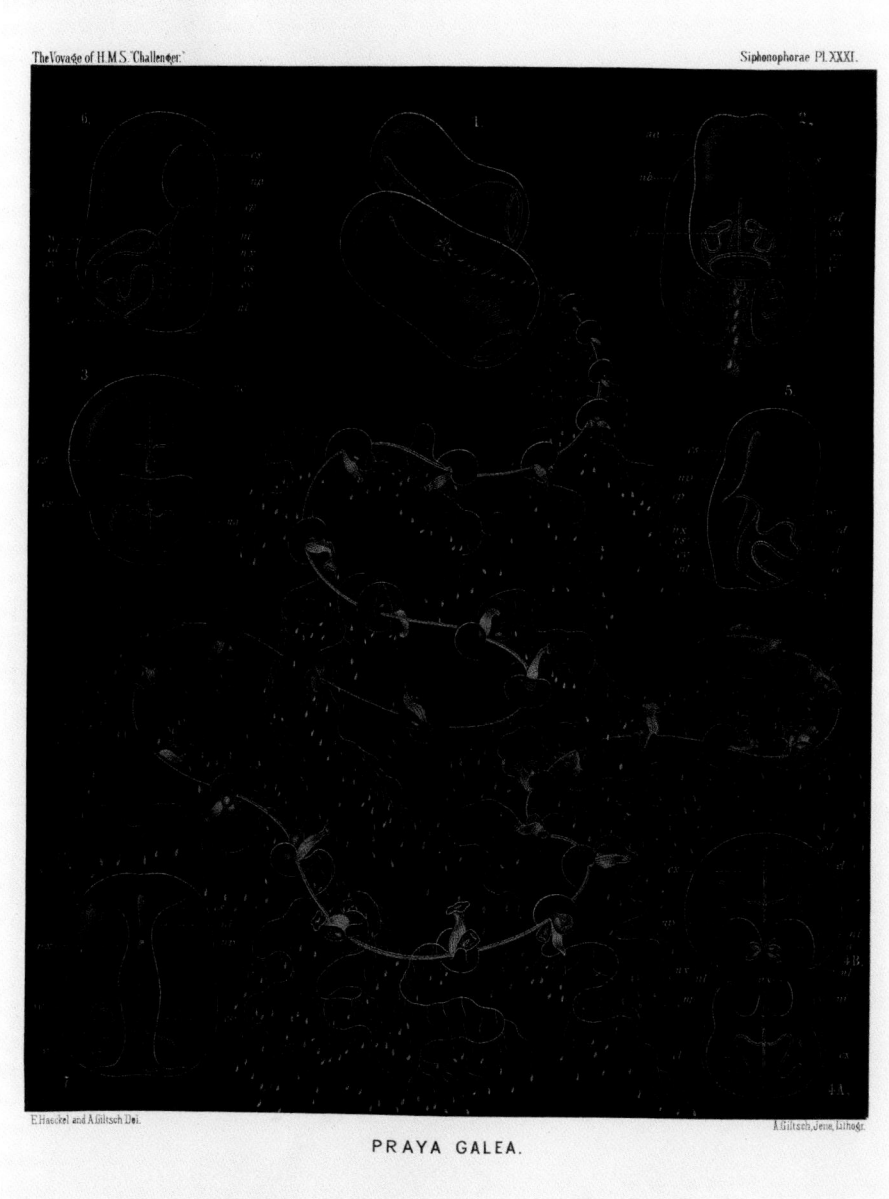

The Voyage of H.M.S. "Challenger."

Siphonophorae Pl. XXXI.

E.Haeckel and A.Giltsch Del.

A.Giltsch, Jena, Lithogr.

PRAYA GALEA.

173

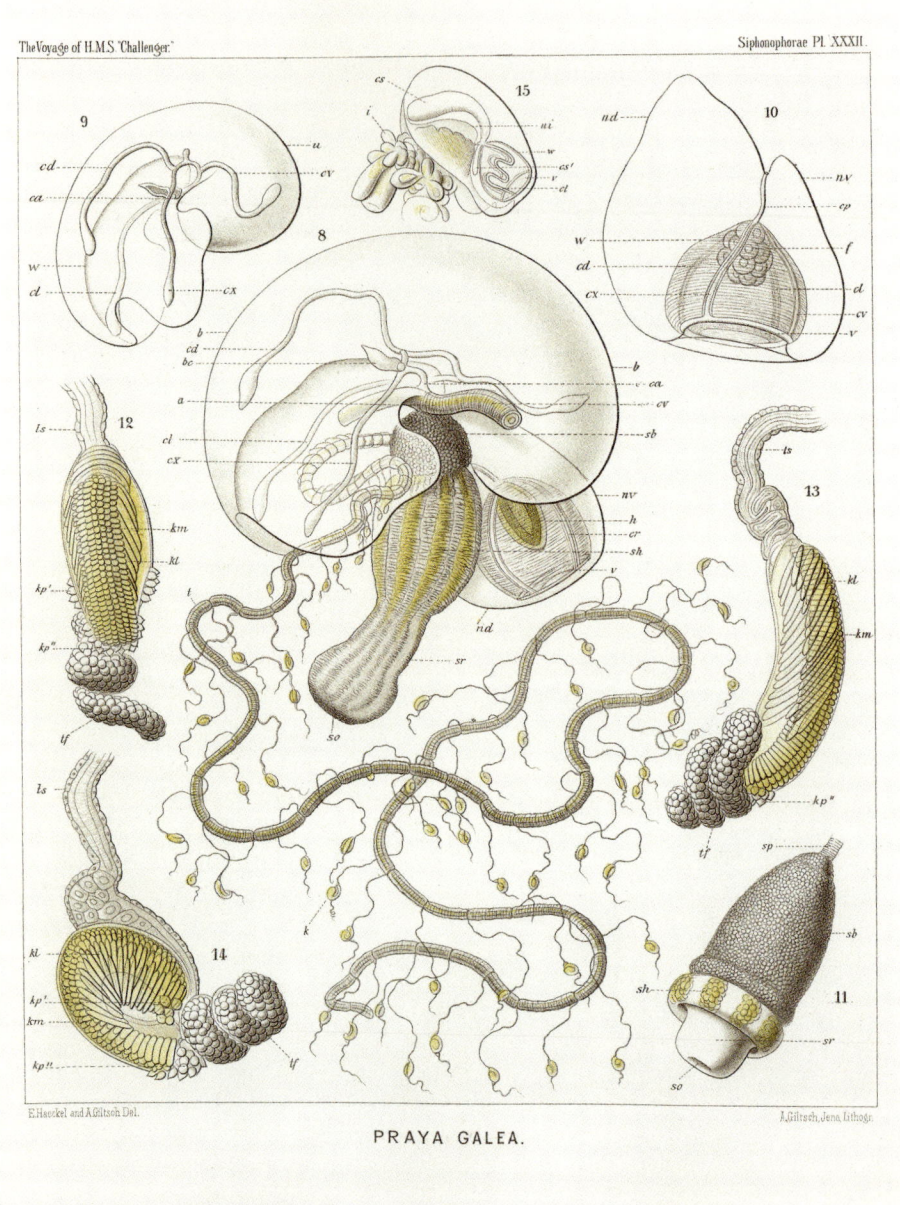

E.Haeckel and A.Giltsch Del.

A.Giltsch, Jena, lithogr.

PRAYA GALEA.

PLATE 32
8–15 Eudoxella galea n. sp. –
Rosacea cymbiformis (DELLE CHIAJE, 1830)

174

DIPHYOPSIS COMPRESSA.

PLATE 33
1–8 Diphyopsis compressa n. sp. –
Diphyes dispar CHAMISSO & EYSENHARDT, 1821

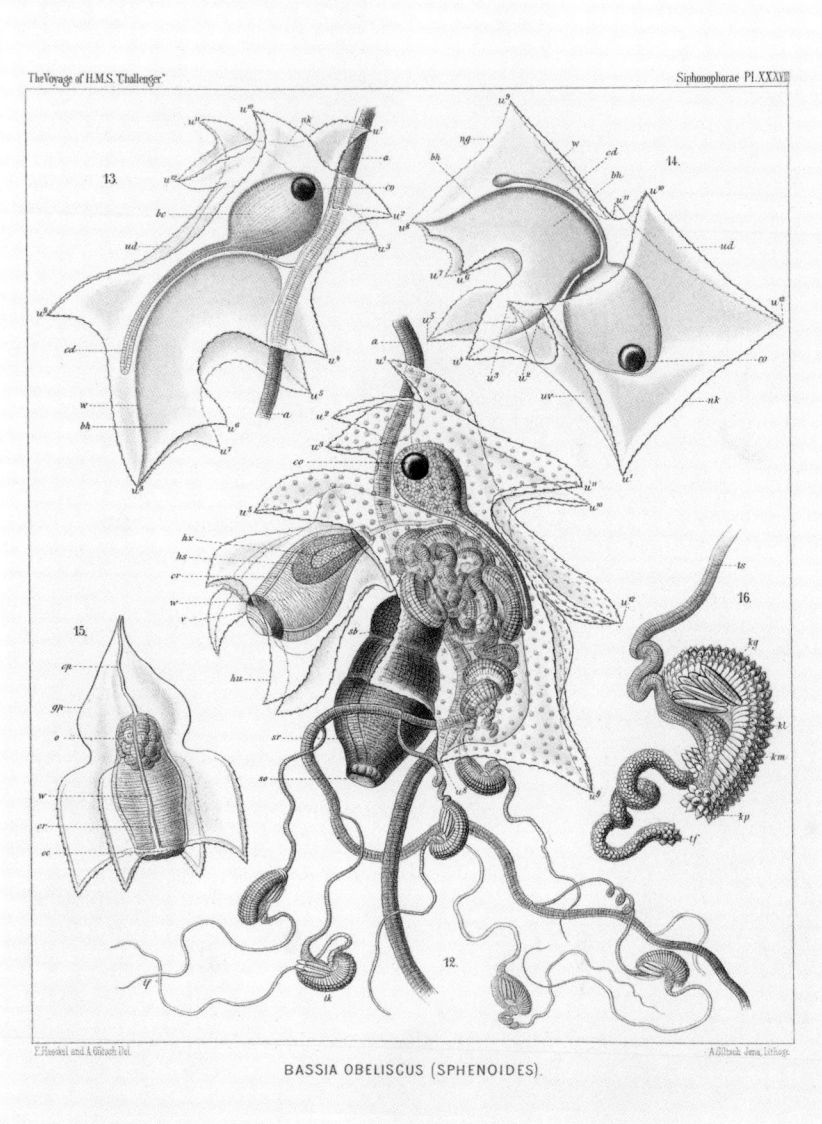

BASSIA OBELISCUS (SPHENOIDES).

PLATE 38
12–16 Sphenoides obeliscus n. sp. –
Bassia bassensis (QUOY & GAIMARD, 1833)

PLATE 39
1–12 Calpe gegenbauri n. sp. –
Abylopsis tetragona (OTTO, 1823)

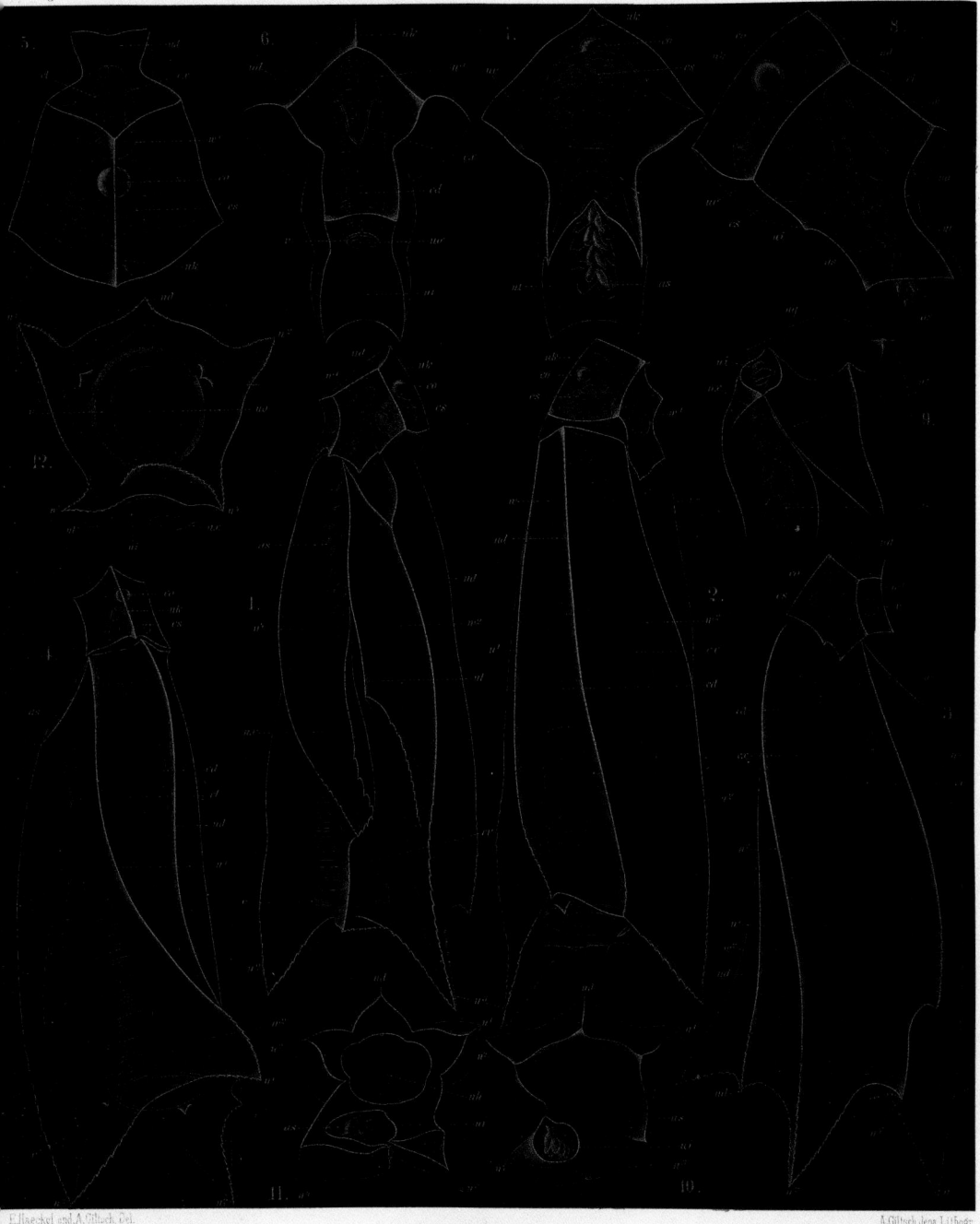

E.Haeckel and A.Giltsch, del. A.Giltsch Jena, Lithogr.

CALPE GEGENBAURI.

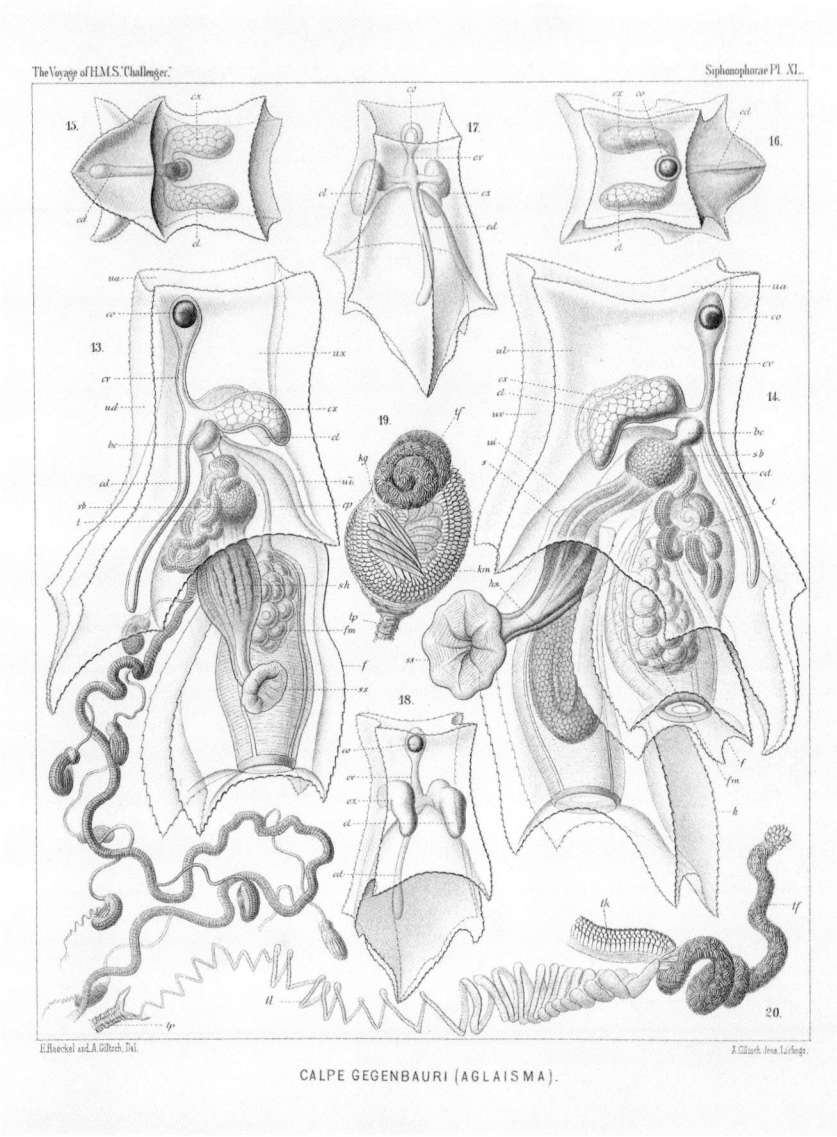

CALPE GEGENBAURI (AGLAISMA).

PLATE 40

13-20 Aglaisma gegenbauri n. sp. –
Abylopsis tetragona (OTTO, 1823)

PLATE 41

1-8 Cymba crystallus n. sp. –
Enneagonum hyalinum QUOY & GAIMARD, 1827

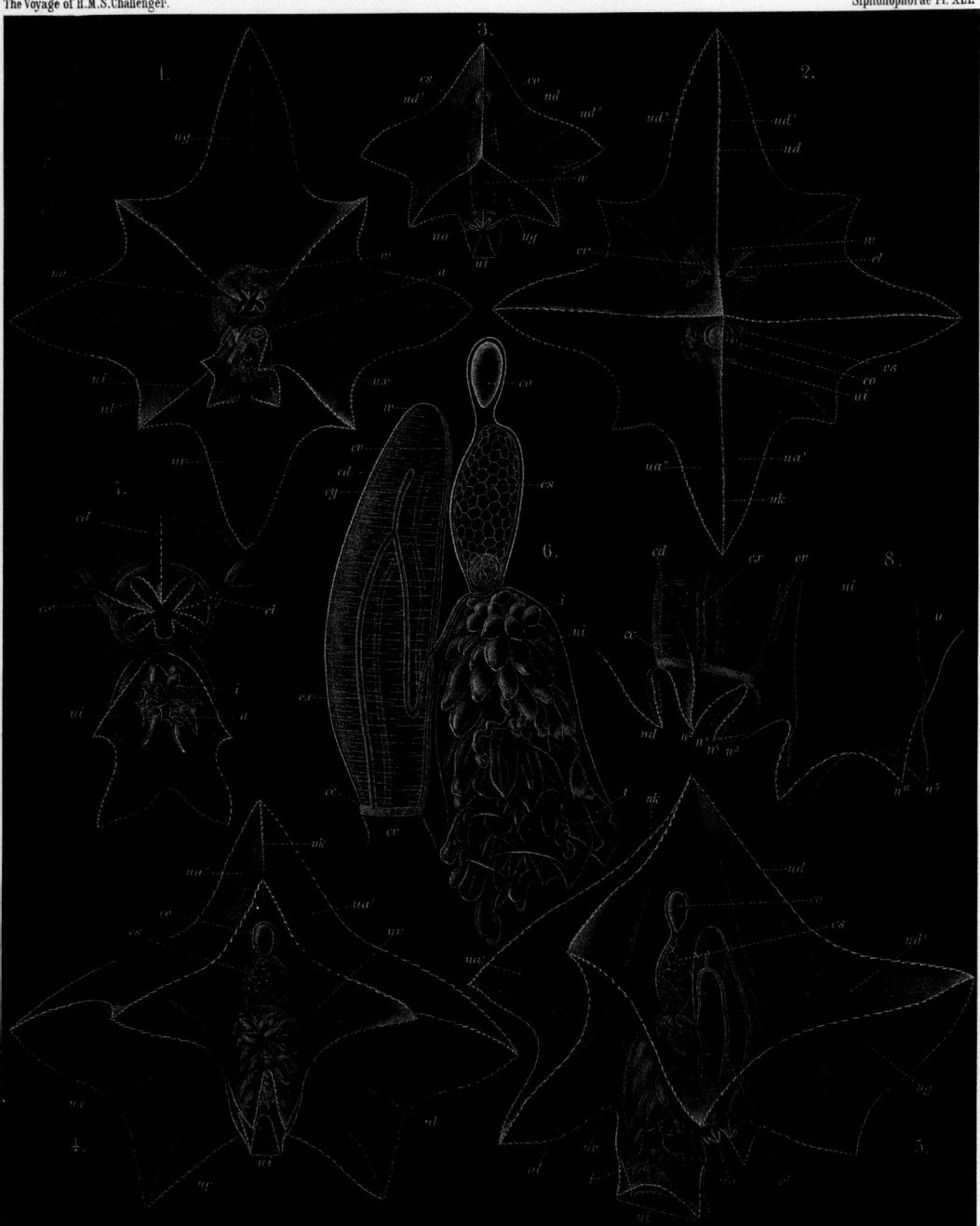

E.Haeckel and A.Giltsch,Del.

A.Giltsch, Jena, Lithogr.

CYMBA CRYSTALLUS

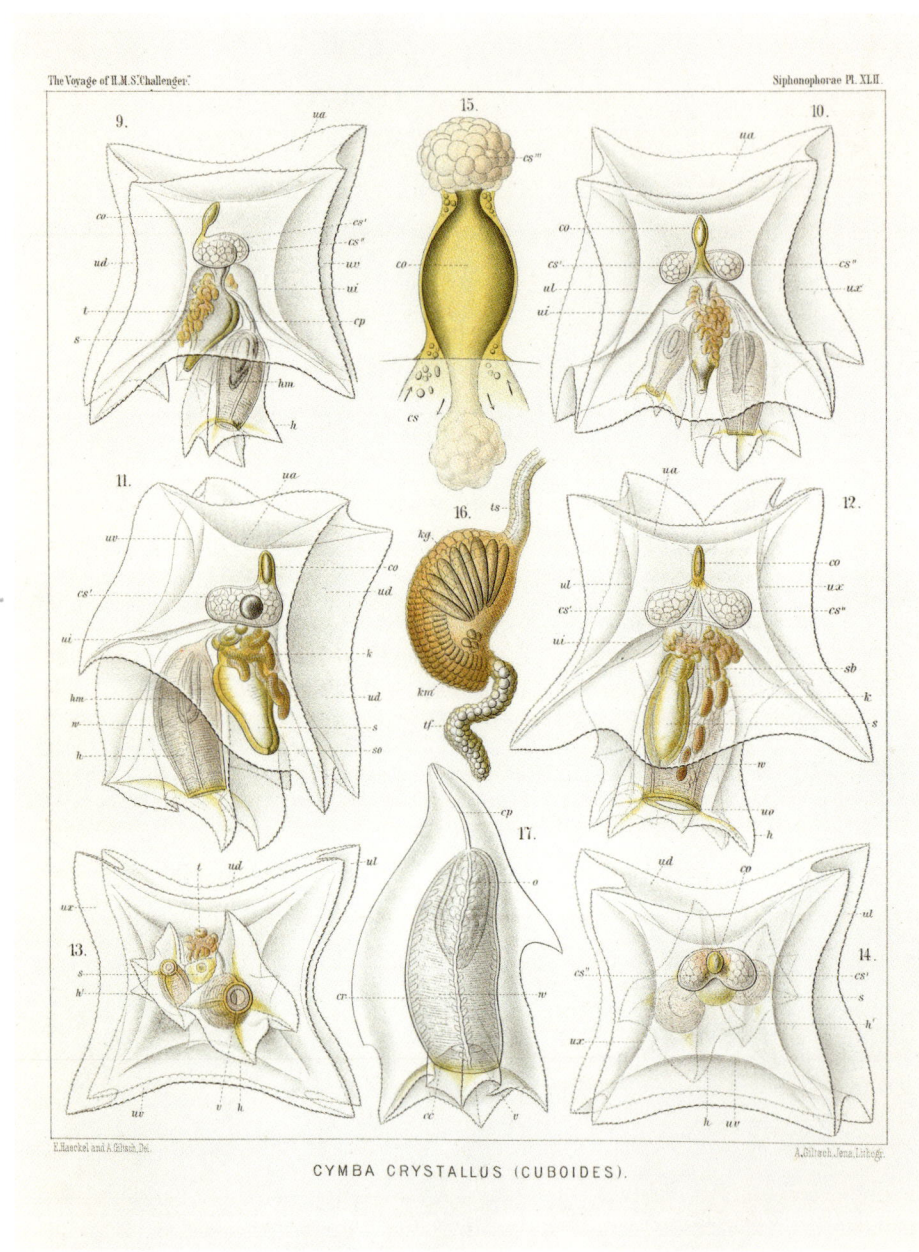

CYMBA CRYSTALLUS (CUBOIDES).

E.Haeckel and A.Gilisch. Del.

A.Gilisch. Jena. Lithogr.

PLATE 42
9–17 Cuboides crystallus n. sp. –
Enneagonum hyalinum QUOY & GAIMARD, 1827

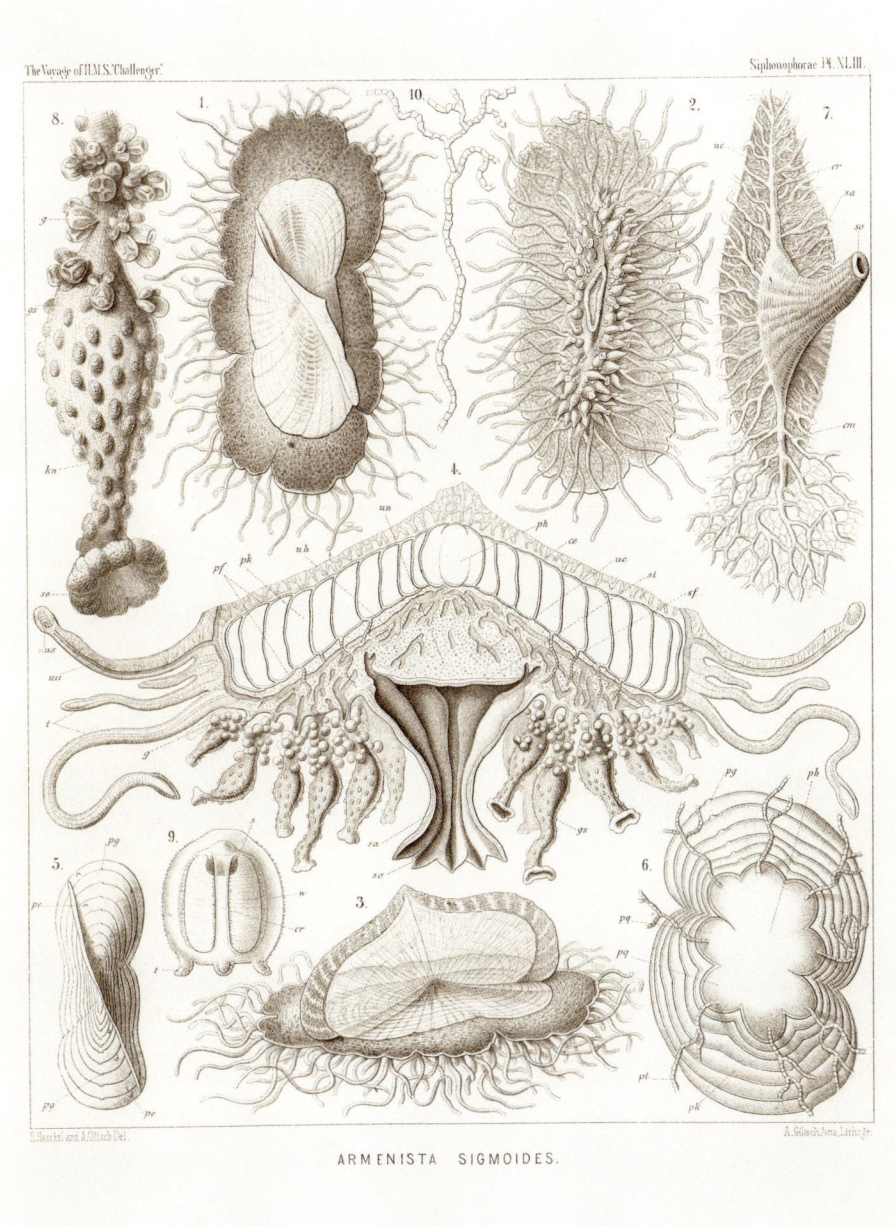

The Voyage of H.M.S. "Challenger".
Siphonophorae Pl. XLIII.

ARMENISTA SIGMOIDES.

E.Haeckel and A.Giltsch.Del.

A.Giltsch.Jena.Lith.gr.

PLATE 43
1–10 Armenista sigmoides n.sp. – *Velella velella* (LINNAEUS, 1758)
By-the-Wind Sailor, Jack Sail-by-the-Wind, Purple Sail

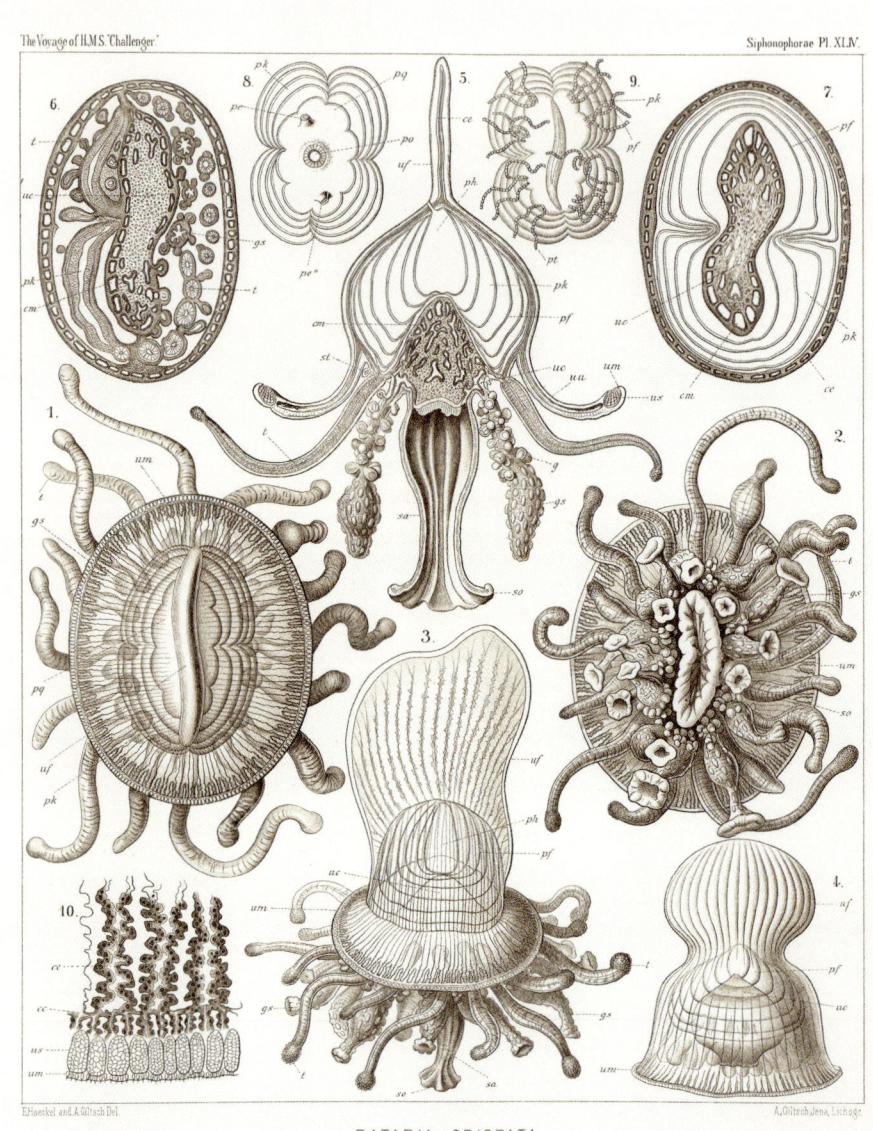

RATARIA CRISTATA.

PLATE 44

1-10 Rataria cristata n. sp. – *Velella velella* LINNAEUS, 1758

By-the-Wind Sailor, Jack Sail-by-the-Wind, Purple Sail

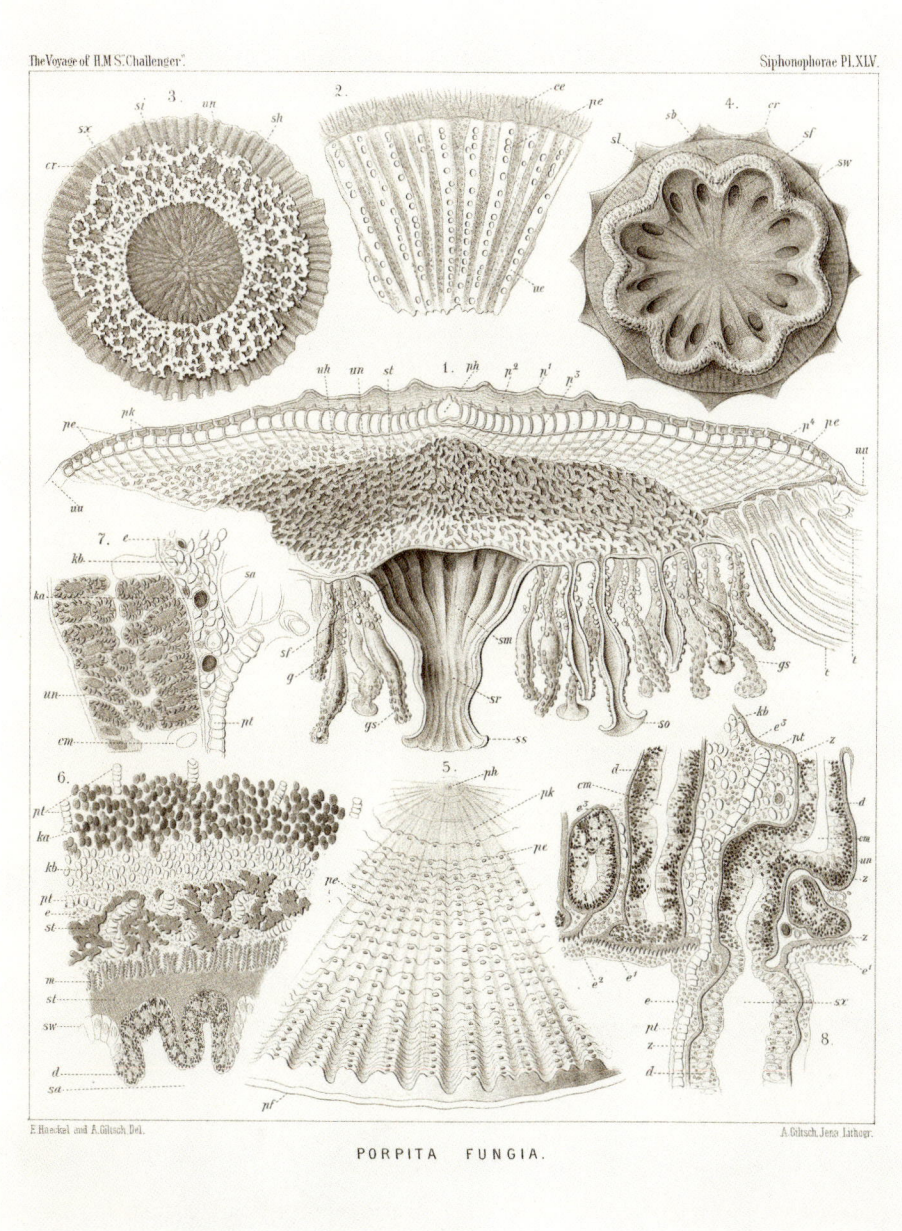

The Voyage of H.M.S. "Challenger".

Siphonophorae Pl.XLV.

E.Haeckel and A.Giltsch.Del.

A.Giltsch, Jena Lithogr.

PORPITA FUNGIA.

PLATE 45

1–8 Porpita fungia n. sp. – *Porpita porpita* (LINNAEUS, 1758)

Blue button

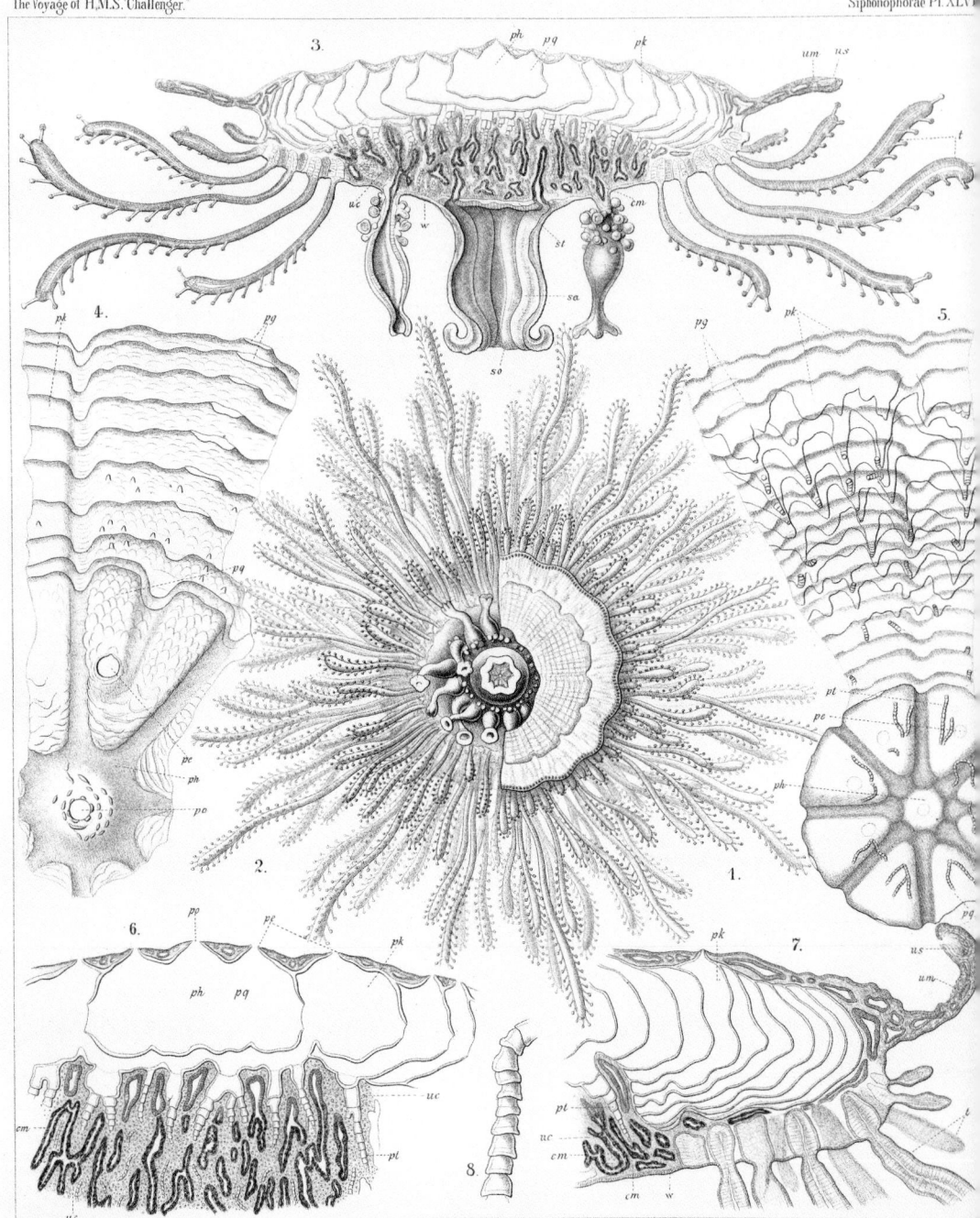

PORPITELLA PECTANTHIS.

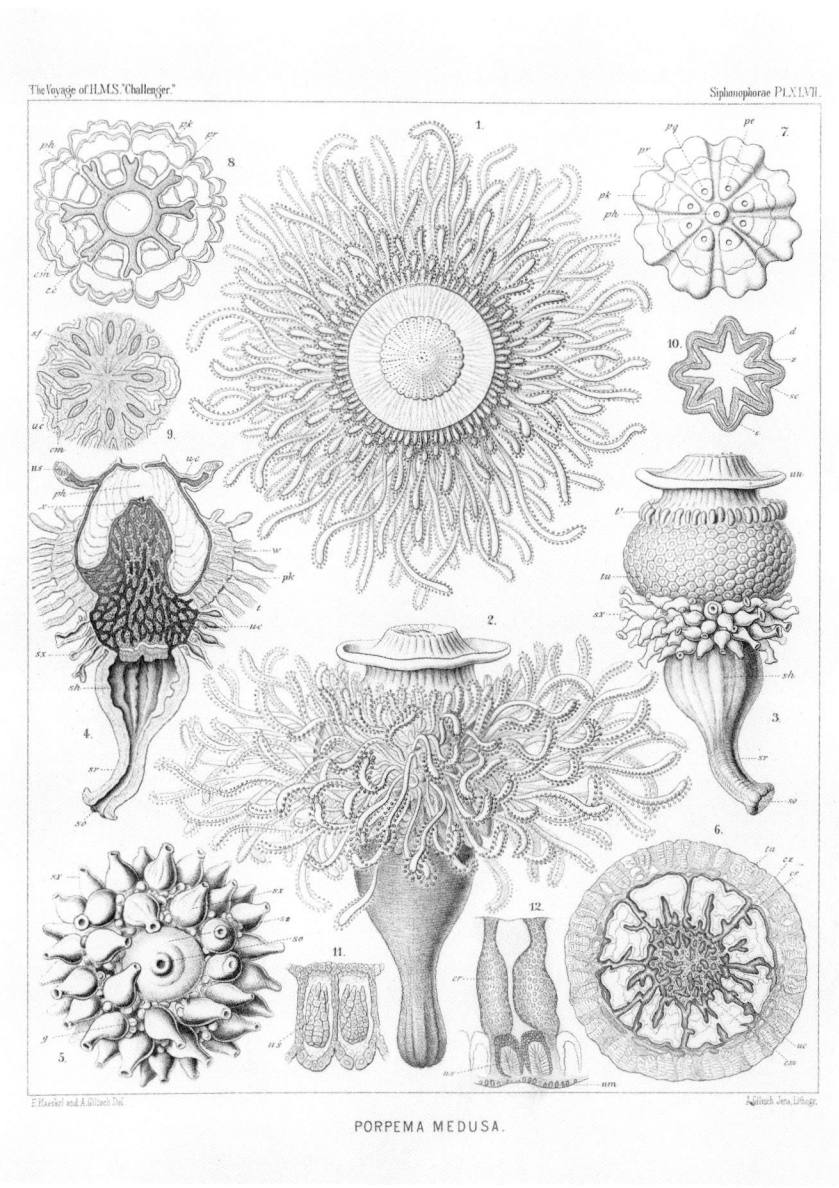

The Voyage of H.M.S. "Challenger."

Siphonophorae PL.XLVII.

E.Haeckel and A.Giltsch Del.

Lith.inst.v. Jena, Lithogr.

PORPEMA MEDUSA.

185

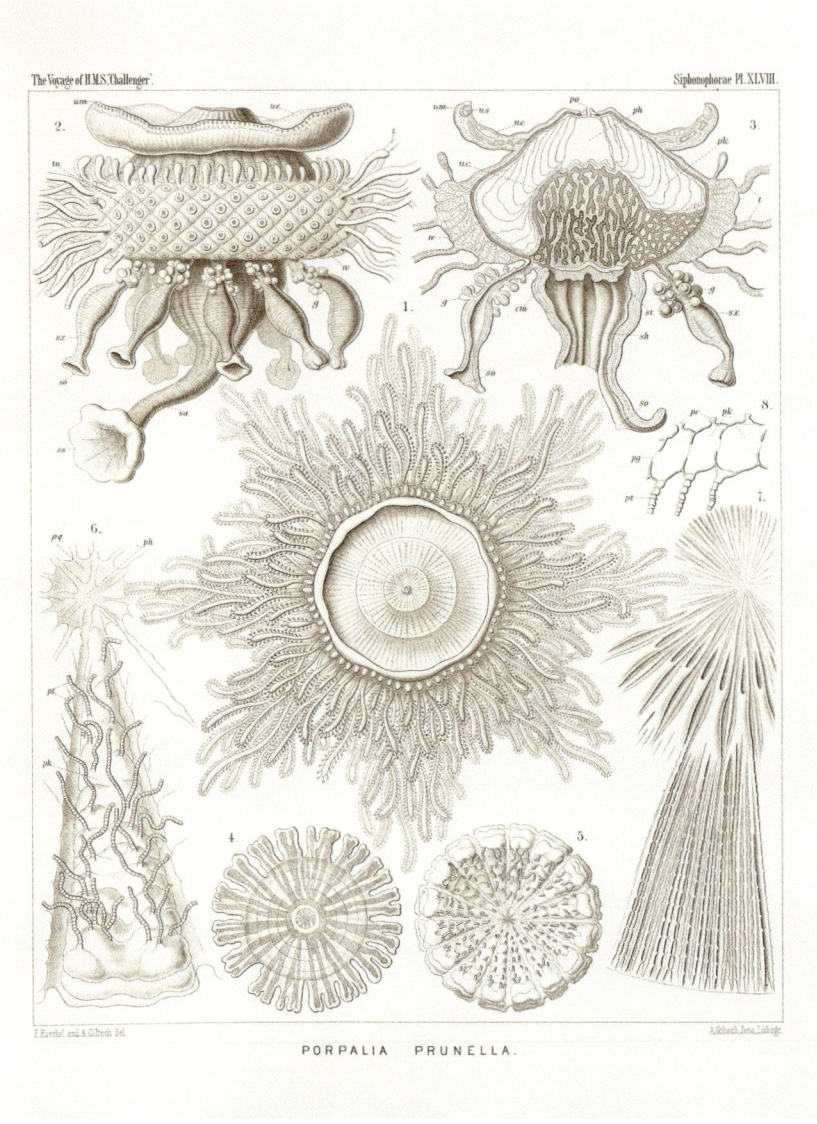

The Voyage of H.M.S.Challenger.
Siphonophorae Pl.XLVIII.

PORPALIA PRUNELLA.

PLATE 48
1–8 Porpalia prunella n. sp. – *Porpema prunella* (HAECKEL, 1888)
(synonym: *Porpita prunella* (HAECKEL, 1888))

PLATE 49
1–6 Discalia medusina n. sp. – *Porpema prunella* HAECKEL, 1888
(synonym: *Porpita prunella* (HAECKEL, 1888))
7–12 Disconalia gastroblasta n. sp. – *Porpita porpita* (LINNAEUS, 1758) Blue button

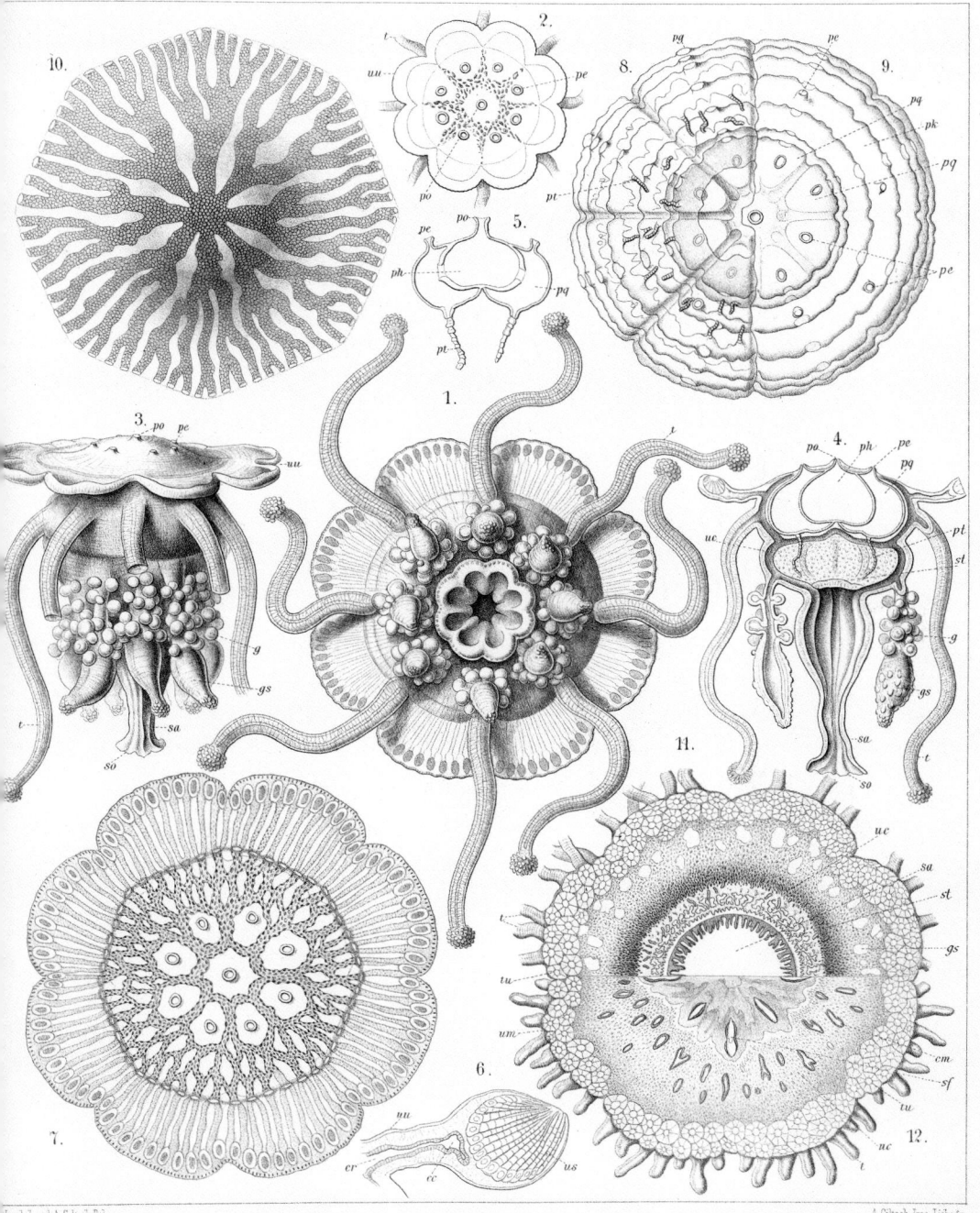

Haeckel and A.Giltsch Del.

A.Giltsch,Jena,Lithogr.

1-6. DISCALIA MEDUSINA. 7-12. DISCONALIA GASTROBLASTA.

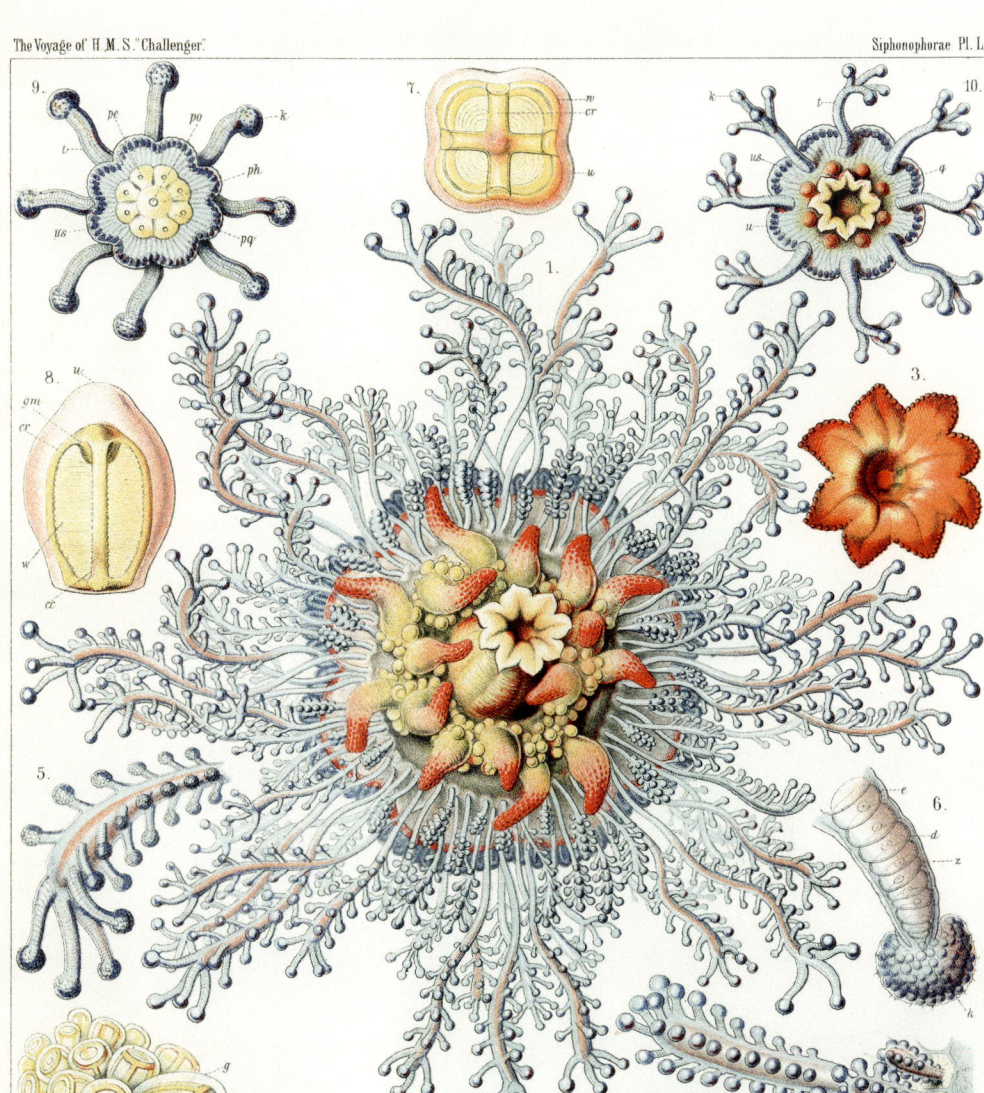

DISCONALIA GASTROBLASTA

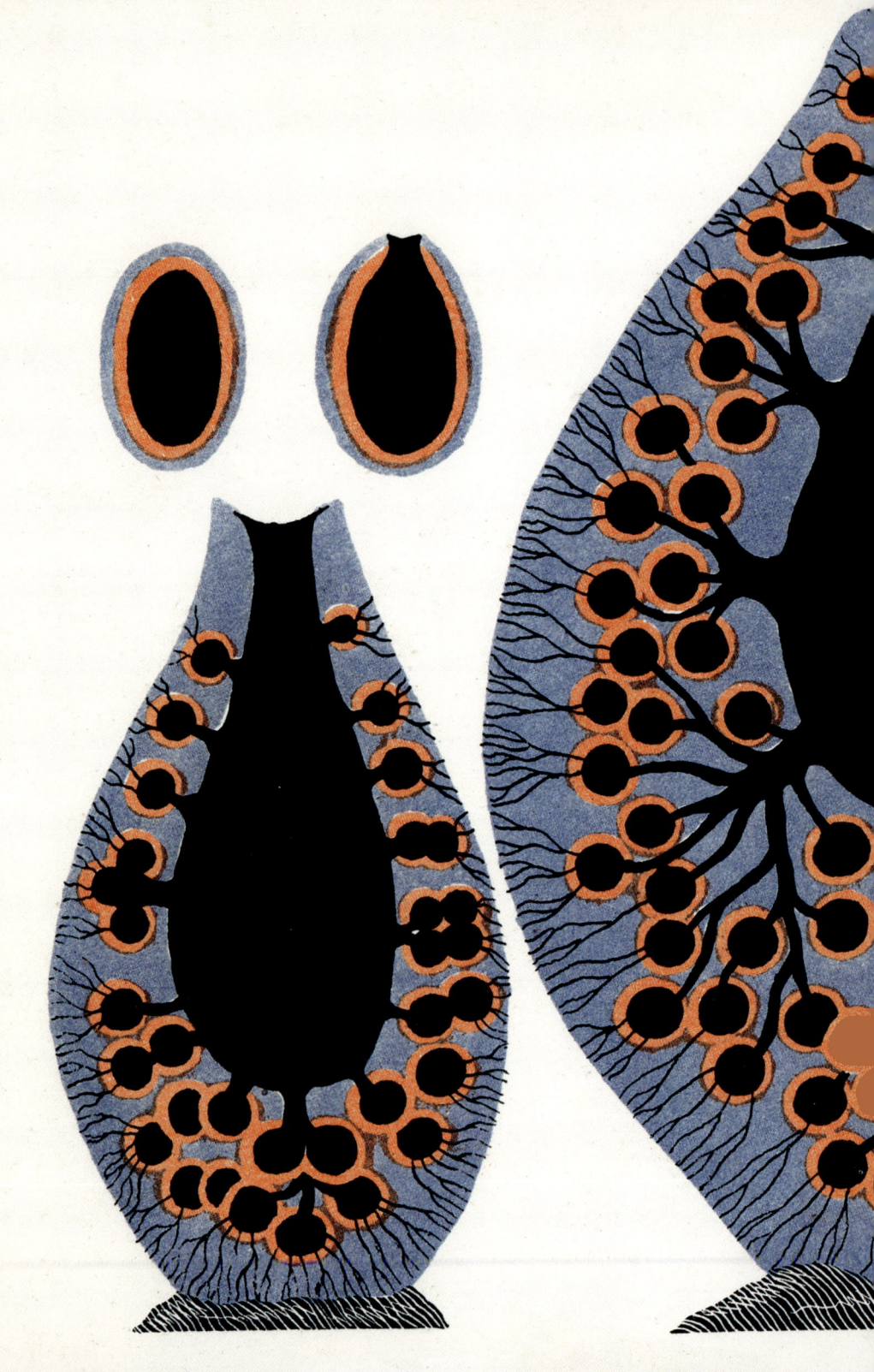

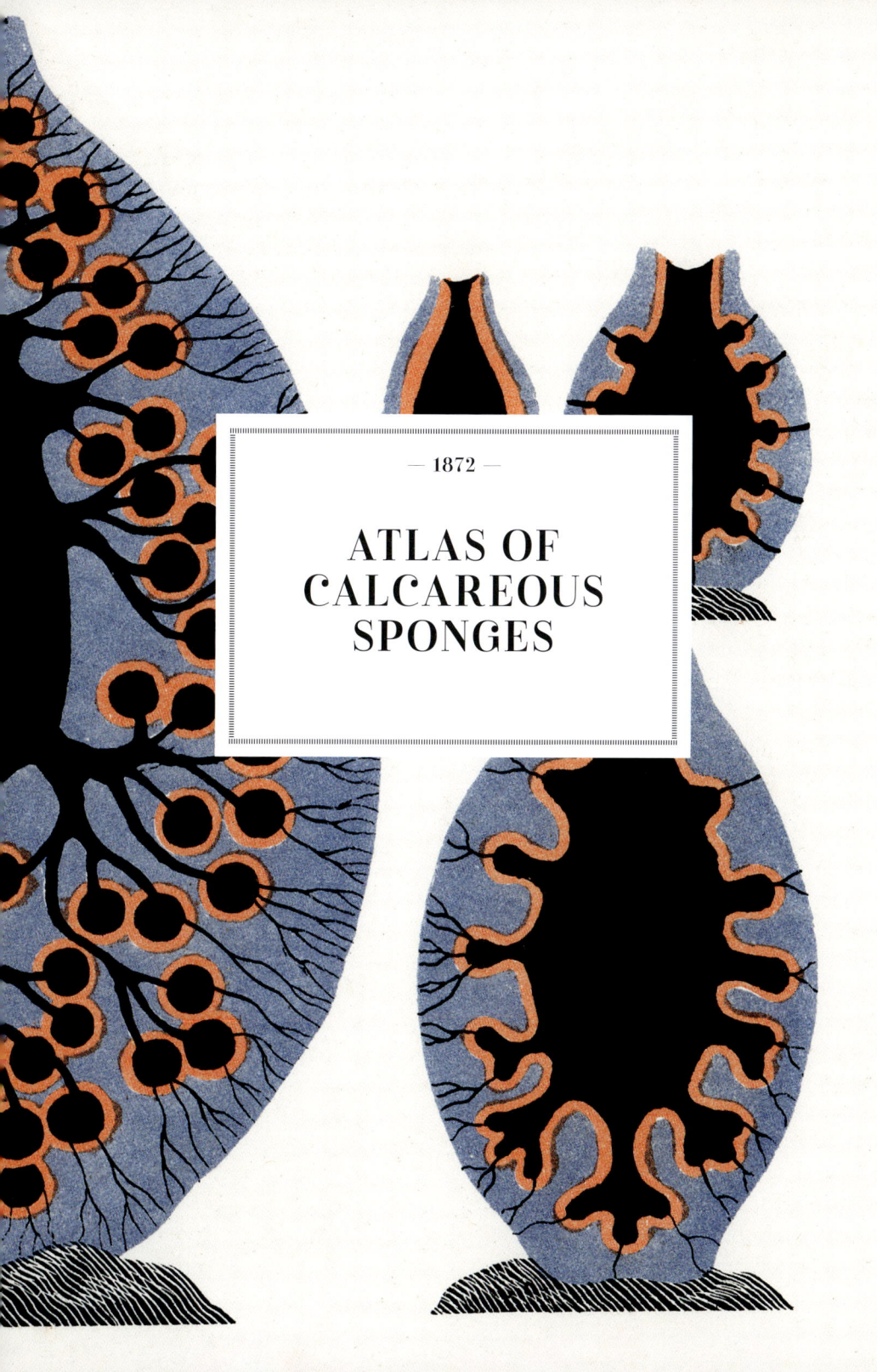

— 1872 —

ATLAS OF CALCAREOUS SPONGES

ATLAS OF CALCAREOUS SPONGES

Sponges are a decidedly primitive group of multicellular organisms and, accordingly, are among the earliest animals appearing in Earth's history. In the supplementary volume to his *Kunstformen der Natur* (*Art Forms in Nature*), Haeckel offered a vivid characterisation of these beings: "Most sponges [...] live firmly fixed on the sea floor, and comprise irregular lumps of indeterminate form, very varied in size (from one or only a few millimetres to over a metre) [...]. By way of numerous microscopic pores (plate 5, fig. 10), water enters the flagellate chamber (a hollow space serving as an effective stomach), which has an inner surface covered with a layer of flagellate cells [...]. The water is then released through a larger opening (*osculum*) usually located at the upper pole of the body's axis (plate 5, figs. 6, 8). The connective tissue of the ectoderm that surrounds and binds the flagellate chambers generates various skeletal elements that provide support. In the case of cork sponges (Malthospongiae), to which the sponges we use in our baths belong, this support takes the form of a firm mesh of elastic keratinous fibres. In the calcareous sponges (Calcispongiae) the support is composed chiefly of delicately shaped spicules, which may be single, three-radiate or four-pronged (plate 5, figs. 10–12). In the case of siliceous sponges (Silicispongiae), the skeletal part is made of silica; these spicules are sometimes monaxial (Monactinella), they sometimes have three or four axes (the Tetractinella), and sometimes six rays arranged in three vertically stacked sets (the Hexactinella, plate 35)."[1]

Because sponges have neither muscles (their slight movements are brought about by way of cells that cover their bodies) nor a nervous system, nor a digestive tract or a stomach, they are regarded as more primitive than other animals. They do, however, possess cells of a sort not to be found in any other animal group. Numerous species of sponges live in freshwater (even in the smallest pools that form on the leaves of plants), and there are very distinctive deep-sea forms.

The grouping of sponges undertaken by Haeckel (see above) has proven to be not entirely tenable. Sponges are, in fact, divided into Hexactinella (glass sponges, around 600 species), Demospongiae (keratinous sponges, around 7,000 species, among them the Homoscleromorpha, often regarded as a high-ranking taxon in its own right), and calcareous sponges (Calcarea or Calcispongiae).

In 1873 Haeckel wrote in the preface to the fourth edition of his *Natürliche Schöpfungsgeschichte* (*The History of Creation*) that he had "[been] carrying out the most painstaking research into this small, but highly instructive, group of animals in all their forms" for five years, and that he might well "maintain that the monograph deriving from this research would present the fullest and the most precise morphological analysis of an entire group of organisms that there had ever been."[2] Naturally, research has further progressed since Haeckel's time and we now know of around 700 species of calcareous sponges. The 60 plates of Haeckel's *Atlas der Kalkschwämme* (Atlas of Calcareous Sponges), published in 1872 as the third and final volume of the monograph *Die Kalkschwämme*, show both complete animals and longitudinal sections to illustrate their internal structure in addition to a great range of details. Haeckel termed sponges "stalks" comprising a number of individual "persons" (in the sense that every individual person has his or her own excretory passage, or *osculum*), the varieties of which he showed in numerous illustrations. With his research into the variability of the "stalks," Haeckel proved that many of the species' names in use at that time did not, in fact, relate to true biological species.

Depicted on plate 4 is an embryo, both as viewed from the outside and in a longitudinal section, and on plates 13 and 30 (not depicted) is a larva, that is to say, a somewhat later stage of development not to be confused with the species shown on plate 4. Larvae may move about freely in the water, whereas embryos are not yet able to live independently. It was Haeckel's research into larval forms (Gastrula larvae) that led him to his *Gastraea Theory* (see pp. 22–23, 25). Numerous plates are devoted to the skeletal spicules. While these may appear to greatly resemble one another, they are actually distinct in significant details, not least on account of the different lengths of their rays and the degree to which their ends diverge. These differences can be characteristic of individual species, yet they are often conditioned by no more than the age of the specimen. Spicules derive their form from the cells that constitute them; but over the course of time they grow and, to certain degrees, also alter their shape. How spicules are stored within the body of the sponge is shown, for example, on plate 6, fig. 1. Plates 20, 40, and 60 provide an overview of the diverse appearance of the canal system of calcareous sponges that Haeckel combines here with a visual explication of the development of young sponges (plate 40, figs. 1–3; plate 60, figs. 1–4).

In order to appreciate what efforts were required of Haeckel in his work on calcareous sponges, one must realise that his illustrations show the spicules, embryos, and larvae sometimes in more than hundredfold magnification. As in the case of the radiolarians or the small crabs that he researched in the 1860s, Haeckel would have needed here as well to spend hour after hour at the microscope to create his drawn records.

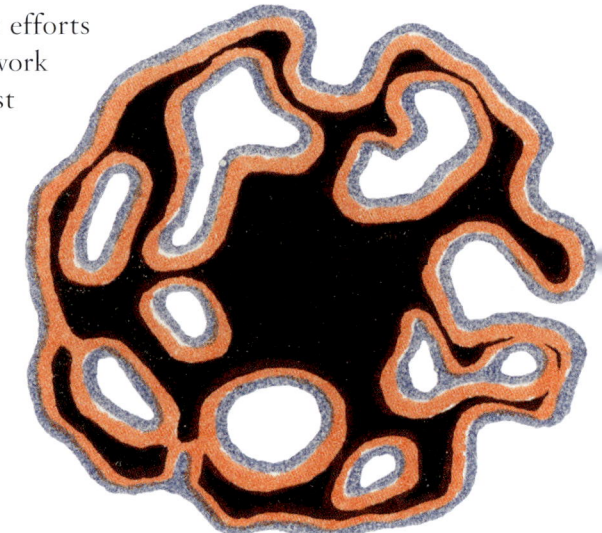

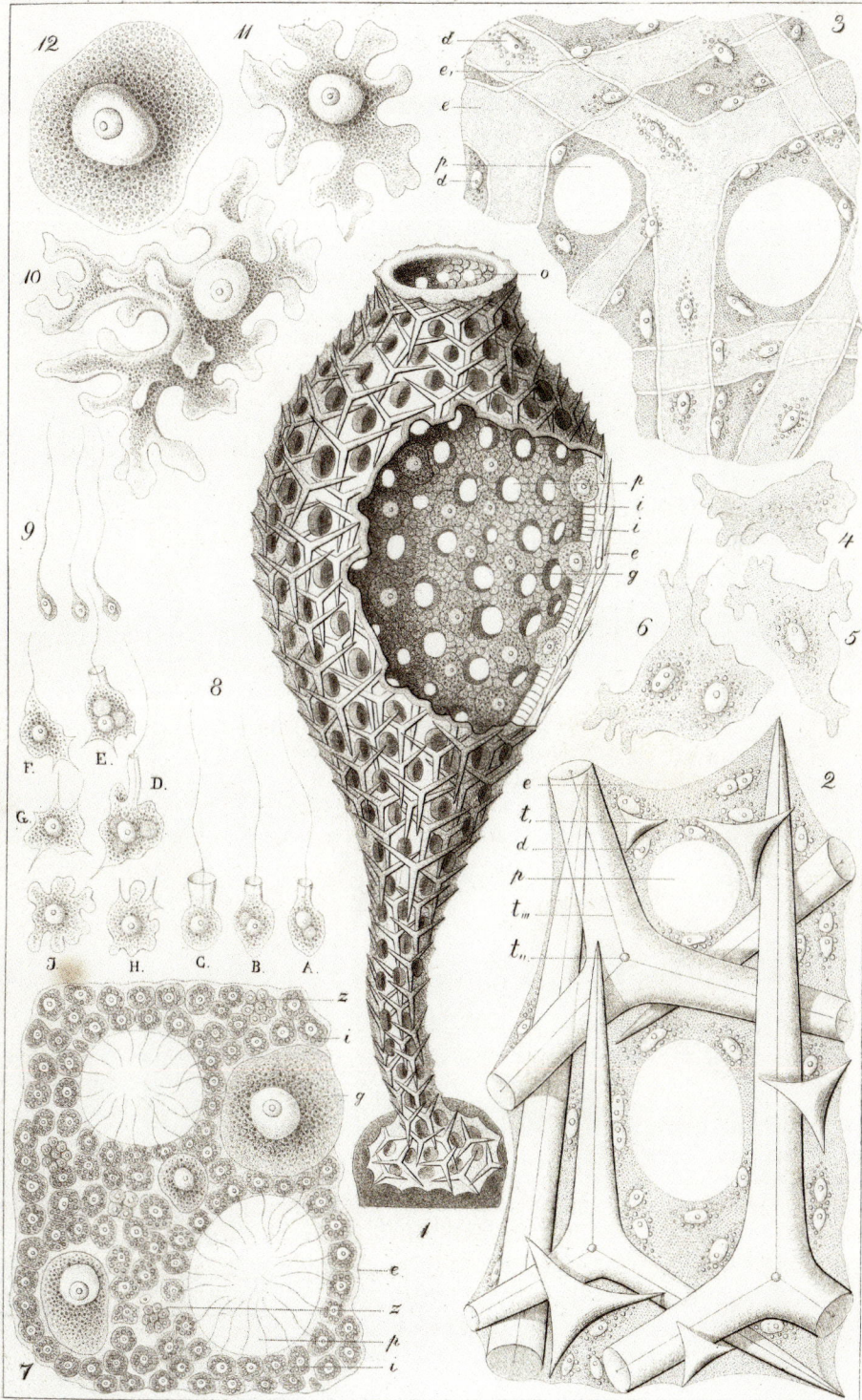

E. Haeckel del.

E. Lange sc.

Taf. 2.

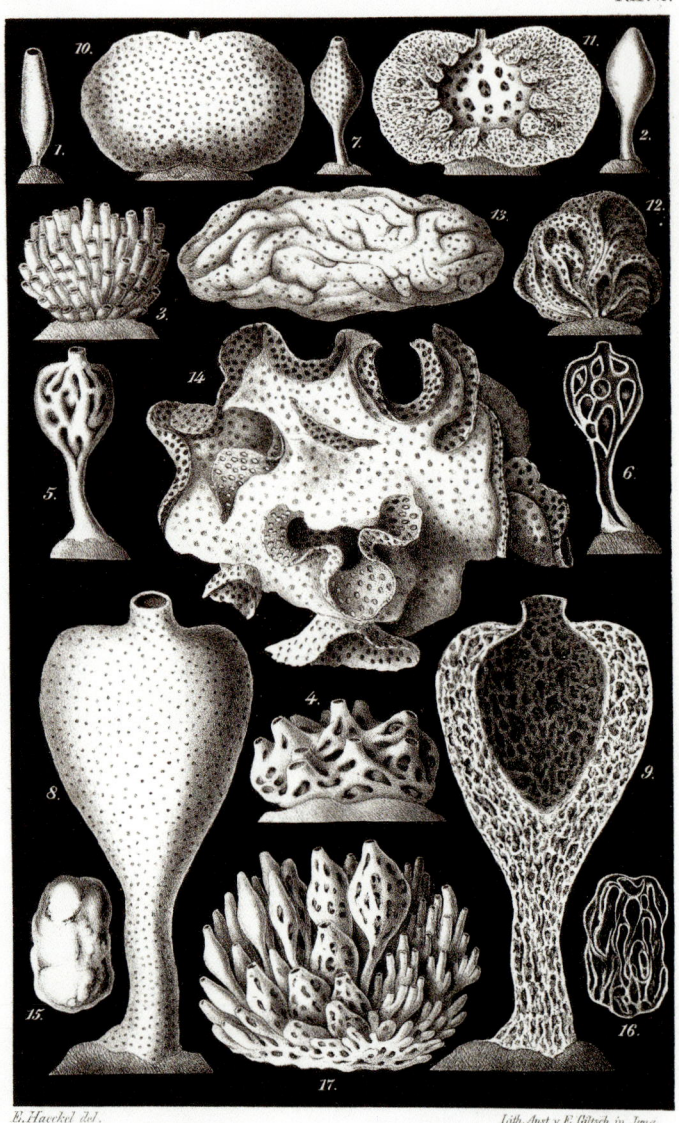

E. Haeckel del.

Lith. Anst. v. E. Giltsch in Jena.

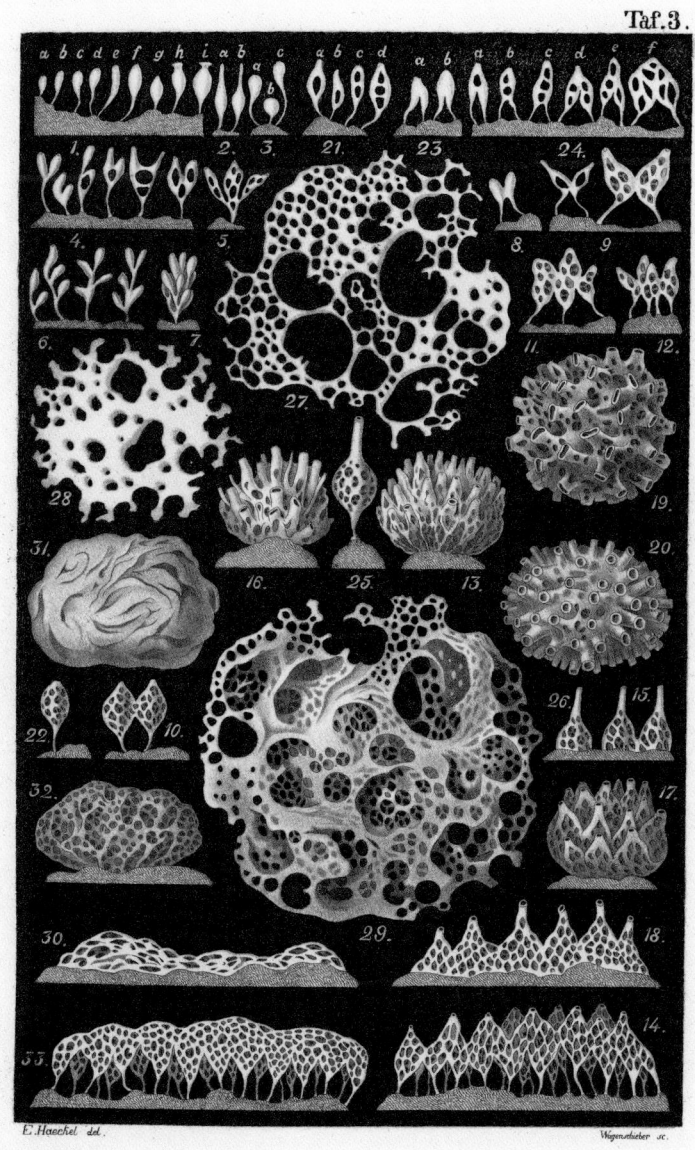

PLATE 3

Ascetta coriacea – *Clathrina coriacea* (MONTAGU, 1814)

White clathrina, White lace sponge

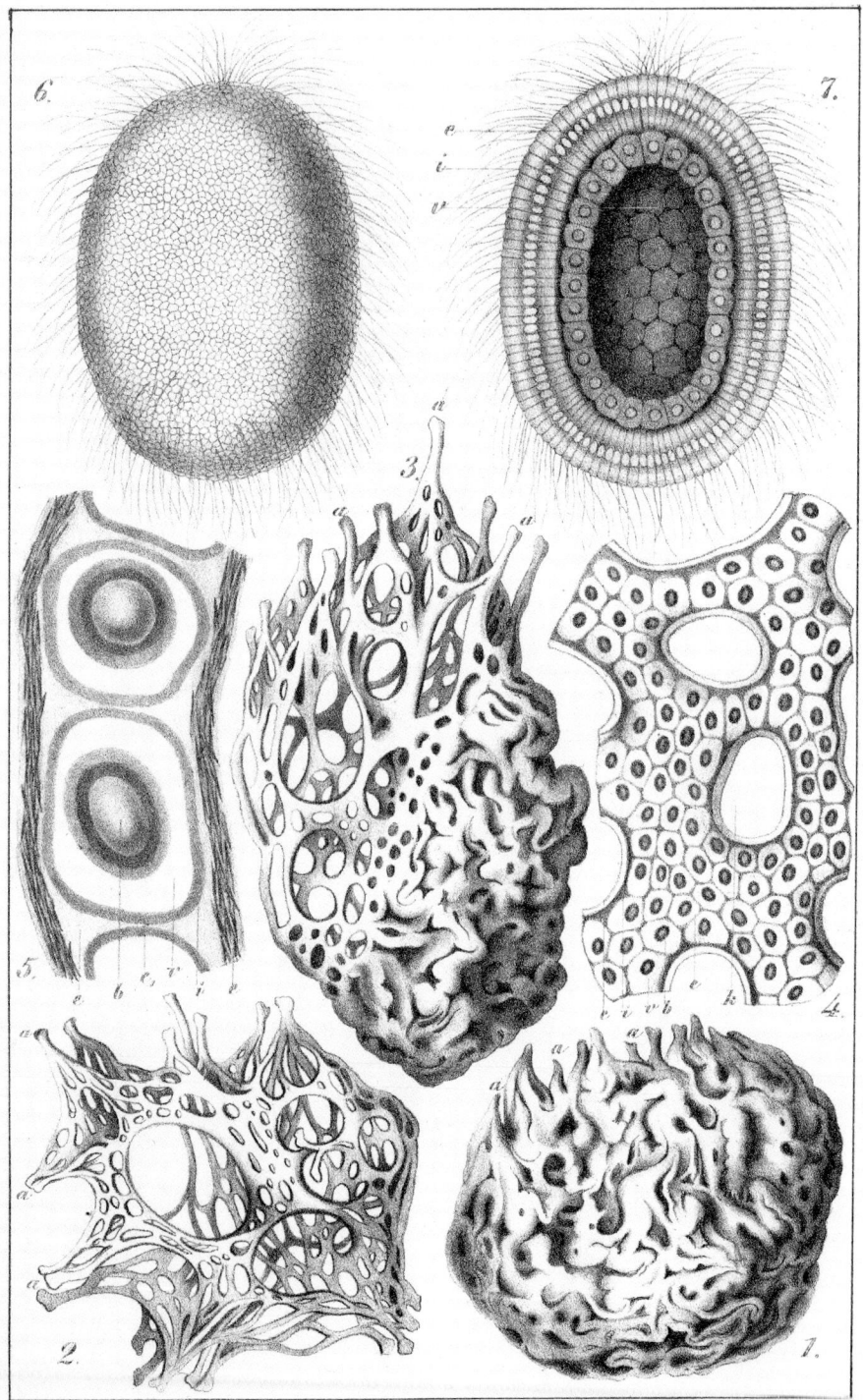

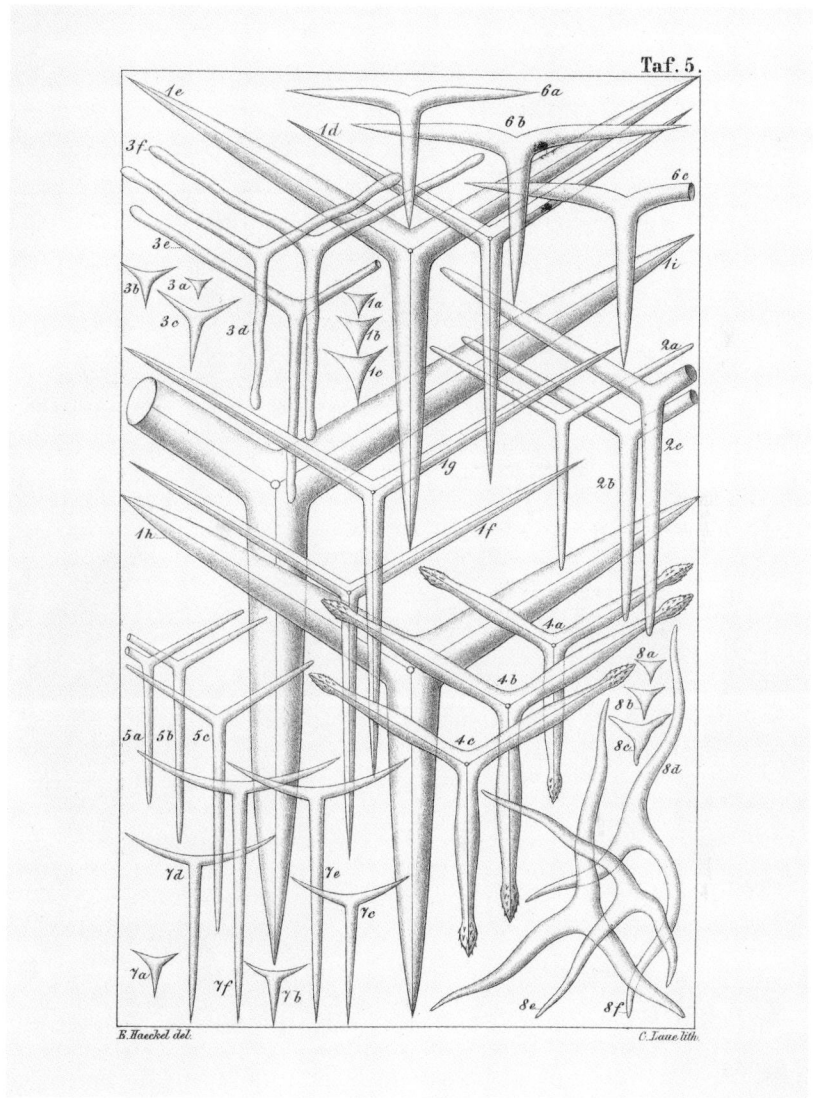

Taf. 5.

E. Haeckel del.   C. Laue lith.

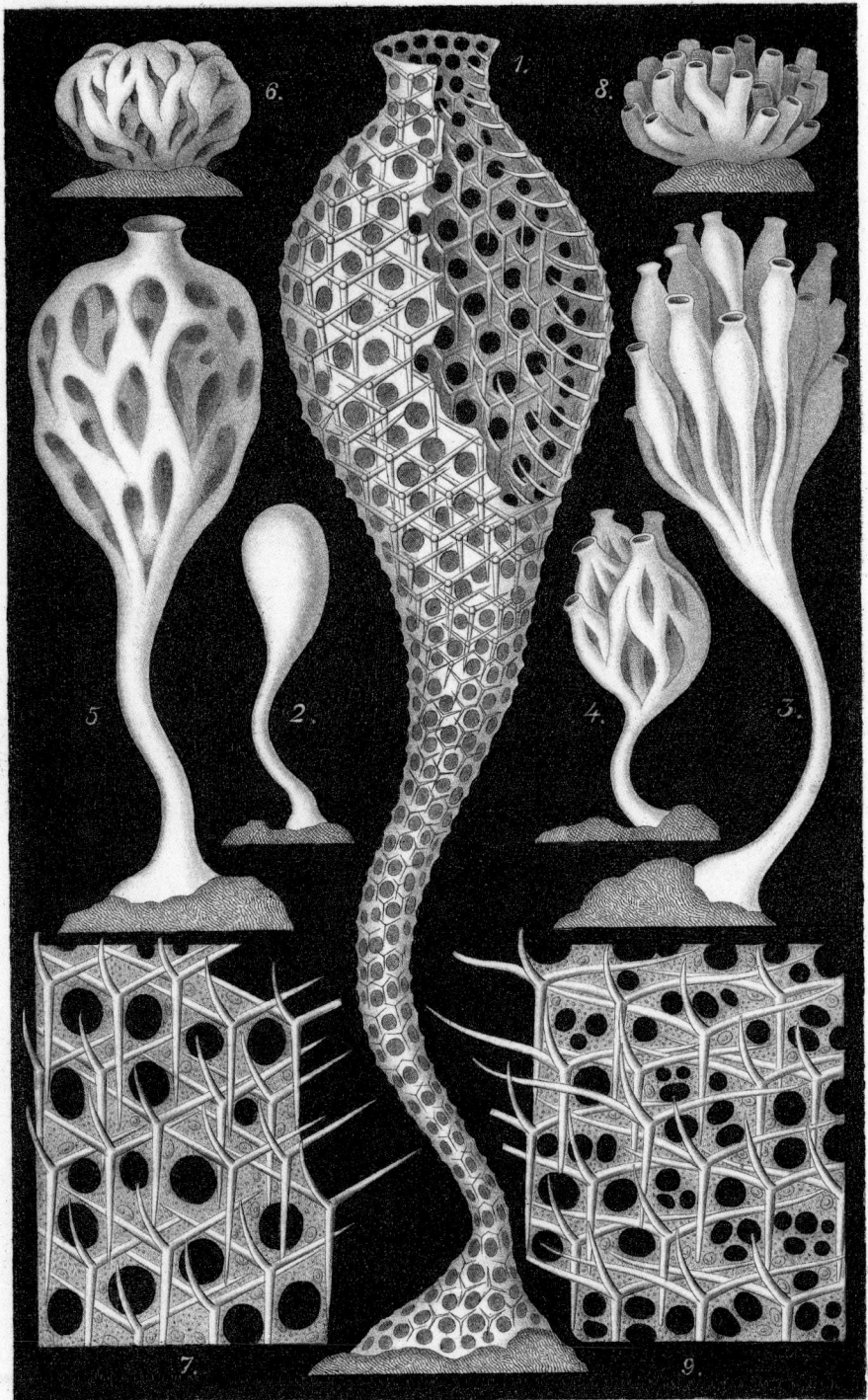

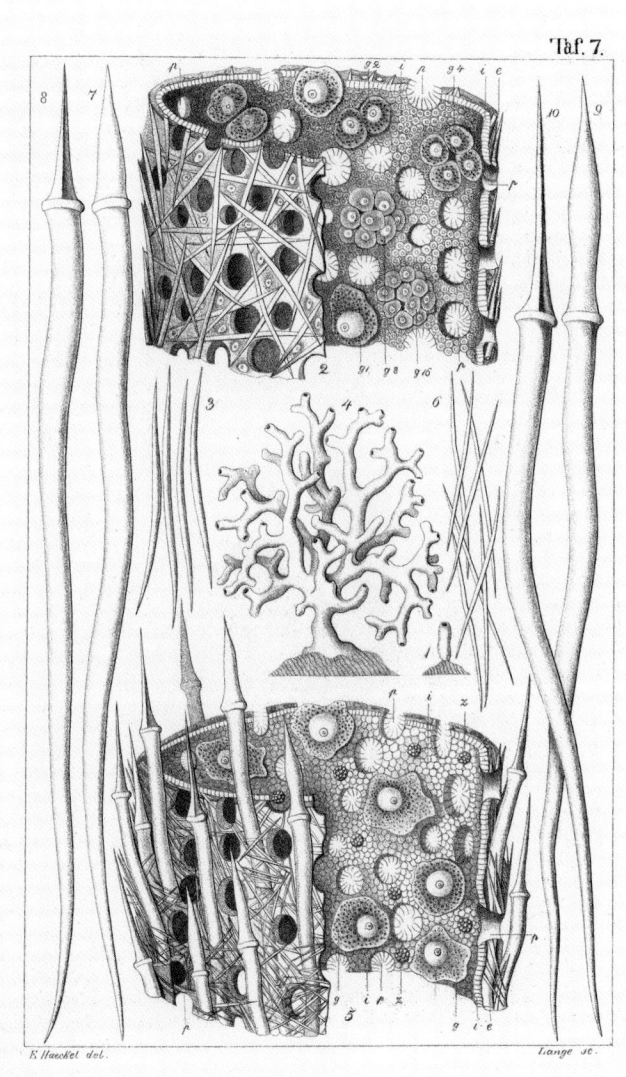

Taf. 7.

PLATE 6
1-7 Ascilla gracilis – *Guancha gracilis* (HAECKEL, 1872)
8-9 Ascilla japonica – *Soleneiscus japonicus* (HAECKEL, 1872)

PLATE 7 ＊
1-3 Ascyssa troglodytes – *Ascyssa troglodytes*
4-10 Ascyssa acufera – *Ascyssa acufera*
＊ *see page 507*

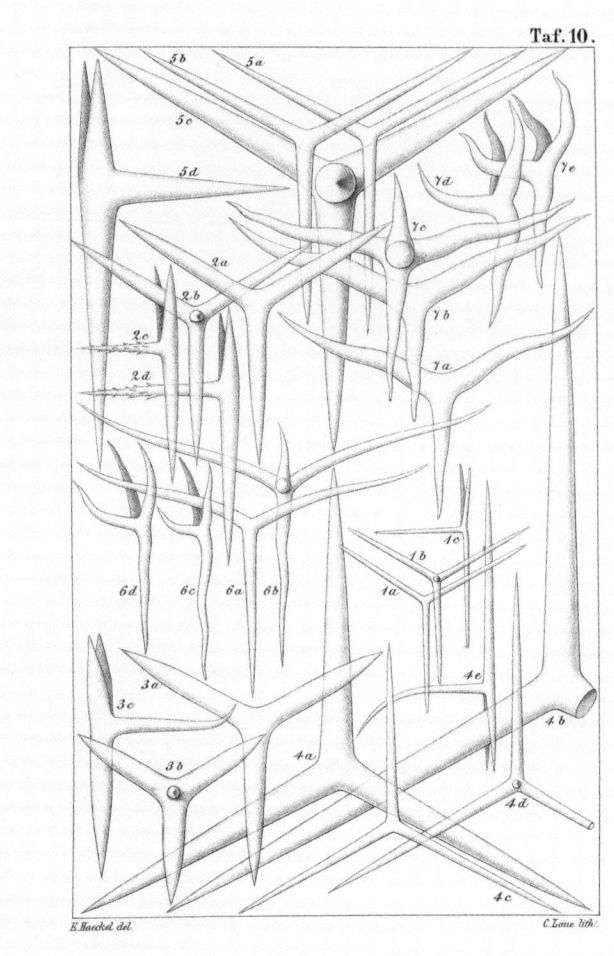

Taf. 10.

E. Haeckel del.   C. Lente lith.

PLATE 10

1 Ascaltis canariensis — *Arthuria canariensis* (MIKLUCHO-MACLAY, 1868) | 2 Ascaltis cerebrum — *Borojevia cerebrum* (HAECKEL, 1872) | 3 Ascaltis Darwinii — *Arthuria darwini* (HAECKEL, 1870) 4 Ascaltis Lamarckii — *Ascaltis lamarcki* (HAECKEL, 1870) | 5 Ascaltis Gegenbauri — *Leucosolenia gegenbauri* (HAECKEL, 1870) | 6 Ascaltis Goethei — *Leucosolenia goethei* (HAECKEL, 1870) 7 Ascaltis botryoides — *Leucosolenia botryoides* (ELLIS & SOLANDER, 1786) Orange pipe sponge

PLATE 11

1 Ascortis horrida — *Leucosolenia horrida* (SCHMIDT IN HAECKEL, 1872) 2 Ascortis lacunosa — *Clathrina lacunosa* (JOHNSTON, 1842) Pedunculate clathrina 3 Ascortis Fabricii — *Leucosolenia complicata* (MONTAGU, 1814) 4 Ascortis corallorrhiza — *Leucosolenia variabilis* HAECKEL, 1870 Calcareous tube-sponge 5 9 Ascortis fragilis — *Leucosolenia fragilis* (HAECKEL, 1870)

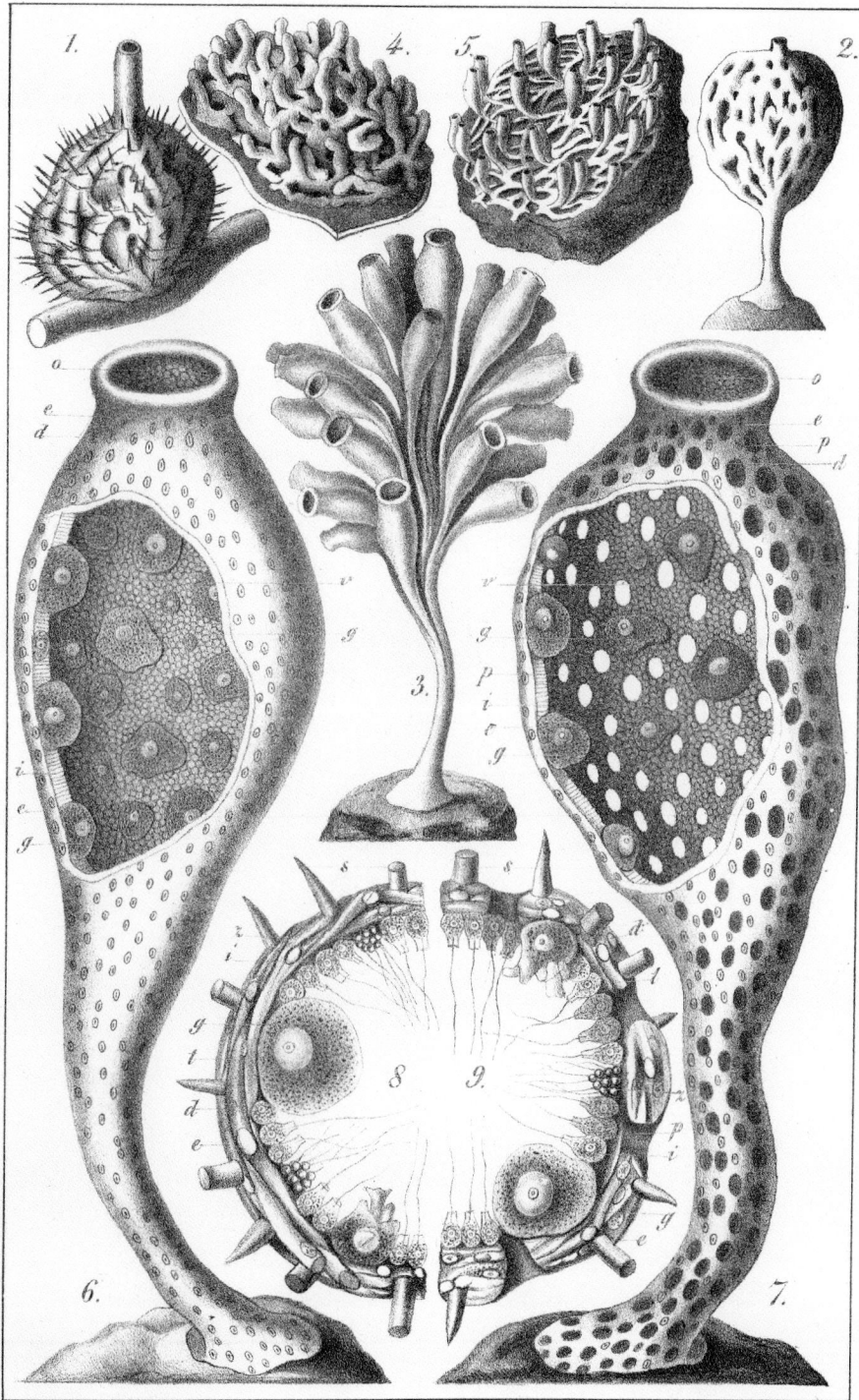

E. Haeckel del.

Lith.Anst. v.E. Giltsch in Jena.

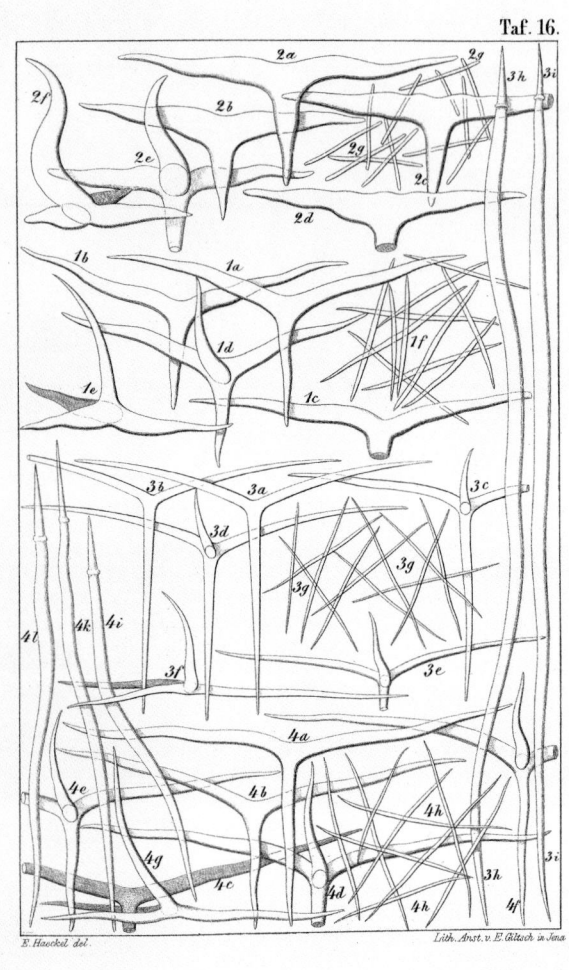

Taf. 16.

E. Haeckel del.

Lith. Anst. v. E. Giltsch in Jena

PLATE 16

1 Ascandra botrys – *Leucosolenia botryoides* (ELLIS & SOLANDER, 1786) Orange pipe sponge
2 Ascandra nitida – *Leucosolenia botryoides* (ELLIS & SOLANDER, 1786) Orange pipe sponge
3 Ascandra pinus – *Leucosolenia complicata* (MONTAGU, 1814)
4 Ascandra variabilis – *Leucosolenia variabilis* HAECKEL, 1870 Calcareous tube-sponge

PLATE 17

1, 4 Ascandra echinoides – *Leucosolenia cyathus* (HAECKEL, 1870) | 2, 6 Ascandra cordata –
Clathrina cordata (HAECKEL, 1872) | 3, 7, 10, 13 Ascandra nitida – *Leucosolenia botryoides*
(ELLIS & SOLANDER, 1786) Orange pipe sponge | 5 Ascandra sertularia – *Ascandra sertularia* HAECKEL, 1872
8, 11, 15 Asacandra falcata – *Ascandra falcata* HAECKEL, 1872 | 9, 12 Ascandra densa – *Ascandra densa*
HAECKEL, 1872 | 14 Ascandra panis – *Clathrina panis* (HAECKEL, 1870)

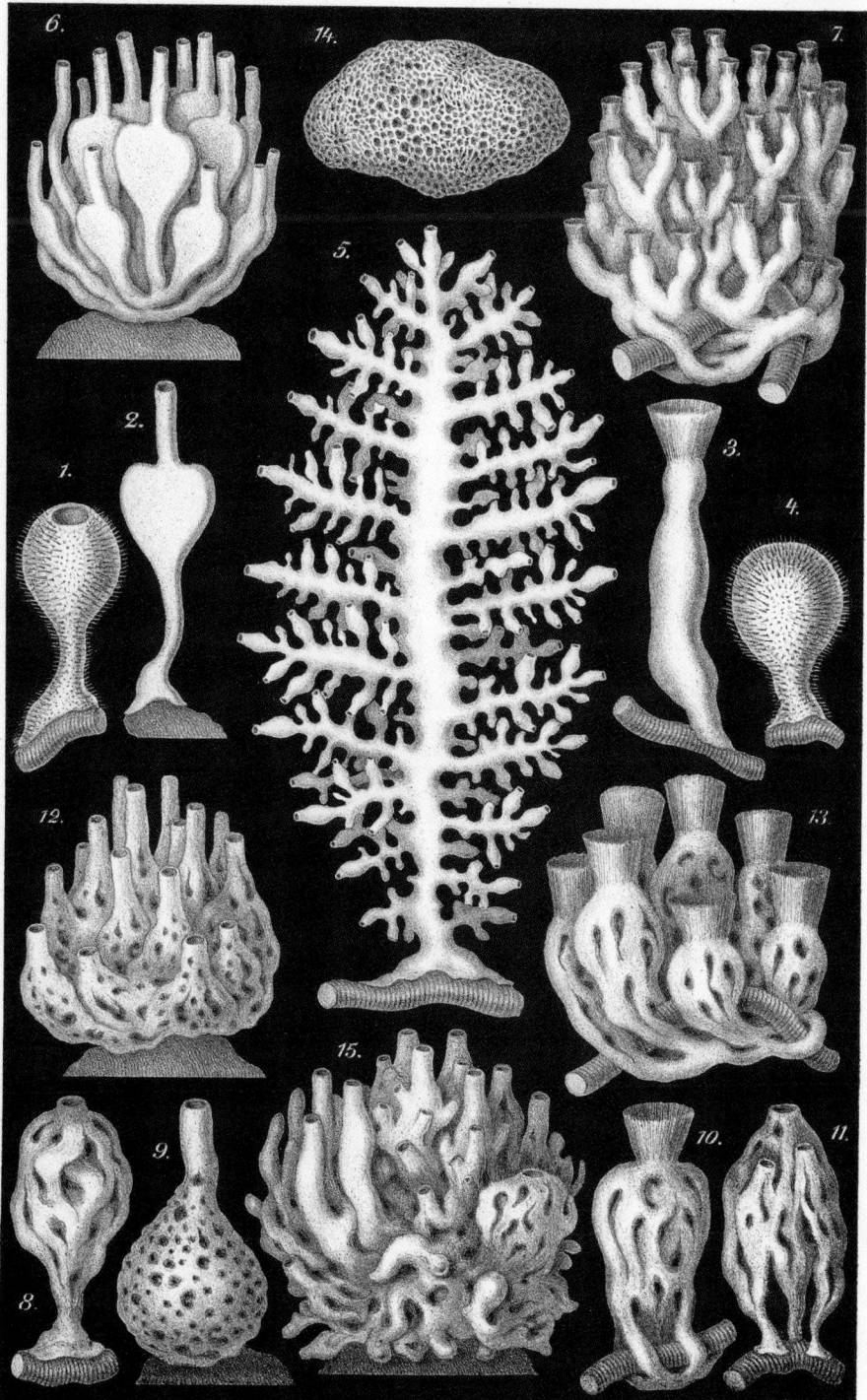

E. Haeckel del.

Alb. Schütze lith. Berlin.

Taf. 18.

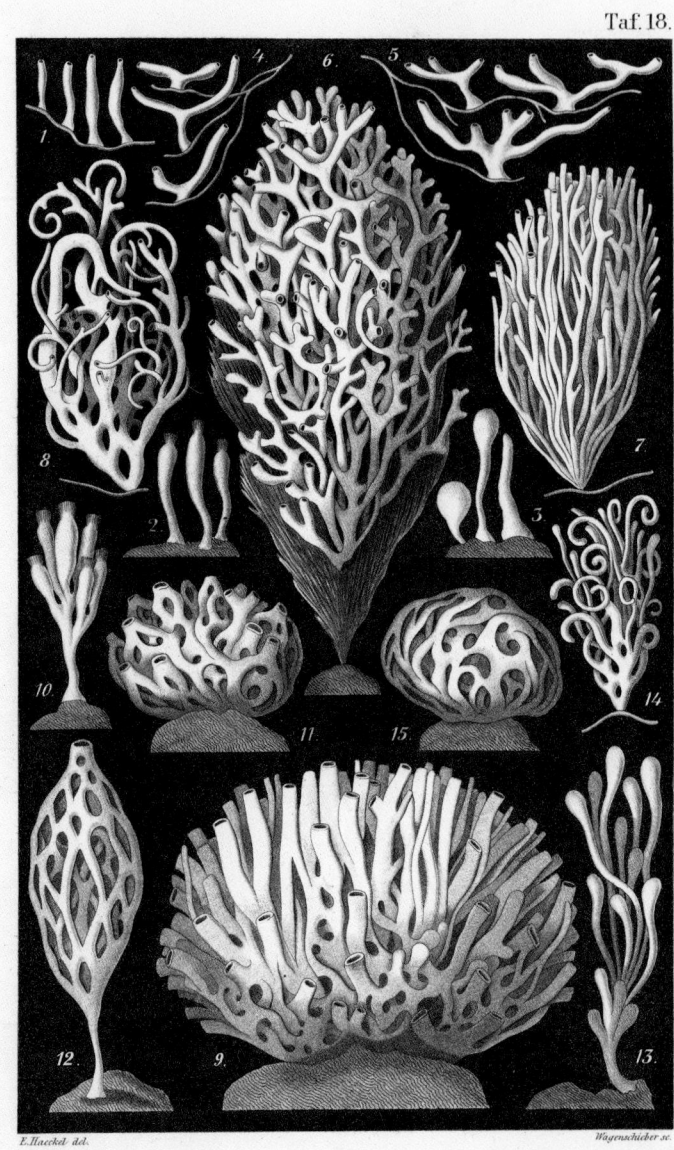

E.Haeckel del.

Wagenschieber sc.

PLATE 18
Ascandra variabilis – *Leucosolenia variabilis* (HAECKEL, 1870) Calcareous tube-sponge

Taf.19.

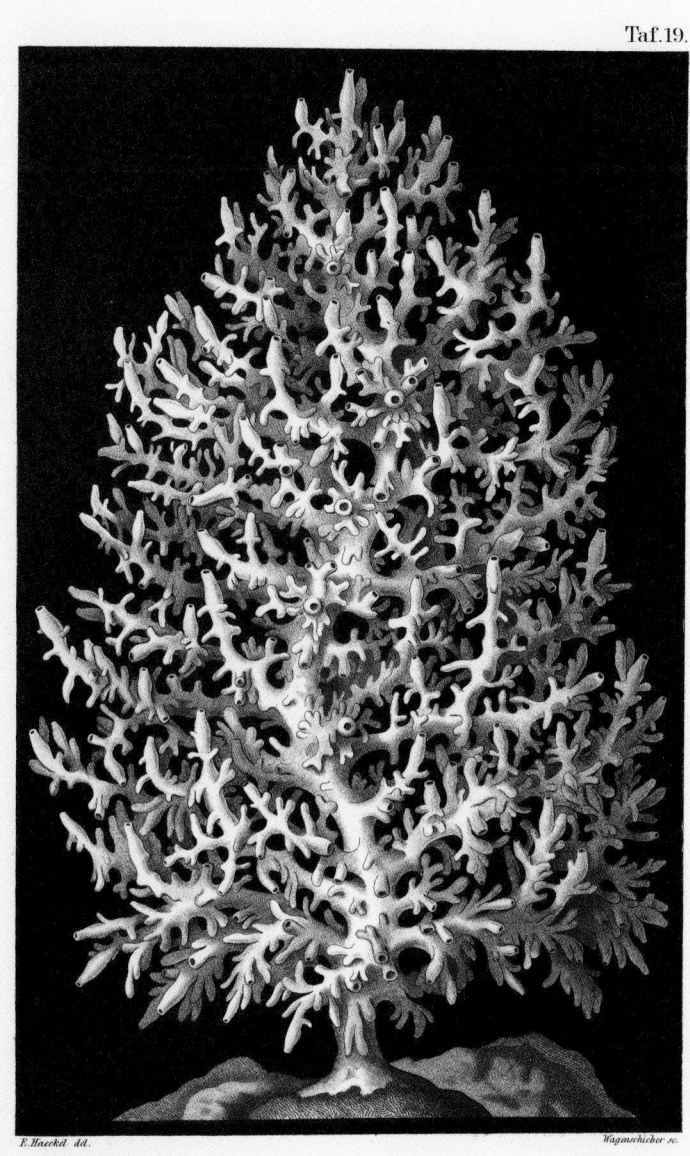

E. Haeckel del.

Wagenschieber sc.

PLATE 19
Ascandra pinus – *Leucosolenia complicata* (MONTAGU, 1814)

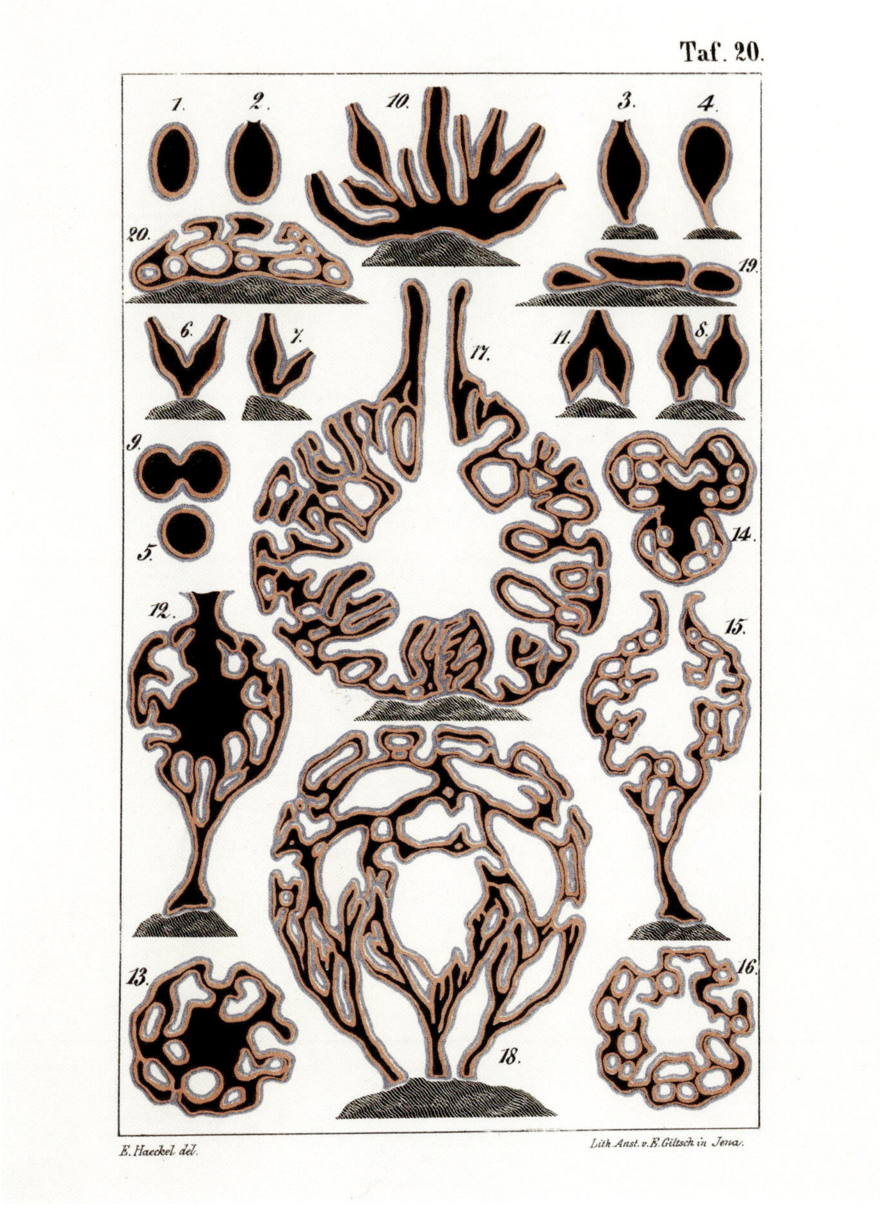

Taf. 20.

PLATE 20
Ascandra reticulum – *Ascaltis reticulum* (SCHMIDT, 1862)

PLATE 21
Leucetta primigenia – *Leucetta primigenia* HAECKEL, 1872

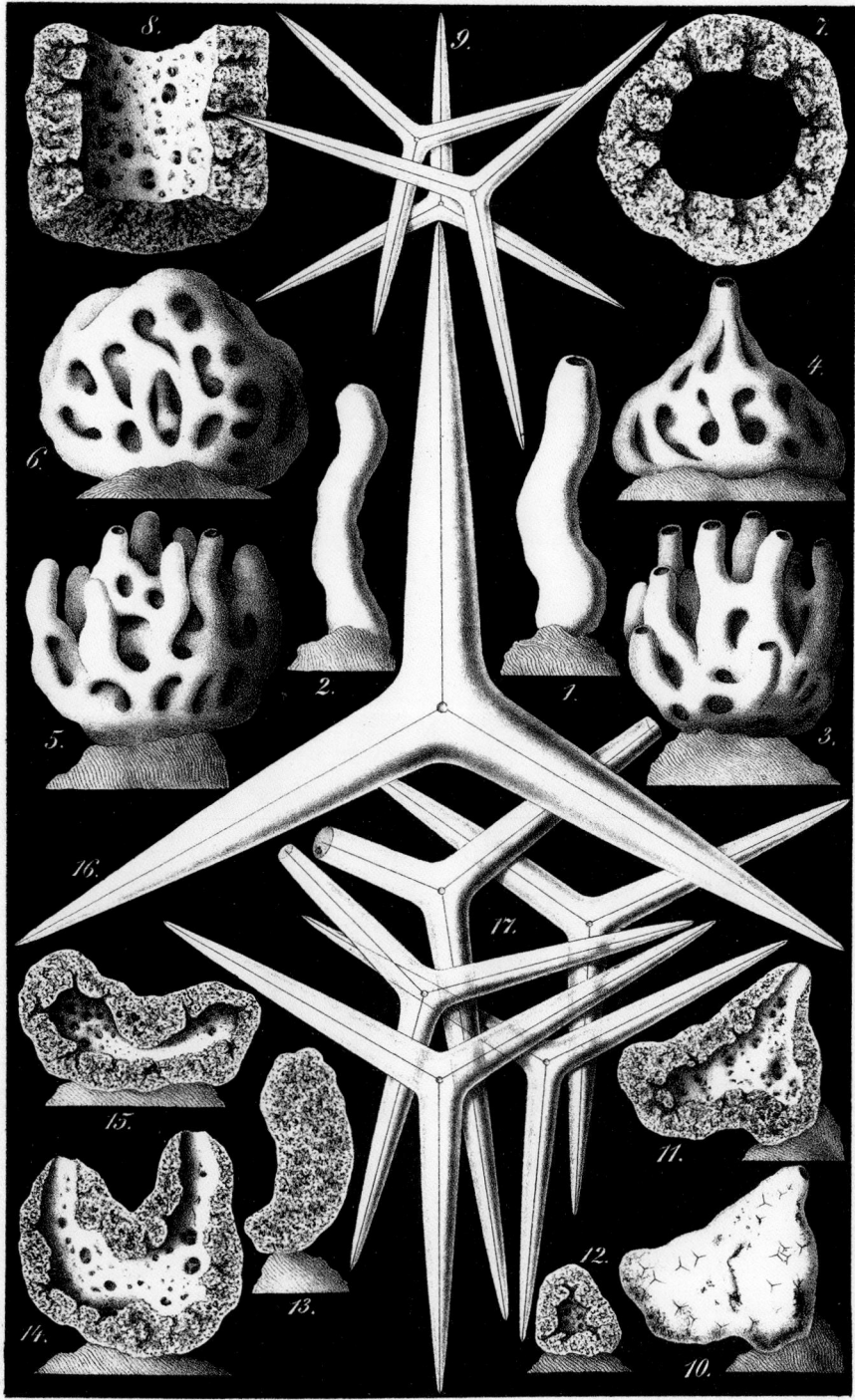

E. Haeckel del.

Lith. Anst. v. E. Giltsch in Jena.

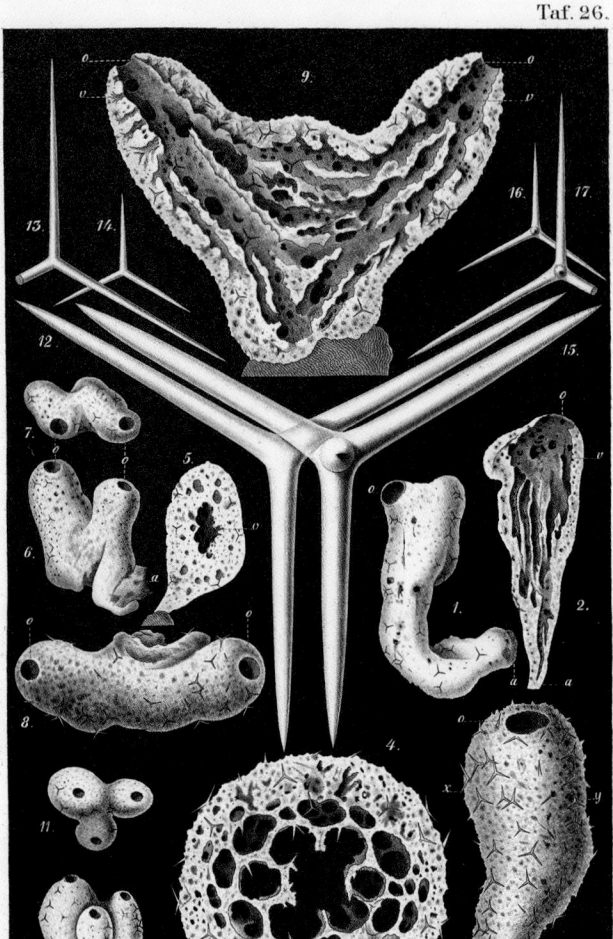

PLATE 26
Leucaltis floridana – *Leucetta floridana* (HAECKEL, 1872)

PLATE 29
Leucortis pulvinar – *Leucandra pulvinar* (HAECKEL, 1870)

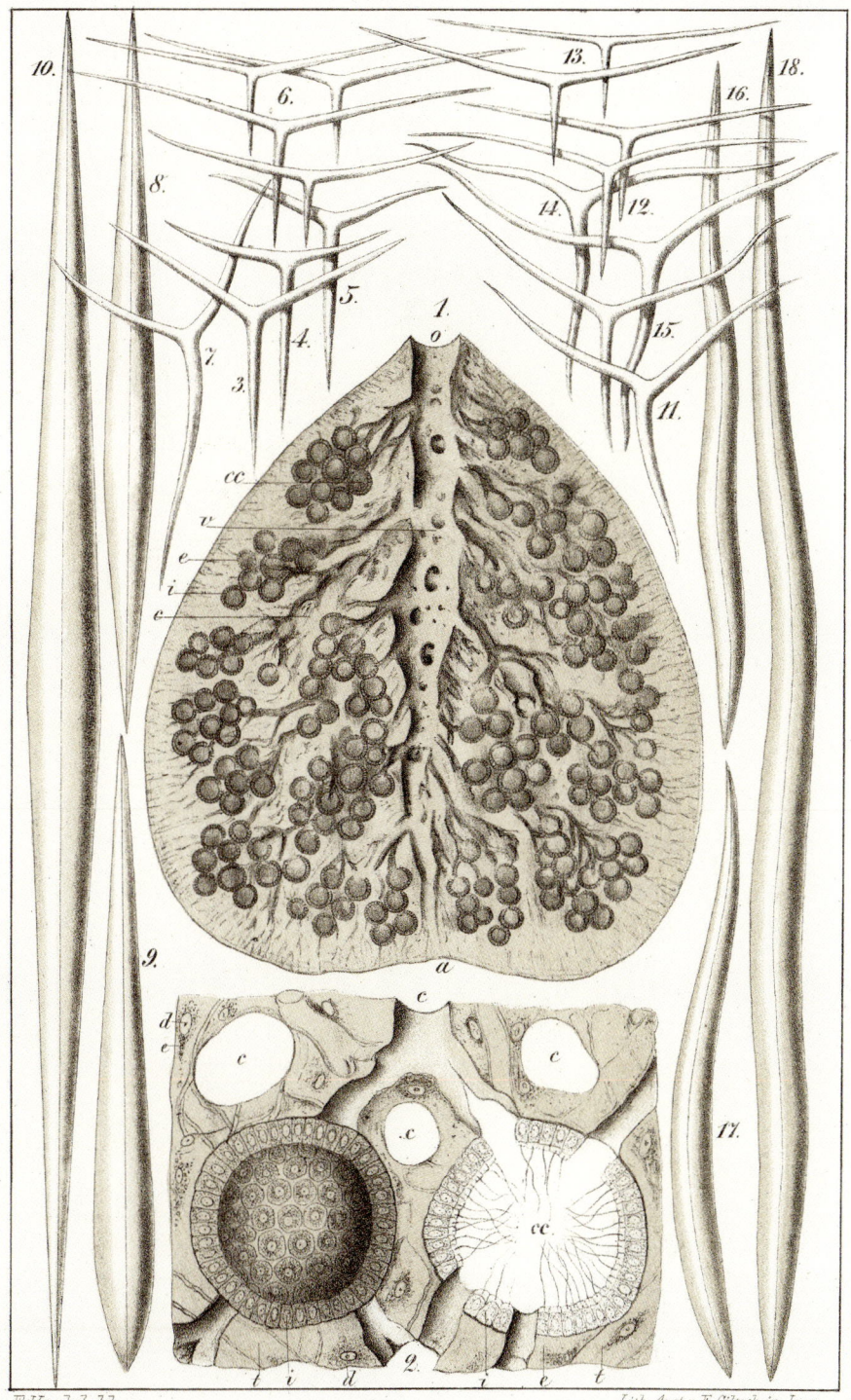

E. Haeckel del.

Lith.Anst.v.E.Giltsch in Jena.

Taf. 34.

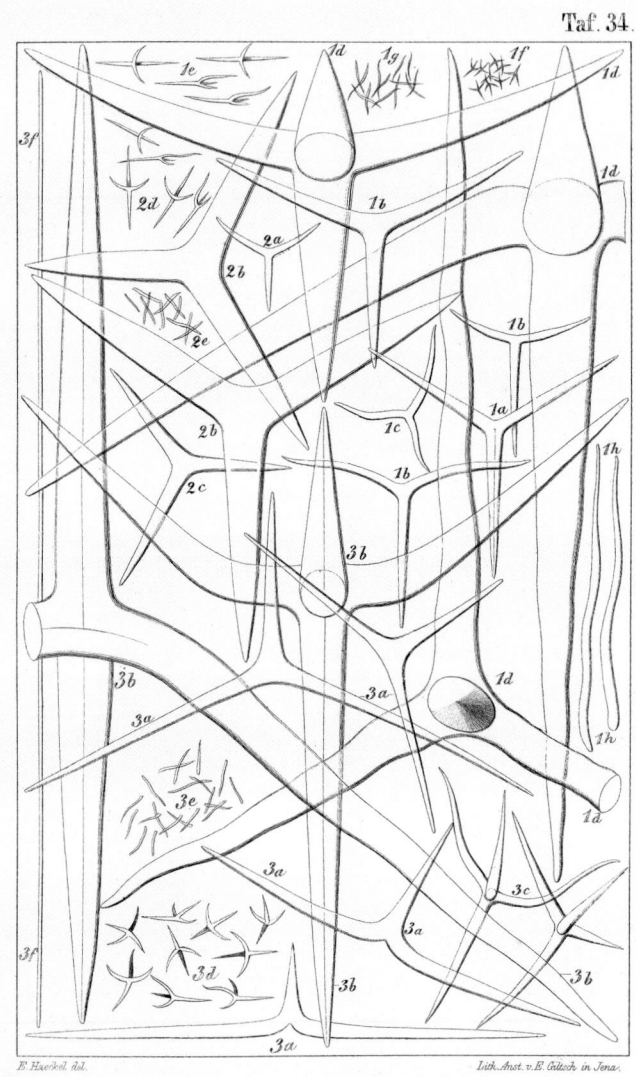

E. Haeckel del.　　　　　　　　　　　Lith. Anst. v. E. Giltsch in Jena.

PLATE 34
1 Leucandra Johnstonii – *Leuconia johnstoni* CARTER, 1871
2 Leucandra nivea – *Leuconia nivea* (GRANT, 1826)
3 Leucandra ochotensis – *Leuconia ochotensis* (MIKLUCHO-MACLAY, 1870)

PLATE 35
Leucandra aspera – *Leucandra aspera* (SCHMIDT, 1862)

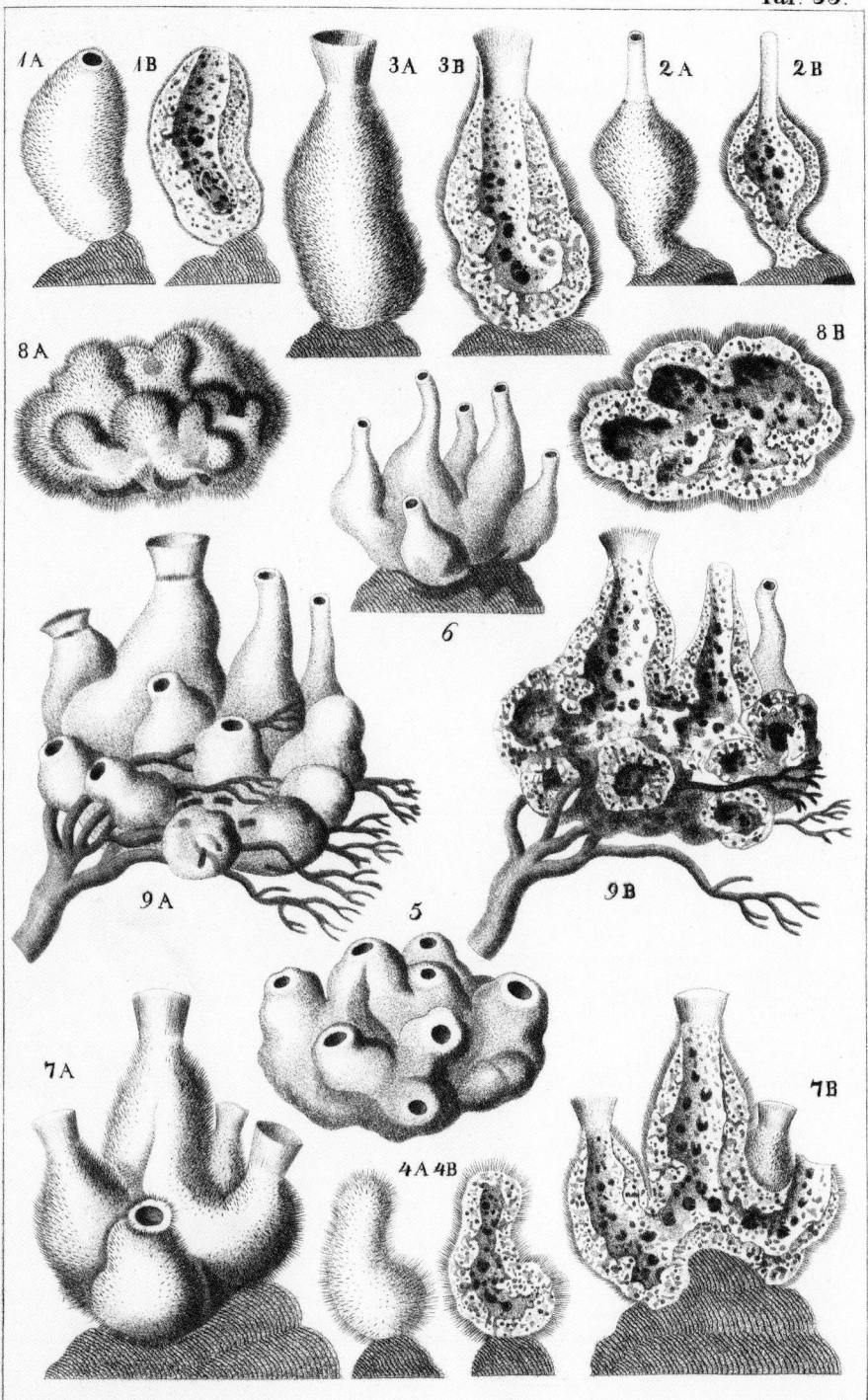

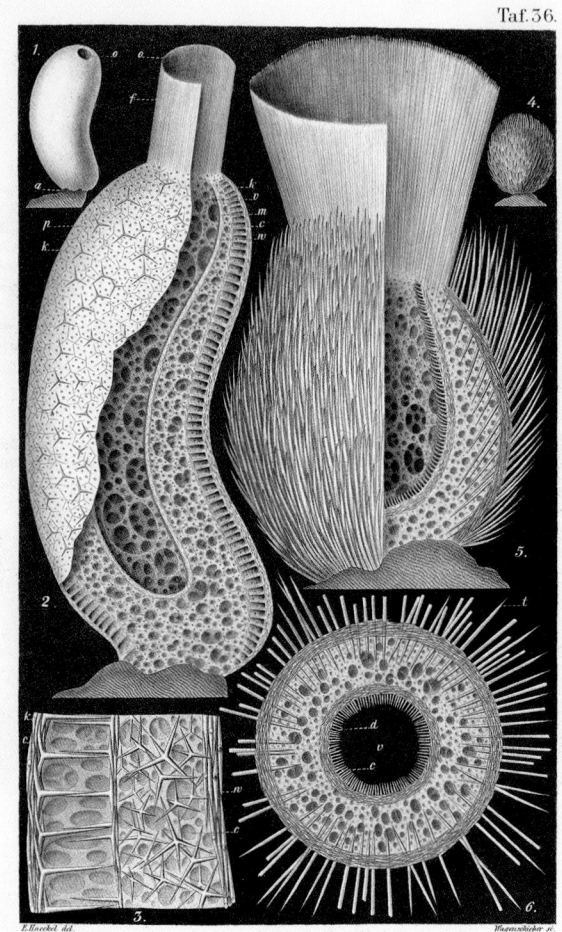

PLATE 36

1–3 Leucandra cucumis – *Paraleucilla cucumis* (HAECKEL, 1872)
4–6 Leucandra aspera – *Leucandra aspera* (SCHMIDT, 1862)

PLATE 37

(Genus: Leucandra)

1 Dyssycus lunulatus – *Sycon lunulatum* (HAECKEL, 1872) | 2 Dyssycus cataphractus – *Aphroceras cataphracta* (HAECKEL, 1872) | 3 Coenostomus alcicornis – *Aphroceras alcicornis* GRAY, 1858 | 4 Artynas alcicornis – *Aphroceras alcicornis* GRAY, 1858 | 5 Coenostomella caminus – *Leucandra caminus* HAECKEL, 1872
6 Artynella caminus – *Leucandra caminus* HAECKEL, 1872 | 7 Coenostomium crambessa – *Leucandra crambessa* HAECKEL, 1872 | 8 Artynium crambessa – *Leucandra crambessa* HAECKEL, 1872 | 9 Aphroceras Gossei – *Leucandra gossei* (BOWERBANK, 1862)

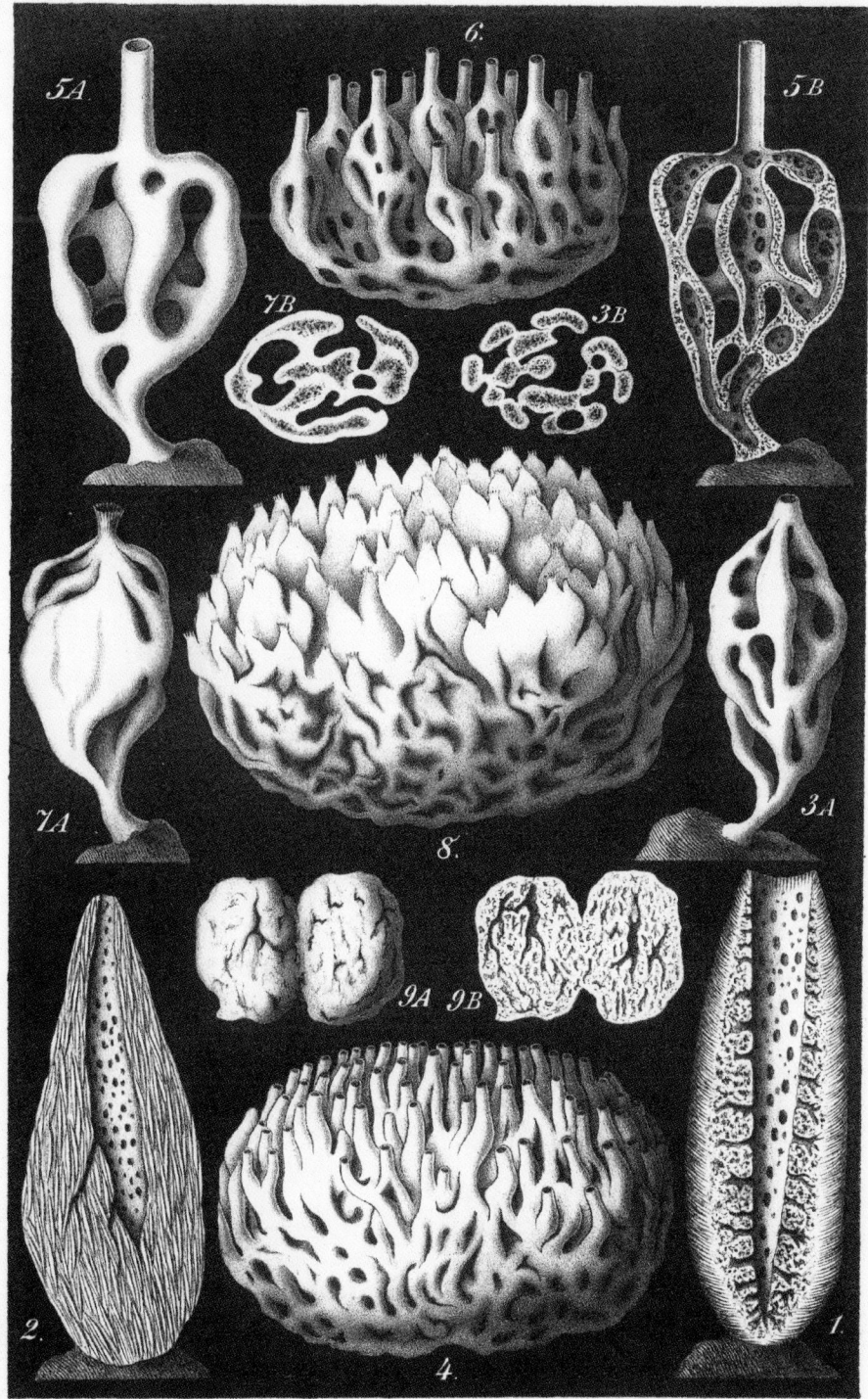

E. Haeckel del.

Lith.Anst.v.E.Giltsch in Jena.

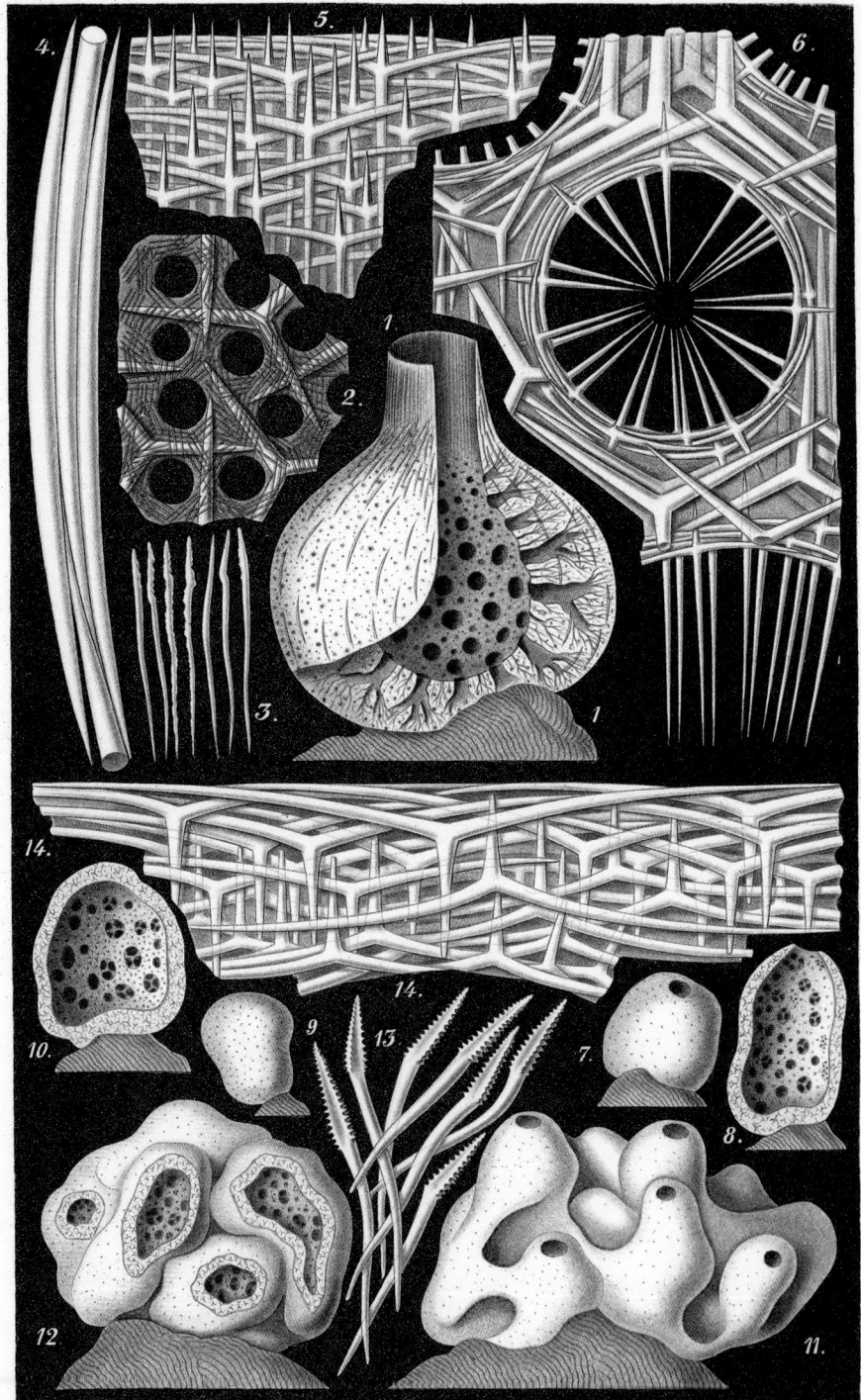

E.Haeckel del.

Wagenschieber sc.

Taf. 39.

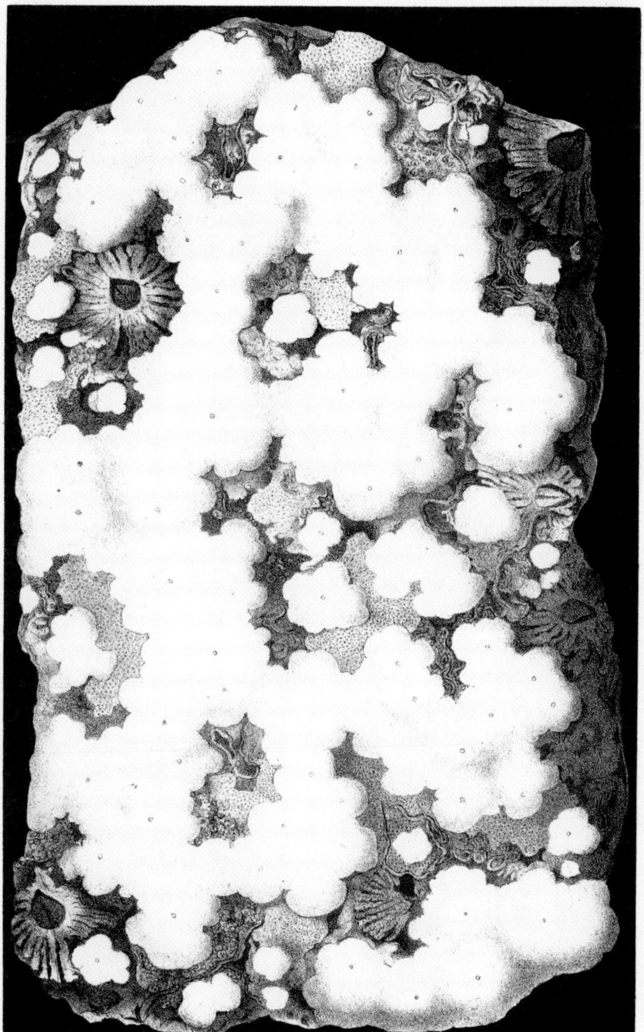

E.Haeckel del.

Lith.Anst.v.E.Giltsch in Jena.

PLATE 38
1-6 Leucandra bomba – *Leucomalthe bomba* HAECKEL, 1872
7-14 Leucandra saccharata – *Paraleucilla saccharata* (HAECKEL, 1872)

PLATE 39
Leucandra nivea – *Leuconia nivea* (GRANT, 1826)

Taf. 40.

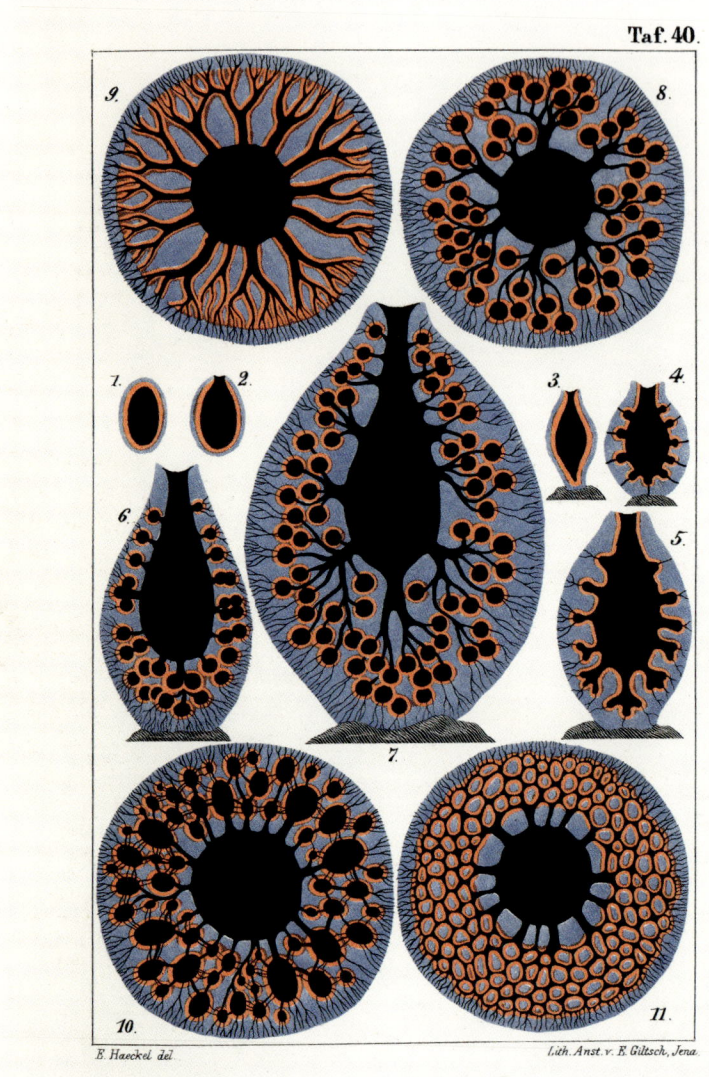

E. Haeckel del.   Lith. Anst. v. E. Giltsch, Jena.

PLATE 40
1–8 Leucandra ananas (Ontogenie) – *Leucandra ananas* (MONTAGU, 1814)
9 Leucandra bomba – *Leucomalthe bomba* HAECKEL, 1872
10 Leucandra fistulosa – *Leucandra fistulosa* (JOHNSTON, 1842)
11 Leucandra stilifera – *Leucopsila stylifera* (SCHMIDT, 1870)

PLATE 41
Sycetta primitiva   *Sycettaga primitiva* (HAECKEL, 1872)

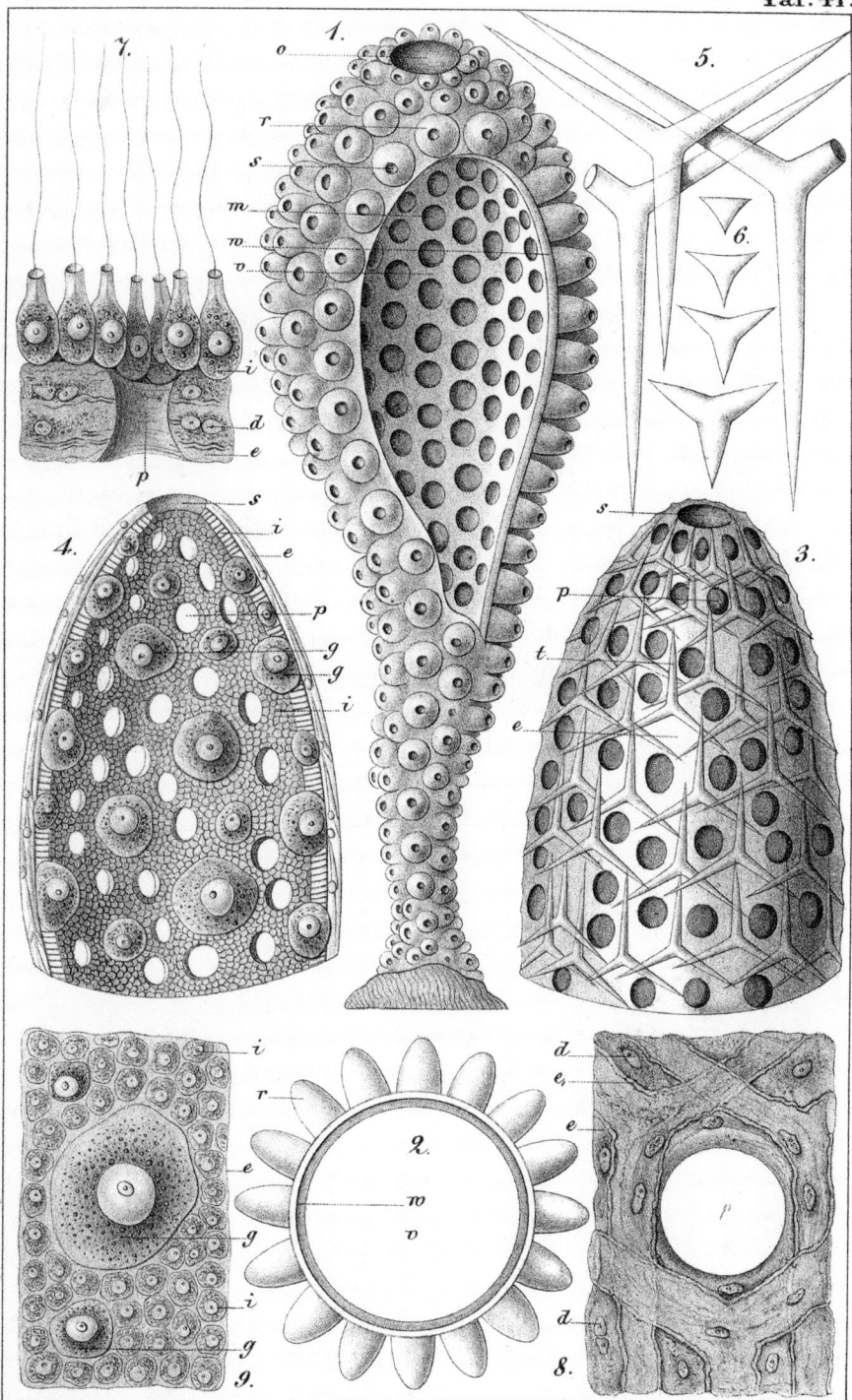

E. Haeckel del.

C. Laue lith.

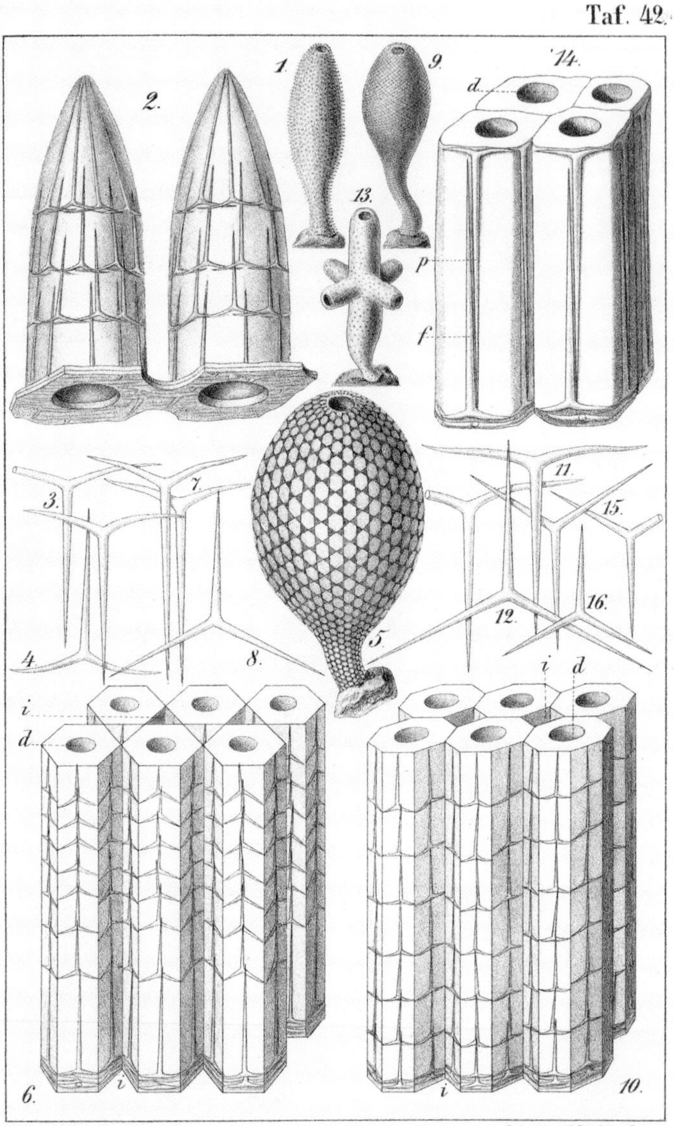

Taf. 42.

E. Haeckel del.

Lith. Anst. v. E. Giltsch in Jena.

PLATE 42
1–4 Sycetta sagittifera – *Sycetta sagittifera* ʜᴀᴇᴄᴋᴇʟ, 1872 | 5–8 Sycetta strobilus –
Grantia strobilus (ʜᴀᴇᴄᴋᴇʟ, 1872) | 9–12 Sycetta cupula – *Grantia cupula* (ʜᴀᴇᴄᴋᴇʟ, 1872)
13–16 Sycetta stauridia – *Sycettusa stauridia* (ʜᴀᴇᴄᴋᴇʟ, 1872)

Taf. 43.

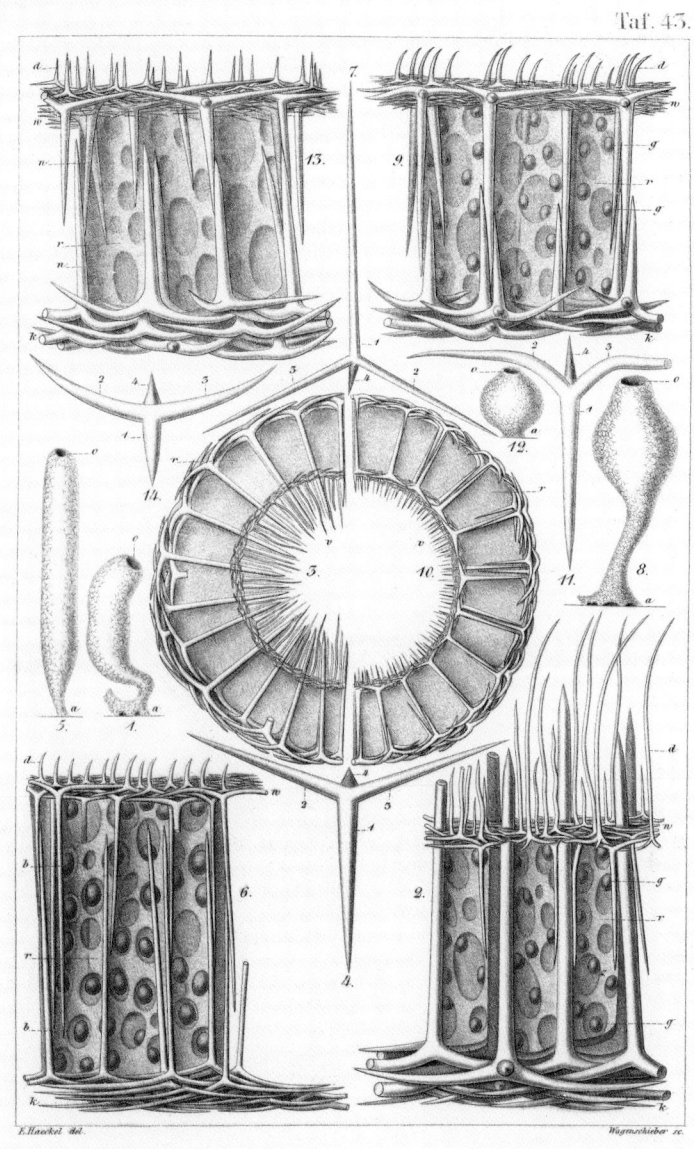

PLATE 43

1–4 Sycilla chrysalis – *Amphoriscus chrysalis* (SCHMIDT, 1864) | 5–7 Sycilla cylindrus – *Amphoriscus cylindrus* (HAECKEL, 1872) | 8–11 Sycilla cyathiscus – *Amphoriscus cyathiscus* (HAECKEL, 1872) 12–14 Sycilla urna – *Amphoriscus urna* HAECKEL, 1872

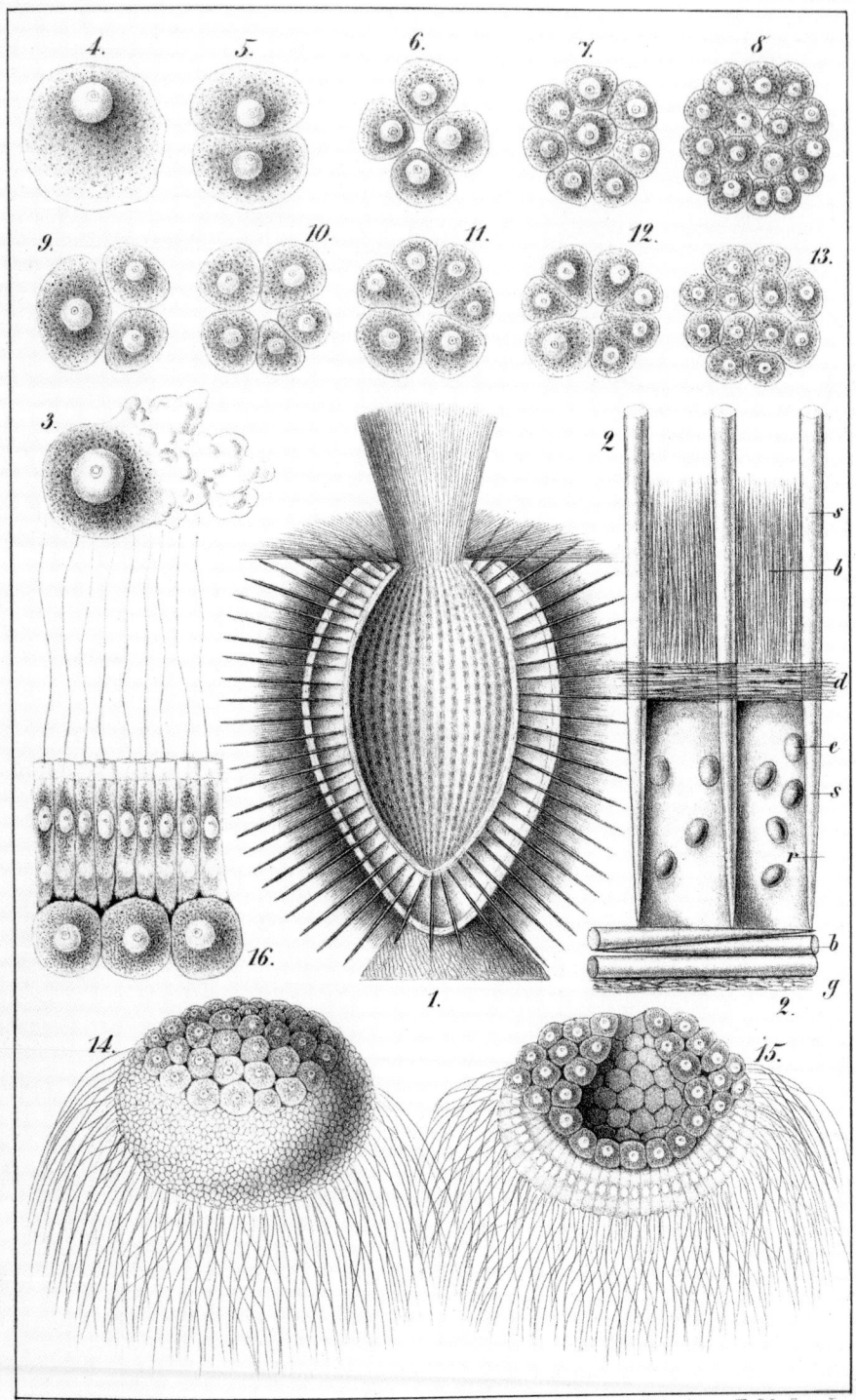

E. Haeckel del.

Lith. Anst. v. E. Giltsch in Jena.

Taf. 45.

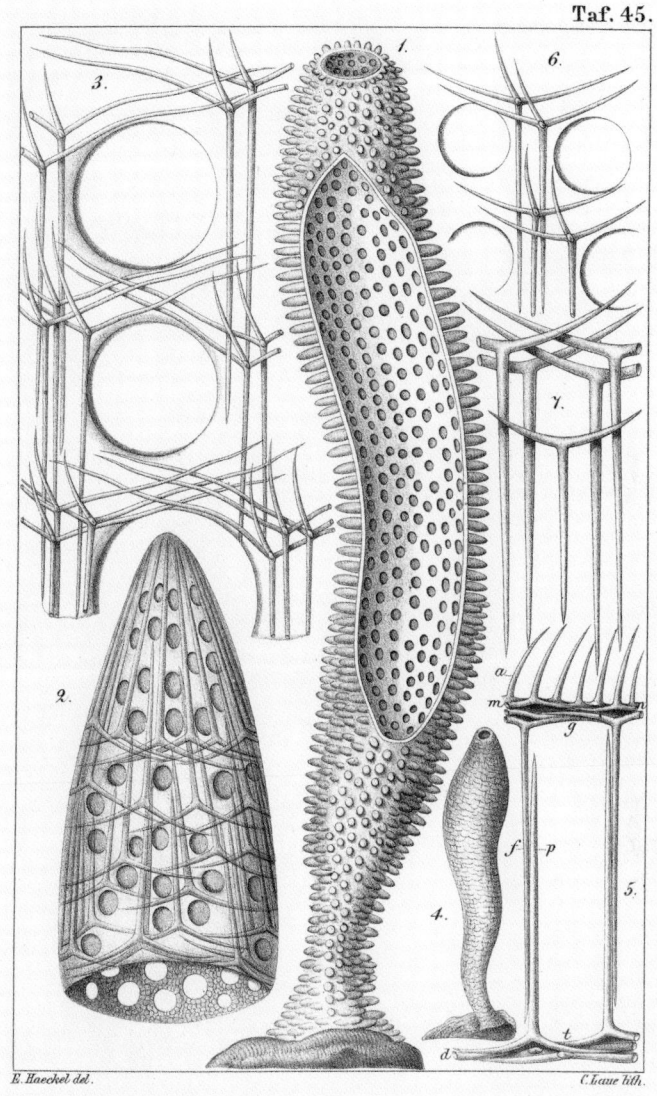

PLATE 44
Sycyssa Huxleyi – *Sycyssa huxleyi* HAECKEL, 1870

PLATE 45
1–3 Sycaltis conifera – *Sycetta conifera* (HAECKEL, 1870)
4–7 Sycaltis glacialis – *Sycettusa glacialis* (HAECKEL, 1870)

Taf. 46.

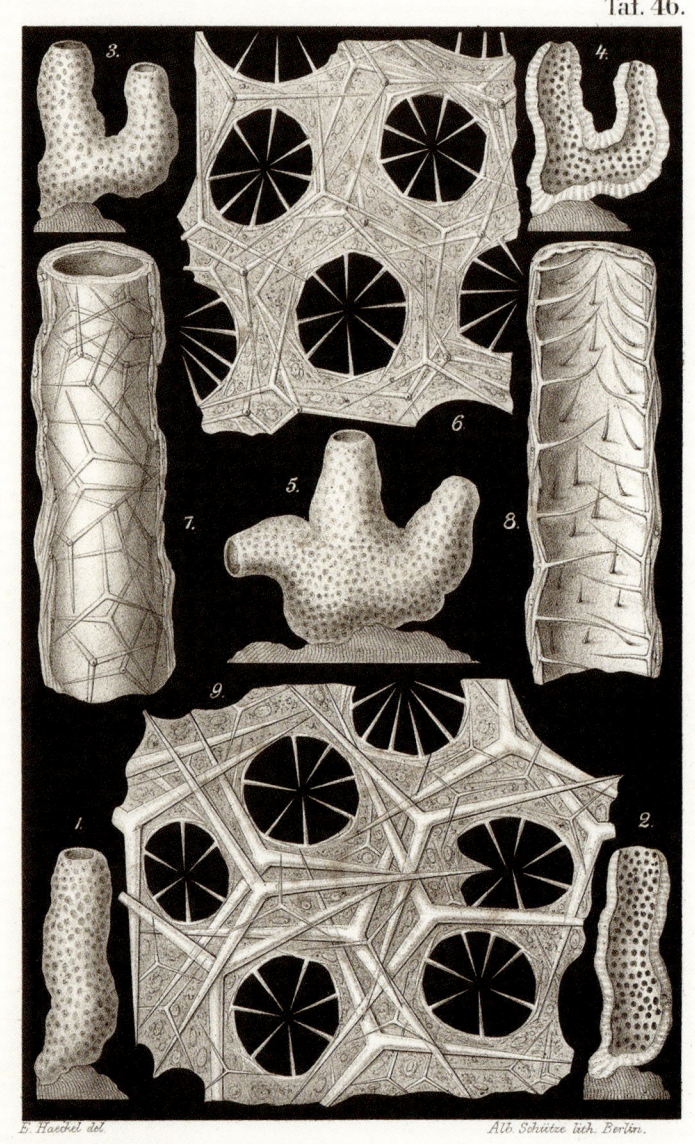

E. Haeckel del.

Alb. Schütze lith. Berlin.

PLATE 46
Sycaltis perforata – *Amphoriscus perforatus* (HAECKEL, 1872)

Taf. 47.

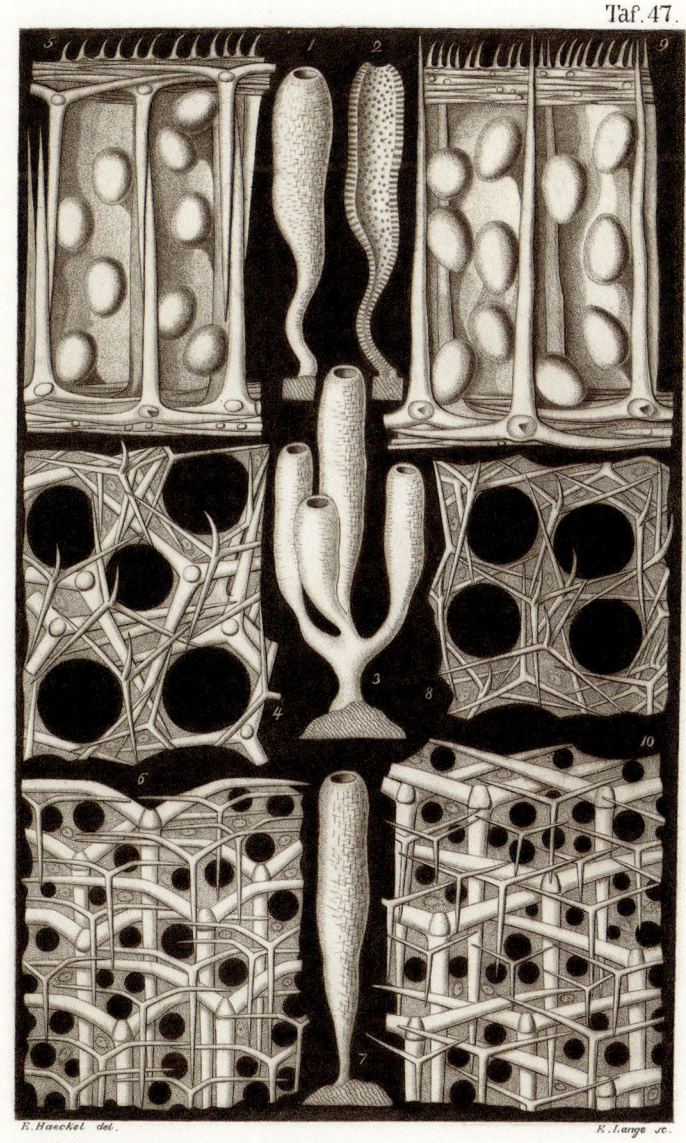

PLATE 47
1–6 Sycaltis testipara – *Amphoriscus testiparus* (HAECKEL, 1872)
7–10 Sycaltis ovipara – *Amphoriscus oviparus* (HAECKEL, 1872)

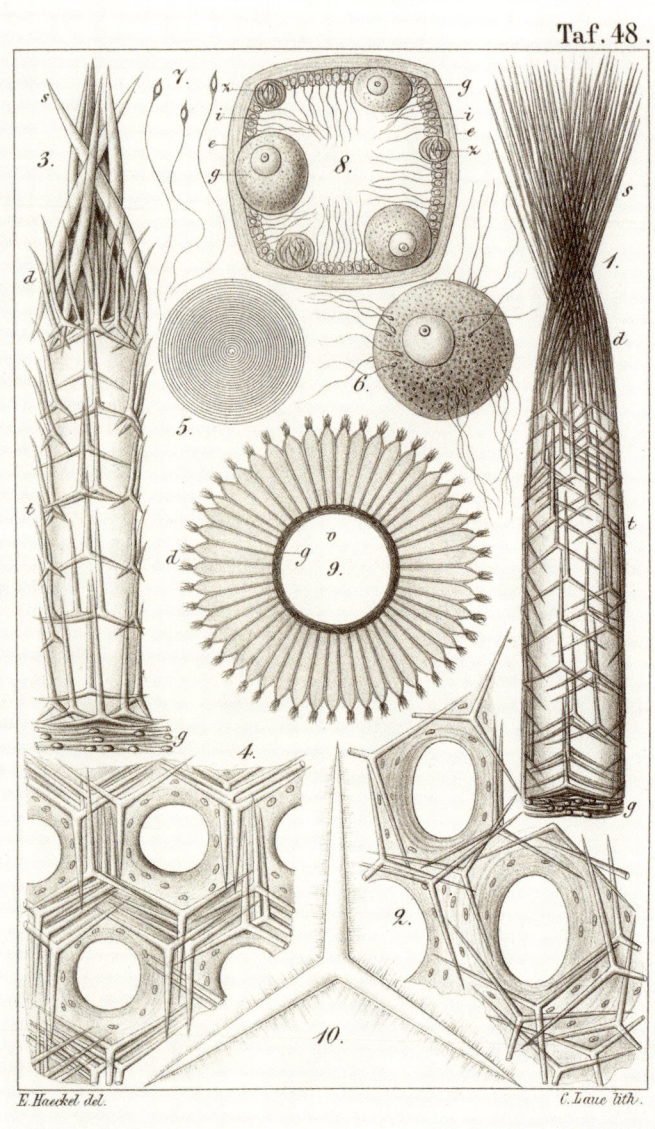

PLATE 48
1–2 Sycortis lingua – *Sycon lingua* (HAECKEL, 1870)
3–10 Sycortis quadrangulata – *Sycon quadrangulatum* (SCHMIDT, 1868)

PLATE 49
Sycortis laevigata – *Grantia laevigata* (HAECKEL, 1872)

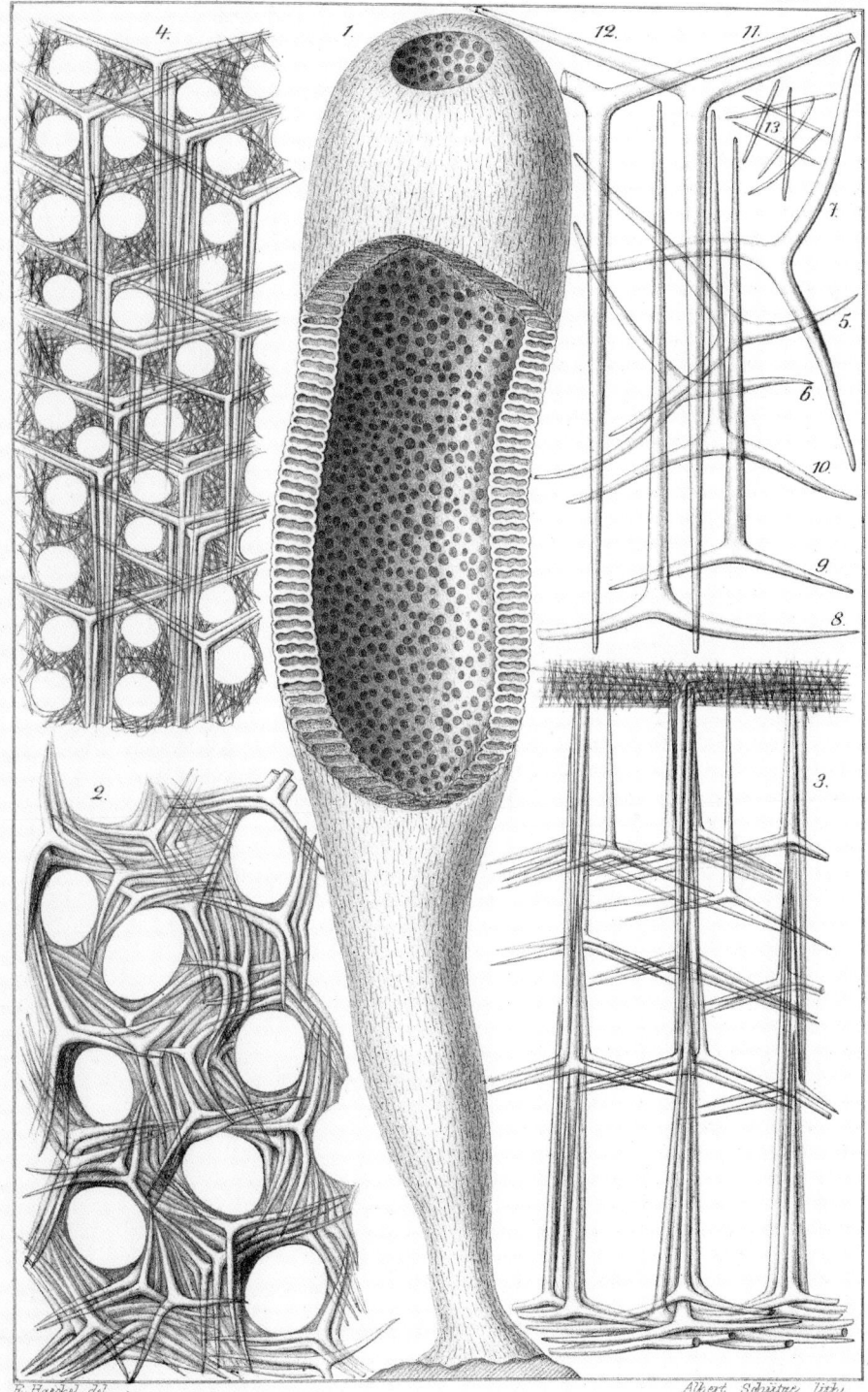

Taf. 49.

E. Haeckel del.   Albert Schütze lith.

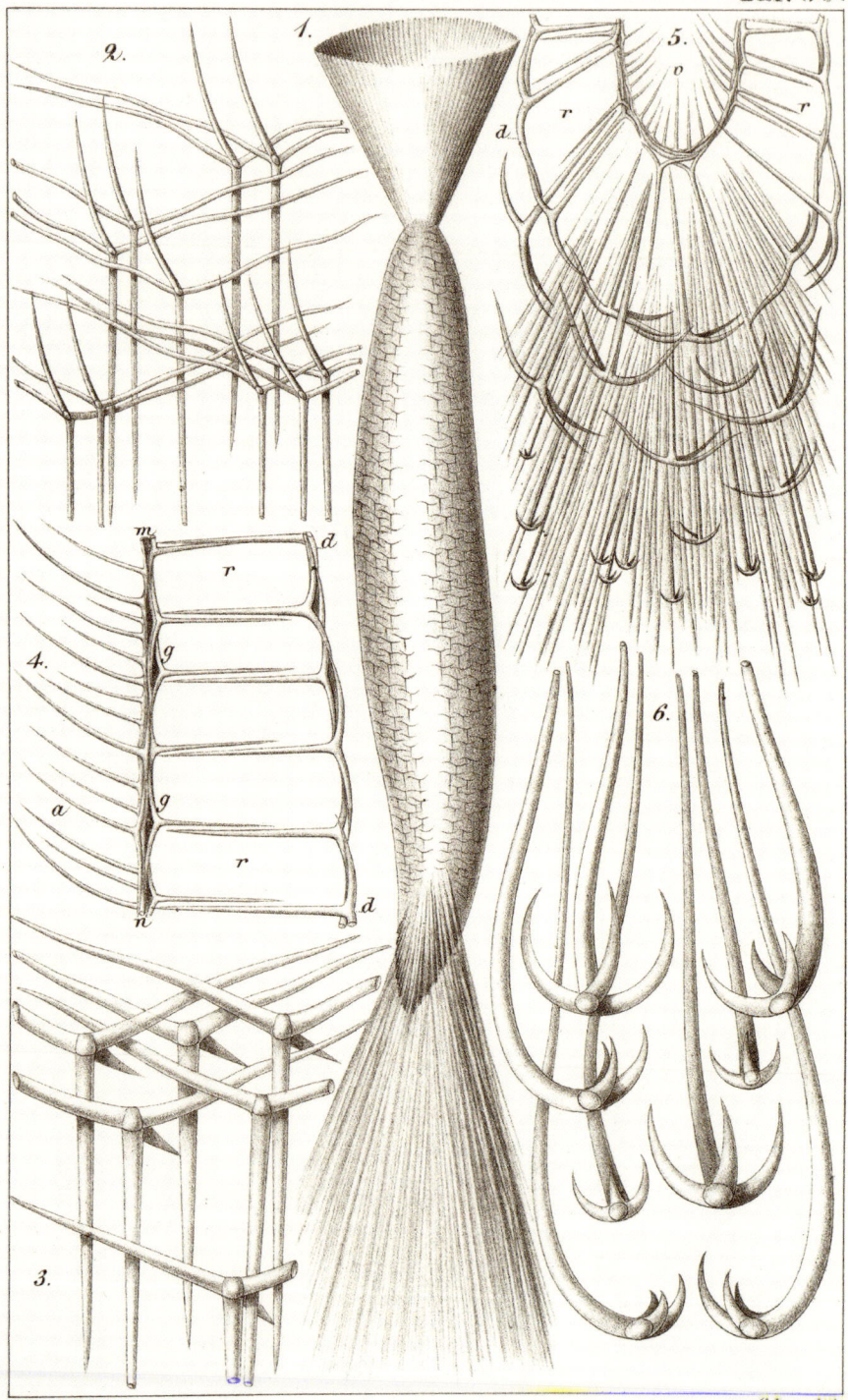

E. Haeckel del.

C. Lone lith.

Taf. 51.

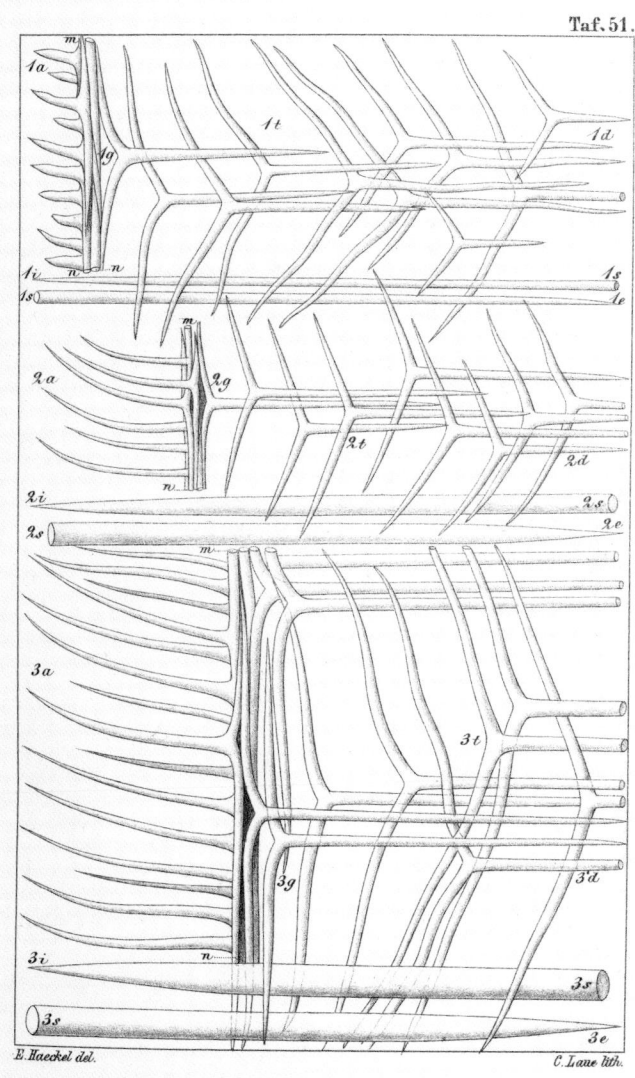

E. Haeckel del.   C. Laue lith.

PLATE 50
Syculmis synapta – *Amphoriscus synapta* (SCHMIDT IN HAECKEL, 1872)

PLATE 51
1 Sycandra ciliata – *Sycon ciliatum* (FABRICIUS, 1780) Vase sponge, Ciliated sponge
2 Sycandra coronata – *Sycon ciliatum* (FABRICIUS, 1780) Vase sponge, Ciliated sponge
3 Sycandra capillosa – *Grantia capillosa* (SCHMIDT, 1862)

Taf. 56.

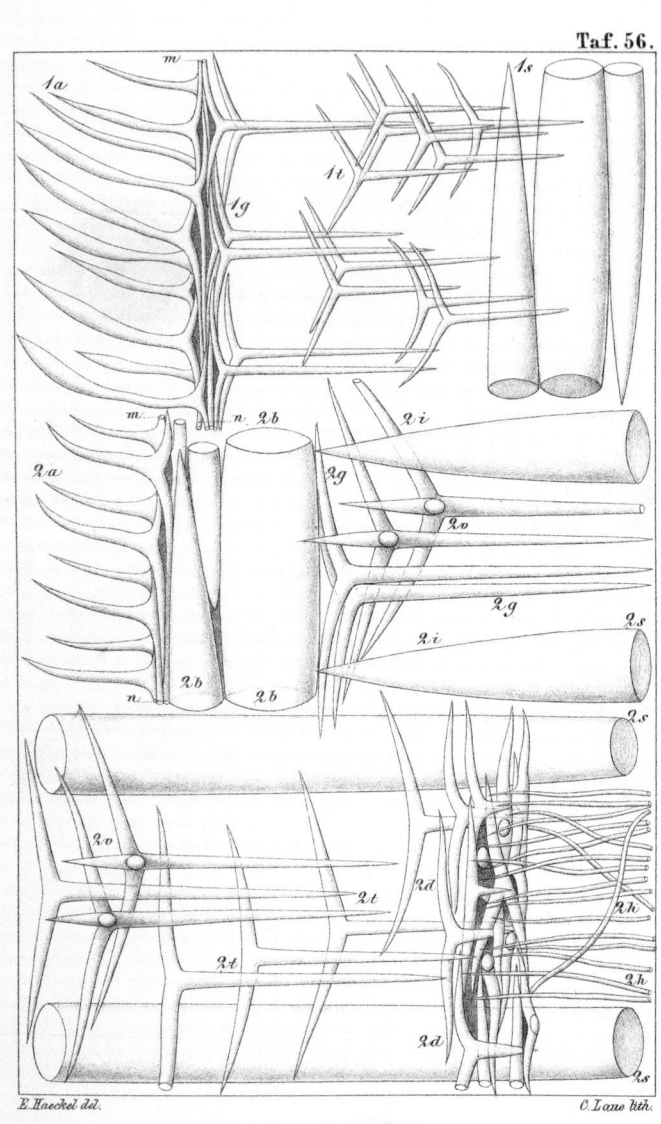

E. Haeckel del.   C. Laue lith.

PLATE 56
1 Sycandra glabra – *Sycettusa glabra* (ROW, 1909)
2 Sycandra hystrix – *Sycodorus hystrix* HAECKEL, 1872

PLATE 57
Sycandra compressa – *Grantia compressa* (FABRICIUS, 1780) Purse sponge

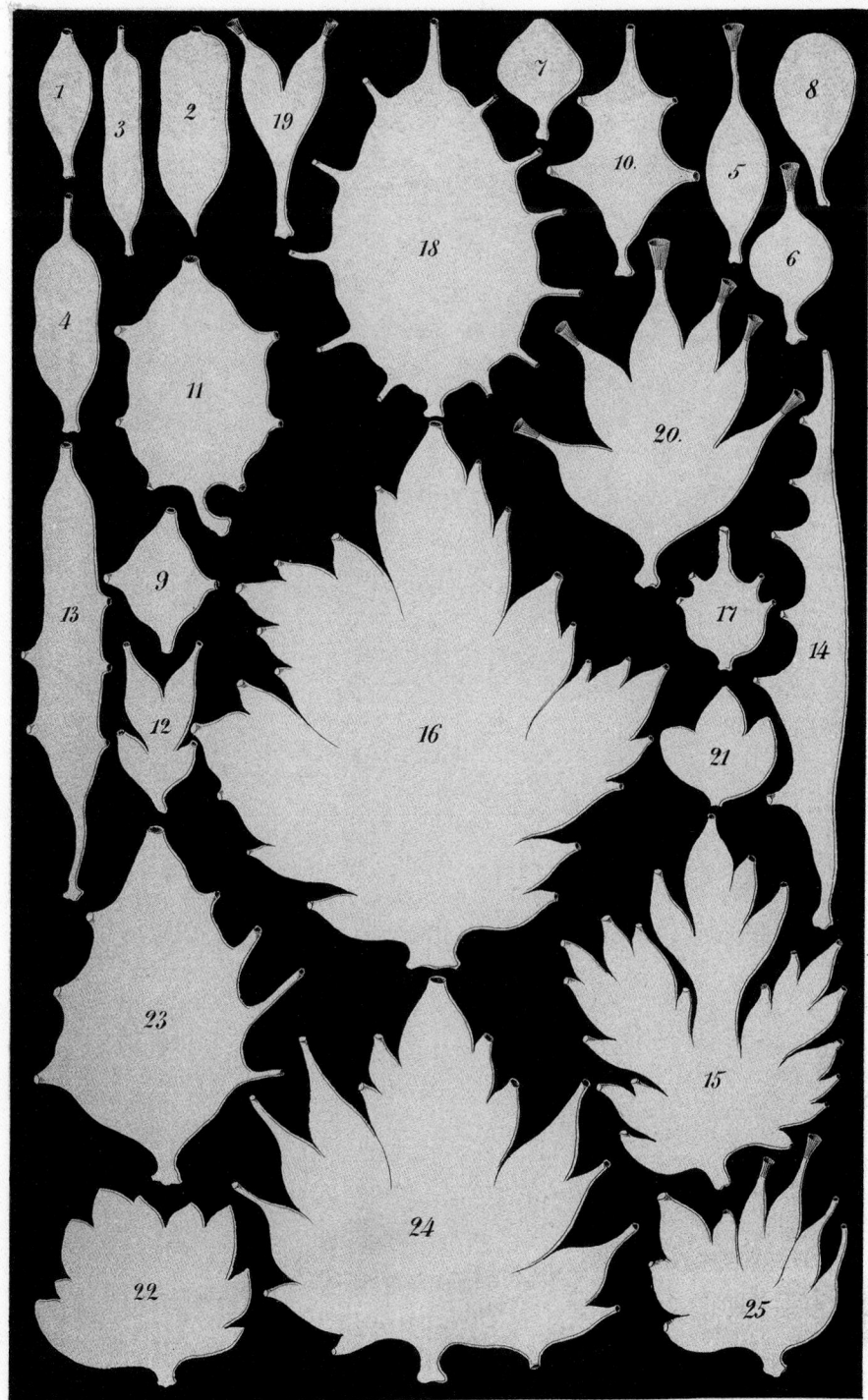

E. Haeckel del.

Lith.Anst. v. E. Giltsch, Jena.

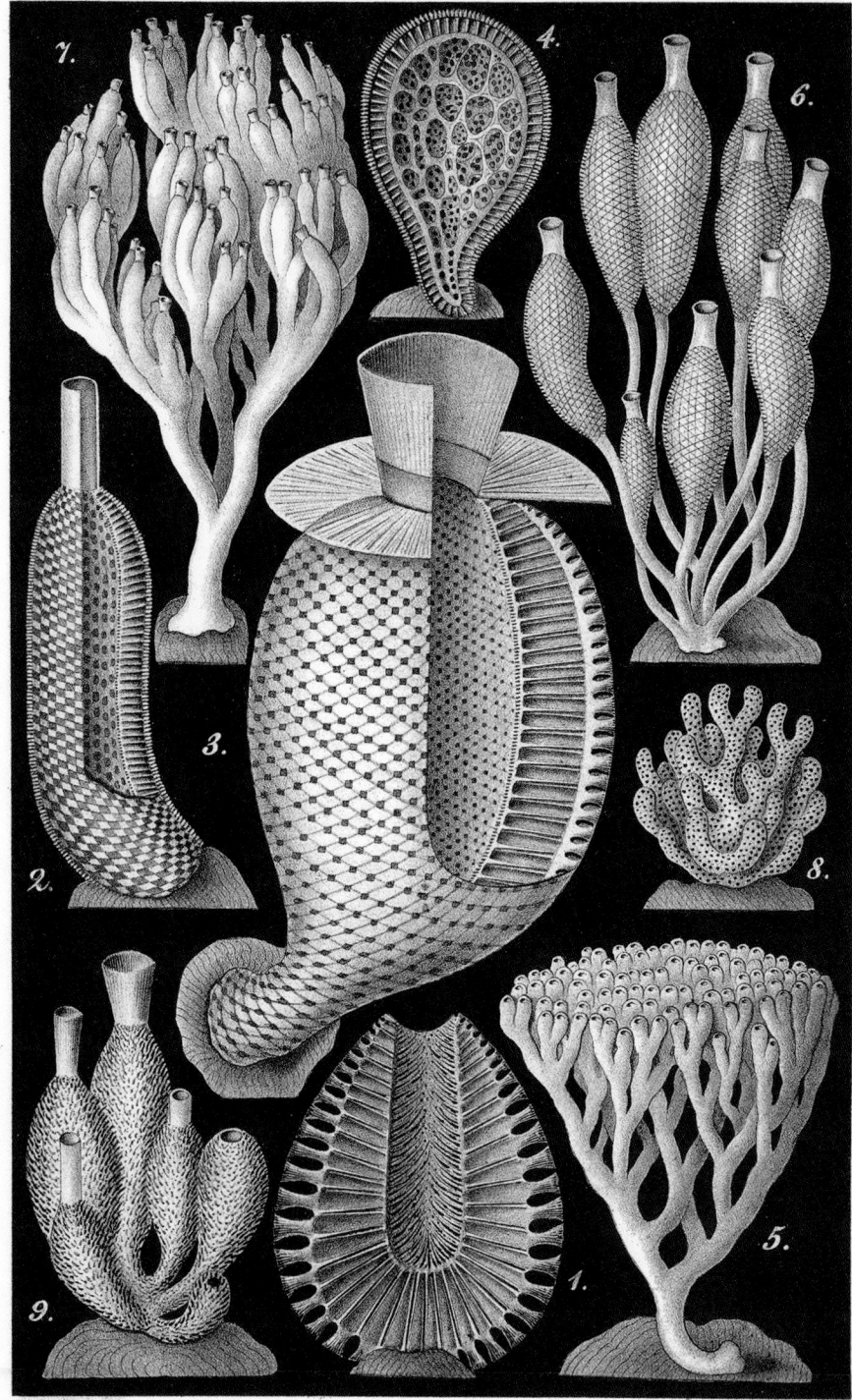

E.Haeckel del.

C.Lane lith.

Taf. 59.

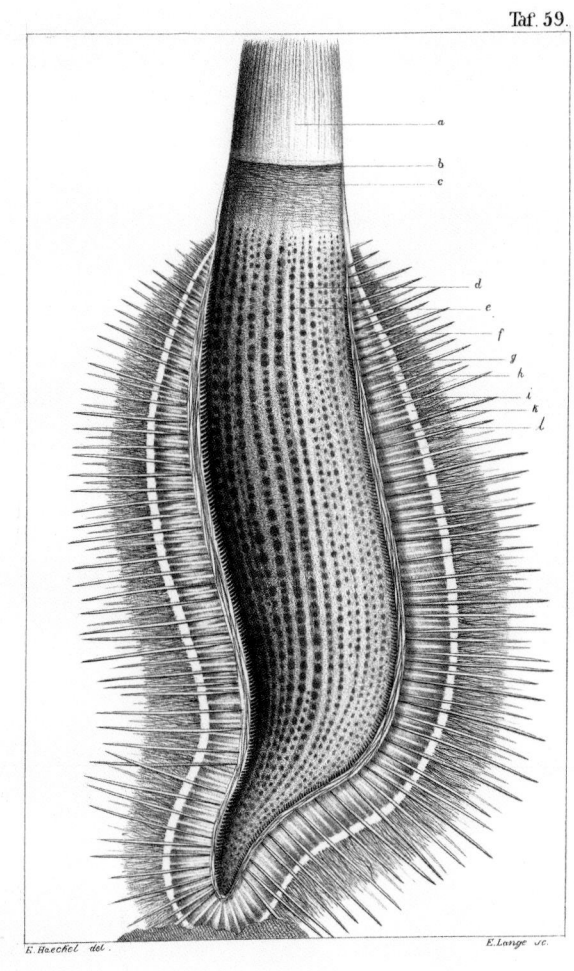

E. Haeckel del.

E. Lange sc.

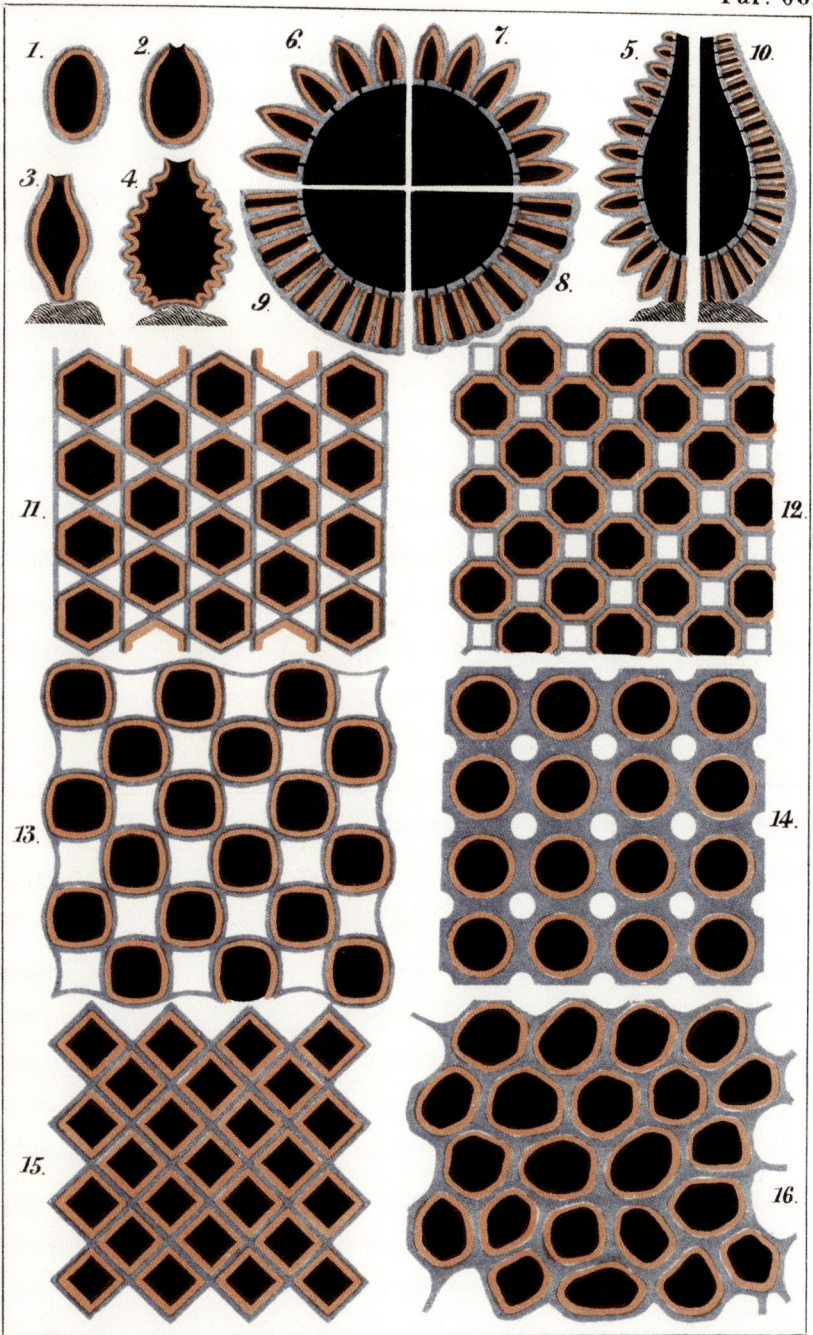

E. Haeckel del.

Lith.Anst. v. E. Giltsch in Jena.

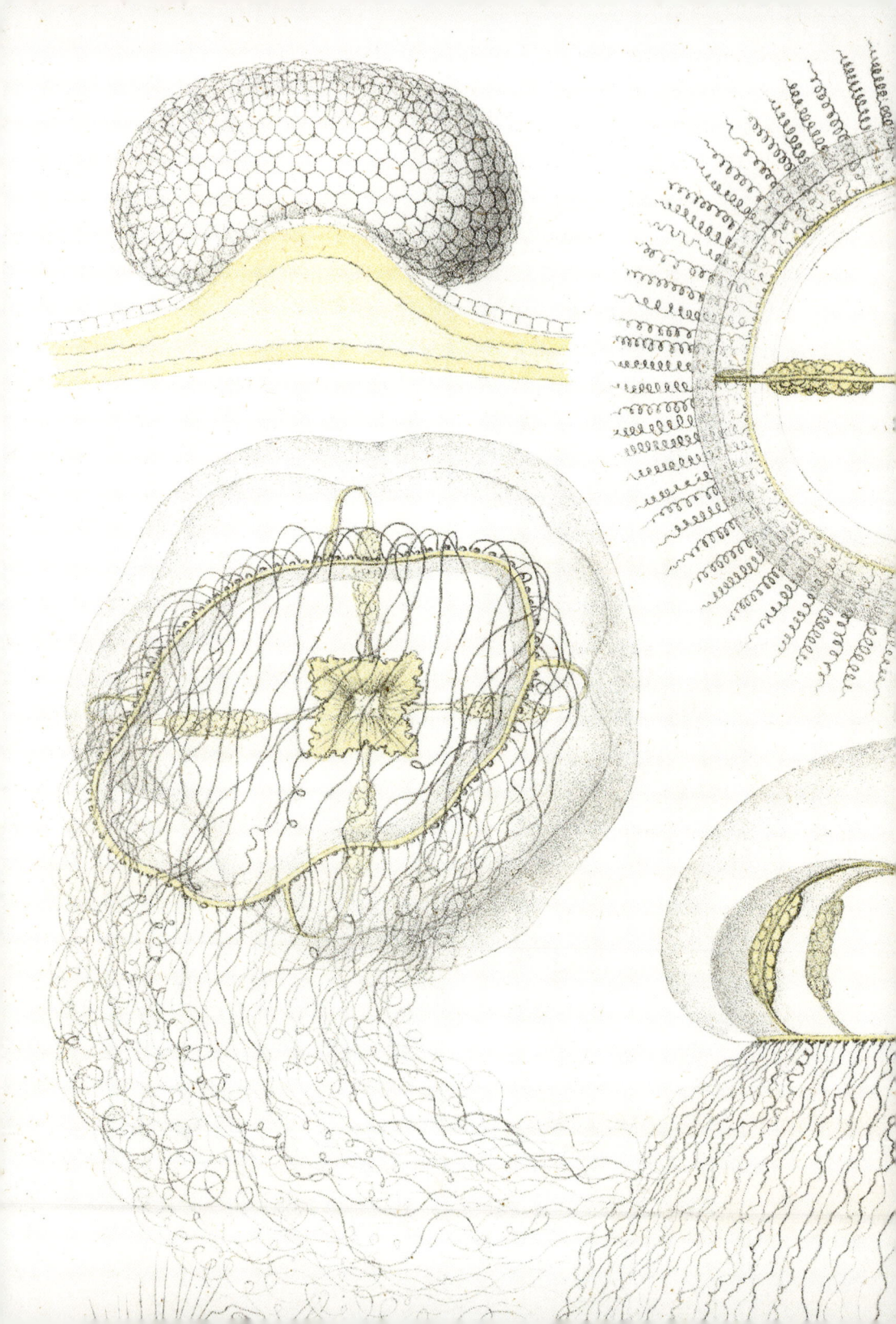

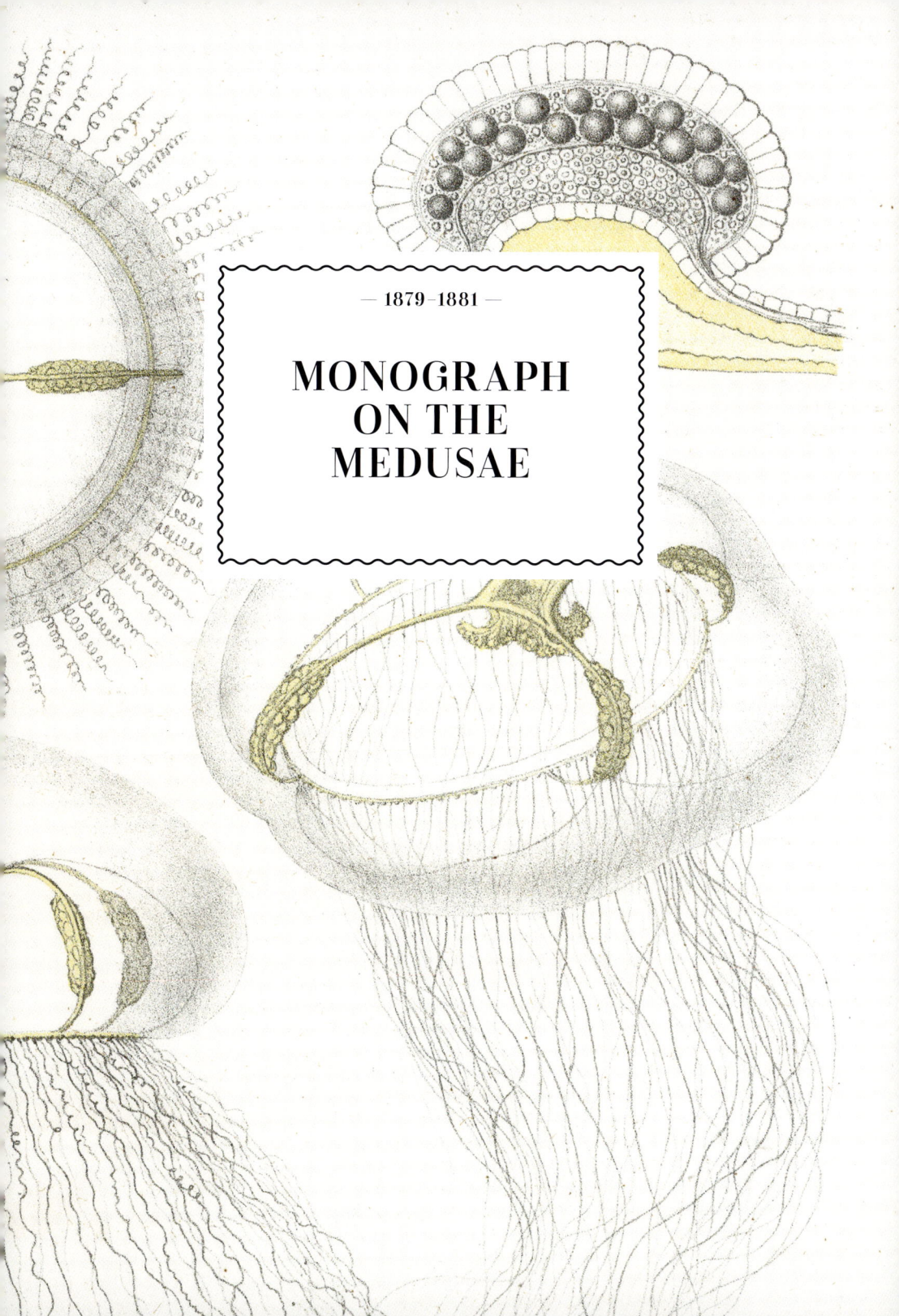

— 1879–1881 —

MONOGRAPH
ON THE
MEDUSAE

MONOGRAPH ON THE MEDUSAE

When Haeckel accompanied his teacher from Berlin, Professor Johannes Müller, on a research trip to the North Sea island of Heligoland in 1854, this was his first encounter with the sea – an experience that was to leave its mark on his entire life. As he was to observe in the Preface to his *Monographie der Medusen* (Monograph on the Medusae) no animals exercised such a power of attraction on him as did the jellyfish: "I will never forget the rapture with which I then, as a 20-year-old student, observed my first Tiara and Irene, my first Chrysaora and Cyanea, and sought with my brush to record their splendid forms and colours."[1] As jellyfish were inadequately researched before the 1860s, Haeckel resolved to devote a comprehensive monograph to them. During his many journeys he collected his own specimens and also visited several great museums of natural history from which he was permitted to borrow numerous other specimens. In addition, he asked the captains and crews of many ships that regularly sailed in the oceans beyond Europe if they would collect jellyfish themselves on his behalf, supplying them with "instructions regarding the appropriate means of conserving of the same."[2] Through these diverse undertakings, Haeckel was able, in preparation for the *Monograph on the Medusae* (appearing in two volumes in 1879 and 1881, with approximately 900 pages of text and two atlases of 40 and 32 plates[3] respectively), to assemble a great wealth of material – more, in fact, than all his predecessors had, combined.

Haeckel knew that this monograph, however valuable it might prove to be would eventually need to be revised, like all such publications. As he also observed in the aforementioned Preface: "All the important publications that have heretofore appeared on Medusae contain numerous errors, and many of them are full of glaring mistakes. And my own 'System of the Medusae' will in this respect resemble all its predecessors. For the organisation of these remarkable creatures in itself; the diverse difficulties involved in obtaining and conserving them; the impossibility of being able to compare all the related forms, whether alive or in a well-conserved state, in addition to many other unavoidable obstacles, create a rich source of potential errors, to which all medusologists, without exception, more or less succumb."[4] Jellyfish are the most ephemeral of creatures; their umbrella- or bell-shaped forms are supported by no skeleton or any sort of firm tissue. In essence, the bodies of jellyfish are a gelatinous mass, more than 95 per cent of which is water. Once cast upon the shore they dry out, and all that remains of them is little more than a paper-thin film.

From the early-21st-century perspective, the choice of title for Haeckel's account of jellyfish was rather unfortunate, for "Medusae" are, in fact, not an animal group in their own right. "Medusa" is rather the name of a generation of particular groups of Cnidaria. A generation of medusae (which are adapted to a swimming mode of life) typically follows on from one of polyps (which are sessile, generally remaining fixed on the seabed), and vice versa.

Of the four large groups of Cnidaria, there are three that have such alternate generations in this fashion: the Hydrozoa (from the Greek *hydra*, sea serpent), Scyphozoa (shield or disc jellyfish), and Cubozoa (box jellyfish). Polyps, in these groups, are generated by older polyps (through asexual reproduction by budding) or arise by way of a larval stage that develops after the fusion of an egg cell and a sperm cell (sexual reproduction). Medusae themselves come about in an asexual fashion. When they mature they generate reproductive cells. The fourth group of Cnidaria is the Anthozoa (from the Greek *anthos*, a flower), comprising floriform animals (anemones, corals). They produce no medusa, only polyps. These develop both from seasonal reproductive cells and through the budding off of new polyps from older ones, most of the latter remaining linked with the mother polyp, thereby enabling the emergence of new colonies or stalks.

Among the Medusae, Haeckel distinguished two sub-groups: the Craspedota and the Acraspedae, both names first introduced in 1856 by Haeckel's colleague in Jena, Professor Carl Gegenbaur (1826–1903). Craspedota are now called Hydrozoa, and Arcraspedae are now comprised of two groups, the Scyphozoa and Cubozoa. The latter two, the so-called disc and box jellyfish, are most closely related with each other, for their own medusae possess organs of a particular type that serve to control balance. Among Cubozoa, the sea wasp is one of the sea animals that is most dangerous to humankind: each year more people die from its extremely venomous sting than from shark attacks. Among Hydrozoa there belongs also, in addition to other groups, the Siphonophora. Haeckel treated the latter in separate essays, and they are not discussed in his monograph on the Medusae (see pp. 132–35).

In the monograph presented here Haeckel published a precise description of two of the species he had named after his first wife Anna Sethe: *Mitrocoma annae* (first described in 1864), and *Desmonema annasethe* (already introduced by him in 1877 as *Cyanantha annasethe*). The illustration of *Desmonema annasethe* in the monograph on the Medusae is not yet coloured (1880, plate 30; here p. 270) but it was supplied with arbitrarily selected colours in *Kunstformen der Natur* (*Art Forms in Nature*, 1899, plate 8; here p. 335). The term *Desmonema* had been introduced in 1862 as a genus named by Louis Agassiz (1807–1873). In 1880, Haeckel had become convinced that certain qualities with which he had justified the nomination of the genus *Cyanantha* in 1877 were insufficient to attest to a distinction between genera and he withdrew this name.

How far Haeckel broke away, in the case of his remarks on *Mitrocoma annae*, from an objective presentation of the species may be convincingly illustrated through a quotation from the text in which he introduced the first of the species to be named in honour of his late wife – "*Mitrocoma annae* is among the most charming and the most graceful of all the Medusae; [...] The movements of this wondrous Eucopid offer a magical sight, and I have spent many happy hours in the contemplation of their tentacles, curling down like a blond hair ornament at the edge of a sweet peaked cap [...]. I name this species the princess among the Eucopides, in memory of my unforgettable dear wife, Anna Sethe. If I am able, during my earthly pilgrimage, to achieve something for science and humanity, then I owe this, in large part, to the ennobling influence of this highly gifted wife, who was torn from me through her sudden death in 1864."[5]

Haeckel's volume *Die Tiefsee-Medusen der Challenger-Reise und der Organismus der Medusen*, with 300 pages of text and 32 plates, and the designation of 18 new species – Haeckel's first work on the material gathered by the research ship named in the title – appeared in 1881, only a year after Haeckel's monograph on the Medusae. Even though Haeckel had access to vast quantities of microscopically small Radiolaria thanks to the HMS *Challenger* Expedition, rapid publication was impossible because his work involved the production of often very time-consuming drawings, so much effort was not required in the case of the Medusae. The nonetheless rather belated publication of his work on Siphonophora, specimens of which he had similarly received in good time (1879), may reasonably be assumed to have had another explanation: that he hoped to treat medusa, his favourite among all animal groups, with particular care. In the case of keratinous sponges (Keratosa), on the other hand, the subject of his last publication to be derived from the HMS *Challenger* material (1889), we may suspect that the publication was delayed simply because these creatures were not among Haeckel's "favourites."

A sense of the problems relating to biological nomenclature, as they repeatedly arise in this branch of research, is to be gleaned through an example from Haeckel's Medusae monograph of 1881. In 1879, Haeckel had described a medusa, which he had termed *Thamnostylus* (a new genus) *dinema* (new species). Haeckel illustrated *Thamnostylus dinema* on the first plate of his monograph on the deep-sea Medusae. In 1907, a new name for this medusa was proposed by the zoologist Gustav Hartlaub (1814–1900) – *Sarsiella*. This name had, however, already been introduced in 1869 for a tiny ostracod, and it was thus invalid for use as the name of a medusa, it being evidently not possible for one and the same name to be employed for two different genera. Haeckel's own proposed name *Thamnostylus*, on the other hand, is a unique one for an animal and valid in principle on that account. Since Haeckel (be it in 1879 or in 1881), the species illustrated has apparently not been researched again; and on this account, a number of authors have assumed that Haeckel's species may not be identifiable now. Since the outstanding quality of Haeckel's illustrations might very well permit an identification, this line of reasoning is inadmissible unless it is based upon new research into Haeckel's original material, which would then need to be compared with research on newly gathered Medusae.

In 1881, Haeckel illustrated numerous species on several plates to show details and the structures of organs. His very precisely documented crown jellyfish *Periphylla periphylla* may serve as an example (plates 18–23). The species is initially shown life-size and viewed from the side. Haeckel shows the chief sensory organs (plate 18); he offers a view from below as well as the rendering of a tentacle (plate 19); he shows the animal in dissected form together with details of its oral tube (plate 20, not depicted)); after this there follows cross-sections and a further longitudinal section (plate 21, not depicted); and the sequence closes with a depiction of a number of organs and their constituent parts, some of these in greatly magnified form through the help of research using a microscope (plates 22–23). The present-day observer will certainly marvel at such an enormous wealth of detail which was rarely been achieved in all the literature of biosystematics.

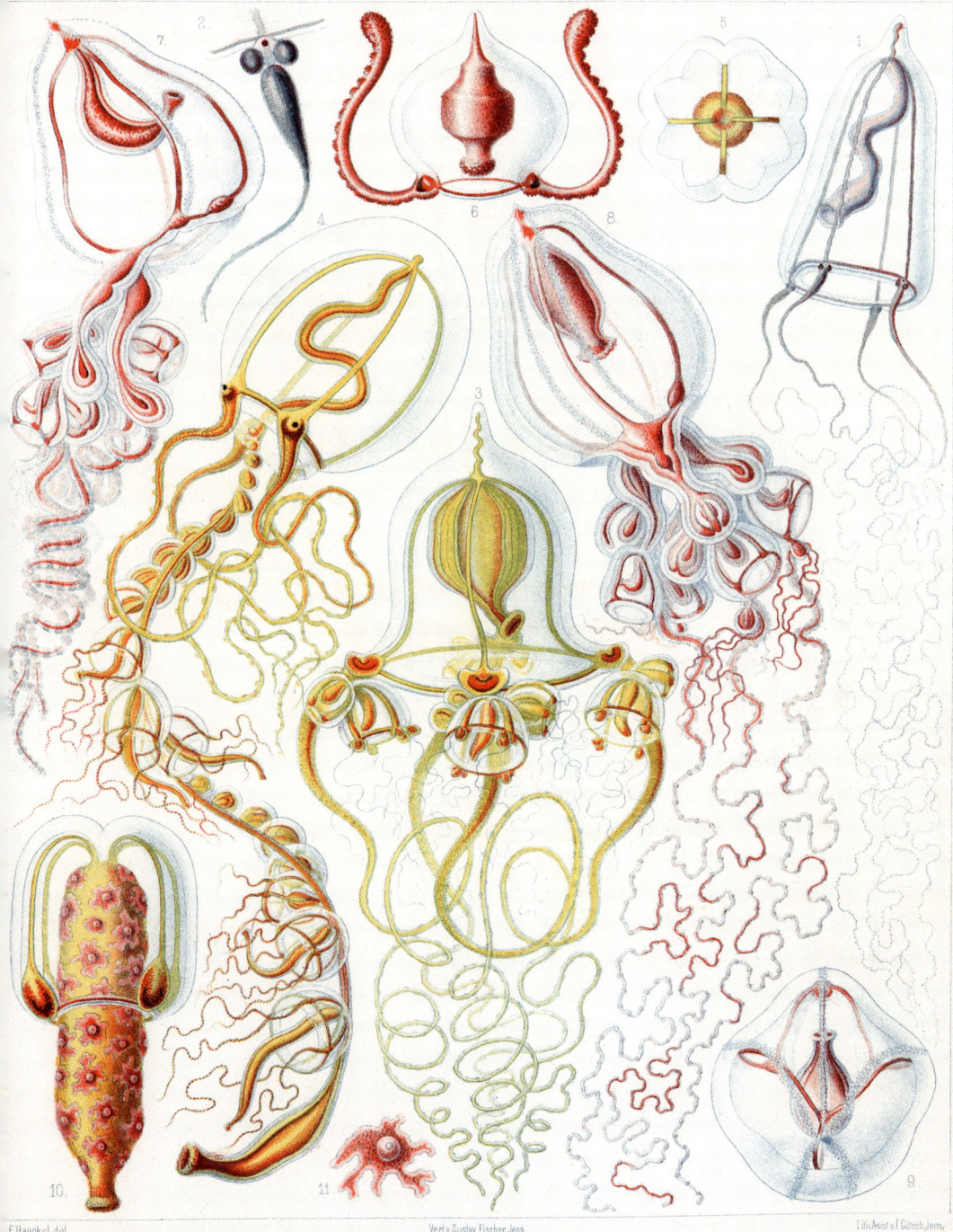

1-3. CODONIUM, 4.5. SARSIA, 6. DICODONIUM, 7-9. AMPHICODON, 10.11. AMALTHAEA.

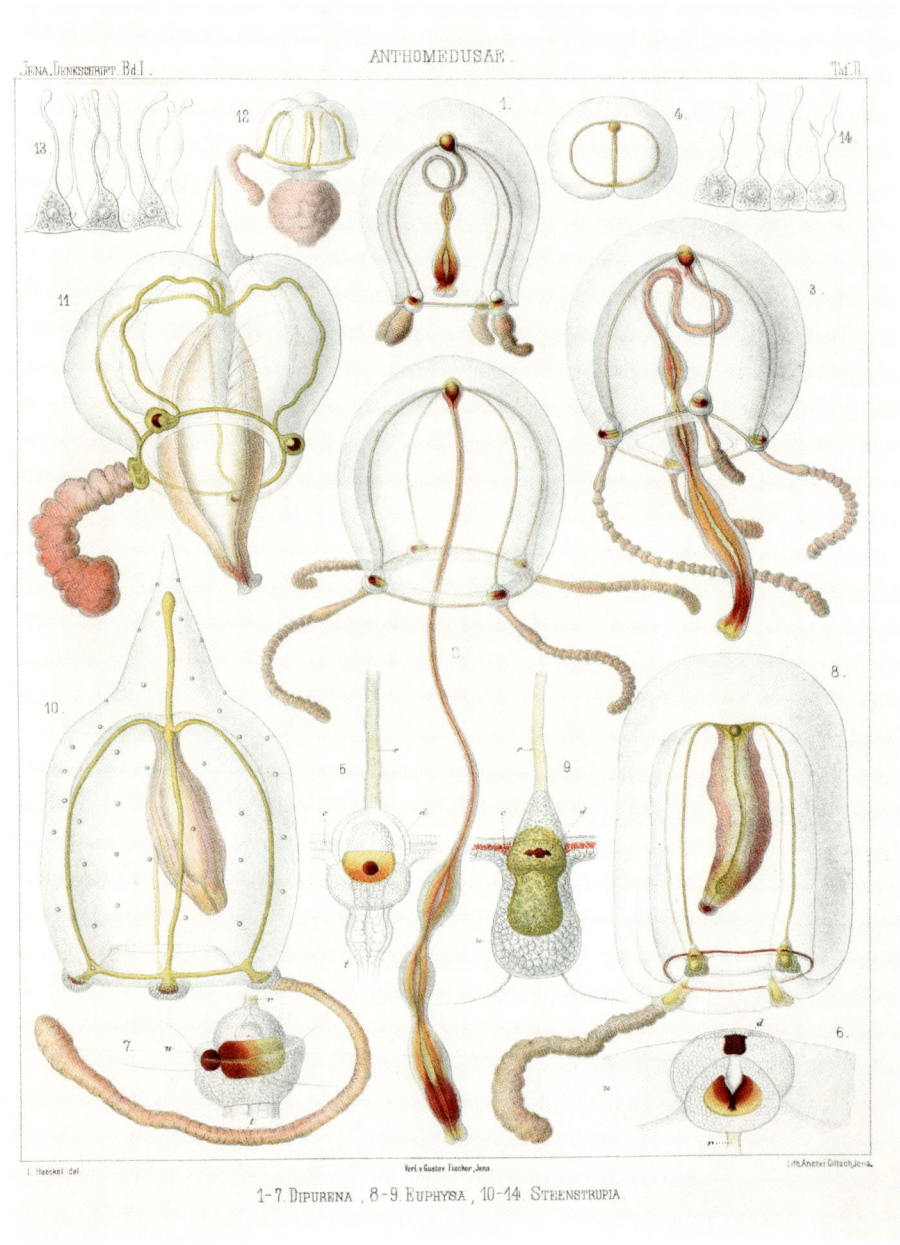

1-7. DIPURENA , 8-9. EUPHYSA , 10-14. STEENSTRUPIA

PLATE 2

1-7 **Dipurena dolichogaster,** HAECKEL — *Slabberia ophiogaster* (HAECKEL, 1864)
8-9 **Euphysa mediterranea,** HAECKEL — *Euphysa aurata* FORBES, 1848
10-14 **Steenstrupia cranoides,** HAECKEL — *Corymorpha nutans* M. SARS, 1835 Nodding hydroid

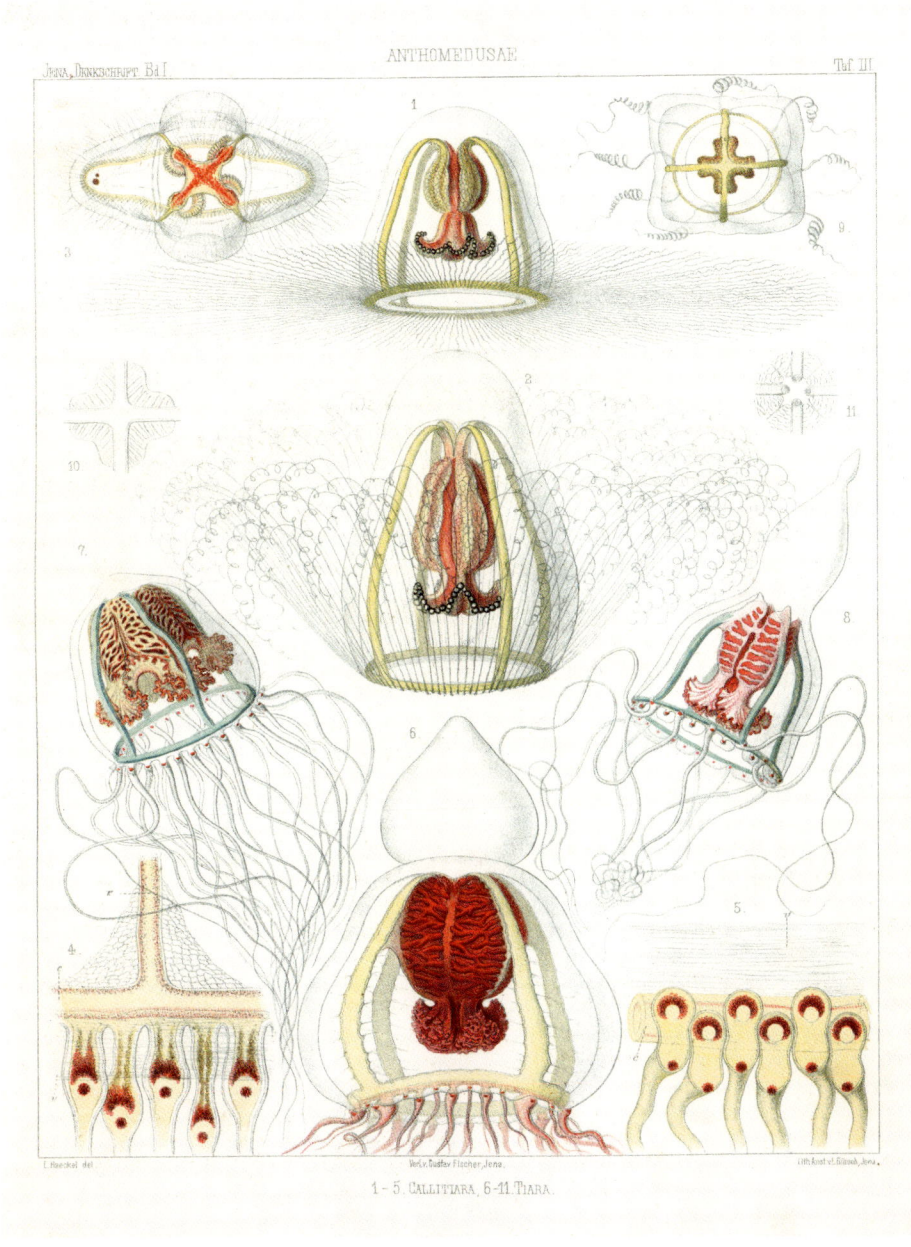

1 - 5. CALLITIARA, 6 -11. TIARA.

PLATE 3

1–5 Callitiara polyophthalma, HAECKEL – *Oceania armata* KÖLLIKER, 1853
6–8 Tiara pileata, L. AGASSIZ – *Neoturris pileata* (FORSSKÅL, 1775) | 9–10 Tiara rotunda, HAECKEL –
Modeeria rotunda (QUOY & GAIMARD, 1827) (= *Tiaranna rotunda* (QUOY & GAIMARD, 1827))
11 Tiara reticulata, HAECKEL – *Pandea conica* (QUOY & GAIMARD, 1827)

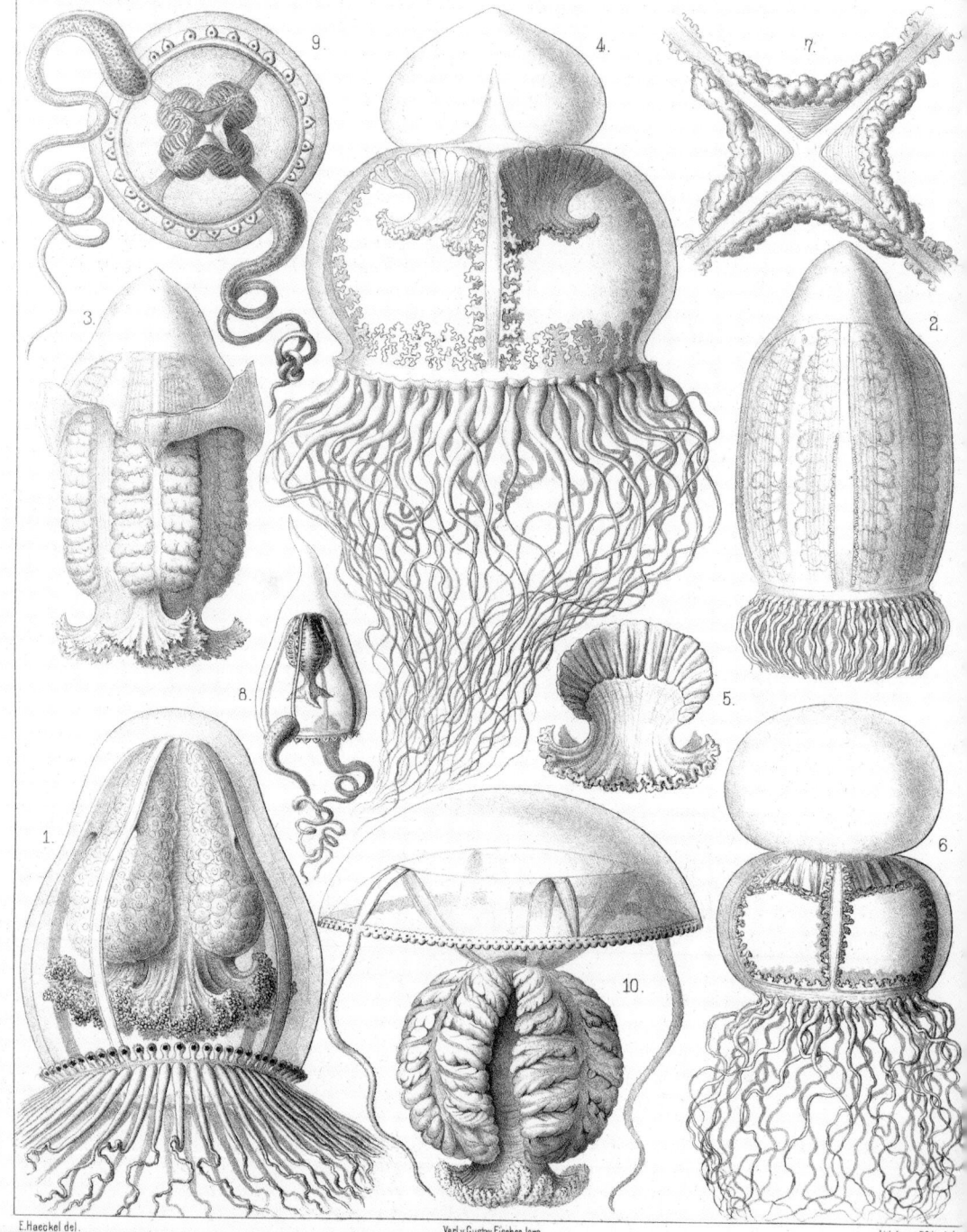

E.Haeckel del.   Verl.v.Gustav Fischer, Jena.   Lith.Anst.v.E.Giltsch Jena

1. CONIS, 2,3. TURRIS, 4-7. CATABLEMA, 8,9. DINEMA, 10. STOMOTOCA.

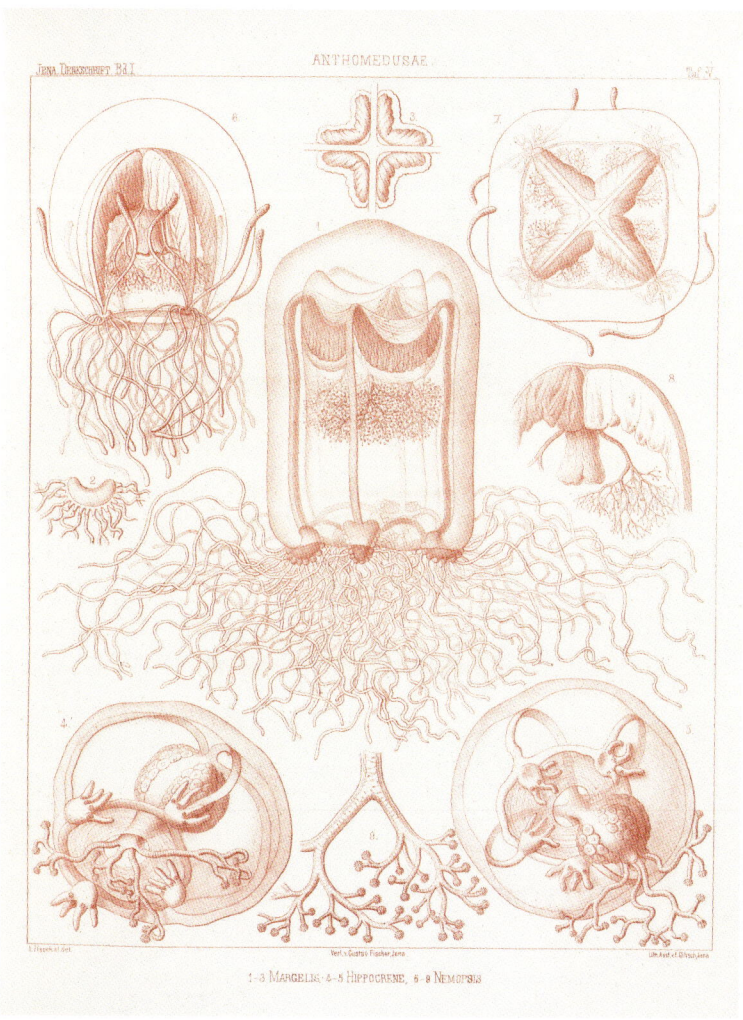

PLATE 4

1 Conis cyclophthalma, HAECKEL – *Oceania armata* KÖLLIKER, 1853 | 2-3 Turris digitalis, FORBES – *Neoturris pileata* (FORSSKÅL, 1775) | 4-5 Catablema campanula, HAECKEL – *Catablema vesicarium* (A. AGASSIZ, 1862) Constricted jellyfish | 6-7 Catablema eurystoma, HAECKEL – *Catablema vesicarium* (A. AGASSIZ, 1862) Constricted jellyfish | 8-9 Amphinema Titania, HAECKEL – *Amphinema dinema* PÉRON & LESSUEUR, 1809 | 10 Stomotoca pterophylla, HAECKEL – *Larsonia pterophylla* (HAECKEL, 1879)

PLATE 5

1-2 Hippocrene macloviana, HAECKEL – *Bougainvillia macloviana* LESSON, 1830

3 Thamnostoma macrostoma, HAECKEL – *Thamnostoma macrostomum* HAECKEL, 1879

4-5 Margelis maniculata, HAECKEL – *Bougainvillia muscus* (ALLMAN, 1863) Sticky (moss) hydroid

6-9 Nemopsis heteronema, HAECKEL – *Nemopsis bachei* L. AGASSIZ, 1849 Clinging jellyfish

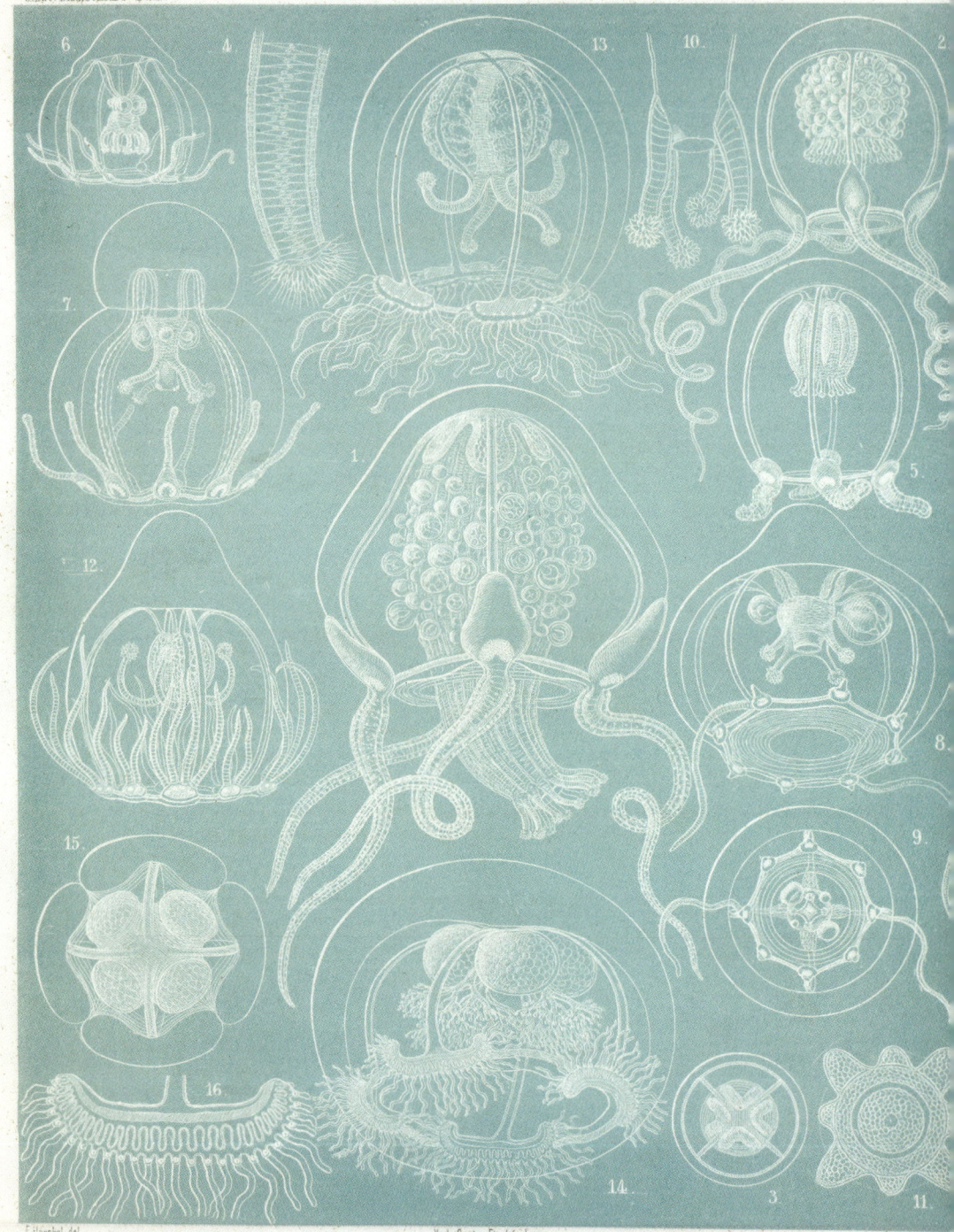

1–5. NIGRITINA, 6.7. BLASTOGASTER, 8–11. CUBOGASTER, 12. LIZUSA, 13. MARGELLIUM, 14–16. MARGELIS.

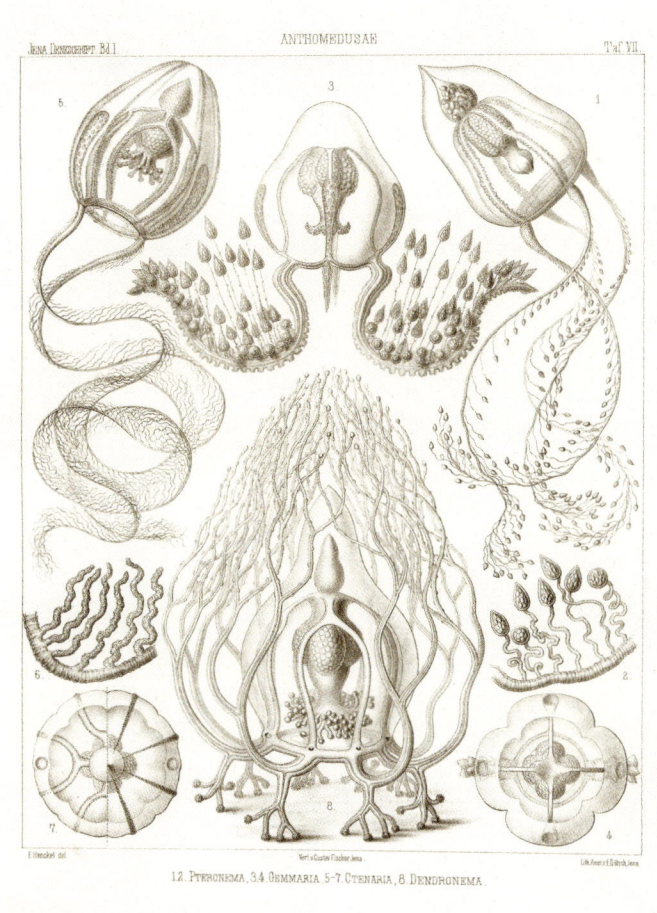

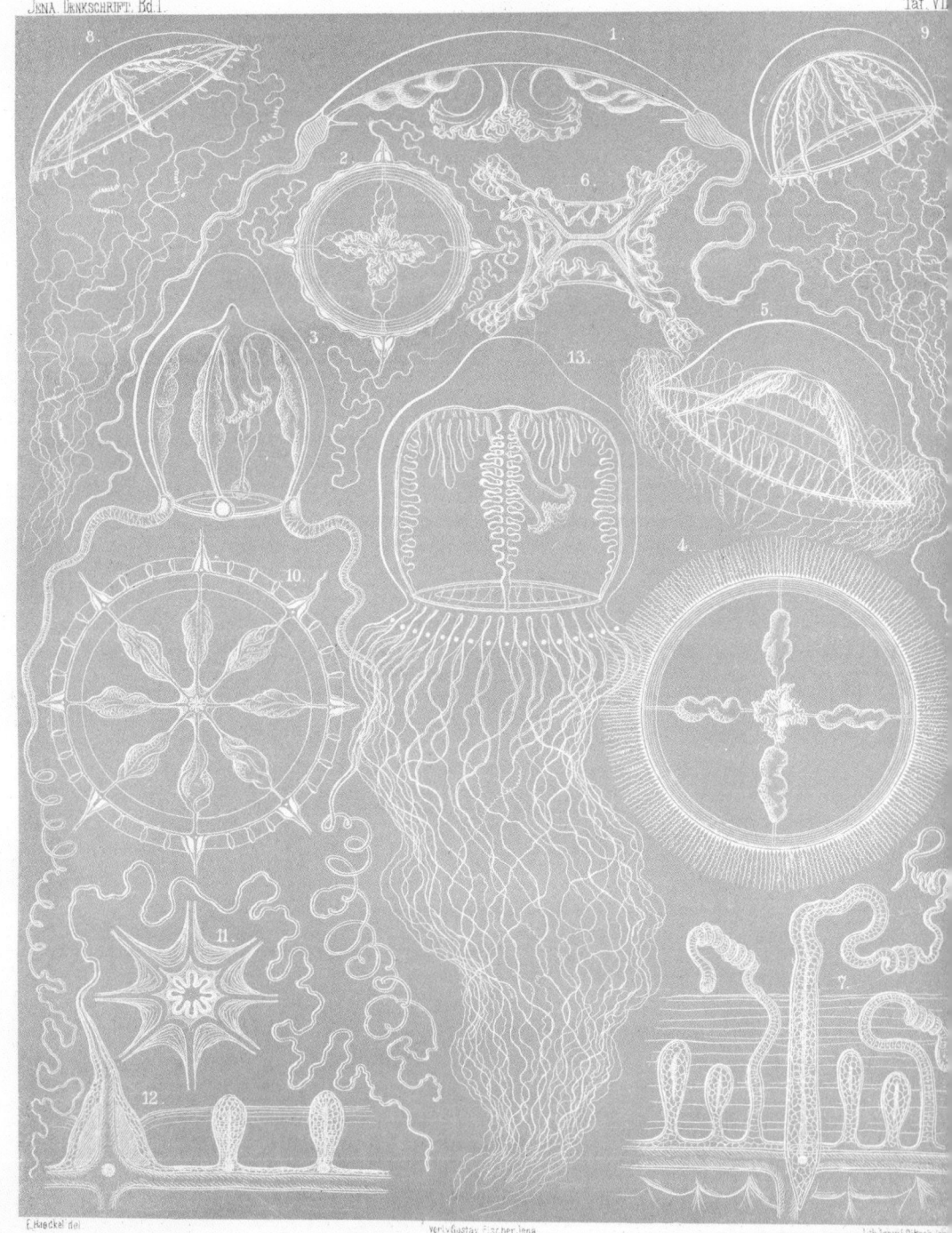

1.2. Tetranema, 3.Dissonema, 4.Thaumantias, 5-7.Cosmetira, 8-12.Melicertella, 13.Polyorchis.

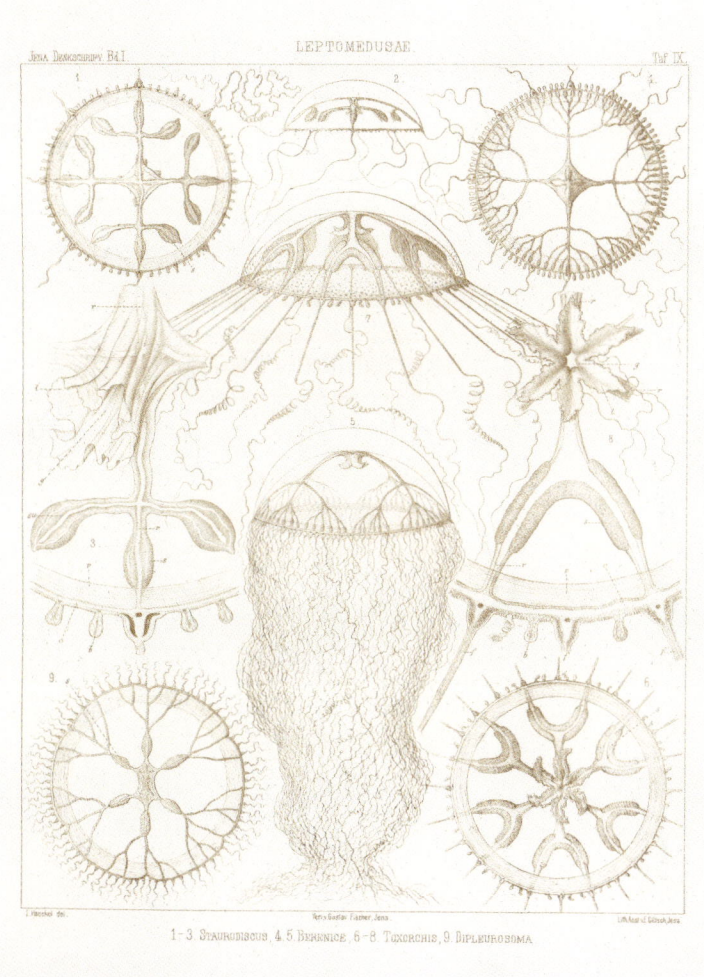

PLATE 8

1–2 **Tetranema eucopium**, HAECKEL (= Prothaumantias eucopium) – *Tetranema eucopium* HAECKEL, 1879

3 **Dissonema saphenella**, HAECKEL (= Prothaumantias dissonema) – *Dissonema saphenella* HAECKEL, 1879

4 **Thaumantias Eschscholtzii**, HAECKEL – *Clytia eschscholtzi* (HAECKEL, 1879) | 5–7 **Laodice ulothrix**, HAECKEL – *Laodicea undulata* (FORBES & GOODSIR, 1853) | 8–12 **Melicertissa clavigera**, HAECKEL (= Melicertella clavigera) – *Melicertissa clavigera* HAECKEL, 1879 | 13 **Polyorchis pinnatus**, HAECKEL – *Polyorchis penicillatus* (ESCHSCHOLTZ, 1829) Penicillate jellyfish

PLATE 9

1–3 **Staurodiscus tetrastaurus**, HAECKEL – *Staurodiscus tetrastaurus* HAECKEL, 1879

4 **Berenice Huxleyi**, HAECKEL – *Cuvieria huxleyi* (HAECKEL, 1879) | 5 **Berenice capillata**, HAECKEL – *Cuvieria carisochroma* PÉRON, 1807 | 6–8 **Toxorchis arcuatus**, HAECKEL – *Staurodiscus arcuatus* (HAECKEL, 1879)

9 **Dipleurosoma amphitheotum**, HAECKEL – *Dipleurosoma amphitheotum* HAECKEL, 1879

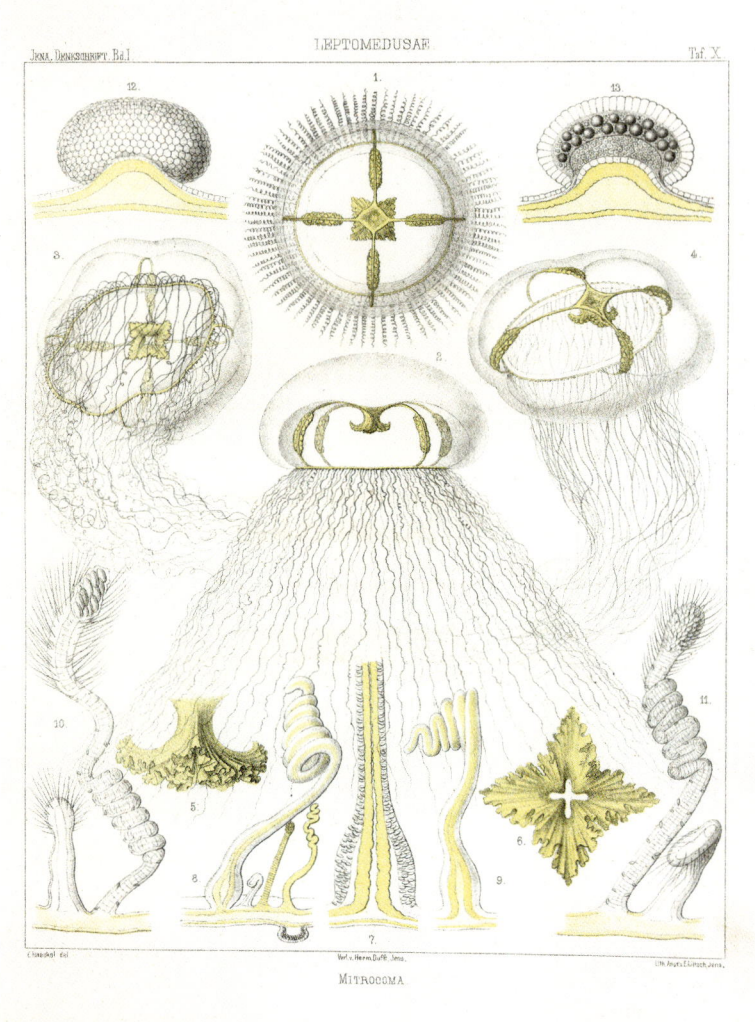

MITROCOMA

PLATE 10
Mitrocoma Annae, HAECKEL – *Mitrocoma annae* HAECKEL, 1864

PLATE 11
1-3 Eucopium primordiale, HAECKEL – *Eucopium primordiale* HAECKEL, 1879
4 Eucope campanulata, GEGENBAUR – *Clytia campanulata* (GEGENBAUR, 1857)
5 Saphenella dissonema, HAECKEL – *Phialella dissonema* (HAECKEL, 1879)
6-7 Obelia gelatinosa, HAECKEL – *Hartlaubella gelatinosa* (PALLAS, 1766)
8 Eutimalphes pretiosa, HAECKEL – *Eutimalphes pretiosa* HAECKEL, 1879
9-11 Mitrocomium cirratum, HAECKEL – *Mitrocomium cirratum* HAECKEL, 1879
12-13 Irenium quadrigatum, HAECKEL – *Irenium quadrigatum* HAECKEL, 1879

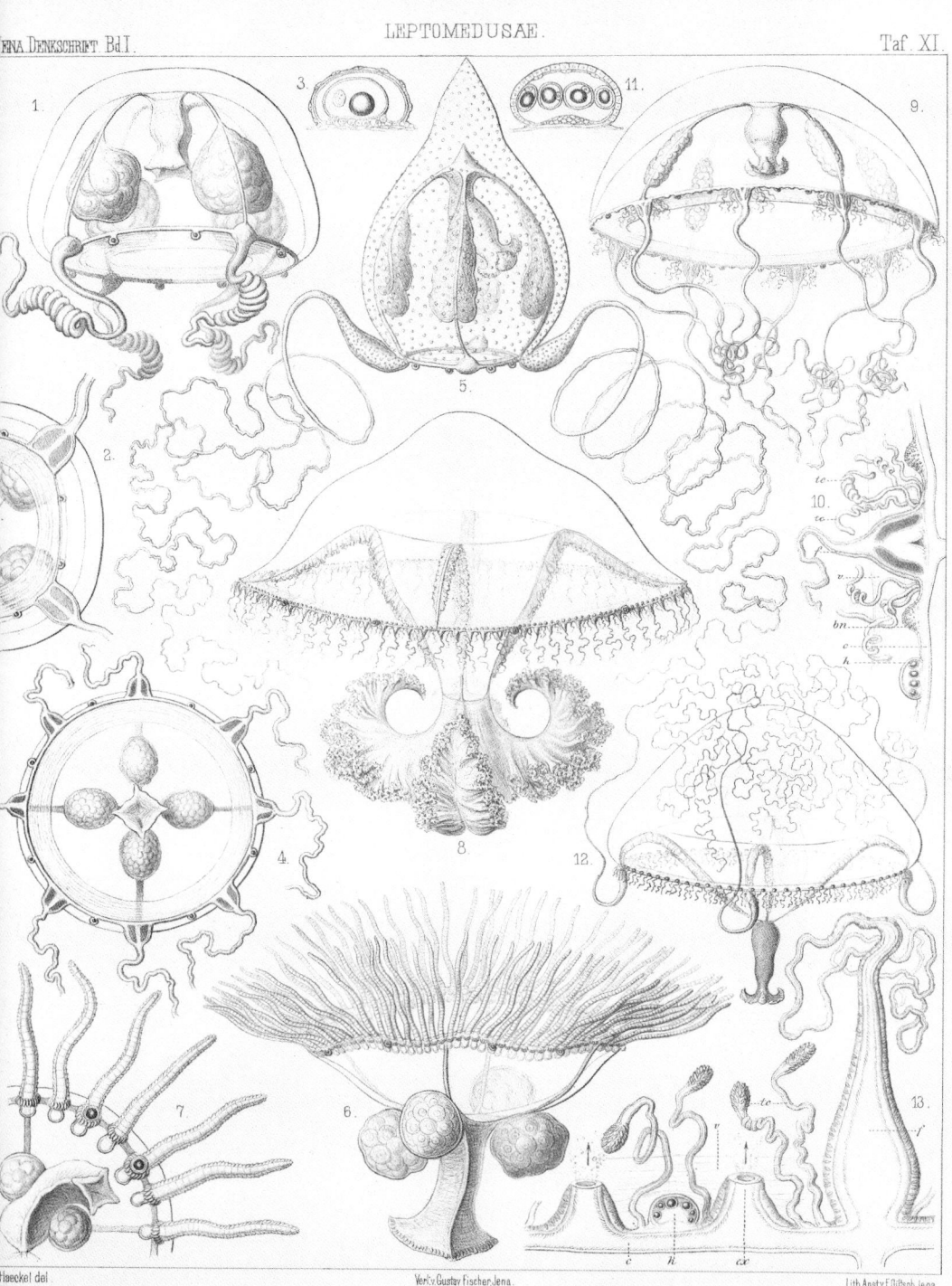

1-3. EUCOPIUM, 4. EUCOPE, 5. SAPHENELLA, 6.7. OBELIA, 8. EUTIMALPHES, 9-11. MITROCOMIUM, 12.13. IRENIUM.

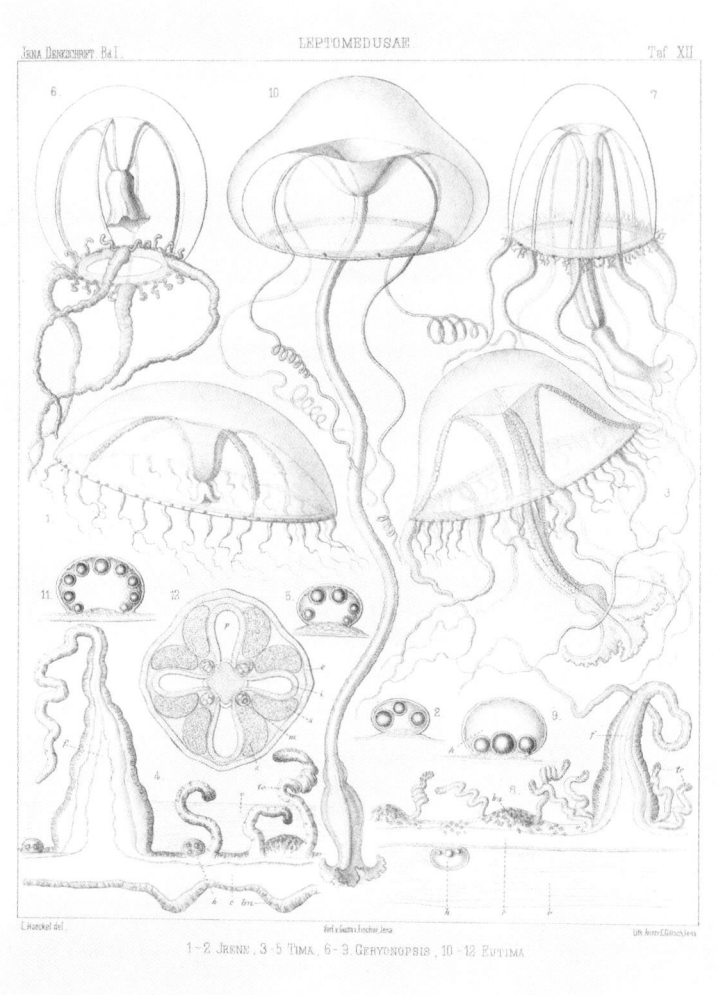

JENA DENKSCHRIFT Bd.I.
LEPTOMEDUSAE
Taf XII

1–2 IRENE, 3–5 TIMA, 6–9 GERYONOPSIS, 10–12 EUTIMA

PLATE 12

1–2 Irene pellucine, HAECKEL – *Eirene pellucine* HAECKEL, 1879 | 3–5 Tima Teuscheri, HAECKEL – *Irenium teuscheri* (HAECKEL, 1879) | 6–9 Eutimeta gentiana, HAECKEL (= Geryonopsis gentiana) – *Eutima gentiana* (HAECKEL, 1879) | 10–12 Eutimium elephas, HAECKEL – *Eutima gracilis* (FORBES & GOODSIR, 1853)

PLATE 13

1 Octorchandra canariensis, HAECKEL – *Eutima canariensis* (HAECKEL, 1879) (= *Eutima gegenbauri* (HAECKEL, 1864)?) | 2 Octorchis campanulata, HAECKEL – *Octorchis campanulata* HAECKEL, 1879 (synonym: *Eutima campanulata* (HAECKEL, 1879)?) | 3 Octorchandra germanica, HAECKEL – *Eutima gegenbauri* (HAECKEL, 1864)? | 4–8 Octorchandra germanica, HAECKEL – *Eutima gegenbauri* (HAECKEL, 1864)?
9 Octorchidium tetranema, HAECKEL – *Octorchidium tetranema* HAECKEL, 1879
10–16 Octorchis Gegenbauri, HAECKEL – *Eutima gegenbauri* (HAECKEL, 1864)

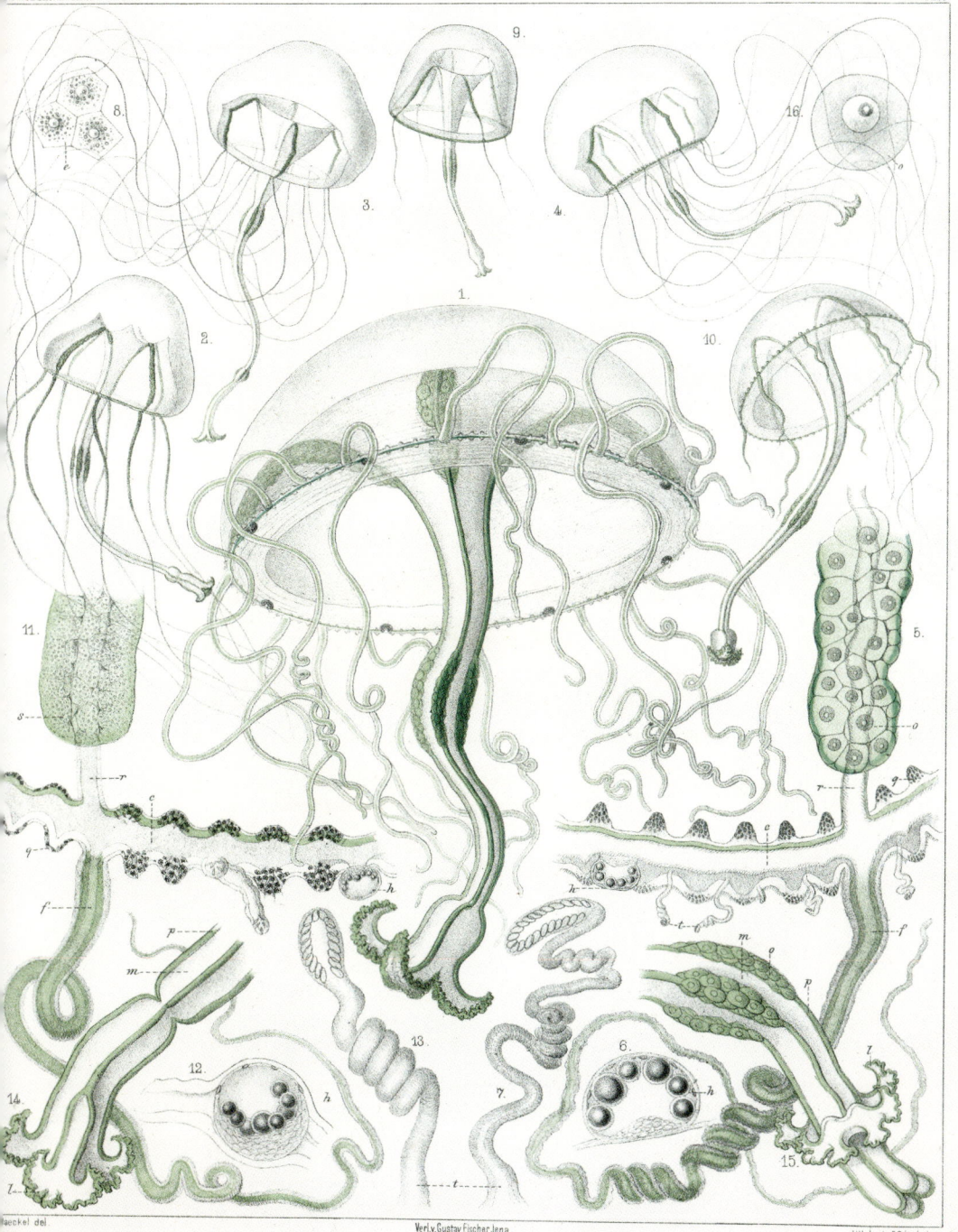

Haeckel del. Verl.v.Gustav Fischer Jena. Lith.Anst.v.E.Giltsch,Jena.

OCTORCHIS.

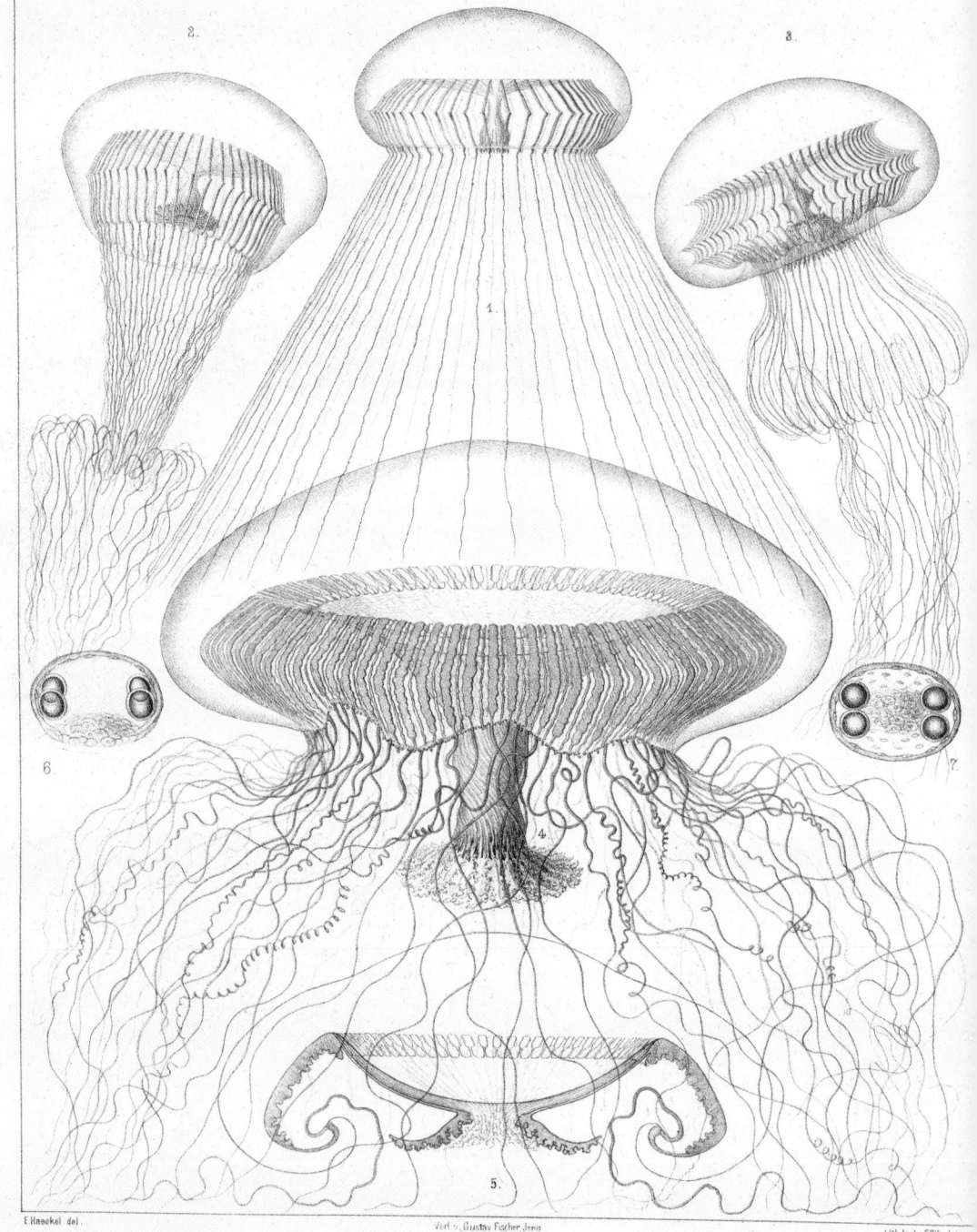

E.Haeckel del.   Verl.v. Gustav Fischer, Jena   Lith.Anst.v.E.Giltsch,Jena

RHEGMATODES.

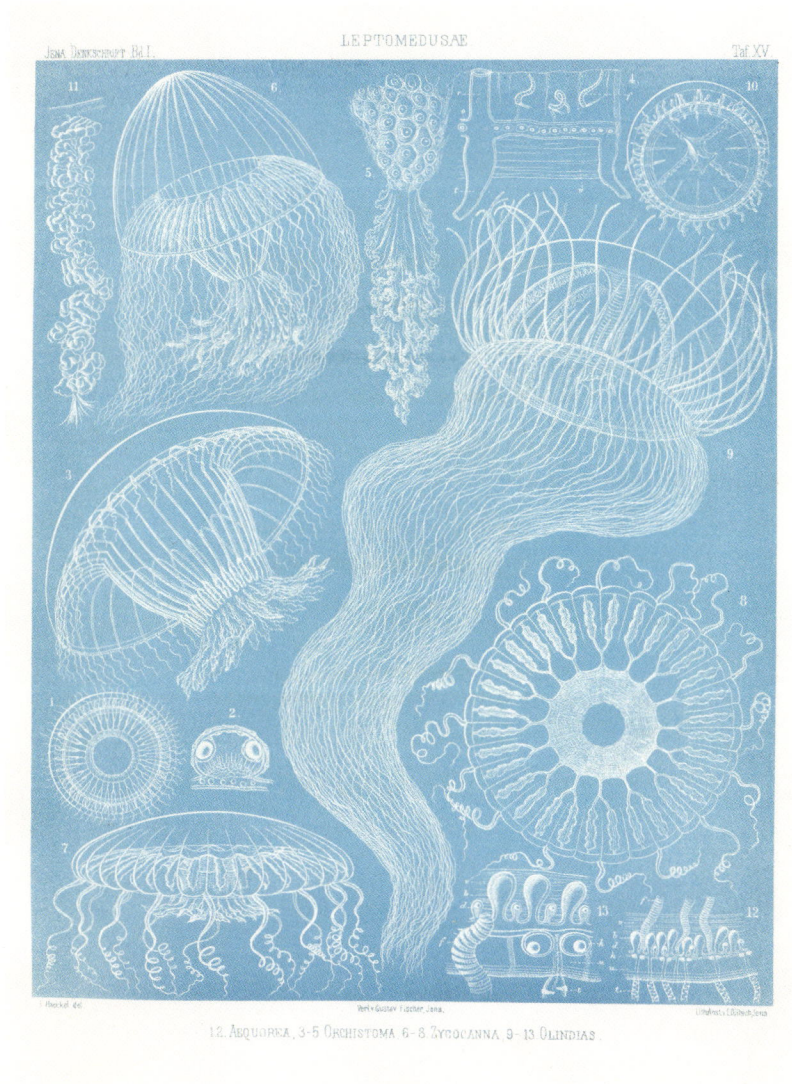

PLATE 14

1–3 Polycanna germanica, HAECKEL – *Aequorea forskalea* PÉRON & LESUEUR, 1810 Many-ribbed jellyfish

4–7 Polycanna fungina, HAECKEL – *Aequorea forskalea* PÉRON & LESUEUR, 1810 Many-ribbed jellyfish

PLATE 15

1–2 Aequorea discus (?), HAECKEL – *Aequorea forskalea* PÉRON & LESUEUR, 1810? | 3–5 Orchistoma Steenstrupii, HAECKEL – *Orchistoma pileus* (LESSON, 1843) | 6–7 Zygocannula diploconus, HAECKEL – *Zygocanna diploconus* (HAECKEL, 1879) | 8 Zygocanna costata, HAECKEL – *Zygocanna pleuronota* (PÉRON & LESUEUR, 1810) | 9–13 Olindias Mülleri, HAECKEL – *Olindias phosphorica* (DELLE CHIAJE, 1841) Cigar jellyfish

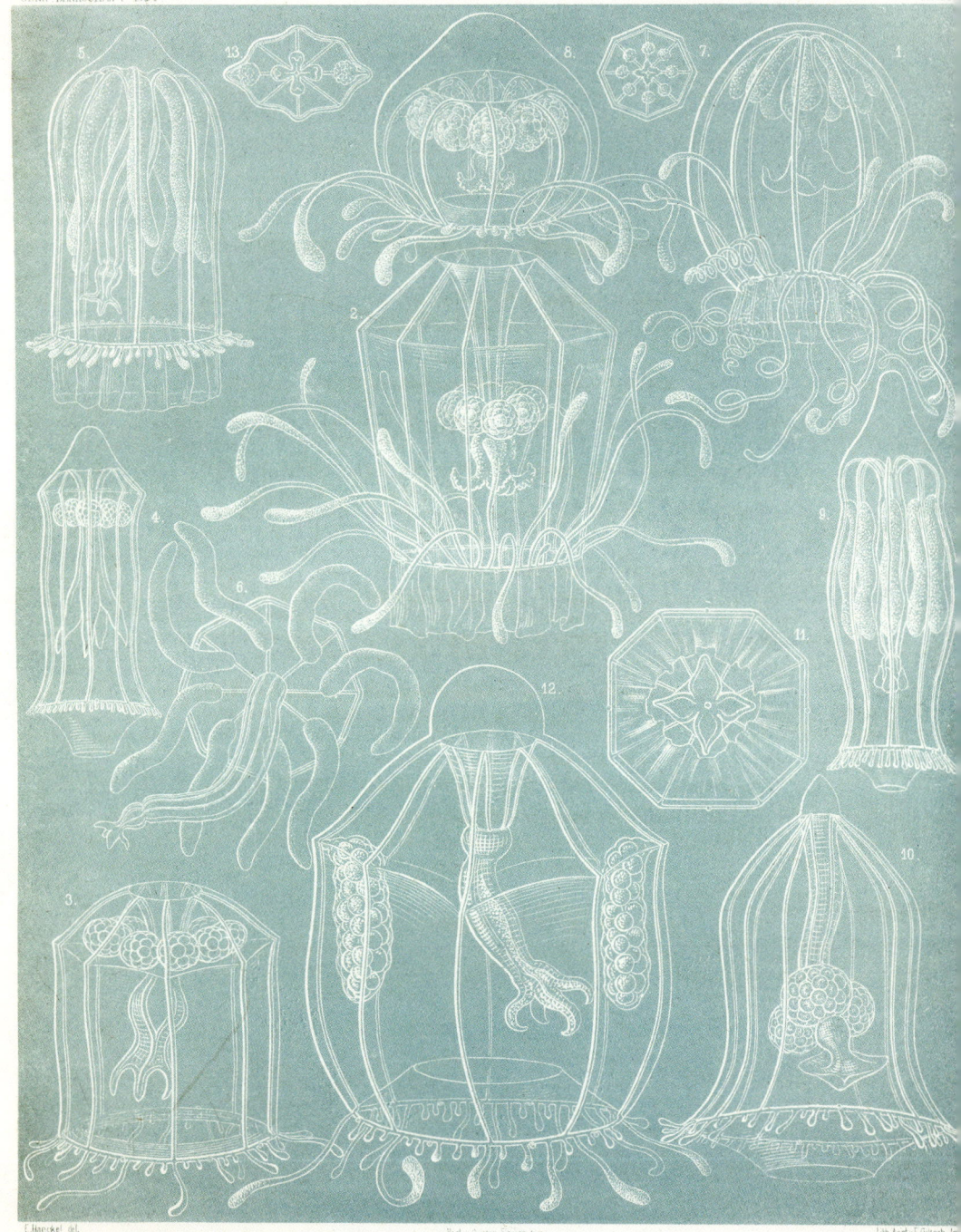

1. Aglaurella, 2-4. Aglaura, 5-8. Circella, 9. Circetta, 10-11. Stauraglaura, 12-13. Persa

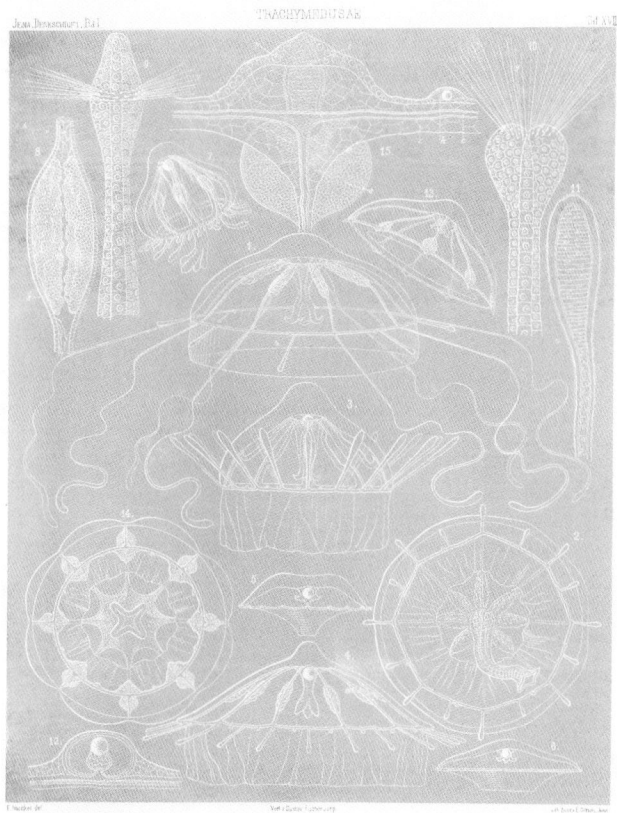

PLATE 16

1 Aglaura Nausicaa, HAECKEL – *Aglaura hemistoma* PÉRON & LESUEUR, 1810 | **2 Aglaura laterna**, HAECKEL – *Aglaura hemistoma* PÉRON & LESUEUR, 1810 | **3–4 Aglaura hemistoma**, PÉRON – *Aglaura hemistoma* PÉRON & LESUEUR, 1810 | **5–7 Aglantha digitalis**, HAECKEL (= Circe rosea = Circella digitalis) – *Aglantha digitale* (O. F. MÜLLER, 1776) Pink helmet **8 Aglantha globuligera**, HAECKEL – *Aglantha globuligera* HAECKEL, 1879 | **9 Agliscra elata**, HAECKEL (= Circetta elata) – *Aglantha elata* (HAECKEL, 1879) | **10–11 Stauraglaura tetragonima**, HAECKEL – *Stauraglaura tetragonima* HAECKEL, 1879 | **12–13 Persa lucerna**, HAECKEL – *Persa lucerna* HAECKEL, 1879

PLATE 17

1–2 Marmanema clavigerum, HAECKEL (= Rhopalonema clavigerum) – *Marmarena clavigerum* HAECKEL, 1879 (= *Rhopalonema velatum* GEGENBAUR, 1857?) | **3–6 Rhopalonema coeruleum**, HAECKEL (= Trachynema coeruleum) – *Rhopalonema coeruleum* HAECKEL, 1879 (= *Rhopalonema velatum* GEGENBAUR, 1857?) **7–12 Rhopalonema polydactylum**, HAECKEL (= Trachynema polydactylum) – *Rhopalonema polydactylum* HAECKEL, 1879 (= *Rhopalonema velatum* GEGENBAUR, 1857?) | **13–15 Marmanema mammaeforme**, HAECKEL (= Sminthonema mammaeforme) – *Sminthea mammaeforme* HAECKEL?

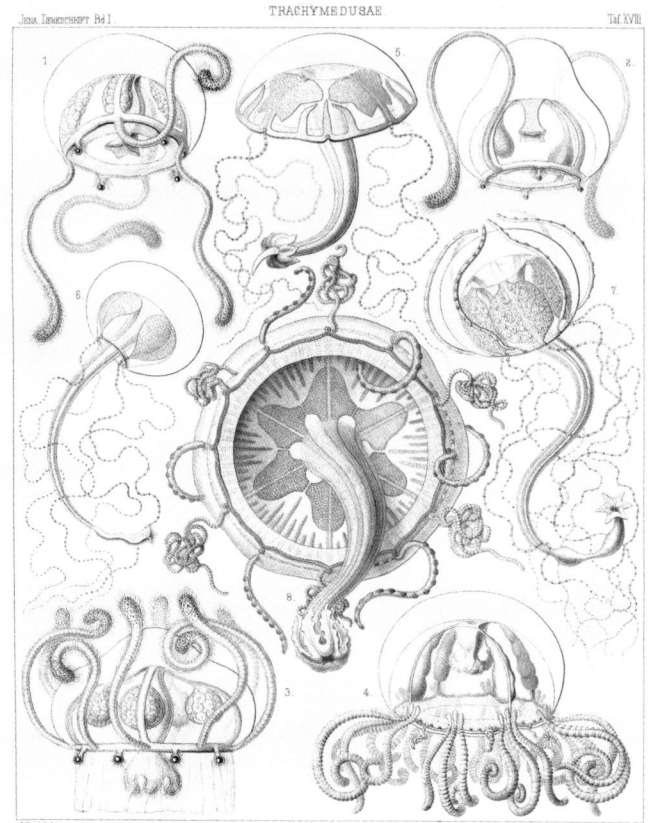

1. PETASUS, 2. DIPETASUS, 3. PETALATA, 4. GOSSEA, 5. GLOSSOCODON, 6. LIRIOPE, 7. GERYONES, 8. CARMARIS

PLATE 18

1 Petasus atavus, HAECKEL – *Petasus atavus* HAECKEL, 1879 | 2 Dipetasus digonimus, HAECKEL – *Petasus digonimus* (HAECKEL, 1879)? | 3 Petasata eucope, HAECKEL – *Petasus eucope* (HAECKEL, 1879)
4 Gossea circinata, HAECKEL – *Gossea corynetes* (GOSSE, 1853) | 5 Glossocodon Lütkenii, HAECKEL – *Liriope tetraphylla* (CHAMISSO & EYSENHARDT, 1821)? | 6 Liriope cerasus, HAECKEL – *Liriope tetraphylla* (CHAMISSO & EYSENHARDT, 1821)? | 7 Geryones elephas, HAECKEL – (= *Geryonia proboscidalis* (FORSSKÅL, 1775)?)
8 Carmaris Giltschii, HAECKEL – *Carmaris giltschi* HAECKEL, 1879 (= *Geryonia proboscidalis* (FORSSKÅL, 1775)?)

PLATE 19

1 Cunantha primigenia, HAECKEL – *Aegina* sp. | 2 Cunoctantha polygonia, HAECKEL – *Cunina polygonia* (HAECKEL, 1879) | 3 Cunina rubiginosa, HAECKEL – *Cunina rhododactyla* (= *Pegantha rubiginosa*)
4-7 Pegantha triloba, HAECKEL – *Pegantha triloba* HAECKEL, 1879 | 8-9 Aeginura myosura, HAECKEL – *Aeginura grimaldii* MAAS, 1904 | 10 Solmundus tetralinus, HAECKEL – *Aegina citrea* ESCHSCHOLTZ, 1829
Golf tee medusa | 11 Solmoneta aureola, HAECKEL – *Pegantha aureola* (HAECKEL, 1879) (nomen dubium)
12 Solmaris Godeffroyi, HAECKEL – *Pegantha godeffroyi* (HAECKEL, 1879) (nomen dubium)

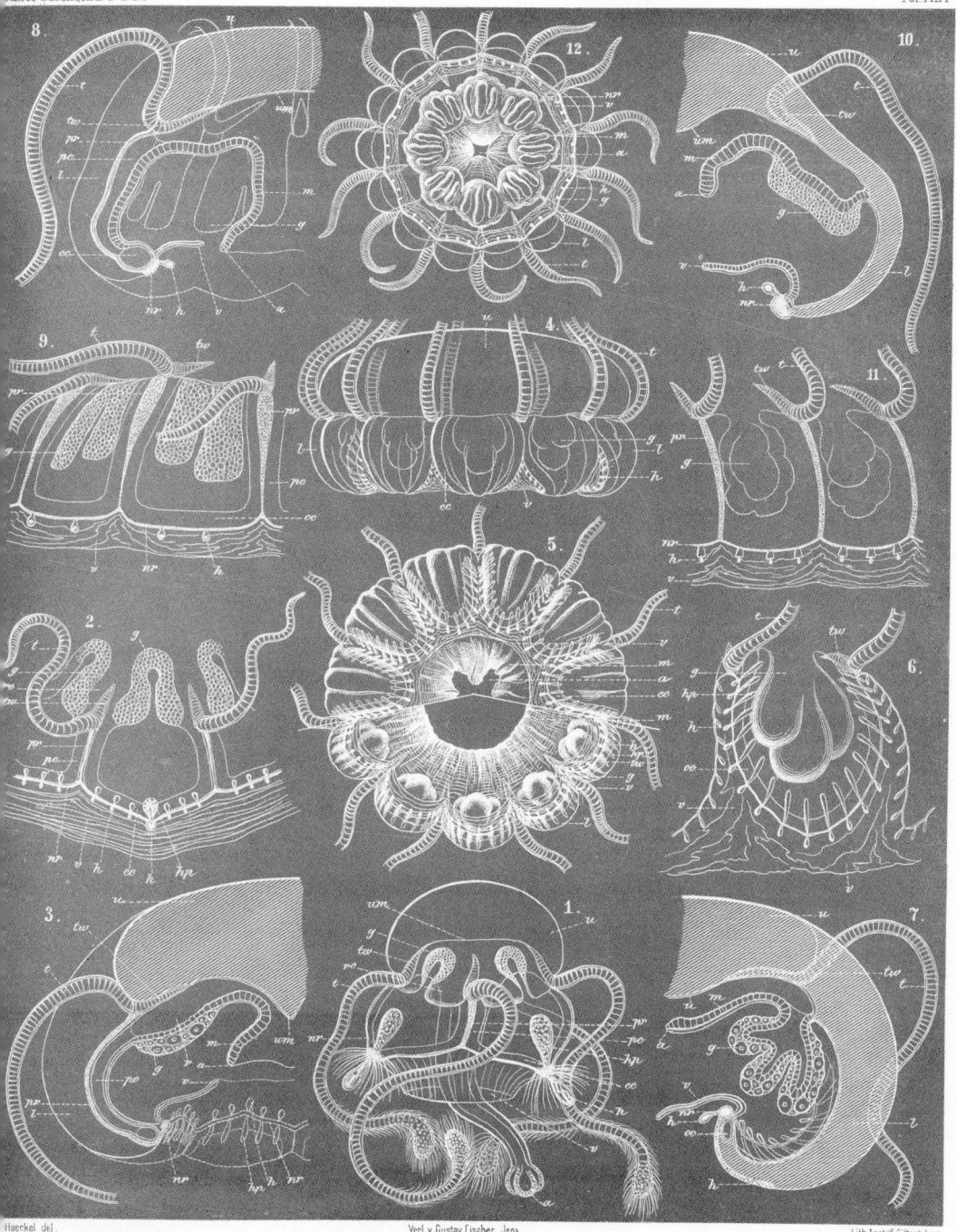

1.Cunantha, 2.Cunoctantha, 3.Cunina, 4—7.Pegantha, 8.9.Aeginura, 10.Solmundus, 11.Solmarium, 12.Solmaris.

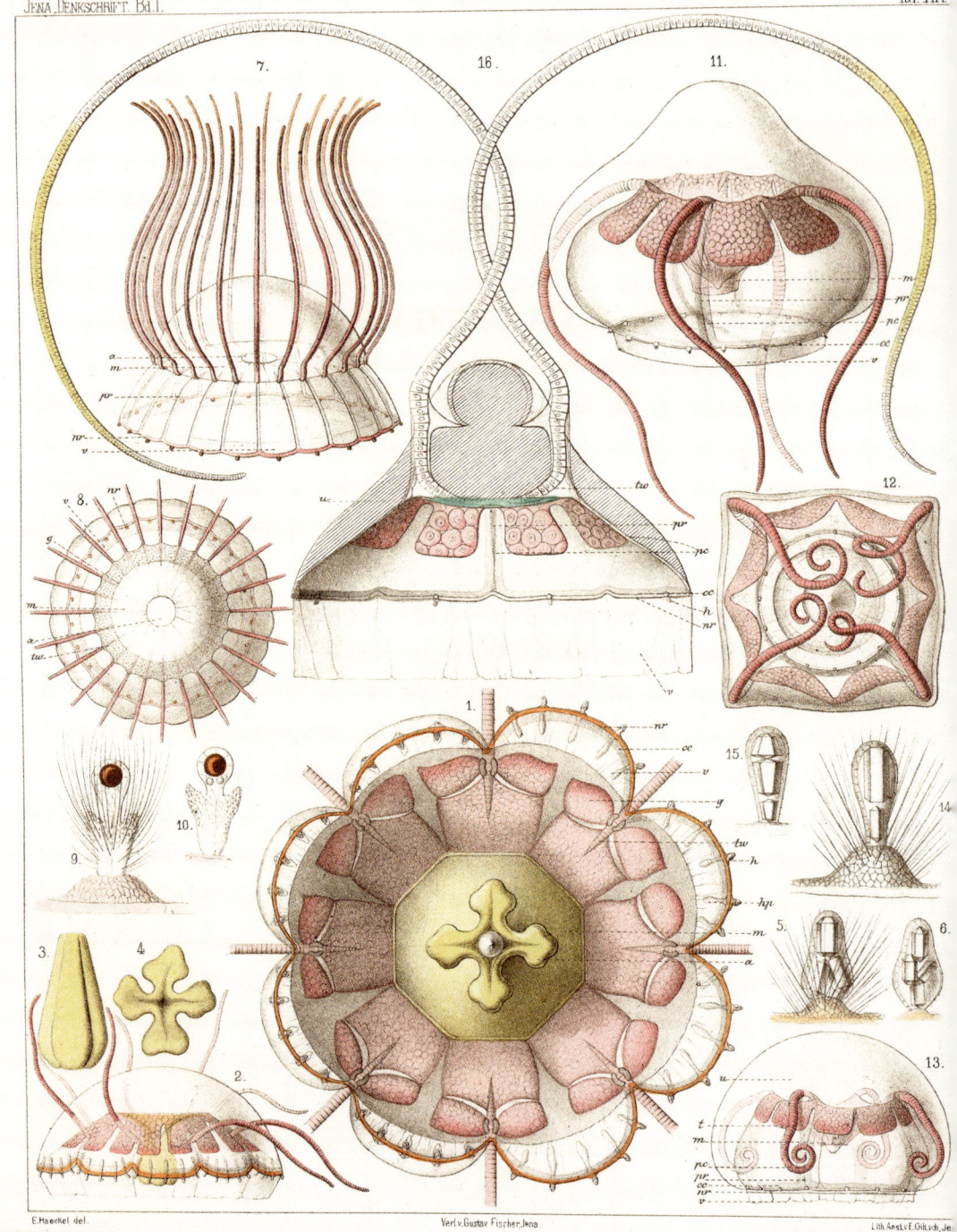

E.Haeckel del.   Verl.v.Gustav Fischer,Jena.   Lith.Anst.v.E.Giltsch, Je.

1-6 CUNINA, 7-10 AEGINETA, 11-15 AEGINA, 16 AEGINOPSIS.

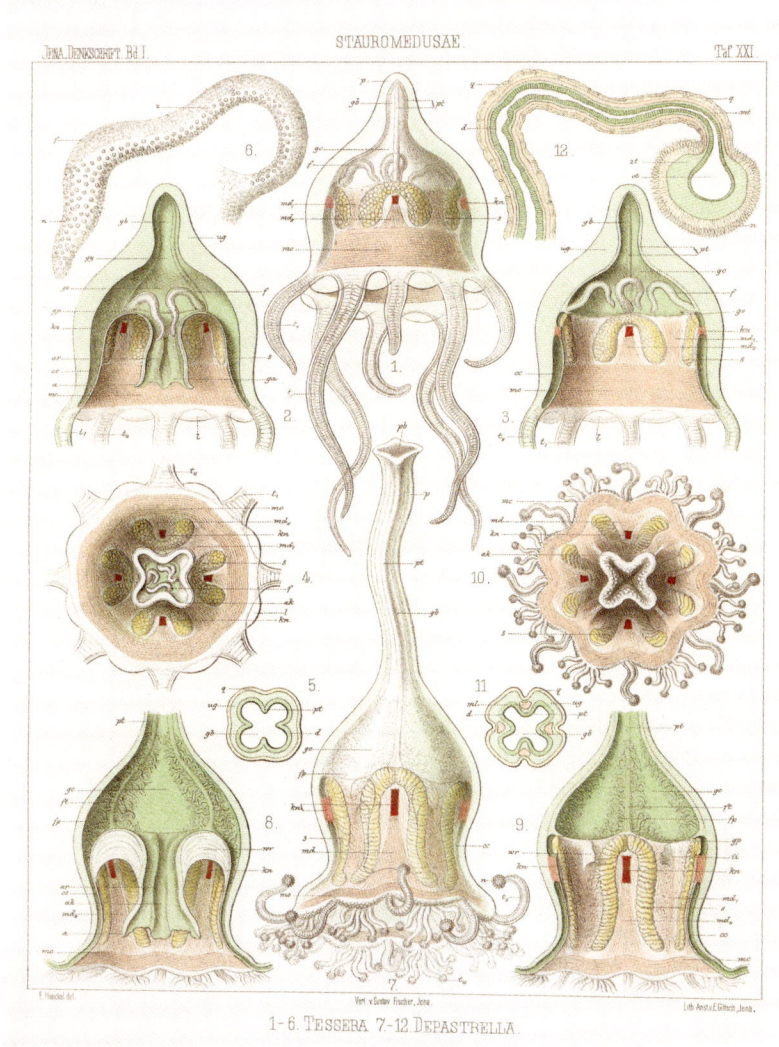

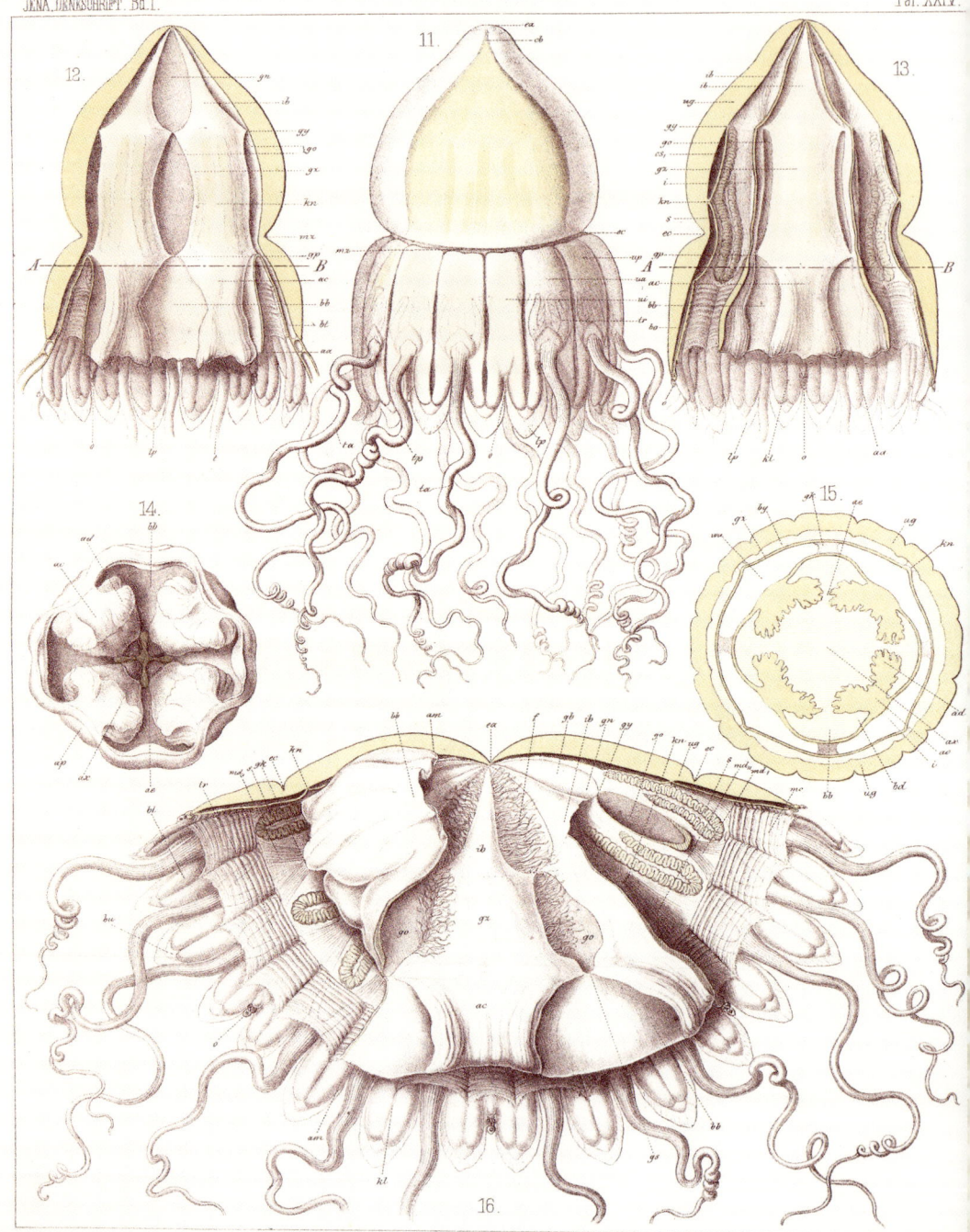

PERIPHYLLA.

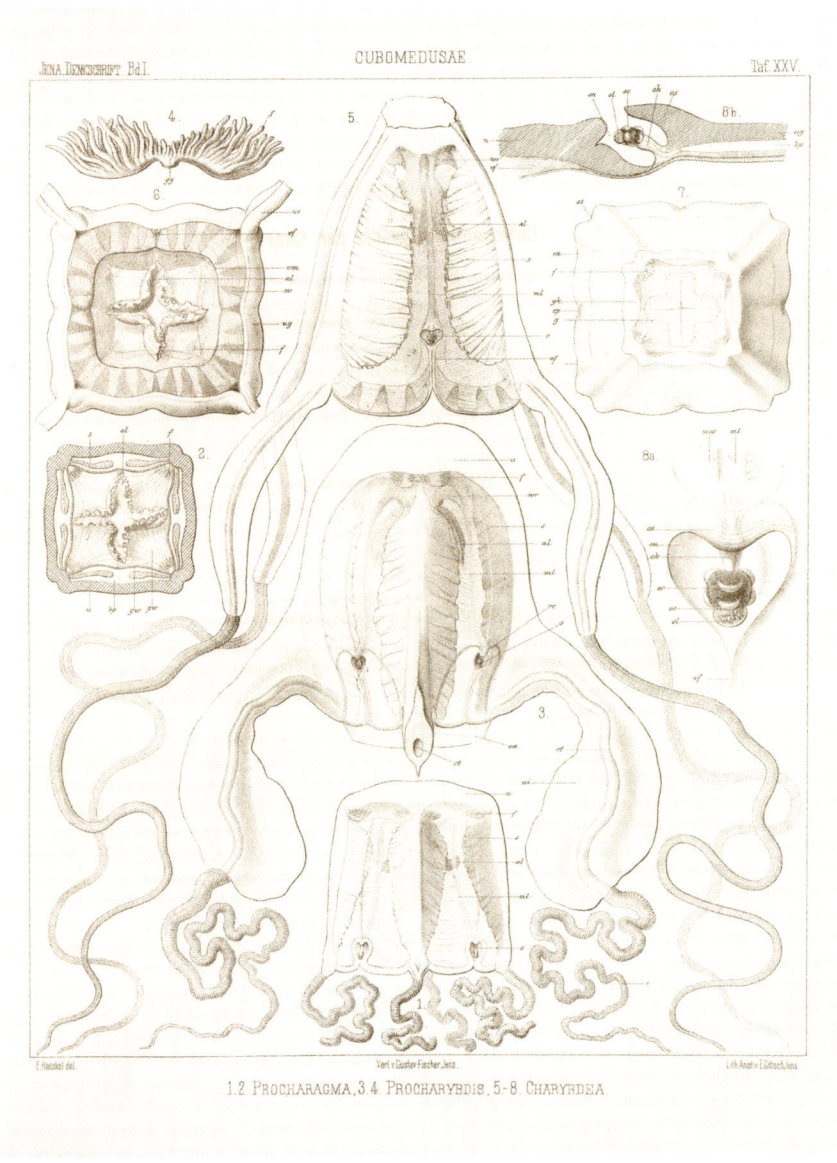

CUBOMEDUSAE.

1.2 PROCHARAGMA, 3.4. PROCHARYBDIS, 5-8. CHARYBDEA.

PLATE 24

Periphylla hyacinthina, STEENSTRUP – *Periphylla periphylla* (PÉRON & LESUEUR, 1810) Merchant-cap

PLATE 25

1-2 Procharagma prototypus, HAECKEL – *Procharagma prototypus* HAECKEL, 1879
3-4 Procharybdis tetraptera, HAECKEL – *Alatina tetraptera* (HAECKEL, 1880)
5-8 Charybdea pyramis, HAECKEL – *Carybdea alata* REYNAUD, 1830?

Jena. Denkschrift. Bd I   Taf XXVI

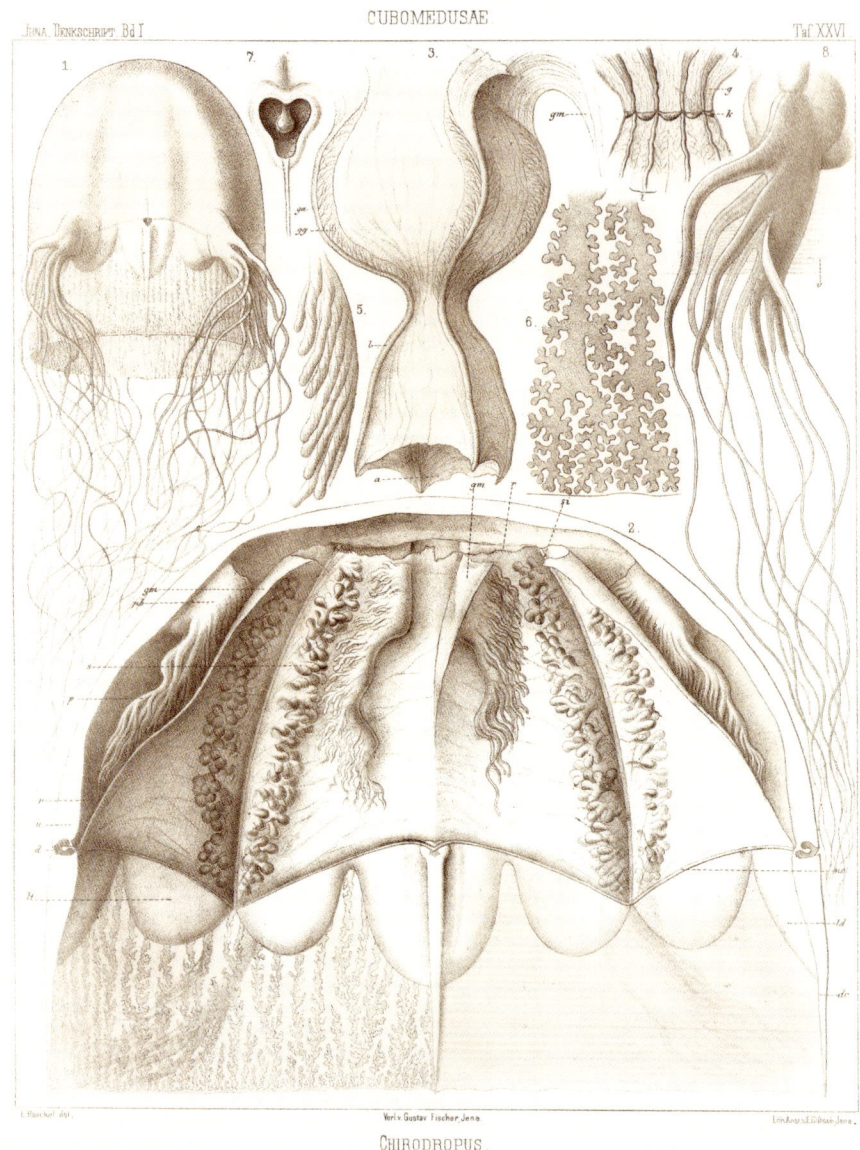

CHIRODROPUS.

PLATE 26

Chirodropus gorilla, HAECKEL – *Chirodropus gorilla* HAECKEL, 1880

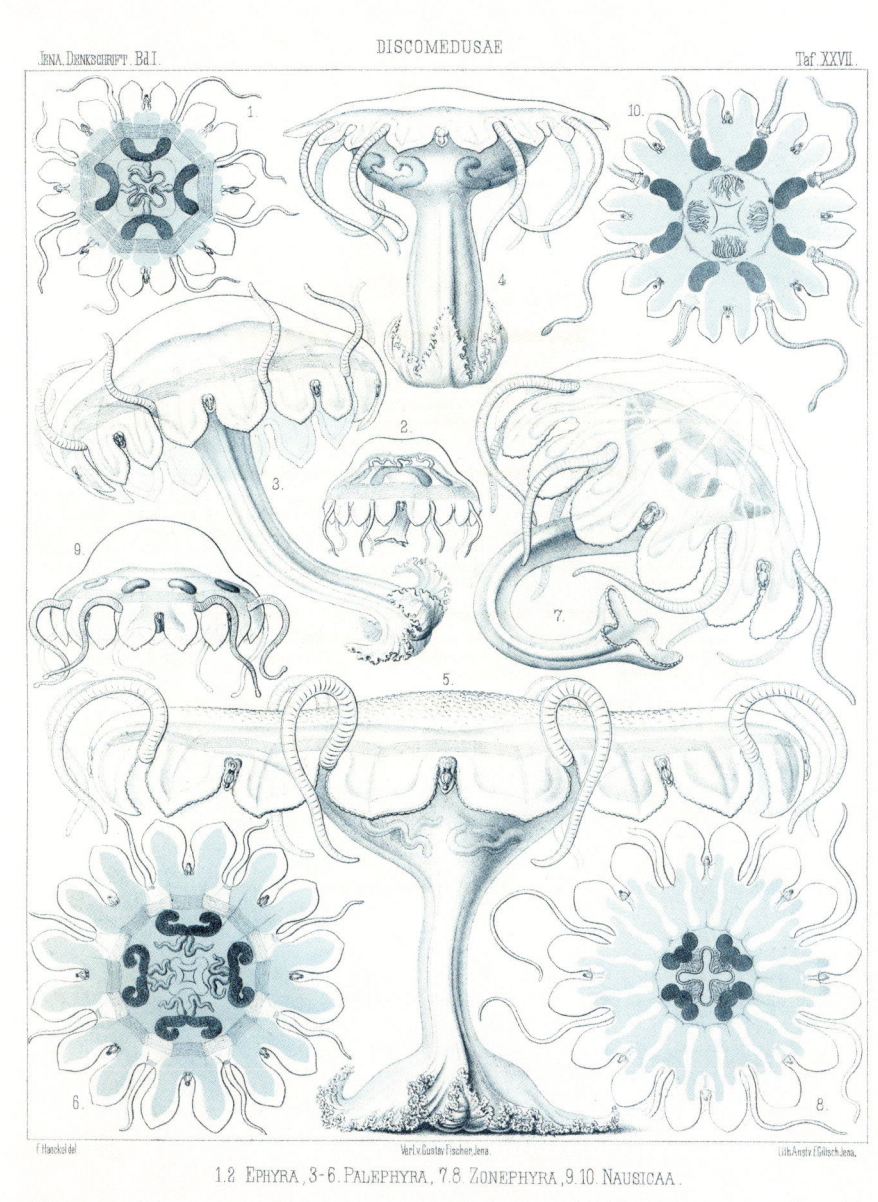

DISCOMEDUSAE

F. Haeckel del.   Verl. v. Gustav Fischer, Jena.   Lith.Anst.v.J.Götsch,Jena.

1.2 EPHYRA, 3–6. PALEPHYRA, 7.8. ZONEPHYRA, 9.10. NAUSICAA.

PLATE 27

1–2 Ephyra prometor, ʜᴀᴇᴄᴋᴇʟ – *Palephyra antiqua* ʜᴀᴇᴄᴋᴇʟ, 1880? | 3–6 Palephyra primigenia, ʜᴀᴇᴄᴋᴇʟ –
Palephyra antiqua ʜᴀᴇᴄᴋᴇʟ, 1880 | 7–8 Zonephyra zonaria, ʜᴀᴇᴄᴋᴇʟ – *Palephyra pelagica* (ʜᴀᴇᴄᴋᴇʟ, 1880)
9–10 Nausicaa Phaeacum, ʜᴀᴇᴄᴋᴇʟ – *Nausicaa phaeacum* ʜᴀᴇᴄᴋᴇʟ, 1879

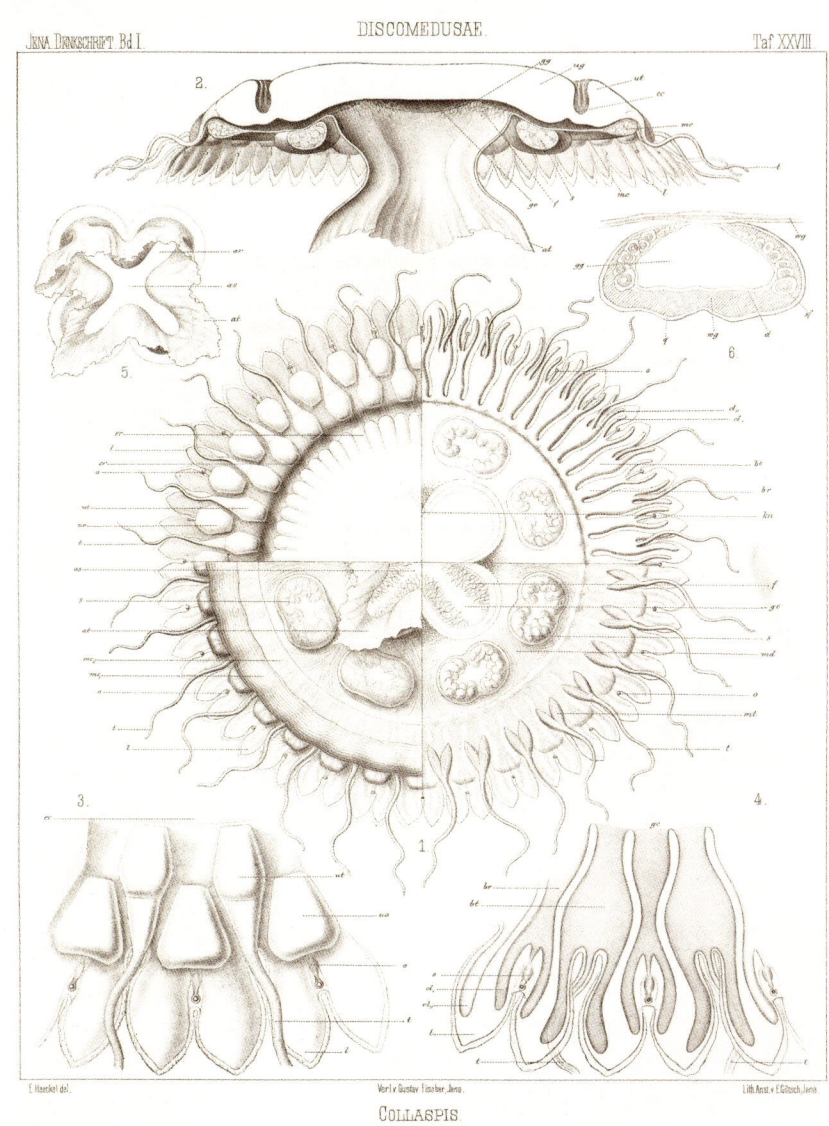

COLLASPIS

PLATE 28
Collaspis Achillis, HAECKEL – *Atolla wyvillei* HAECKEL, 1880 Wyville's crownjelly

PLATE 29
1-3 Linantha lunulata, HAECKEL – *Linantha lunulata* HAECKEL, 1880 (nomen dubium)
4-6 Linerges mercurius, HAECKEL – *Linuche unguiculata* (SCHWARTZ, 1788) Thimble jellyfish

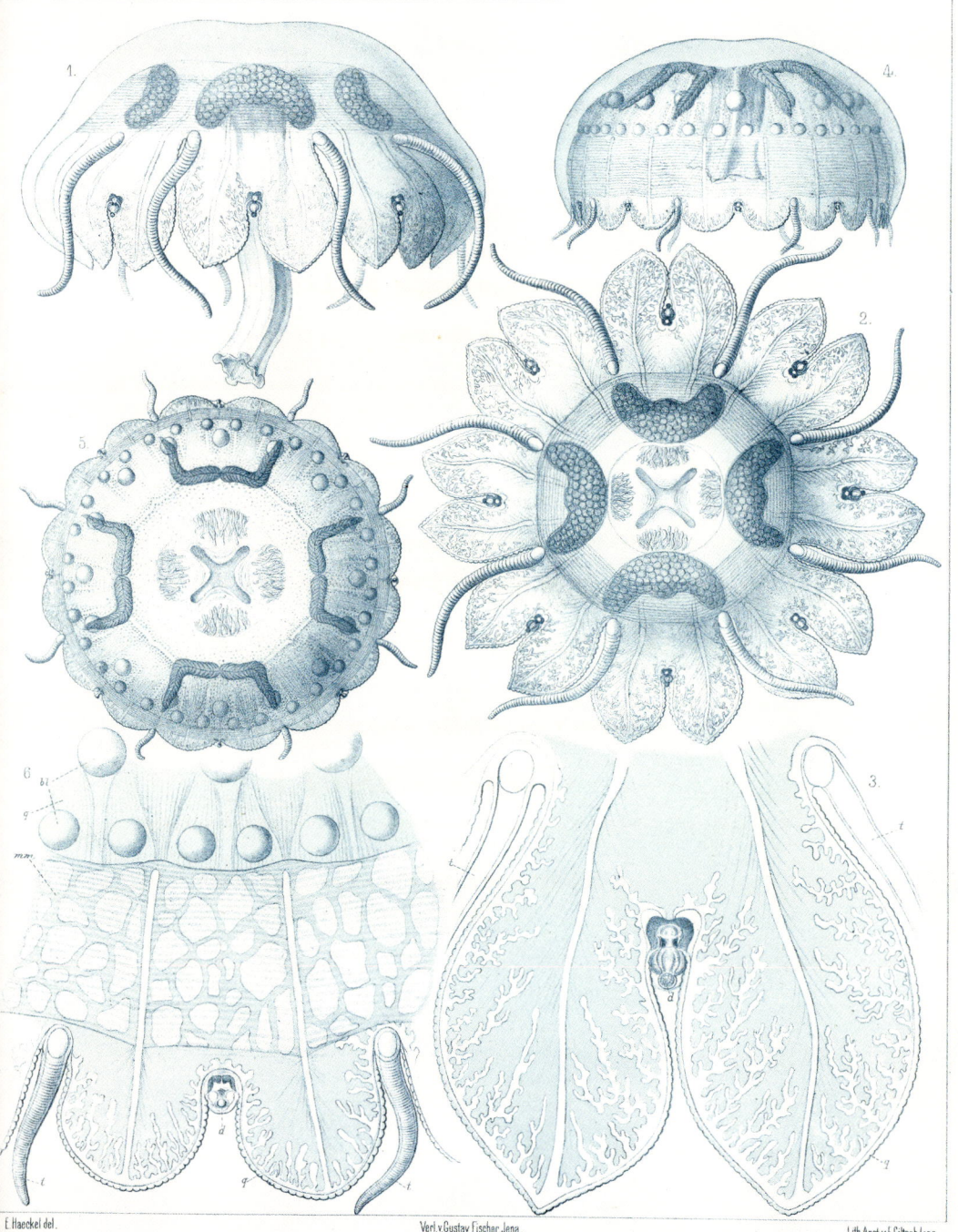

1.-3. LINANTHA, 4.-6. LINERGES.

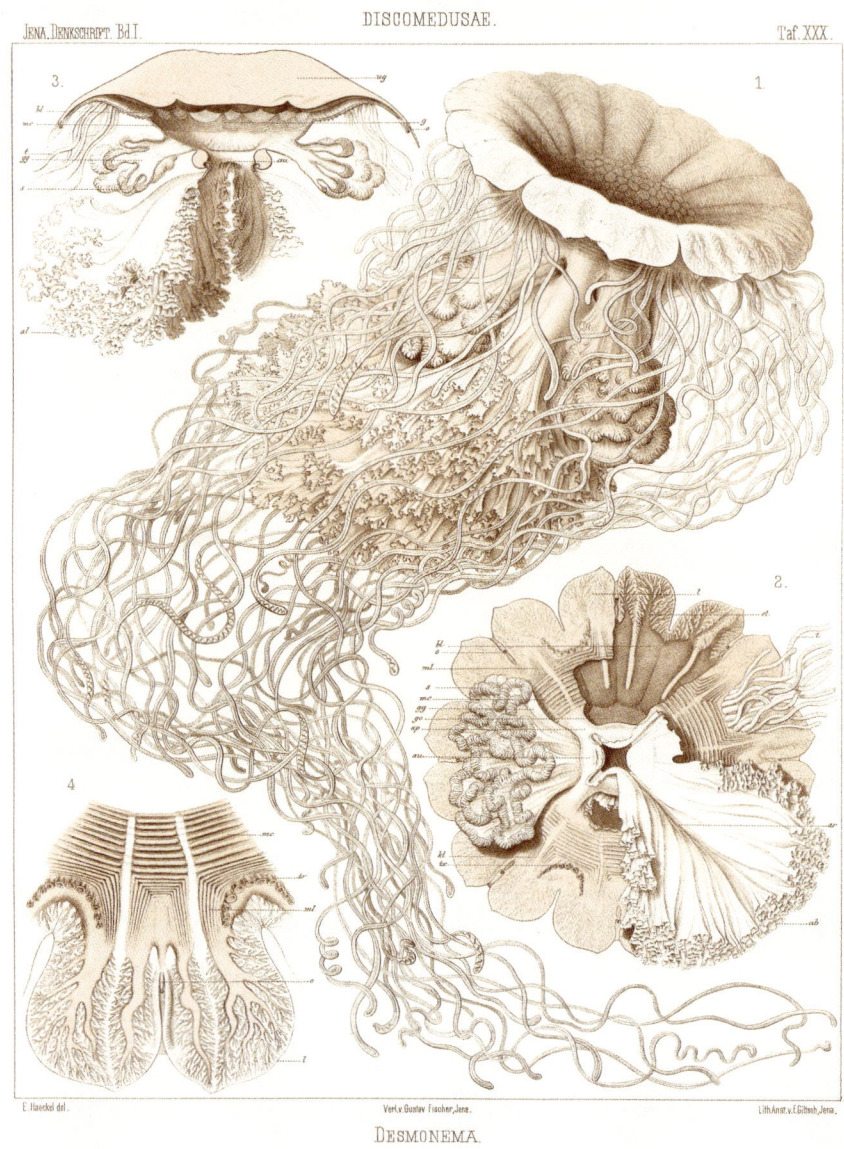

DESMONEMA.

PLATE 30
Desmonema Annasethe, HAECKEL – *Cyanea? annasethe* HAECKEL, 1880 Lion's mane jellyfish

PLATE 31
Chrysaora mediterranea, HAECKEL – *Chrysaora hysoscella* LINNAEUS, 1767 Compass jellyfish

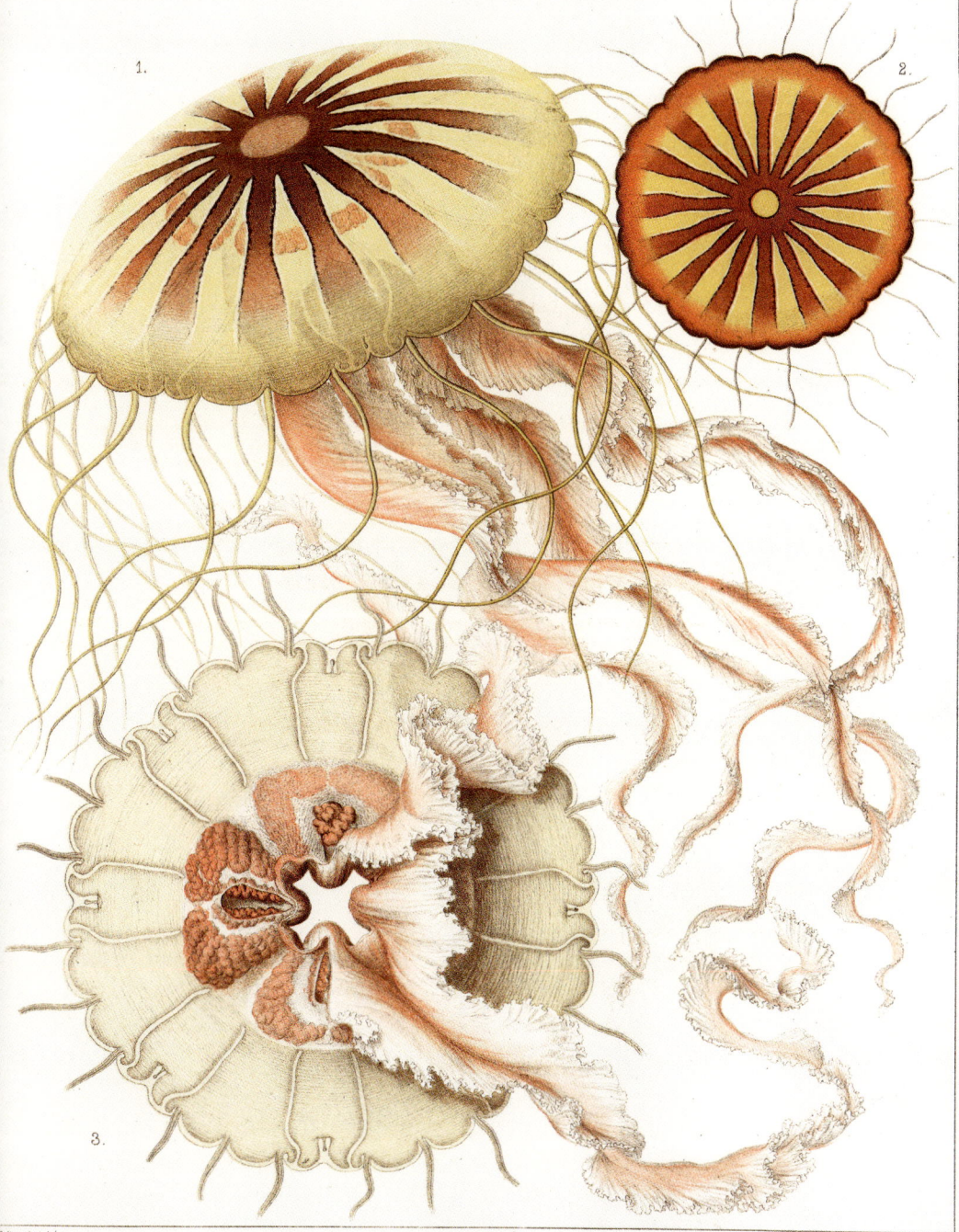

POLYBOSTRICHA.

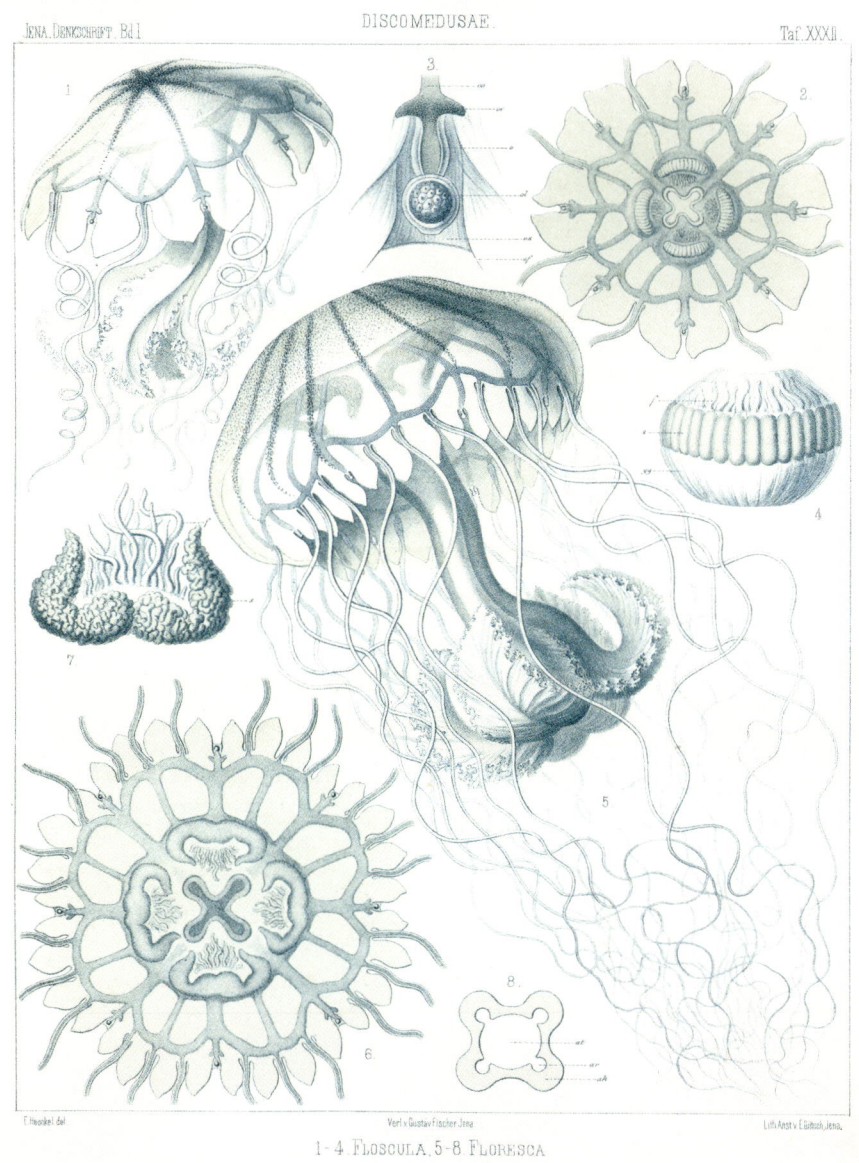

Jena.Denkschrift. Bd.1. DISCOMEDUSAE. Taf.XXXII.

1–4 FLOSCULA. 5–8 FLORESCA.

PLATE 32
1–4 Floscula Promethea, HAECKEL – *Floresca parthenia* HAECKEL, 1880?
5–8 Floresca Parthenia – *Floresca parthenia* HAECKEL, 1880

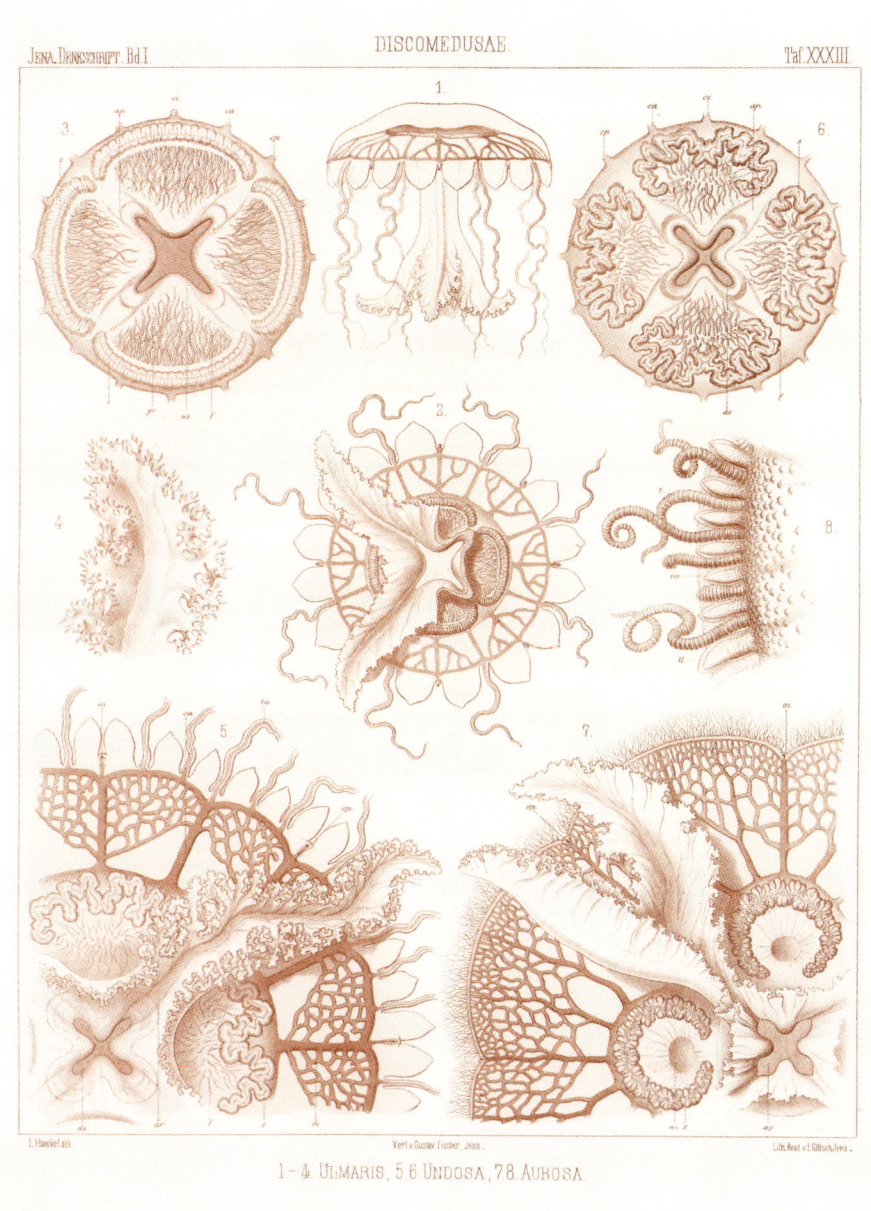

PLATE 33
1-4 Ulmaris prototypus, HAECKEL – *Ulmaris prototypus* HAECKEL, 1880
5-6 Undosa undulata, HAECKEL – *Undosa undulata* HAECKEL, 1880 (after ROSS)
7-8 Aurosa furcata, HAECKEL – *Aurosa furcata* HAECKEL, 1880

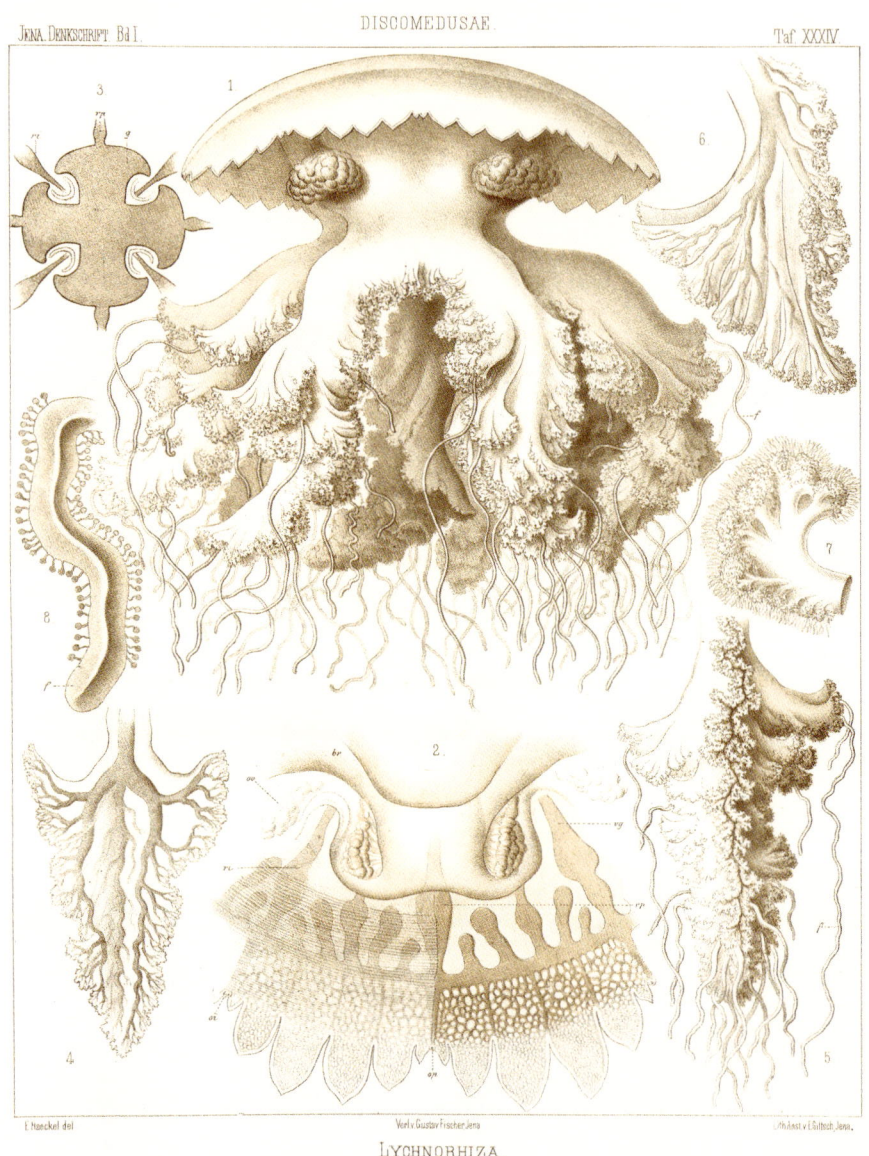

LYCHNORHIZA.

PLATE 34
Lychnorhiza lucerna, HAECKEL – *Lychnorhiza lucerna* HAECKEL, 1880

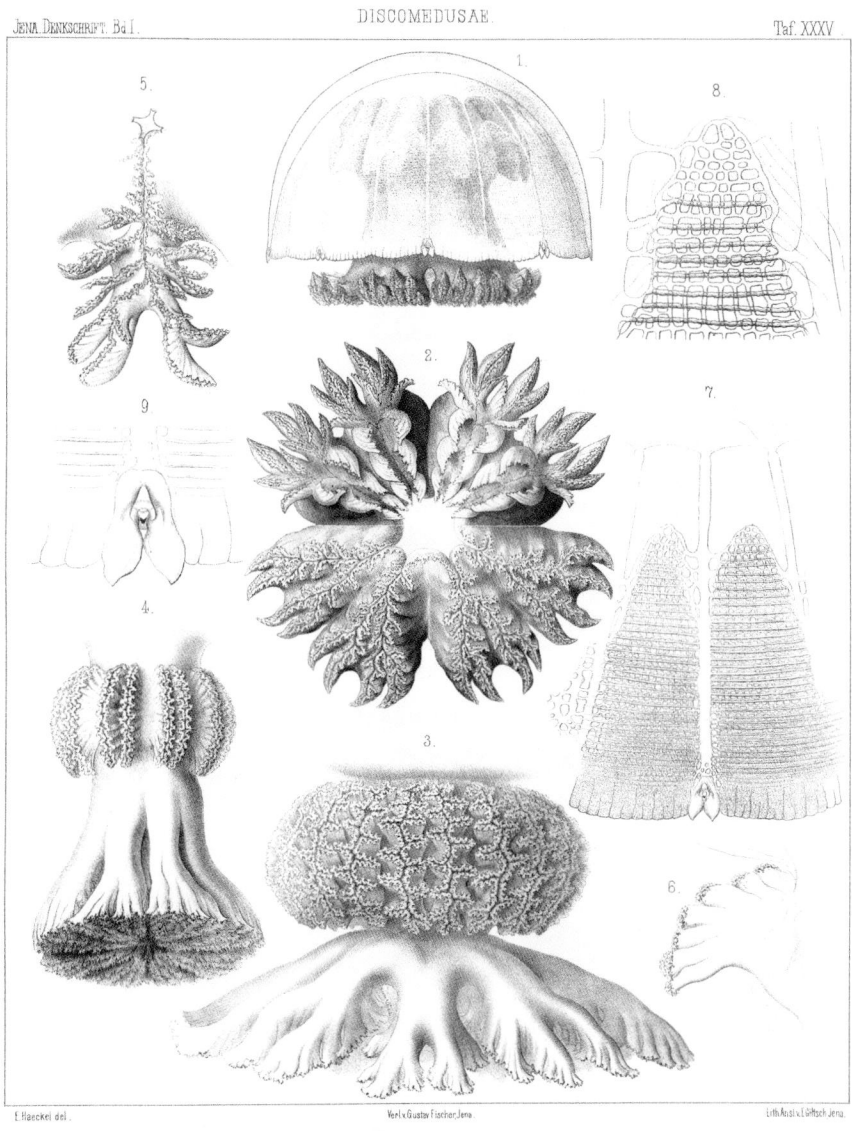

E. Haeckel del.   Verl.x.Gustav Fischer,Jena.   Lith.Anst.v.J.Wittsch.Jena.

STOMOLOPHUS.

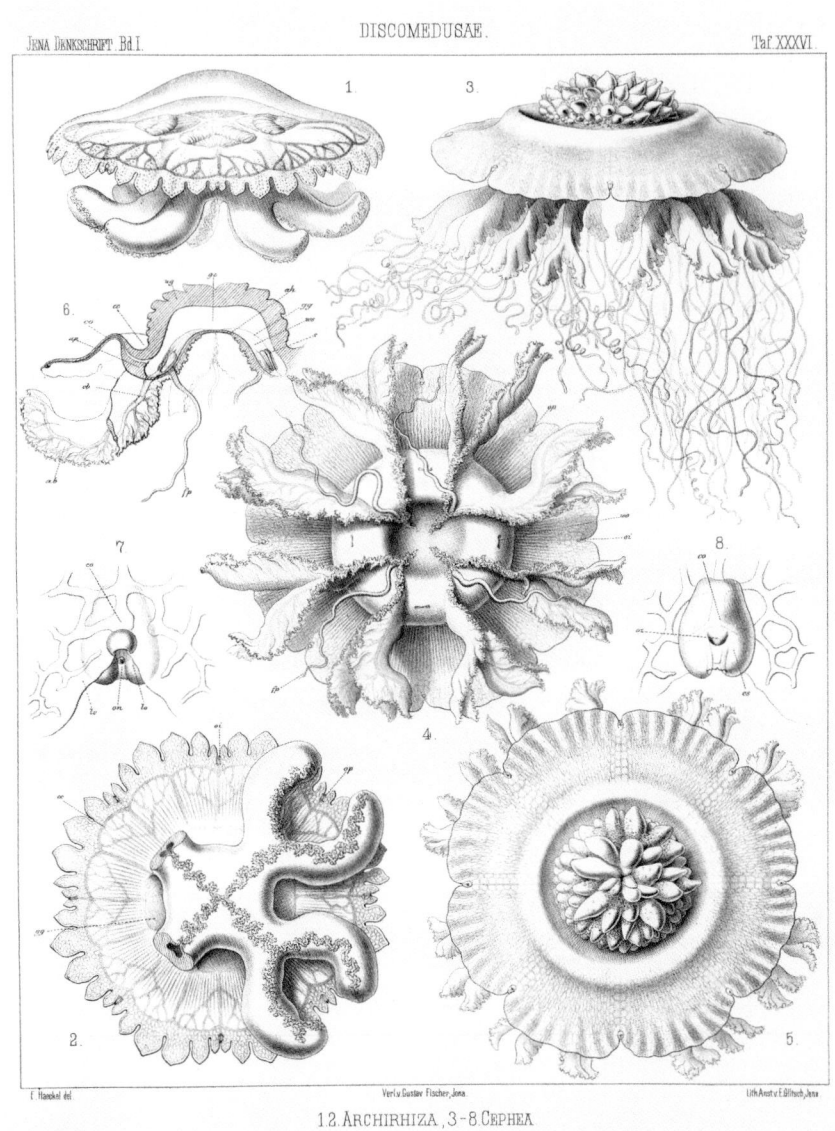

F. Haeckel del.　　　　Verl.v.Gustav Fischer,Jena.　　　　Lith.Anst.v.E.Giltsch,Jena

1.2. ARCHIRHIZA, 3-8.CEPHEA

PLATE 36
1–2 Archirhiza primordialis, HAECKEL – *Archirhiza primordialis* HAECKEL, 1880
3–8 Cephea conifera, HAECKEL – *Cephea cephea* (FORSKÅL, 1775) Crowned jellyfish, Cauliflower jellyfish, Crown sea jelly

PLATE 37
Cassiopea ornata, HAECKEL – *Cassiopea ornata* HAECKEL, 1880 Upside down jellyfish

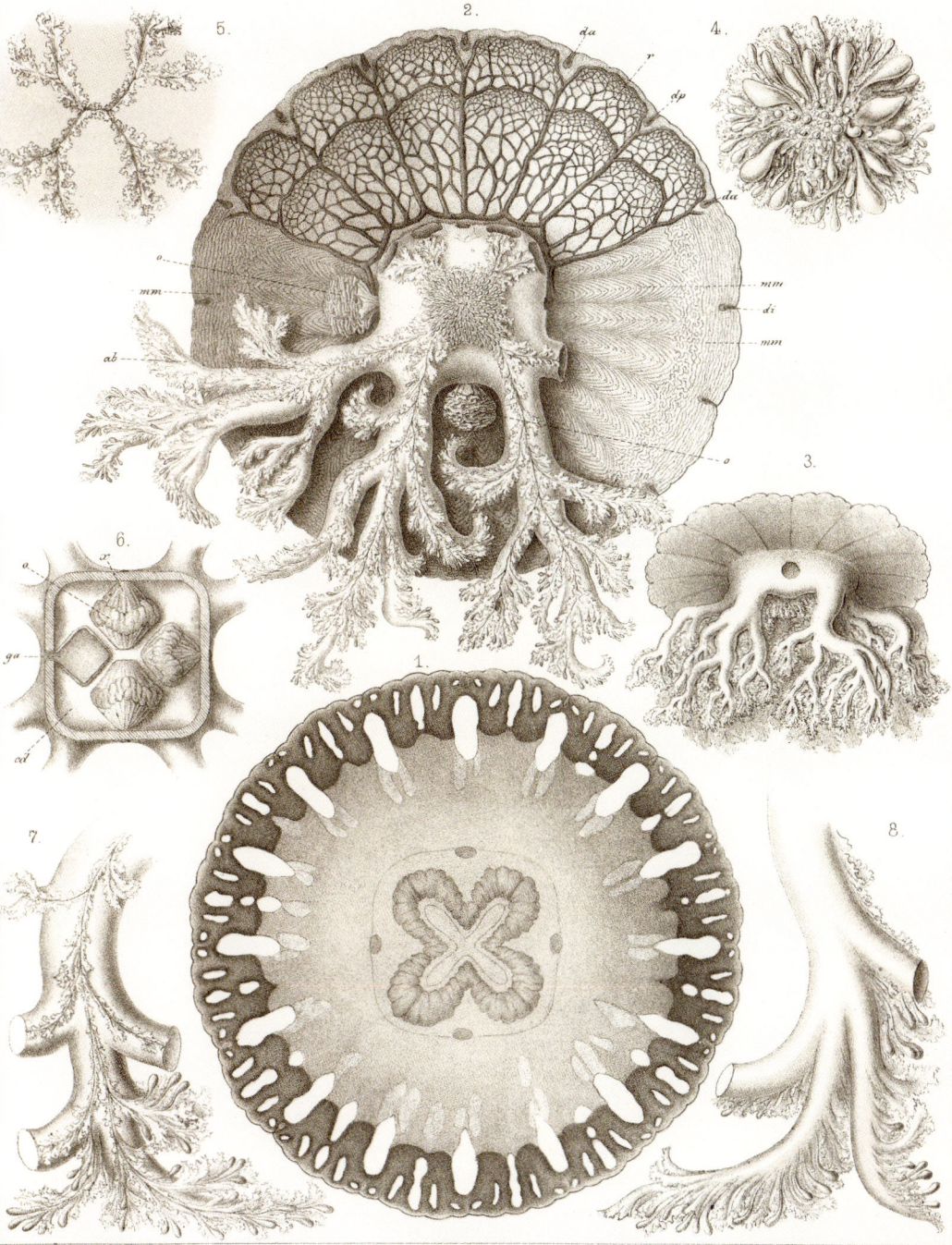

Haeckel del.   Verl.v.Gustav Fischer Jena.   Lith.Anst.v.f.Gütsch,Jena.

BRYOCLONIA.

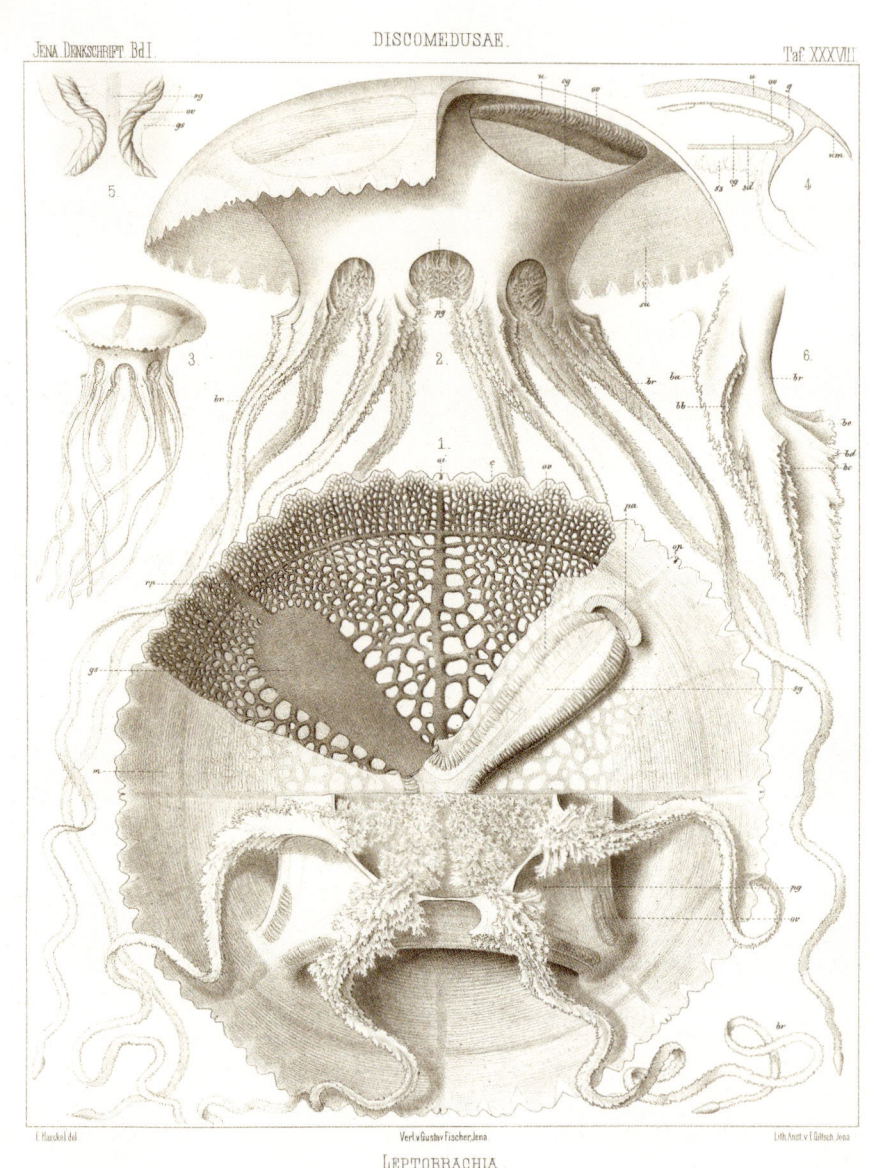

LEPTOBRACHIA.

PLATE 38

Himantostoma lorifera, HAECKEL (= *Leptobranchia lorifera* L. AGASSIZ = *Rhizostoma lorifera* EHRENBERG) — *Thysanostoma loriferum* (EHRENBERG, 1835) Purple jellyfish

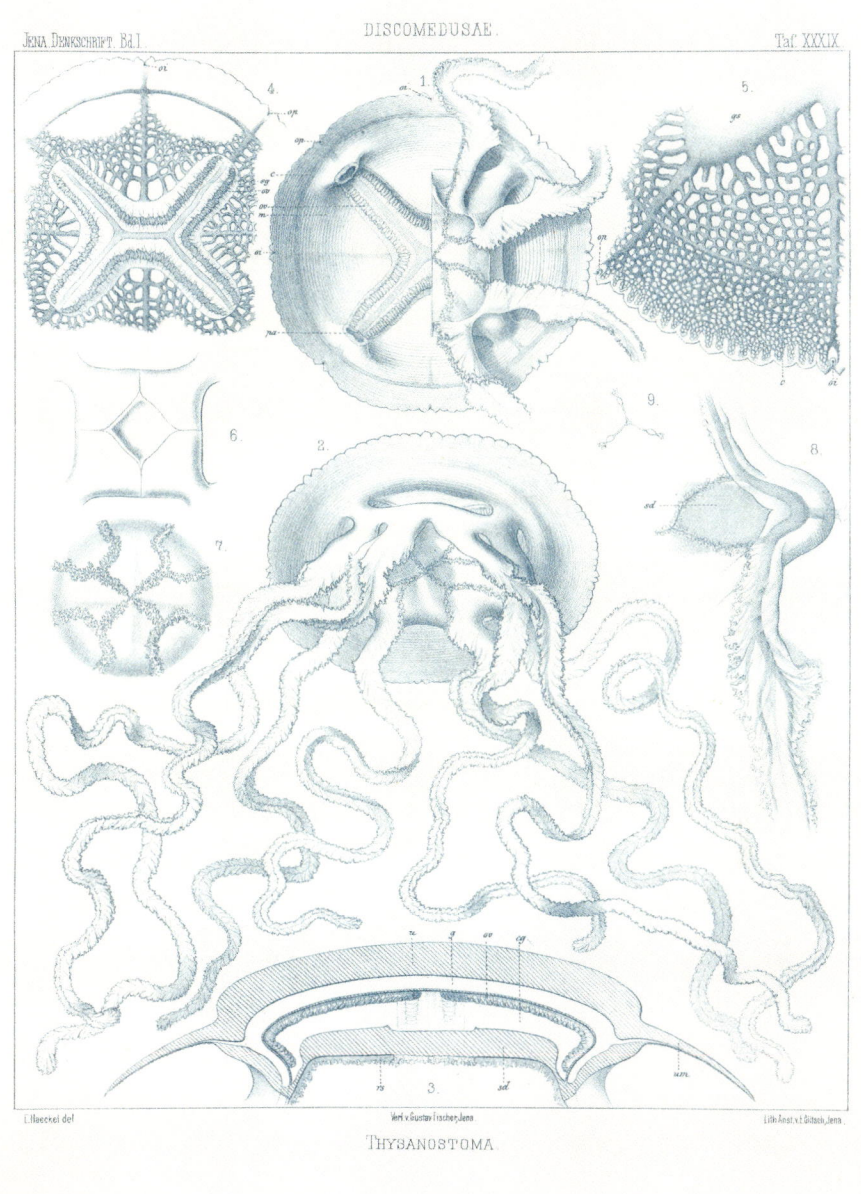

C. Haeckel del.   Verl. v. Gustav Fischer, Jena.   Lith.Anst.v.f.Gitsch, Jena.

THYSANOSTOMA.

PLATE 39

Thysanostoma thysanura, HAECKEL — *Thysanostoma thysanura* HAECKEL, 1880

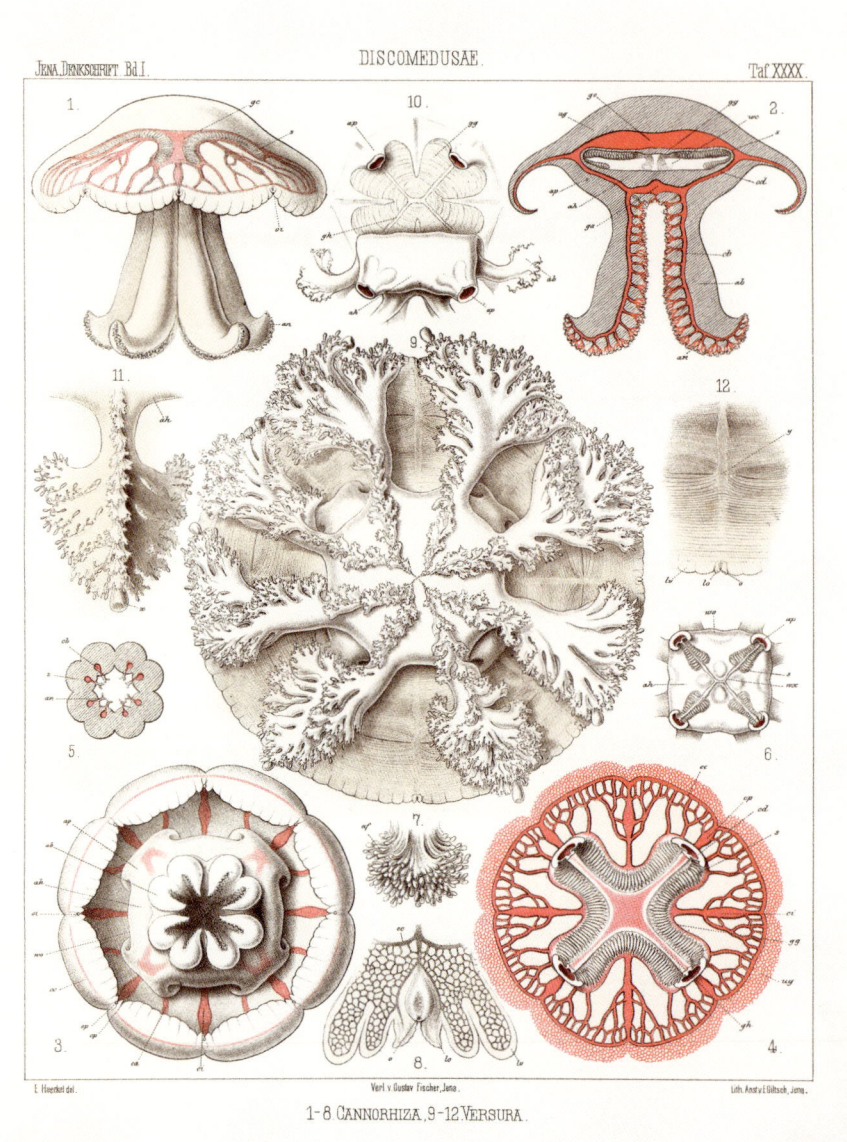

PLATE 40
1–8 Cannorhiza connexa, HAECKEL – *Cannorhiza connexa* HAECKEL, 1880
9–12 Versura palmata, HAECKEL – *Mastigias ocellatus* (MODEER, 1791)? Golden medusa, Spotted jellyfish

PLATE I
Thamnostylus dinema – *Thamnostylus dinema* HAECKEL, 1879

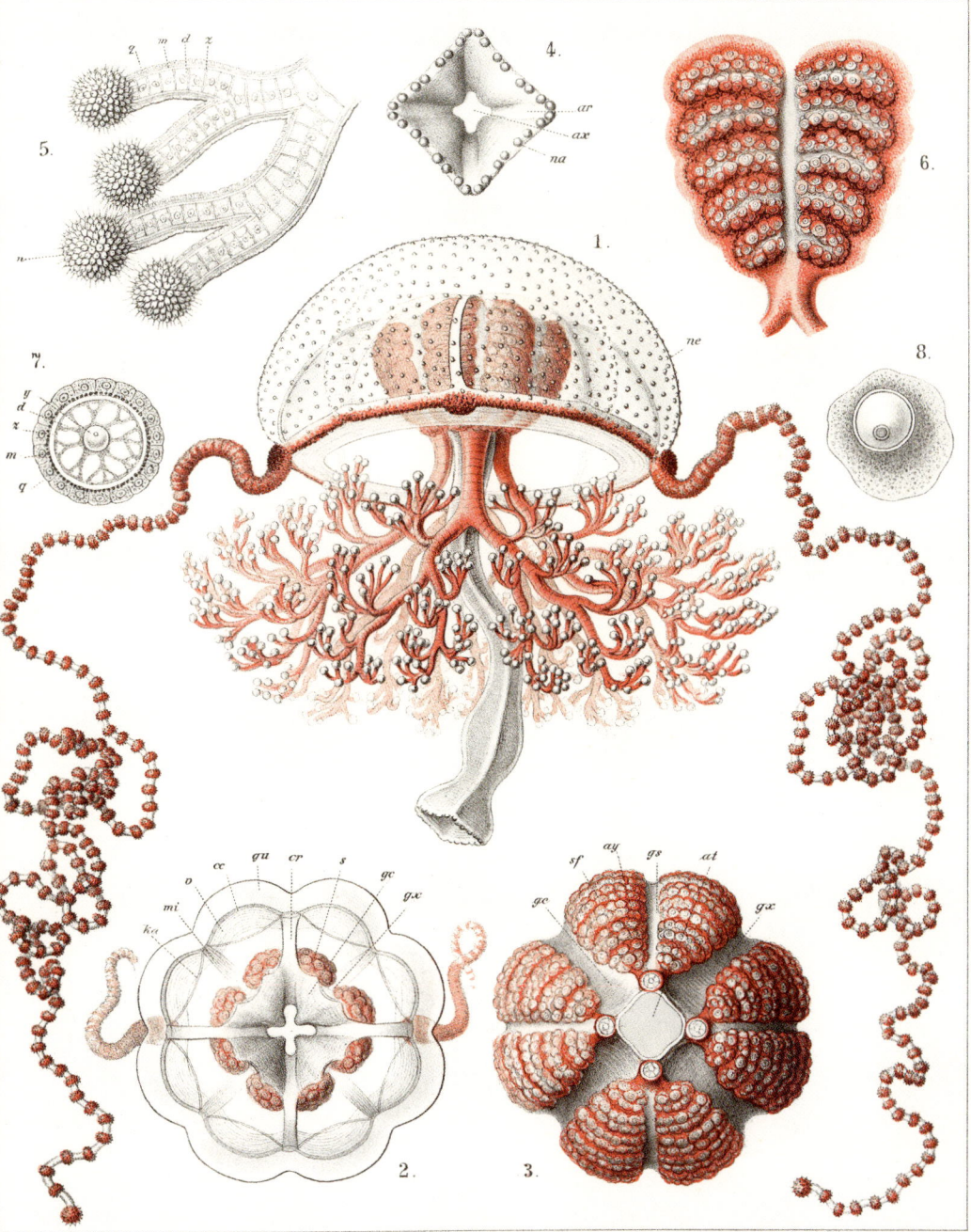

aeckel and A.Giltsch Del.

E.Giltsch,Jena,Litho&r.

THAMNOSTYLUS DINEMA.

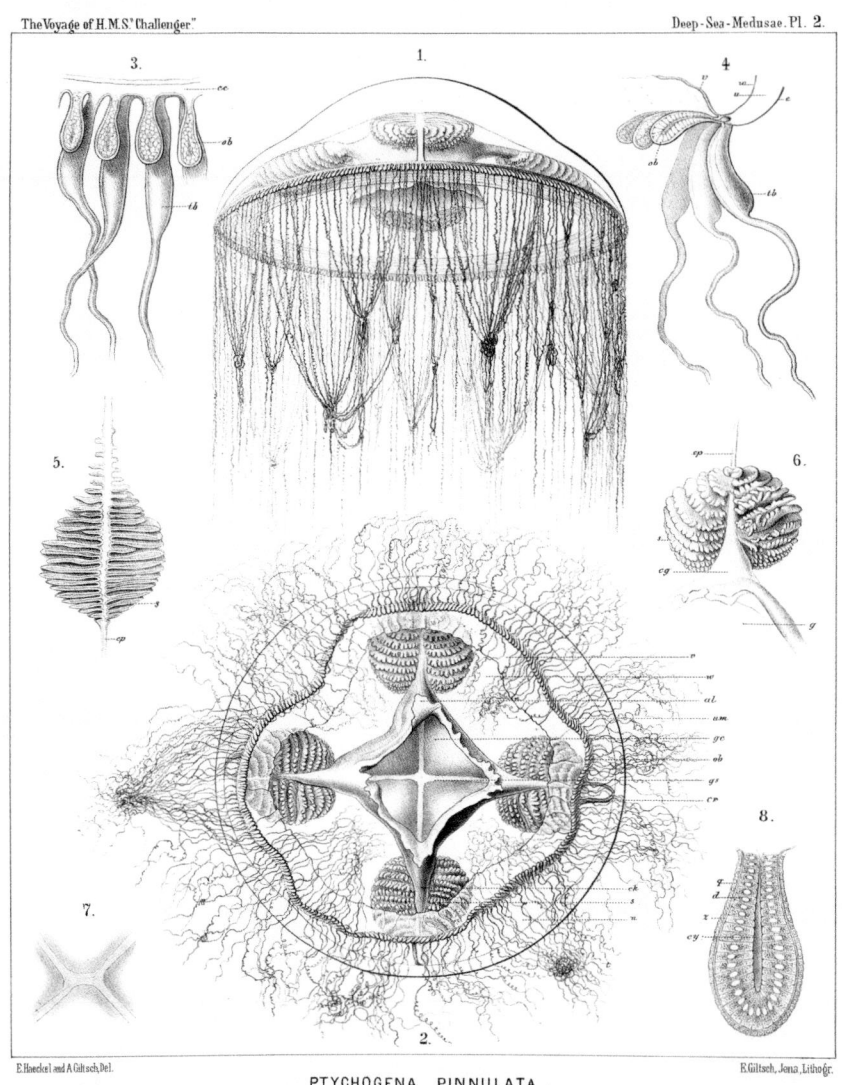

E.Haeckel and A.Giltsch,Del. F.Giltsch, Jena ,Lithogr.

PTYCHOGENA PINNULATA .

PLATE 2

Ptychogena pinnulata – *Ptychogena lactea* AGASSIZ, 1865

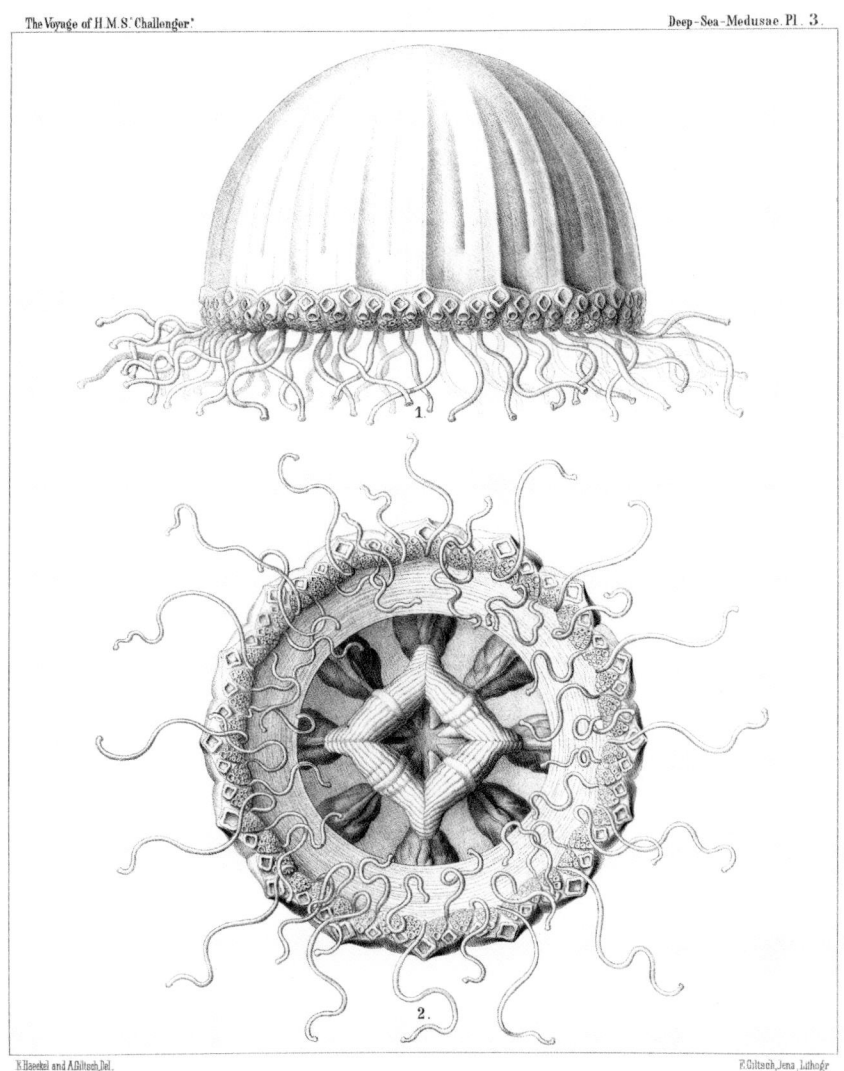

R.Haeckel and A.Giltsch,Del.

F.Giltsch, Jena, Lithogr

PECTYLLIS ARCTICA.

PLATE 3
Pectyllis arctica – *Ptychogastria polaris* ALLMAN, 1878

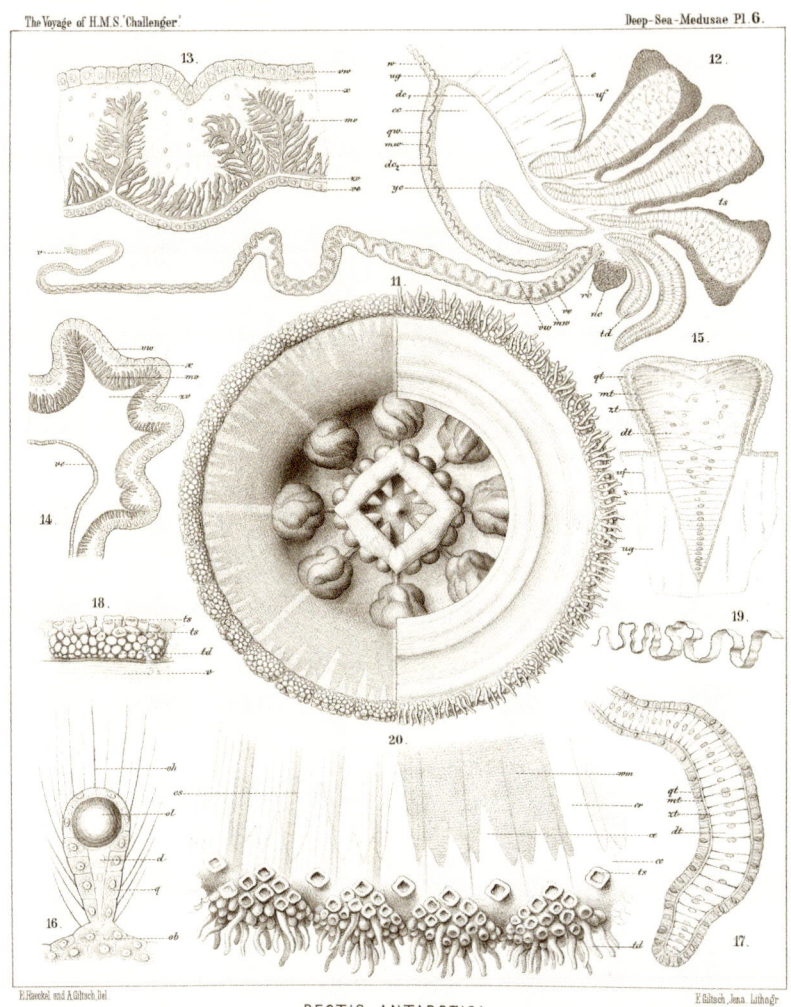

PECTIS ANTARCTICA.

E.Haeckel and A.Giltsch,Del.

F.Giltsch ,Jena ,Lithogr.

PLATE 6
Pectis antarctica –
Ptychogastria antarctica (HAECKEL, 1879)

PLATE 7
Pectanthis asteroides –
Ptychogastria asteroides (HAECKEL, 1879)

Haeckel and A.Giltsch Del.

E.Giltsch, Jena, Lithogr.

PECTANTHIS ASTEROIDES.

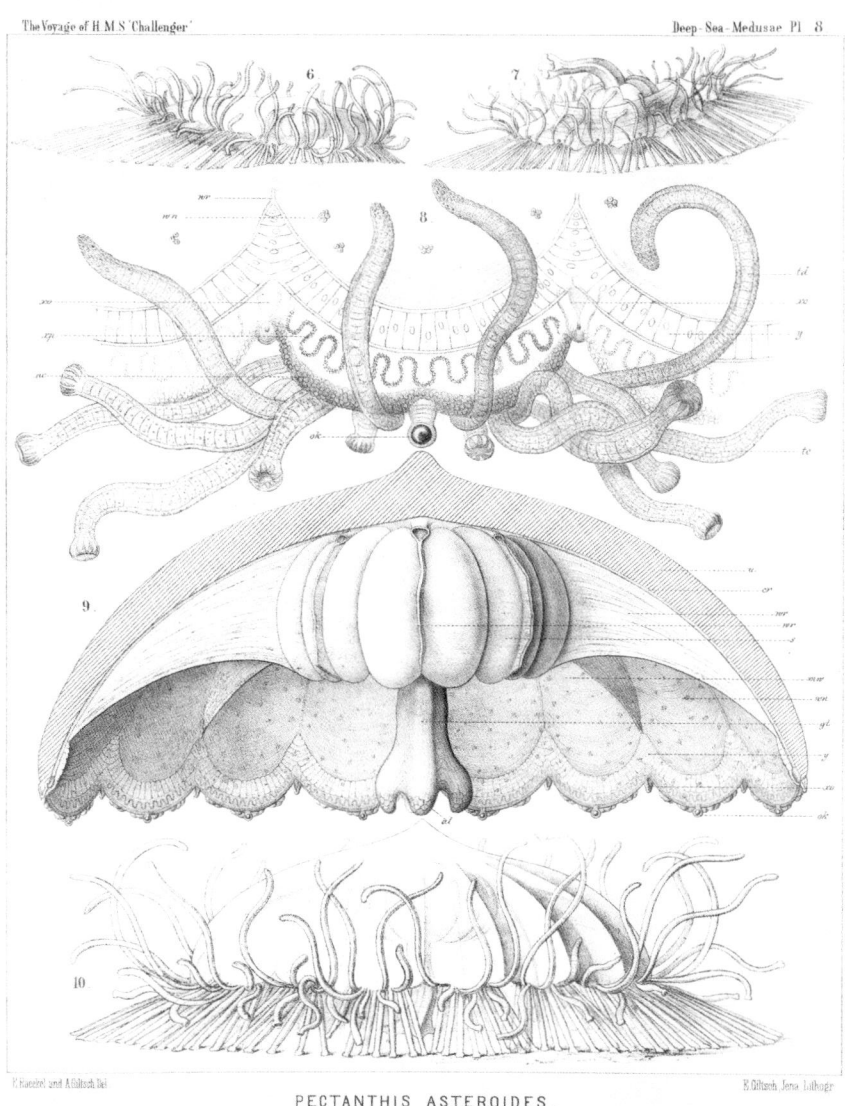

E. Haeckel and A.Giltsch Del.

E.Giltsch Jena Lithogr.

PECTANTHIS ASTEROIDES.

PLATE 8
Pectanthis asteroides – *Ptychogastria asteroides* (HAECKEL, 1879)

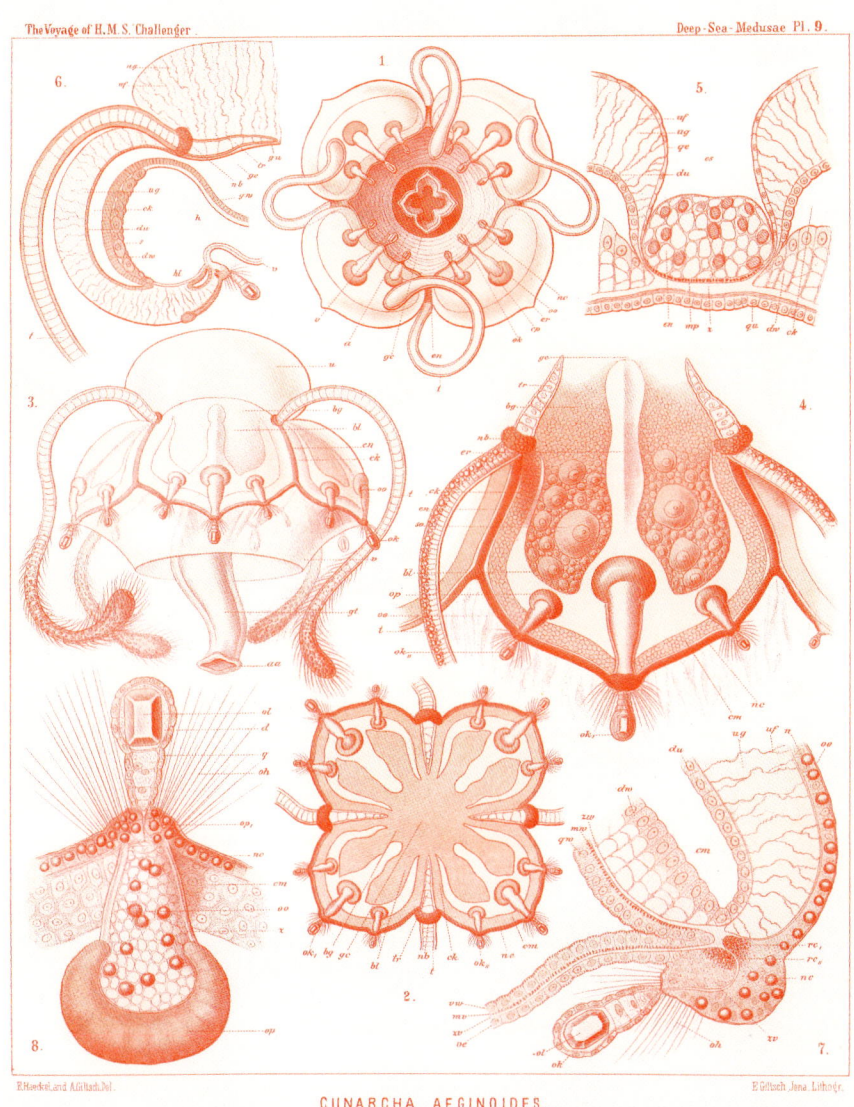

CUNARCHA AEGINOIDES.

PLATE 9
Cunarcha aeginoides – *Aegina citrea* ESCHSCHOLTZ, 1829 Golf tee medusa

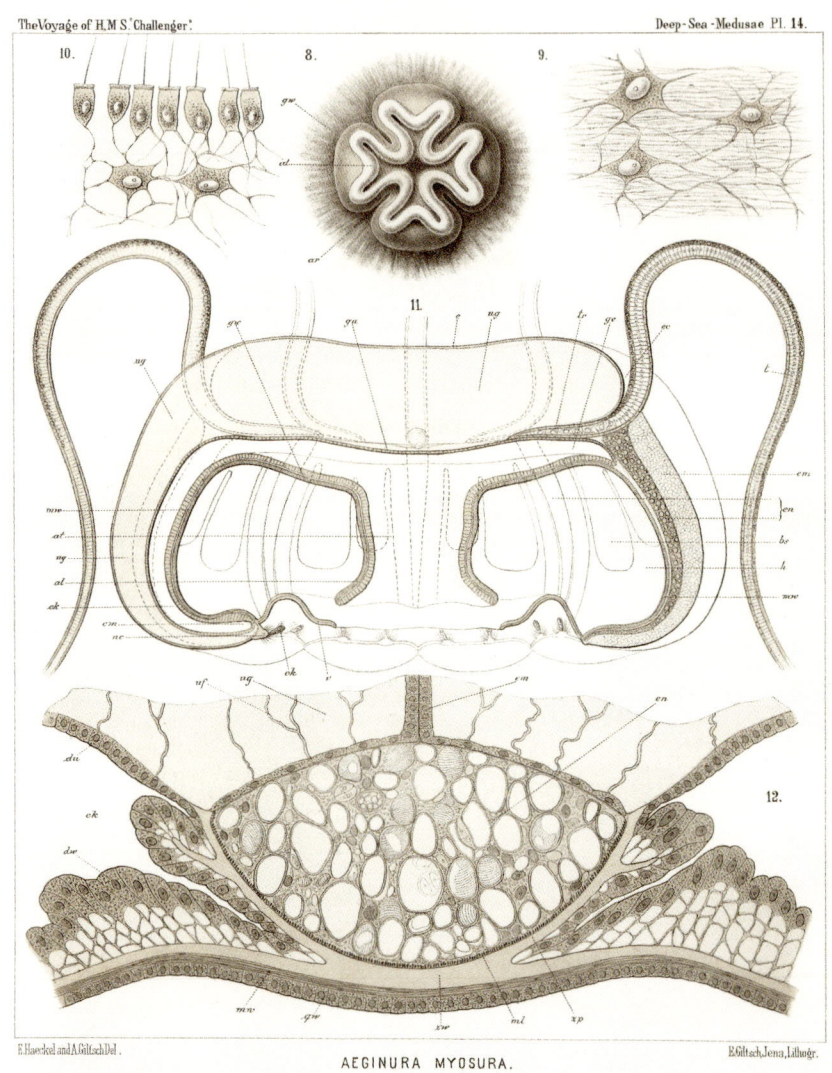

E.Haeckel and A.Giltsch Del.

AEGINURA MYOSURA.

E.Giltsch,Jena,Lithogr.

PLATE 14

Aeginura myosura – *Aeginura myosura* HAECKEL, 1879

PLATE 15

Tesserantha connectens – *Tesserantha connectens* HAECKEL, 1880

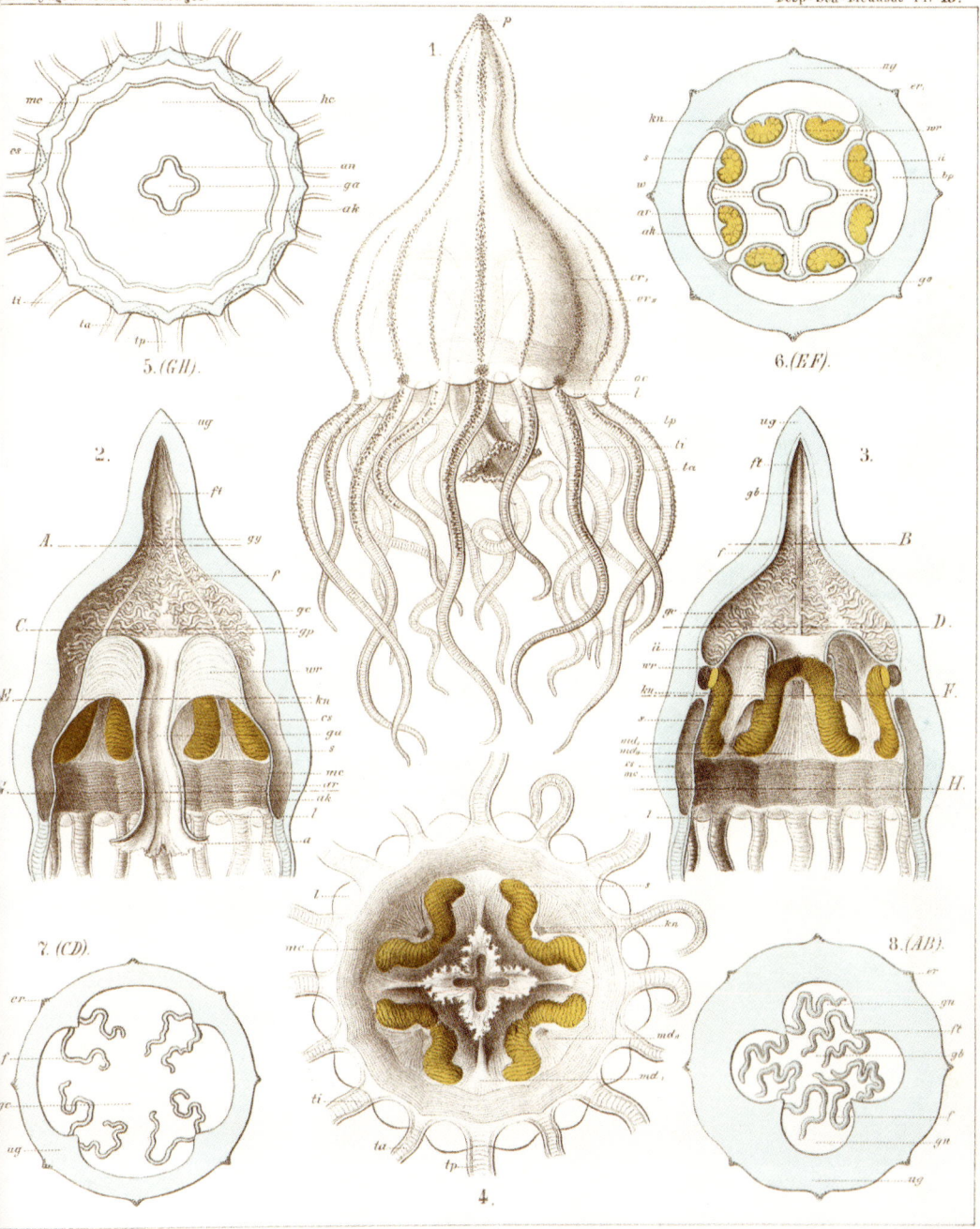

TESSERANTHA CONNECTENS.

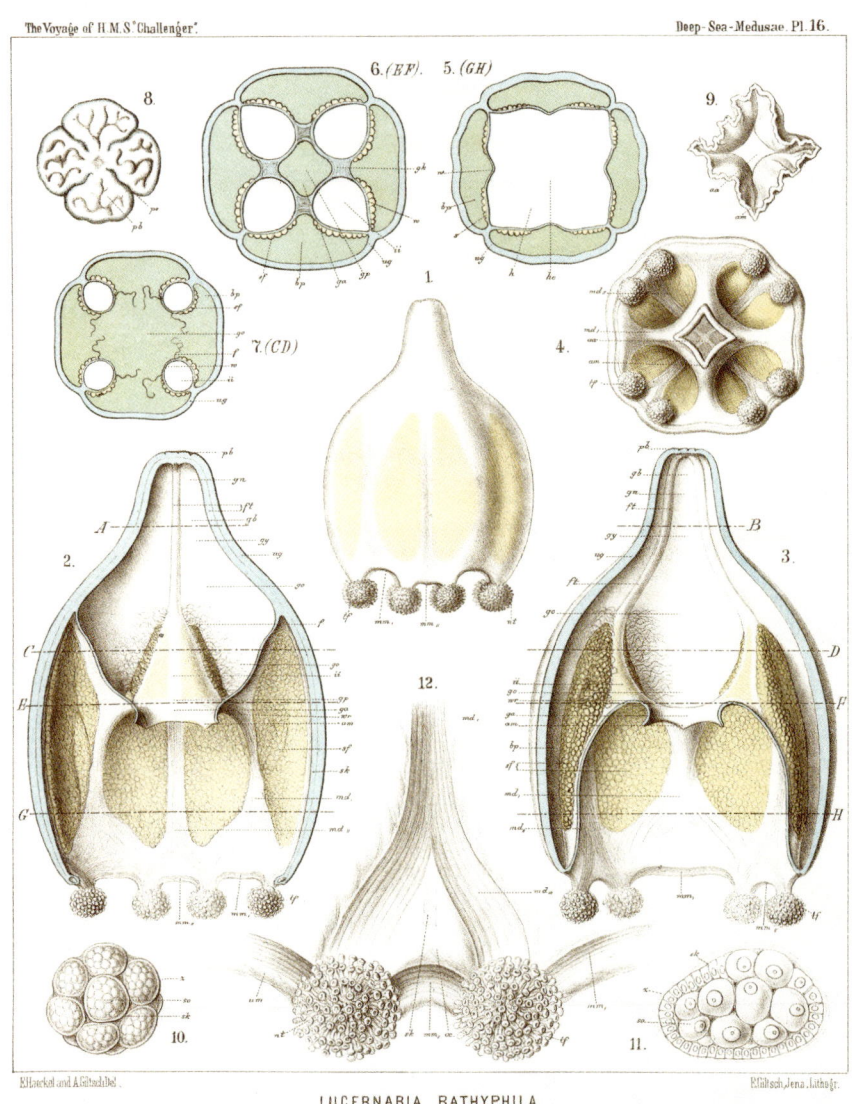

LUCERNARIA BATHYPHILA.

PLATE 16
Lucernaria bathyphila – *Lucernaria bathyphila* HAECKEL, 1880

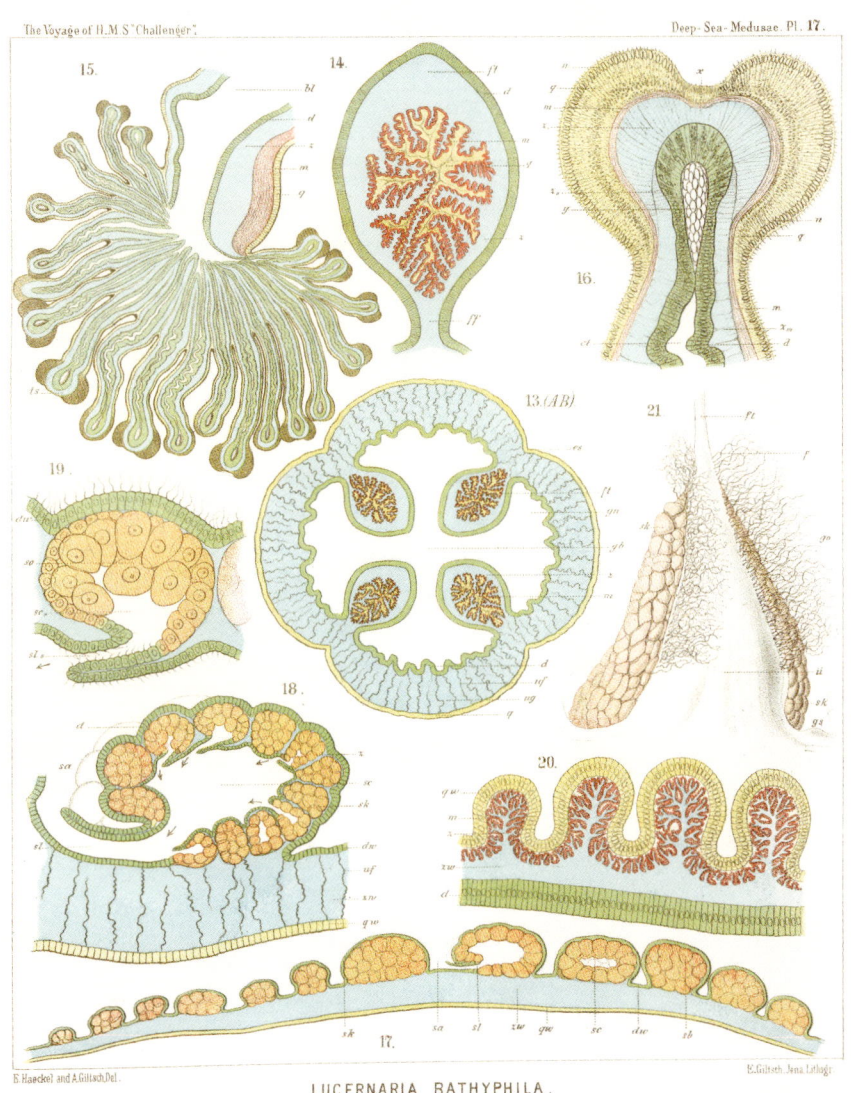

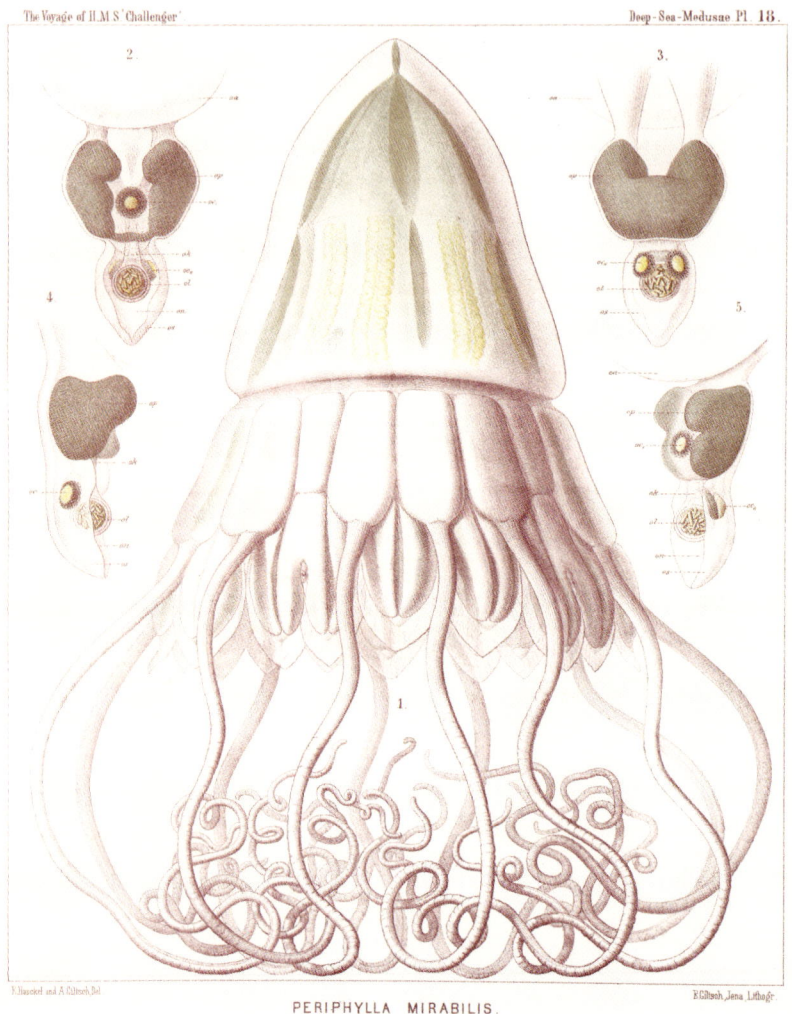

PERIPHYLLA MIRABILIS.

PLATE 18
Periphylla mirabilis – *Periphylla periphylla* (PÉRON & LESUEUR, 1810)
Helmet jelly, Helmet jellyfish

PLATE 19
Periphylla mirabilis – *Periphylla periphylla* (PÉRON & LESUEUR, 1810)
Helmet jelly, Helmet jellyfish

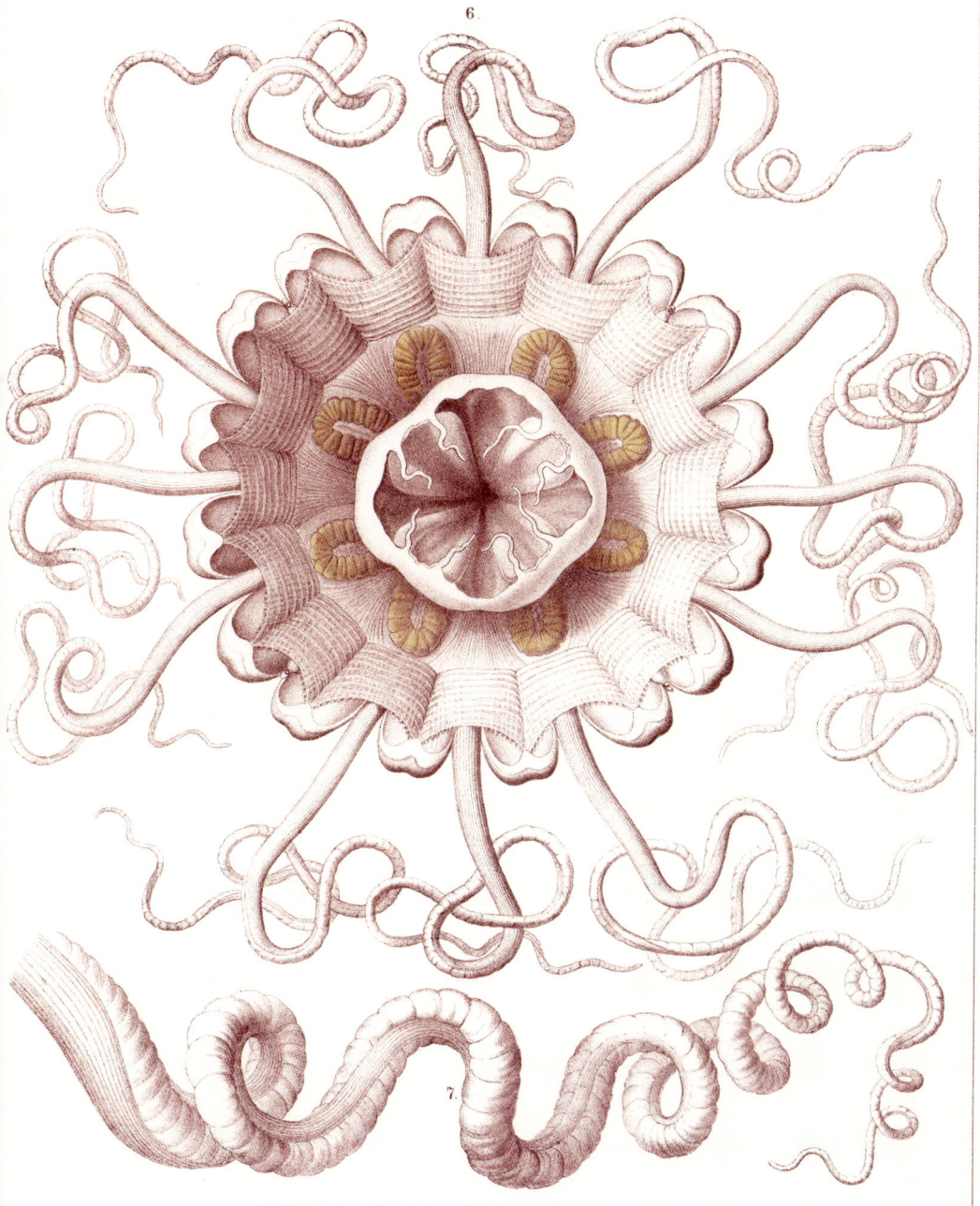

PERIPHYLLA MIRABILIS.

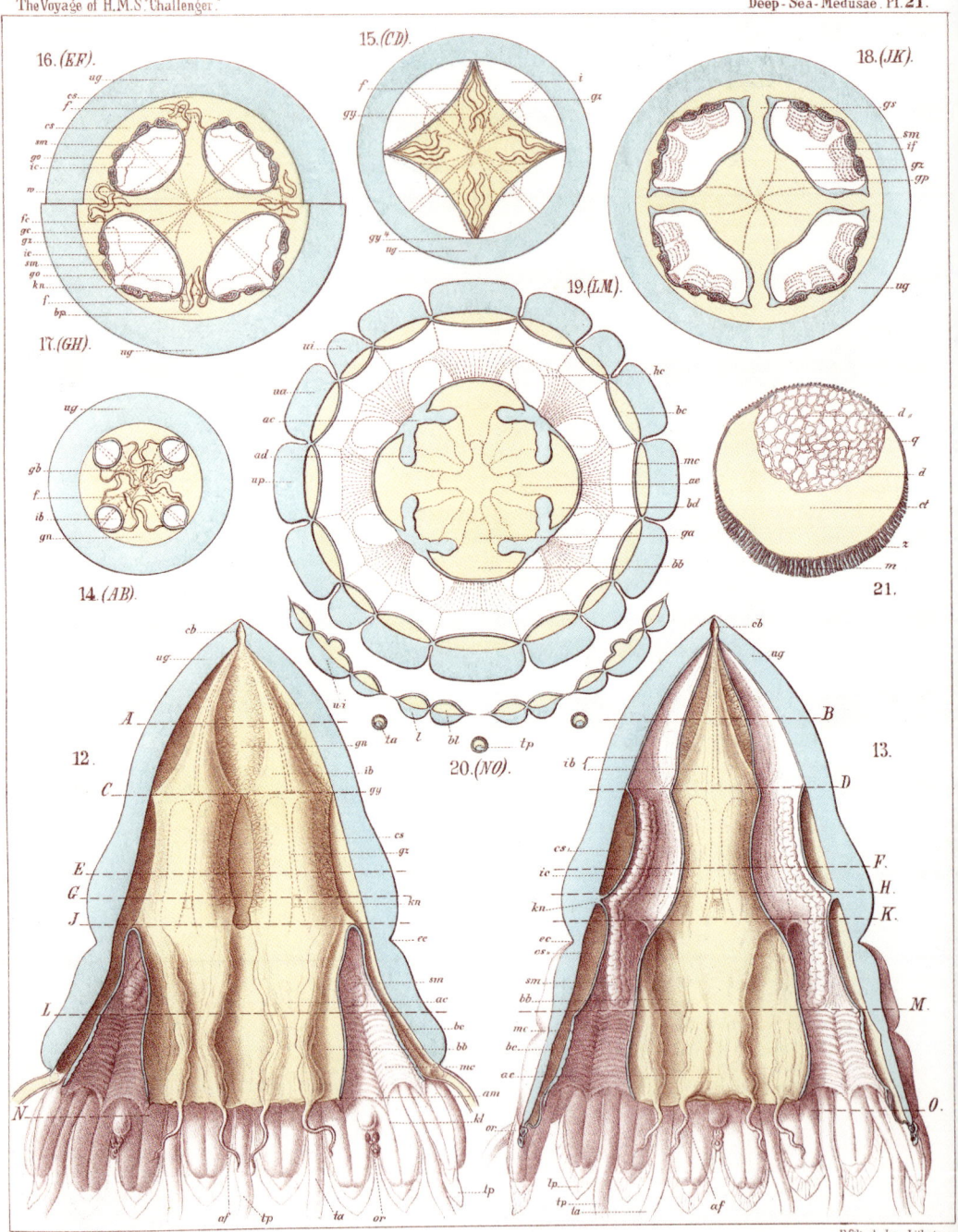

E.Haeckel and A.Giltsch Del.

E.Giltsch, Jena, Lithogr.

PERIPHYLLA MIRABILIS.

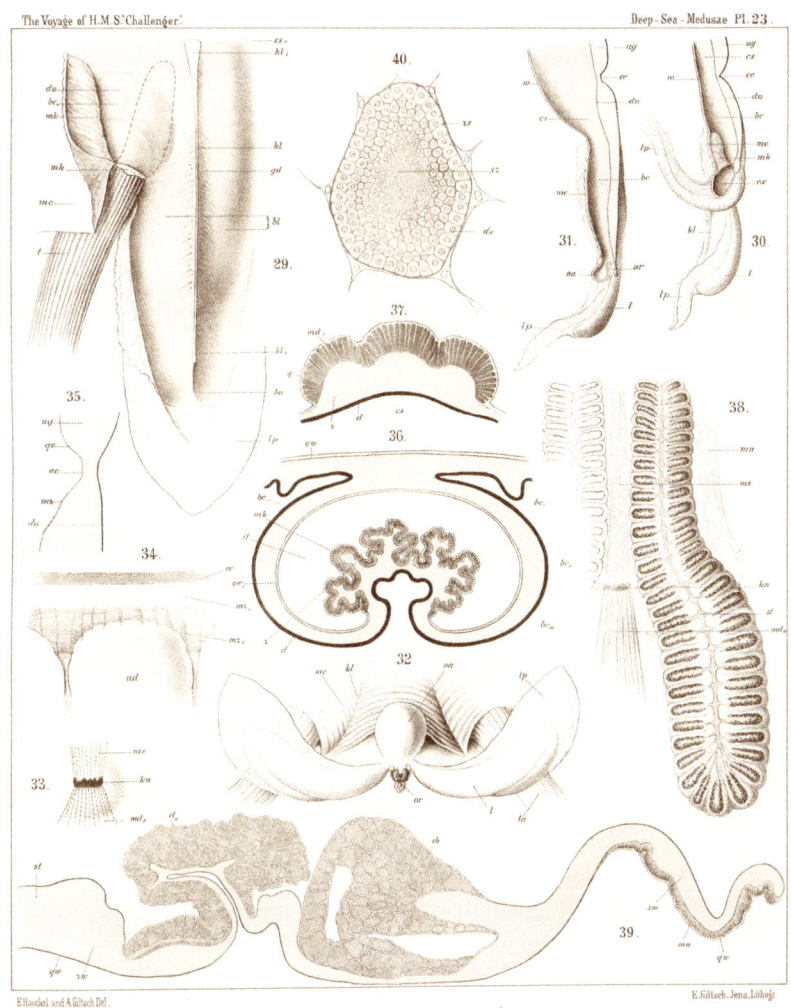

E.Haeckel and A.Giltsch Del.

E.Giltsch.Jena.Lith⌐

PERIPHYLLA MIRABILIS.

PLATE 22

Periphylla mirabilis – *Periphylla periphylla* (PÉRON & LESUEUR, 1810)

Helmet jelly, Helmet jellyfish

PLATE 23

Periphylla mirabilis – *Periphylla periphylla* (PÉRON & LESUEUR, 1810)

Helmet jelly, Helmet jellyfish

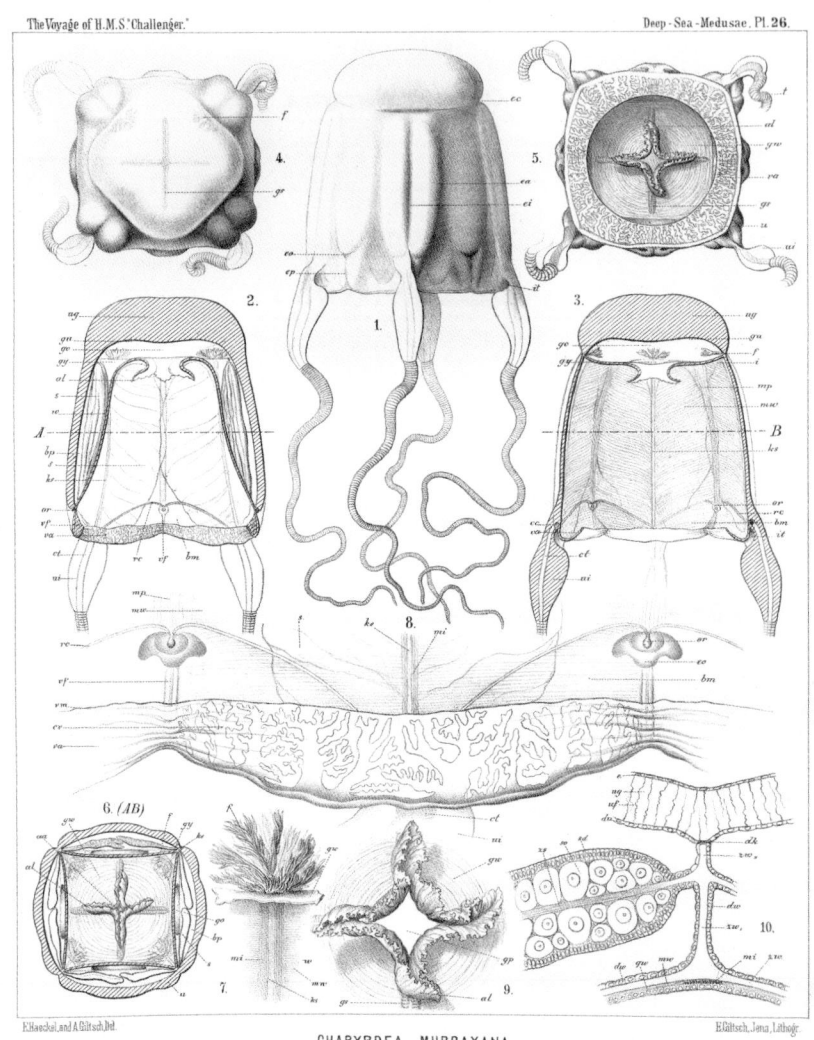

E.Haeckel. and A.Giltsch,lith.

E.Giltsch, Jena, Lithogr.

CHARYBDEA MURRAYANA.

PLATE 26
Charybdea murrayana (HAECKEL) –
Carybdea murrayana HAECKEL, 1880 (non *Charybdea*)

PLATE 27
Nauphanta Challengeri – *Nausithoe challengeri* (HAECKEL, 1880)

296

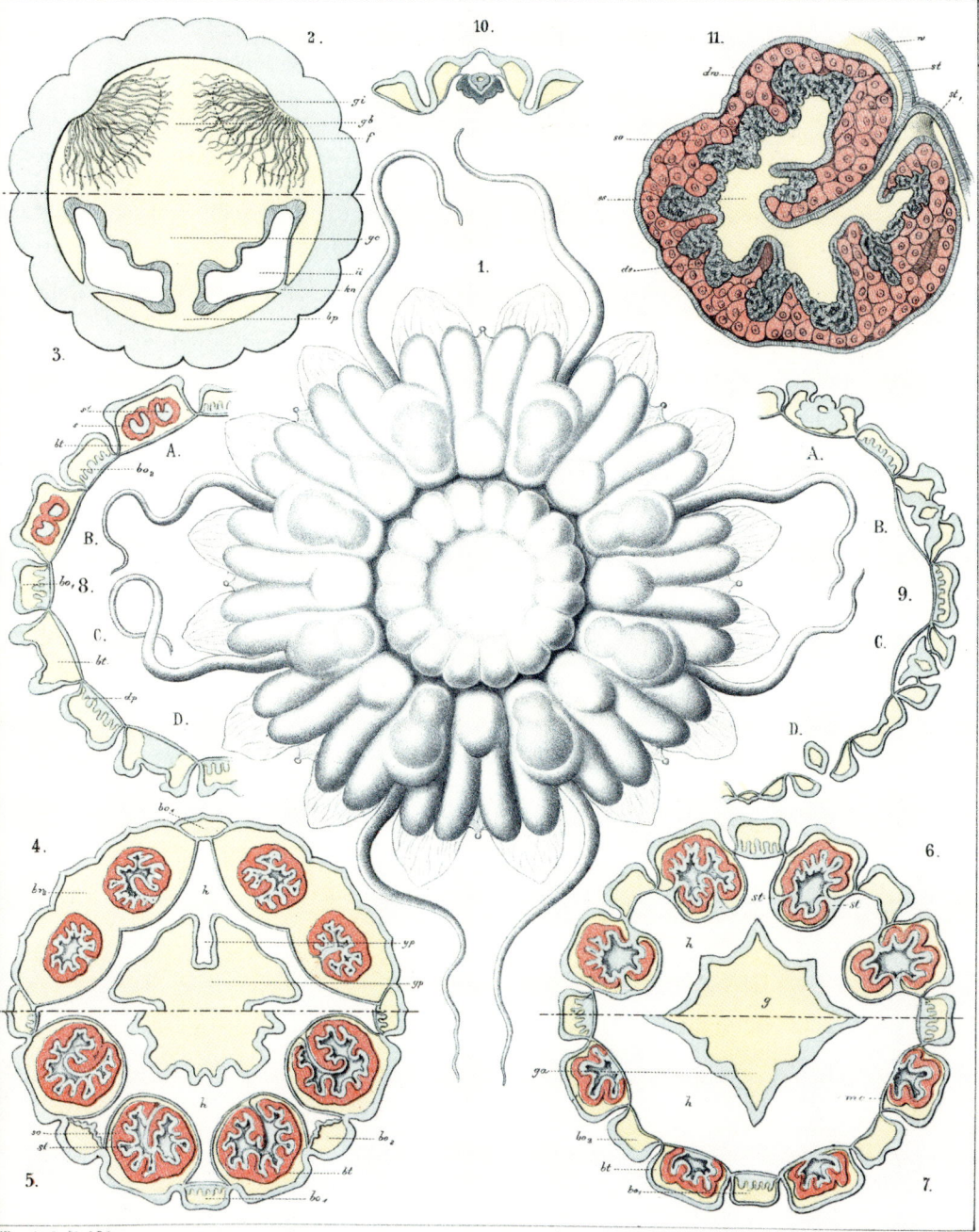

E.Haeckel and A.Giltsch Del.

E.Giltsch Jena, Lithogr.

NAUPHANTA CHALLENGERI.

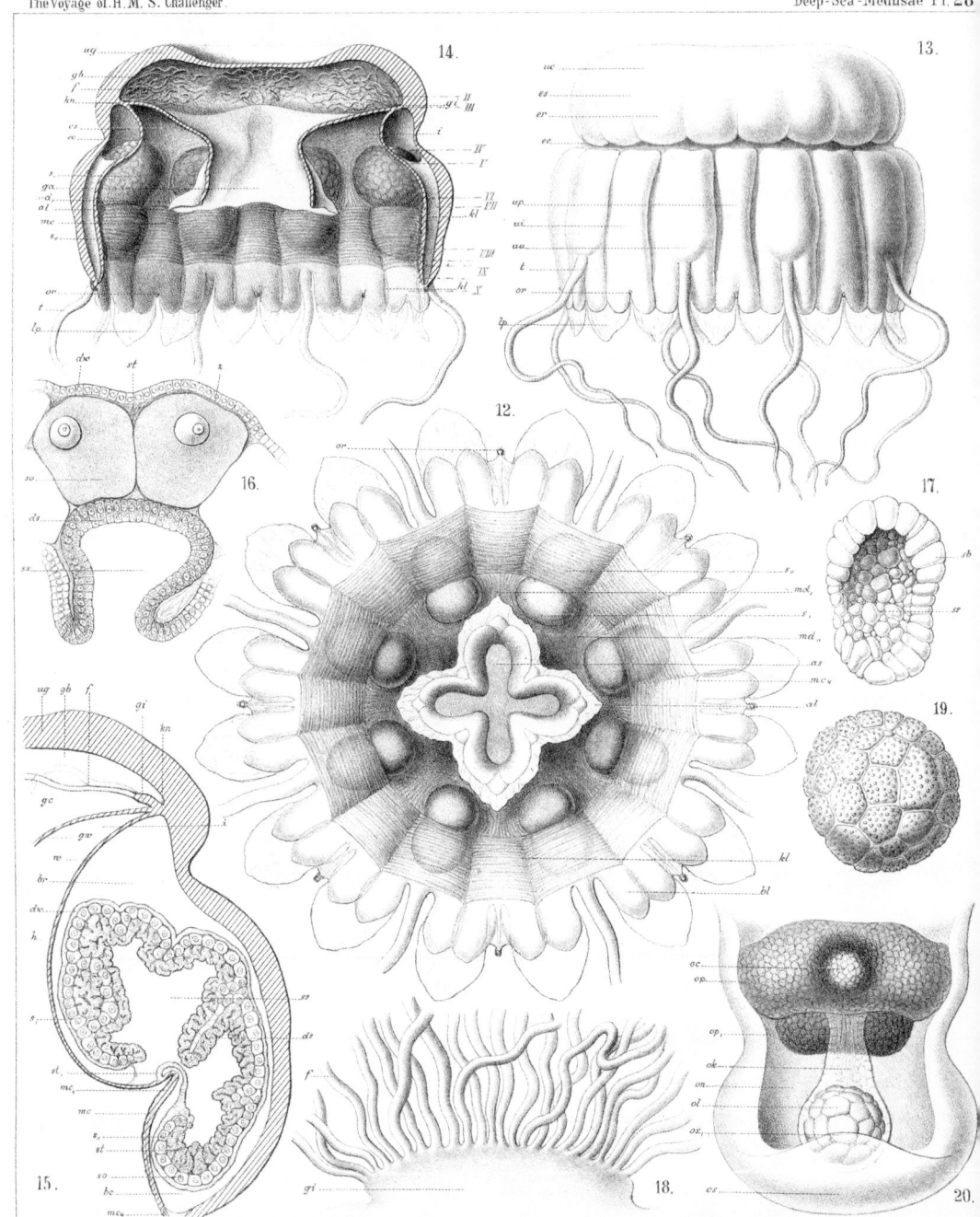

E. Haeckel and A. Giltsch Del.

E. Giltsch, Jena. Lith. gr.

NAUPHANTA CHALLENGERI.

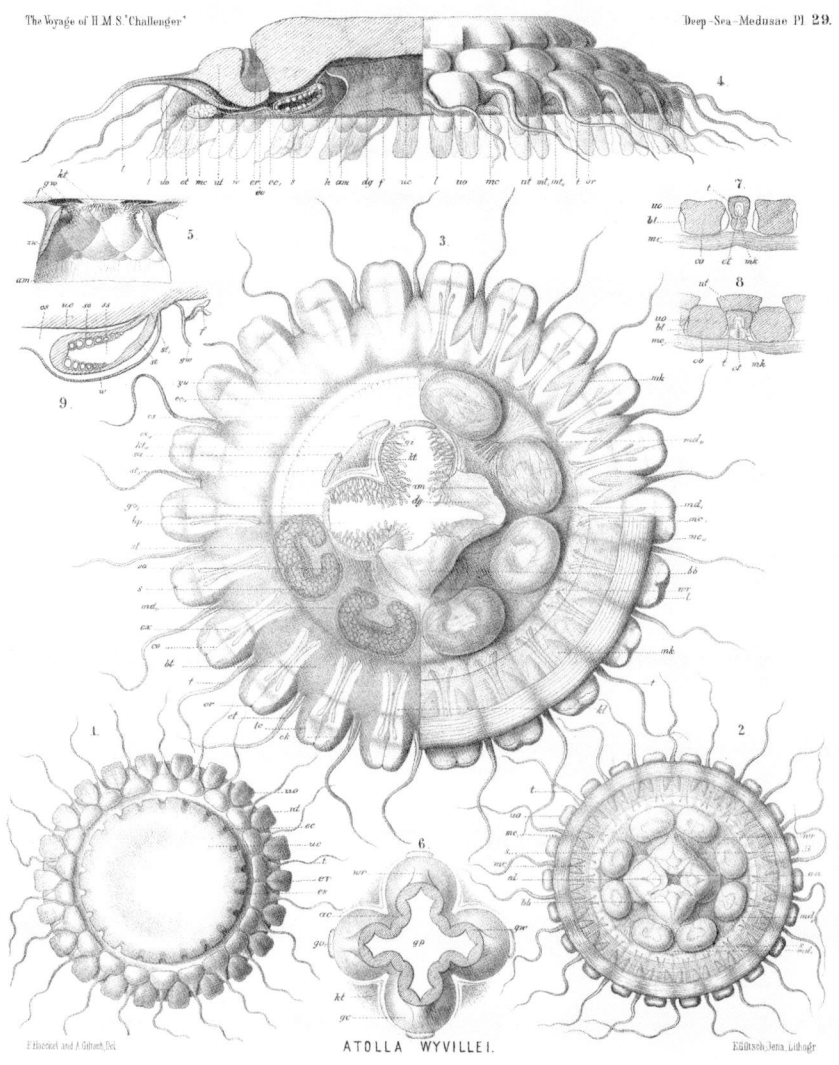

ATOLLA WYVILLEI.

PLATE 28

Nauphanta Challengeri – *Nausithoe challengeri* (HAECKEL, 1880)

PLATE 29

Atolla Wyvillei – *Atolla wyvillei* HAECKEL, 1880 Wyville's crownjelly

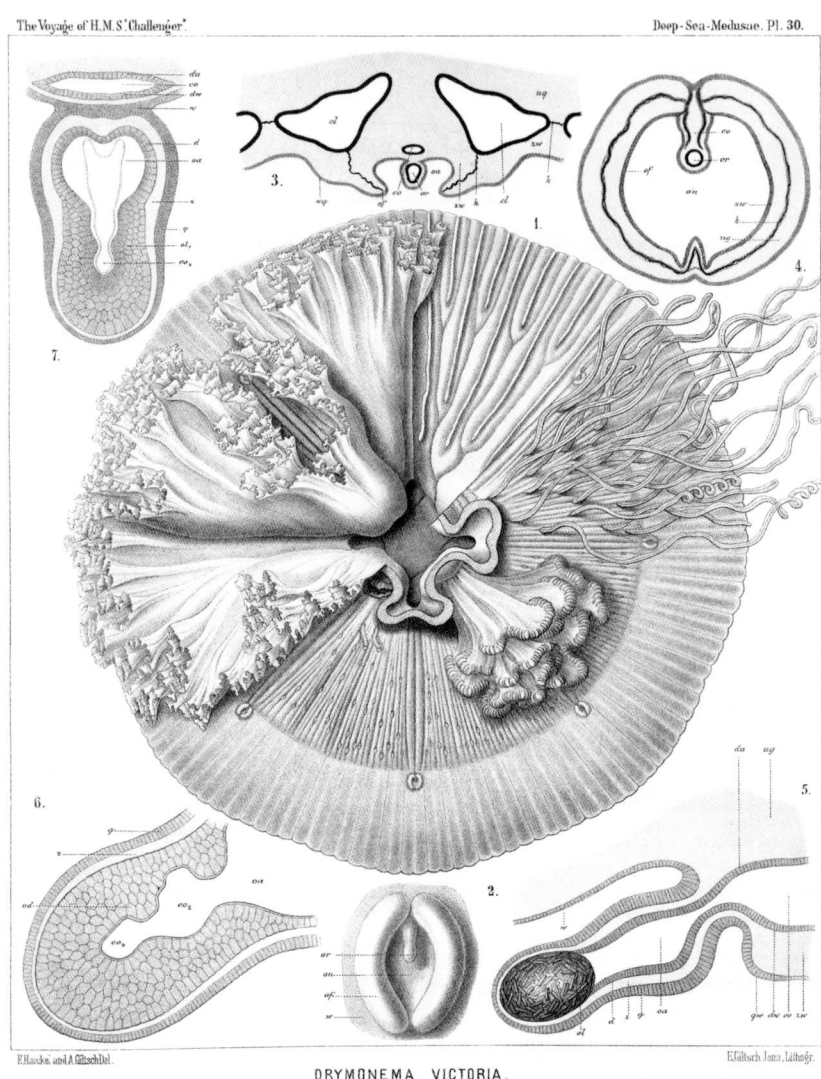

The Voyage of H.M.S 'Challenger'.

Deep-Sea-Medusae. Pl. 30.

F.Haeckel and A.Giltsch Del.

F.Giltsch Jena, Lith.gr.

DRYMONEMA VICTORIA.

PLATE 30
Drymonema victoria – *Drymonema dalmatinum* HAECKEL, 1880

PLATE 31
Drymonema victoria – *Drymonema dalmatinum* HAECKEL, 1880

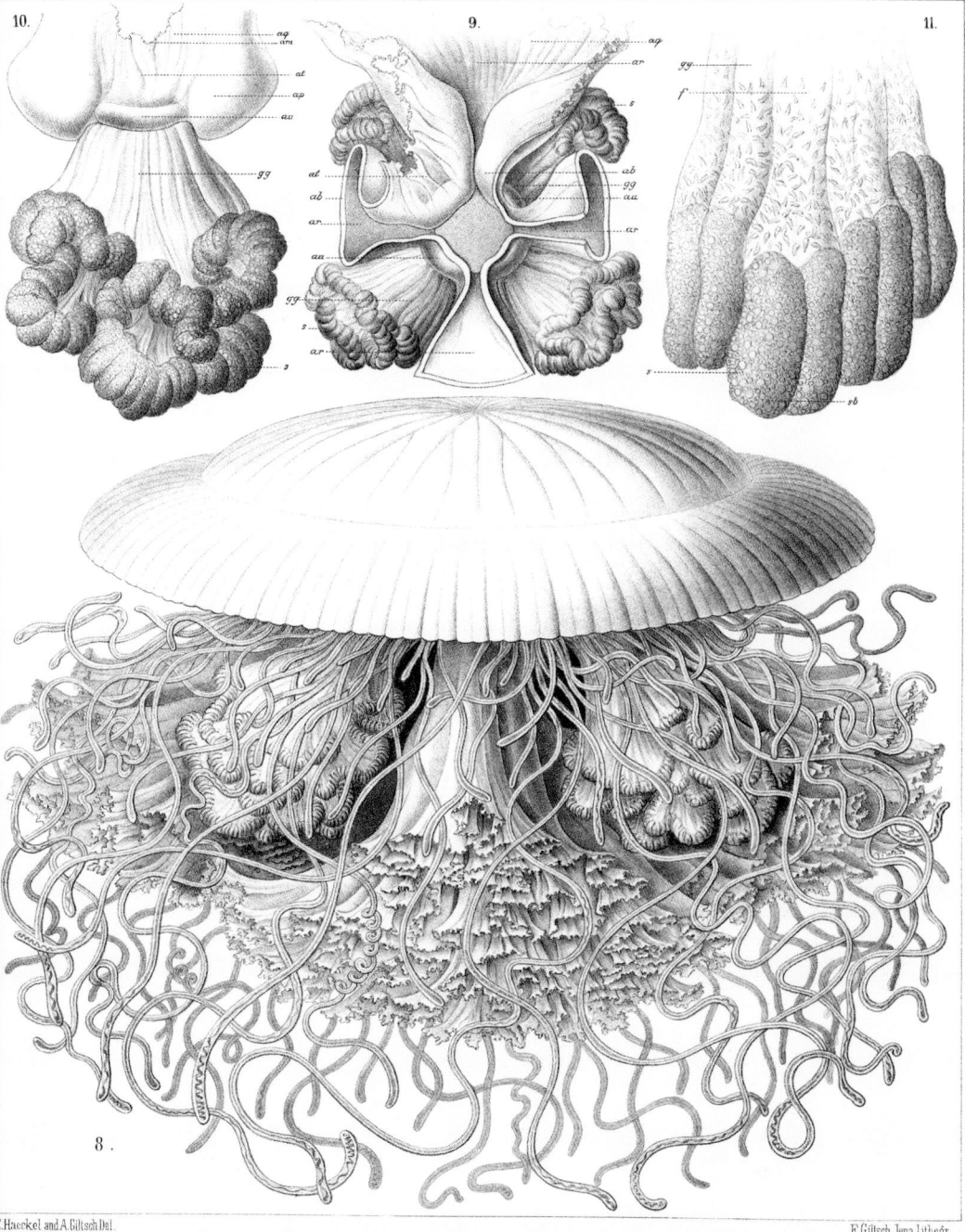

DRYMONEMA VICTORIA

PLATE 32
Leonura terminalis –
Leonura terminalis HAECKEL, 1880

302

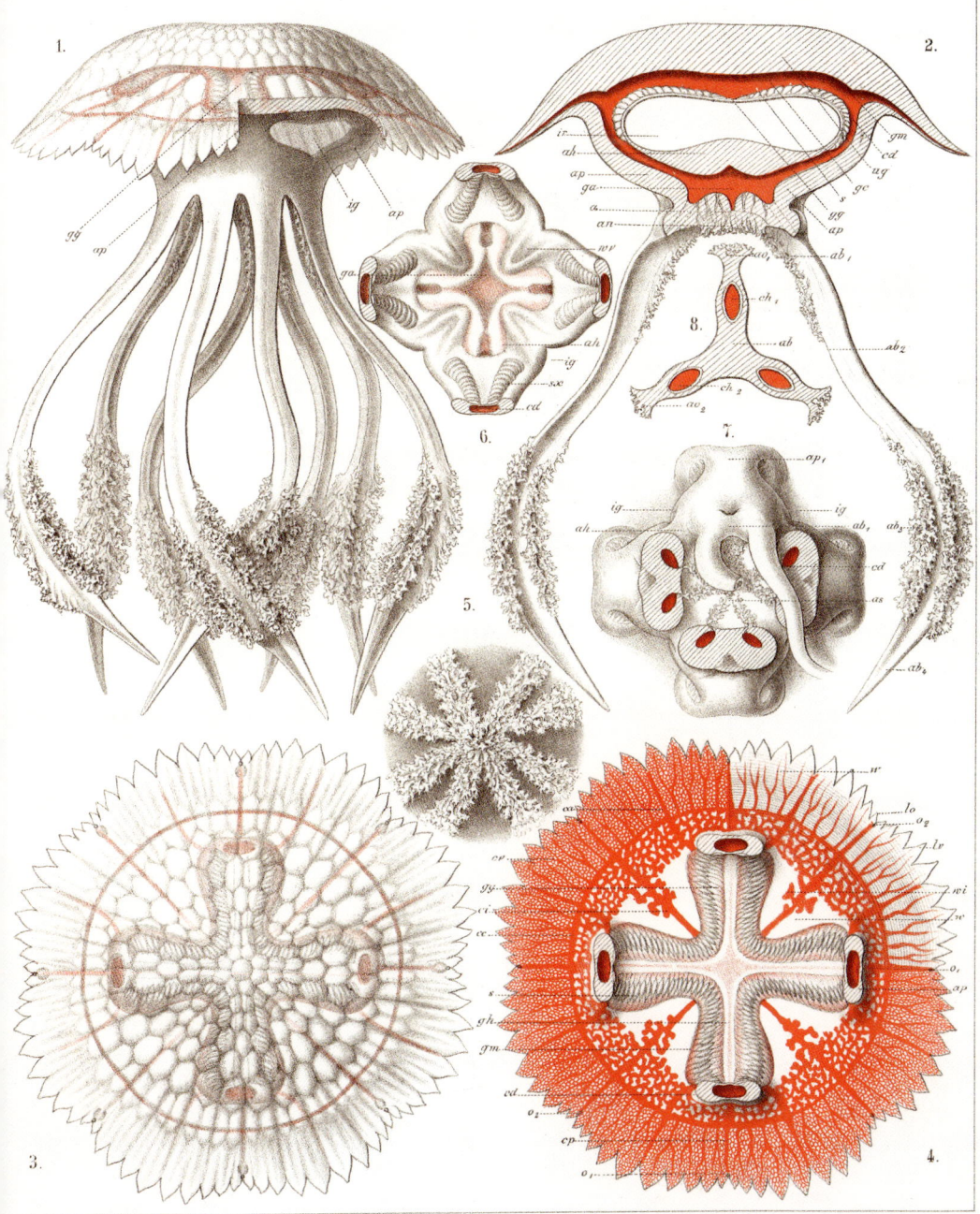

E. Haeckel and A.Giltsch Del.

E. Giltsch, Jena Lithogr.

LEONURA TERMINALIS.

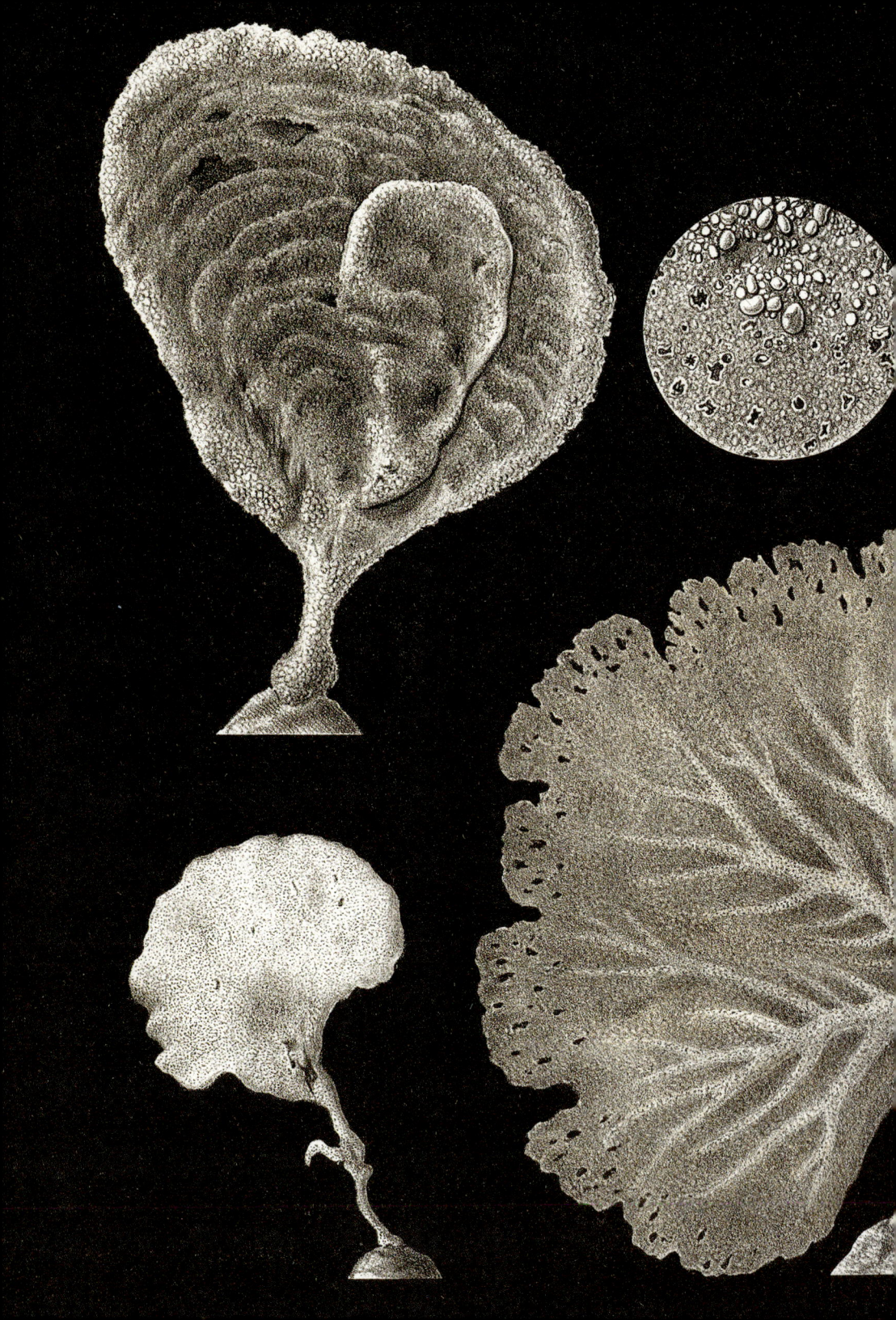

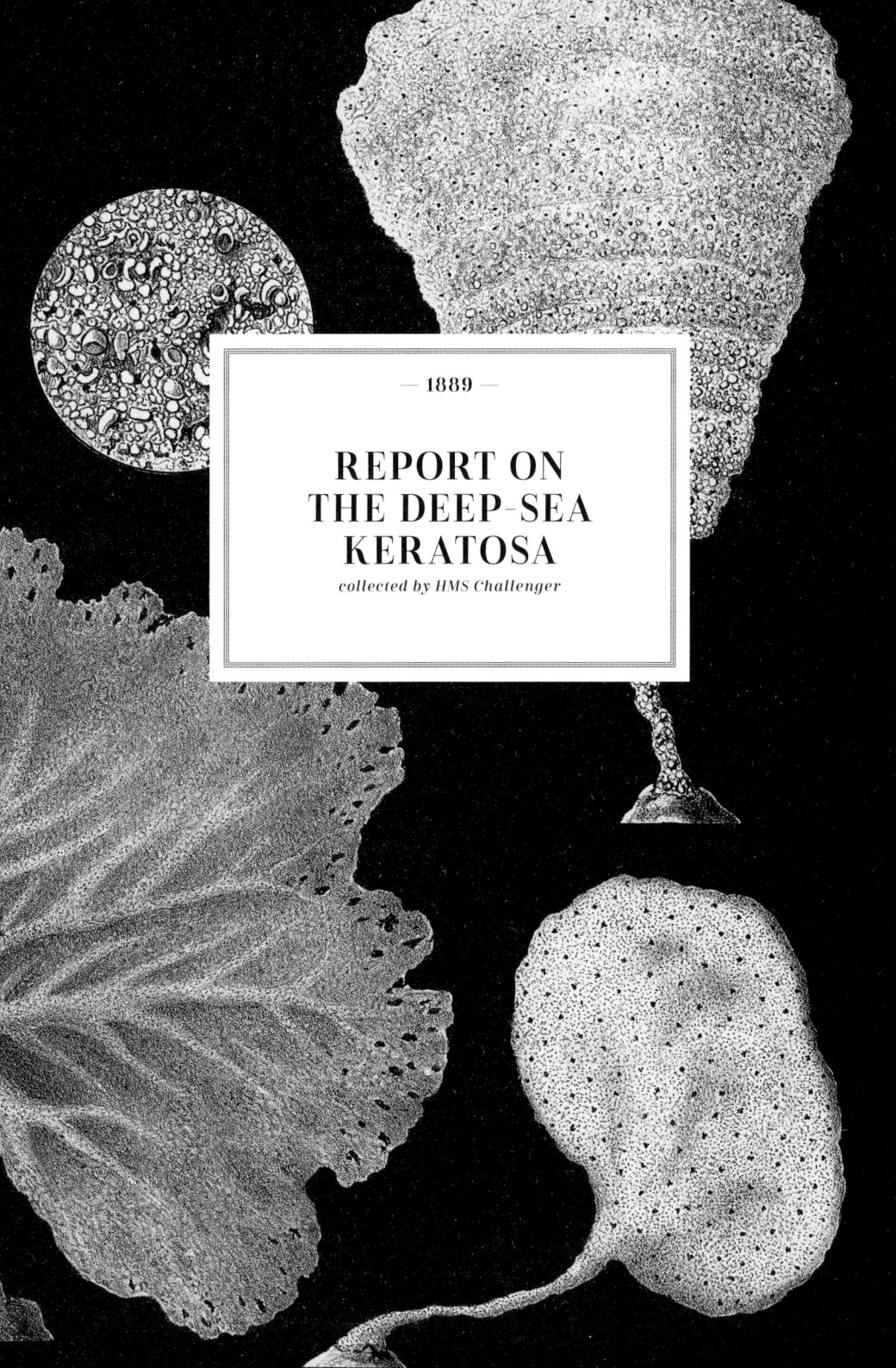

— 1889 —

REPORT ON
THE DEEP-SEA
KERATOSA

collected by HMS Challenger

REPORT ON
THE DEEP-SEA KERATOSA

COLLECTED BY HMS CHALLENGER

In publishing the results of his research into deep-sea Keratosa gathered by the HMS *Challenger* (*Report on the Deep-sea Keratosa*, 92 text pages, 8 plates) in 1889, Haeckel brought to an end his connection with this expedition.

Among sponges, Keratosa constitute a group of Demospongia or keratino-siliceous sponges. As presented in the overview of Haeckel's System of Organisms (pp. 492–505), sponges are inhabitants of the sea and, on very rare occasions, of freshwater. They remain fixed in a single location and filter the waters in which they inhabit. Keratosa (from the Greek *keras*, horn) possess a skeleton comprising of fibres of spongin, a keratinous substance (The casual designation "keratinous sponges" is, however, used for Demospongiae in general, which has led to Keratosa being re-ferred to on occasion as "true keratinous sponges").

The different species of sponges are often indistinguishable from each other through characteristic shapes they assume as they grow; and many eventually have an irregular, asymmetrical form. It is therefore hardly surprising that the plates Haeckel devoted to Keratosa are very distinct aesthetically from those he devoted to other organisms. As Keratosa – in contrast with, for example, calcareous sponges – do not even possess symmetrical small structures, such as skeletal spicules, Haeckel resolved to exclude even a single species of them in his *Kunstformen der Natur* (*Art Forms in Nature*;

other species of other groups of sponges are, however, illustrated there: see plates 5 and 35, pp. 330 and 370).

As is so often the case in biological systematics, the meaning of the designation "Keratosa," first introduced in 1861, has altered over the course of time. The term is now used to refer to two groups: the Dendroceratida and the Dictyoceratida.[1] Among those belonging to the Dictyoceratida is a particular species: *Vaceletia crypta*. This species, unknown to Haeckel, is the only representative of Keratosa to possess a mineralised skeleton, in this case a calcareous basal plate.

While Haeckel devoted numerous plates to calcareous sponges in his monograph (1872), even to the representation of skeletal spicules that support the body of sponges, such spicules are not to be found in Keratosa. Haeckel provides, nonetheless, several illustrations of details in which we find the spicules of other sponges present as foreign elements (e. g. plate 4, figs. 2 and 6). Grains of sand or radiolaria skeletons particles are also to be found within the bodies of Keratosa (plate 2, fig. 2; plate 4, fig. 2; plate 8) – where they have become woven into the sponge by means of its fibres (plates 5 and 8).

The colours employed by Haeckel in his plates devoted to Keratosa do not correspond on the whole to the colours of the living organisms found in nature. Rather they serve primarily to elucidate particular structural aspects.

.

PLATE I [⊕]
1 Stannophyllum zonarium – *Stannophyllum zonarium*
2 Stannophyllum radiolarium – *Stannophyllum radiolarium*
3 Stannophyllum pertusum – *Stannophyllum pertusum*
4 Stannophyllum venosum – *Stannophyllum venosum*
5 Stannophyllum globigerinum – *Stannophyllum globigerinum*
[⊕] *see page 507*

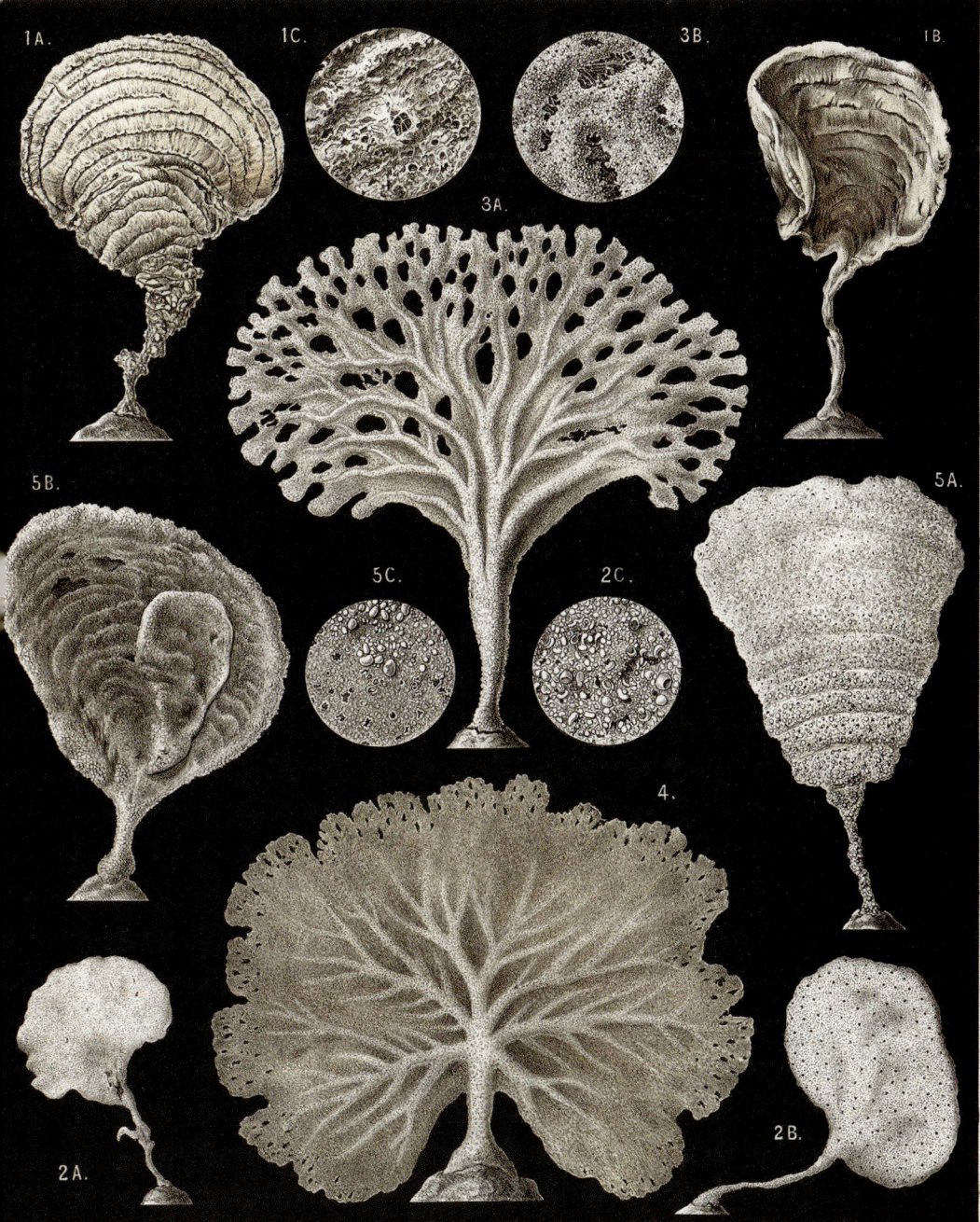

E.Haeckel and A.Giltsch Del.   A.Giltsch Jena Lithogr.

1-5. STANNOPHYLLUM, 1. S. ZONARIUM, 2. S. RADIOLARIUM,
3. S. PERTUSUM, 4. S. VENOSUM, 5. S. GLOBIGERINUM.

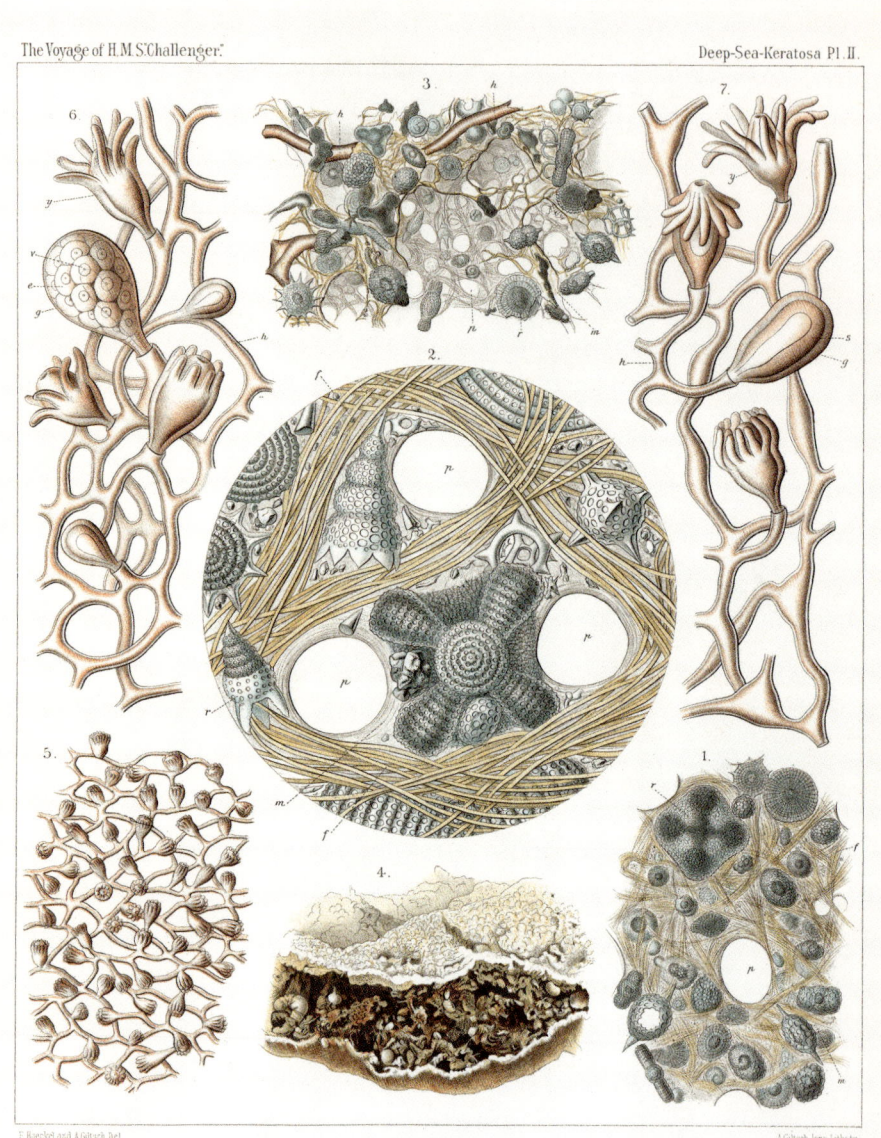

E. Haeckel and A.Giltsch del.   A.Giltsch Jena Lith.gr.

1–4. STANNOPHYLLUM ZONARIUM,
5–7. STYLACTELLA, 5,6. S.SPONGICOLA, 7 S.ABYSSICOLA.

PLATE 2

1–4 Stannophyllum zonarium – *Stannophyllum zonarium* ʜᴀᴇᴄᴋᴇʟ, 1889
5–6 Stylactella spongicola – *Perarella spongicola* (ʜᴀᴇᴄᴋᴇʟ, 1889)
7 Stylactella abyssicola – *Perarella abyssicola* (ʜᴀᴇᴄᴋᴇʟ, 1889)

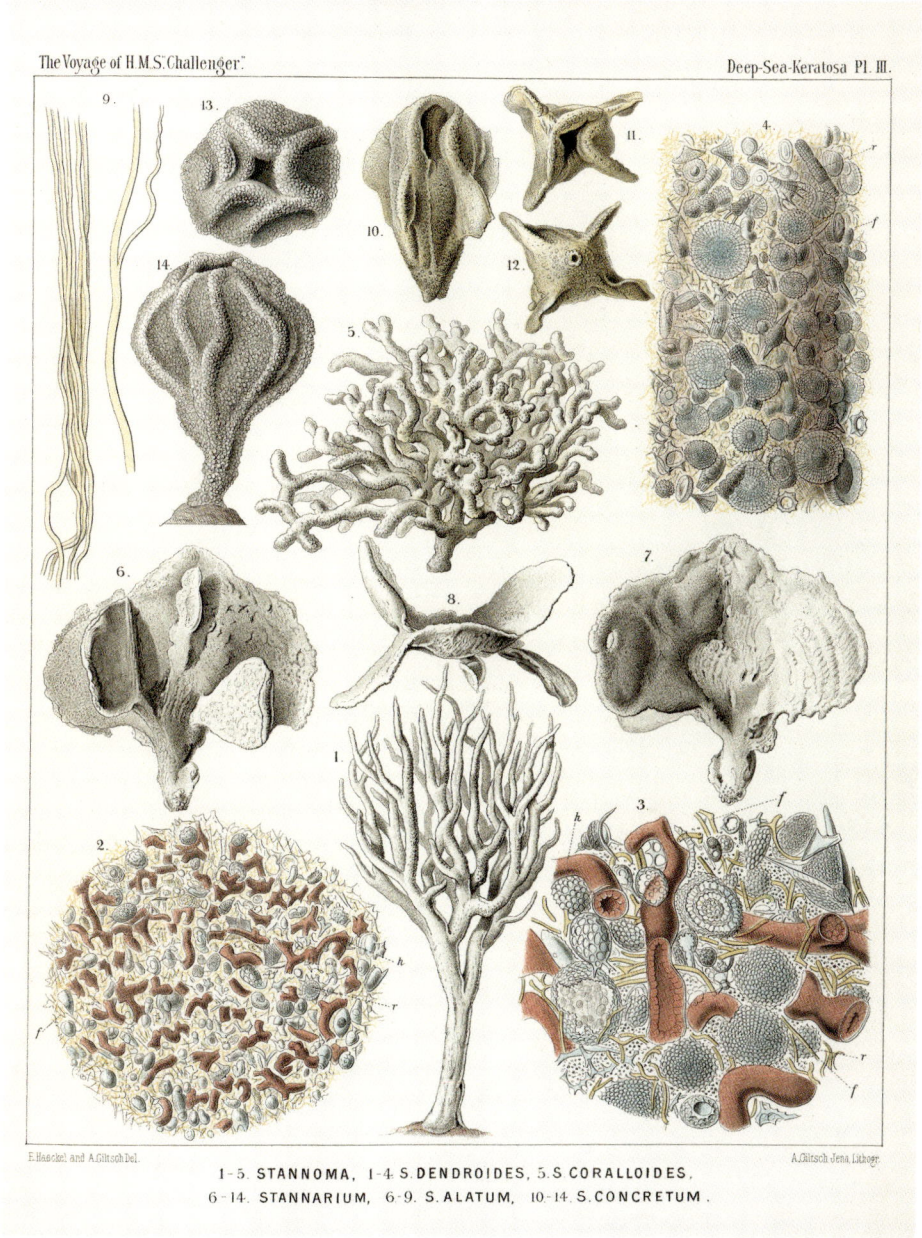

The Voyage of H.M.S. Challenger.

Deep-Sea-Keratosa Pl. III.

E.Haeckel and A.Giltsch Del.

A.Giltsch Jena lith.gr.

1-5. STANNOMA, 1-4. S. DENDROIDES, 5. S. CORALLOIDES,
6-14. STANNARIUM, 6-9. S. ALATUM, 10-14. S. CONCRETUM.

PLATE 3
1-4 Stannoma dendroides – *Stannoma dendroides* HAECKEL, 1889 | 5 Stannoma coralloides –
Stannoma coralloides HAECKEL, 1889 | 6-9 Stannarium alatum – *Stannophyllum alatum* (HAECKEL, 1889)
10-14 Stannarium concretum – *Stannophyllum concretum* (HAECKEL, 1889)

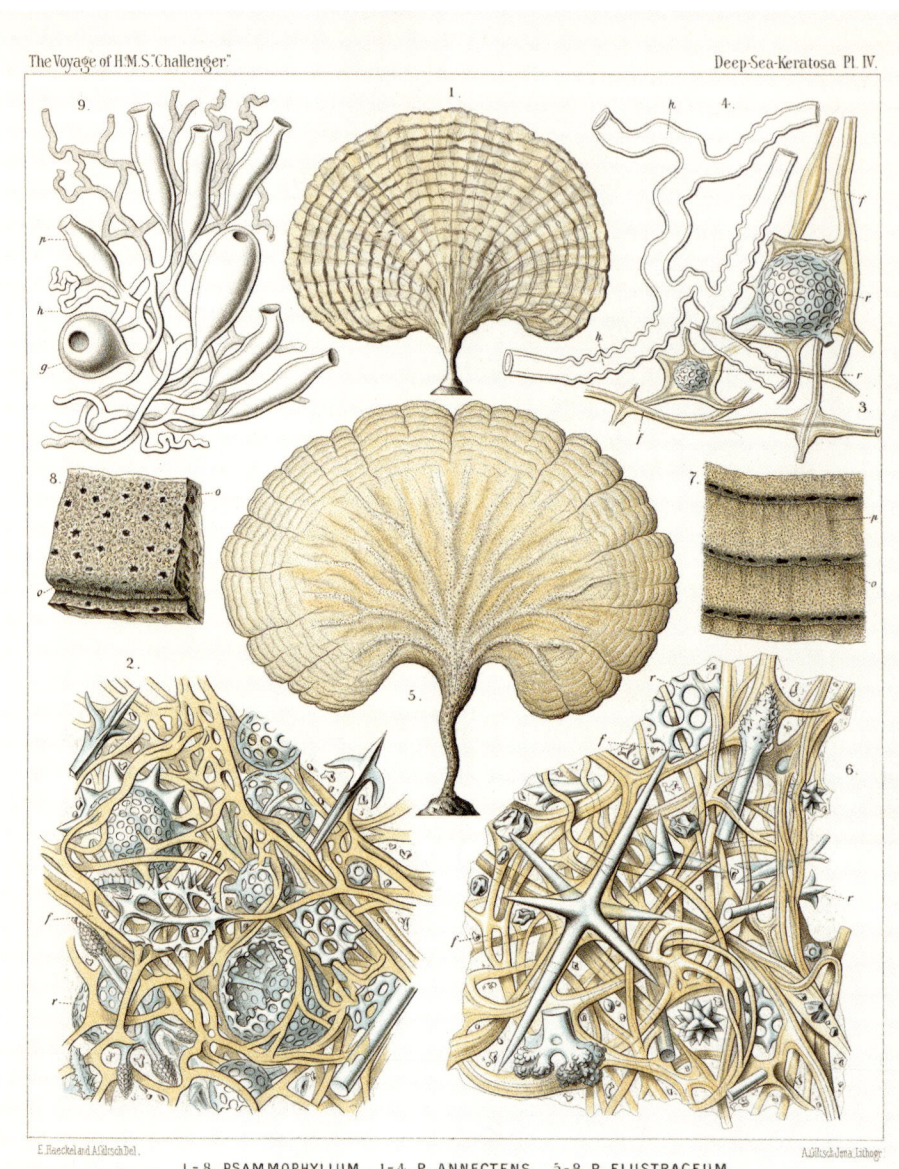

E.Haeckel and A.Giltsch.Del.

A.Giltsch.Jena.lithogr.

1–8. PSAMMOPHYLLUM, 1–4. P. ANNECTENS, 5–8. P. FLUSTRACEUM.
9. HALISIPHONIA SPONGICOLA.

PLATE 4
1–4 Psammophyllum annectens – *Psammophyllum annectens* HAECKEL, 1889
5–8 Psammophyllum flustraceum – *Stannophyllum flustraceum* (HAECKEL, 1889)
9 Halisiphonia spongicola – *Halisiphonia spongicola* HAECKEL, 1889

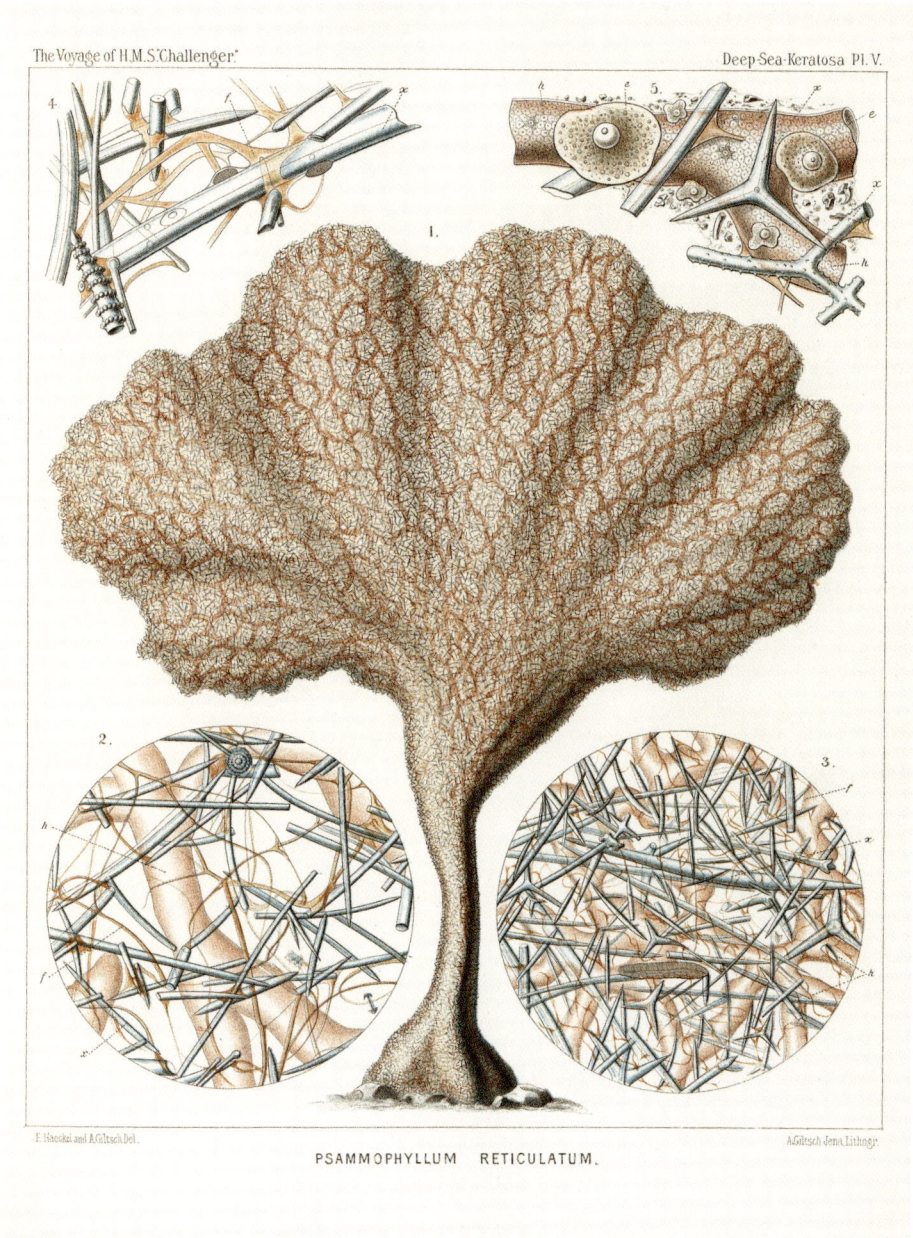

E. Haeckel and A.Giltsch Del.

A.Giltsch Jena Lithogr.

PSAMMOPHYLLUM RETICULATUM.

PLATE 5

1–4 Psammophyllum reticulatum – *Stannophyllum reticulatum*
(HAECKEL, 1889) (= *Psammina reticulatum* (HAECKEL, 1889))
5 Psammophyllum flustraceum – *Stannophyllum flustraceum* (HAECKEL, 1889)

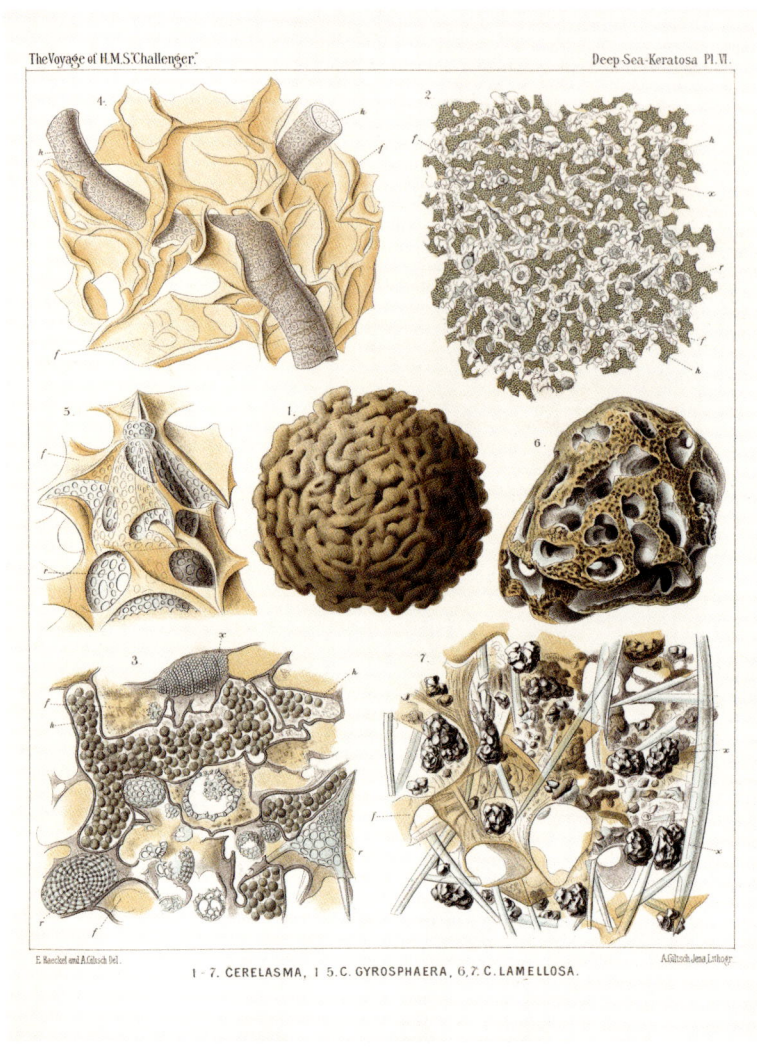

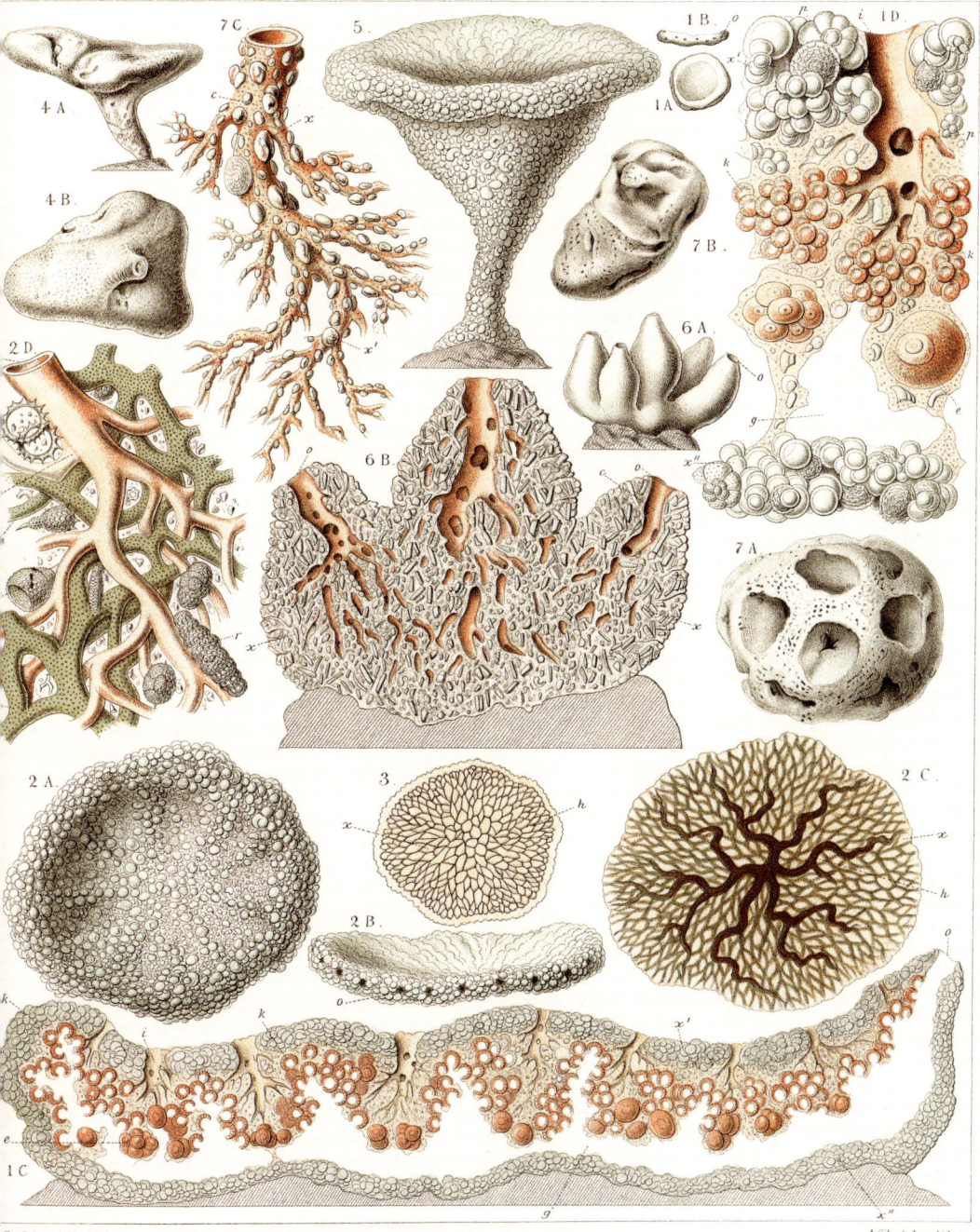

1-3. PSAMMINA, 1. P. PLAKINA, 2. P. GLOBIGERINA, 3. P. NUMMULINA,

4,5. PSAMMOPEMMA, 4. P. RADIOLARIUM, 5. P. CALCAREUM,

6,7. HOLOPSAMMA, 6. H. ARGILLACEUM, 7. H. CRETACEUM.

PLATE 8

1 Ammolynthus prototypus – *Ammolynthus prototypus*
2 Ammolynthus haliphysema – *Ammolynthus haliphysema*
3 Ammosolenia rhizammina – *Ammosolenia rhizammina*
4 Ammoconia auloplegma – *Ammoconia auloplegma*
5 Ammoconia sagenella – *Ammoconia sagenella*

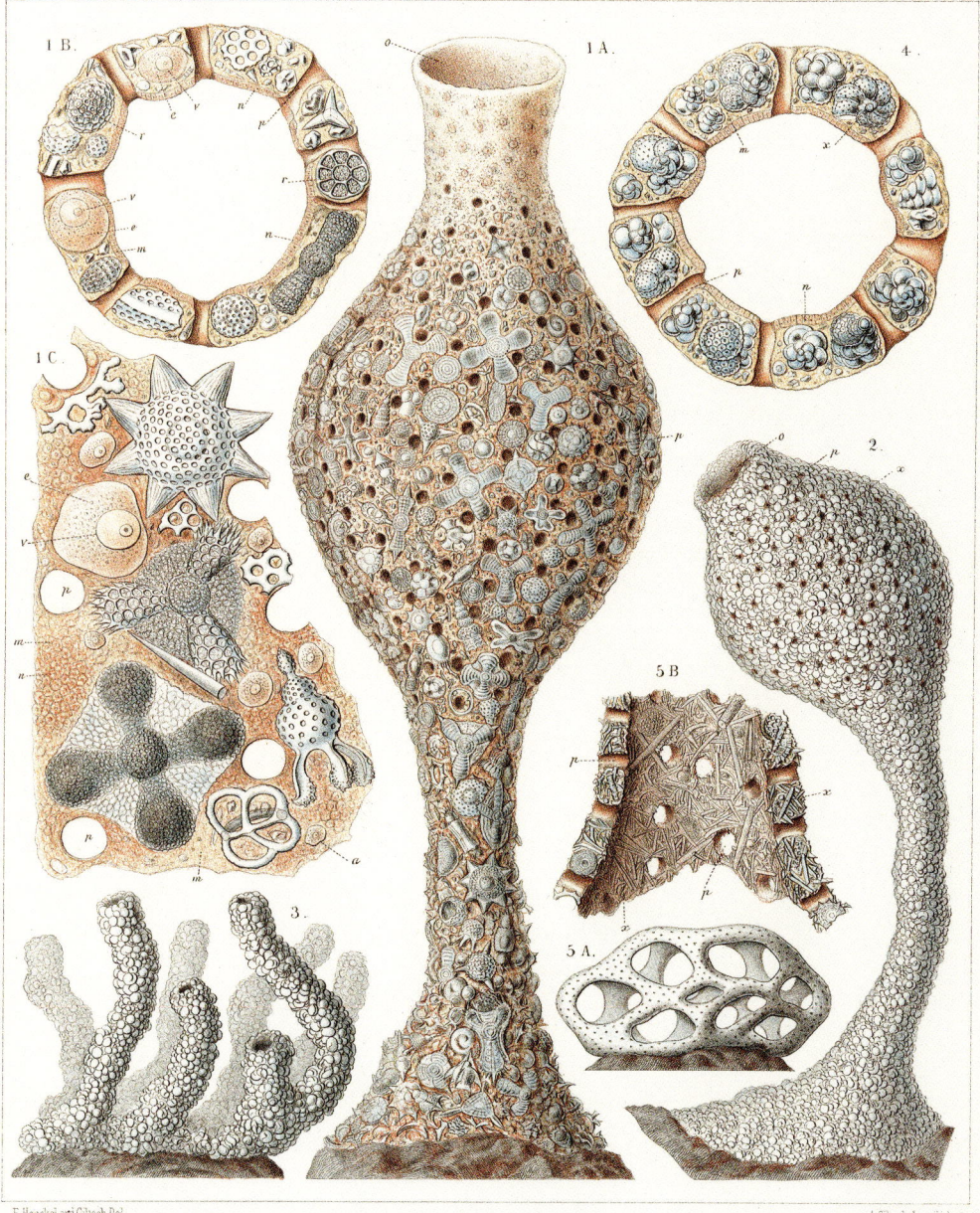

E.Haeckel and Giltsch Del.

A.Giltsch Jena lithogr.

1.2. AMMOLYNTHUS, 1.A.PROTOTYPUS, 2.A.HALIPHYSEMA, 3. AMMOSOLENIA RHIZAMMINA.
4,5. AMMOCONIA, 4.A.AULOPLEGMA, 5.A.SAGENELLA.

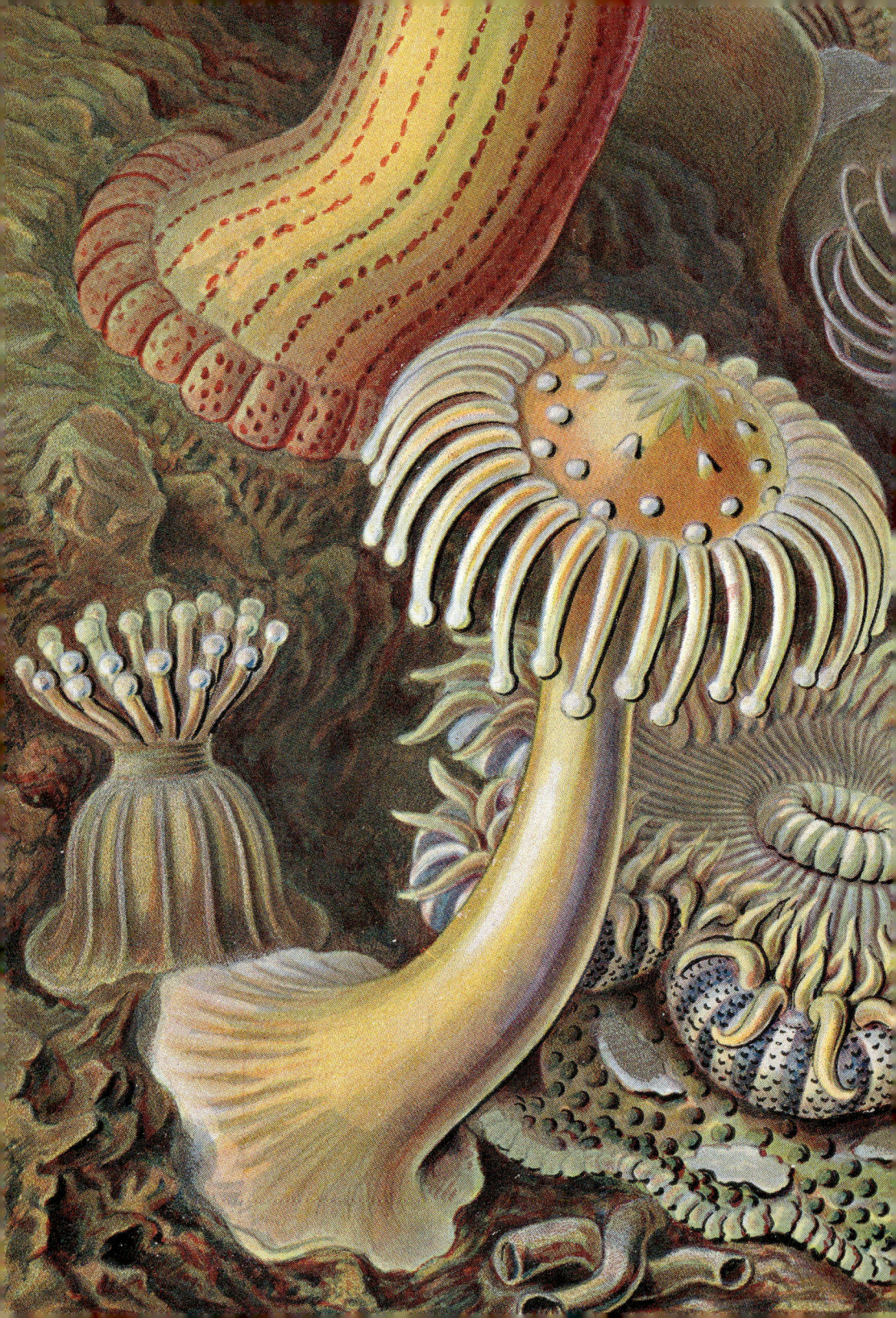

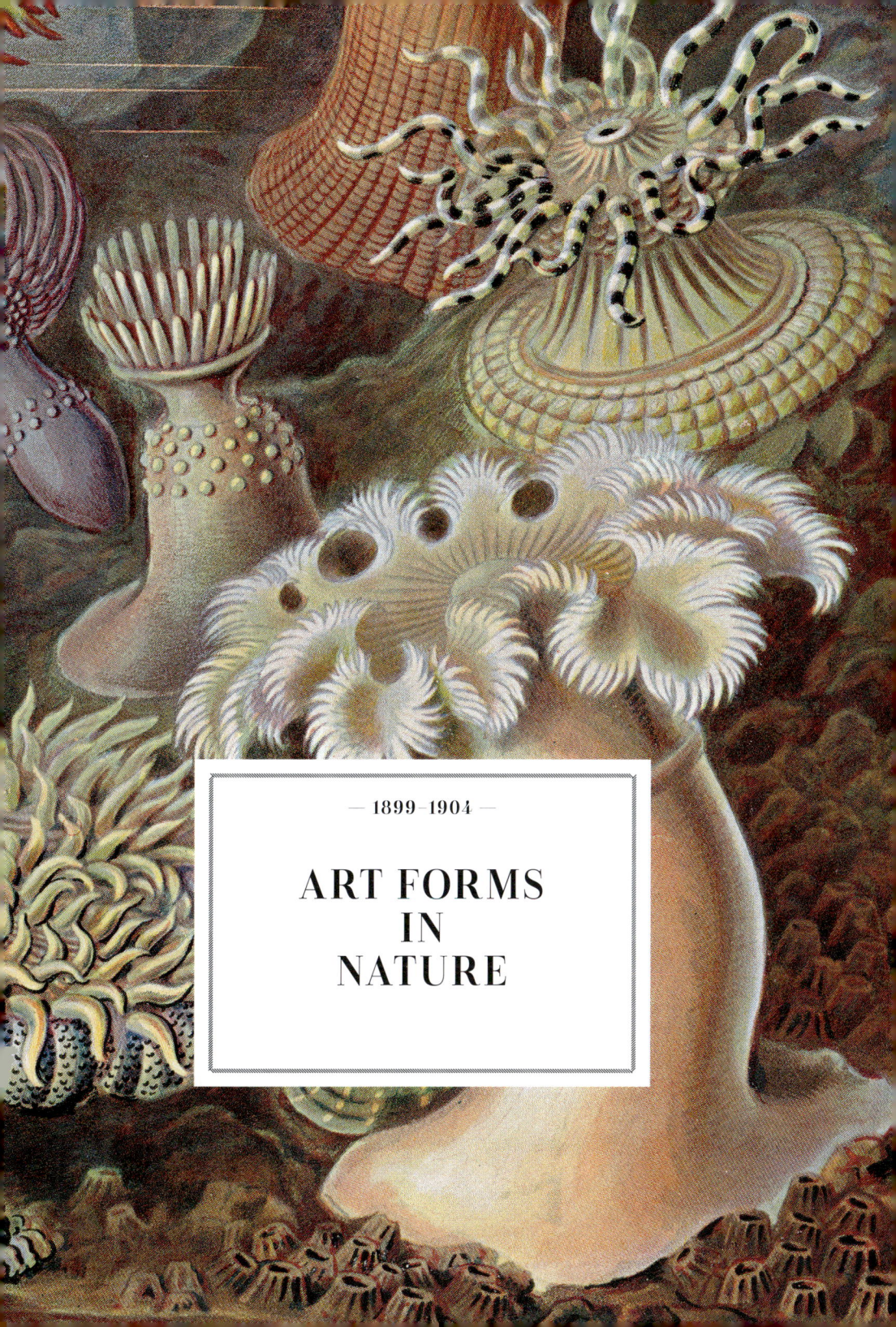

— 1899–1904 —

ART FORMS
IN
NATURE

ART FORMS
IN NATURE

In 1899, Ernst Haeckel embarked on the publication of a series of what were eventually to number 100 splendid plates (grouped in ten instalments) depicting diverse groups of organisms (plates 13, 20, 48, 52, 73, 76 not depicted). When finishing his work in 1904, he wrote of this undertaking: "The chief purpose of my *Kunstformen der Natur* was aesthetic. I wished to make accessible to far more of the educated general public those marvellous treasures of beauty that lie hidden in the depths of the ocean or which, on account of their diminutive size, can be viewed only through a microscope. Associated with this purpose, however, was the scientific aim of conveying an insight into the truly astonishing structure of the organisation of these natural forms."[1] Yet Haeckel's *Kunstformen der Natur* (*Art Forms in Nature*) did not actually fulfil an emphatically scientific aim, for almost all of its illustrations of scientific significance had already appeared – accompanied by detailed descriptions of the species presented, and a consideration of the relevant literature – either in scholarly journals or in monographs. The aim, however, of reaching a broad segment of the educated general public was certainly achieved: *Kunstformen der Natur* proved, indeed, to be one of Haeckel's "bestsellers." One reason for this lies perhaps in the thematic range of this publication.

For here, in addition to revealing the beauties to be found in the depths of the ocean, Haeckel devoted many plates to plants and animals to be found on land. Nor did he overlook fossils.

In his Postscript to the full series of plates Haeckel explained that he had intended "to combine exquisite beauty with the greatest possible truth to nature. Accordingly, all the 'art forms' presented here are forms that really exist in nature; and any sort of idealisation and stylisation has been eschewed."[2] In fact, Haeckel had presented each organism – as would indeed be a matter of course in publications on biology – in such a way as to render especially clearly its distinguishing features, also using shading and other such graphic devices to emphasise particular aspects of its structure. In the case of the fossils – as is, of course, usual in scientific publications intended for a general public – he avoided recording the damage accompanying a poor state of preservation or resulting from the way an item had been treated during preparation. From the start, moreover, Haeckel had selected examples that, in terms of their state of preservation, had seemed especially well suited for his purpose.

The approach that Haeckel adopted in *Kunstformen der Natur*, both through his selection of objects and through his preferred emphases, reveals that the title of this publication concealed a contradiction. If, by the term "form in art" one understands the way in which an entity is artistically shaped, it is clear that in nature there are no such consciously shaped forms: "created by nature" and "shaped by art" are fundamentally opposing notions. Haeckel himself recognised this; and in his essay of 1913 "Die Natur als Künstlerin" (Nature as an Artist) he emphasised that, notwithstanding the similarities between the skeletal forms of Radiolaria "and highly sophisticated products of human ingenuity" (crowns, diadems, necklaces, helmets, etc.), it was important not to forget that "we can no more impute consciousness to the single cell of a radiolarian than we can impute a life of the psyche to plants and most of the lower animals."[3] In line with his critical remarks on the widespread tendency among scientists to impose an anthropocentric point of view, Haeckel maintained his objection to any attempt of equating the art of humanity with the "admirable arts of the animal kingdom." In the context of sexual selection, even the most appealing and attractive structures and colours had evolved to serve as signals in the search for a mate. Here, one was unconcerned with works of art, although – as Darwin had already demonstrated – creatures of the same species would effectively be perceiving their beauty in receiving these signals, and thus did possess in that respect what might justifiably be understood as "aesthetic" sensitivity. Haeckel also made this point in his commentary on plate 99 of *Kunstformen der Natur*, in which hummingbirds are depicted.

As *Kunstformen der Natur* was also a work of scientific pretensions, one might have expected that Haeckel, as a naturalist, would avoid the use of such a contradictory title. But he was not solely in pursuit of scientific accuracy in this publication. With such a title he sought to secure the attention of those with an interest in the beauties of nature, and to emphasise, through this rare instance of the interplay of science and aesthetics, the proximity of these two realms. And in so doing, he had his eye on a particular category of potential readers: Thanks to the decorative elaboration of his own drawings by his lithographer Adolf Giltsch (1852–1911), Haeckel believed that his plates would provide inspiration for both artists and craftsmen. As he also observed in his Preface: "[...] the visual arts of our own day, as well as the powerfully emerging applied arts, will find a wealth of new and beautiful motifs in these true 'art forms of Nature'."[4] And this did indeed occur in a most direct fashion when Frida von Uslar-Gleichen (1864–1903) lent some of Haeckel's plates to a Göttingen goldsmith, who found in them new motifs for his work.

In his Postscript to *Kunstformen der Natur* Haeckel wrote: "The endlessly various beauty that adorns the important and widely recognised forms of the higher plants and animals has been familiar to humanity for millennia, and has been greatly exploited in the visual arts. By contrast, the no less rich, and to a degree unparalleled, forms of the lower Metaphyta and Metazoa are still largely unknown to most of the educated general public, and yet these very much deserve our aesthetic interest and our study."[5] Haeckel's aim was to bring to attention those forms of life that were less widely familiar. And in accordance with this aim he devoted more space in his publication to these than to life forms that were far better known.

Haeckel had wanted to conclude the tenth instalment of *Kunstformen der Natur* and thus the sequence as a whole with a plate that was in some sense special. At this time he was still deeply committed to a notion of the diversity of life forms, to a vision of nature in which mankind was a truly exceptional animal – notwithstanding his vehement rejection of every manifestation of anthropocentrism in the sciences. In devising and publishing his *Kunstformen der Natur*, Haeckel was, however, not acting exclusively in his capacity as a scientist. Here, it was Haeckel the artist who was effectively "in charge"; and Haeckel as an artist had been deeply moved emotionally, above all, by those surprisingly strong feelings aroused during his relationship with Frida von Uslar-Gleichen. As the highpoint of beauty in nature, Haeckel accordingly resolved to reserve plate 100 for a rendering of the "eternal feminine" – a rendering of "the ideal of Eve and the Virgin Mary, of Helen and Aspasia – and of Frida."[6] Haeckel prepared a sketch of his idealised version of woman, whom he showed emerging from a circle of other primates. As Haeckel knew, however, that his own artistic skills were not equal to such a task, he asked his friend the painter Gabriel von Max (1840–1915; who had given him his celebrated painting of the posited, evolutionary, "missing link," *Pithecanthropus alalus* in 1894 to mark Haeckel's 60th birthday) to provide an improved final version of the composition. As is revealed, however, in a letter sent to Haeckel from Frida von Uslar-Gleichen in September 1903,[7] his publishers (Hans and Arndt Meyer) did not dare use this composition, fearing that it would provoke a scandal. Haeckel therefore eventually replaced it with an image of antelopes.

The image originally intended to serve as plate 100 of *Kunstformen der Natur* was finally published in 1905 in a supplement to the volume devoted to the paintings Haeckel had produced while on his extensive travels (*Wanderbilder*; ill. p. 46).

PLATE 1 *(Page 326)*

PHAEODARIA

1 Circogonia icosahedra (HAECKEL) – *Circogonia icosahedra* HAECKEL, 1887

2 Circostephanus coronarius (HAECKEL) – *Circostephanus coronarius* HAECKEL, 1887

3 Haeckeliana porcellana (JOHN MURRAY) – *Haeckeliana porcellana* MURRAY, 1885

4 Cortinetta tripodiscus (HAECKEL) – *Cortinetta tripodiscus* HAECKEL, 1887

5 Medusetta tetranema (HAECKEL) – *Medusetta tetranema* HAECKEL, 1887

6 Challengeria murrayi (HAECKEL) – *Protocystis murrayi* (HAECKEL, 1887)

PLATE 2

FORAMINIFERA
Foraminiferans, Forams

1 Nodosaria spinicosta (D'ORBIGNY) – *Laevidentalina badenensis* (D'ORBIGNY, 1846)
or *Amphicoryna spinicosta* (D'ORBIGNY, 1846)

2 Uvigerina aculeata (D'ORBIGNY) – *Uvigerina aculeata* (D'ORBIGNY, 1846)
(synonym: *Euuvigerina aculeata* (D'ORBIGNY, 1846))

3 Bolivina alata (SEGUENZA) – *Bolivina alata* (SEGUENZA, 1862)
(synonym: *Brizalina alata* (SEGUENZA, 1862))

4 Cristellaria echinata (D'ORBIGNY) – *Lenticulina costata* (FICHTEL & MOLL, 1798)

5 Cristellaria siddalliana (BRADY) – *Planularia siddalliana* (BRADY, 1881)

6 Cristellaria compressa (D'ORBIGNY) – *Lenticulina compressa* (D'ORBIGNY, 1846)

7 Polystomella aculeata (D'ORBIGNY) – *Elphidium aculeatum* (D'ORBIGNY, 1846)

8 Polystomella venusta (MAX SCHULTZE) – *Elphidium venustum* (SCHULTZE, 1854)

9 Nummulites orbiculatus (EHRENBERG) – *Nummulites orbiculatus* (EHRENBERG)?

10 Globigerina bulloides (D'ORBIGNY) – *Globigerina bulloides* D'ORBIGNY, 1826

11 Pavonina flabelliformis (D'ORBIGNY) – *Pavonina flabelliformis* D'ORBIGNY, 1826

12 Bulimina inflata (SEGUENZA) – *Bulimina inflata* SEGUENZA, 1862

13 Frondicularia alata (D'ORBIGNY) – *Frondicularia complanata* (DEFRANCE, 1824)

14 Calcarina clavigera (D'ORBIGNY) – *Calcarina* sp.

15 Tinoporus baculatus (CARPENTER) – *Baculogypsina sphaerulata* (PARKER & JONES, 1860)?

16 Orbulina universa (D'ORBIGNY) – *Orbulina universa* D'ORBIGNY, 1839

17 Lagena alata (BRADY) – cf. *Fissurina alata* (MÖBIUS, 1880)

18 Lagena interrupta (WILLIAMSON) – *Lagena interrupta* WILLIAMSON, 1848

19 Lagena acuticosta (REUSS) – *Homalohedra acuticosta* (REUSS, 1862)

20 Lagena spiralis (BRADY) – *Cushmanina spiralis* (BRADY, 1884)

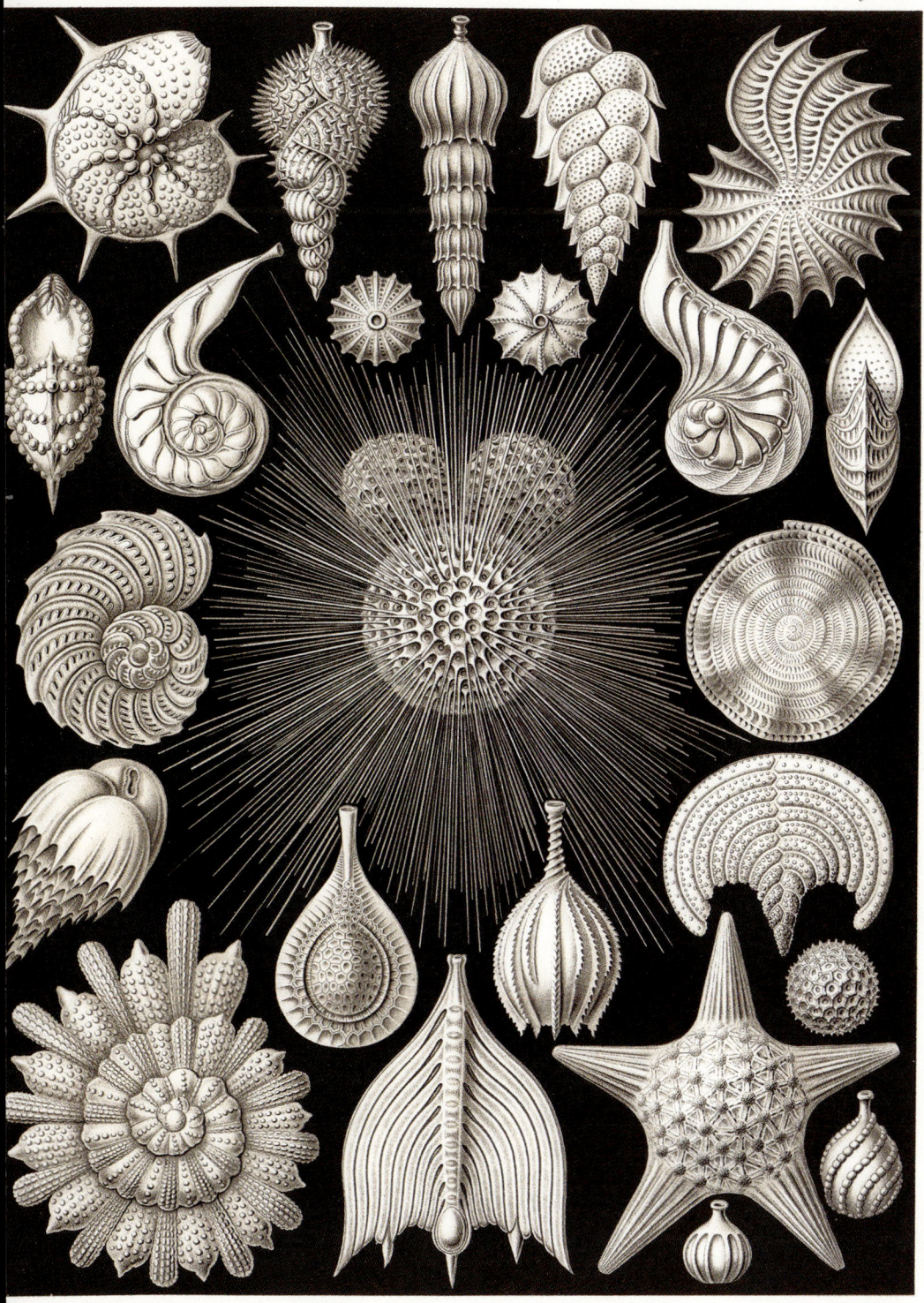

Thalamophora. — Kammerlinge.

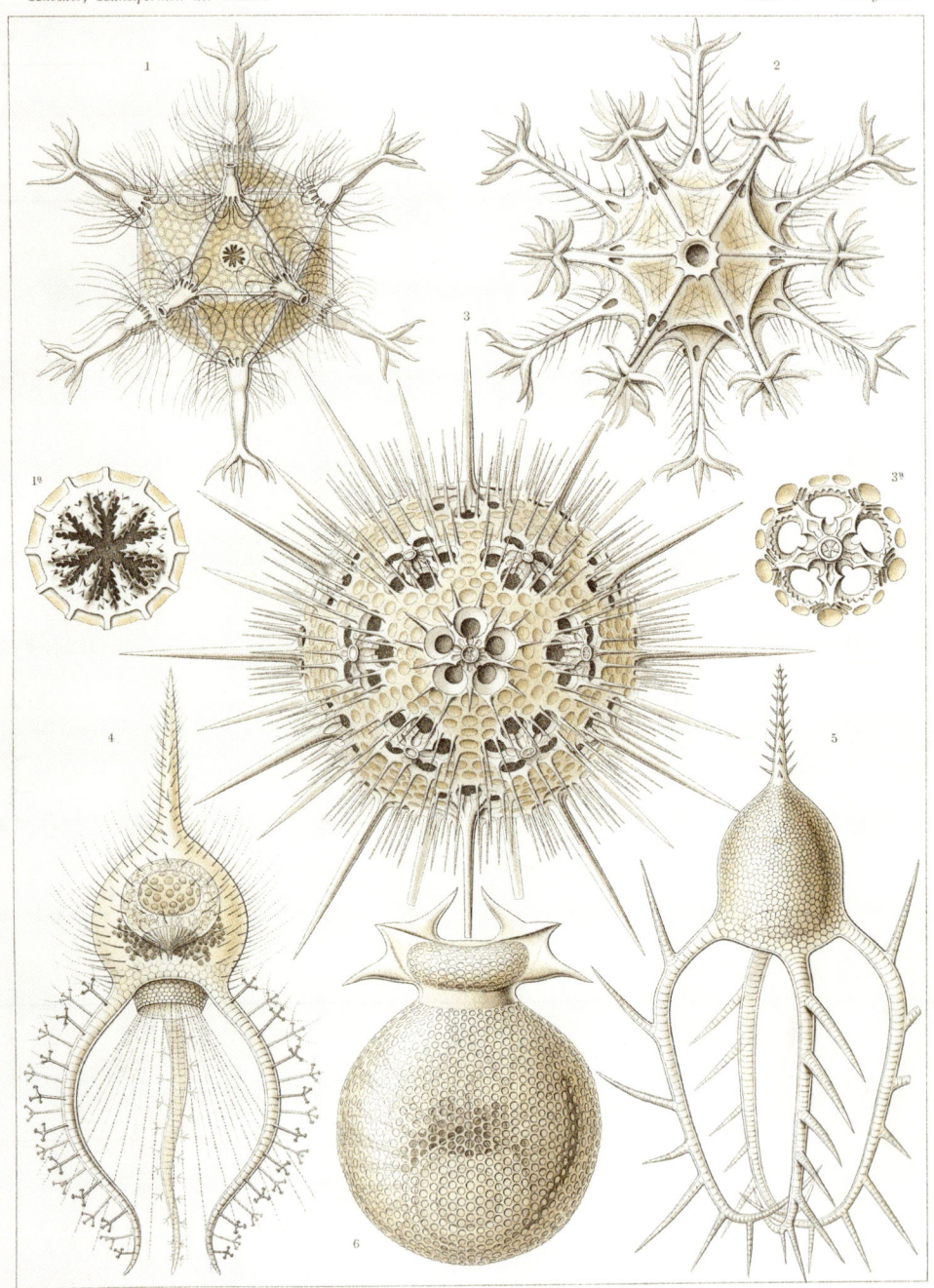

Phaeodaria. — Rohrstrahlinge.

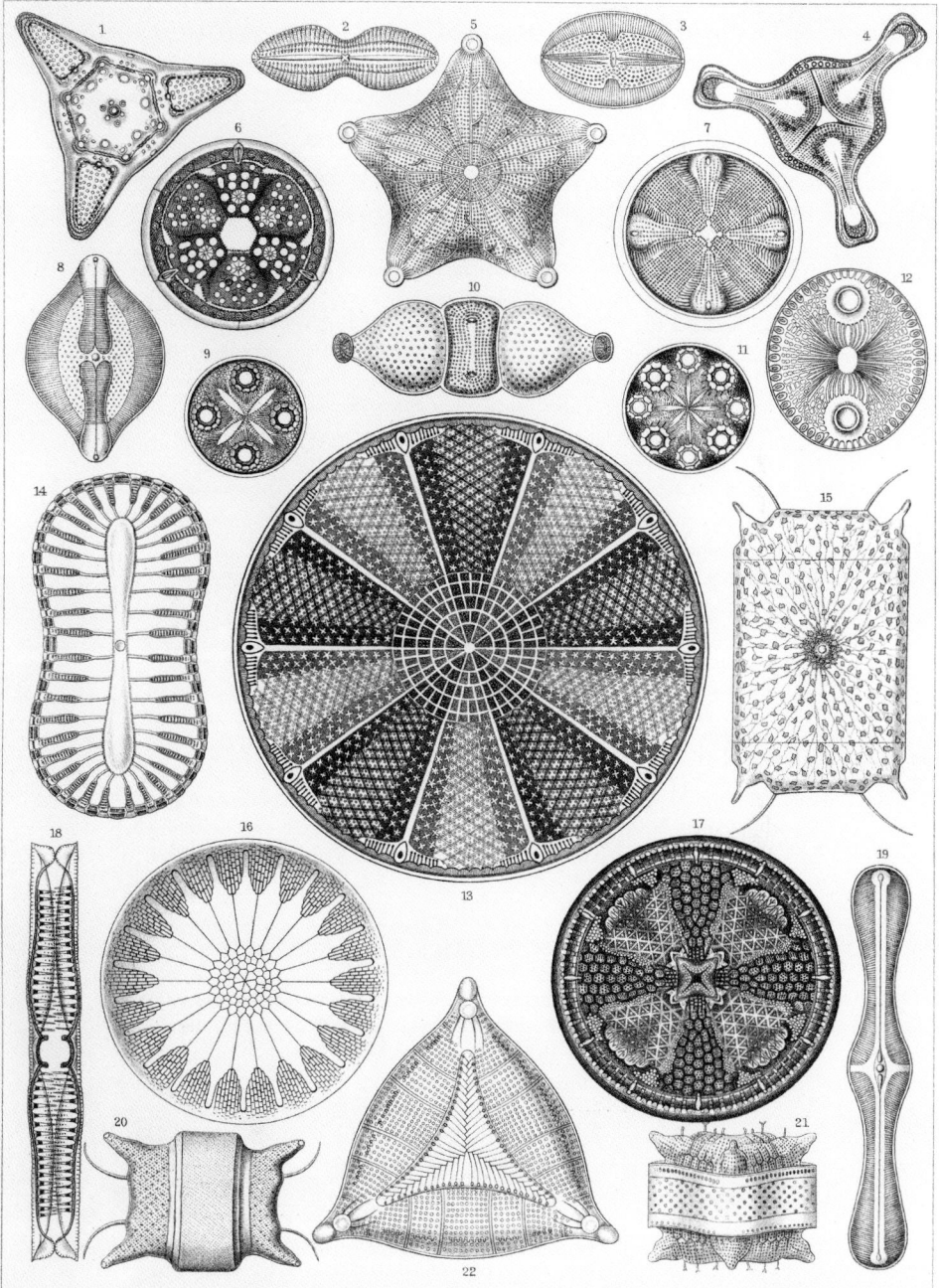

Diatomea. — Schachtellinge.

PLATE 4 *(Page 327)*
DIATOMEAE
Diatoms

1 Triceratium digitale (BRUN) – cf. *Triceratium digitale* BRUN
2 Navicula lyra (EHRENBERG) – *Lyrella lyra* (EHRENBERG, 1841) KARAJEVA, 1978
(synonym: *Navicula lyra* EHRENBERG, 1841*)*
3 Navicula excavata (GREVILLE) – *Lyrella excavata* (GREVILLE, 1866) MANN, 1990
(synonym: *Navicula excavata* GREVILLE, 1866)
4 Triceratium mirificium (BRUN) – *Triceratium mirificium* (BRUN)
5 Triceratium pentacrinus (WALLICH) – *Triceratium pentacrinus* (EHRENBERG) WALLICH, 1858
6 Actinoptychus constellatus (BRUN) – *Actinoptychus constellatus* BRUN
7 Aulacodiscus mammosus (GREVILLE) – *Aulacodiscus mammosus* GREVILLE
8 Navicula Wrightii (MEARA) – *Navicula wrightii* O'MEARA, 1867
9 Auliscus crucifer (BRUN) – *Auliscus* sp.
10 Biddulphia pulchella (GRAY) – *Biddulphia biddulphiana* (J. E. SMITH, 1807) BOYER, 1900
11 Auliscus craterifer (BRUN) – *Auliscus* cf. *johnsonianus* var. *craterifer* BRUN
12 Auliscus mirabilis (GREVILLE) – *Auliscus mirabilis* GREVILLE
13 Aulacodiscus Grevilleanus (NORMAN) – *Aulacodiscus Grevilleanus* NORMAN EX GREVILLE
14 Surirella Macraeana (GREVILLE) – *Surirella macraeana* GREVILLE
15 Denticella regia (MAX SCHULTZE) – *Trieres regia* (M. SCHULTZE, 1858) ASHWORTH & THERIOT 2013
(synonym: *Odontella regia* (M. SCHULTZE, 1858) SIMONSEN, 1974)
16 Asterolampra eximia (GREVILLE) – *Asterolampra eximia* GREVILLE
17 Actinoptychus heliopelta (BRUN) – *Actinoptychus heliopelta* GRUNOW, 1883
18 Plagiogramma barbadense (BRUN) – *Rutilaria barbadensis* (RALFS) RATABOUL & BRUN
19 Pinnularia Mülleri (HAECKEL) – *Pinnularia* sp.
20 Biddulphia granulata (SMITH) – *Odontella granulata* (ROPER, 1859) ROSS
21 Triceratium pentacrinus (WALLICH) – *Triceratium pentacrinus* (EHRENBERG) WALLICH, 1858
22 Triceratium moronense (GREVILLE) – *Triceratium moronense* GREVILLE

PLATE 3
CILIATA
Ciliates

1 Codonella campanella (HAECKEL) – *Tintinnopsis campanula* (EHRENBERG, 1840)
2 Dictyocysta tiara (HAECKEL) – *Dictyocysta elegans* EHRENBERG, 1854
3 Dictyocysta templum (HAECKEL) – *Dictyocysta elegans* EHRENBERG, 1854
4 Tintinnopsis campanula (CLAPARÈDE) – *Tintinnopsis campanula* (EHRENBERG, 1840)
5 Cyttarocylis cistellula (FOL) – *Codonaria cistellula* (FOL, 1884)
6 Petalotricha galea (HAECKEL) – *Codonella aspera* KOFOID & CAMPBELL, 1829
7 Stentor polymorphus (EHRENBERG) – *Stentor polymorphus* (O. F. MÜLLER, 1773)
8 Stentor polymorphus (EHRENBERG) – *Stentor polymorphus* (O. F. MÜLLER, 1773)
9 Freia ampulla (CLAPARÈDE) – *Folliculina ampulla* O. F. MÜLLER, 1783
10 Vorticella convallaria (EHRENBERG) – *Vorticella convallaria* LINNAEUS, 1758
11–12 Carchesium polypinum (EHRENBERG) – *Carchesium polypinum* LINNAEUS, 1758
13 Epistylis flavicans (EHRENBERG) – *Campanella umbellaria* LINNÉ, 1767
14–15 Zoothamnium arbuscula (EHRENBERG) – *Zoothamnium arbuscula* EHRENBERG, 1839

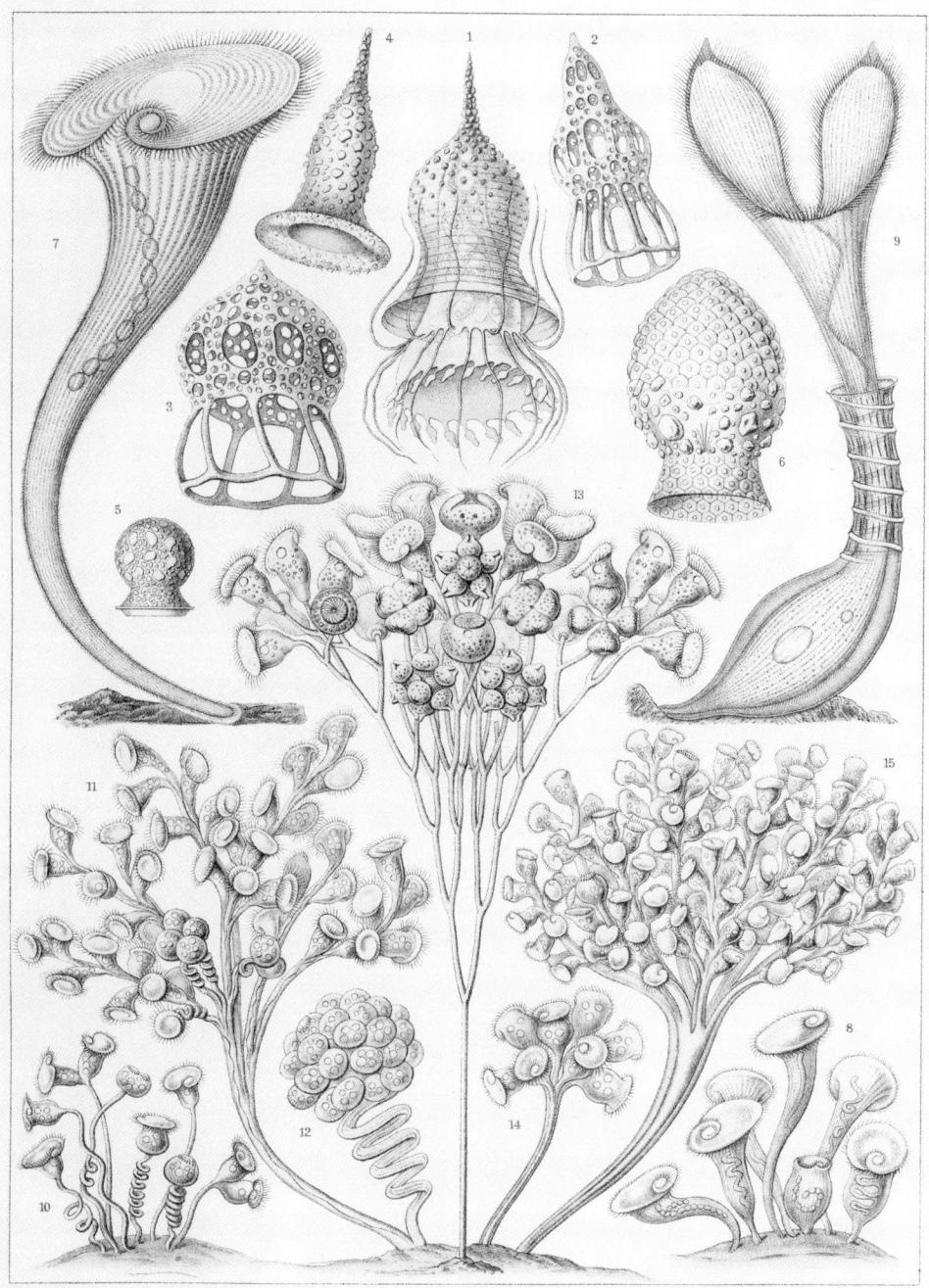

Ciliata. — Wimperlinge.

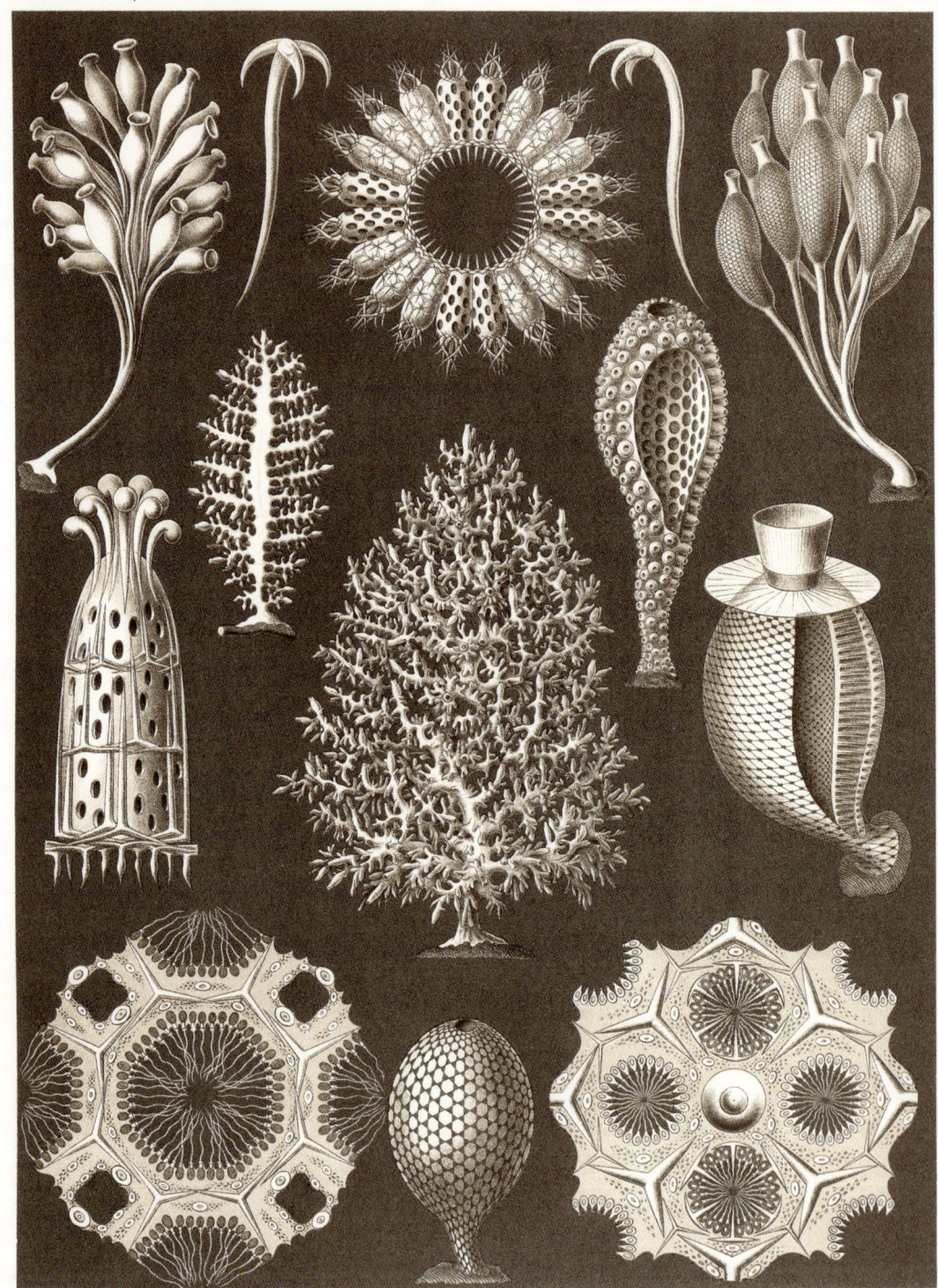

Calcispongiae. — Kalkschwämme.

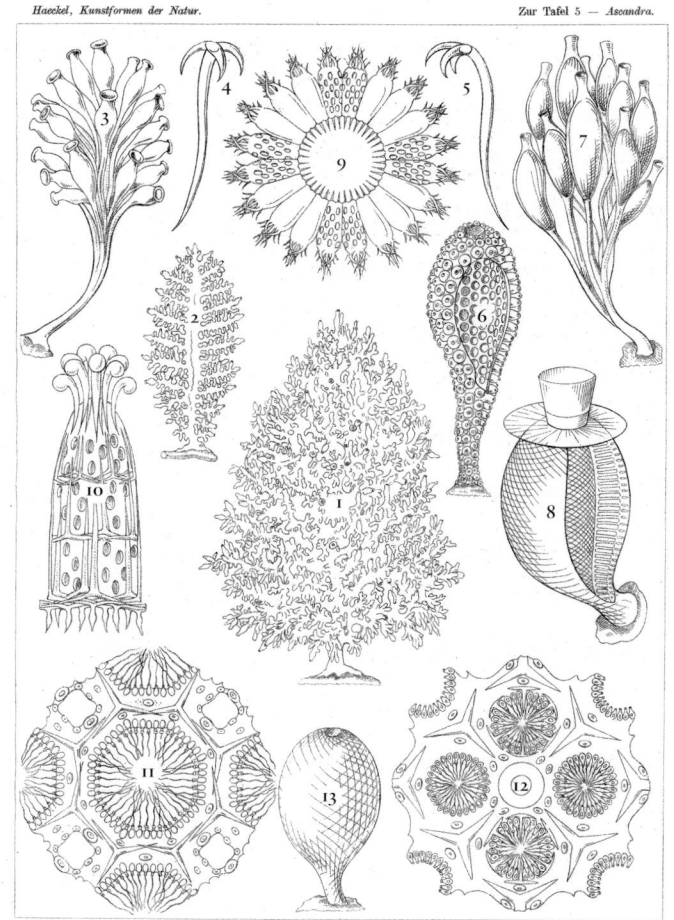

PLATE 5

PORIFERA

Sponges

1 Ascandra pinus (HAECKEL) – *Leucoselenia complicata* (MONTAGU, 1818) | **2** Ascandra sertularia (HAECKEL) – *Leucoselenia sertularia* (HAECKEL, 1872) | **3** Ascilla gracilis (HAECKEL) – *Guancha gracilis* (HAECKEL, 1872) | **4-5** Syculmis synapta (HAECKEL) – *Amphoriscus synapta* (SCHMIDT, 1872 IN HAECKEL) **6** Sycurus primitivus (HAECKEL) – *Sycettaga primitiva* (HAECKEL, 1872) | **7** Sycodendron ampulla (HAECKEL) – *Sycon ampulla* (HAECKEL, 1870) | **8** Sycarium elegans (HAECKEL) – *Sycon elegans* (BOWERBANK, 1845) **9** Sycortis quadrangulata (HAECKEL) – *Sycon quadrangulatum* (SCHMIDT, 1868) | **10** Sycandra compressa (HAECKEL) – *Grantia compressa* (FABRICIUS, 1780) | **11** Sycarium elegans (HAECKEL) – *Sycon elegans* (BOWERBANK, 1845) | **12** Sycaltis perforata (HAECKEL) – *Amphoriscus perforatus* (HAECKEL, 1872) **13** Sycetta strobilus (HAECKEL) – *Grantia strobilus* (HAECKEL, 1872)

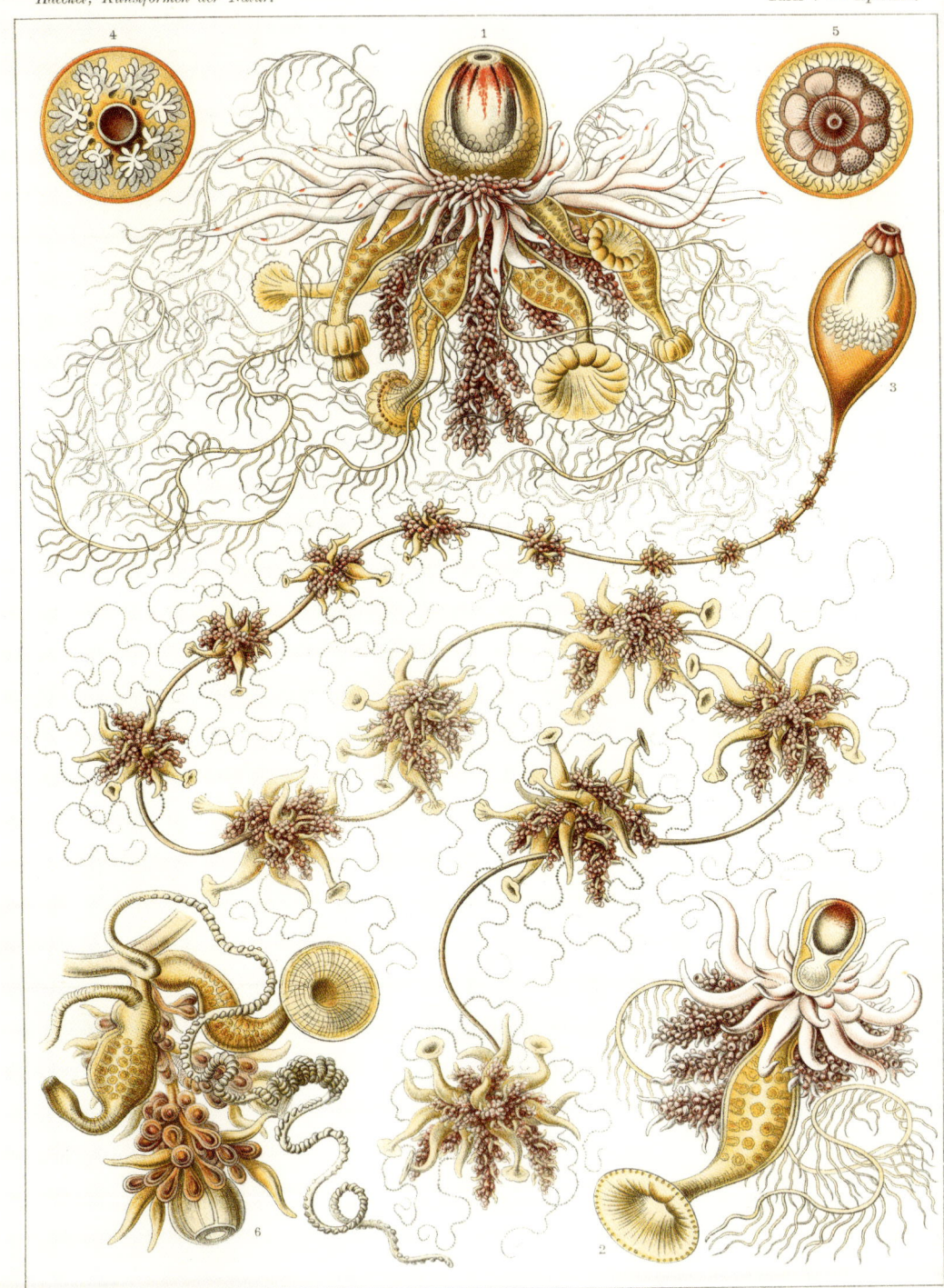

Siphonophorae. — Staatsquallen.

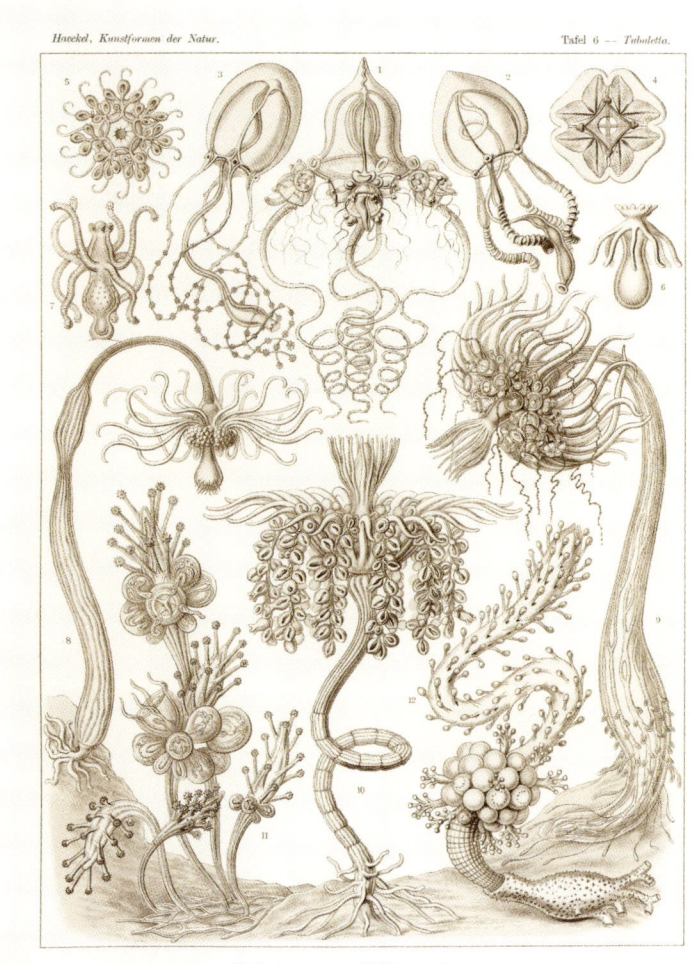

Haeckel, Kunstformen der Natur.　　　　　　　　　Tafel 6 — Tubuletta.

Tubulariae. — Röhrenpolypen.

PLATE 6
CNIDARIA – HYDROZOA
Cnidarians – Hydrozoans

1 Codonium codonophorum (HAECKEL) – *Codonium codonophorum* HAECKEL, 1879; synonym: *Codonium proliferum* (FORBES, 1848)? | 2 Dipurena dolichogaster (HAECKEL) – *Stauridiosarsia ophiogaster* (HAECKEL, 1877) | 3 Sarsia tubulosa (LESSON) – *Sarsia tubulosa* (M. SARS, 1835) | 4 Sarsia tubulosa (LESSON) – *Sarsia tubulosa* (M. SARS, 1835) | 5-7 Thamnocnidia coronata (L. AGASSIZ) – *Ectopleura larynx* (ELLIS & SOLANDER, 1786) | 8 Monocaulus pendulus (ALLMAN) – *Corymorpha pendula* L. AGASSIZ, 1862 | 9 Corymorpha nutans (SARS) – *Corymorpha nutans* M. SARS, 1835 | 10 Tubuletta splendida (HAECKEL) – *Tubuletta splendida* HAECKEL, 1899 | 11 Syncoryne pulchella (ALLMAN) – *Sarsia pulchella* (ALLMAN, 1865) | 12 Myriothela phrygia (FABRICIUS) – *Candelabrum phrygium* (FABRICIUS, 1780)

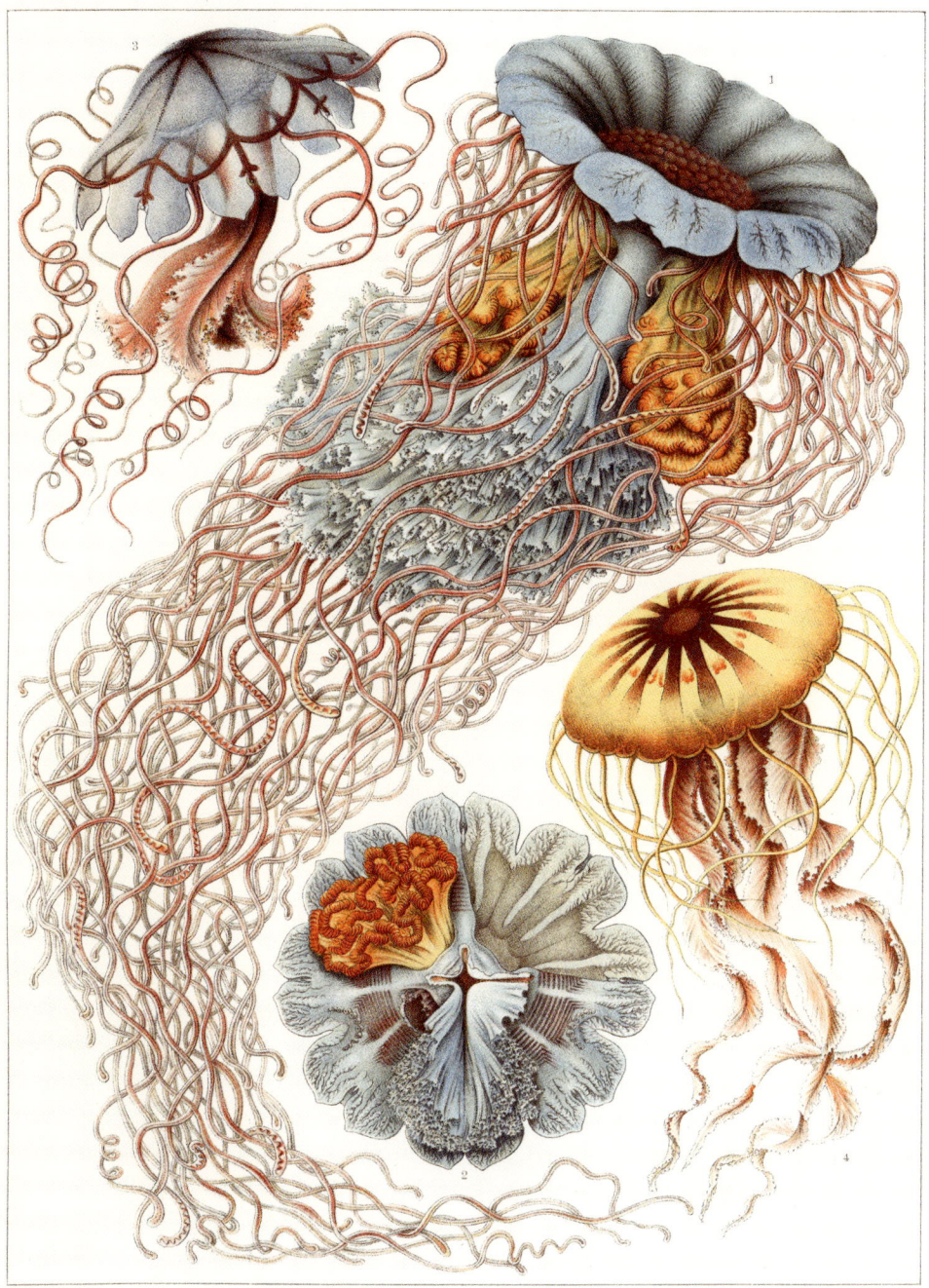

Discomedusae. — Scheibenquallen.

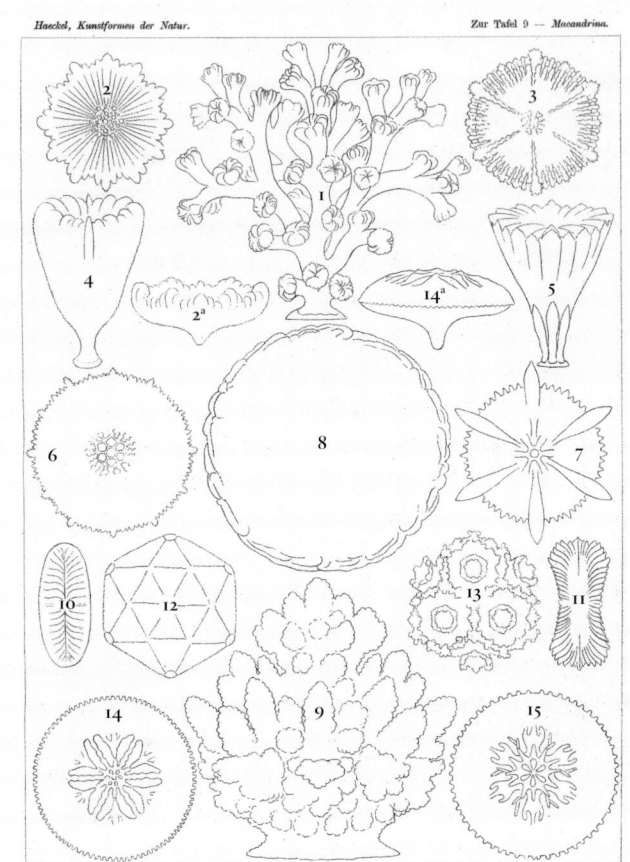

Haeckel, Kunstformen der Natur.   Zur Tafel 9 — Maeandrina.

PLATE 9
CNIDARIA – ANTHOZOA
Cnidarians – Anthozoans, Flower-like animals

1 Lophohelia prolifera (PALLAS) – *Lophelia pertusa* (LINNAEUS, 1758) (synonym: *Lophelia prolifera* (PALLAS, 1766)) 2 Leptocyathus elegans (MILNE-EDWARDS) – *Leptocyathus elegans* MILNE-EDWARDS & HAIME, 1850 | 3 Cyathina cylindrica – *Caryophyllia cylindrica* PHILIPPS, 1839 | 4 Balanophyllia floridana (POURTALES) – *Balanophyllia floridana* POURTALÈS, 1868 Porous cup coral | 5 Rhizotrochus fragilis (POURTALES) – *Polymyces fragilis* PORTALÈS, 1871 6 Stephanophyllia elegans (MILNE-EDWARDS) – *Stephanophyllia elegans* (BRONN, 1837) | 7 Astrocyathus paradoxus (POURTALES) – *Caryophyllia paradoxus* ALCOCK, 1898 | 8 Maeandrina filograna (LAMARCK) – *Meandrina filograna* (ESPER, 1791) | 9 Madrepora fruticosa (BROOK) – *Acropora humilis* (DANA, 1846) | 10 Flabellum australe (MOSELEY) – *Flabellum (Flabellum) australe* MOSELEY, 1881 | 11 Flabellum alabastrum (MOSELEY) – *Flabellum (Ulocyathus) alabastrum* MOSELEY, 1873 IN THOMPSON | 12 Thamnastraea arachnoides (MILNE-EDWARDS) – *Thamnastraea arachnoides* (PARKINSON, 1808) | 13 Porites furcata (LAMARCK) – *Porites furcata* LAMARCK, 1816 14 Stephanophyllia complicata (MOSELEY) – *Stephanophyllia complicata* MOSELEY, 1876 15 Leptopenus discus (MOSELEY) – *Leptopenus discus* MOSELEY, 1881

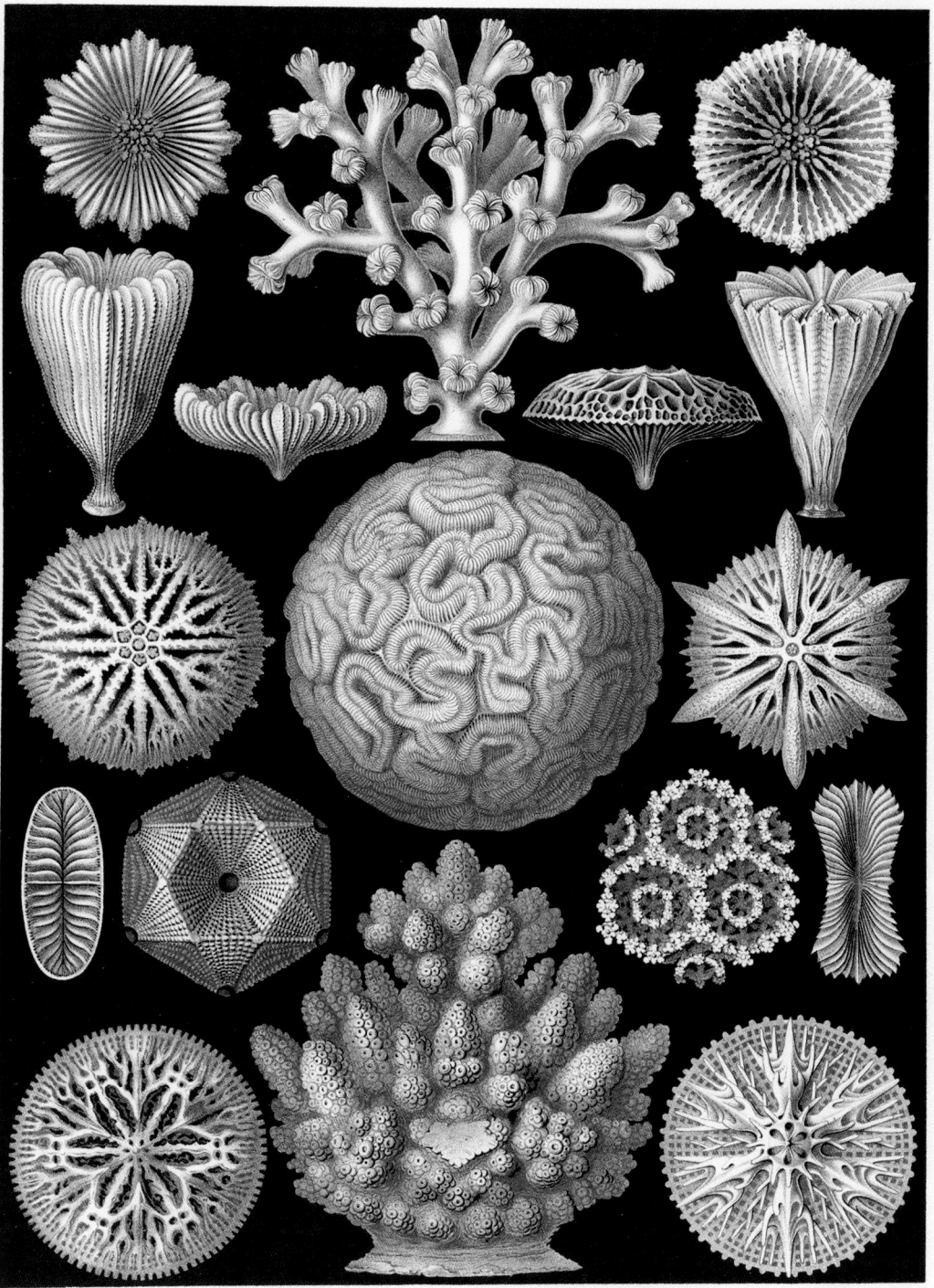

Hexacoralla. — Sechsstrahlige Sternkorallen.

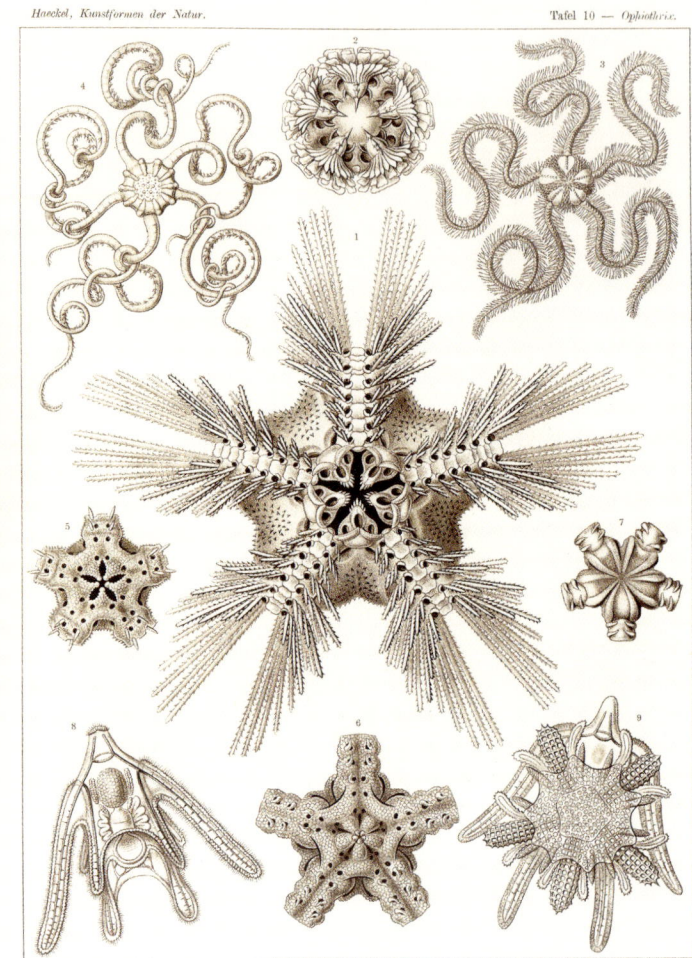

Haeckel, Kunstformen der Natur. Tafel 10 — Ophiothrix.

Ophiodea. — Schlangensterne.

PLATE 10
ECHINODERMATA – OPHIOIDEA
Echinoderms – Brittle stars

1 Ophiothrix capillaris (LYMAN) – *Macrophiothrix capillaris* (LYMAN, 1879) | 2 Ophiotholia supplicans (LYMAN) – *Ophiotholia supplicans* LYMAN, 1880 | 3 Ophiocoma rosula (LINK) – *Ophiothrix fragilis* (ABILDGARD, 1789) Common brittle star | 4 Astroschema brachiatum (LYMAN) – *Asteroschema brachiatum* LYMAN, 1879 | 5 Astroschema horridum (LYMAN) – *Asteroschema horridum* LYMAN, 1879 | 6 Astroschema rubrum (LYMAN) – *Asteroschema rubrum* LYMAN, 1879 | 7 Ophiocreas oedipus (LYMAN) – *Ophiocreas oedipus* LYMAN, 1879 | 8-9 Pluteus paradoxus (JOHANNES MÜLLER) – *Ophiura albida* FORBES, 1839 Serpent's table brittle star

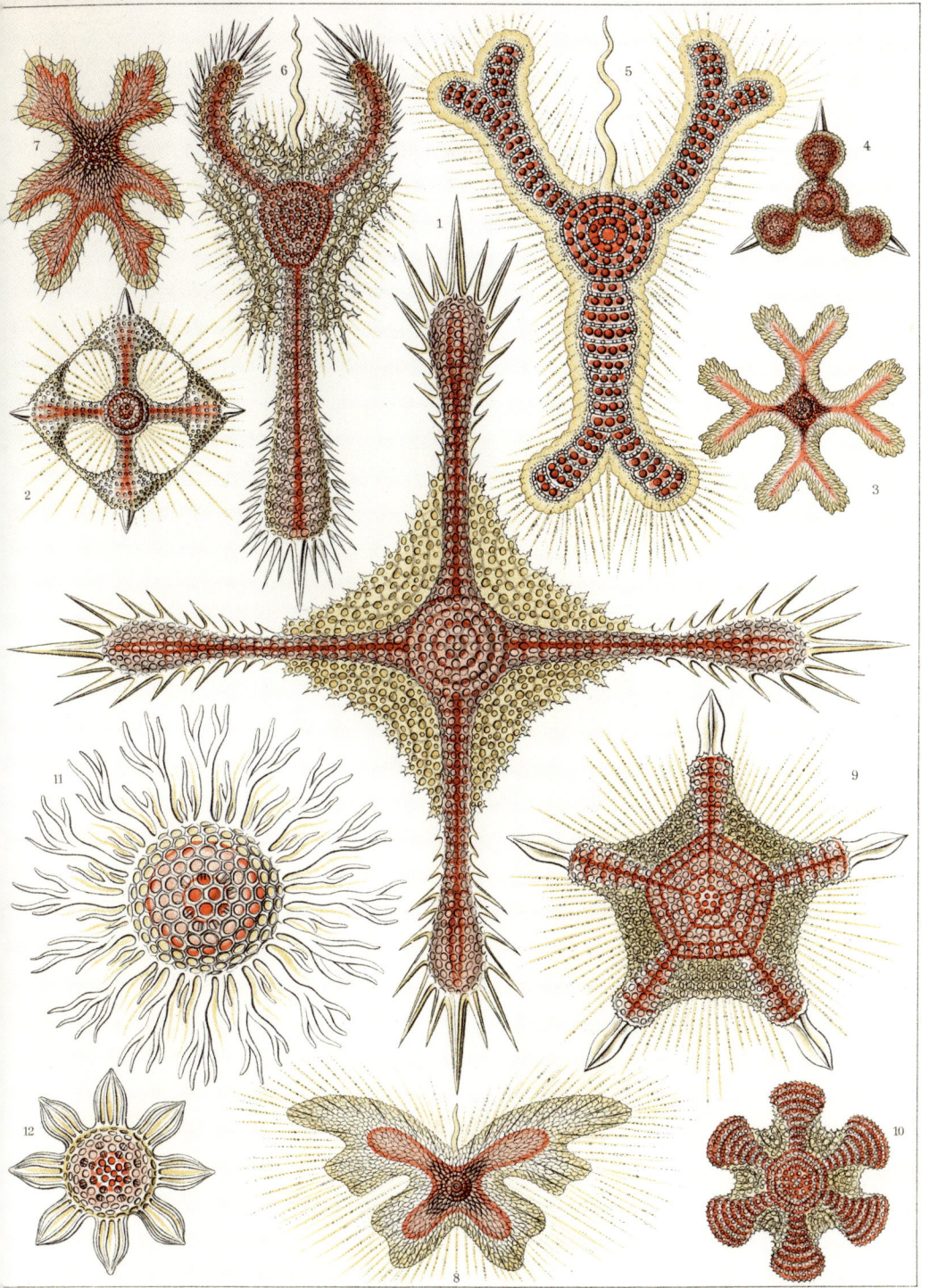

Discoidea. — Scheiben-Strahlinge.

PLATE 11 *(Page 339)*

RADIOLARIA SPUMELLARIA
Radiolarians

1 Histiastrum Boseanum (HAECKEL) – *Histiastrum boseanum* HAECKEL, 1887

2 Stephanastrum quadratum (HAECKEL) – *Stephanastrum quadratum* HAECKEL, 1887

3 Dicranastrum furcatum (HAECKEL) – *Dicranastrum furcatum* HAECKEL, 1887

4 Rhopalastrum trispinosum (HAECKEL) – *Dictyastrum trispinosum* (HAECKEL, 1887)

5 Chitonastrum lyra (HAECKEL) – *Amphirhopalum virchowii lyra* (HAECKEL, 1887)

6 Euchitonia carcinus (HAECKEL) – *Euchitonia carcinus* HAECKEL

7 Myelastrum dodecaceros (HAECKEL) – *Myelastrum* sp.?

8 Myelastrum papilio (HAECKEL) – *Myelastrum papilio* HAECKEL, 1887

9 Pentinastrum asteriscus (HAECKEL) – *Pentinastrum asteriscus* HAECKEL, 1887

10 Hexinastrum geryonidum (HAECKEL) – *Hexinastrum geryonidum* (HAECKEL, 1879)

11 Heliodrymus dendrocylus (HAECKEL) – *Heliodrymus dendrocyclus* (HAECKEL, 1881)

12 Heliodiscus glyphodon (HAECKEL) – *Heliodiscus glyphodon* (HAECKEL, 1881)

PLATE 12

FORAMINIFERA
Foraminiferans, Forams

1 Miliola parkeri (BRADY) – *Quinqueloculina parkeri* (BRADY, 1881)

2 Miliola reticulata (LAMARCK) – *Quinqueloculina* sp.

3 Miliola striolata (REUSS) – *Miliolinella fichteliana* (D'ORBIGNY, 1839)
(synonym: *Triloculina fichteliana* (D'ORBIGNY, 1839))

4 Cornuspira planorbis (MAX SCHULTZE) – *Cornuspira planorbis* SCHULTZE, 1853/1854

5 Articulina sagra (D'ORBIGNY) – *Articularia sagra* (D'ORBIGNY, 1839)

6 Spiroloculina nitida (D'ORBIGNY) – *Spiroloculina nitida* D'ORBIGNY, 1826/1839

7 Alveolina melo (D'ORBIGNY) – *Borelis melo* (FICHTEL & MOLL, 1798)

8 Peneroplis planata (MONTFORT) – *Peneroplis planatus* (FICHTEL & MOLL, 1798)

9 Hauerina circinata (BRADY) – *Polysegmentina circinata* (BRADY, 1881)

10 Hauerina ornatissima (KÄRRER) – *Hauerina ornatissima* (KÄRRER, 1868)

11 Vertebralina mucronata (D'ORBIGNY) – *Articulina mucronata* (D'ORBIGNY, 1826)

12 Vertebralina insignis (BRADY) – *Vertebralina insignis* BRADY, 1884

13 Vertebralina catena (HAECKEL) – *Milioda* gen. sp.

14 Vertebralina furcata (HAECKEL) – *Miliolida* gen. sp.

15 Biloculina comata (BRADY) – *Pyrgo comata* (BRADY, 1881)

16 Orbiculina adunca (LAMARCK) – *Marginopora vertebralis* (QUOY & GAIMARD, 1830)
(*Marginopora vertebralis* var. *laciniata* (DANA, 1848))

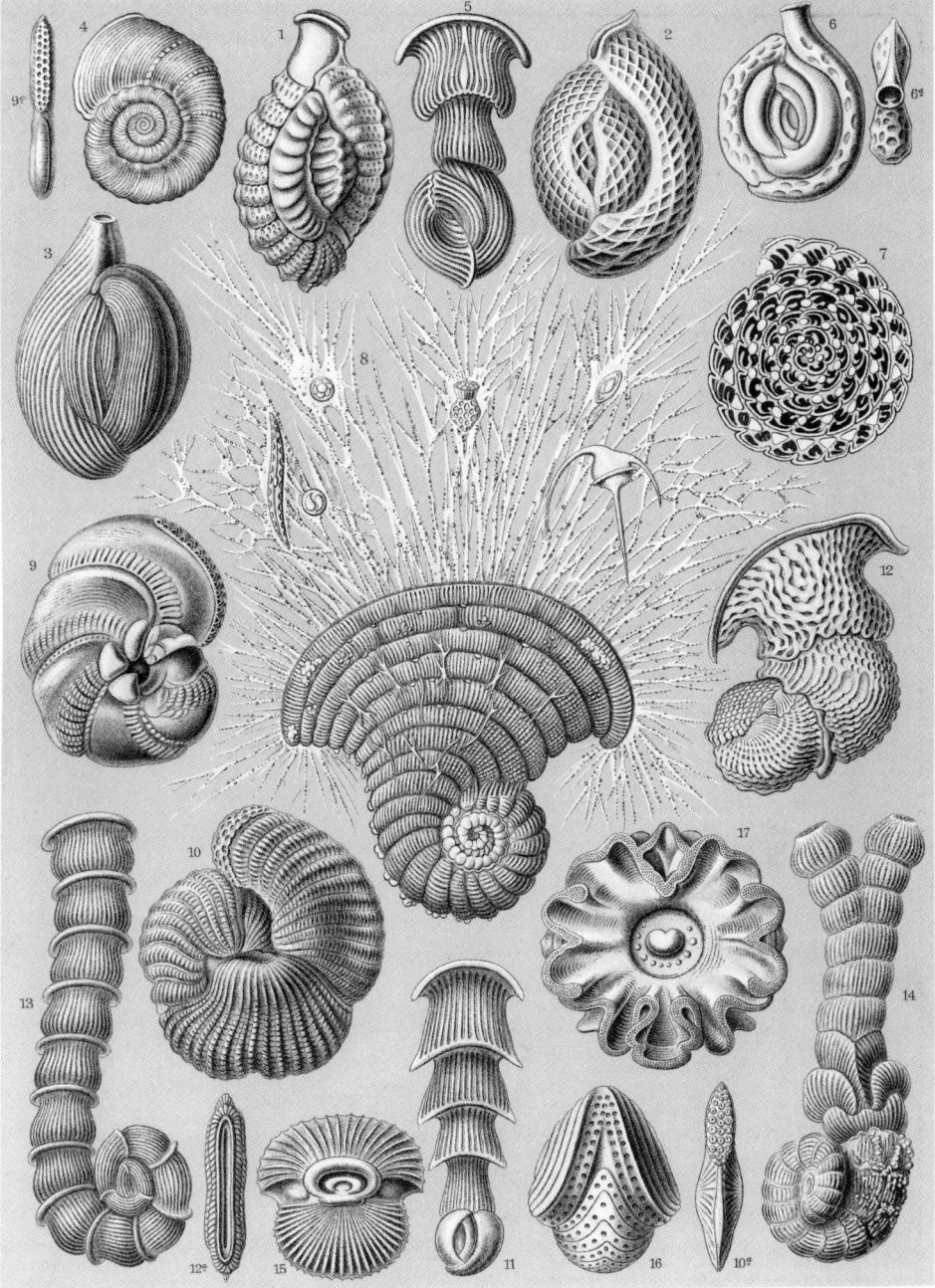

Talamophora. — Kammerlinge.

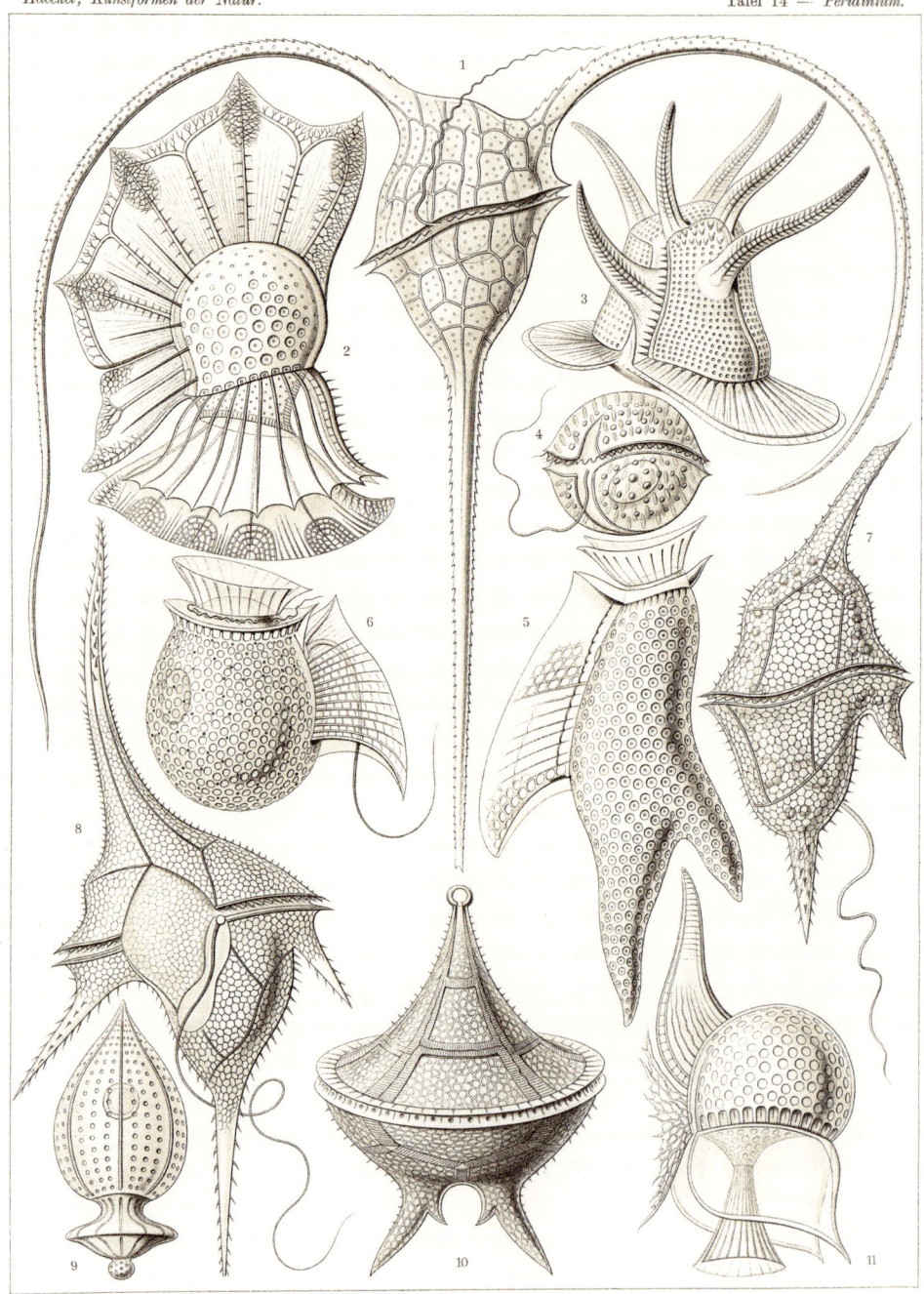

Peridinea. — Geißelhütchen.

PLATE 14
DINOFLAGELLATA – PERIDINEA
Dinoflagellates

1 Ceratium tripos (NITSCH) – *Neoceratium tripos* (O. F. MÜLLER) GOMEZ,
MOREIRA & LOPEZ-GARCIA (synonym: *Ceratium tripos* (O. F. MÜLLER) NITZSCH, 1817)
2 Ornithocerus magnificus (STEIN) – *Ornithocerus magnificus* STEIN, 1883
3 Ceratocorys horrida (STEIN) – *Ceratocorys horrida* STEIN, 1883
4 Goniodoma acuminatum (STEIN) – *Goniodoma acuminatum* (EHRENBERG) STEIN, 1883
5 Dinophysis homunculus (STEIN) – *Dinophysis caudata* SAVILLE-KENT, 1881
6 Dinophysis sphaerica (STEIN) – *Dinophysis sphaerica* STEIN, 1883
7 Ceratium cornutum (CLAPARÈDE) – *Ceratium cornutum* (EHRENBERG) CLAPARÈDE & LACHMANN, 1859
8 Ceratium macroceros (SCHRANK) – *Tripos macroceros* (EHRENBERG) GÓMEZ, 2013
9 Pyrigidium pyriforme (HAECKEL) – *Pyrigidium pyriforme* HAECKEL, 1899
10 Peridinium divergens (EHRENBERG) – *Protoperidinium divergens* (EHRENBERG) BALECH, 1974
11 Histioneis remora (STEIN) – *Histioneis remora* STEIN, 1883

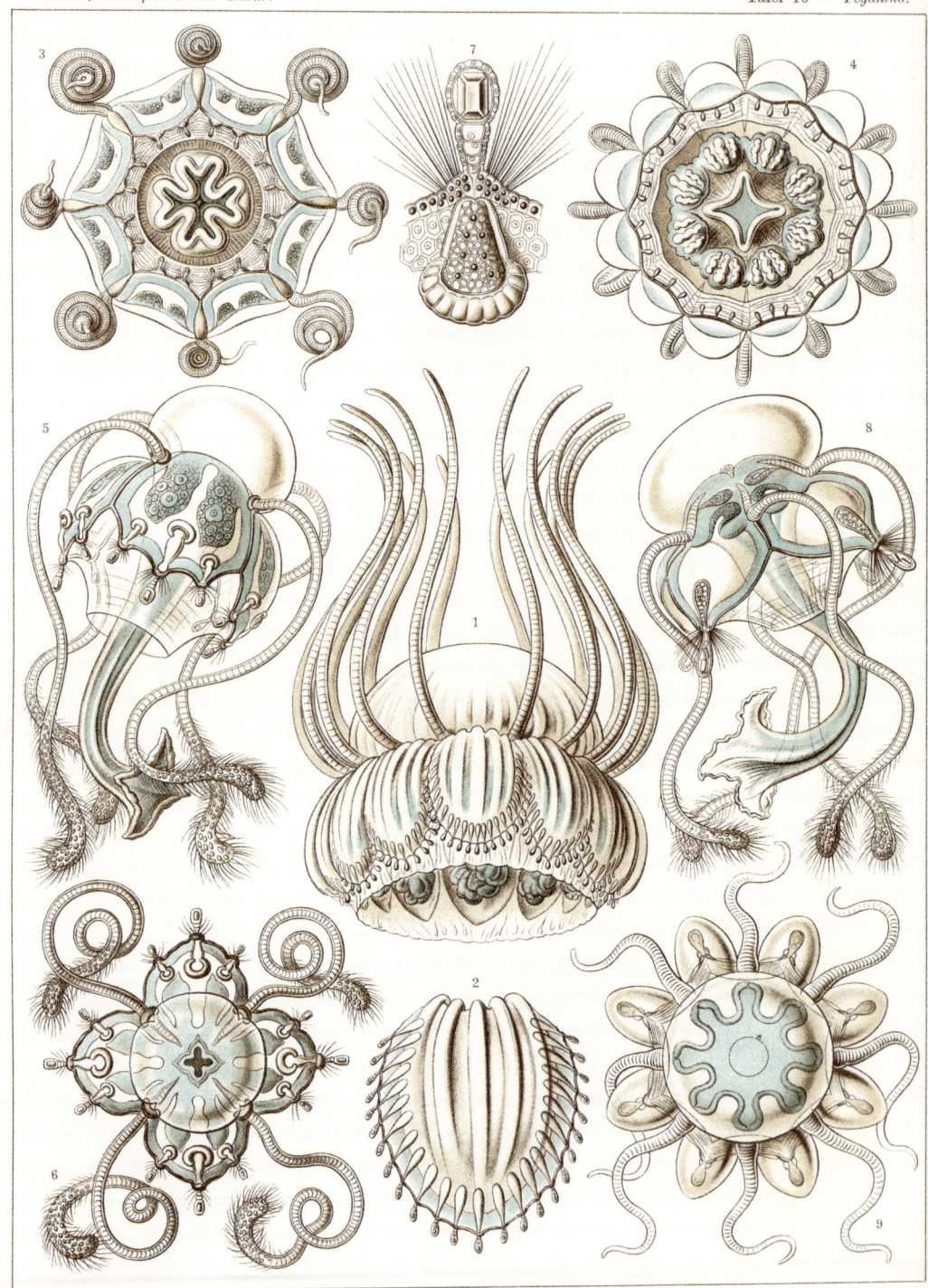

Narcomedusae. — Spangenquallen.

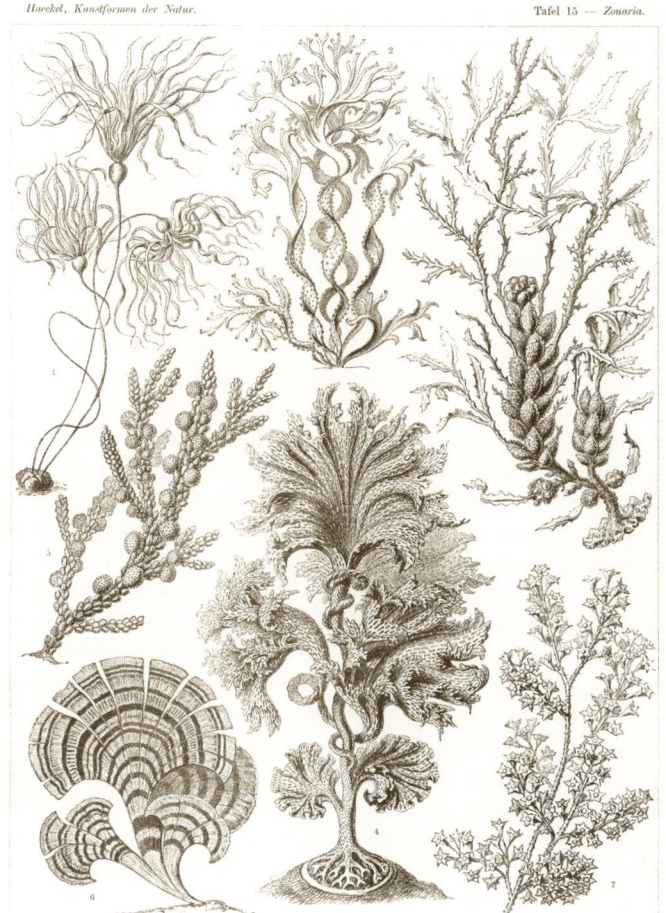

Fucoideae. — Brauntange.

PLATE 15
PHAEOPHYCEAE
Brown Algae

1 **Nereocystis lütkeana** (MERTENS) – *Nereocystis luetkeana* (K. MERTENS) POSTELS & RUPRECHT, 1840
Ribbon Kelp, Giant Kelp, Bull Whip Kelp, Sea Whip, Horsetail Kelp, Sea Otter's Cabbage | 2 **Cutleria multifida** (GREY) –
Cutleria multifida (TURNER) GREVILLE, 1830 Cutler's Many Cleft Weed | 3 **Cystosira erica** (NACCARI) –
Cystoseira tamariscifolia (HUDSON, 1762) PAPENFUSS, 1950 (synonym: *Cystoseira erica-marina* (GMELIN, 1798)
NACCARI, 1828; *Cystoseira spinosa* SAUVAGEAU, 1912) | 4 **Thalassophyllum clathrus** (POSTELS) – *Agarum clathrus*
(S. G. GMELIN) GREVILLE, 1830 | 5 **Scaberia Agardhi** (GREVILLE) – *Scaberia agardhii* GREVILLE, 1830
Brown fingerweed (austr.) | 6 **Zonaria pavonia** (AGARDH) – *Padina pavonica* (LINNAEUS) THIVY, 1960 Peacock's tail
7 **Turbinaria gracilis** (SONDER) – *Turbinaria gracilis* SONDER, 1845

PLATE 16 *(Page 344)*
CNIDARIA
Cnidarians

1 Pegantha pantheon (HAECKEL) – *Pegantha pantheon* HAECKEL, 1879 | 2 Pegantha pantheon (HAECKEL) – *Pegantha pantheon* HAECKEL, 1879 | 3 Aeginura myosura (HAECKEL) – *Aeginura myosura* HAECKEL, 1879 | 4 Solmaris Godeffroyi (HAECKEL) – *Pegantha godeffroyi* (HAECKEL, 1879) | 5-7 Cunarcha aeginoides (HAECKEL) – *Aegina citrea* ESCHSCHOLTZ, 1829 Golf tee medusa | 8 Cunantha primigenia (HAECKEL) – *Aegina* sp. | 9 Cunoctantha discoidalis (HAECKEL) – *Cunoctantha discoidalis* (KEFERSTEIN & EHLERS, 1861) (synonym: *Cunina octonaria* MCCRADY, 1857?)

PLATE 17
CNIDARIA – SIPHONOPHORA
Cnidarians – Siphonophores

1-4 Porpema medusa (HAECKEL) – *Porpalia prunella* (HAECKEL, 1888) | 5 Porpalia prunella (HAECKEL) – *Porpita prunella* (HAECKEL, 1888) | 6 Discalia medusina (HAECKEL) – *Porpita prunella* (HAECKEL, 1888) 7 Discalia medusina (HAECKEL) – *Porpita prunella* (HAECKEL, 1888) | 8-12 Disconalia gastroblasta (HAECKEL) – *Porpita porpita* (LINNAEUS, 1758) Blue button

PLATE 18 *(Page 348)*
CNIDARIA – SCYPHOZOA
Cnidarians – Scyphozoans, True jellyfish

1 Linantha lunulata (HAECKEL) – *Linantha lunulata* HAECKEL, 1880 | 2 Linantha lunulata (HAECKEL) – *Linantha lunulata* HAECKEL, 1880 | 3-5 Palephyra primigenia (HAECKEL) – *Palephyra antiqua* HAECKEL, 1880 6 Zonephyra zonaria (HAECKEL) – *Zonephyra zonaria* (HAECKEL, 1880) | 7 Strobila monodisca (HAECKEL) – ? (*Strobila monodisca* (HAECKEL)) | 8 Nauphanta Challengeri (HAECKEL) – *Nausithoe challengeri* (HAECKEL, 1880) 9 Atolla Wyvillei (HAECKEL) – *Atolla wyvillei* HAECKEL, 1880 Wyville's crownjelly

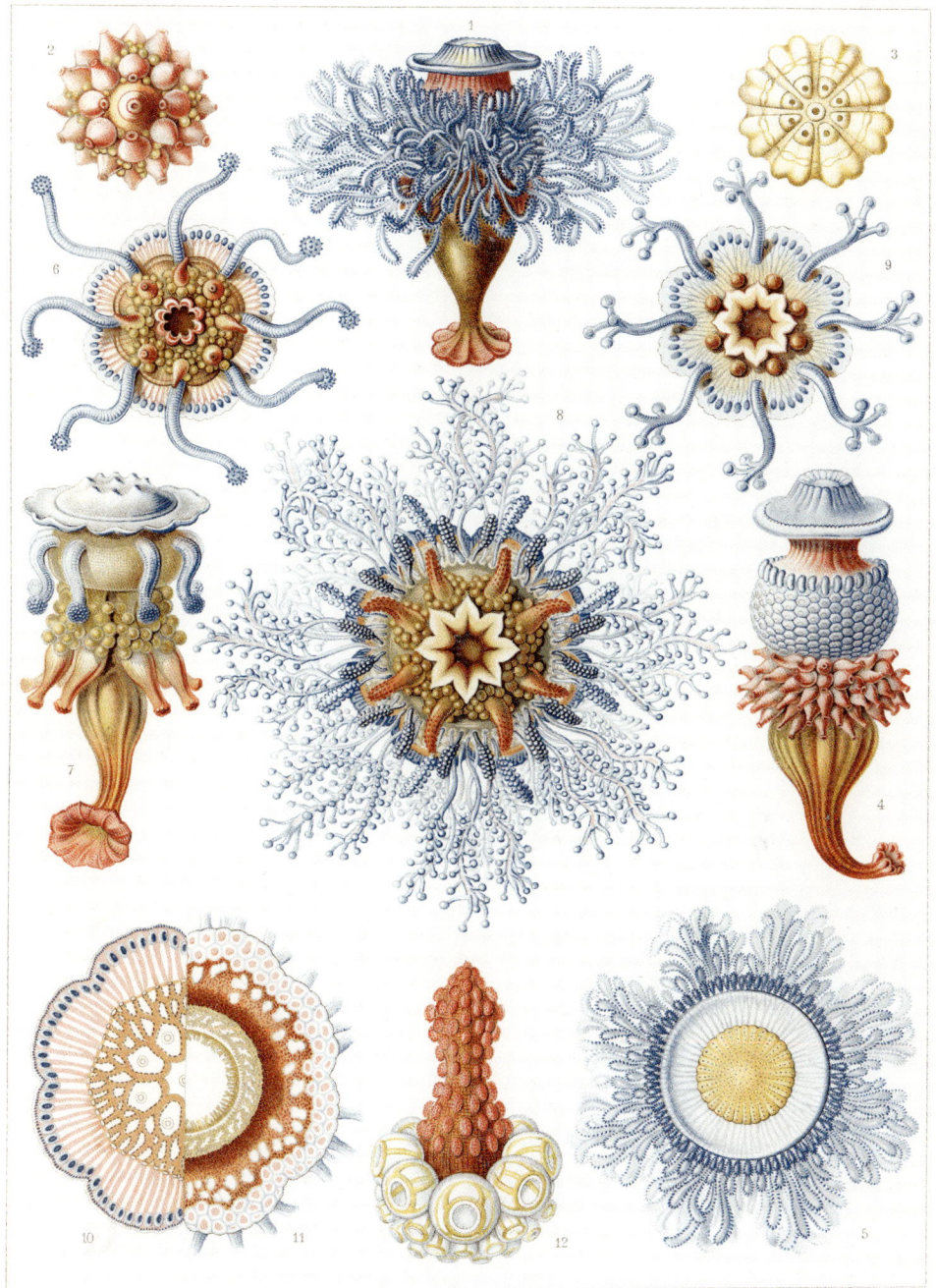

Siphonophorae. — Staatsquallen.

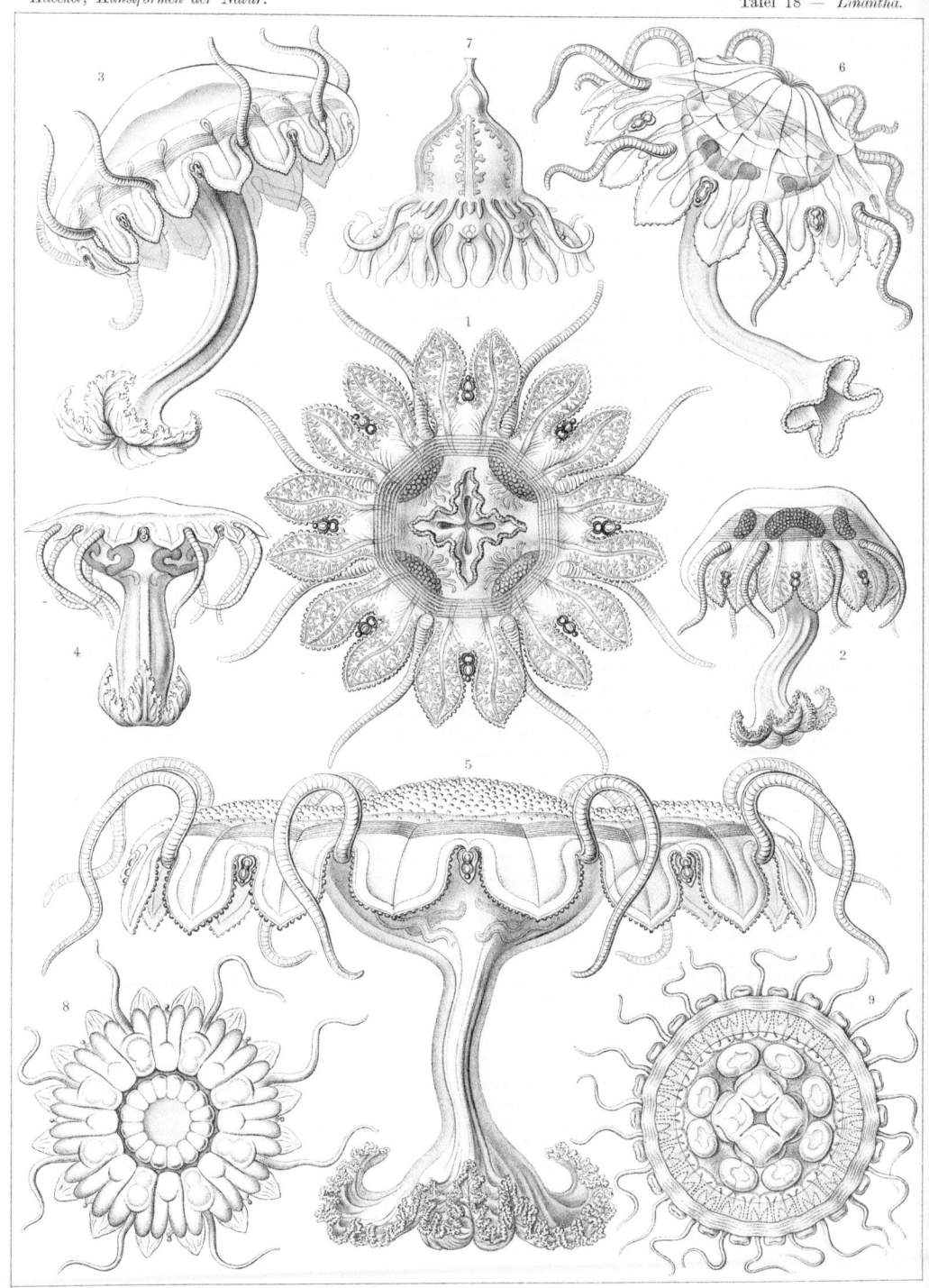

Discomedusae. — Scheibenquallen.

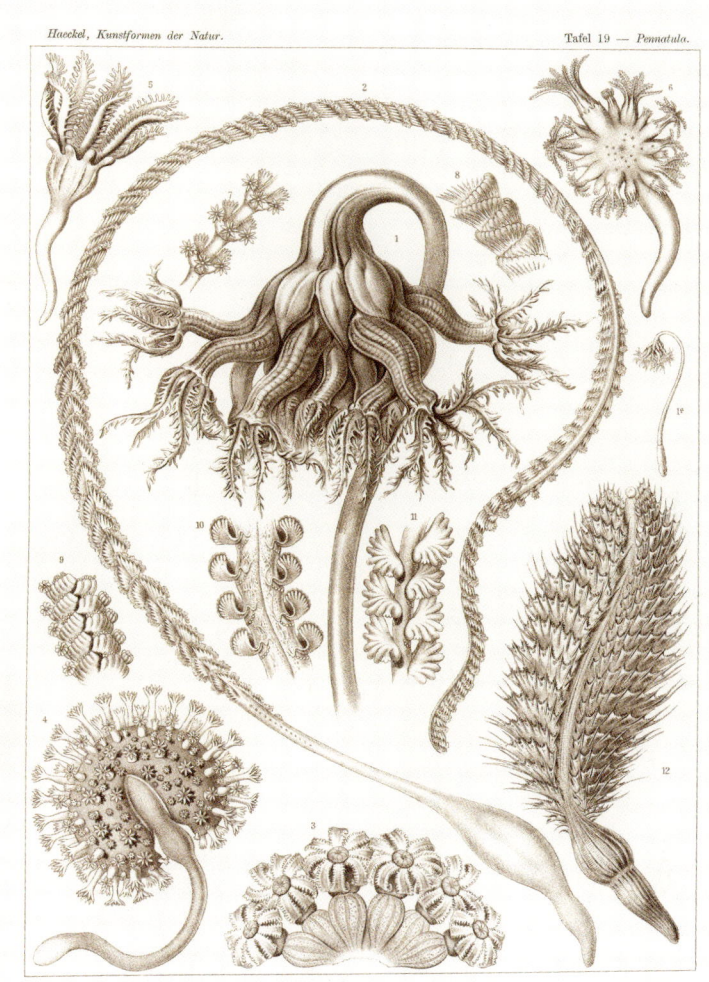

Haeckel, Kunstformen der Natur.   Tafel 19 — Pennatula.

Pennatulida. — Federkorallen.

PLATE 19
CNIDARIA – ANTHOZOA
Cnidarians – Anthozoans, Flower-like animals

1 **Umbellula encrinus** (LINNÉ) – *Umbellula encrinus* LINNAEUS, 1758 | 2 **Stylatula Finmarchica** (SARS) – *Halipteris finmarchica* (SARS, 1851) Sea whip | 3 **Virgularia Leuckarti** (RICHIARDI) – *Kophobelemnon leukarti* KÖLLIKER, 1872
4–6 **Renilla reniformis** (PALLAS) – *Renilla reniformis* (PALLAS, 1766) Sea pansy | 7 **Stylatula elegans** (DANA) – *Stylatula elegans* (DANIELSSEN, 1860) | 8 **Stylatula Kinbergii** (KÖLLIKER) – *Stylatula kinbergi* KÖLLIKER, 1870
9 **Virgularia glacialis** (SARS) – *Virgularia glacialis* KÖLLIKER, 1870 | 10 **Virgularia Rumphii** (KÖLLIKER) – *Virgularia rumphi* KÖLLIKER, 1870 | 11 **Virgularia mirabilis** (LAMARCK) – *Virgularia mirabilis* (MÜLLER, 1776)
12 **Pennatula spinosa** (ELLIS) – *Pteroeides spinosum* (ELLIS, 1764)

RADIOLARIA – ACANTHARIA
Radiolarians

1 Xiphacantha ciliata (HAECKEL) – *Xiphacantha ciliata* HAECKEL, 1900?
2 Xiphacantha spinulosa (HAECKEL) – *Stauracantha spinulosa* (HAECKEL, 1860)
3 Stauracantha quadrifurca (HAECKEL) – *Stauracantha quadrifurca* HAECKEL, 1887
4 Pristacantha polyodon (HAECKEL) – *Pristacantha polyodon* HAECKEL, 1887
5 Lithoptera dodecaptera (HAECKEL) – *Lithoptera dodecaptera* HAECKEL, 1887
6 Acantholonche peripolaris (HAECKEL) – *Acantholonche peripolaris* HAECKEL, 1887
7 Acantholonche favosa (HAECKEL) – *Acantholonche favosa* HAECKEL, 1899?

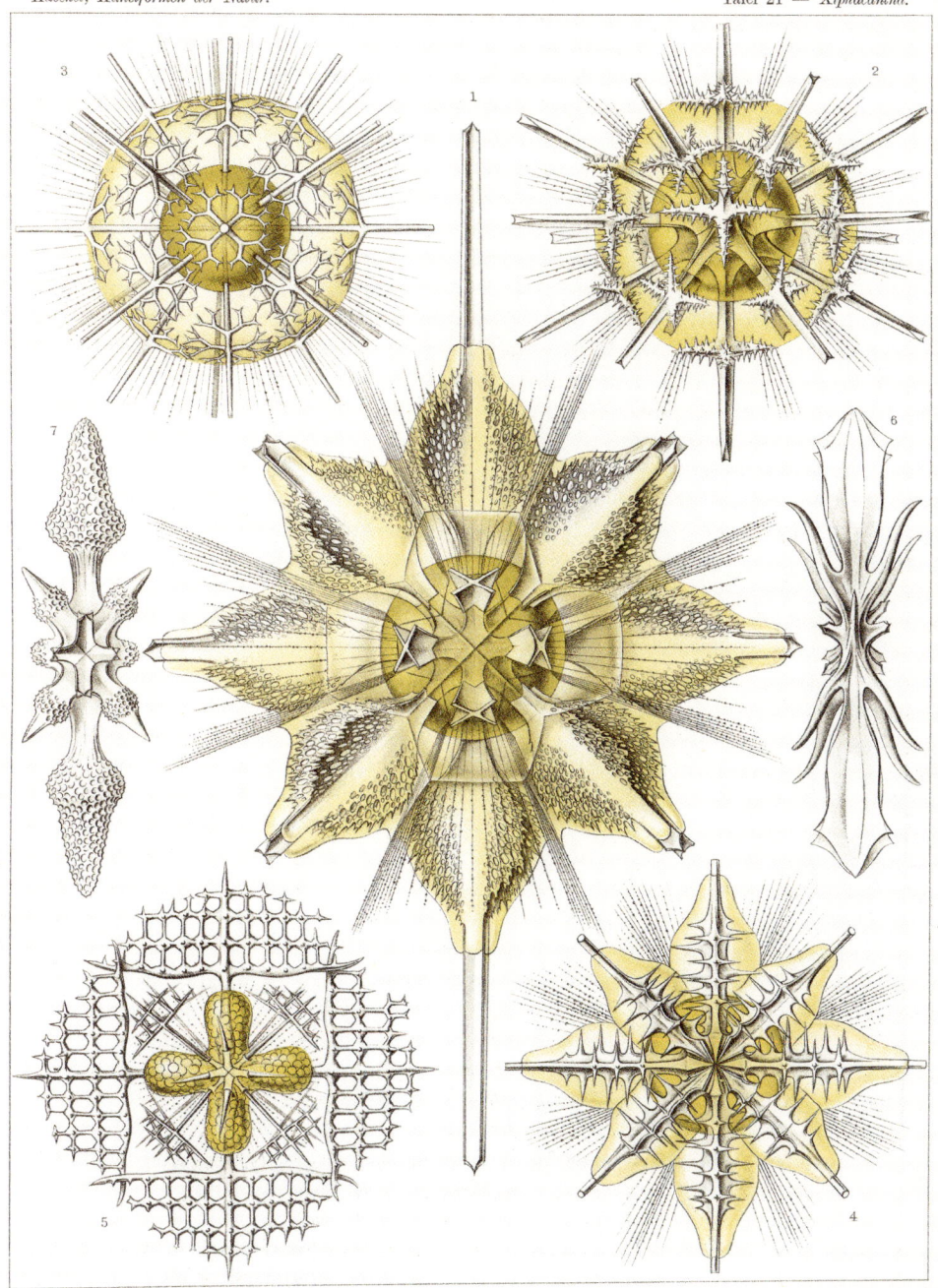

Acanthometra. — Stachelstrahlinge.

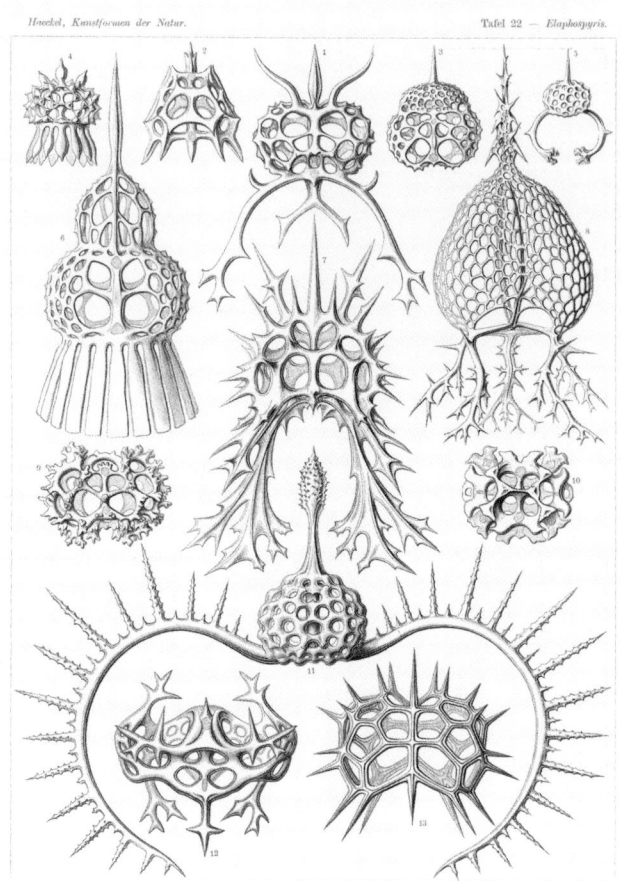

Haeckel, Kunstformen der Natur.   Tafel 22 — *Elaphospyris.*

Spyroidea. — Flüßchenstraßlinge.

PLATE 22
RADIOLARIA – NASSELARIA
Radiolarians

1 Triceraspyris gazella (HAECKEL) – *Triceraspyris gazella* HAECKEL | 2 Clathrospyris pyramidalis (HAECKEL) – *Clathrospyris pyramidalis* HAECKEL, 1887 | 3 Pylospyris canariensis (HAECKEL) – *Pylospyris canariensis* HAECKEL, 1887 4 Anthospyris mammillata (HAECKEL) – *Anthospyris mammillata* HAECKEL, 1887 | 5 Dendrospyris polyrrhizza (HAECKEL) – *Dendrospyris polyrrhizza* HAECKEL | 6 Sepalospyris pagoda (HAECKEL) – *Sepalospyris pagoda* HAECKEL 7 Elaphospyris cervicornis (HAECKEL) – *Elaphospyris cervicornis* HAECKEL, 1881 (synonym: *Giraffospyris cervicornis* (HAECKEL)) | 8 Tholospyris cupola (HAECKEL) – *Tholospyris ramosa* HAECKEL, 1887 9 Dictyospyris stalactites (HAECKEL) – *Dictyospyris stalactites* HAECKEL, 1887 | 10 Dictyospyris anthophora (HAECKEL) – *Tholospyris anthophora* (HAECKEL, 1887) | 11 Dorcadospyris dinoceras (HAECKEL) – *Dorcadospyris dinoceras* (HAECKEL) | 12 Triceraspyris damaecornis (HAECKEL) – *Corythospyris stapedius* (HAECKEL) GOLL, 1978 13 Ceratospyris Strasburgeri (HAECKEL) – *Lophospyris pentagona* (EHRENBERG) PETRUSHEVSKAYA, 1971

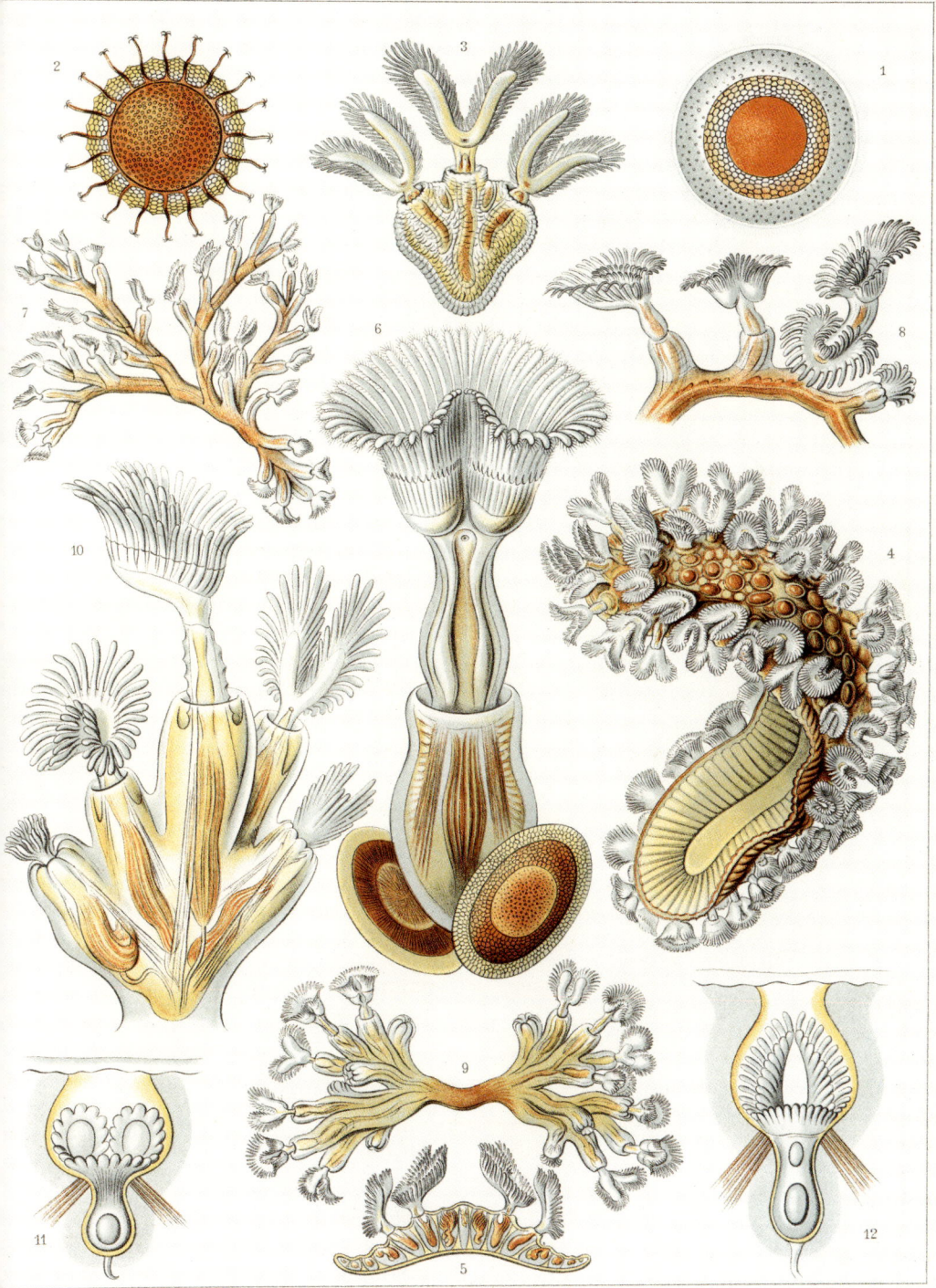

Bryozoa. — Moostiere.

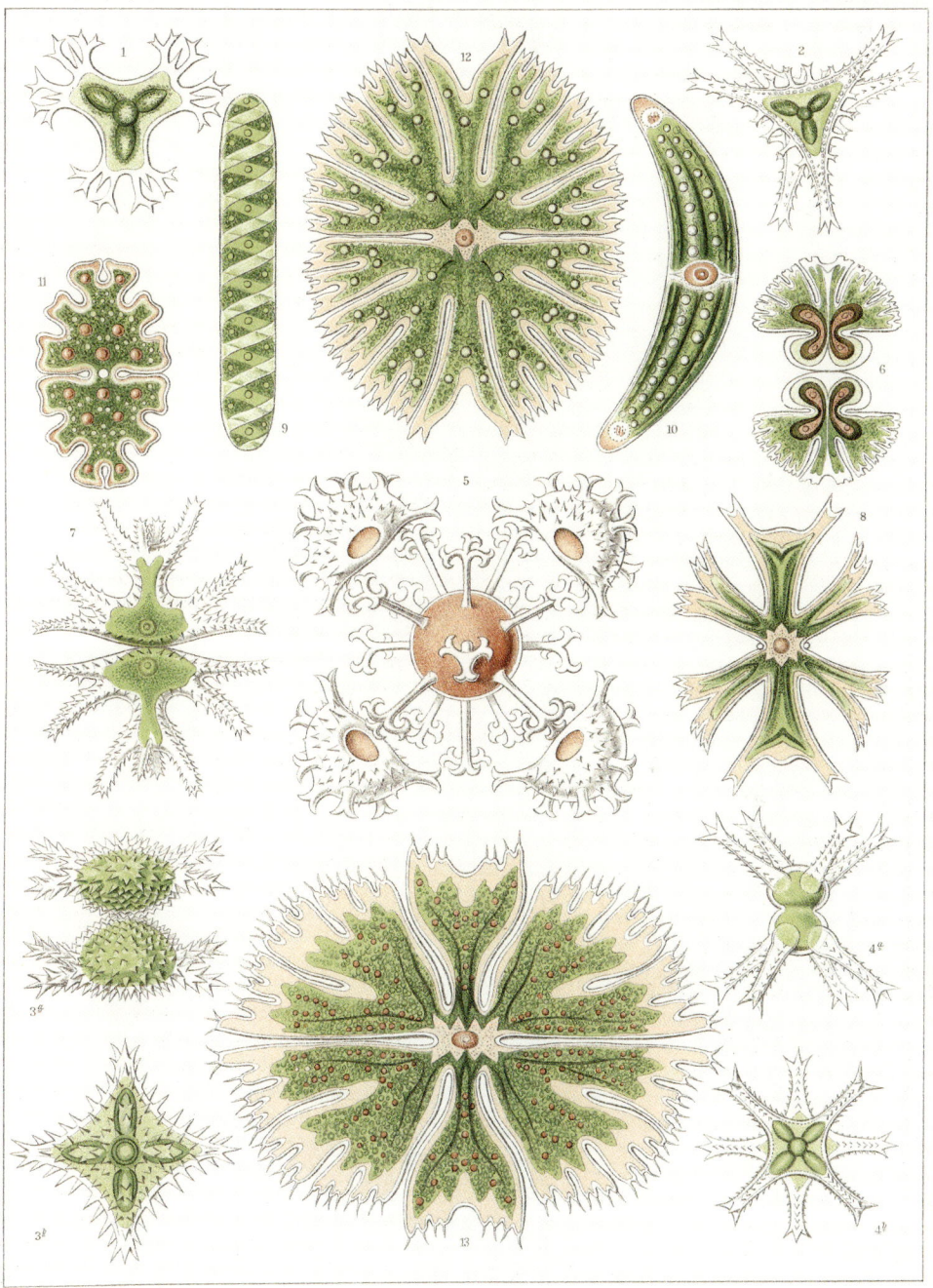

Desmidiea. — Zierdinge.

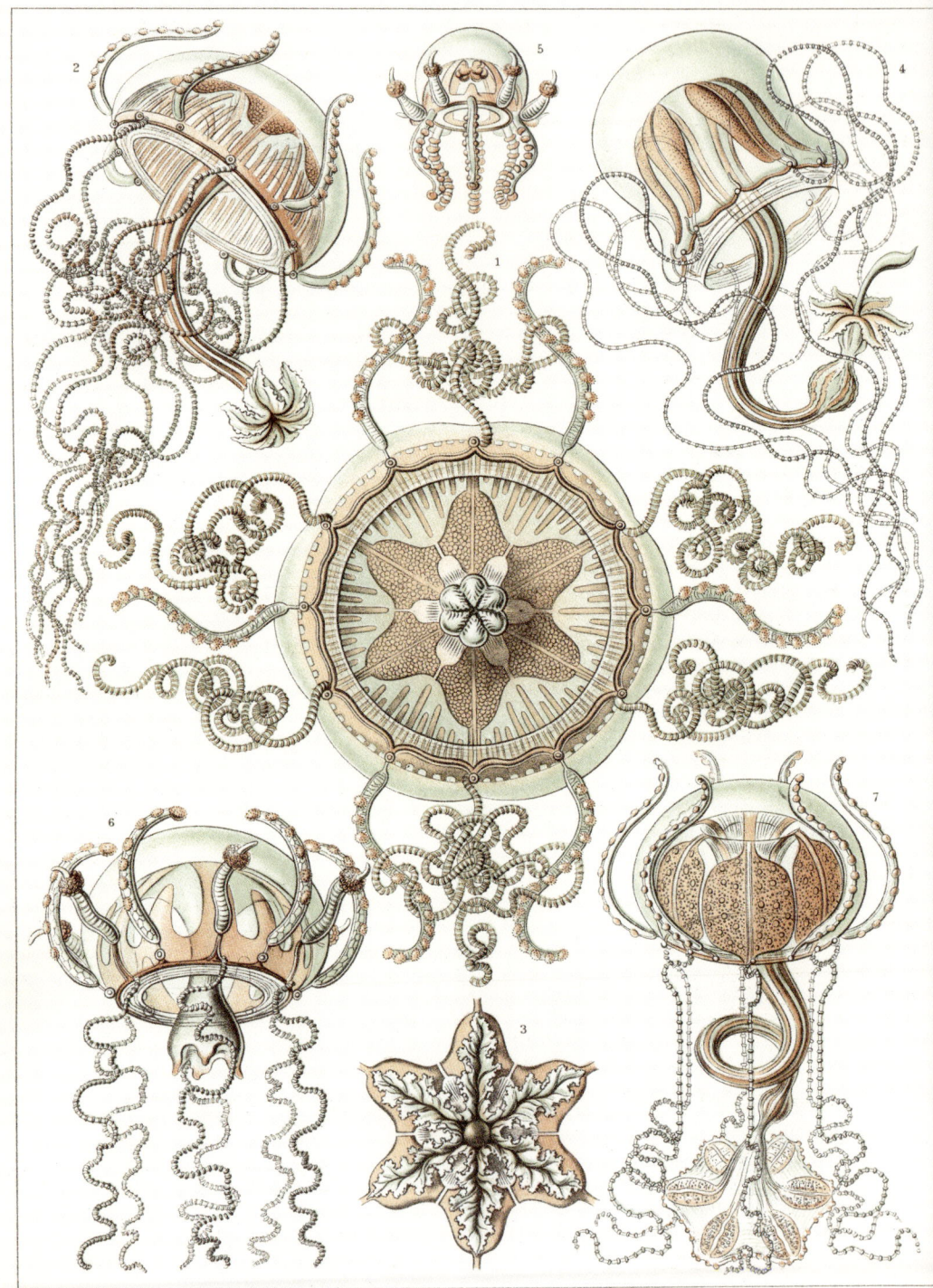

Trachomedusae. — Kolbenquallen.

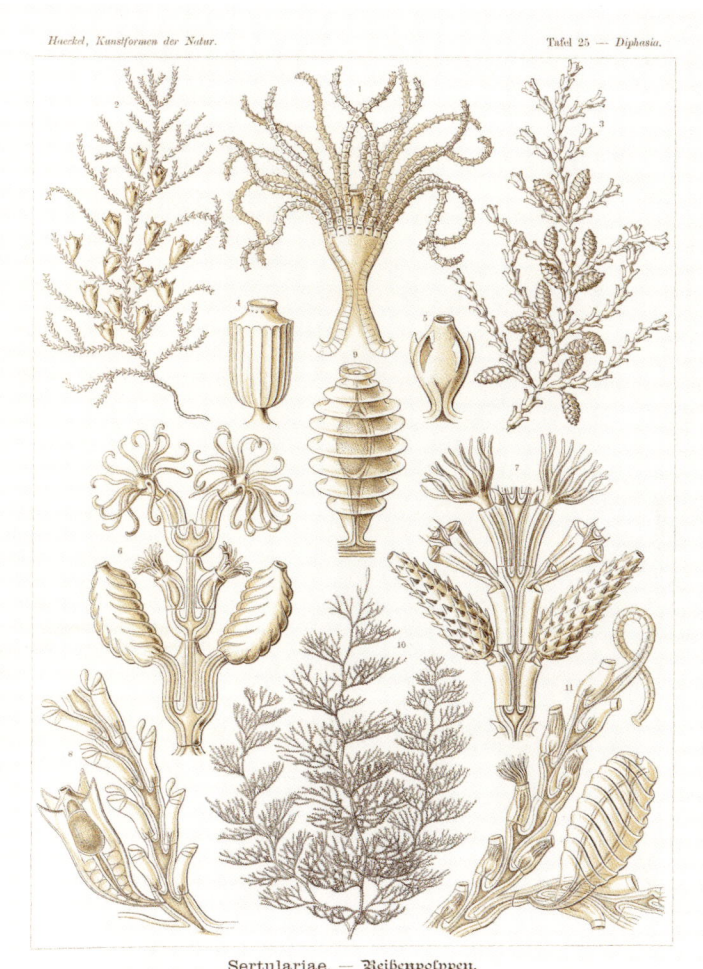

PLATE 25
CNIDARIA – HYDROZOA
Cnidarians – Hydrozoans

1–2 Diphasia pinaster (L. AGASSIZ) – *Diphasia margareta* (HASSALL, 1841) | 3 Synthecium elegans (ALLMAN) – *Synthecium elegans* ALLMAN, 1872 | 4 Idia pristis (LAMOUROUX) – *Idiellana pristis* (LAMOUROUX, 1816)
5 Thuiaria quadridens (ALLMAN) – *Sertularella quadrifida* HARTLAUB, 1901 | 6 Synthecium campylocarpum (ALLMAN) – *Synthecium campylocarpum* ALLMAN, 1888 | 7 Desmoscyphus acanthocarpus (ALLMAN) – ? (*Diphasia digitalis* (BUSK, 1852)?) | 8 Diphasia pinaster (L. AGASSIZ) – *Diphasia margareta* (HASSALL, 1841)
9 Eusertularia exserta (ALLMAN) – *Symplectoscyphus exsertus* (ALLMAN, 1888) | 10 Dynamena argentea (FLEMING) – *Sertularia argentea* LINNAEUS, 1758 Squirrel's tail hydroid, Squirrel's tail
11 Thecocladium flabellum (ALLMAN) – *Sertularella flabellum* (ALLMAN, 1885)

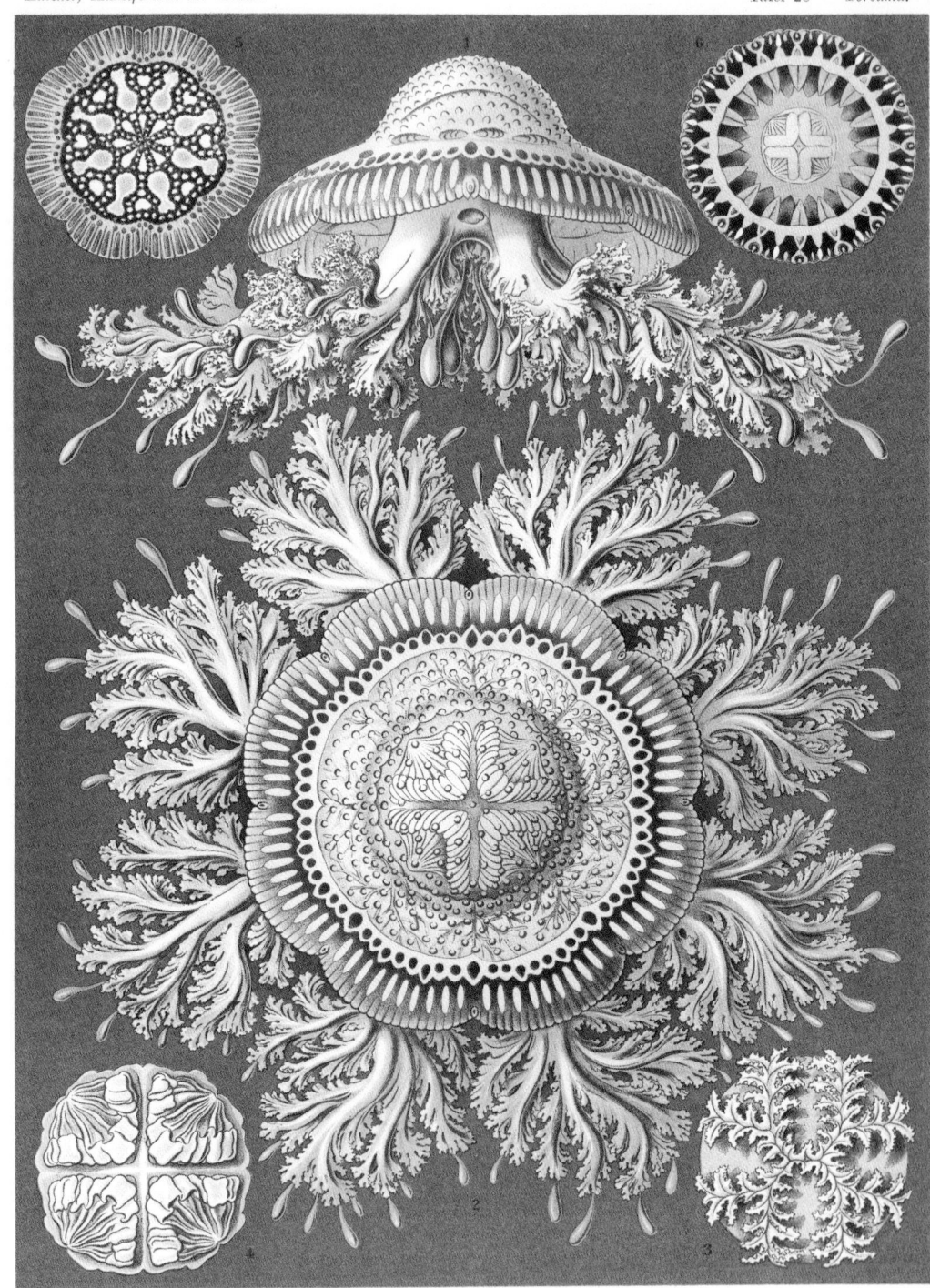

Discomedusae. — Scheibenquallen.

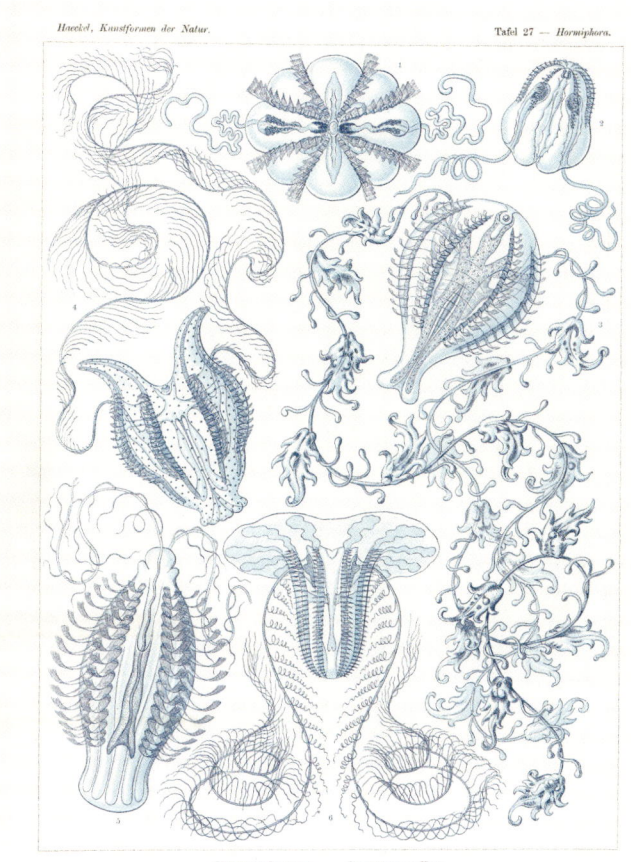

Ctenophorae. — Rammquallen.

PLATE 28
CNIDARIA – SCYPHOZOA
Cnidarians – Scyphozoans, True jellyfish

1–4 Toreuma bellagemma (HAECKEL) – *Toreuma bellagemma* HAECKEL, 1899 | 5 Toreuma thamnostoma
(HAECKEL) – *Toreuma thamnostoma* HAECKEL, 1880 | 6 Cassiopeja cyclobalia (LEO SCHULTZE) –
Cassiopea andromeda (FORSSKÅL, 1775) Upside-down jellyfish

PLATE 27
CTENOPHORA
Comb jellies

1–2 Haeckelia rubra (VICTOR CARUS, 1862) – *Haeckelia rubra* (GEGENBAUR, KÖLLIKER & MÜLLER, 1853)
3 Hormiphora foliosa (HAECKEL) – *Hormiphora foliosa* HAECKEL | 4 Callianira bialata (DELLE CHIAJE) –
Callianira bialata DELLE CHIAJE, 1841 | 5 Tinerfe cyanea (CHUN) – *Tinerfe cyanea* (CHUN, 1889)
6 Lampetia pancerina (CHUN) – *Lampea pancerina* (CHUN, 1879)

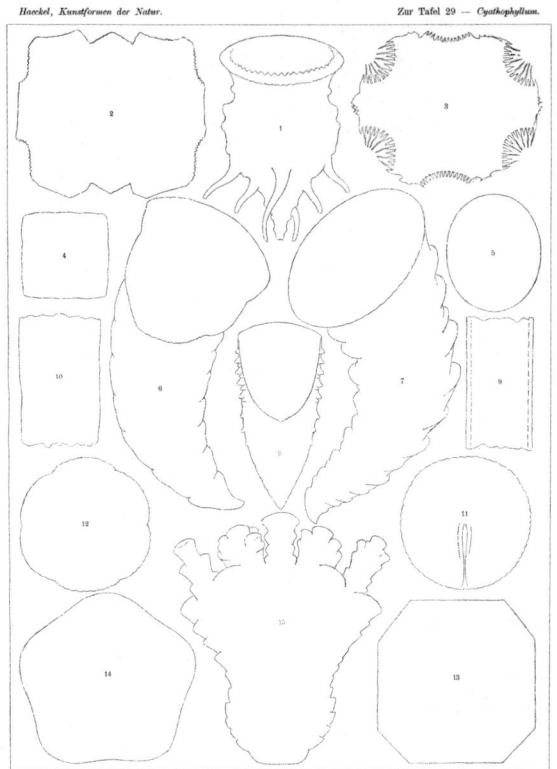

Haeckel, Kunstformen der Natur.　　　　Zur Tafel 29 — *Cyathophyllum.*

PLATE 29
CNIDARIA – ANTHOZOA
Cnidarians – Anthozoans, Flower-like animals

1 Omphyma turbinata (MILNE EDWARDS) – *Omphyma turbinata* (LINNAEUS, 1761)

2 Cyathophyllum Marmini (MILNE EDWARDS) – *Marisastrum marmini* (MILNE-EDWARDS & HAIME, 1851)

3 Pachyphyllum devoniense (MILNE EDWARDS) – *Phillipsastrea devoniensis* MILNE-EDWARDS & HAIME, 1851

4 Goniophyllum pyramidale (MILNE EDWARDS) – *Goniophyllum pyramidale* (HISINGER, 1831)

5 Menophyllum tenuimarginum (MILNE EDWARDS) – *Menophyllum tenuimarginatum* MILNE-EDWARDS & HAIME, 1850

6 Zaphrentis cornicula (LESUEUR) – *Zaphrentis phrygia* RAFINESQUE & CLIFFORD, 1820

7 Cyathophyllum expansum (D'ORBIGNY) – *Palaeosmilia murchisoni* (MILNE-EDWARDS & HAIME, 1851)

8 Cyathaxonia cynodon (RAFINESQUE) – *Cyathaxonia cynodon* (RAFINESQUE & CLIFFORD, 1820)

9 Lithostrotion irregulare (MILNE EDWARDS) – *Siphonodendron irregulare* (PHILIPS, 1836)

10 Alveolites Battersbyi (MILNE EDWARDS) – *Caliapora battersbyi* (HUXLEY, 1851)

11 Hadrophyllum multiradiatum (MILNE EDWARDS) – Hadrophyllidae?

12 Clisiophyllum turbinatum (JAMES THOMPSON) – *Dibunophyllum bipartitum turbinatum* THOMPSON, 1874

13 Acervularia ananas (SCHWEIGGER) – *Acervularia ananas* (LINNAEUS, 1758)

14 Syringophyllum organum (MILNE EDWARDS) – *Sarcinula organum* LINNÉ, 1767

15 Cyathophyllum articulatum (MILNE EDWARDS) – *Entelophyllum articulatum* (WAHLENBERG, 1821)

360

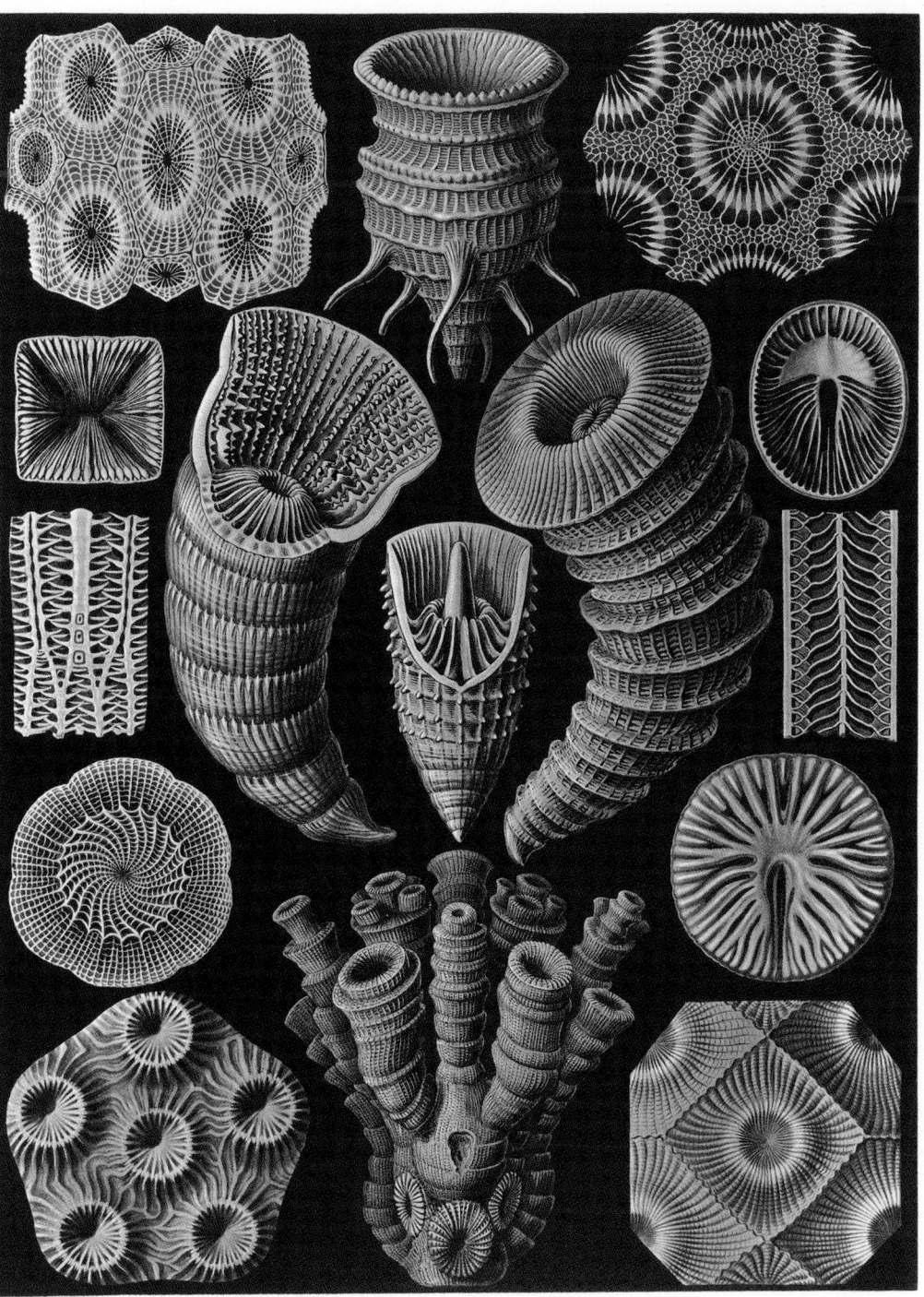

Tetracoralla. — Vierstrahlige Sternkorallen.

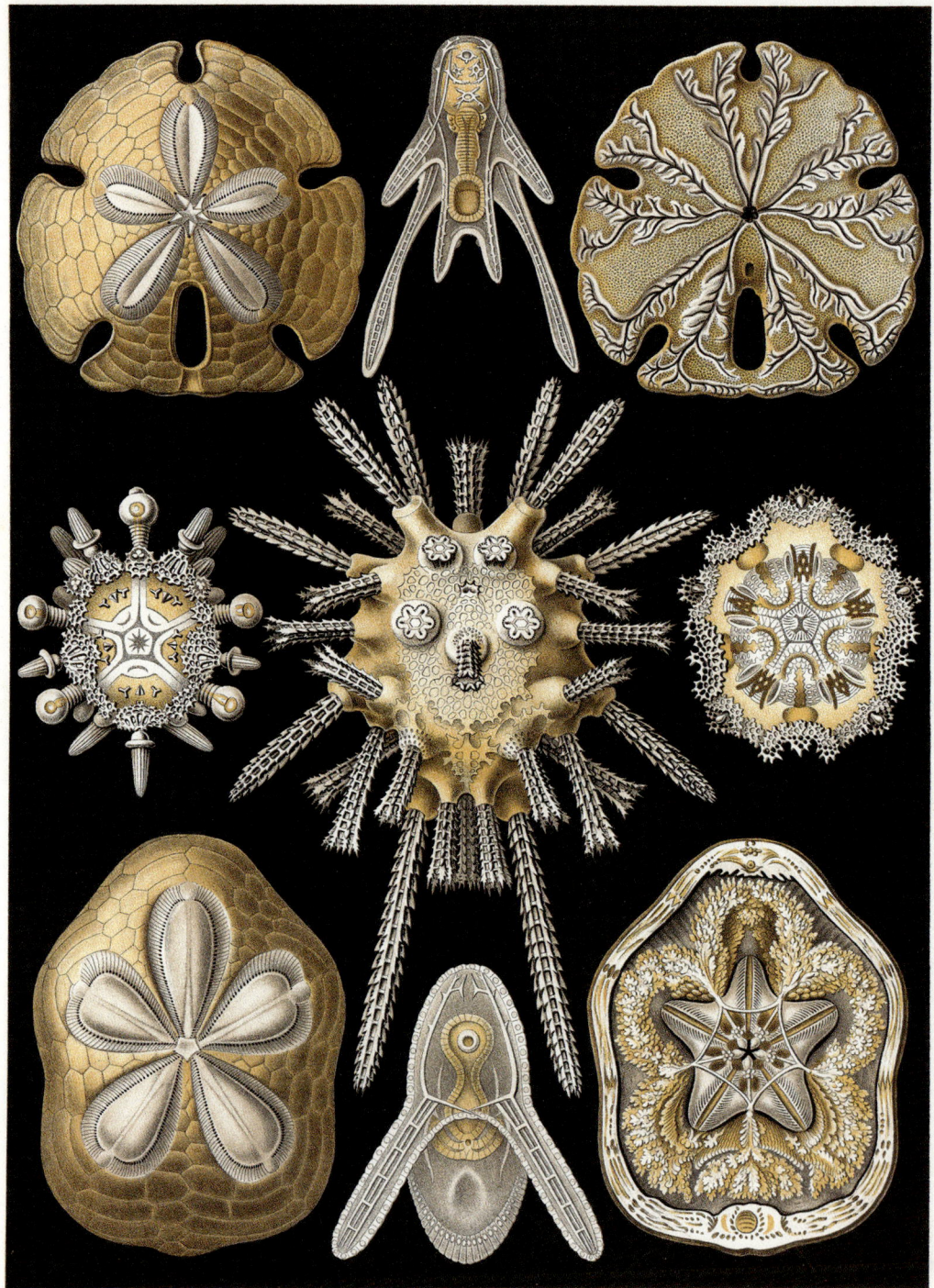

Echinidea. — Igelsterne.

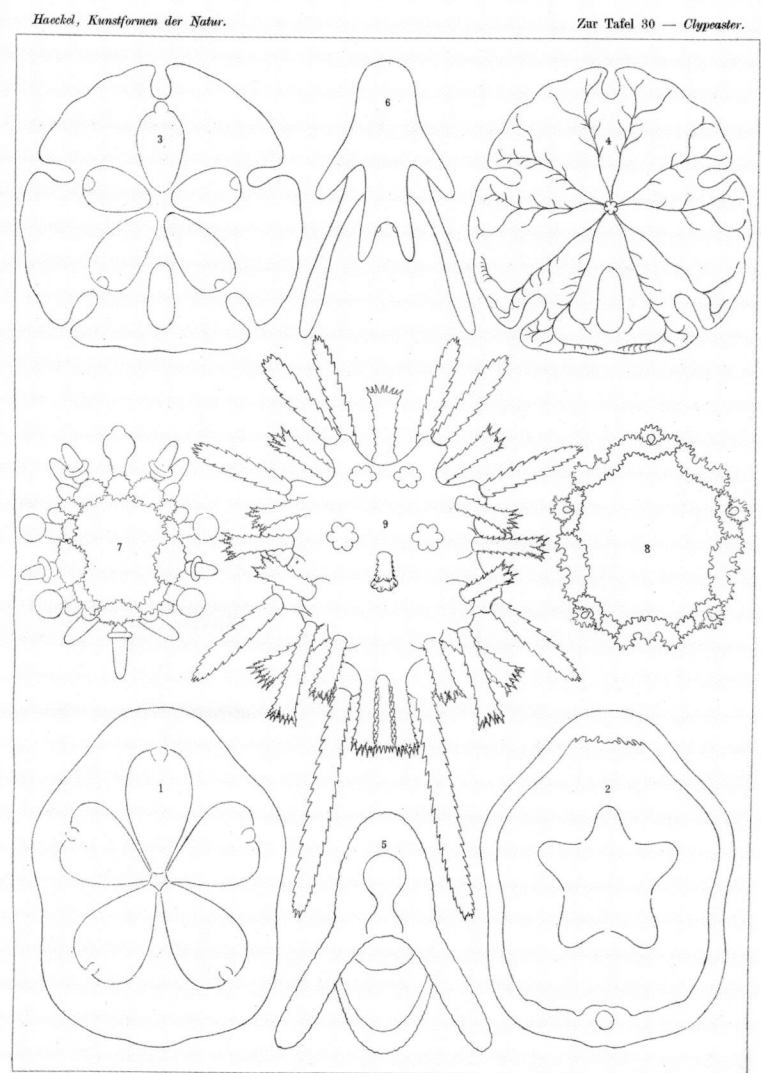

PLATE 30

ECHINODERMATA – ECHINOIDEA
Echinoderms – Sea urchins

1-2 Clypeaster rosaceus (LAMARCK) – *Clypeaster rosaceus* (LINNAEUS, 1758) Sea biscuit
3-4 Encope emarginata (LESKE) – *Encope emarginata* (LESKE, 1778)
5-9 Echinocyamus pusillus (MÜLLER) – *Echinocyamus pusillus* (O. F. MÜLLER, 1776)
Green sea urchin, Broad beau of sea

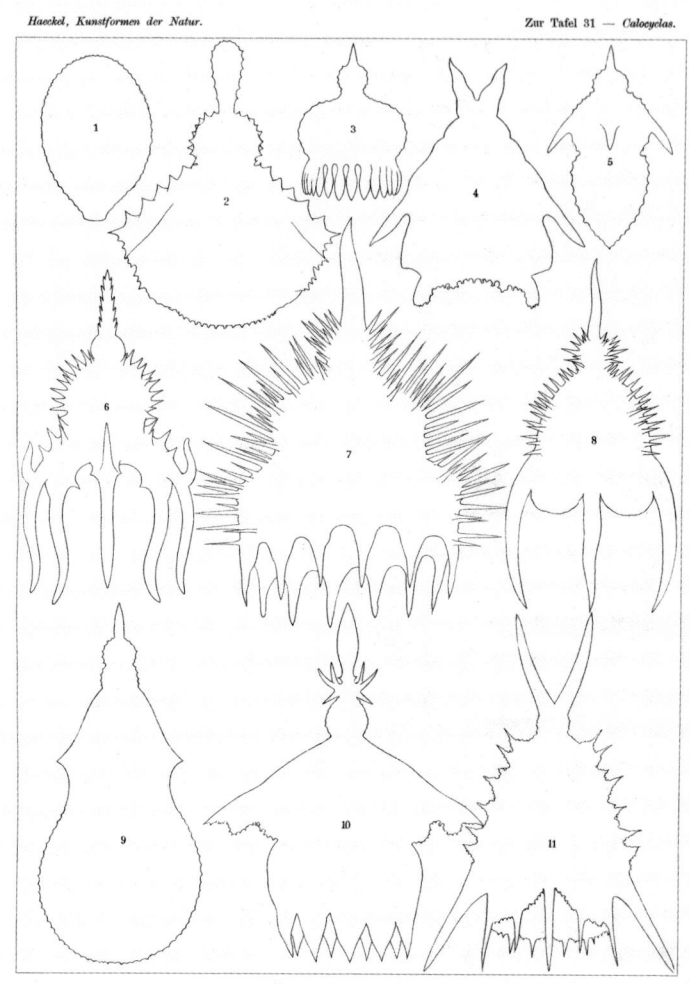

Haeckel, Kunstformen der Natur.   Zur Tafel 31 — Calocyclas.

PLATE 31
RADIOLARIA – NASSELARIA
Radiolarians

1 Cyrtophormis spiralis (HAECKEL) – *Cyrtophormis spiralis* HAECKEL, 1887 | 2 Clathrocanium reginae (HAECKEL) – *Clathrocanium reginae* HAECKEL, 1887 | 3 Anthocyrtium campanula (HAECKEL) – *Anthocyrtium campanula* HAECKEL, 1887 | 4 Pterocorys rhinoceros (HAECKEL) – *Pterocorys rhinoceros* HAECKEL, 1887 | 5 Lithornithium falco (HAECKEL) – *Lithornithium falco* HAECKEL, 1887 | 6 Alacorys Bismarckii (HAECKEL) – *Alacorys bismarckii* HAECKEL, 1887 | 7 Calocyclas monumentum (HAECKEL) – *Calocyclas momentum* HAECKEL, 1887 | 8 Pterocanium trilobum (HAECKEL) – *Pterocanium charybdeum* (MÜLLER, 1858) | 9 Stichophaena Ritteriana (HAECKEL) – *Stichophaena ritteriana* HAECKEL | 10 Dictyocodon Annasethe (HAECKEL) – *Dictyocodon annasethe* HAECKEL, 1887 | 11 Artopilium elegans (HAECKEL) – *Pterocanium elegans* (HAECKEL, 1887)

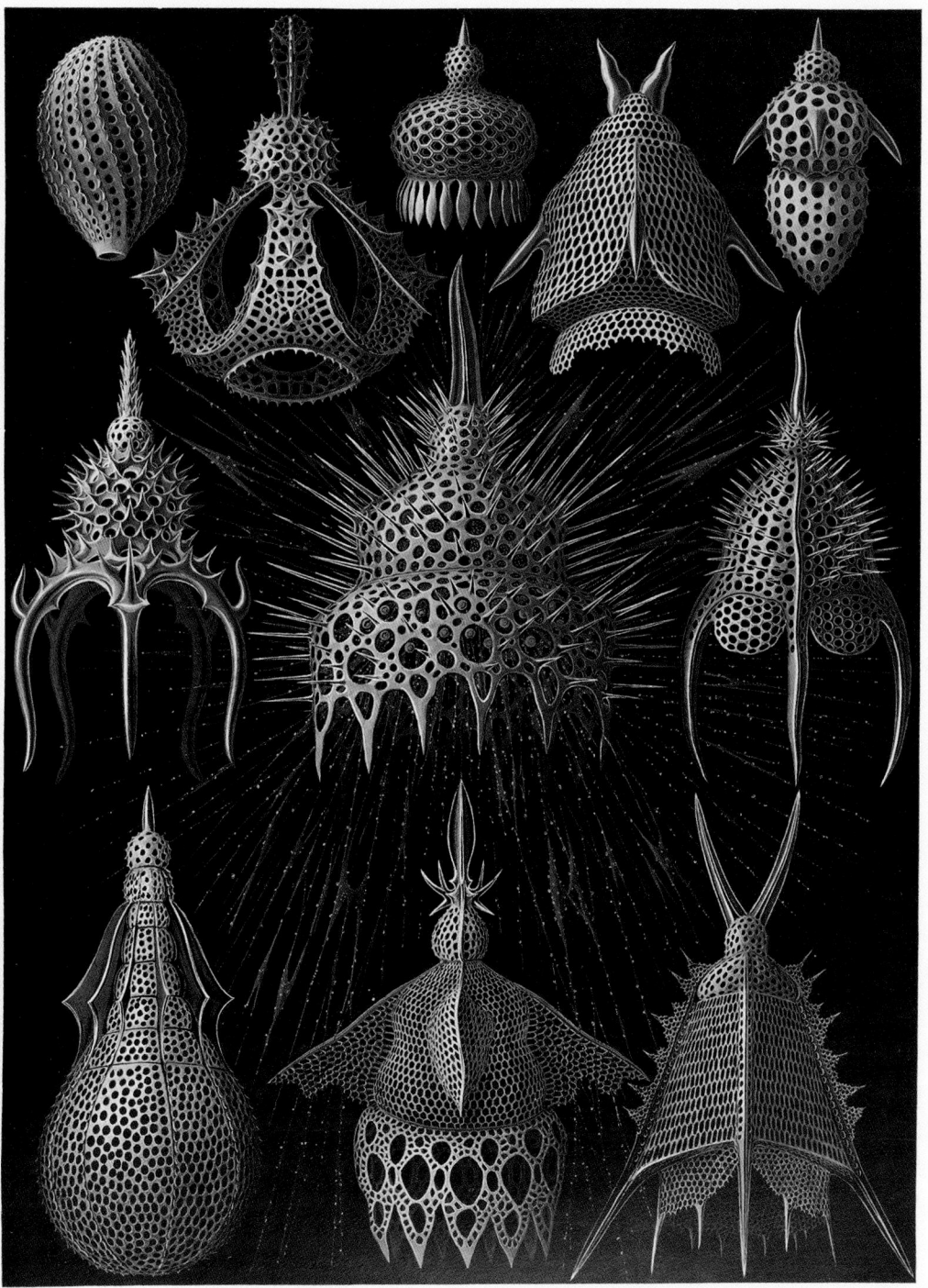

Cyrtoidea. — Flaſchenſtrahlinge.

PLATE 32
ROTATORIA, ROTIFERA
Rotifers

1 Pedalion mirum (HUDSON) – *Hexarthra mira* (HUDSON, 1871)
2 Lacinularia socialis (EHRENBERG) – *Lacinularia* sp.?
3 Polyarthra platyptera (EHRENBERG) – *Polyarthra cf. platyptera* EHRENBERG, 1838
4 Pterodina patina (EHRENBERG) – *Testudinella patina* (HERMANN, 1783)
5 Stephanoceros Eichhornii (EHRENBERG) – *Stephanoceros fimbriatus* (GOLDFUSS, 1820)
6 Euchlanis dilatata (LEYDIG) – *Euchlanis dilatata* EHRENBERG, 1832
7 Noteus Leydigii (HAECKEL) – *Platyias quadricornis* (EHRENBERG, 1832)
8 Brachionus Bakeri (EHRENBERG) – *Brachionus quadridentatus* HERMANN, 1783

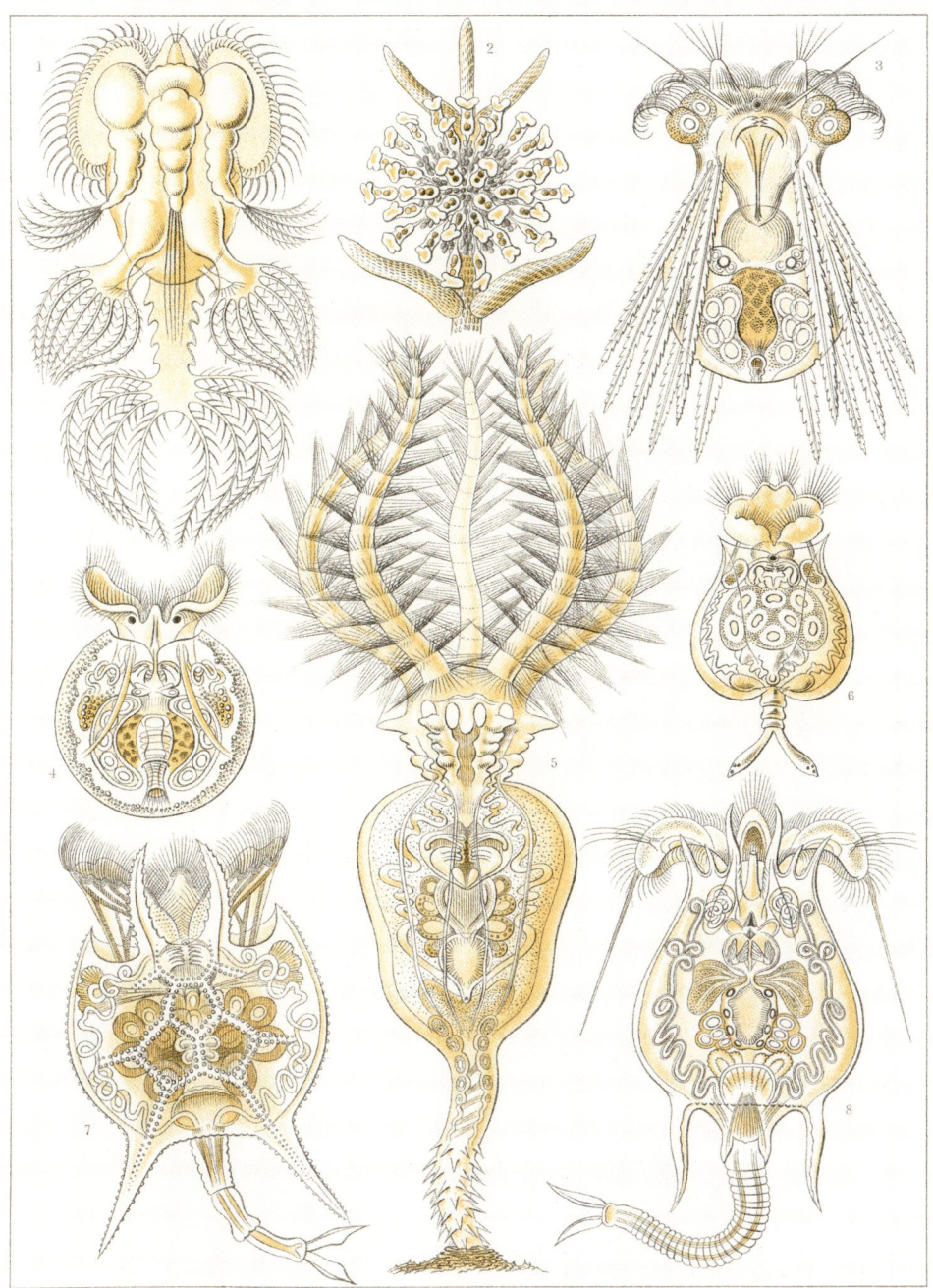

Rotatoria. — Rädertiere.

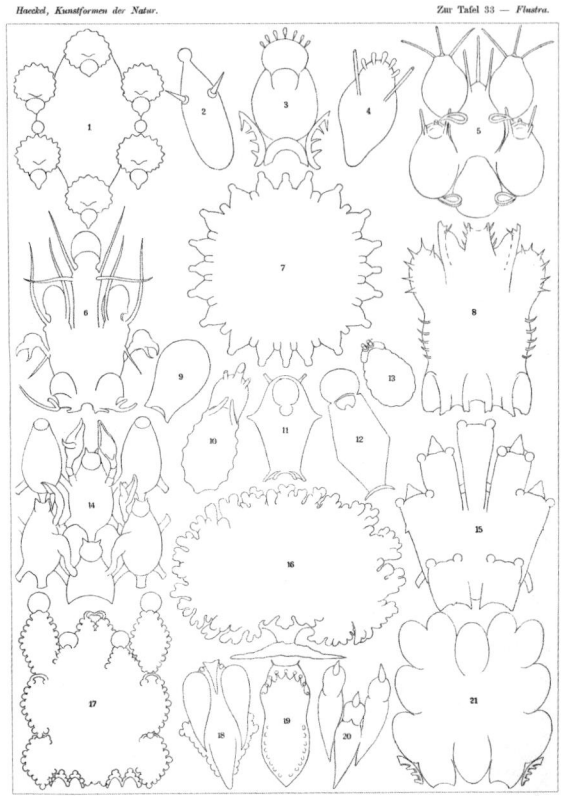

Haeckel, Kunstformen der Natur.

Zur Tafel 33 — Flustra.

PLATE 33
BRYOZOA
Moss animals

1 Lepralia spinifera (JOHNSTON) – *Phaeostachys spinifera* (JOHNSTON, 1847) | 2 Cribrilina punctata (HASSALL) – *Cribrilina punctata* (HASSALL, 1841) | 3 Umbonula verrucosa (HINCKS) – *Umbonula verrucosa* (ESPER, 1790) 4 Cribrilina radiata (SMITT) – *Puellina radiata* (MOLL, 1803) (synonym: *Colletosia radiata* (MOLL, 1803)) 5 Lepralia alata (BUSK) – *Umbonula alvareziana* (D'ORBIGNY, 1842) | 6 Bugula flabellata (BUSK) – *Bugulina flabellata* (THOMPSON,1848) | 7 Cupularia stellata (BUSK) – *Cupuladria canariensis* (BUSK, 1859) 8 Farciminaria aculeata (BUSK) – *Farciminaria aculeata* BUSK, 1852 | 9 Umbonula reticulata (HINCKS) – *Umbonula* sp.? | 10 Cribrilina costata (BUSK) – *Beania costata* (BUSK, 1876) | 11 Smittia Landsborovii (HINCKS) – *Smittina landsborovii* (JOHNSTON, 1847) | 12 Smittia reticulata (HINCKS) – *Smittina reticulata* (MACGILLIVRAY, 1842) 13 Lepralia annulata (JOHNSTON) – *Cribrilina annulata* (O.FABRICIUS, 1780) | 14 Diachoris magellanica (BUSK) – *Beania magellanica* (BUSK, 1852) | 15 Diachoris crotali (BUSK) – *Beania crotali* (BUSK, 1852) | 16-17 Flustra Gayi (SAVIGNY) – *Gemelliporina glabra* (SMITT, 1873) | 18 Schizoporella hyalina (HINCKS) – *Celleporella hyalina* (LINNÉ, 1767) | 19 Lepralia variolosa (JOHNSTON) – *Escharella variolosa* (JOHNSTON, 1838) 20 Chorizopora Brongniartii (AUDOUIN) – *Chorizopora brongniartii* (AUDOUIN, 1826) 21 Flustra Aragoi (SAVIGNY) – *Klugerella aragoi* (AUDOUIN, 1826)

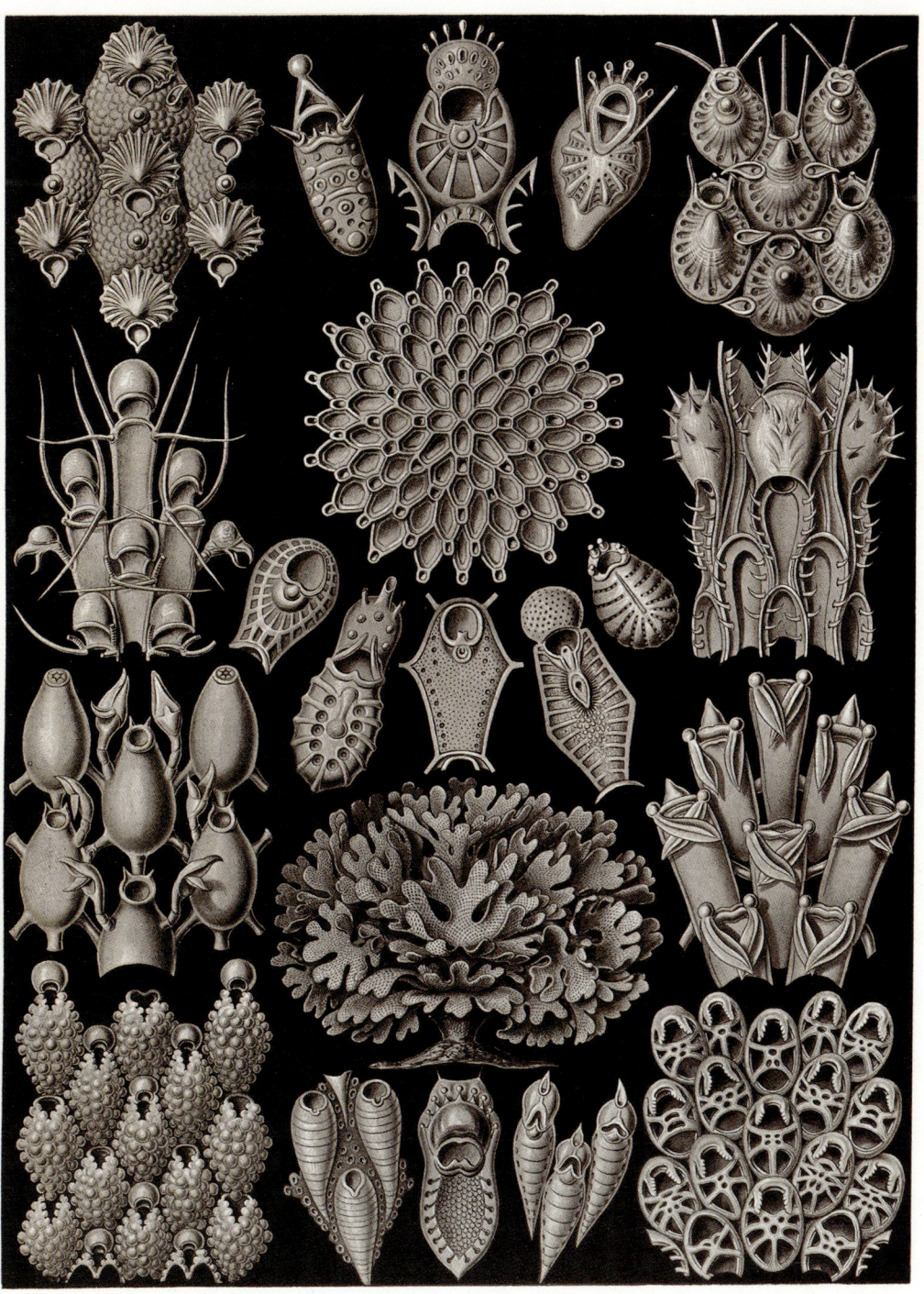

Bryozoa. — Moostiere.

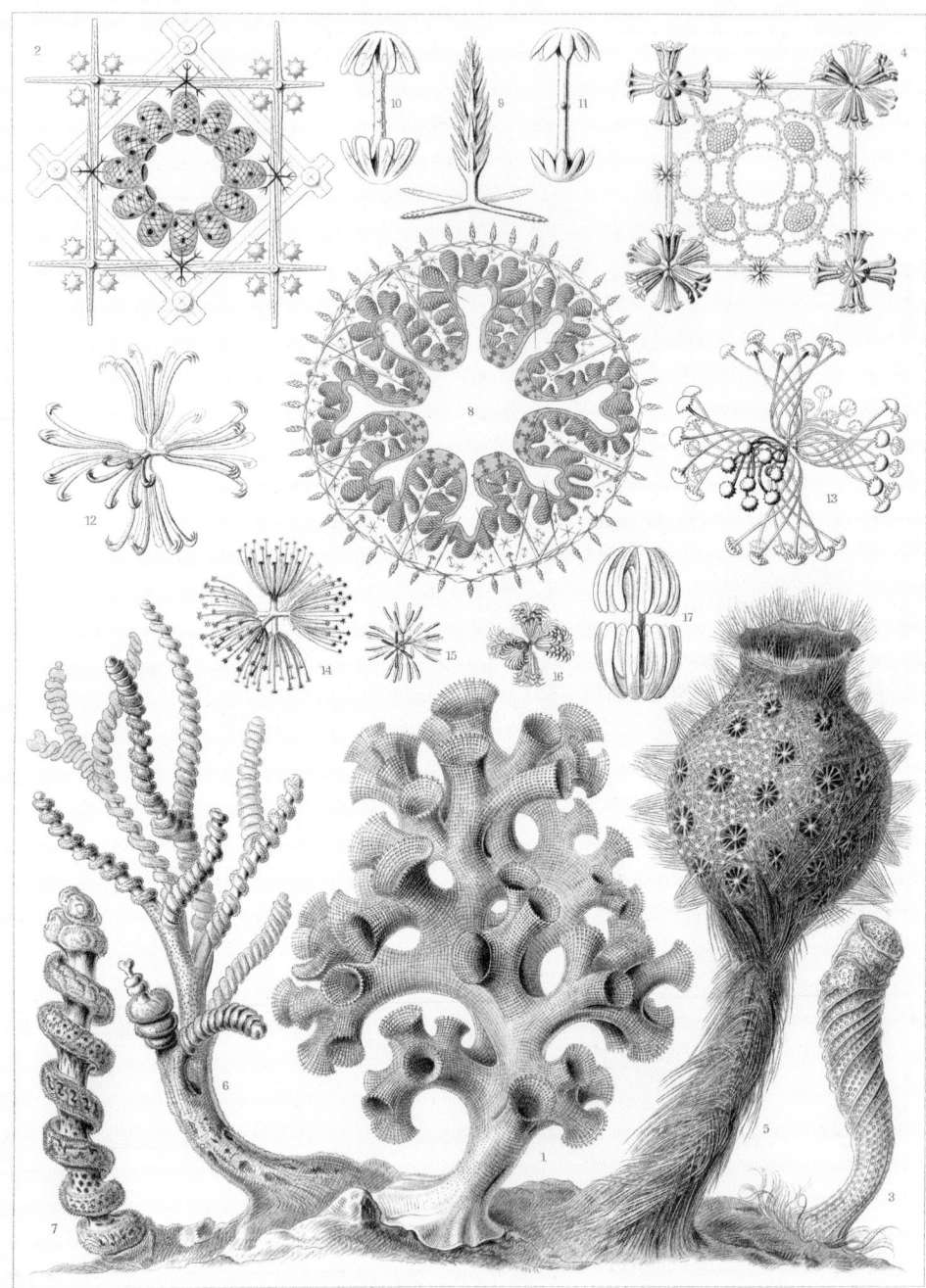

Hexactinellae. — Glasschwämme.

PLATE 35
PORIFERA
Sponges

1–2 Farrea Haeckelii (F. E. SCHULZE) – *Farrea occa* BOWERBANK, 1862
3–4 Euplectella aspergillum (OWEN) – *Euplectella aspergillum* OWEN, 1841 Venus's flower basket
5 Holtenia crateromorpha (WYVILLE THOMPSON) – *Vazella* sp.?
6–7 Sclerothamnus spiralis (MARSHALL) – *Sclerothamnus* sp.?
8 Polyopogon amadu (WYVILLE THOMPSON) – *Poliopogon amadou* THOMSON, 1878
9 Pheronema rhaphanus (FRANZ EILHARD SCHULZE) – *Pheronema raphanus* SCHULZE, 1895
10 Hyalonema indicum (FRANZ EILHARD SCHULZE) – *Hyalonema (Coscinonema) indicum* SCHULZE, 1895
11 Hyalonema conus (F. E. SCHULZE) – *Hyalonema (Coscinonema) conus* SCHULZE, 1886
12 Regadrella phoenix (OSKAR SCHMIDT) – *Regadrella phoenix* SCHMIDT, 1880
13 Saccocalyx pedunculata (F. E. SCHULZE) – *Saccocalyx pedunculatus* SCHULZE, 1896
14 Crateromorpha Meyeri (GRAY) – *Crateromorpha (Crateromorpha) meyeri* GRAY, 1872
15 Hyalostylus dives (FRANZ EILHARD SCHULZE) – *Hyalostylus dives* SCHULZE, 1886
16 Polylophus philippinensis (GRAY) – *Lophocalyx philippinensis* (GRAY, 1872)
17 Stylocalyx tenera (FRANZ EILHARD SCHULZE) – *Hyalonema tenerum* SCHULZE, 1886

PLATE 34 *(Page 372)*
CHLOROPHYTA
Green algae

1 Pediastrum tetras (EHRENBERG) – *Stauridium tetras* (EHRENBERG) HEGEWALD, 2005
2 Pediastrum rotula (KÜTZING) – *Parapediastrum biradiatum* (MEYEN, 1829) HEGEWALD, 2005
3 Pediastrum granulatum (KÜTZING) – *Pseudopediastrum boryanum* (TURPIN) HEGEWALD, 2005 (forma *granulatum*)
4 Pediastrum octonum (HAECKEL) – *Pediastrum octonum* HAECKEL, 1900
5 Pediastrum cruciatum (HAECKEL) – *Pseudopediastrum boryanum* (TURPIN) HEGEWALD, 2005
6 Pediastrum selenaea (KÜTZING) – *Pediastrum duplex* MEYEN, 1829
7 Pediastrum pertusum (KÜTZING) – *Pediastrum duplex* MEYEN, 1829
8 Pediastrum elegans (HAECKEL) – *Pediastrum elegans* HAECKEL, 1900 (non *Pediastrum elegans* HASSALL)
9 Pediastrum lunatum (HAECKEL) – *Pediastrum lunatum* HAECKEL, 1900?
10 Pediastrum furcatum (HAECKEL) – *Pediastrum furcatum* HAECKEL, 1900?
11 Pediastrum Braunii (HAECKEL) – *Pediastrum braunii* WARTMANN, 1862
12 Pediastrum ellipticum (EHRENBERG) – *Pediastrum ellipticum* EHRENBERG EX RALFS, 1848
13 Pediastrum Darwinii (HAECKEL) – *Pediastrum darwinii* HAECKEL, 1900?
14 Pediastrum trochiscus (HAECKEL) – *Pediastrum trochiscus* HAECKEL, 1900?
15 Pediastrum solare (HAECKEL) – *Pediastrum solare* HAECKEL, 1900?

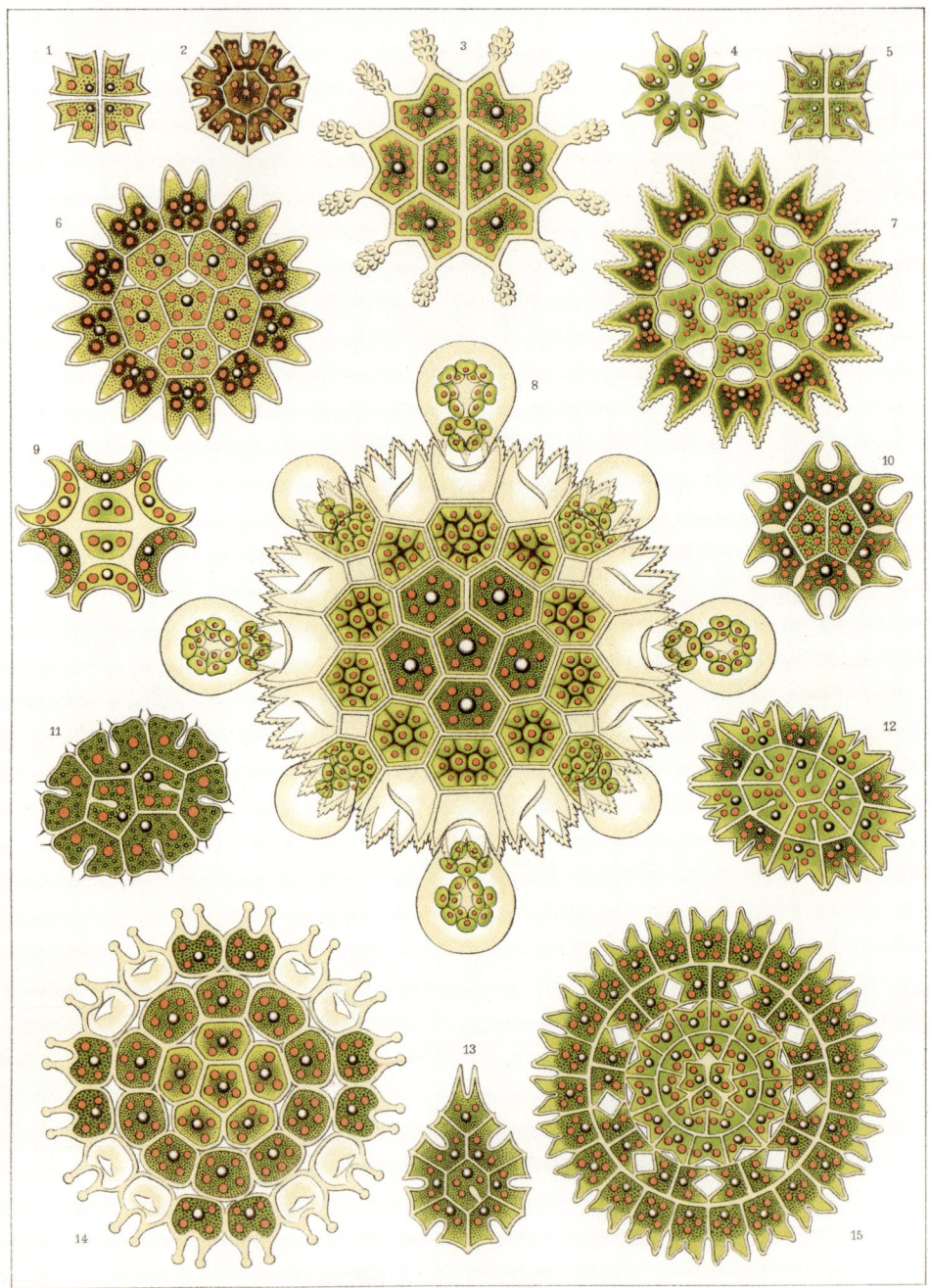

Melethallia. — Gesellige Algetten.

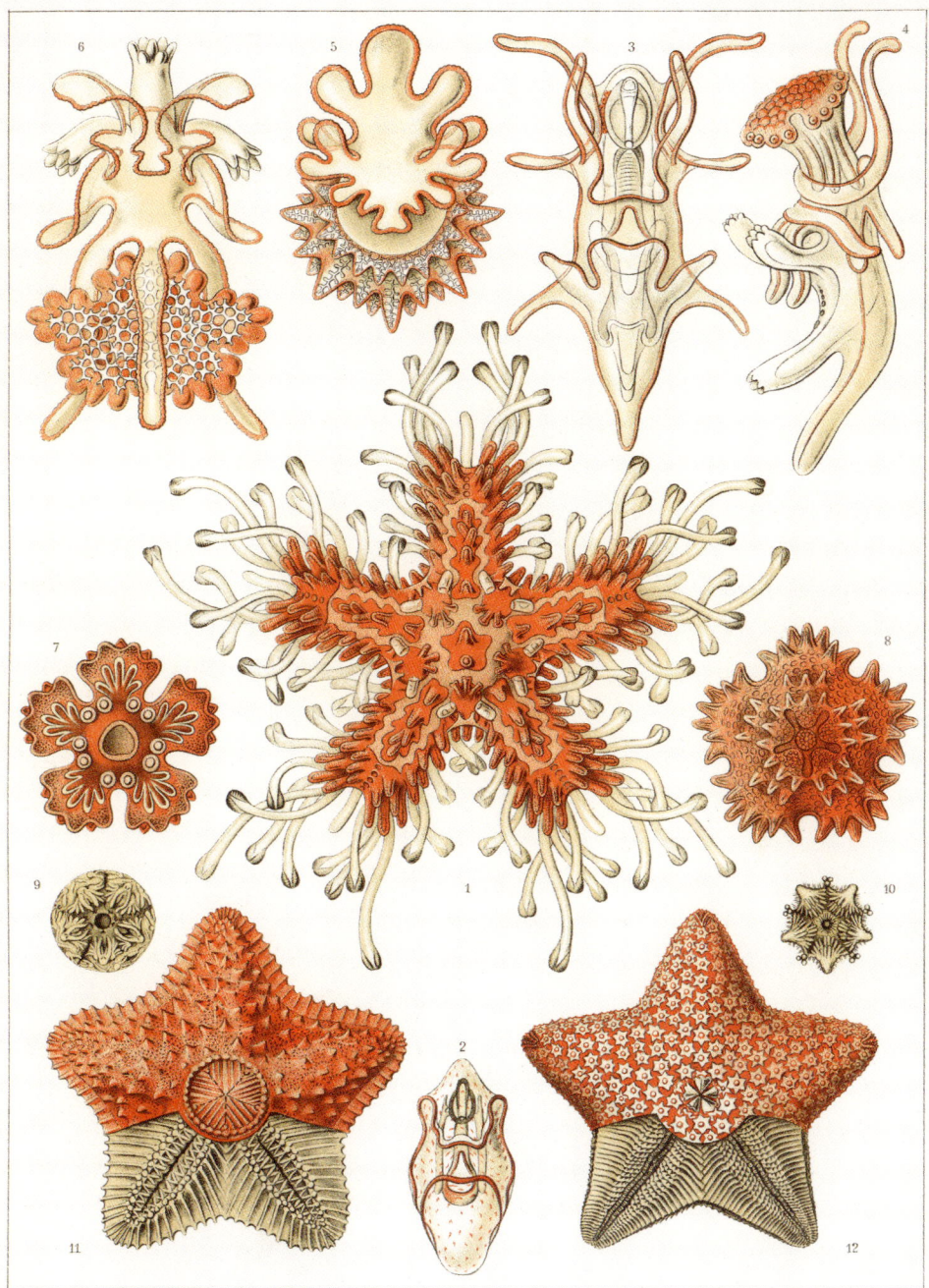

Asteridea. — Seesterne.

PLATE 40 *(Page 373)*
ECHINODERMATA – ASTEROIDEA
Echinoderms – Starfish, Sea stars

1 Asterias rubens (LINNÉ) – *Asterias rubens* LINNAEUS, 1758 Common starfish
2–6 *Asterias rubens,* LARVAE | 7–8 *Asterias rubens,* JUVENIL
9, 11 Hymenaster echinulatus (PERCY SLADEN) – *Hymenaster echinulatus* SLADEN, 1882
10, 12 Pteraster stellifer (PERCY SLADEN) – *Pteraster stellifer* SLADEN, 1882

PLATE 38
CNIDARIA – SCYPHOZOA
Cnidarians – Scyphozoans, True jellyfish

1–2 Periphylla mirabilis (HAECKEL) – *Periphylla periphylla* (PÉRON & LESUEUR, 1810) Merchant-cap
3 Periphylla Peronii (HAECKEL) – *Periphylla periphylla* (PÉRON & LESUEUR, 1810) Merchant-cap, Helmet jelly, Helmet jellyfish
4 Periphylla hyacinthina (STEENTRUPP) – *Periphylla periphylla* (PÉRON & LESUEUR, 1810) Merchant-cap
5–7 Periphylla mirabilis (HAECKEL) – *Periphylla periphylla* (PÉRON & LESUEUR, 1810) Merchant-cap

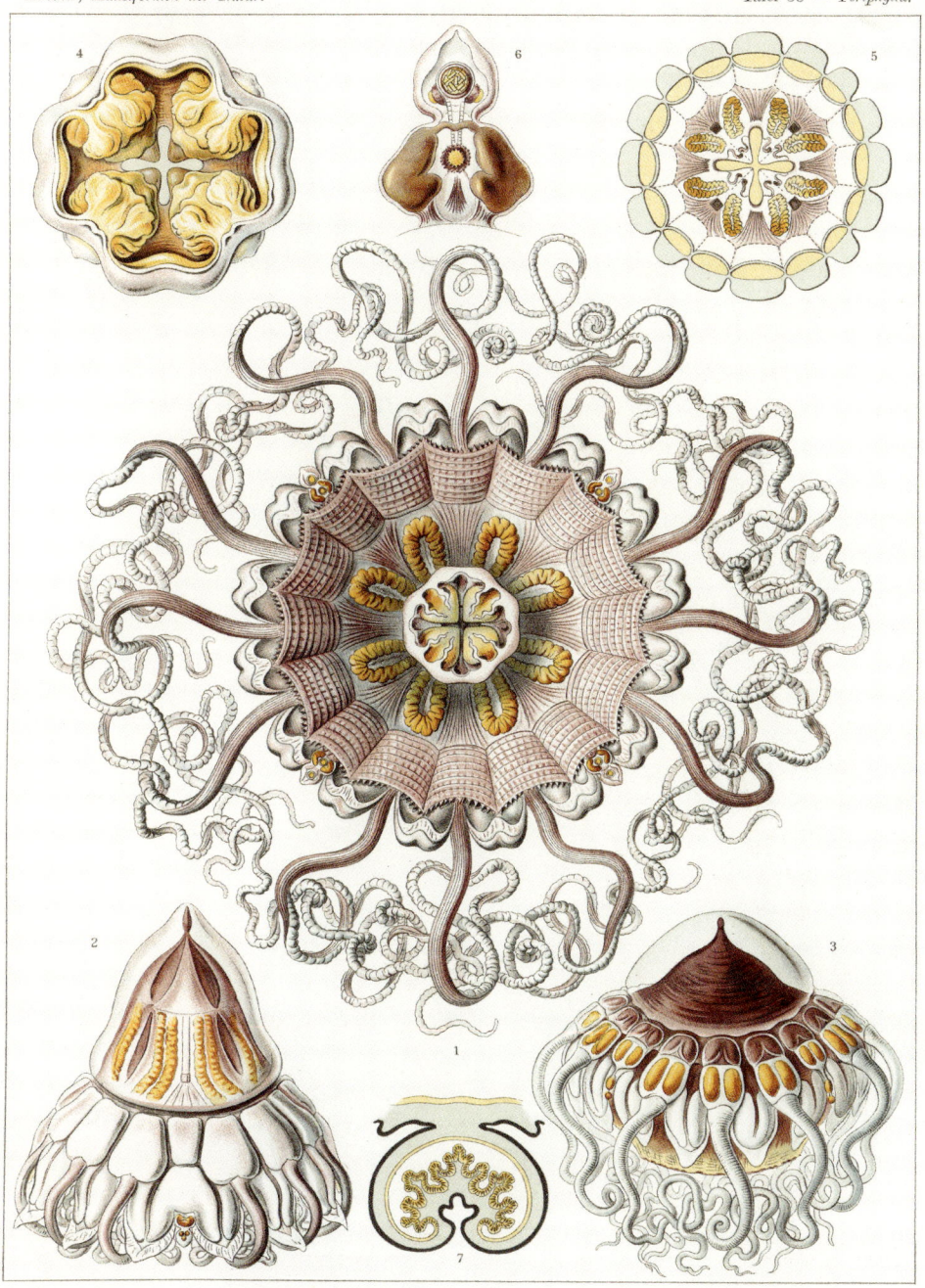

Peromedusae. — Taſchenquallen.

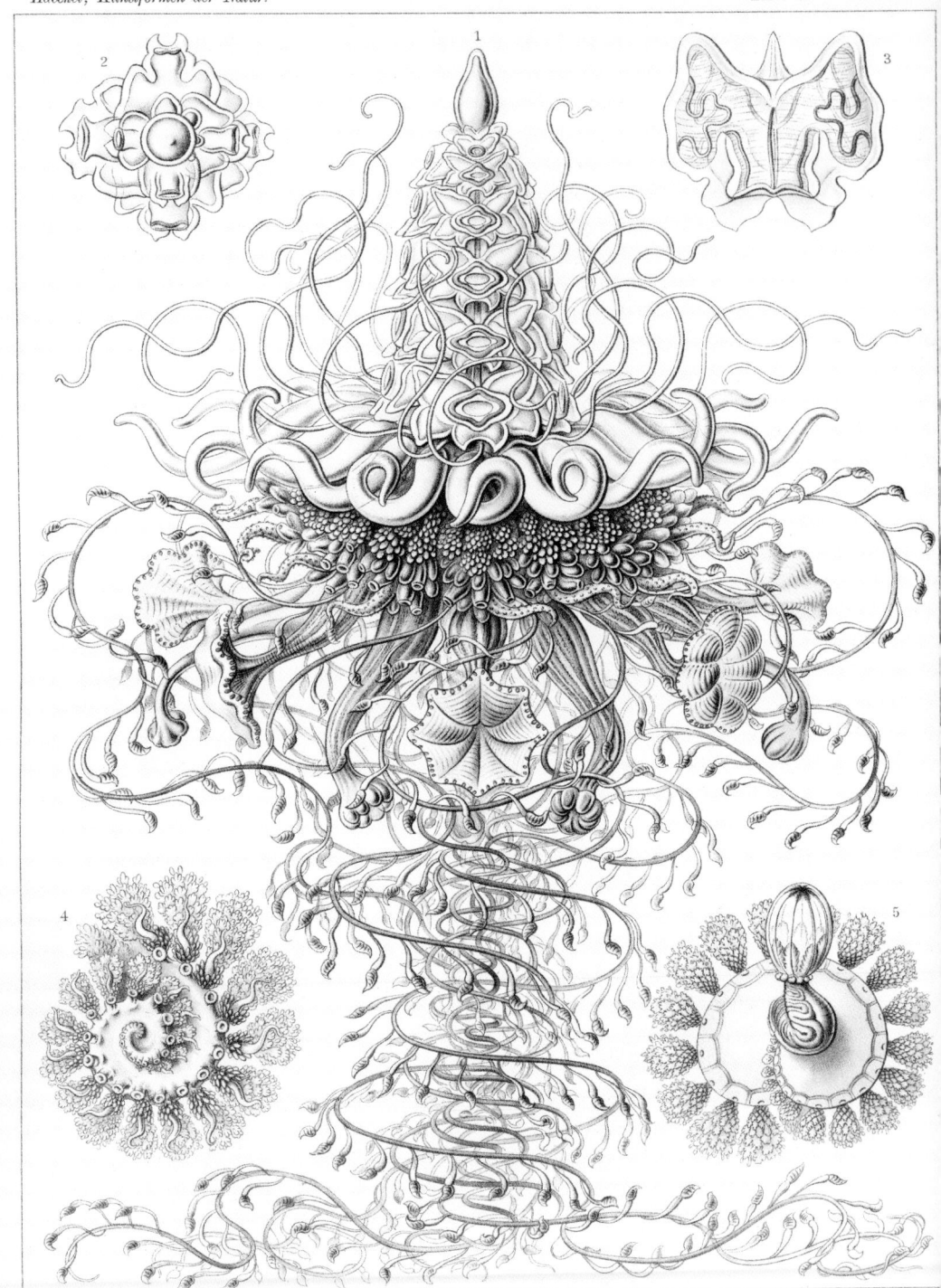

Siphonophorae. — Staatsquallen.

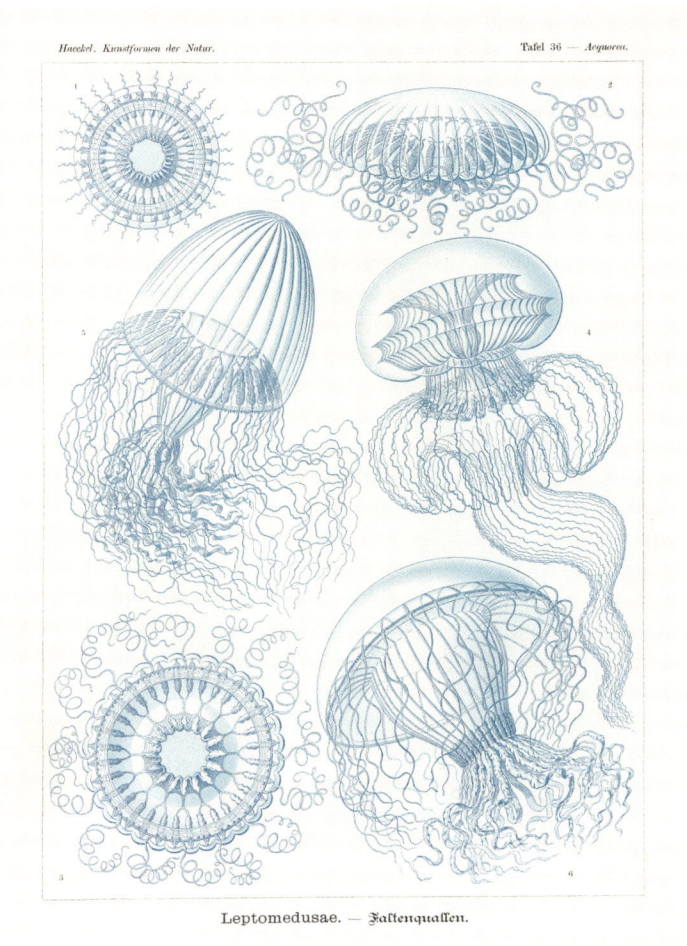

Haeckel. Kunstformen der Natur.   Tafel 36 — Aequorea.

Leptomedusae. — Faltenquallen.

PLATE 37
CNIDARIA – SIPHONOPHORA
Cnidarians – Siphonophores

Discolabe quadrigata (HAECKEL) – *Physophora hydrostatica* FORSSKÅL, 1775

PLATE 36
CNIDARIA – HYDROZOA
Cnidarians – Hydrozoans

1 Aequorea discus (HAECKEL) – *Aequorea pensilis* (ESCHSCHOLTZ, 1829)
2–3 Zygocanna diploconus (HAECKEL) – *Zygocanna diploconus* (HAECKEL, 1879)
4 Polycanna germanica (HAECKEL) – *Aequorea forskalea* PÉRON & LESUEUR, 1810 Many-ribbed jellyfish
5 Zygocannula diploconus (HAECKEL) – *Zygocanna diploconus* (HAECKEL, 1879)
6 Orchistoma elegans (HAECKEL) – *Orchistoma elegans* HAECKEL, 1879

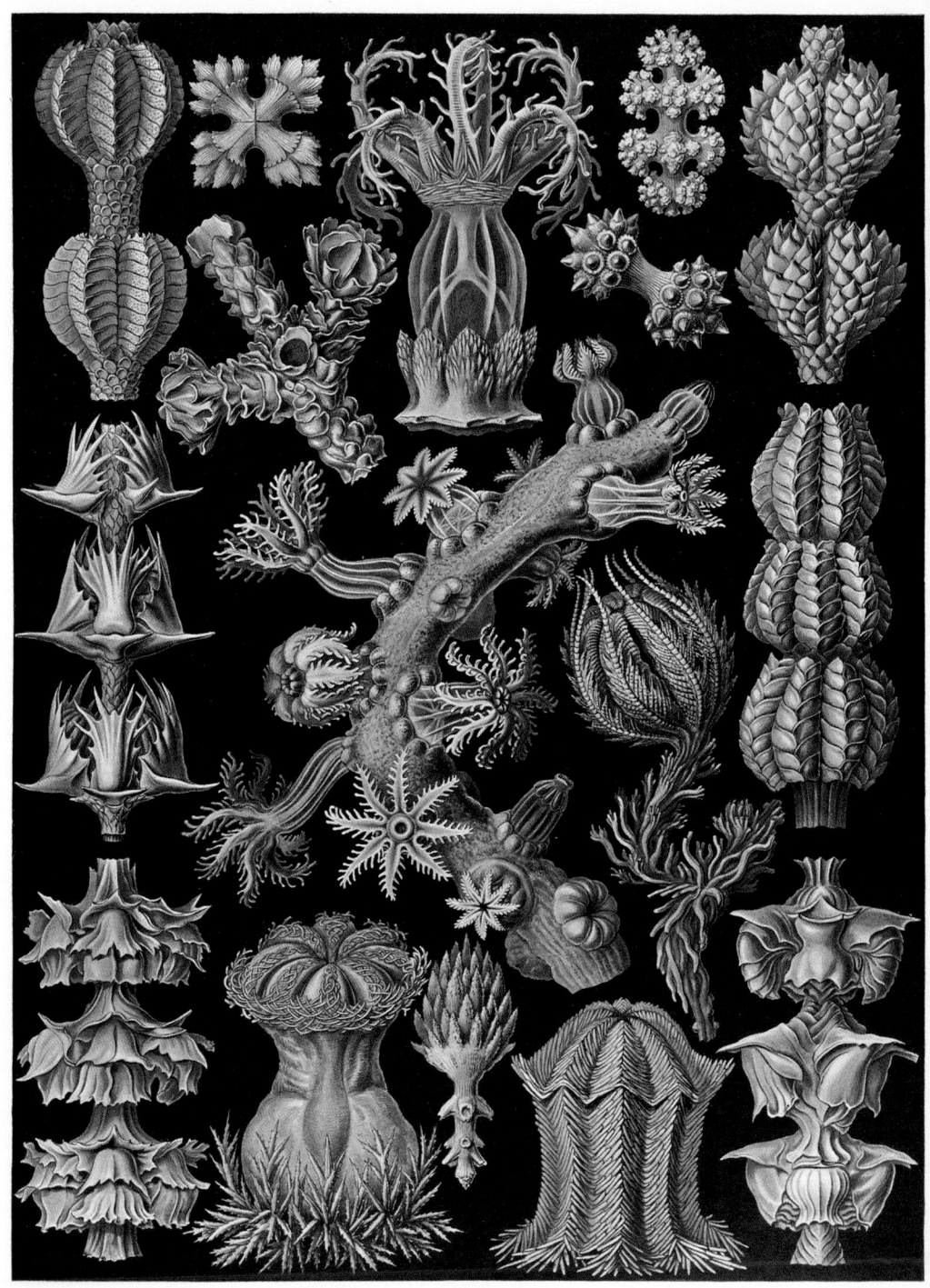

Gorgonida. — Rindenkorallen.

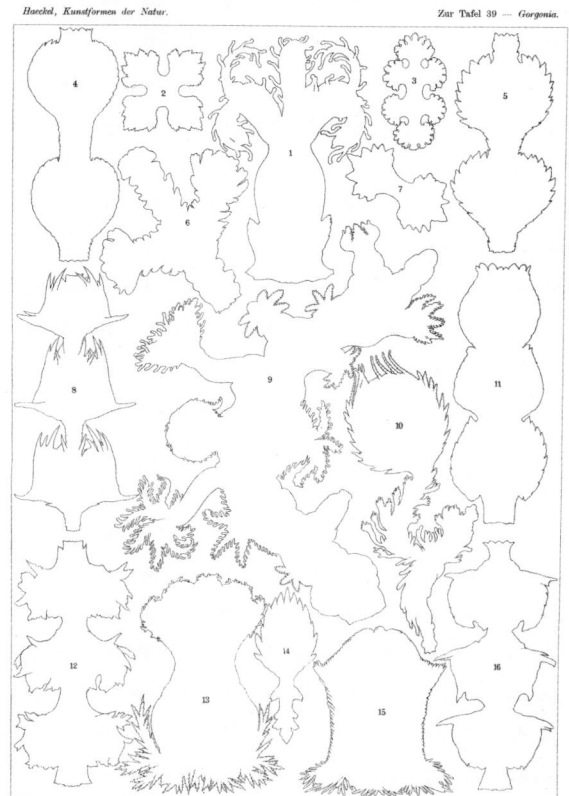

Haeckel, Kunstformen der Natur.   Zur Tafel 39 — Gorgonia.

PLATE 39
CNIDARIA – ANTHOZOA
Cnidarians – Anthozoans, Flower-like animals

1 Gorgonia Verrucosa (PALLAS) – *Eunicella verrucosa* (PALLAS, 1766) Pink sea fan | 2 Platycaulos Danielsseni
(PERCEVAL WRIGHT) – *Swiftia* sp.? | 3 Euplexaura parciclados (PERCEVAL WRIGHT) – *Euplexaura parciclados*
WRIGHT & STUDER, 1889 | 4 Primnoella biserialis (PERCEVAL WRIGHT) – *Primnoella chilensis* (PHILLIPI, 1894)
5 Primnoella Murrayi (PERCEVAL WRIGHT) – *Convexella murrayi* (WRIGHT & STUDER, 1889)
6 Stenella spinosa (PERCEVAL WRIGHT) – *Parastenella spinosa* (WRIGHT & STUDER, 1889) | 7 Junceella juncea
(PALLAS) – *Junceella juncea* (PALLAS, 1766) | 8 Calyptrophora japonica (GRAY) – *Calyptrophora japonica* GRAY, 1866
9 Gorgonia verrucosa (PALLAS) – *Eunicella verrucosa* (PALLAS, 1766) Pink sea fan
10 Acanthogorgia longiflora (PERCEVAL WRIGHT) – *Acanthogorgia longiflora* WRIGHT & STUDER, 1889
11 Primnoella Australasiae (GRAY) – *Primnoella australasiae* (GREY, 1849) Southern sea whip
12 Calypterinus Allmani (PERCEVAL WRIGHT) – *Narella allmani* (WRIGHT & STUDER, 1889) | 13 Paramuricea spinosa
(KÖLLIKER) – *Paramuricea spinosa* KÖLLIKER, 1865 | 14 Juncea barbadensis (DUCHASSAING) – *Ctenocella barbadensis*
(DUCHASSAING & MICHELOTTI, 1864) (synonym: *Ellisella barbadensis* (DUCHASSAING & MICHELOTTI, 1864))
Devil's sea whip | 15 Anthomuricea argentea (PERCEVAL WRIGHT) – *Anthomuricea argentea* WRIGHT & STUDER, 1889
16 Calyptrophora Wyvillei (PERCEVAL WRIGHT) – *Calyptrophora wyvillei* WRIGHT, 1885

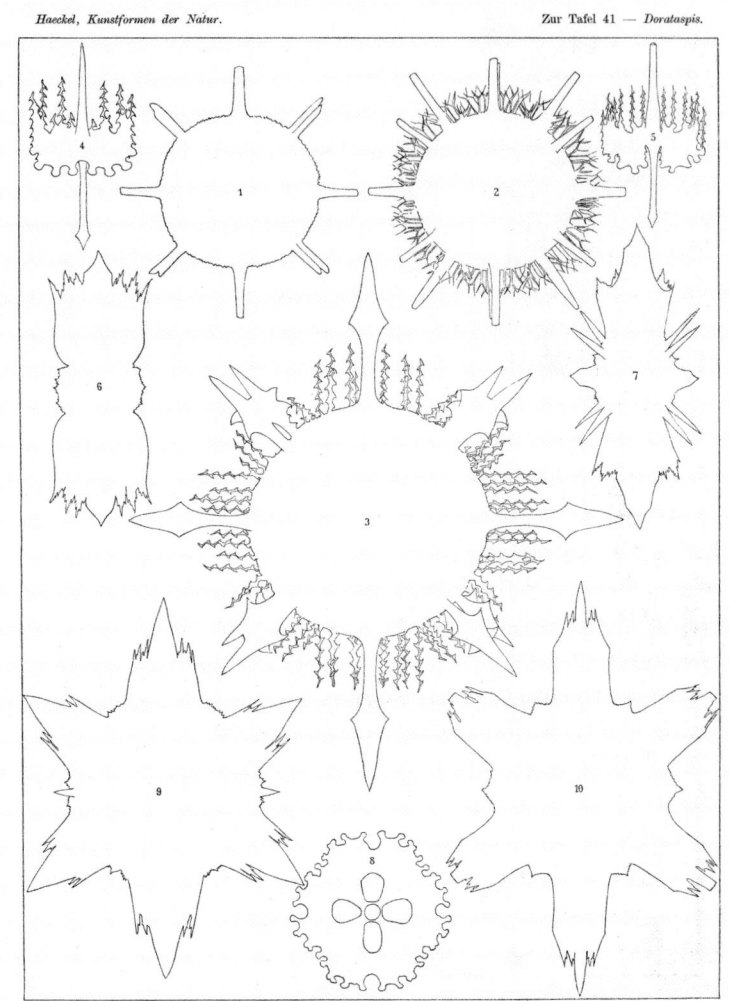

Haeckel, Kunstformen der Natur.　　　　　　　　　　Zur Tafel 41 — Dorataspis.

PLATE 41
RADIOLARIA – ACANTHARIA
Radiolarians

1 Dorataspis typica (HAECKEL) – *Dorataspidae* genus et species indet. | 2 Dorataspis nephropora (HAECKEL) – *Dorataspis nephropora* HAECKEL | 3 Lychnaspis miranda (HAECKEL) – *Lychnaspis miranda* HAECKEL | 4 Lychnaspis polyancistra (HAECKEL) – *Lychnaspis polyancistra* HAECKEL, 1860 | 5 Echinaspis echinoides (HAECKEL) – *Echinaspis echinoides* HAECKEL, 1887 | 6 Diplocolpus costatus (HAECKEL) – *Diplocolpis costatus* HAECKEL, 1887 7 Diploconus hexaphyllus (HAECKEL) – *Diploconus hexaphyllus* HAECKEL, 1887 | 8 Icosaspis elegans (HAECKEL) – *Icosaspis elegans* HAECKEL, 1881 | 9 Hexaconus serratus (HAECKEL) – *Hexaconus serratus* HAECKEL, 1887 10 Hexacolpus nivalis (HAECKEL) – *Hexaconus nivalis* HAECKEL, 1887

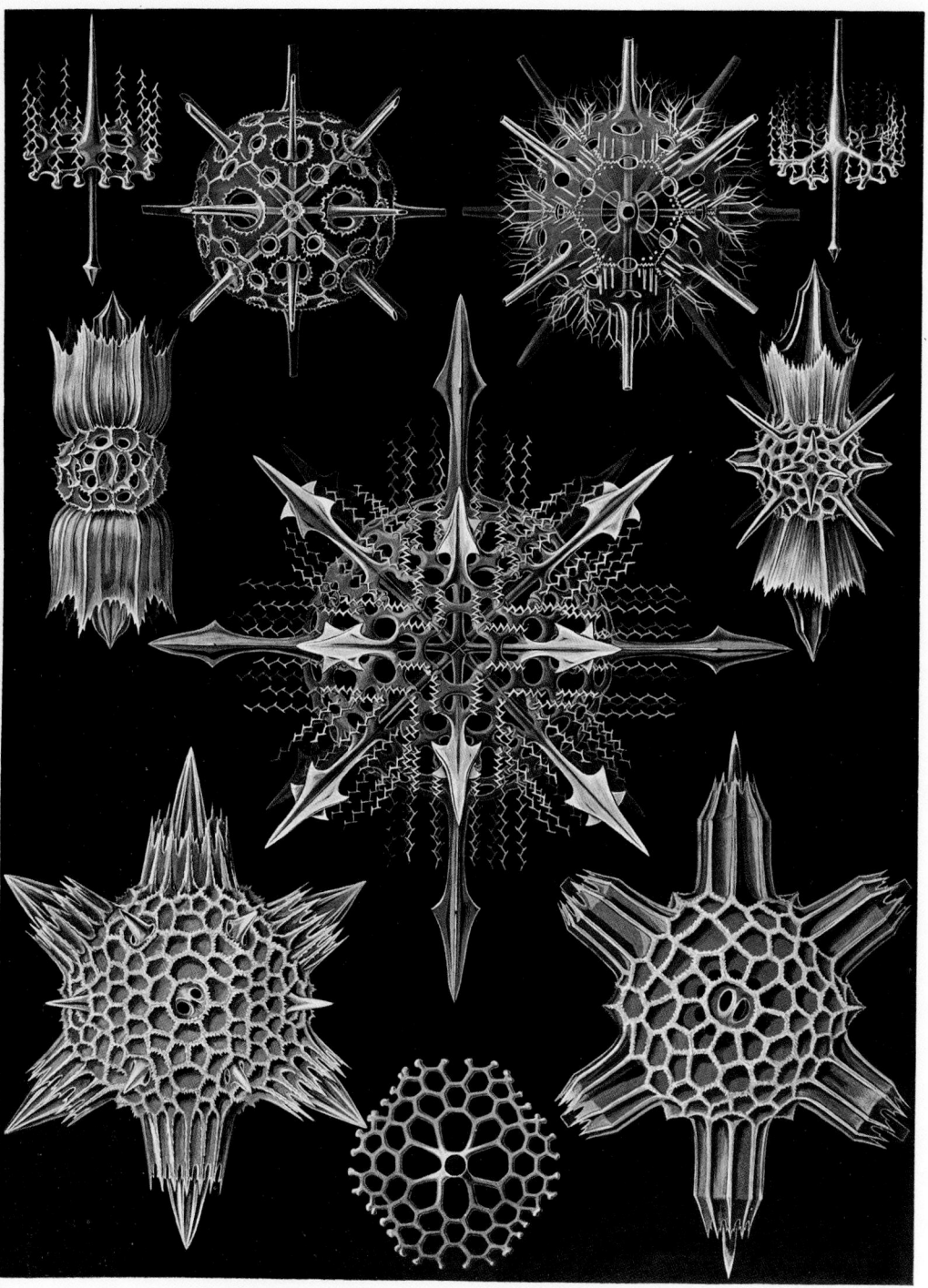

Acanthophracta. — Wunderstrahlinge.

PLATE 42
VERTEBRATA – ACTINOPTERYGII
Vertebrates – Ray-finned fishes

1–5 Ostracion cornutus (LINNÉ) – *Lactoria cornuta* (LINNAEUS, 1758) Longhorn cowfish
6–8 Ostracion quadricornis (LINNÉ) – *Acanthostracion quadricornis* (LINNAEUS, 1758) Scrawled cowfish
9 Ostracion auritus (SHAW) – *Aracana aurita* (SHAW, 1798) Striped cowfish
10 Ostracion turritus (SWAINSON) – *Tetrosomus gibbosus* (LINNAEUS, 1758) Humpback turretfish

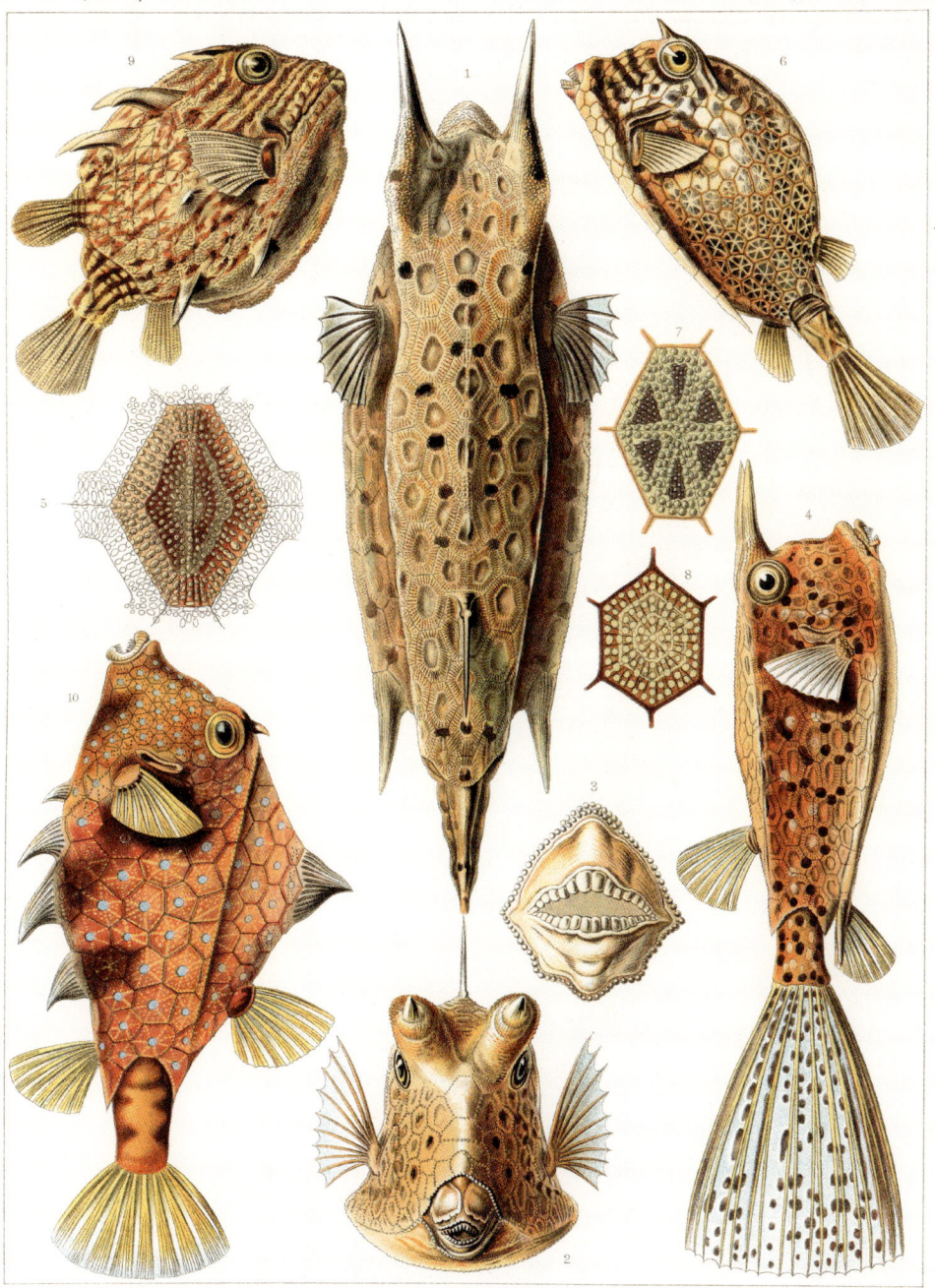

Ostraciontes. — Kofferfiſche.

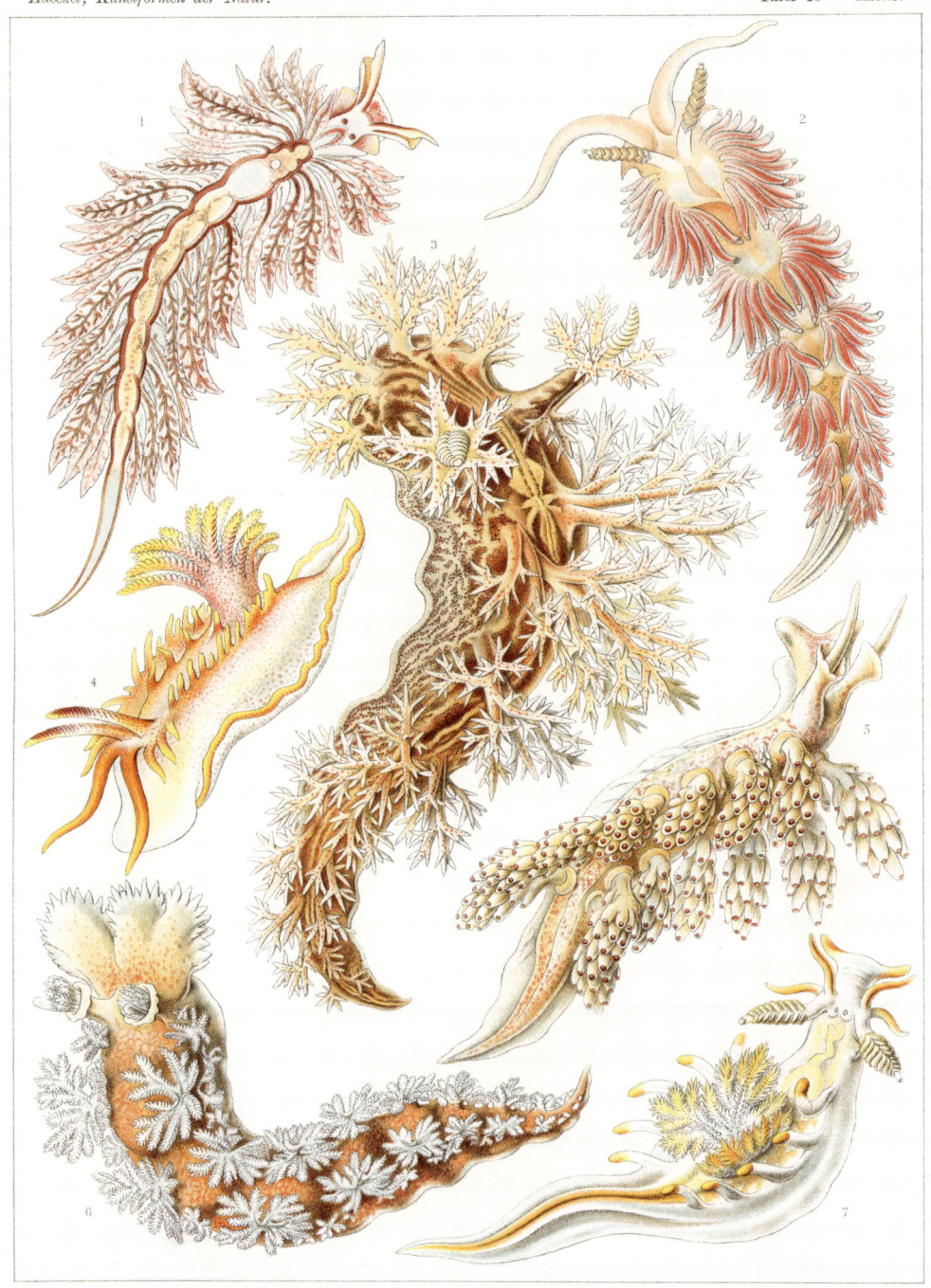

Nudibranchia. — Nacktkiemen-Schnecken.

PLATE 43
MOLLUSCA – GASTROPODA
Mollusc – Snails

1 Hermaea bifida (LOVÉN) – *Hermaea bifida* (MONTAGU, 1816)
2 Aeolis coronata (FORBES) – *Facelina auriculata* (MÜLLER, 1776)
(synonym: *F. coronata* (FORBES & GOODSIR, 1839))
3 Dendronotus arborescens (ALDER) – *Dendronotus frondosus* (ASCANIUS, 1774) Frond-aeolis, Frond eolis
4 Idalia elegans (LEUCKART) – *Okenia elegans* (LEUCKART, 1828)
5 Doto coronata (LOVÉN) – *Doto coronata* (GMELIN, 1791) Crowned doto, Crown doto, Coronate doto
6 Tritonia Hombergii (CUVIER) – *Tritonia hombergii* CUVIER, 1803
7 Ancula cristata (LOVÉN) – *Ancula gibbosa* (RISSO, 1818) Atlantic ancula

385

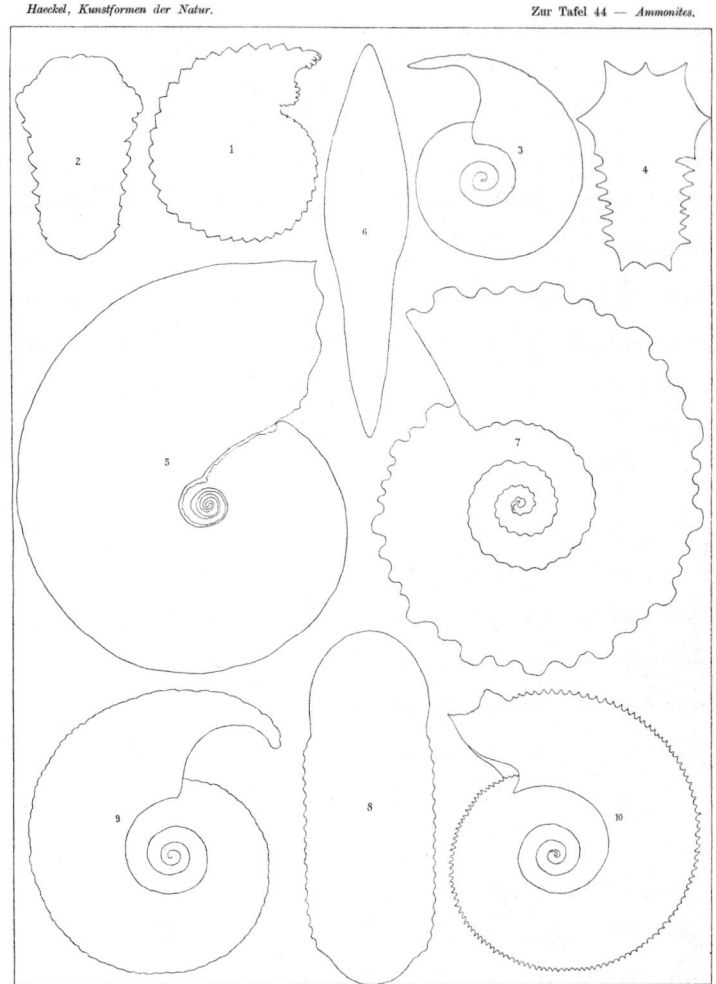

Haeckel, Kunstformen der Natur. Zur Tafel 44 — Ammonites.

PLATE 44
MOLLUSCA – CEPHALOPODA – AMMONOIDEA
Mollucs – Cephalopods – Ammonoids

1-2 Ammonites (Cardioceras) cordatus (QUENSTEDT) – *Cardioceras cordatum* SOWERBY, 1813
3-4 Ammonites (Schloenbachia) Coupei (BRONGNIART) – *Schloenbachia cf. varians* (SOWERBY, 1813)
5-6 Ammonites (Ptychites) opulentus (MOJSISOVICH) – *Ptychites opulentus* MOJSISOVICH, 1882
7 Ammonites (ornatus) mammillaris (SCHLOTHEIM) – *Douvilleiceras mammillatum* (SCHLOTHEIM, 1813)
8 Ammonites (planulatus) cavernosus (QUENSTEDT) – *Puzosia planulatus* (SOWERBY, 1827)
9 Ammonites (amaltheus) rotula (SCHLOTHEIM) – *Amaltheus margaritatus* MONTFORT, 1808
10 Ammonites (stephanoceras) Humphryi (SOWERBY) – *Stephanoceras humphriesianum* (SOWERBY, 1825)

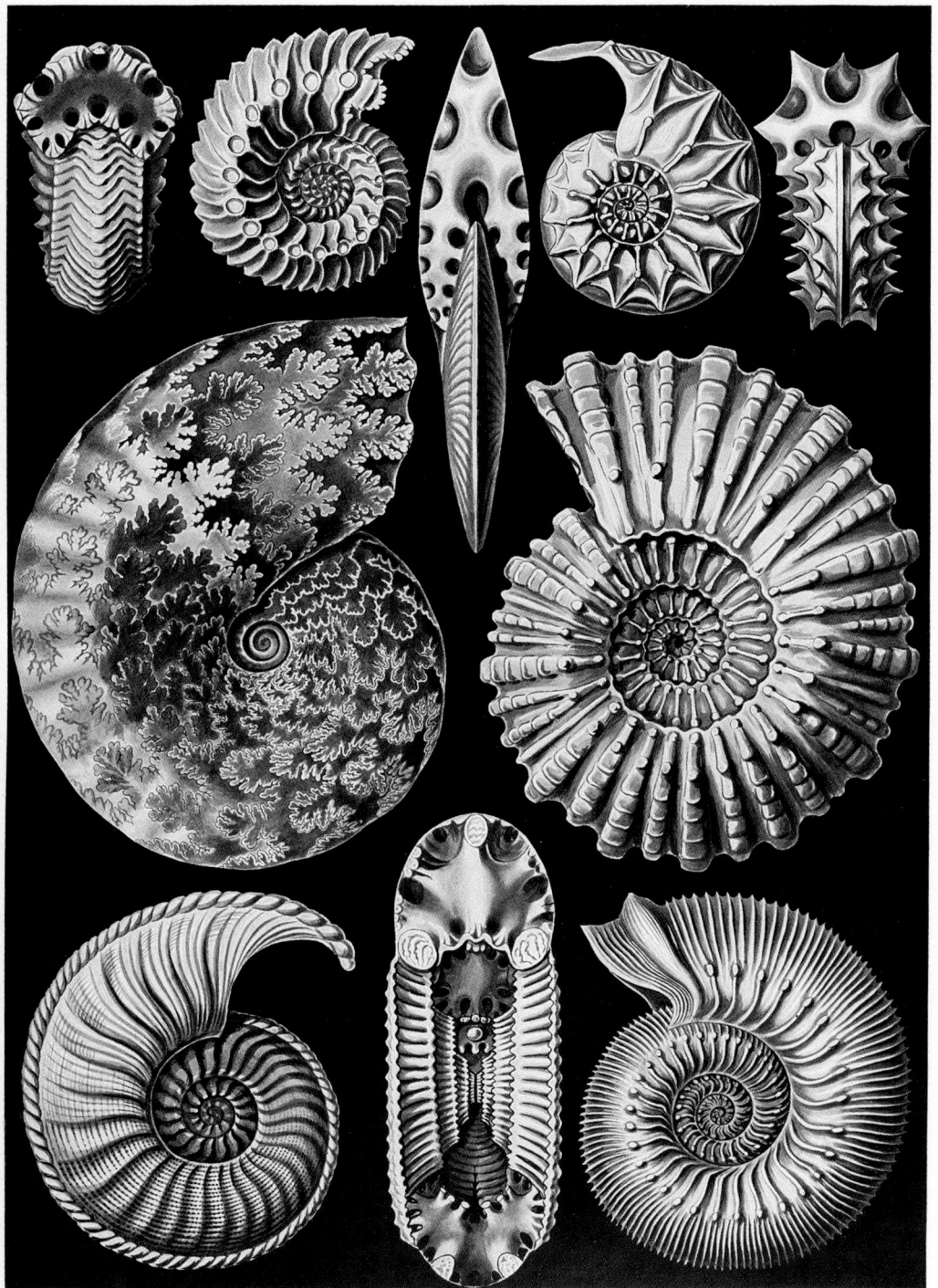

Ammonitida. — Ammonshörner.

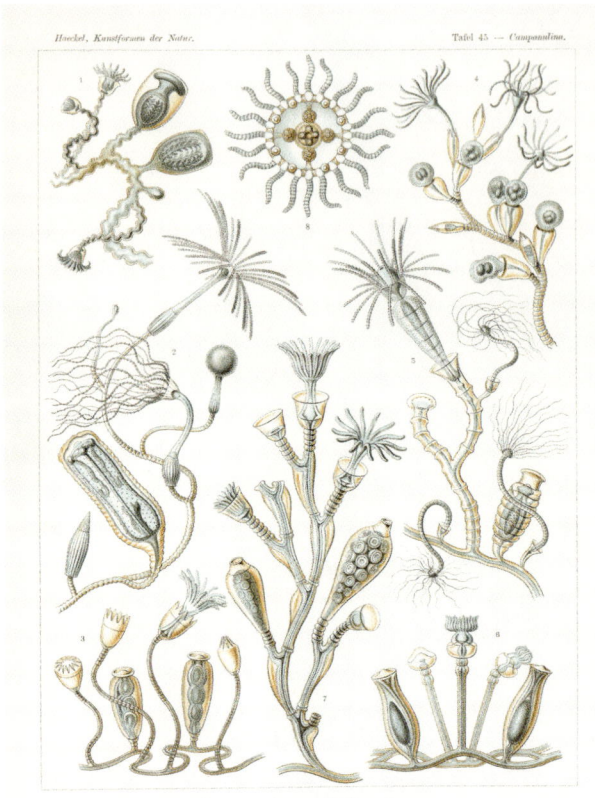

PLATE 45
CNIDARIA – HYDROZOA
Cnidarians – Hydrozoans

1 Campanulina pinnata (HAECKEL) – *Campanulariidae* sp. | 2 Campanulina tenuis (VAN BENEDEN) – *Campanulina tenuis* VAN BENEDEN, 1847 | 3 Campanularia ptychocyathus (ALLMAN) – *Clytia noliformis* MCCRADY, 1859 | 4 Opercularella lacerata (HINCKS) – *Opercularella lacerata* (JOHNSTON, 1847) 5 Ophiodes mirabilis (HINCKS) – *Hydrodendron mirabile* (HINCKS, 1866) | 6 Hypanthea hemisphaerica (ALLMAN) – *Silicularia hemisphaerica* ALLMAN, 1888 | 7 Obelaria geniculata (HAECKEL) – *Obelia geniculata* (LINNAEUS, 1758) Knotted thread hydroid, Bell hydroid | 8 Obelia lucifera (HAECKEL) – *Obelia lucifera* FORBES, 1848

PLATE 46
CNIDARIA
Cnidarians

1 Gemmaria sagittaria (HAECKEL) – *Zanclea sagittaria* (HAECKEL, 1879) | 2 Rathkea fasciculata (HAECKEL) – *Koellikerina fasciculata* (PÉRON & LESUEUR, 1810) | 3-4 Tiara pileata (L. AGASSIZ) – *Neoturris pileata* (FORSKÅL, 1775) | 5 Stomotoca pterophylla (HAECKEL) – *Larsonia pterophylla* HAECKEL, 1879 6 Thamnostylus dinema (HAECKEL) – *Sarsiella dinema* (HAECKEL, 1879)

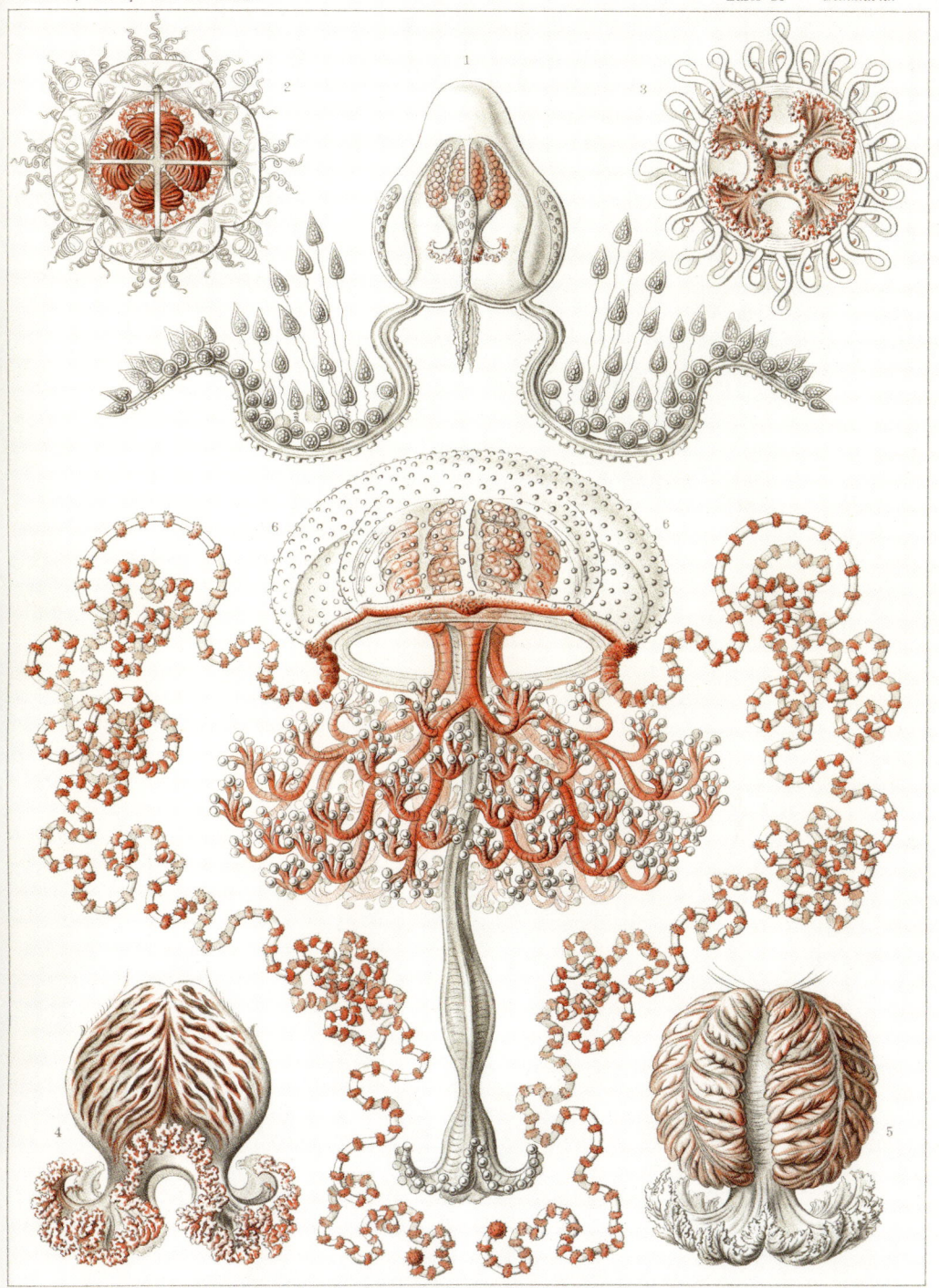

Anthomedusae. — Blumenquallen.

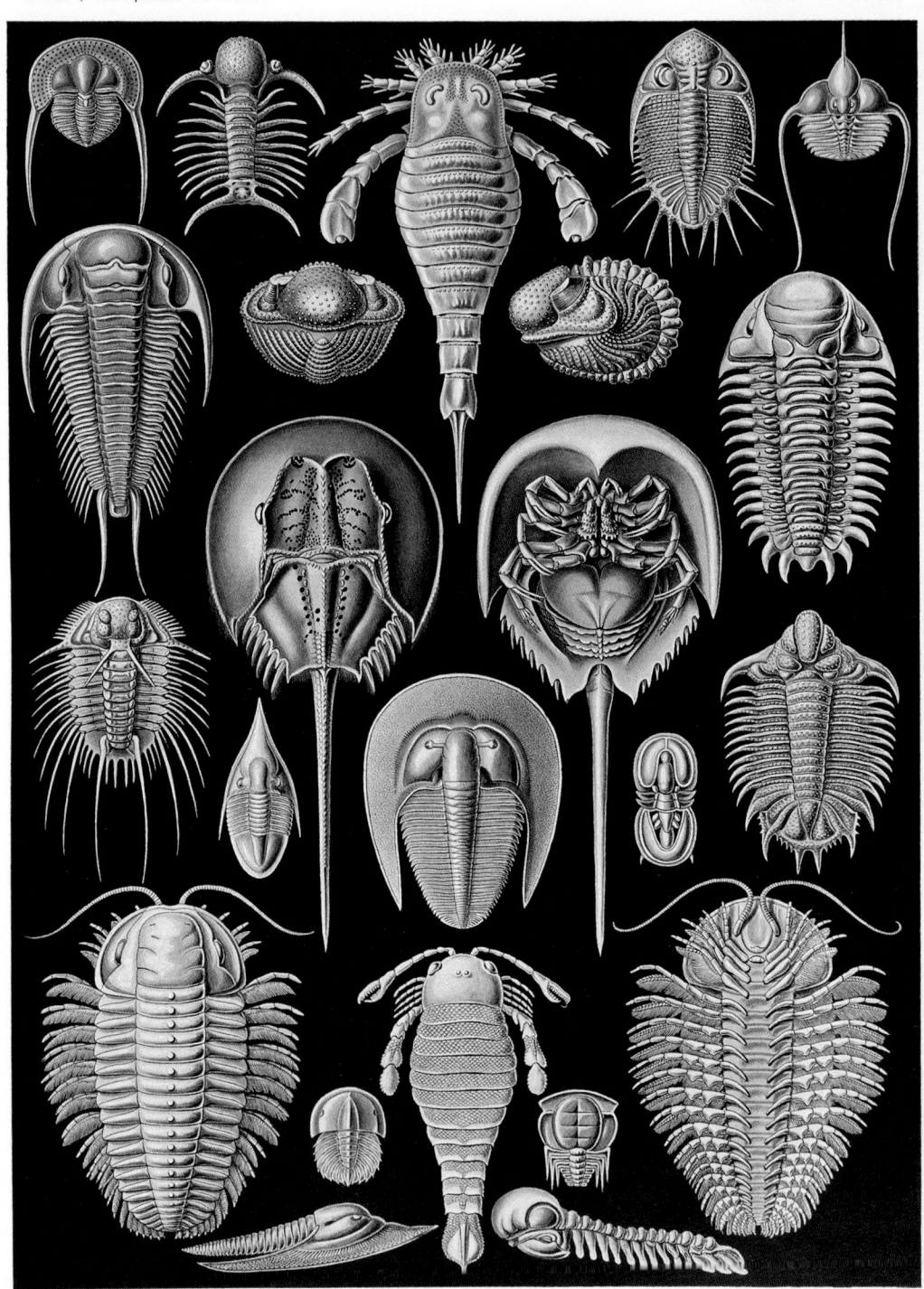

Aspidonia. — Schildtiere.

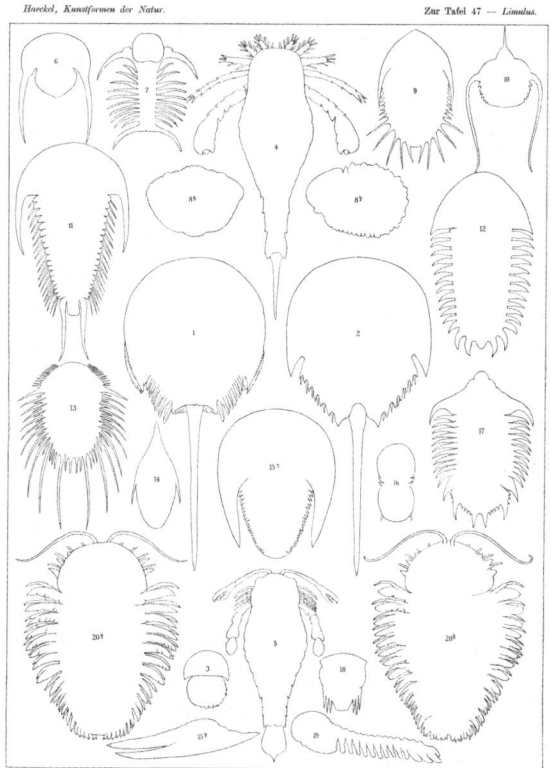

Haeckel, Kunstformen der Natur.   Zur Tafel 47 — Limulus.

PLATE 47
ARTHROPODA
Arthropods

1–3 Limulus moluccanus (CLUSIUS) – *Tachypleus gigas* (O. F. MÜLLER, 1785) Indian horseshoe crab,
Chinese horseshoe crab | 4 Eurypterus Fischeri (EICHWALDT) – *Eurypterus tetragonophthalmus* (FISCHER, 1839)
(synonym: *Baltoeurypterus tetragonophthalmus* (FISCHER, 1839)) | 5 Pterygotus anglicus (AGASSIZ) – *Pterygotus
anglicus* AGASSIZ, 1844 | 6–20 Trilobita | 6 Trinucleus Goldfussi (BARRANDE) – *Onnia goldfussi* (BARRANDE, 1846) |
7 Deiphon Forbesi (BARRANDE) – *Deiphon forbesi* BARRANDE, 1850 | 8 Phacops latifrons (BRONN) – *Phacops
latifrons* (BRONN, 1825) | 9 Dalmania punctata (BARRANDE) – *Asteropyge punctata* (STEININGER, 1831) | 10 Ampyx
Rouaulti (BARRANDE) – *Raphiophorus rouaulti* (BARRANDE, 1852) | 11 Paradoxides bohemicus (BOECK) –
Paradoxides bohemicus (BOECK, 1828) | 12 Cheirurus insignis (BEYRICH) – *Cheirurus insignis* BEYRICH, 1845 |
13 Acidaspis Dufresnoyi (BARRANDE) – *Selenopeltis buchi* (BARRANDE, 1846) | 14 Megalaspis extenuatus
(ANGELIN) – *Megistaspidella extenuata* (WAHLENBERG, 1821) | 15 Harpes ungula (STERNBERG) – *Bohemoharpes ungula*
(STERNBERG, 1833) (synonym: *Bohemoharpes [Unguloharpes] ungula*) | 16 Agnostus pisiformis (LINNÉ) – *Agnostus
pisiformis* (LINNÉ, 1768) | 17 Lichas palmata (BARRANDE) – *Trochurus speciosus* BEYRICH, 1845 | 18 Hydrocephalus
saturnoides (BARRANDE) – *Hydrocephalus saturnoides* BARRANDE, 1846 or *Paradoxides (Eccaparadoxides) pusillus*
(BARRANDE, 1846) | 19 Sphaerexochus mirus (BEYRICH) – *Sphaerexochus mirus* BEYRICH, 1845 |
20 Triarthrus Becki (BEECHER) – *Triarthrus becki* GREEN, 1832

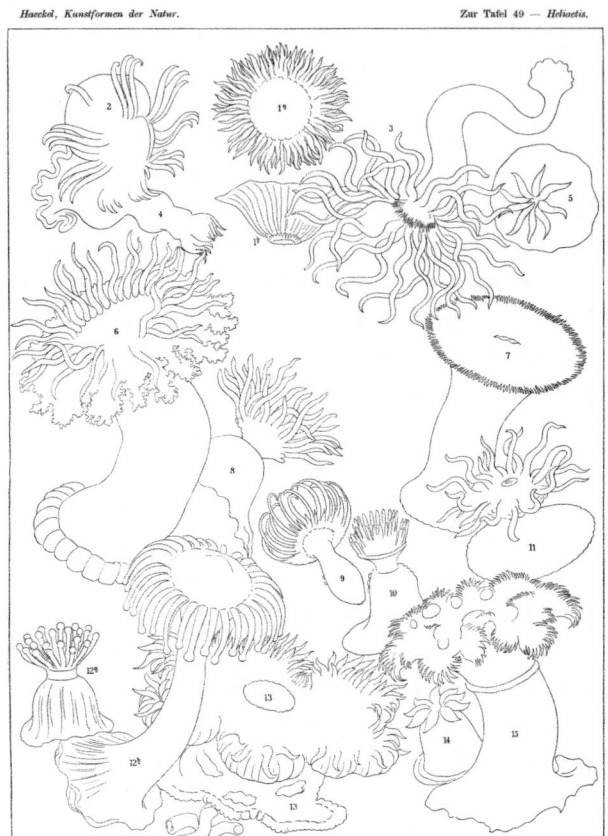

Haeckel, Kunstformen der Natur.   Zur Tafel 49 — Heliactis.

PLATE 49
CNIDARIA – ANTHOZOA
Cnidarians – Anthozoans, Flower-like animals

1 Heliactis bellis (THOMPSON) – *Cereus pedunculatus* (PENNANT, 1777) Daisy anemone | **2 Mesacmaea stellata** (ANDRES) – *Mesacmea mitchelli* GOSSE, 1853 (synonym: Mesacmaea stellata (ANDRÈS, 1881)) | **3 Aiptasia Couchii** (GOSSE) – *Aiptasia mutabilis* (GRAVENHORST, 1831) Trumpet anemone | **4 Cylista impatiens** (DANA) – *Paractis impatiens* (COUTHOUY IN DANA, 1846) | **5 Bunodes thallia** (GOSSE) – *Anthopleura thallia* (GOSSE, 1854) | **6 Metridium praetextum** (COUTHOUY) – *Phyllactis praetexta* (COUTHOUY IN DANA, 1846) or *Actinostella flosculifera* (LE SUEUR, 1817) Collared sand anemone | **7 Heliactis troglodytes** (THOMPSON) – *Sagartia troglodytes* (PRICE IN JOHNSTON, 1847) Mud sagartia | **8 Anthea cereus** (GOSS) – *Anemonia sulcata* (PENNANT, 1777) (synonym: *Anthea cereus* GÄRTNER) Snakelocks anemone | **9-10 Aiptasia undata** (MARTENS) – *Aiptasia diaphana* (RAPP, 1829) Yellow aiptasia | **11 Bunodes monilifera** (DANA) – *Paractis monilifera* (DRAYTON IN DANA, 1846) | **12 Corynactis viridis** (ALLMAN) – *Corynactis viridis* ALLMAN, 1846 Jewel anemone | **13 Metridium concinnatum** (DANA) – *Oulactis concinnata* (DRAYTON IN DANA, 1846) | **14 Sagartia chrysosplenium** (GOSSE) – *Chrysoela chrysosplenium* (COCKS IN JOHNSON, 1847) | **15 Actinoloba dianthus** (BLAINVILLE) – *Metridium dianthus* (ELLIS, 1768) Plumose anemone

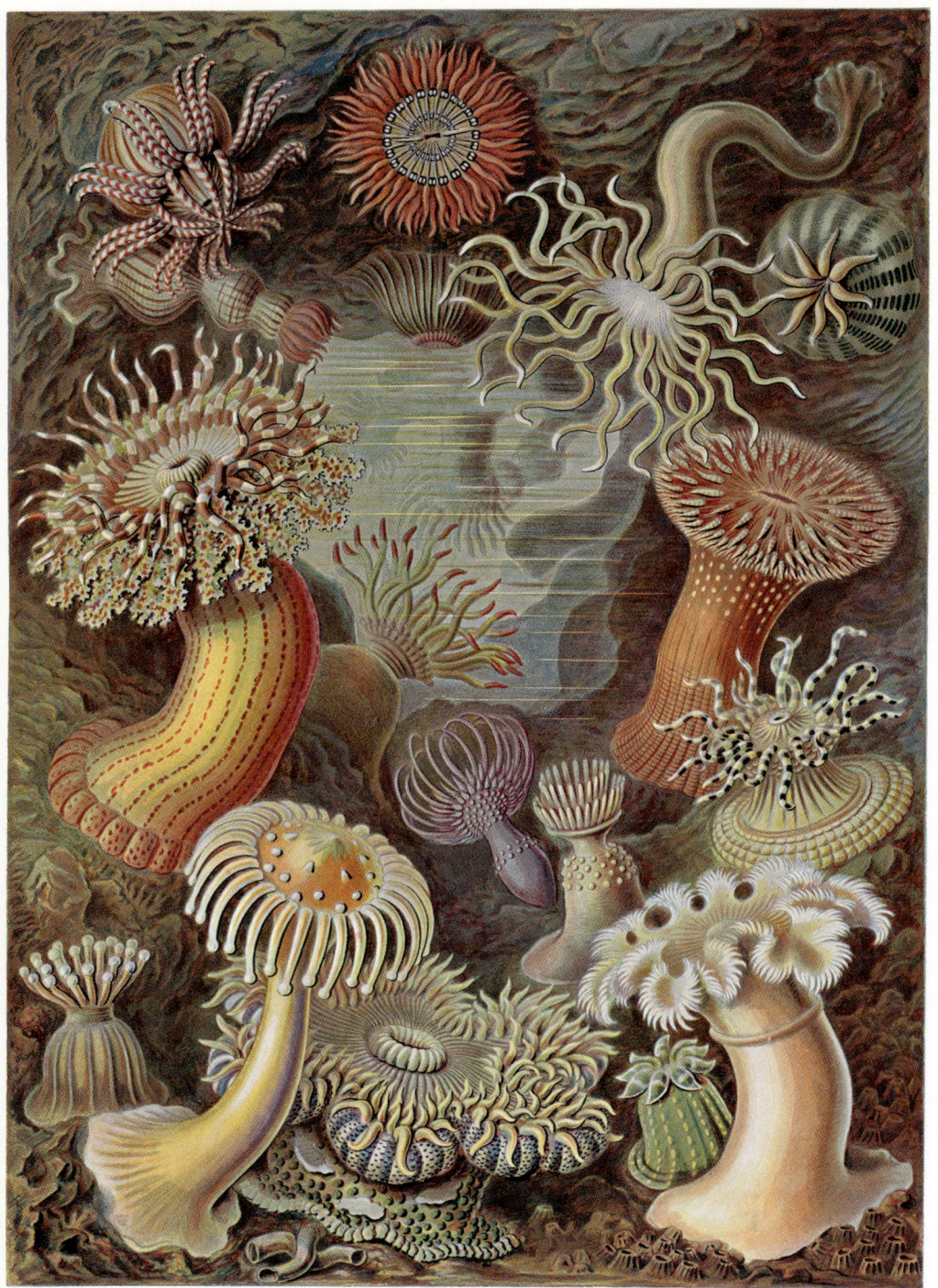

Actiniae. — Seeanemonen.

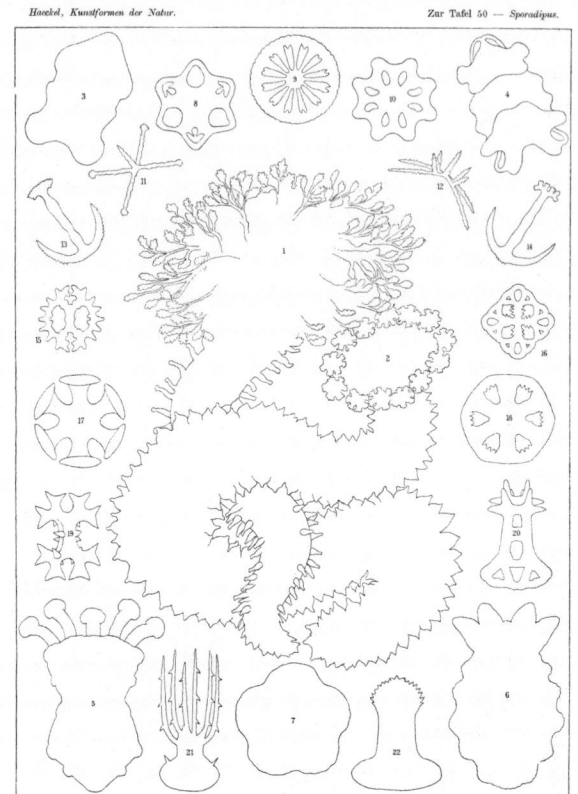

PLATE 50

ECHINODERMATA – HOLOTHUROIDEA
Echinoderms – Sea cucumbers

1 Phyllophorus urna (GRUBE) – *Phyllophorus urna* GRUBE, 1840 | 2 Sporadipus botellus (SELENKA) – *Holothuria (Thymiosycia) impatiens* (FORSKÅL, 1775) Bottleneck sea cucumber | 3-7 Synapta digitatat – *Oestergrenia digitata* (MONTAGU, 1815) | 8 Stichopus Murrayi (THEEL) – *Mesothuria murrayi* (THÉEL, 1886) | 9 Myriotrochus Rinkii (STEENSTRUP) – *Myriotrochus rinkii* STEENSTRUP, 1851 | 10 Caudina coriacea (HUTTON) – *Paracaudina coriacea* (HUTTON, 1872) | 11 Paelopatides aspera (THEEL) – *Galatheathuria aspera* (THÉEL, 1886) | 12 Elpidia rigida (THEEL) – *Psychroplanes rigida* (THÉEL, 1882) | 13 Synapta aculeata (THEEL) – *Protankyra aculeata* (THÉEL, 1886) | 14 Synapta glabra (SEMPER) – *Opheodesoma glabra* (SEMPER, 1867) | 15 Colochirus inornatus (MARENZELLER) – *Plesiocolochirus inornatus* (MARENZELLER, 1881) | 16 Stichopus Moebii (SEMPER) – *Isostichopus badionotus* (SELENKA, 1867) Chocolate chip cucumber, Cookie dough sea cucumber, Three-rowed sea cucumber | 17-18 Chirodota venusta (SEMON) – *Taeniogyrus venustus* (SEMON, 1887) | 19 Cucumaria crucifera (SEMPER) – *Trachasina crucifera* (SEMPER, 1869) | 20 Thelonota atra (JAEGER) – *Holothuria atra* JAEGER, 1833 Black sea cucumber, Lollywfish | 21 Arbacia pustulosa (SEMON) – *Arbacia lixula* (LINNAEUS, 1758) Black sea urchin | 22 Stichopus Moebii (SEMPER) – *Isostichopus badionotus* (SELENKA, 1867) Chocolate chip cucumber, Cookie dough sea cucumber, Three-rowed sea cucumber

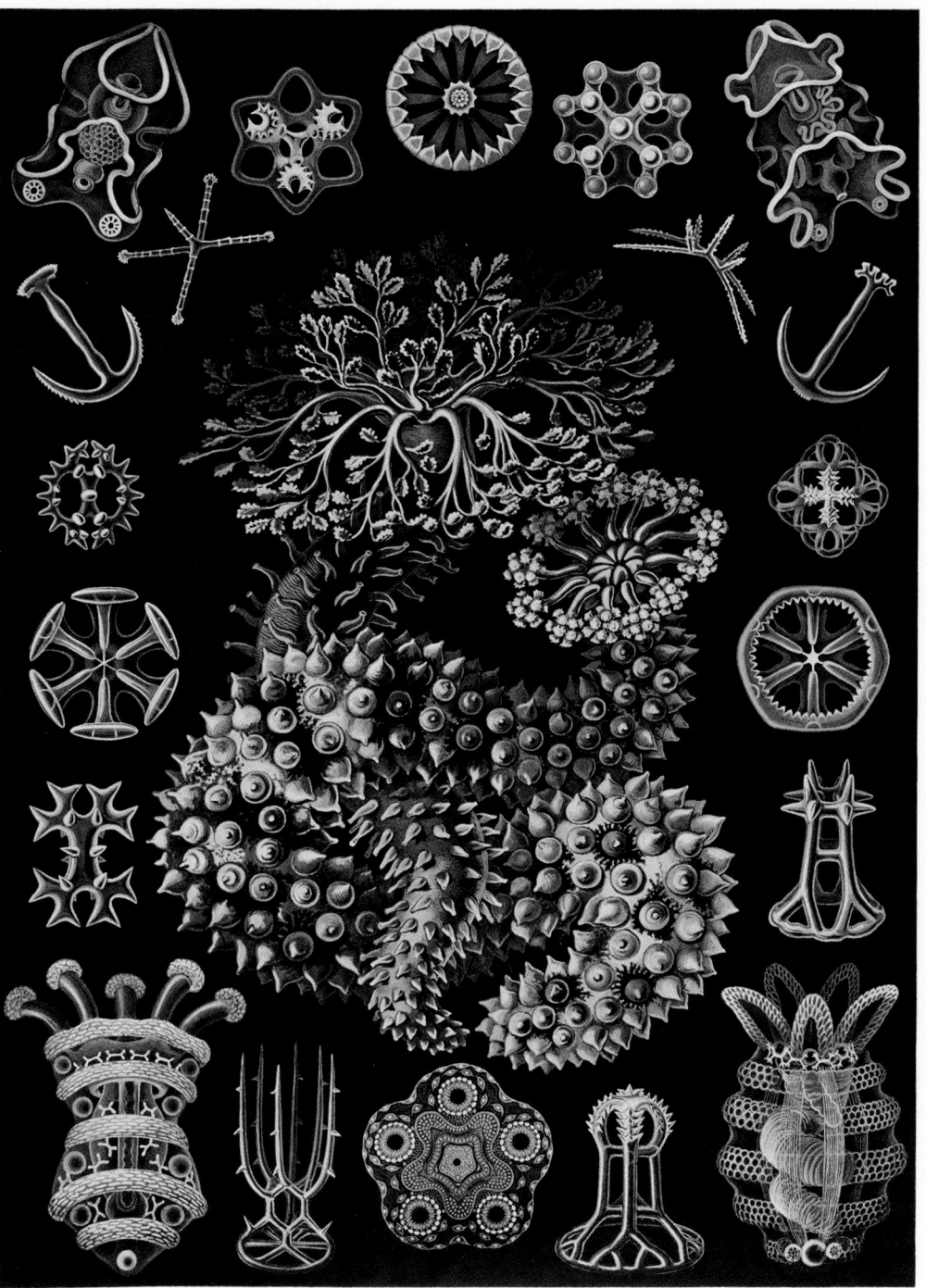

Thuroidea. — Gurkensterne.

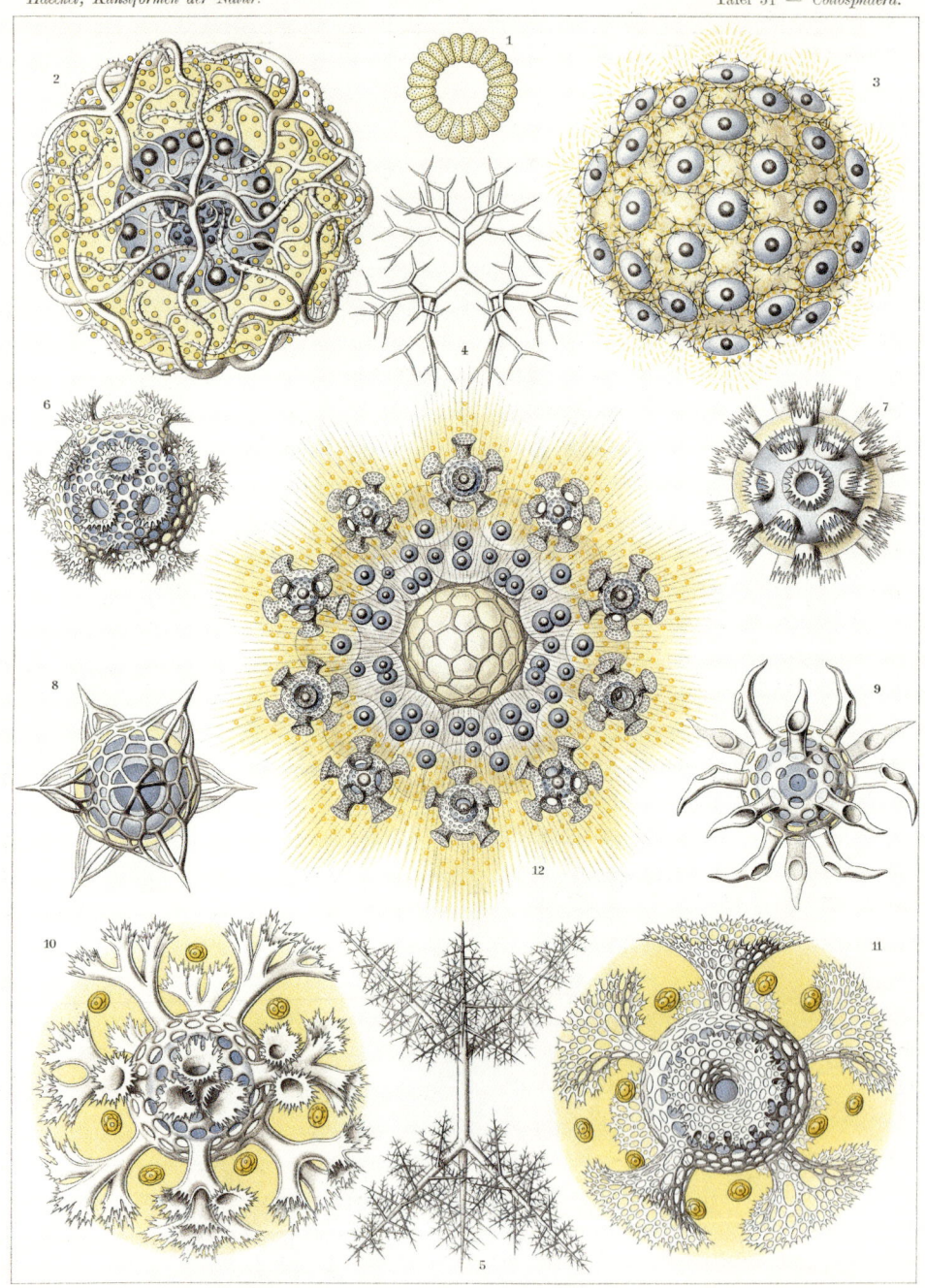

Polycyttaria. — Vereins-Strahlinge.

PLATE 51
RADIOLARIA – SPUMELLARIA
Radiolarians

1 Collosphaera primordialis (HAECKEL) – *Collosphaera (Eucollosphaera) primordialis* HAECKEL, 1887
2 Thalassoxanthium medusinum (HAECKEL) – *Thalassosphaera medusinum* (HAECKEL, 1887)
3 Sphaerozoum ovodimare (HAECKEL) – *Sphaerozoum ovodimare* HAECKEL, 1862
4 Thalassoxanthium cervicorne (HAECKEL) – *Thalassosphaera (Thalassoxanthella) cervicorne* HAECKEL, 1887
5 Sphaerozoum spinosissimum (HAECKEL) – *Sphaerozoum spinosissum* HAECKEL, 1902
6 Coronosphaera diadema (HAECKEL) – *Coronosphaera diadema* HAECKEL, 1887
7 Trypanosphaera trepanata (HAECKEL) – *Acrosphaera trepanata* (HAECKEL, 1887)
8 Acrosphaera inflata (HAECKEL) – *Acrosphaera inflata* (HAECKEL, 1887)
9 Mazosphaera lagotis (HAECKEL) – *Mazosphaera lagotis* HAECKEL, 1887
10 Caminosphaera dendrophora (HAECKEL) – *Caminosphaera dendrophora* HAECKEL, 1887
11 Coronosphaera calycina (HAECKEL) – *Coronosphaera calycina* HAECKEL, 1887
12 Solenosphaera familiaris (HAECKEL) – *Solenosphaera familiaris* (HAECKEL, 1887)

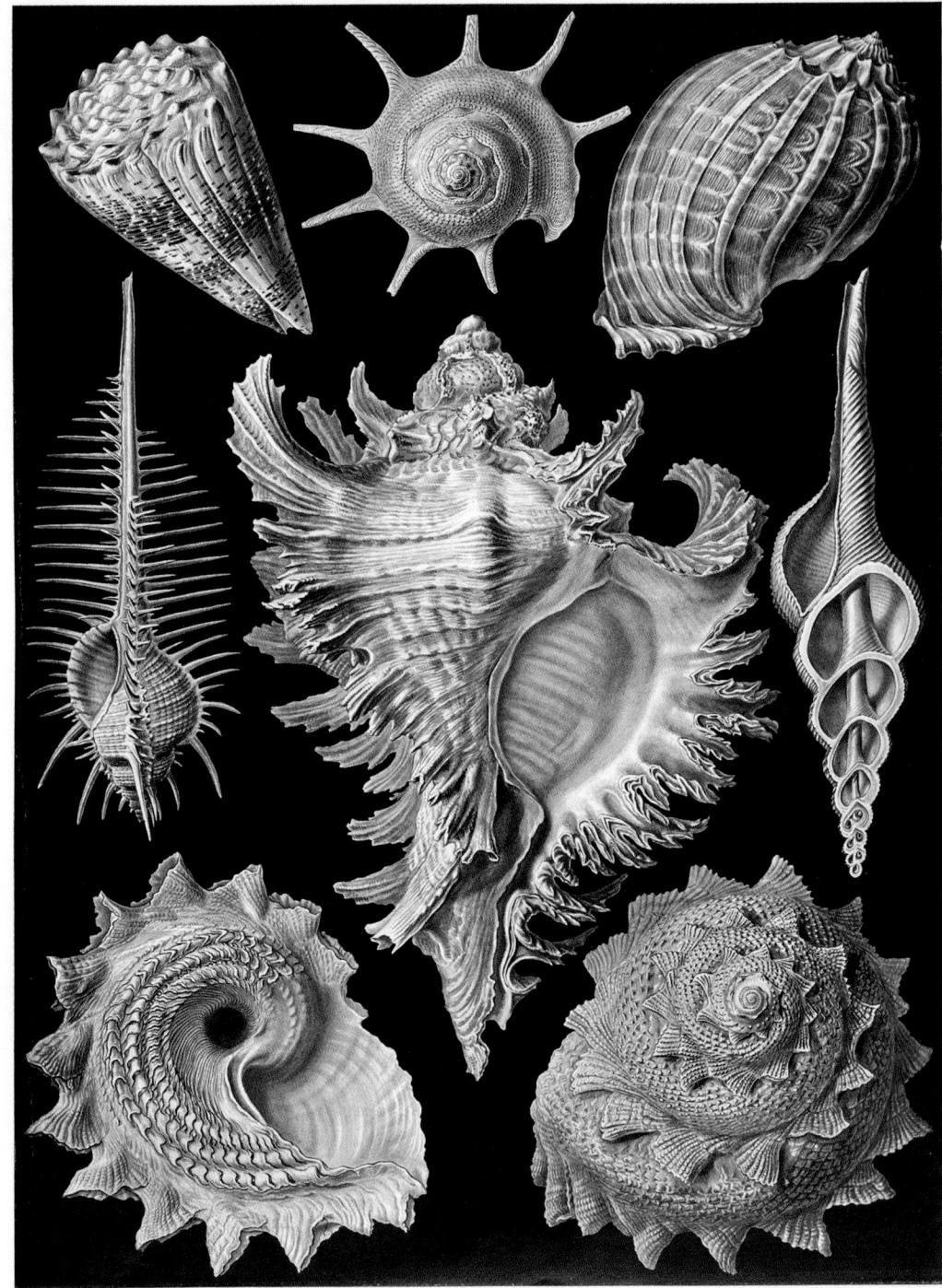

Prosobranchia. — Vorderkiemen-Schnecken.

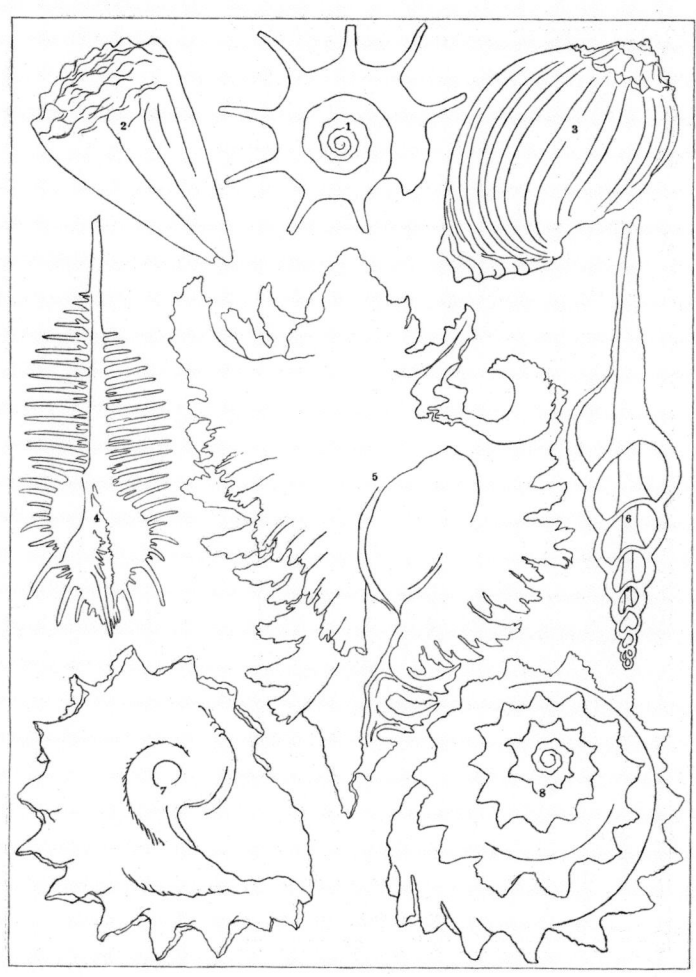

PLATE 53
MOLLUSCA – GASTROPODA
Mollucs – Snails

1 **Calcar triumphans** (PHILIPPI) – *Guildfordia triumphans* (PHILIPPI, 1841) Triumphant star turban
2 **Conus imperialis** (LINNÉ) – *Conus imperialis* LINNAEUS, 1758 Imperial cone | 3 **Harpa ventricosa** (LAMARCK) –
Harpa davidis RÖDING, 1798 (synonym: *Harpa ventricosa* (LAMARCK, 1801) Madras harp, David harp, Ventral harp
4 **Murex tenuispinus** (LAMARCK) – *Murex pecten* LIGHTFOOT, 1786 (synonym: *Murex tenuispina* LAMARCK, 1822)
Venus comb murex, Thorny woodcock | 5 **Murex inflatus** (LAMARCK) – *Chicoreus ramosus* (LINNAEUS, 1758) Ramose murex,
Branched murex | 6 **Fusus longicauda** (LAMARCK) – *Fusinus colus* (LINNAEUS, 1758) Distaff spindle, Long-tailed spindle
7-8 **Astralium imperiale** (CHEMNITZ) – *Astraea heliotropium* MARTYN, 1784 Sunburst star turban, Circular saw shell

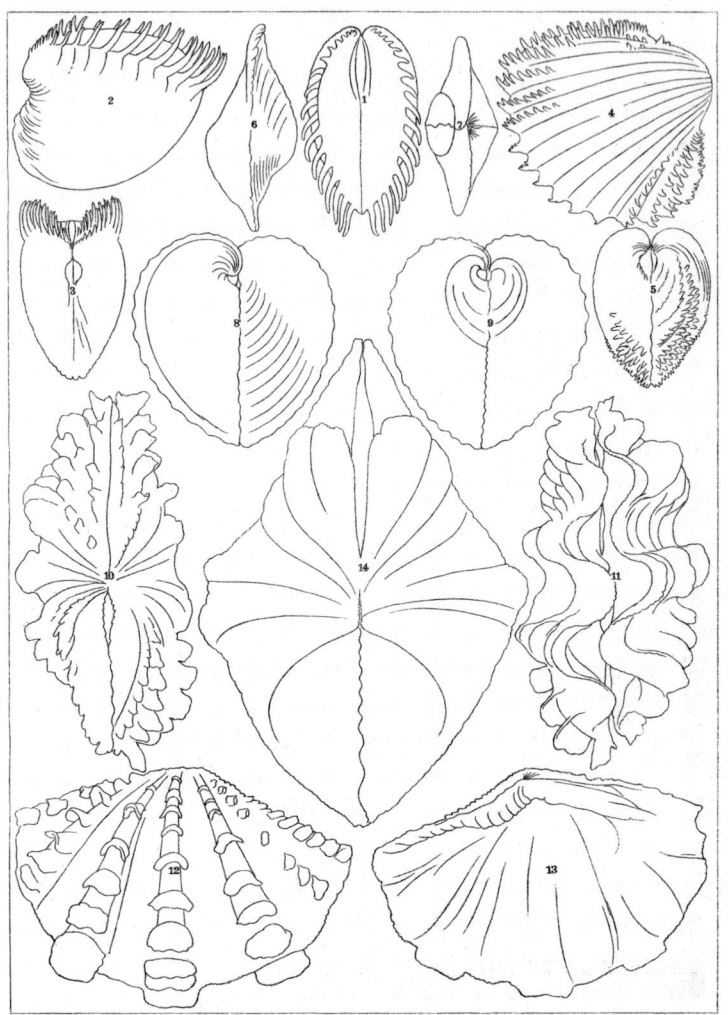

PLATE 55
MOLLUSCA – BIVALVIA
Mollucs – Bivalves – Bivalved shells

1–3 Cytherea Dione (LAMARCK) – *Hysteroconcha (Pitar) dione* (LINNAEUS, 1758) Elegant Venus clam
4–5 Cardium aculeatum (LINNÉ) – *Acanthocardia aculeata* (LINNÉ, 1767) Spiny cockle, Red nose
6–9 Hemicardium cardissa (LINNÉ) – *Corculum cardissa* (LINNAEUS, 1758) Heart cockle
10–13 Tridacna squamosa (LAMARCK) – *Tridacna squamosa* LAMARCK, 1819 Fluted giant clam, Scaly clam
14 Hippopus maculatus (LAMARCK) – *Hippopus hippopus* (LINNAEUS, 1758) Horse's hoof clam, Bear paw clam, Strawberry clam

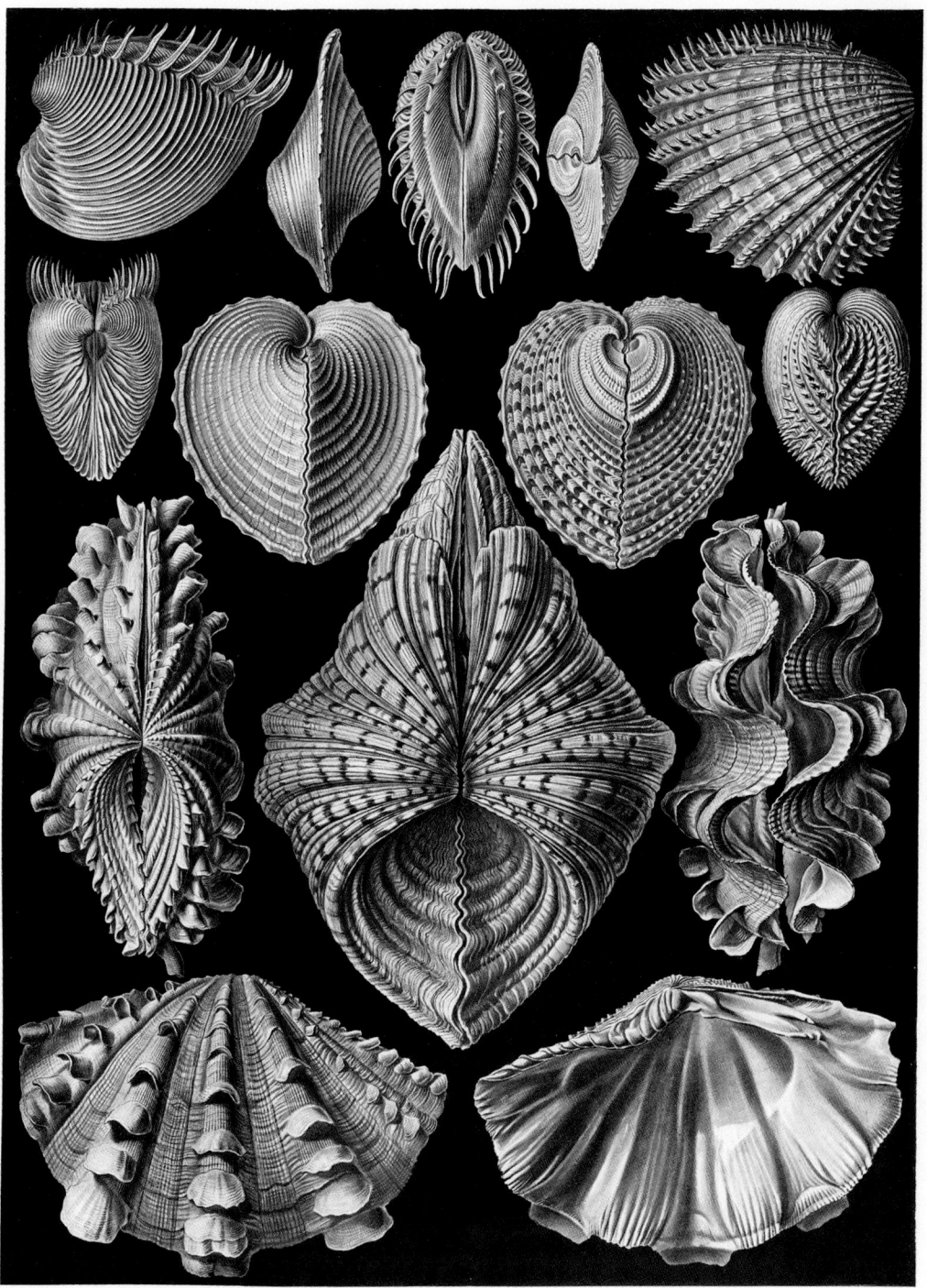

Acephala. — Muſcheln.

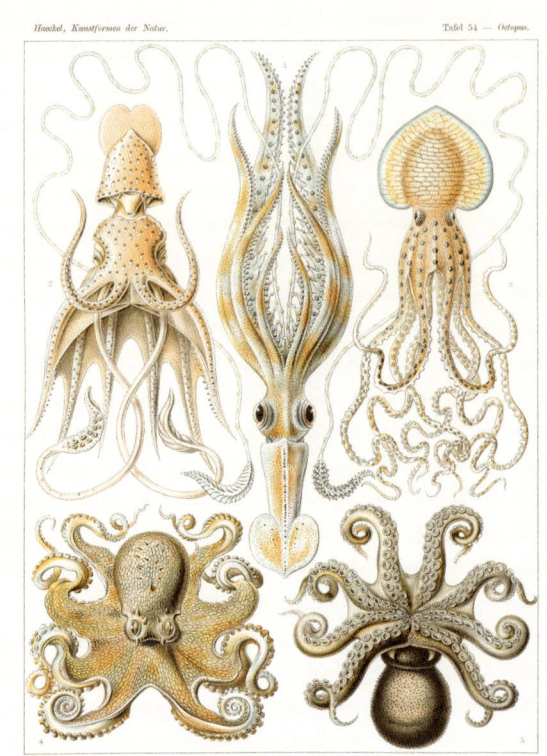

Haeckel, Kunstformen der Natur.   Tafel 54 — Octopus.

Gamochonia. — Trichterkrakeu.

PLATE 54

MOLLUSCA – CEPHALOPODA
Mollucs – Cephalopods

1 Chiroteuthis Veranyi (FÉRUSSAC) – *Chiroteuthis veranyi* (FÉRUSSAC, 1834) Long-armed squid
2 Histioteuthis Rüppellii (VERANY) – *Histioteuthis bonnellii* (FERUSSAC, 1835) Umbrella squid
3 Pinnoctopus cordiformis (GAIMARD) – *Pinnoctopus cordiformis* QUOY & GAIMARD, 1832
4 Octopus vulgaris (LAMARCK) – *Octopus vulgaris* CUVIER, 1797 Scuttle, Common octopus
5 Octopus granulatus (LAMARCK) – *Amphioctopus granulatus* (LAMARCK, 1799)

PLATE 56

CRUSTACEA
Crustaceans

1 Calanus pavo (DANA) – *Calocalanus pavo* (DANA, 1852) | 2 Clytemnestra scutellata (DANA) – *Clytemnestra scutellata* DANA, 1847 | 3 Oncaea venusta (PHILIPPI) – *Oncaea venusta* PHILIPPI, 1843
4 Cryptopontius thorelli (GIESBRECHT) – *Cryptopontius thorelli* (GIESBRECHT, 1895) | 5 Acontiophorus scutatus (BRADY) – *Acontiophorus scutatus* (BRADY & ROBERTSON, 1873) | 6 Corycaeus venustus (DANA) – *Corycaeus crassiusculus* DANA, 1849 | 7 Sapphirina Darwinii (HAECKEL) – *Sapphirina darwini* HAECKEL, 1864
8 Augaptilus filigerus (GIESBRECHT) – *Euaugaptilus filigerus* (CLAUS, 1863)

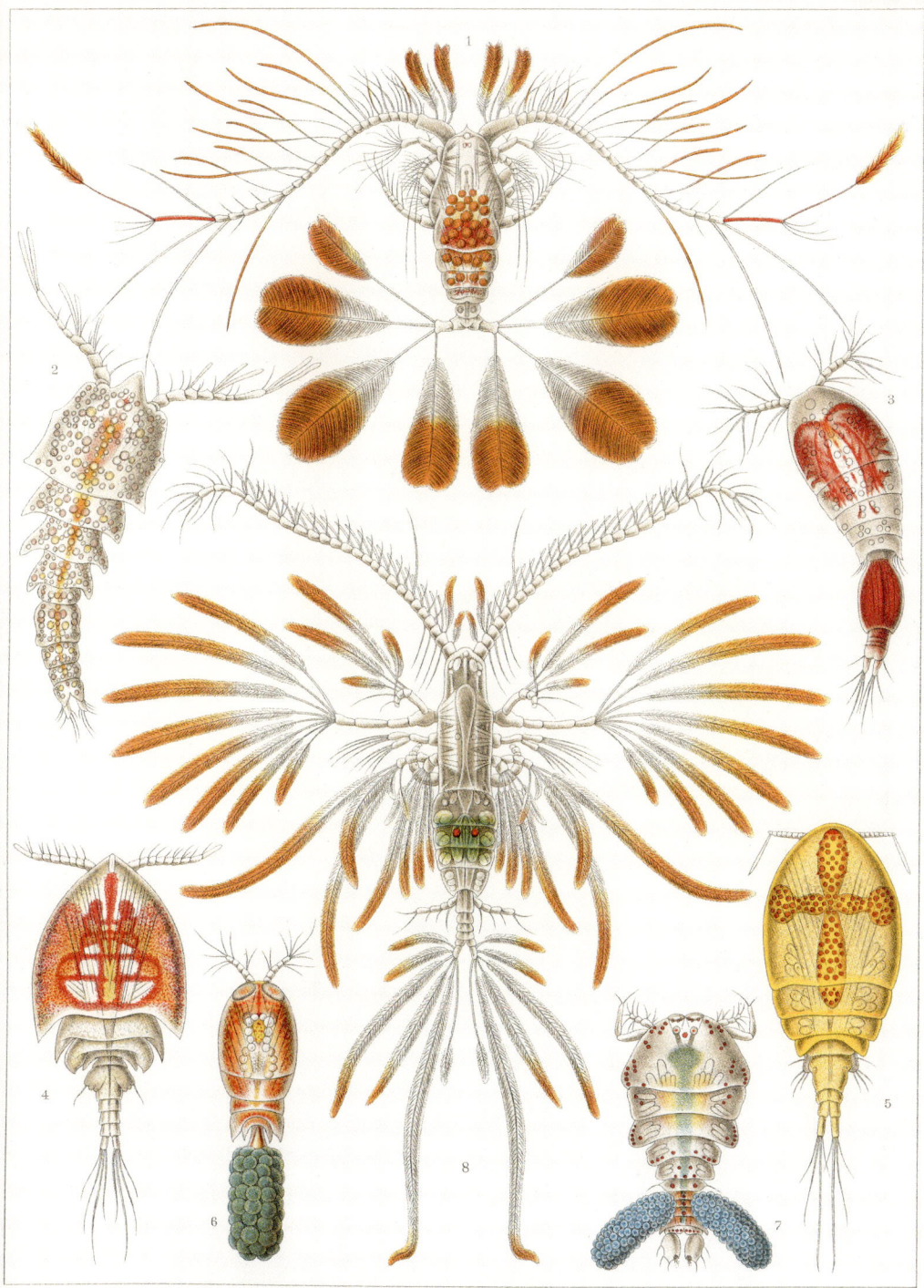

Copepoda. — Ruderkrebfe.

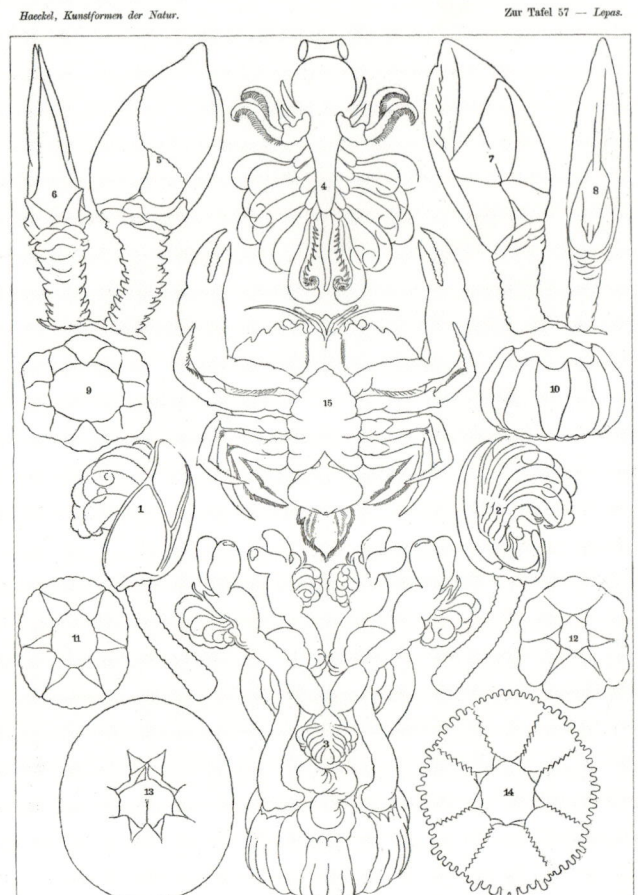

Haeckel, Kunstformen der Natur.   Zur Tafel 57 — Lepas.

PLATE 57
CRUSTACEA
Crustaceans

1–2 Lepas anatifera (LINNÉ) – *Lepas (Anatifa) anatifera* LINNAEUS, 1758 Duck barnacle, Common goose barnacle
3 Conchoderma auritum (OLFERS) – *Conchoderma auritum* (LINNÉ, 1767) Rabbit-ear barnacle
4 Pentalasmis vitrea (LEACH) – *Dosima fascicularis* (ELLIS & SOLANDER, 1786) (synonym: *Lepas fascicularis*
ELLIS & SOLANDER, 1786) Buoy barnacle | **5–6 Scalpellum eximium** (HOEK) – *Arcoscalpellum michelottianum*
(SEGUENZA, 1876) | **7–8 Scalpellum vitreum** (HOEK) – *Amigdoscalpellum vitreum* (HOEK, 1883) | **9–10 Coronula**
diadema (LAMARCK) – *Coronula diadema* (LINNÉ, 1767) Humpback whale barnacle | **11 Coronula reginae** (DARWIN) –
Coronula reginae DARWIN, 1854 | **12 Chthamalus antennatus** (DARWIN) – *Chthamalus antennatus* DARWIN, 1854
Six-plated barnacle | **13 Catophragmus polymerus** (DARWIN) – *Catomerus polymerus* (DARWIN, 1854)
Surf barnacle | **14 Octomeris angulosa** (SOWERBY) – *Octomeris angulosa* SOWERBY, 1825
15 Sacculina carcini (THOMPSON) – *Sacculina carcini* THOMPSON, 1836 Parasitic barnacle, Parasitic castrator

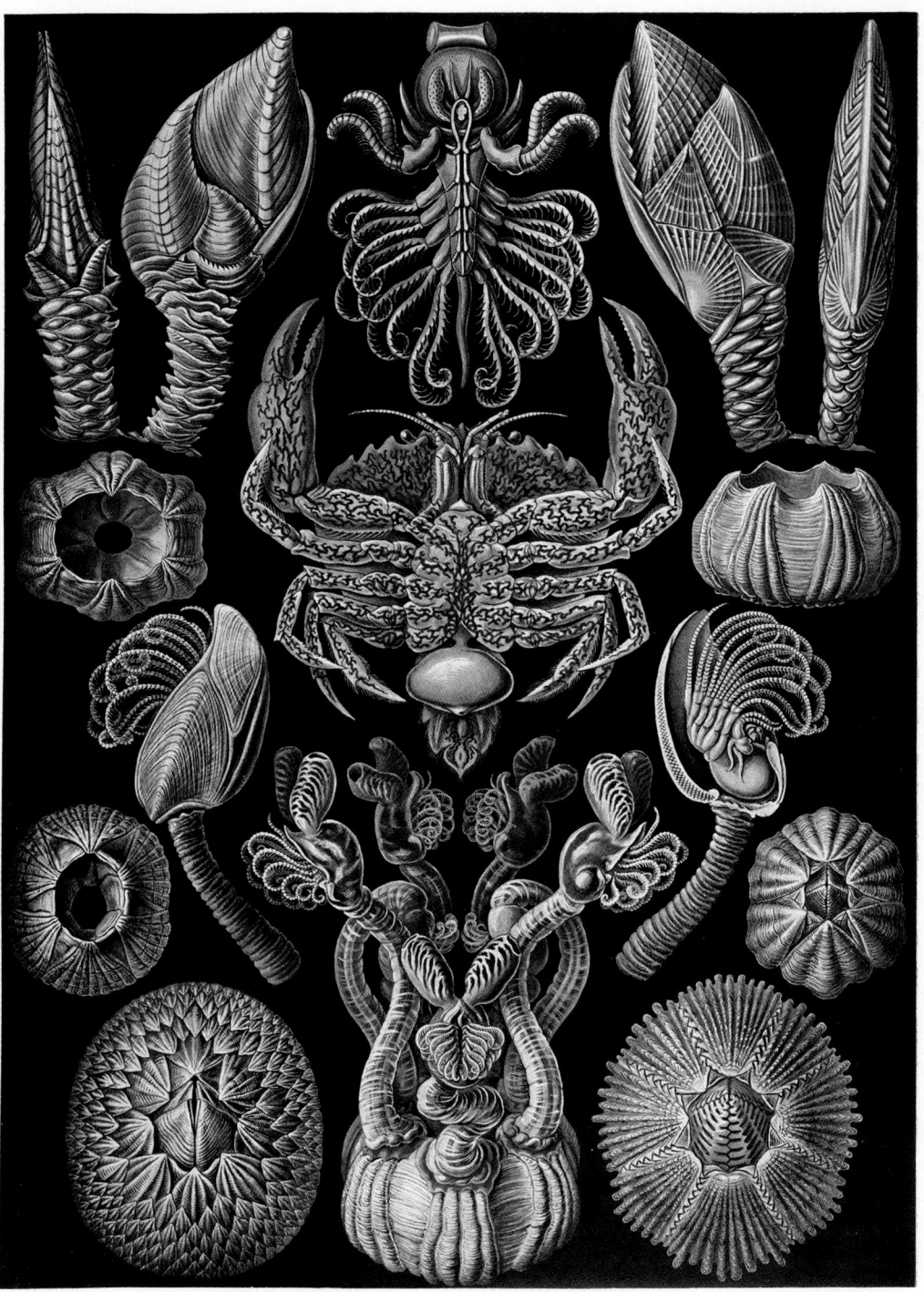

Cirripedia. — Rankenkrebſe.

Haeckel, Kunstformen der Natur.   Zur Tafel 58 — Alucita.

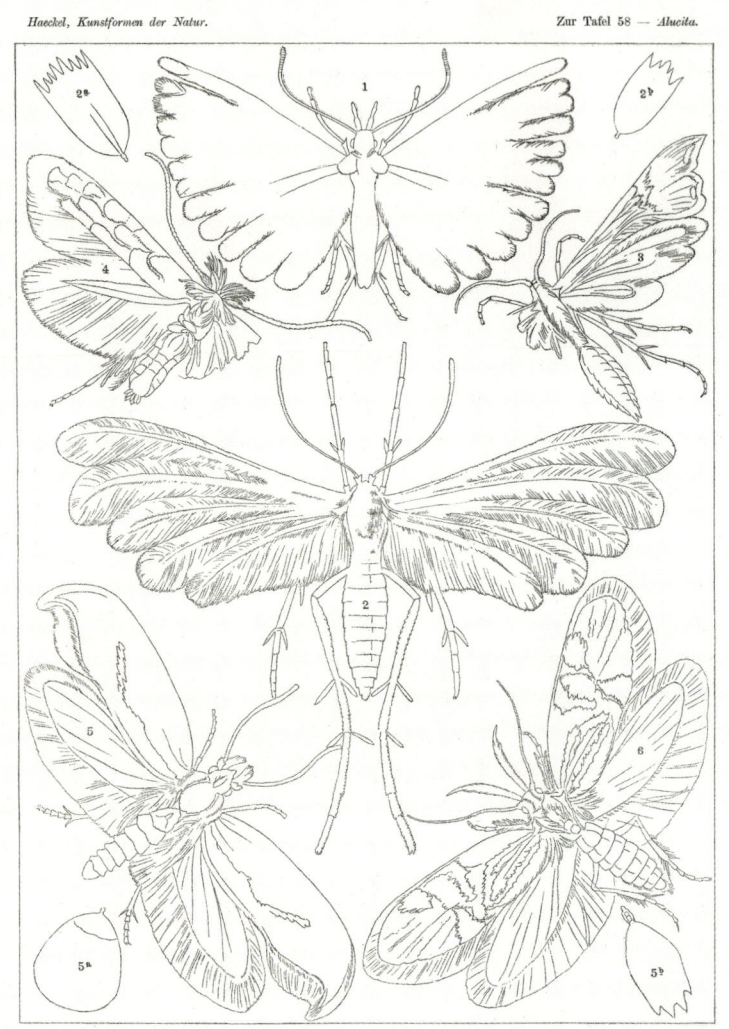

PLATE 58
INSECTA – LEPIDOPTERA
Insects, Hexapods – Butterflies and Moths

1 Alucita hexadactyla (LINNÉ) – *Alucita hexadactyla* LINNAEUS, 1758 Twenty-plume moth | 2 Pterophorus
pentadactylus (LINNÉ) – *Pterophorus pentadactyla* (LINNAEUS, 1758) White plume moth | 3 Pterophorus
rhododactylus (LINNÉ) – *Cnaemidophorus rhododactyla* (DENIS & SCHIFFERMÜLLER, 1775) Rose plume mothe
4 Lithocolletis populifolia (TREITSCHKE) – *Phyllonorycter populifoliella* (TREITSCHKE, 1833)
5 Plutella xylostella (ZELLER) – *Plutella xylostella* (LINNAEUS, 1758) Diamondback moth, Cabbage moth
6 Harpella geoffroyella (SCHRANCK) – *Alabonia geoffrella* (LINNÉ, 1767)

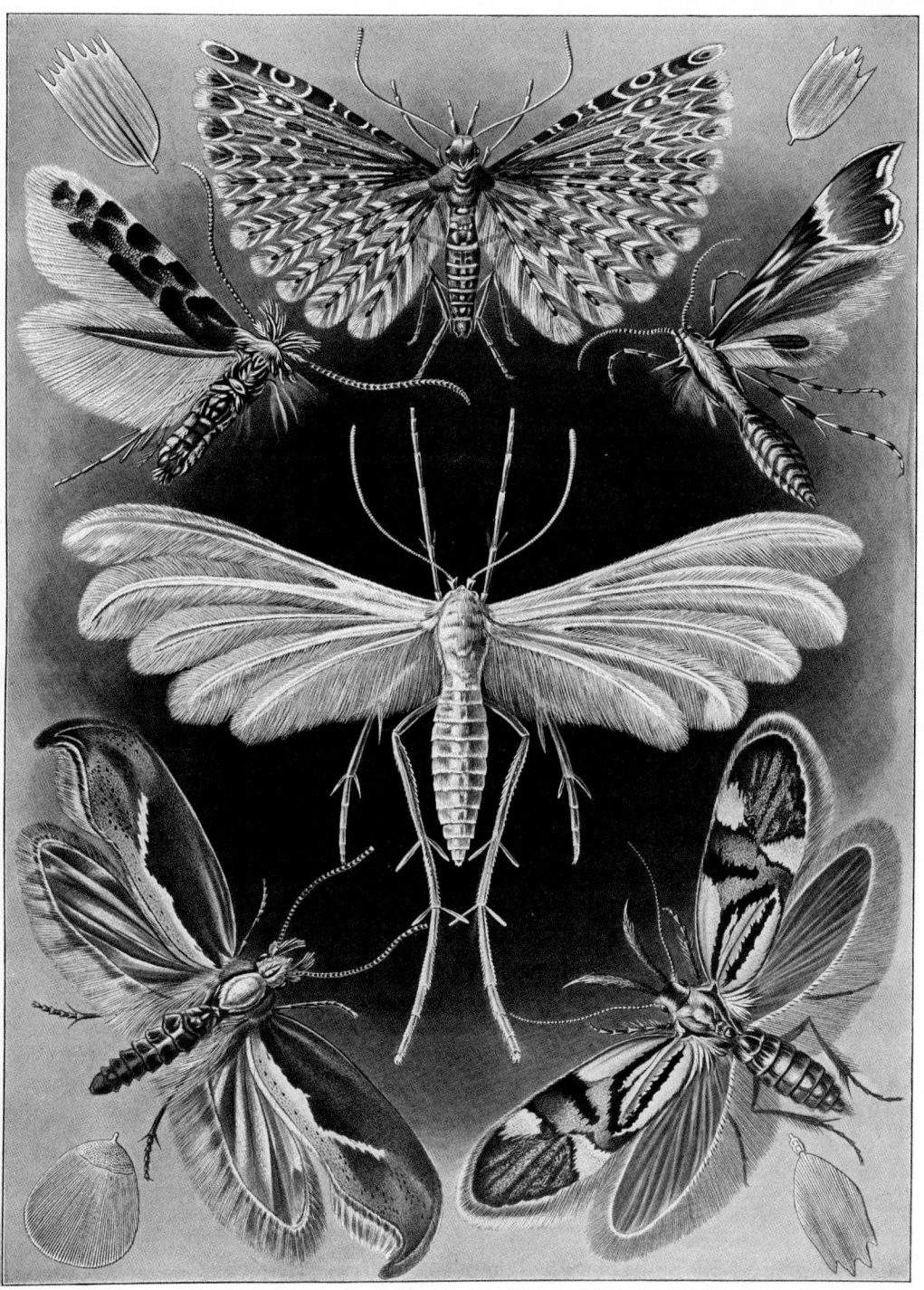

Tineida. — Motten.

PLATE 59

CNIDARIA – SIPHONOPHORA
Cnidarians – Siphonophores

1-9 Strobalia cupola (HAECKEL) – *Strobalia cupola* HAECKEL, 1902
(*Forobalia cupola* (HAECKEL, 1902)?)

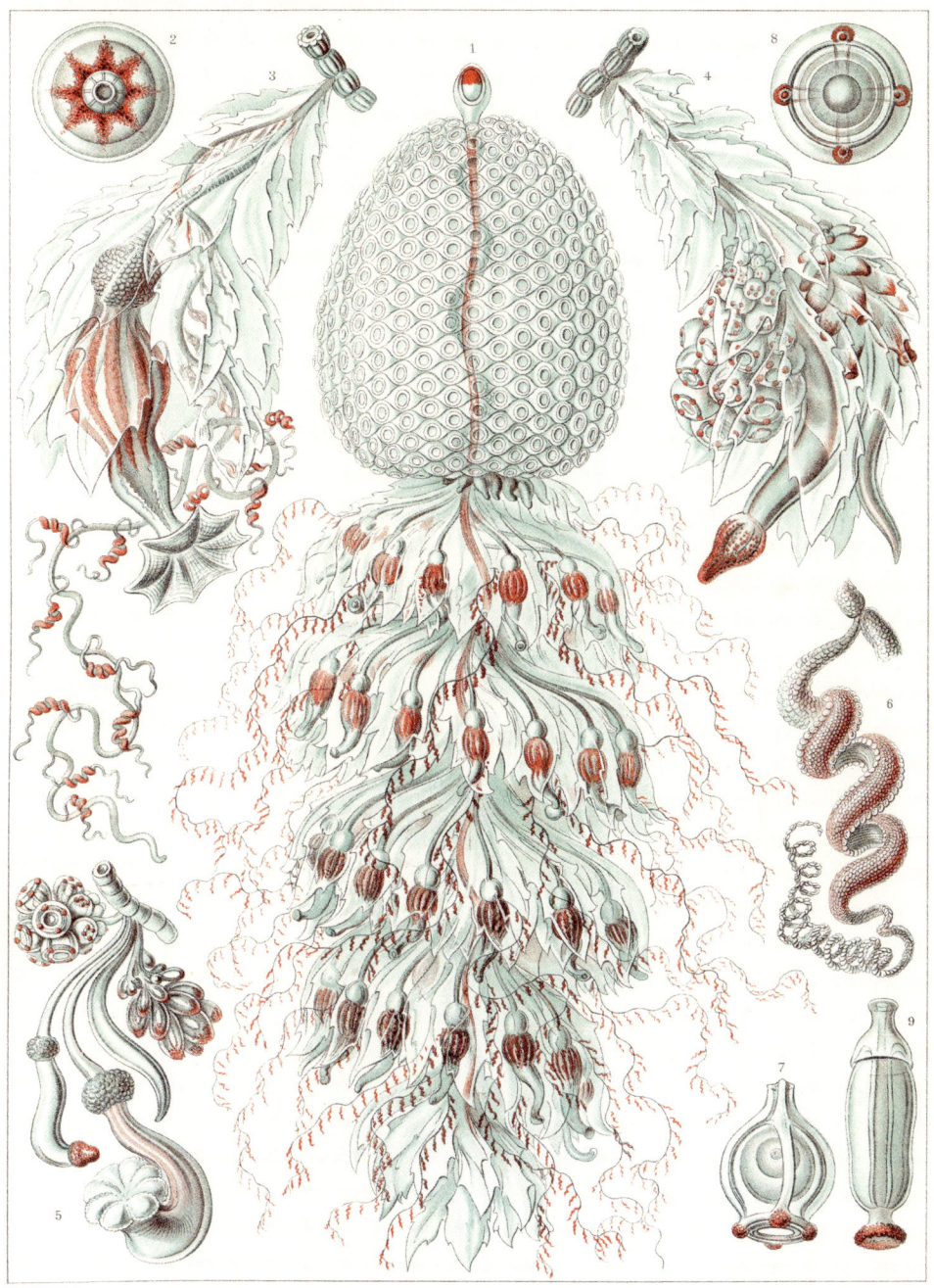

Siphonophorae. — Staatsquallen.

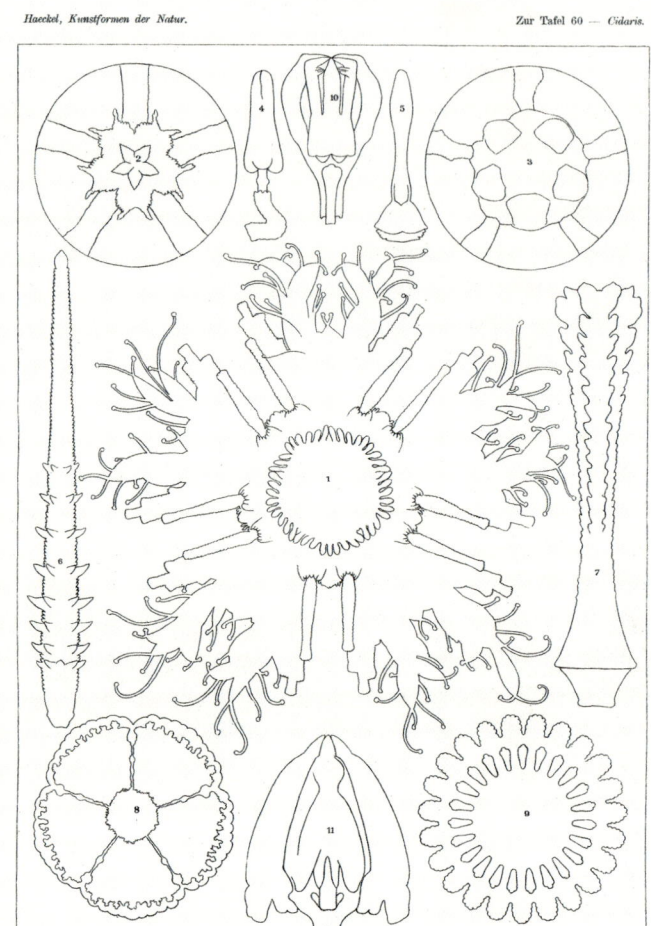

Haeckel, *Kunstformen der Natur.*   Zur Tafel 60 — *Cidaris.*

PLATE 60
ECHINODERMATA – ECHINOIDEA
Echinoderms – Sea urchins

1 Cidaris tribuloïdes (LAMARCK) – *Eucidaris tribuloides* (LAMARCK, 1816) Slate pencil urchin | 2 Cidaris baculosa (LAMARCK) – *Prionocidaris baculosa* (LAMARCK, 1816) | 3 Cidaris baculosa (LAMARCK) – *Prionocidaris baculosa* (LAMARCK, 1816) | 4 Dorocidaris papillata (AGASSIZ) – *Cidaris cidaris* (LINNAEUS, 1758) Long-spine slate pen sea urchin 5 Strongylocentrus nudus (AGASSIZ) – *Mesocentrotus nudus* (A. AGASSIZ, 1864) (synonym: *Strongylocentrotus nudus* (A. AGASSIZ, 1864)) | 6 Phyllacanthus annulifera (AGASSIZ) – *Prionocidaris baculosa annulifera* (A. AGASSIZ, 1873) 7 Phyllacanthus baculosa (AGASSIZ) – *Prionocidaris baculosa* (LAMARCK, 1816) | 8 Psammechinus miliaris (AGASSIZ) – *Psammechinus miliaris* (P.L.S. MÜLLER, 1771) Green sea urchin, Sand sea urchin, Sand urchin | 9 Centrostephanus longispinus (PETERS) – *Centrostephanus longispinus* (PHILIPPI, 1845) Long-spined urchin | 10-11 Sphaerechinus esculentus (DESOR) – *Echinus esculentus* LINNAEUS, 1758 Common sea urchin, European edible sea urchin

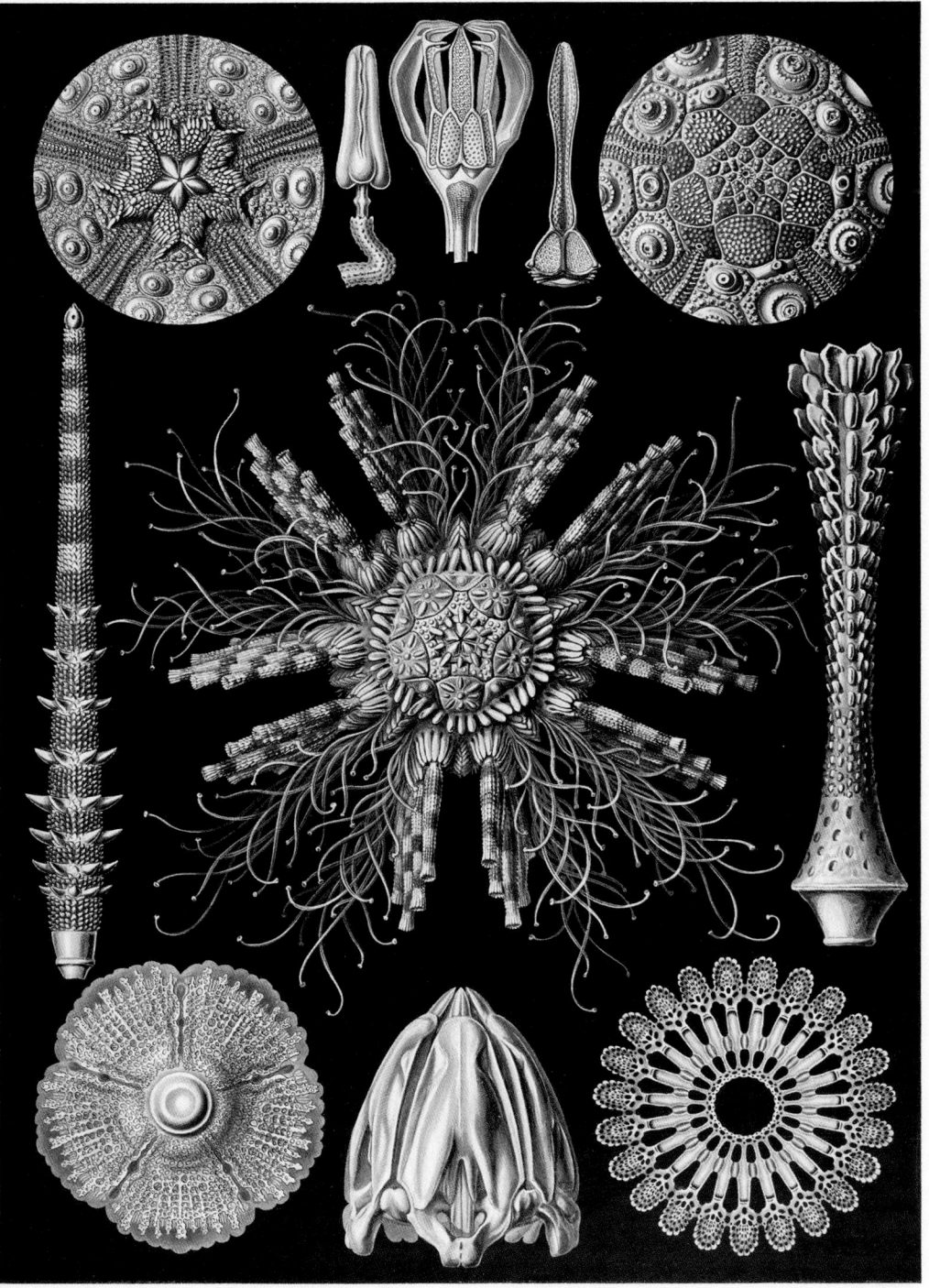

Echinidea. — Igelfterne.

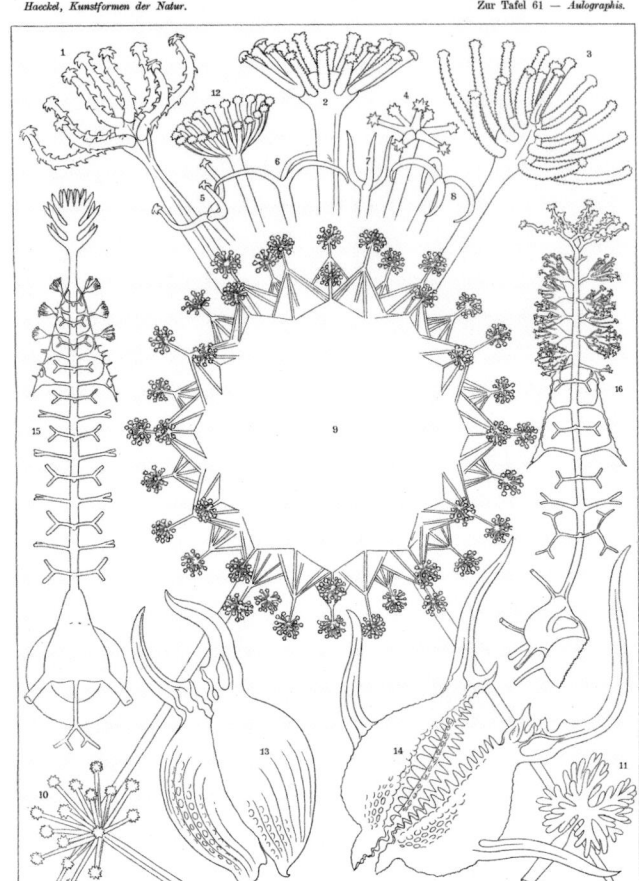

Haeckel, Kunstformen der Natur.　　　　　　　Zur Tafel 61 — Aulographis.

PLATE 61

PHAEODARIA

1 Aulographis candelabrum (HAECKEL) – *Aulographis (Aulographonium) candelabrum* HAECKEL, 1887
2 Aulographis pulvinata (HAECKEL) – *Aulographis pulvinata* HAECKEL, 1887 | 3 Aulographis verticillata (HAECKEL) – *Aulographis verticillata* HAECKEL, 1887 | 4 Aulographis asteriscus (HAECKEL) – *Aulographis asteriscus* HAECKEL, 1887 | 5 Aulographis furcula (HAECKEL) – *Aulographis furcula* HAECKEL, 1887 | 6 Aulographis triglochin (HAECKEL) – *Aulographis triglochin* HAECKEL, 1887 | 7 Aulographis bovicornis (HAECKEL) – *Aulographis bovicornis* HAECKEL, 1887 | 8 Aulographis ancorata (HAECKEL) – *Aulographis ancorata* HAECKEL, 1887 | 9–10 Sagenoscena stellata (HAECKEL) – *Sagenoscena stellata* HAECKEL, 1887 | 11 Sagenoscena ornata (HAECKEL) – *Sagenoscena ornata* HAECKEL, 1887 | 12 Auloscena mirabilis (HAECKEL) – *Auloscena mirabilis* HAECKEL, 1887) | 13 Conchoceras cornutum (HAECKEL) – *Conchoceras cornutum* HAECKEL, 1887 | 14 Conchonia quadricornis (HAECKEL) – *Conchonia quadricornis* HAECKEL, 1887 | 15 Coelographis regina (HAECKEL) – *Coelographis regina* HAECKEL, 1887 | 16 Coelospathis ancorata (HAECKEL) – *Coelospathis ancorata* HAECKEL, 1887

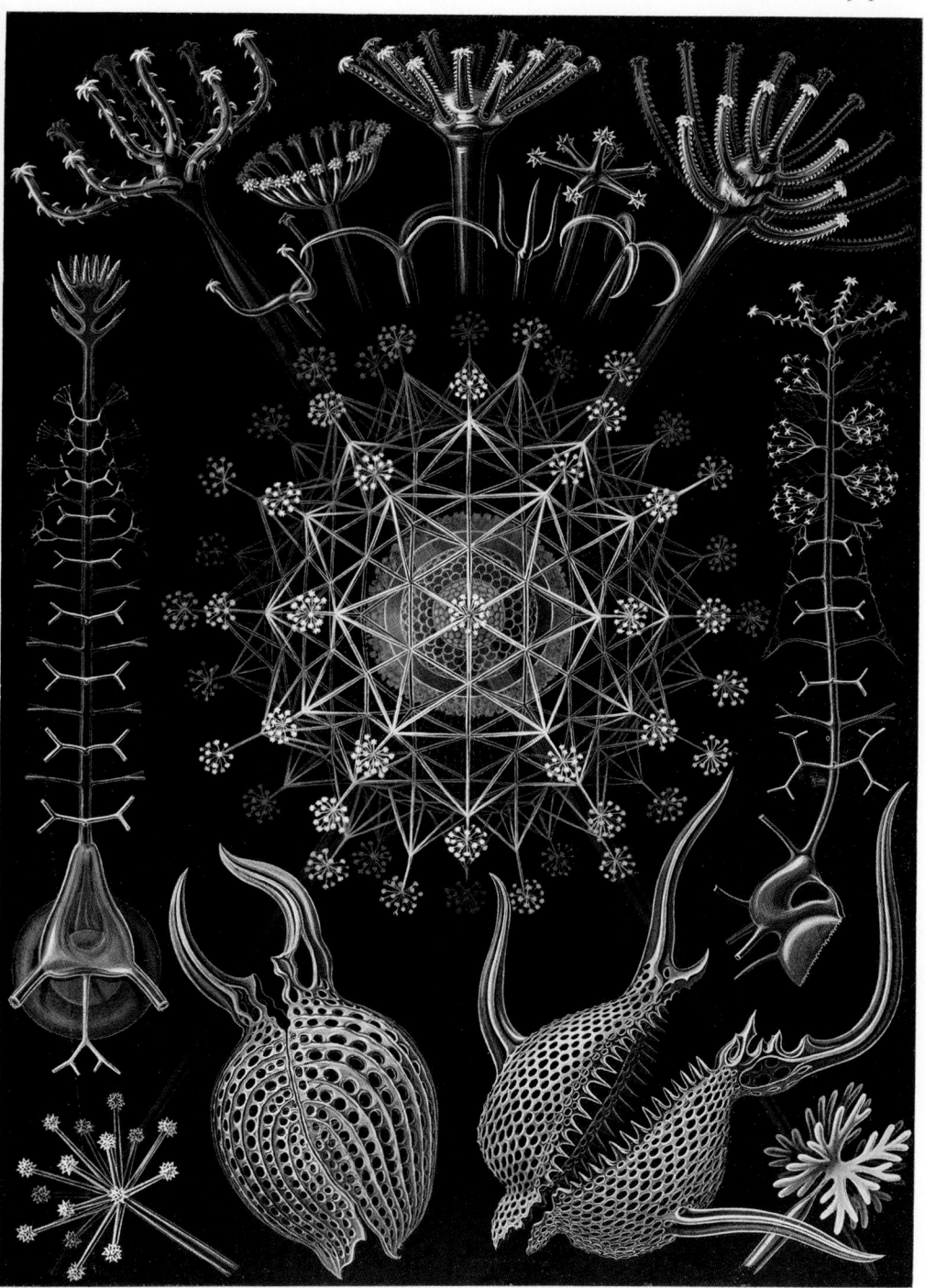

Phaeodaria. — Rohrstrahlinge.

PLATE 62
ANGIOSPERMAE - NEPENTHACEA
Angiosperms – Pitcher plants

Nepenthes melamphora (REINWARD) – *Nepenthes gymnamphora Reinwardt* EX NEES, 1824 Pitcher plant

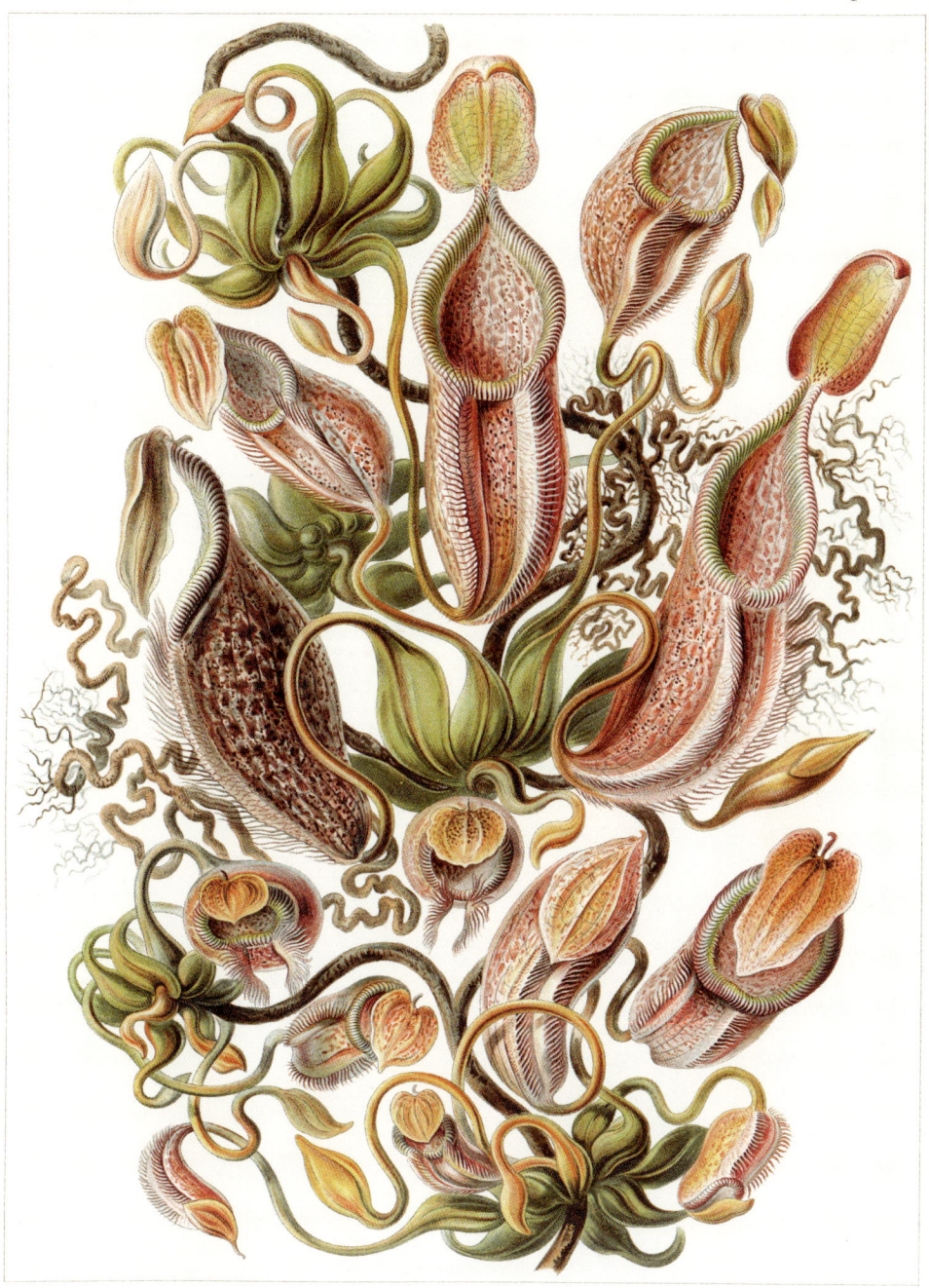

Nepenthaceae. — Kannenpflanzen.

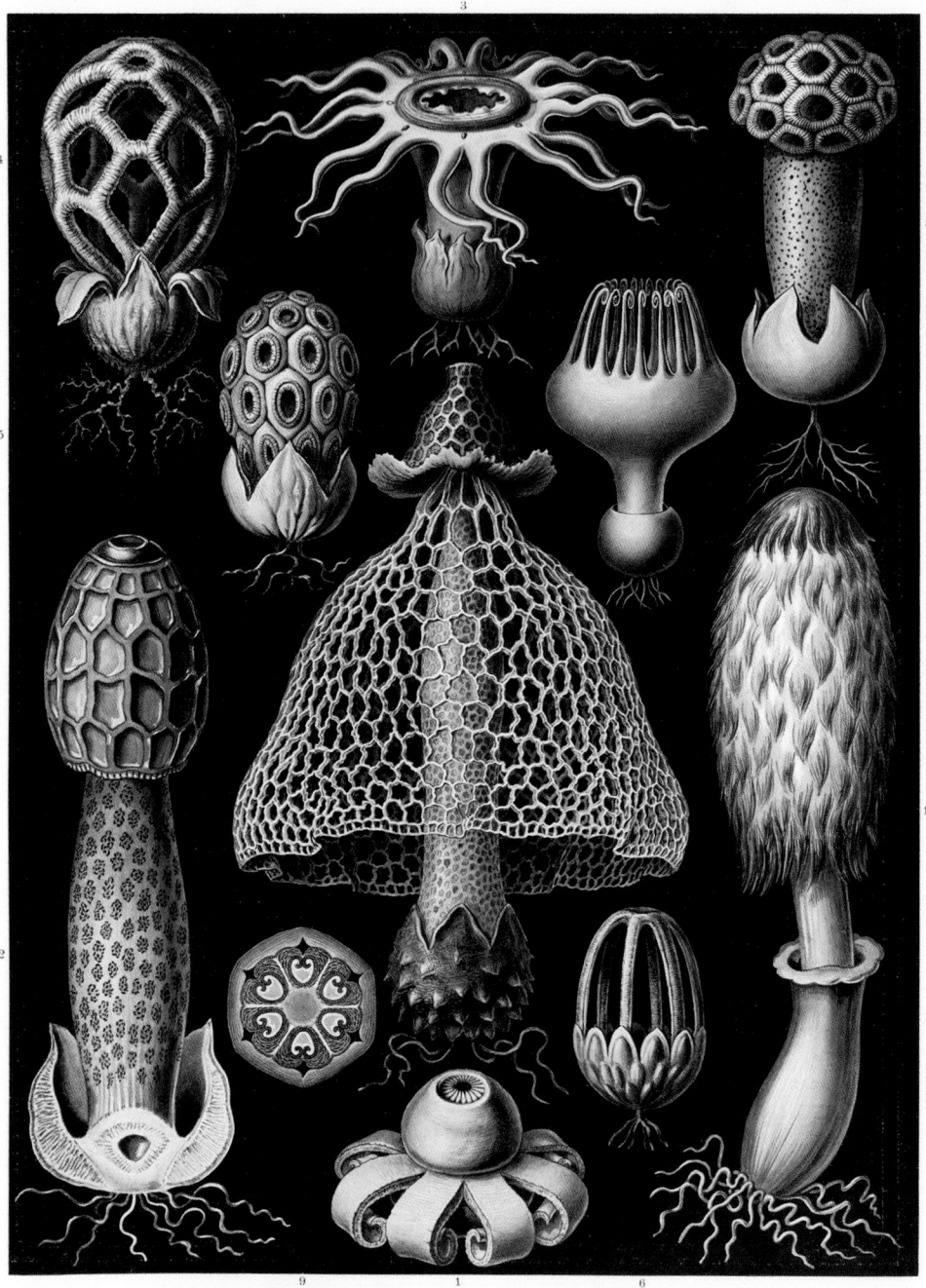

Basimycetes. — Schwammpilze.

PLATE 63

FUNGI – BASIDIOMYCETES
Fungi – Club fungi

1 Dictyophora madonna (HAECKEL) – *Dictyophora madonna* HAECKEL, 1901
2 Phallus impudicus (LINNÉ) – *Phallus impudicus* LINNAEUS, 1753 Common stinkhorn | **3 Aseroë rubra** (BILLARDIÈRE) –
Aseroë rubra LABILLARDIÈRE, 1800 Anemone stinkhorn | **4 Clathrus cancellatus** (TOURNEFORT) – *Clathrus ruber* MICHELI
EX PERSOON, 1801 Latticed stinkhorn, Basket stinkhorn, Red cage | **5 Clathrella crispa** (E. FISCHER) – *Clathrella crispa* (TURPIN)
FISCHER 1886 | **6 Clathrella pusilla** (E. FISCHER) – *Colus pusillus* (BERKELEY, 1845) REICHERT Craypot stinkhorn
7 Calathiscus sepia (MONTAGNE) – *Calathiscus sepia* MONTAGNE, 1841 | **8 Simblum sphaerocephalum** (KLOTSCH) –
Lysurus periphragmoides (KLOTZSCH) DRING, 1980 Stalked lattice stinkhorn, Chambered stinkhorn
9 Anthurus borealis (BURTON) – *Lysurus cruciatus* (LEPRIEUR & MONTAGNE, 1845) HENNINGS, 1902 (synonym:
Lysurus borealis (BURTON, 1894)) | **10 Geaster multifidus** (MICHELI) – *Geastrum fornicatum var. multifidum*
(PERSOON) FRIES, 1829 (synonym: *Geastrum multifidus* PERSOON, 1794) Acrobatic earthstar, Arched earthstar
11 Coprinus comatus (MÜLLER) – *Coprinus comatus* (O. F. MÜLLER) PERSOON, 1797 Shaggy ink cap, Lawyer's wig

PLATE 64 *(Page 418)*

CHLOROPHYCEAE
Green Algae

1 Caulerpa racemosa (AGARDH) – *Caulerpa racemosa* (FORSSKÅL) J. AGARDH, 1873 Sea grapes | **2 Caulerpa uvifera**
(AGARDH) – *Caulerpa racemosa* (FORSSKÅL) J. AGARDH, 1873 Sea grapes | **3 Caulerpa pinnata** (WEBER VAN BOSSE) –
Caulerpa mexicana SONDER EX KÜTZING, 1849 (synonym: *Caulerpa pinnata* C. AGARDH, 1817 var. *mexicana*)
4 Caulerpa peltata (LAMOUROUX) – *Caulerpa chemnitzia* ESPER J.V.LAMOUROUX, 1809
5 Caulerpa paspaloïdes (HARVEY) – *Caulerpa paspaloides* (BORY DE SAINT-VINCENT) GREVILLE, 1830
6 Caulerpa macrodisca (DECAISNE) – *Caulerpa macrodisca* DECAISNE, 1842 (synonym: *Caulerpa peltata* var.
macrodisca (DECAISNE) WEBER-VAN BOSSE) | **7 Struvea plumosa** (SONDER) – *Struvea plumosa* SONDER, 1845
Green veinweed | **8-9 Neomeris Kelleri** (CRAMER) – *Neomeris annulata* DICKIE, 1874 | **10 Acetabularia mediterranea**
(LAMARCK) – *Acetabularia acetabulum* (LINNAEUS) P. C. SILVA, 1952 Mermaid's wine glass | **11 Bornetella capitata**
(AGARDH) – *Bornetella capitata* (HARVEY EX E. P. WRIGHT) J. AGARDH, 1887

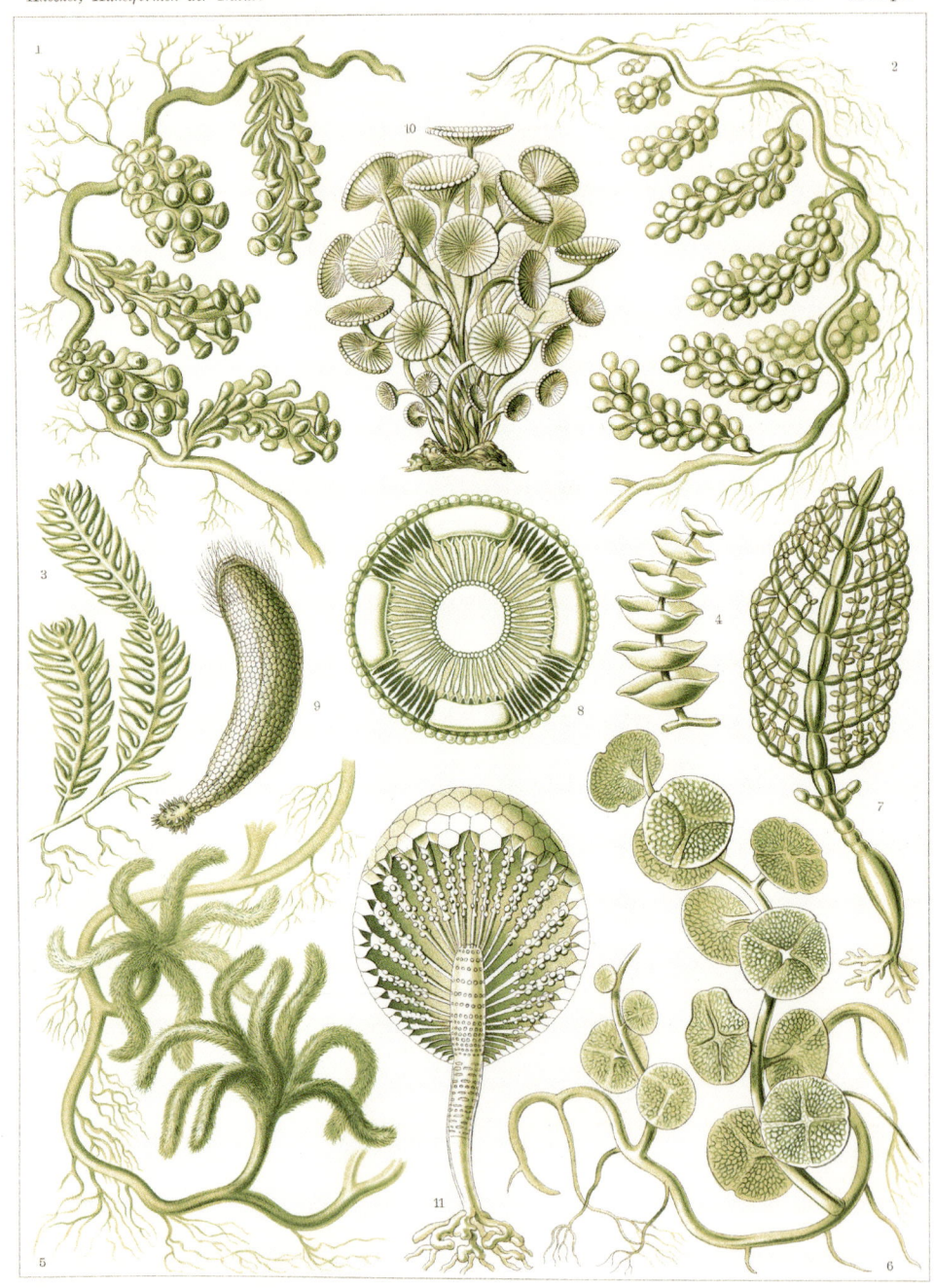

Siphoneae. — Riesen-Algetten.

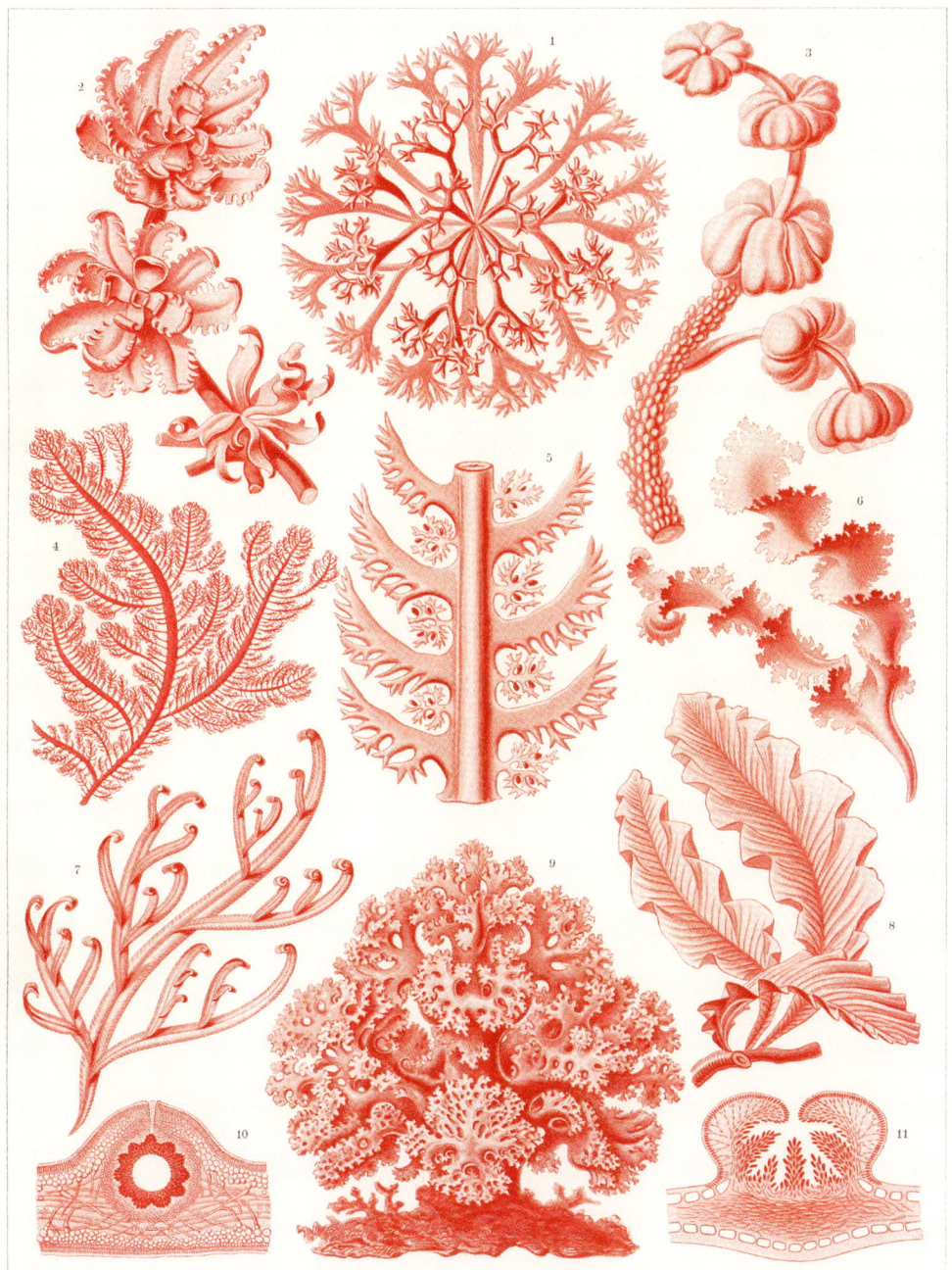

Florideae. — Rotalgen.

PLATE 65 *(Page 419)*

RHODOPHYCEAE
Red algae

1 **Chondrus crispus** (LINNÉ) – *Chondrus crispus* STACKHOUSE, 1797 Carrageen, Irish moss | 2 **Amansia glomera** (AGARDH) – *Melanamansia glomerata* (C. AGARDH) NORRIS, 1995 | 3 **Constantinea rosamarina** (POSTELS) – *Constantinea rosa-marina* (S. G. GMELIN) POSTELS & RUPRECHT, 1840 | 4 **Ptilota serrata** (KÜTZING) – *Ptilota serrata* KÜTZING, 1847 | 5 **Ptilota densa** (AGARDH) – *Neoptilota densa* (C. AGARDH) KYLIN EX ABBOTT & HOLLENBERG, 1966 6 **Rissonella verruculosa** (AGARDH) – *Rissonella verruculosa* (BERTOLONI) J. AGARDH, 1851 | 7 **Delesseria involvens** (HARVEY) – *Hypoglossum involvens* (HARVEY) J. AGARDH, 1898 | 8 **Delesseria sanguinea** (LINNÉ) – *Delesseria sanguinea* (HUDSON) LAMOUROUX, 1813 Sea beech | 9 **Nemastoma cervicorne** (AGARDH) – *Platoma cyclocolpum* (MONTAGNE) F. SCHMITZ, 1894 | 10 **Solieria chordalis** (AGARDH) – *Solieria chordalis* (C. AGARDH) J. AGARDH, 1842 11 **Binderella neglecta** (SCHMITZ) – *Amphiplexia hymenocladioides* J. AGARDH, 1892

PLATE 66

CHELICERATA – ARACHNIDA
Chelicerates – Spiders and their relatives

1 **Tegeocranus hericius** (MICHAEL) – *Protocepheus hericius* (MICHAEL, 1888) | 2 **Tegeocranus latus** (KOCH) – *Cepheus latus* KOCH, 1836 | 3 **Tegeocranus cepheiformis** (NICOLET) – *Cepheus cepheiformis* (NICOLET, 1855) 4 **Leiosoma palmicinctum** (MICHAEL) – *Tereticepheus palmicinctum* (MICHAEL, 1880) 5 **Phrynus reniformis** (OLIVIER) – *Phrynichus reniformis* (LINNAEUS, 1758) (synonym: *Phrynichus ceylonicus* (KOCH, 1843) | 6 **Arkys cordiformis** (WALCKENAER) – *Gnolus cordiformis* (NICOLET, 1849) | 7 **Gasteracantha cancriformis** (LATREILLE) – *Gasteracantha cancriformis* (LINNAEUS, 1758) Star spider, Spiny-backed orbweaver, Spiny orbweaver spider, Crab-like orbweaver spider, Jewel spider, Double-spotted spiny spider | 8 **Gasteracantha acrosomoïdes** (KOCH) – *Acrosomoides acrosomoides* (O. PICKARD-CAMBRIDGE, 1879) | 9 **Gasteracantha geminata** (KOCH) – *Gasteracantha geminata* (FABRICIUS, 1798) Spiny(-backed) orbweaver | 10 **Gasteracantha arcuata** (KOCH) – *Macracantha arcuata* (FABRICIUS, 1793) Long-horned orbweaver, Curved spiny spider | 11 **Acrosoma hexacanthum** (HAHN) – *Gasteracantha cancriformis* (LINNAEUS, 1758) Star spider, Spiny-backed orbweaver, Spiny orbweaver spider, Crab-like orbweaver spider, Jewel spider 12 **Acrosoma spinosum** (KOCH) – *Micrathena schreibersi* (PERTY, 1833) | 13 **Acrosoma bifurcatum** (HAHN) – *Micrathena furcata* (HAHN, 1822) | 14 **Oxyopes variegatus** (HAHN) – *Oxyopes ramosus* (MARTINI & GOEZE, IN LISTER, 1778) | 15 **Epeira diadema** (LINNÉ) – *Araneus diadematus* CLERCK, 1757

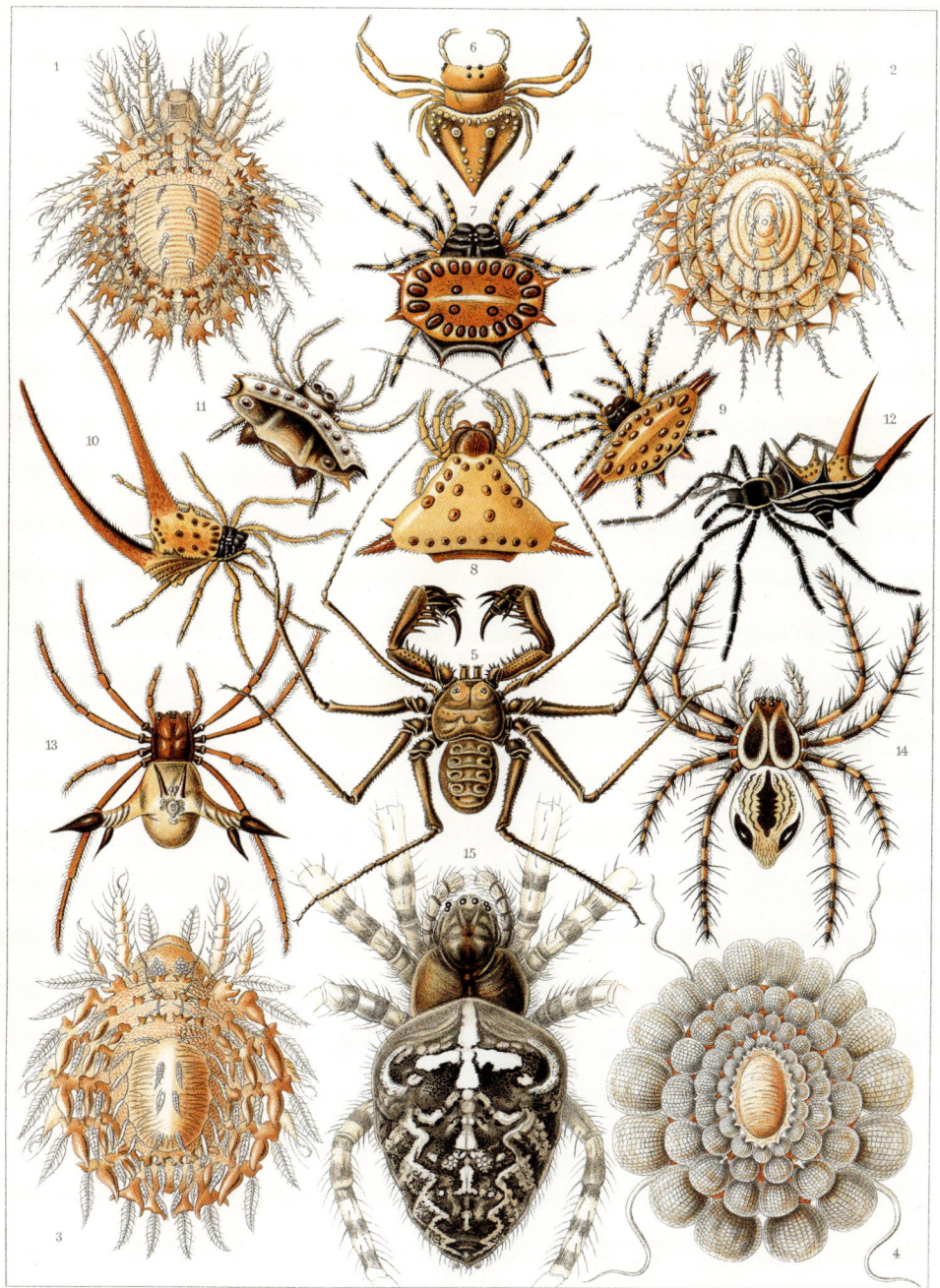

Arachnida. — Spinnentiere.

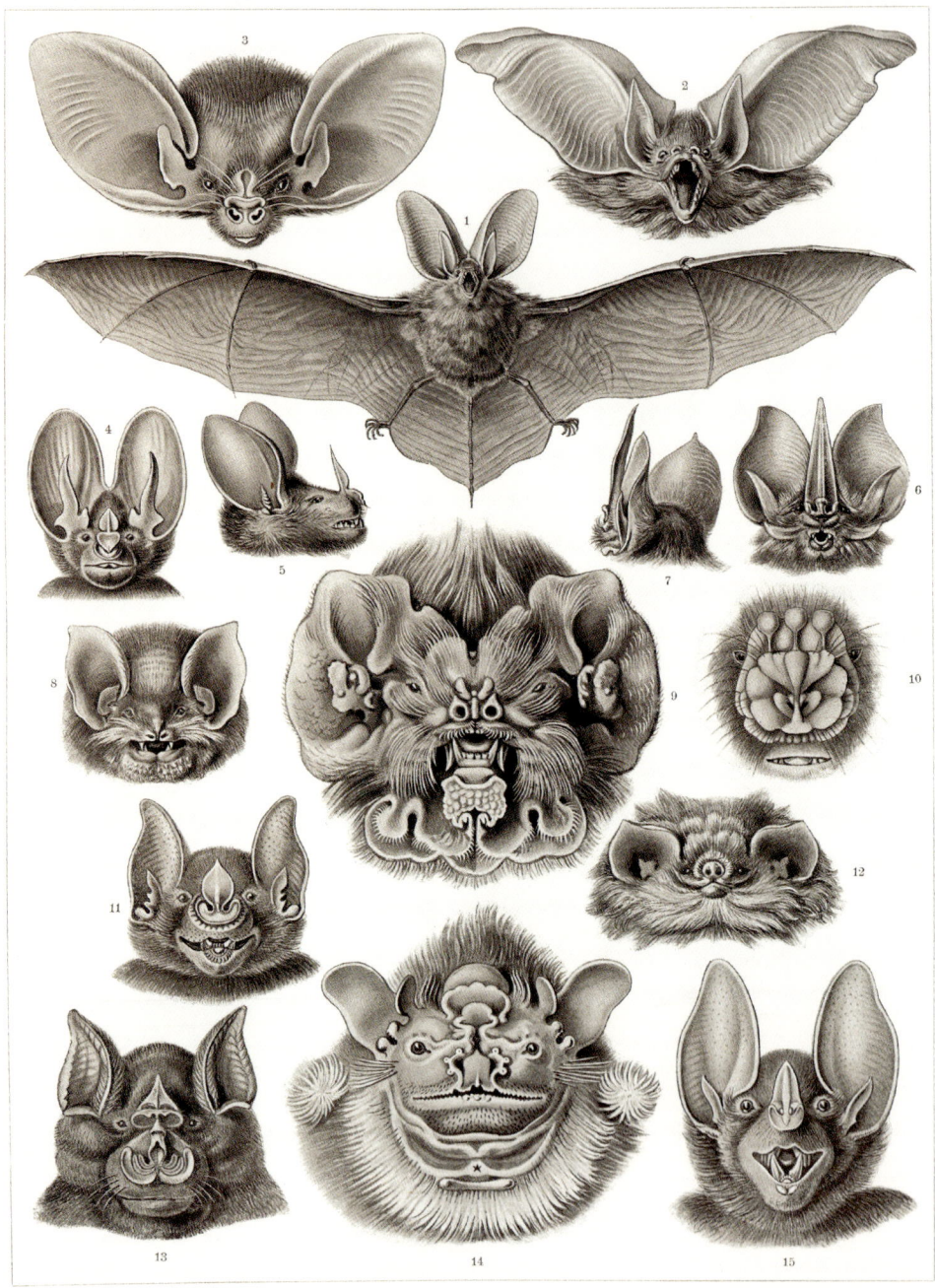

Chiroptera. — Fledertiere.

PLATE 67

MAMMALIA – CHIROPTERA
Mammals – Bats

1–2 **Plecotus auritus** (GEOFFROY) – *Plecotus auritus* (LINNAEUS, 1758)
Garden cross spider, Cross orbweaver, Diadem spider, Brown long-eared bat, Brown big-eared bat, Common long-eared bat
3 **Nyctophilus australis** (PETERS) – *Nyctophilus geoffroyi* LEACH, 1821 Lesser long-eared bat
4 **Megaderma trifolium** (GEOFFROY) – *Megaderma spasma trifolium* E. GEOFFROY, 1810
Megaderma spasma (LINNAEUS, 1758) Long eared false vampire bat, Lesser false vampire bat
5 **Vampyrus auritus** (PETERS) – *Chrotopterus auritus* (PETERS, 1856) Big-eared woolly bat, Woolly false vampire bat
6–7 **Lonchorhina aurita** (TOMES) – *Lonchorhina aurita* TOMES, 1863 Tomes's sword-nosed bat, Sword-nosed bat
8 **Natalus stramineus** (GRAY) – *Natalus stramineus* GRAY, 1838 Mexican greater funnel-eared bat, Mexican funnel-eared bat
9 **Mormops blainvillei** (PETERS) – *Mormoops blainvillei* (LEACH, 1821) Antillean ghost-faced bat, Blainville's ghost-faced bat
10 **Anthops ornatus** (THOMAS) – *Anthops ornatus* THOMAS, 1888 Flower-faced bat, Solomons leaf-nosed bat
11 **Phyllostoma hastatum** (PALLAS) – *Phyllostomus hastatus* (PALLAS, 1767) Greater spear-nosed bat
12 **Furipterus coerulescens** (TOMES) – *Furipterus horrens* (F.CUVIER, 1828)
(synonym: *Furipterus coerulescens* TOMES, 1856) Thumbless bat
13 **Rhinolophus equinus** (SCHREBER) – *Rhinolophus ferrumequinum* (SCHREBER, 1774) Greater horseshoe bat
14 **Centurio flavigularis** (PETERS) – *Centurio senex* GRAY, 1842 Wrinkle-faced bat
15 **Vampyrus spectrum** (GEOFFROY) – *Vampyrum spectrum* (LINNAEUS, 1758) Spectral bat

PLATE 68
AMPHIBIA
Amphibians

1 Notodelphys ovifera (WEINLAND) – *Gastrotheca ovifera* (LICHTENSTEIN & WEINLAND, 1854)
Giant marsupial frog, Pouched frog
2 Hyla meridionalis (BOULENGER) – *Hyla meridionalis* BOETTGER, 1874
Mediterranean tree frog, Stripeless tree frog
3 Hyla tuberculosa (BOULENGER) – *Ecnomiohyla tuberculosa* (BOULENGER, 1882)
Canelos tree frog
4 Amphignathodon Güntheri (BOULENGER) – *Gastrotheca guentheri* (BOULENGER, 1882)
Gunther's marsupial frog, Dentate marsupial frog
5 Rhacophorus pardalis (WALLACE) – *Rhacophorus pardalis* GÜNTHER, 1859
Harlequin tree frog, Gliding tree frog, Panther tree frog
6 Hylodes lineatus (SCHNEIDER) – *Craugastor lineatus* (BROCCHI, 1879)
(synonym: *Eleutherodactylus lineatus*) or *Lithodytes lineatus* (SCHNEIDER, 1799)
(synonym: *Leptodactylus lineatus* (SCHNEIDER, 1799)) Montane robber frog
7 Limnodytes erythraeus (DUMÉRIL) – *Hylarana erythraea* (SCHLEGEL, 1837)
Common green frog, Common greenback, Green paddy frog, Golden-lined frog, Green lotus frog, Red-eared frog
8 Ceratobatrachus Güntheri (boulenger) – *Cornufer guentheri* (BOULENGER, 1884)
(= *Ceratobatrachus guentheri* BOULENGER, 1884 = *Platymantis guentheri* (BOULENGER, 1882))
Gunther's triangle frog, Solomon Island eyelash frog, Guenther's forest frog, Gunther's wrinkled ground frog
9 Breviceps mossambicus (PETERS) – *Breviceps mossambicus* PETERS, 1854
Mozambique rain frog, Flat-face frog, Mozambique short-headed frog frog
10 Rana pipiens (LINNÉ) – *Rana pipiens* SCHREBER, 1782
Northern leopard frog, Leopard frog

424

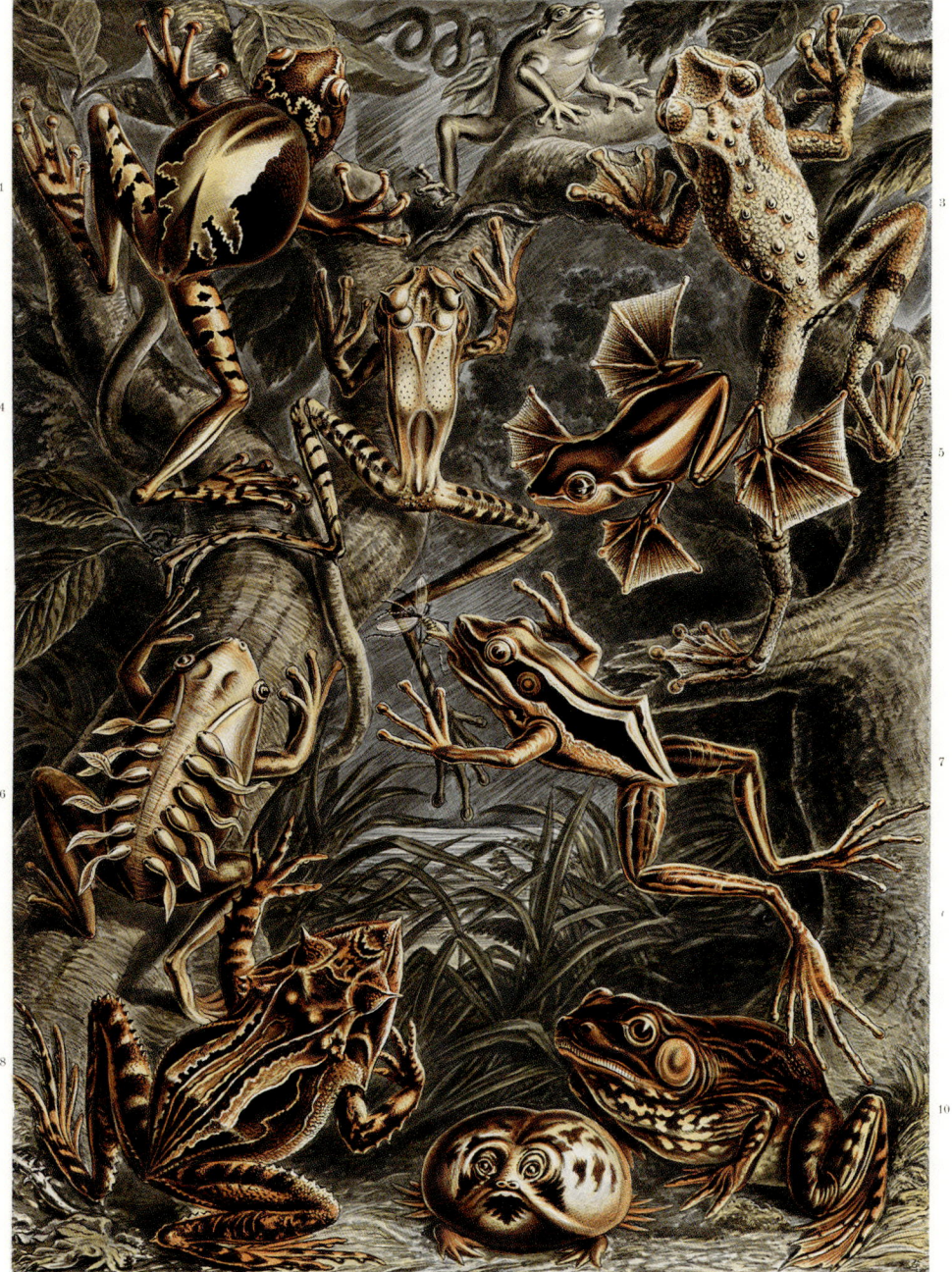

Batrachia. — Frösche.

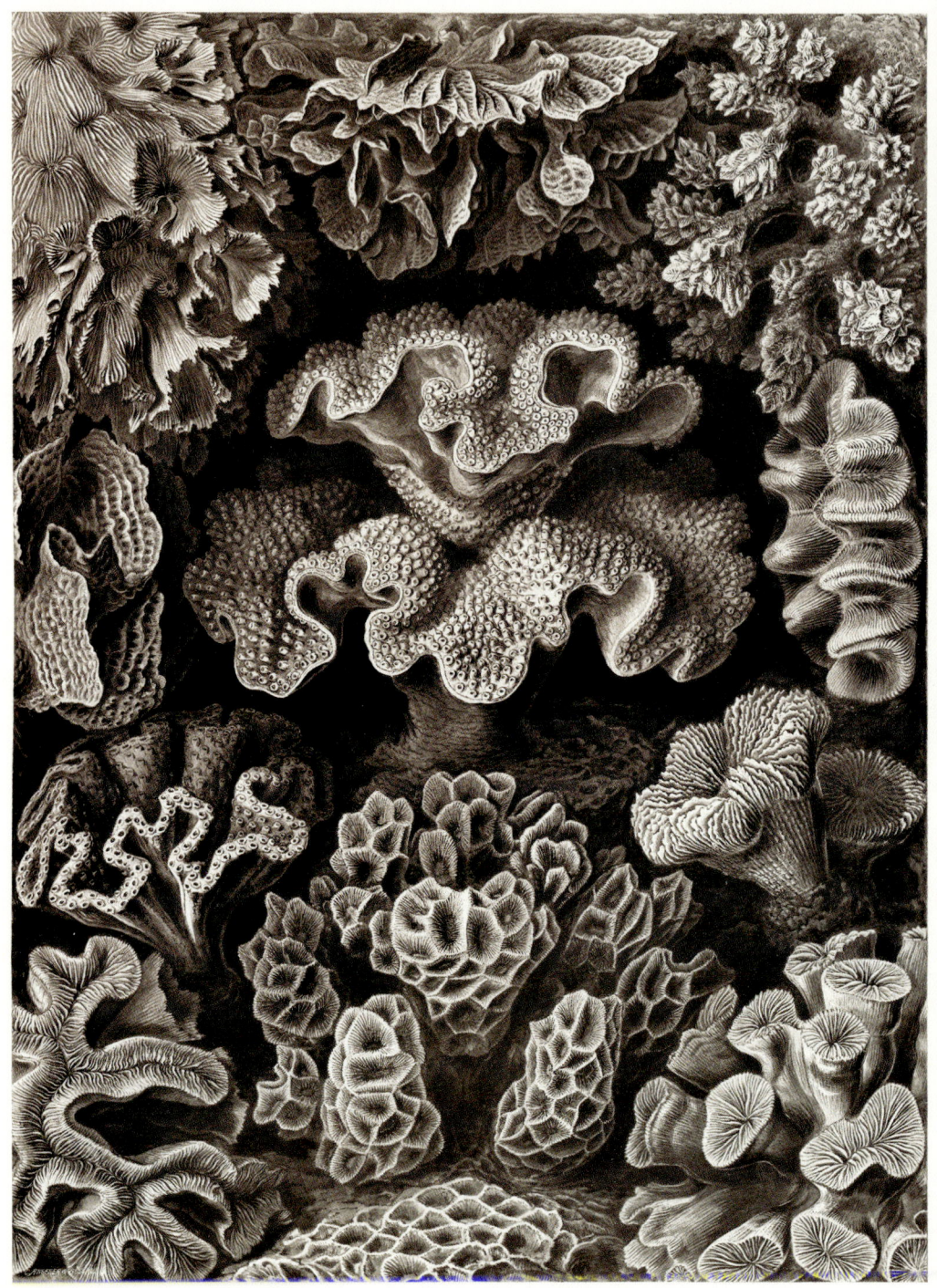

Hexacoralla. — Sechsstrahlige Sternkorallen.

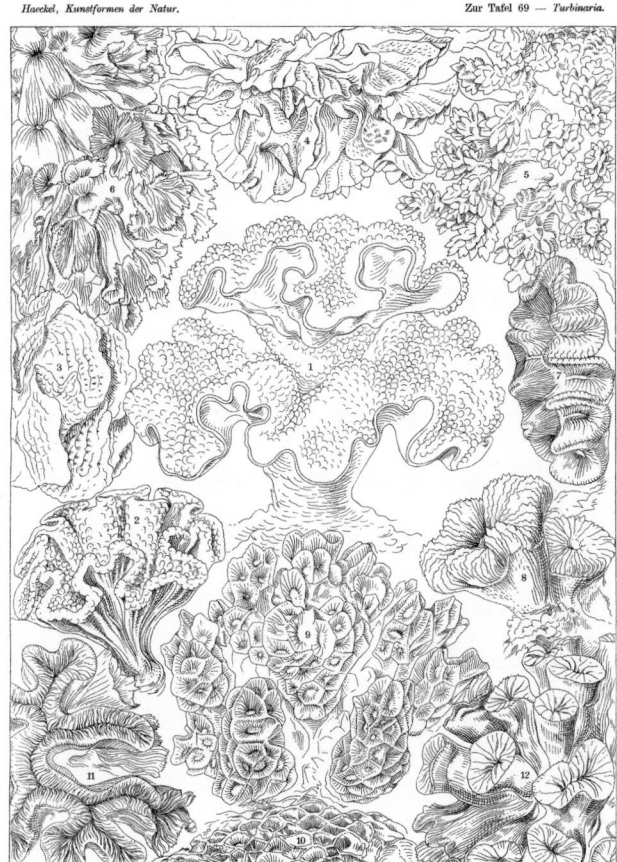

PLATE 69

CNIDARIA – ANTHOZOA
Cnidarians – Flower-like animals

1 Turbinaria transformis (HAECKEL) – *Dendrophylliidae* gen. sp. Lettuce coral | 2 Turbinaria robusta (HENRY BERNARD) – *Turbinaria patula* (DANA, 1846) Disc coral | 3 Lophoseris frondifera (MILNE-EDWARDS) – *Pavona frondifera* (LAMARCK, 1816) Leaf coral | 4 Lophoseris divaricata (MILNE-EDWARDS) – *Pavona divaricata* LAMARCK, 1816 Leaf coral | 5 Hydnophora racemosa (HAECKEL) – *Hydnophora exesa* (PALLAS, 1766) | 6 Tridacophyllia lactuca (BLAINVILLE) – *Pectinia lactuca* (PALLAS, 1766) Lettuce coral, Deep valley hard coral | 7 Manicina crispata (MILNE-EDWARDS) – *Mancinia* sp.? | 8 Lithophyllia lacera (OKEN) – *Scolymia lacera* (PALLAS, 1766) Atlantic mushroom coral, Large-cupped fungus coral, Fleshy disk coral | 9 Astraea magnifica (DANA) – *Coelastrea aspera* (VERRILL, 1866) (synonym: *Goniastrea aspera* VERRILL, 1856) Lesser star coral | 10 Astraea expansa (MILNE-EDWARDS) – *Favia* sp.? 11 Plerogyra laxa (MILNE-EDWARDS) – *Plerogyra sinuosa* (DANA, 1846) (synonym: *Plerogyra laxa* MILNE EDWARDS & HAIME, 1848) Bubble coral, Grape coral | 12 Euphyllia striata (MILNE-EDWARDS) – *Euphyllia glabrescens* (CHAMISSO & EYSENHARDT, 1821) Torch coral, Joker coral

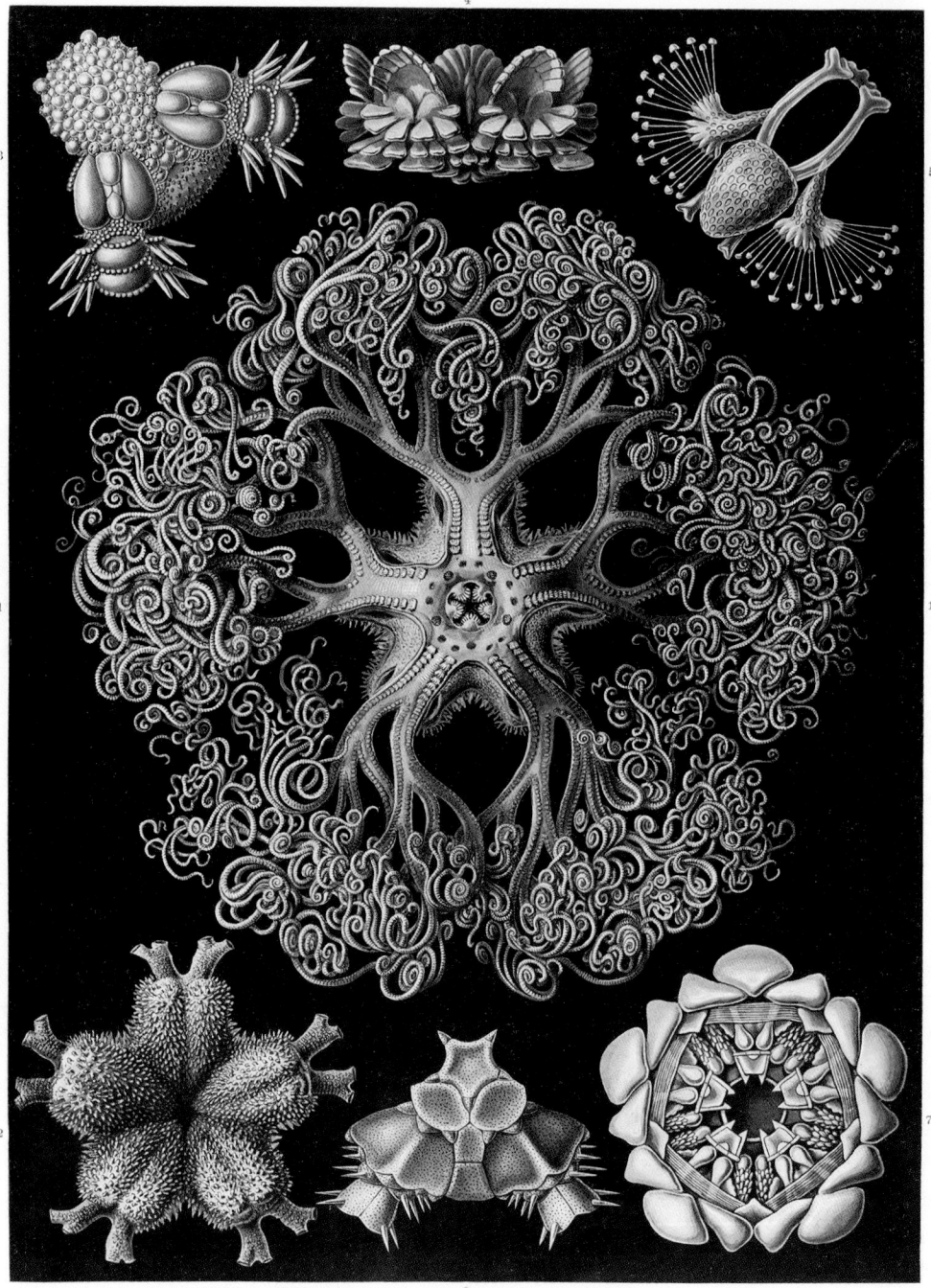

Ophiodea. — Schlangensterne.

PLATE 70

ECHINODERMATA – OPHIOIDEA
Echinoderms – Brittle stars

1–2 Astrophyton darwinium (HAECKEL) – *Astrophyton* sp.
3 Ophiopholis japonica (LYMAN) – *Ophiopholis japonica* LYMAN, 1879
4 Ophiotholia supplicans (LYMAN) – *Ophiotholia supplicans* LYMAN, 1880
5 Ophiohelus umbella (LYMAN) – *Ophiohelus umbella* LYMAN, 1880
6 Ophiglypha minuta (LYMAN) – *Aspidophiura minuta* (LYMAN, 1878)
7 Hemipholis cordifera (LYMAN) – *Hemipholis cordifera* (BOSC, 1802)
(synonym: *Hemipholis elongata* (SAY, 1825))

PLATE 71
RADIOLARIA – NASSELARIA
Radiolarians

1 Lithocircus magnificus (HAECKEL) – *Lithocircus magnificus* HAECKEL
2 Semantis sigillum (HAECKEL) – *Semantis sigillum* HAECKEL, 1887
3 Acanthodesmia corona (HAECKEL) – *Acanthodesmia corona* HAECKEL, 1887
4 Tristephanium dimensivum (HAECKEL) – *Tristephanium dimensivum* HAECKEL, 1887
5 Trissocyclus sphaeridium (HAECKEL) – *Trissocyclus sphaeridium* HAECKEL, 1887
6 Octotympanum cervicorne (HAECKEL) – *Acanthodesmia viniculata* (MÜLLER, 1858)
7 Microcubus zonarius (HAECKEL) – *Amphispyris zonarius* (HAECKEL, 1887)
8 Tympaniscus tripodiscus (HAECKEL) – *Tympaniscus tripodiscus* HAECKEL, 1887
9 Tympaniscus quadrupes (HAECKEL) – *Tympaniscus quadrupes* HAECKEL, 1887
10 Tympanidium foliosum (HAECKEL) – *Tympanidium foliosum* HAECKEL, 1887
11 Lithotympanum tuberosum (HAECKEL) – *Lithotympanum tuberosum* HAECKEL, 1887
12 Circotympanum octogonium (HAECKEL) – *Circotympanum octogonium* HAECKEL, 1887
13 Lithocubus astragalus (HAECKEL) *Lithocubus astragalus* HAECKEL, 1887

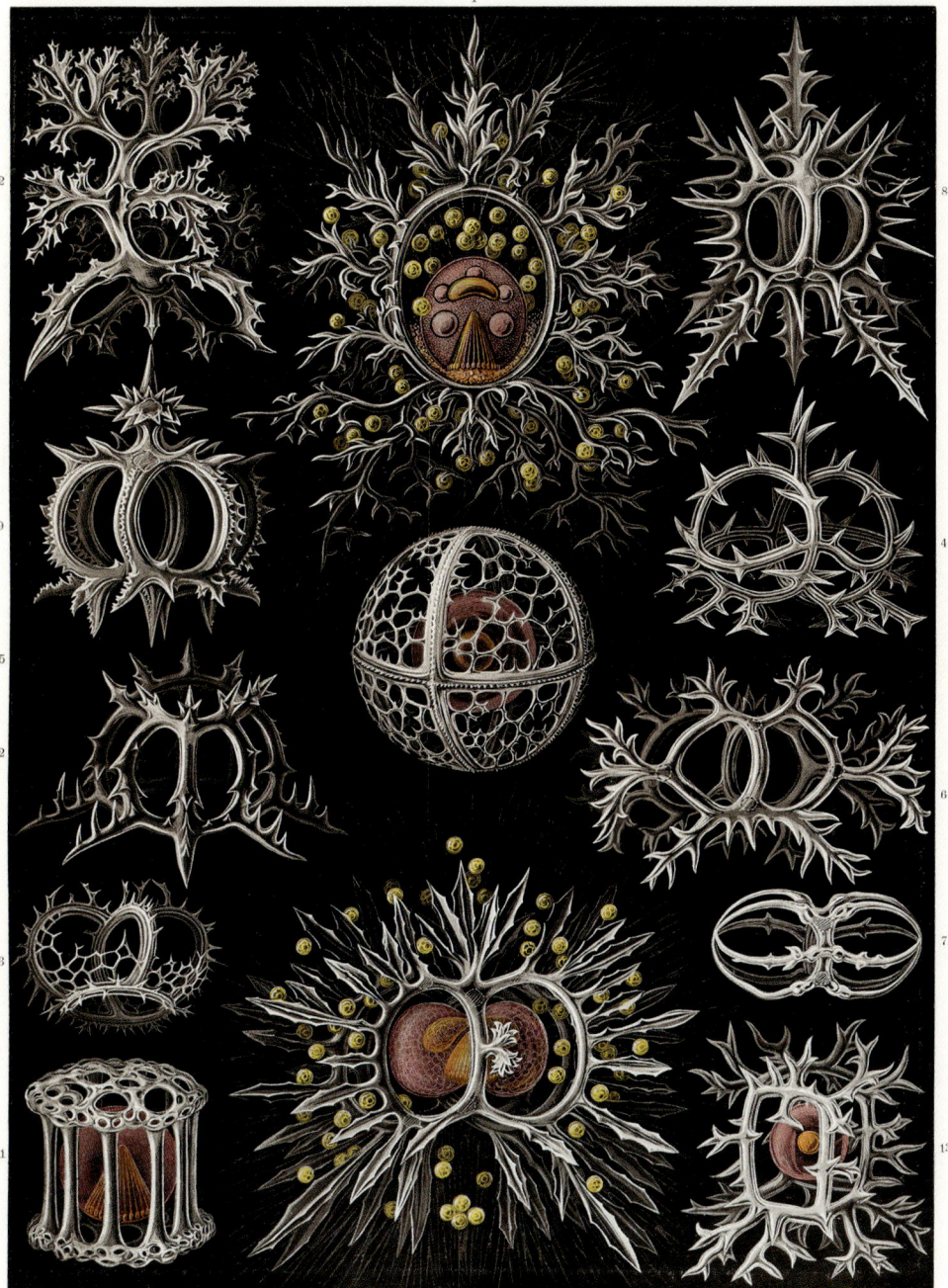

Stephoidea. — Ringelstrahlinge.

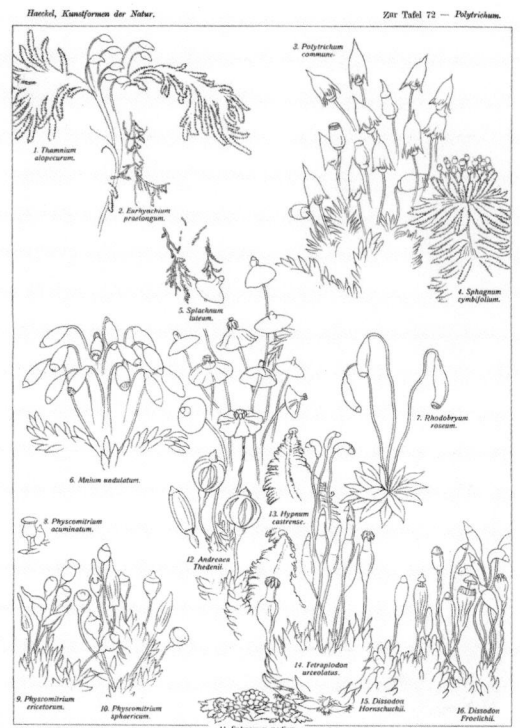

PLATE 72
MUSCINAE
Mosses

1 **Thamnium alopecurum** (LINNÉ) – *Thamnobryum alopecurum* (HEDWIG) NIEUWLAND EX GANGULEE
2 **Eurhynchium praelongum** (LINNÉ) – *Kindbergia praelonga* (HEDWIG) OCHYRA, 1982 (synonym: *Eurhynchium praelongum* (HEDWIG) SCHIMPER) Common feather moss | 3 **Polytrichum commune** (LINNÉ) – *Polytrichum commune* HEDWIG Common haircap moss, Common hair moss, Great gold headed, Great goldilocks | 4 **Sphagnum cymbifolium** (EHRHARD) – *Sphagnum palustre* LINNAEUS, 1753 (synonym: *S. cymbifolium* ERHARD) Prairie sphagnum, Blunt-leaved bog-moss
5 **Splachnum luteum** (LINNÉ) – *Splachnum luteum* HEDWIG Yellow moosedung moss | 6 **Mnium undulatum** (HEDWIG) – *Plagiomnium undulatum* HEDWIG Hart's-tongue thyme moss | 7 **Rhodobryum roseum** (SCHREBER) – *Rhodobryum roseum* (HEDWIG) LIMPRICHT Rose moss, Rose rhodobryum moss | 8 **Physcomitrium acuminatum** (SCHLEICH) – *Physcomitrium acuminatum* BRUCH & SCHIMPER, 1841 | 9 **Physcomitrium ericetorum** (NOTARIS) – *Physcomitrium ericetorum* (DE NOT.) BRUCH & SCHIMPER | 10 **Physcomitrium sphaericum** (SCHWANG) – *Physcomitrium sphaericum* (C.F. LUDW.) FÜRNR. | 11 **Sphagnum medium** (LIMPRICHT) – *Sphagnum magellanicum* BRID. Magellan's peatmoss, Magellan's sphagnum | 12 **Andreaea Thedenii** (SCHIMPER) – *Andreaea obovata* THEDENIUS, 1849 Obovate rock moss, Obovate Andreaea moss | 13 **Hypnum castrense** (LINNÉ) – *Ptilium crista-castrensis* HEDWIG Knights plume moss | 14 **Tetraplodon urceolatus** (SCHIMPER) – *Tetraplodon urceolatus* (HEDWIG) BRUCH & SCHIMPER 1844 Urceolate nitrogen moss
15 **Dissodon Hornschuchii** (GREVILLE) – *Tayloria hornschuchii* (GREV. & ARNOTT) BROTH. Hornschuch's dung moss
16 **Dissodon Froelichii** (HEDWIG) – *Tayloria froelichiana* MITTEN EX BROTHERUS, 1903 Froelich's dung moss

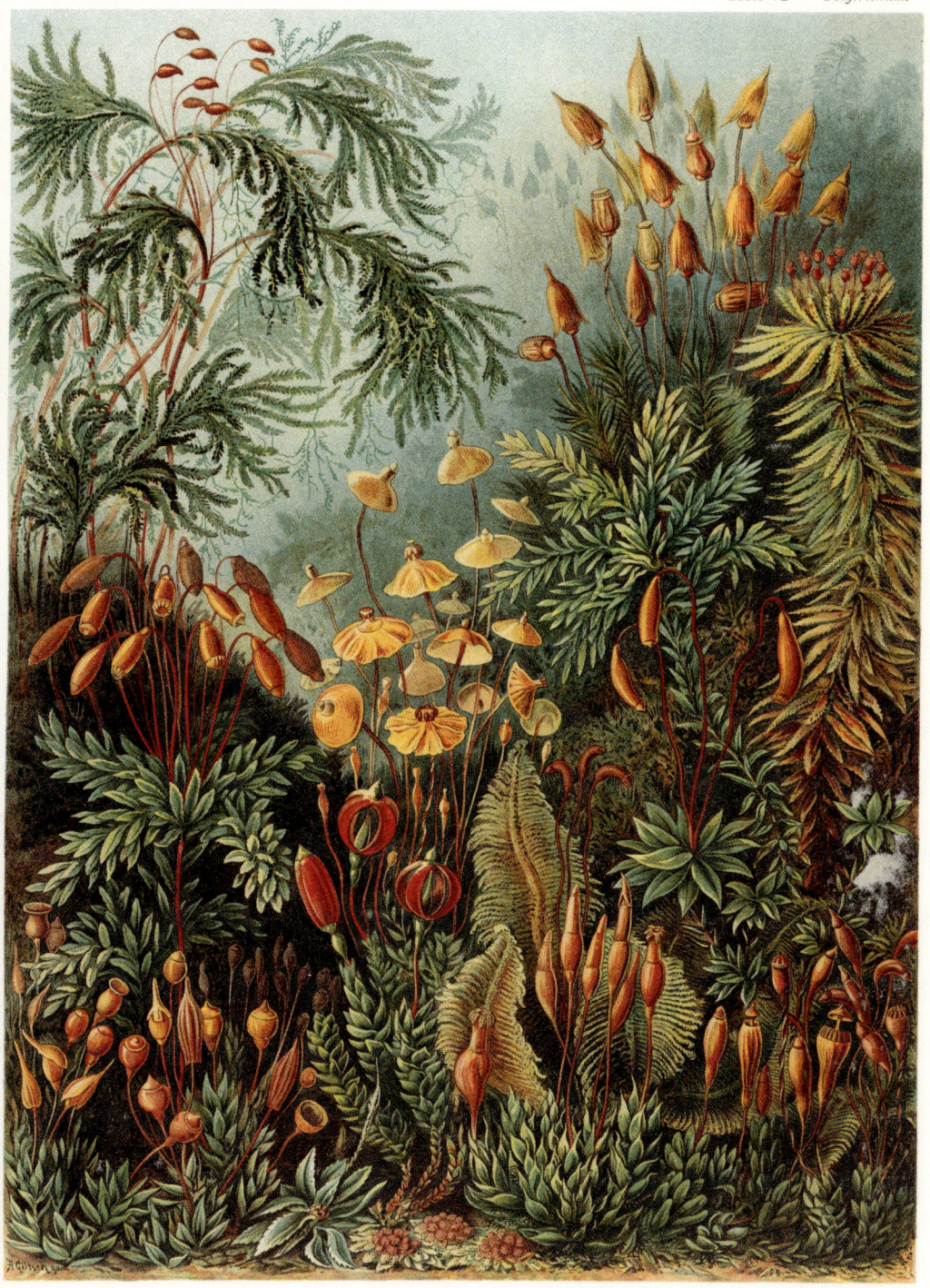

Muscinae. — Laubmoose.

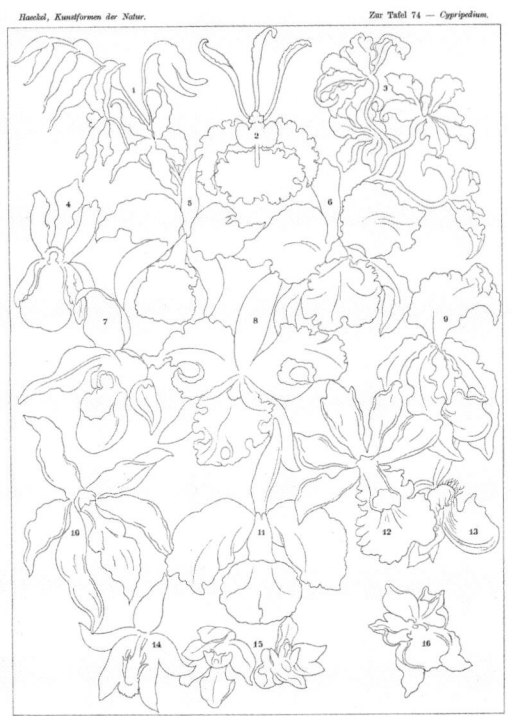

Haeckel, Kunstformen der Natur.   Zur Tafel 74 — Cypripedium.

PLATE 74
ANGIOSPERMAE – ORCHIDACEAE
Flowering plants – Orchids

1 Odontoglossum naevium – *Odontoglossum naevium* LINDLEY, 1850 (synonym: *Oncidium naevium* (LINDLEY) BEER, 1854) Spotted Odontoglossum | 2 Oncidium kramerianum – *Psychopsis krameriana* (REICHENBACH F.) H. G. JONES Kramer's Psychopsis | 3 Odontoglossum ramosissimum – *Cyrtochilum ramosissimum* (LINDLEY) DALSTRÖM Many branched cyrtochilum | 4 Odontoglossum schroederianum – *Oncidium schroederianum* (O'BRIEN) GARAY & STACY Schroeder's miltonia | 5 Cattleya ballantiniana – *Cattleya x ballantiniana* REICHENBACH F. natural hybrid: *Cattleya x ballantiniana* REICHENBACH F. (*C. trianae* LINDEN & REICHENBACH F. X *C. warscewiczii* REICHENBACH F.) | 6 Cattleya mendellii (sic!) – Cattleya mendelii DOMBRAIN Mendel's cattleya | 7 Cypripedium lemoinieri – *Phragmipedium x sedenii* (REICHENBACH F.), ROLFE (*P. longifolium* (WARSZ. & REICHENBACH F.), ROLFE X *P. schlimii* (LINDEN EX REICHENBACH F.) ROLFE) | 8 Cattleya rochellensis – *Cattleya warscewiczii* REICHENBACH F. San Juanes, Warscewicz's cattleya, Warscewicz's cattley's orchid | 9 Cypripedium leeanum – *Paphiopedilum insigne* (WALL. EX LINDLEY), PFITZER X *P. spicerianum* (REICHENBACH F.) PFITZER Splendid paphiopedilum (hybrid) | 10 Odontoglossum wattianum (sic!) – *Oncidium wyattianum* (A. G. WILSON) CHASE & WILLIAMS Wyatt's Odontoglossum | 11 Cattleya labiata – *Cattleya labiata* (LINDLEY) Crimson cattleya, Ruby-lipped cattleya | 12 Epidendrum atropurpureum – *Encyclia cordigera* (KUNTH) DRESSLER, 1964 Peacock orchid, Large-lipped encyclia | 13 Cypripedium argus – *Paphiopedilum argus* (REICHENBACH F.) STEIN Argus paphiopedilum | 14 Paphinia rugosa – *Paphinia rugosa* REICHENBACH F. Wrinkly paphinia | 15 Zygopetalum xanthinum – *Promenaea xanthina* (LINDLEY) LINDLEY Yellow promenaea | 16 Oncidium laxense (sic!) – *Cyrtochilum loxense* (LINDLEY) KRAENZL Loja cyrtochilum

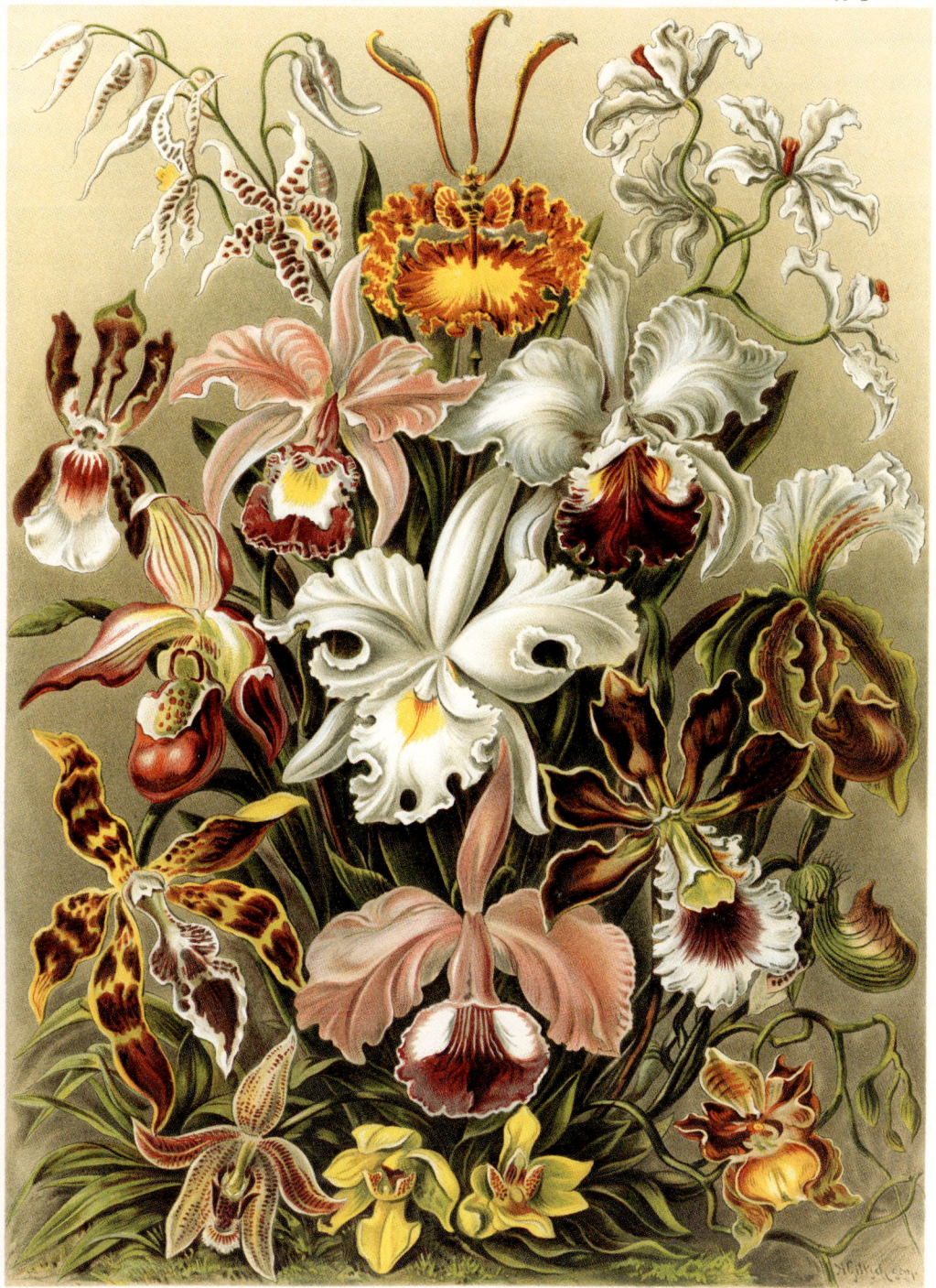

Orchideae. — Venusblumen.

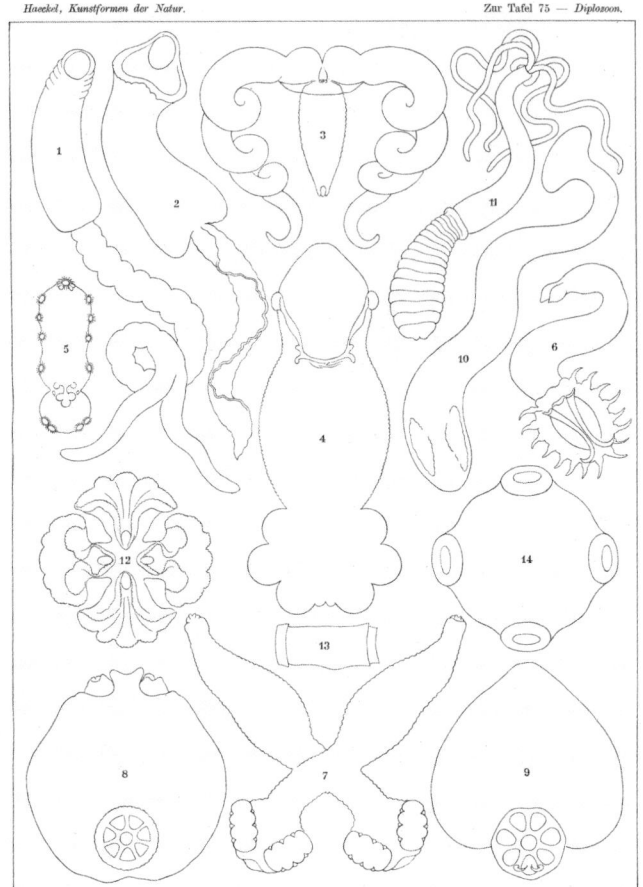

PLATE 75
PLATHYELMINTHES
Flatworms

1 Cercaria dichotoma (JOHANNES MÜLLER) – *Cercaria dichotoma* LA VALETTE, 1855 | 2 Cercaria spinifera
(LA VALETTE) – *Echinostoma echinatum* (ZEDER, 1803) | 3 Cercaria bucephalus (ERCOLANI) – *Bucephalus
polymorphus* BAER, 1827 | 4–5 Polystomum integerrimum (RUDOLPHI) – *Polystoma integerrimum* (FRÖHLICH, 1791)
6 Gyrodactylus elegans (NORDMANN) – *Gyrodactylus elegans* VON NORDMANN, 1832 | 7 Diplozoon paradoxum
(NORDMANN) – *Diplozoon paradoxum* VON NORDMANN, 1832 | 8 Tristomum coccineum (CUVIER) – *Tristoma
coccineum* (CUVIER, 1817) | 9 Callicotyle Kroyeri (DIESING) – *Calicotyle kroyeri* DIESING, 1850
10 Caryophyllaeus mutabilis (RUDOLPHI) – *Caryophyllaeus laticeps* (PALLAS, 1781) | 11 Tetrarhynchus longicollis
(CUVIER) – *Tetrarhynchus longicollis* VAN BENEDEN, 1849 (synonym: *Halysiorhynchus longicollis* (VAN BENEDEN, 1849))
12 Phyllobothryon gracile (VAN BENEDEN) – *Phyllobothrium gracile* WEDL, 1855 (after ROSS)
13 14 Taenia solium (RUDOLPHI) – *Taenia solium* LINNAEUS, 1758 Pork tapeworm, Pig tapeworm

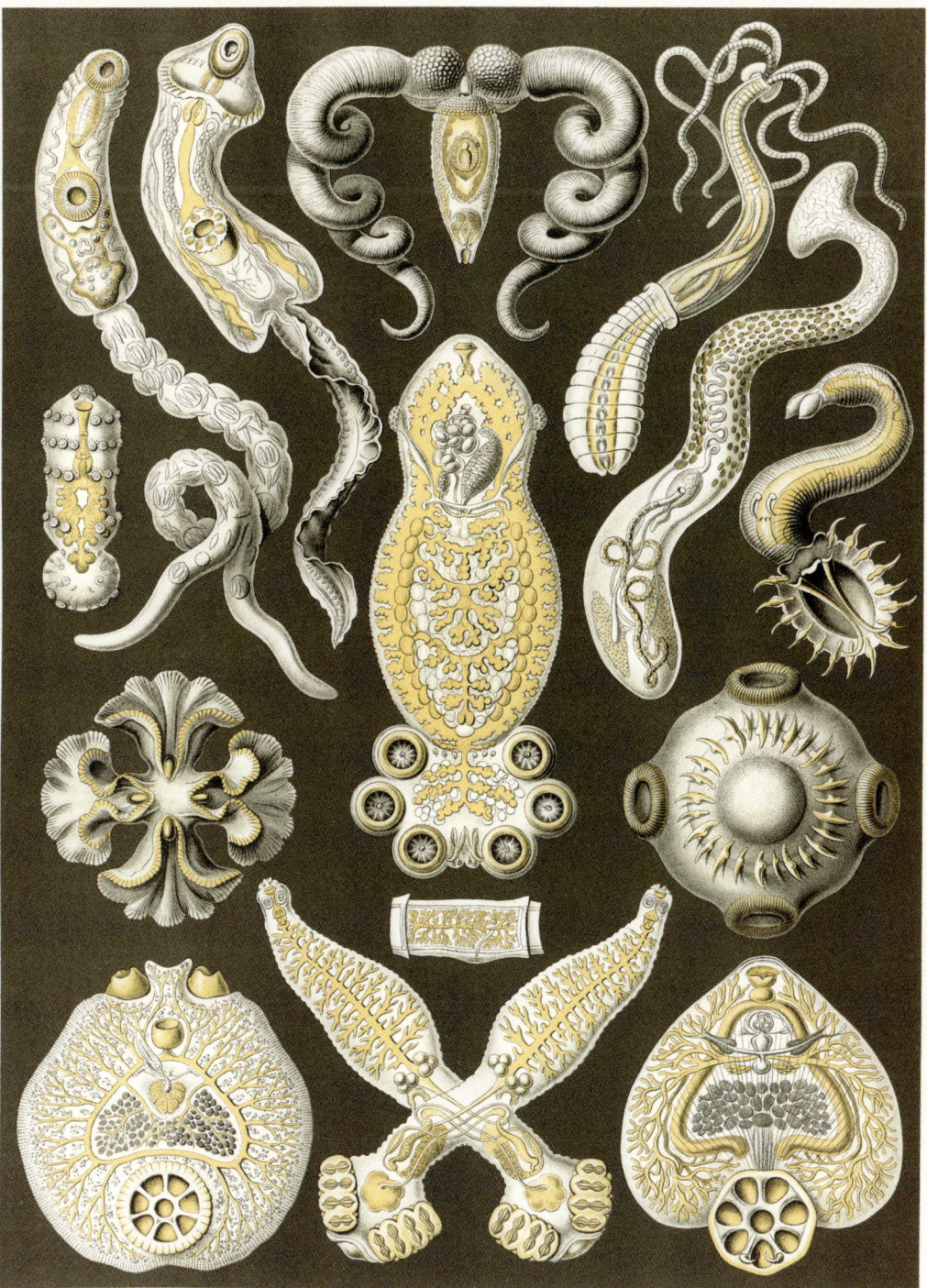

Platodes. — Plattentiere.

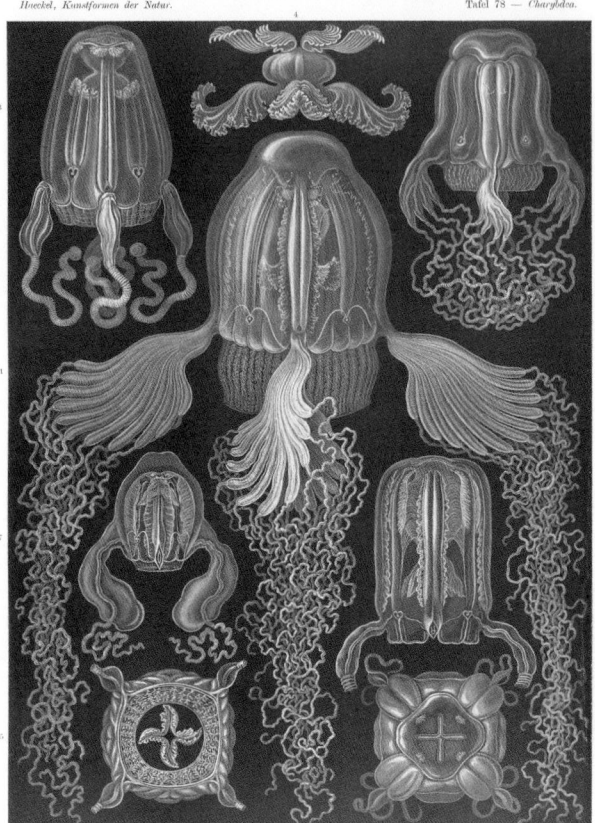

Cubomedusae. — Würfelquallen.

PLATE 78

CNIDARIA – CUBOZOA

Cnidarians – Box jellyfish

1 Chirodropus palmatus (HAECKEL) – *Chirodropus palmatus* HAECKEL, 1880 | 2 Chiropsalmus quadrigatus (HAECKEL) – *Chiropsoides quadrigatus* (HAECKEL, 1880) Box jellyfish, Fire medusa, Indringa
3-4 Charybdea obeliscus (HAECKEL) – *Alatina obeliscus* (HAECKEL, 1880) | 5-6 Charybdea murrayana (HAECKEL) – *Carybdea murrayana* HAECKEL, 1880 | 7 Procharybdis tetraptera (HAECKEL) – *Alatina tetraptera* (HAECKEL, 1880) 8 Tamoya prismatica (HAECKEL) – *Tamoya haplonema* F. MÜLLER, 1859

PLATE 77

CNIDARIA – SIPHONOPHORA

Cnidarians – Siphonophores

1-2 Praya galea (HAECKEL) – *Rosacea cymbiformis* (DELLE CHIAJE, 1830)
3-8 Bassia obeliscus (HAECKEL) – *Bassia bassensis* (QUOY & GAIMARD, 1833)

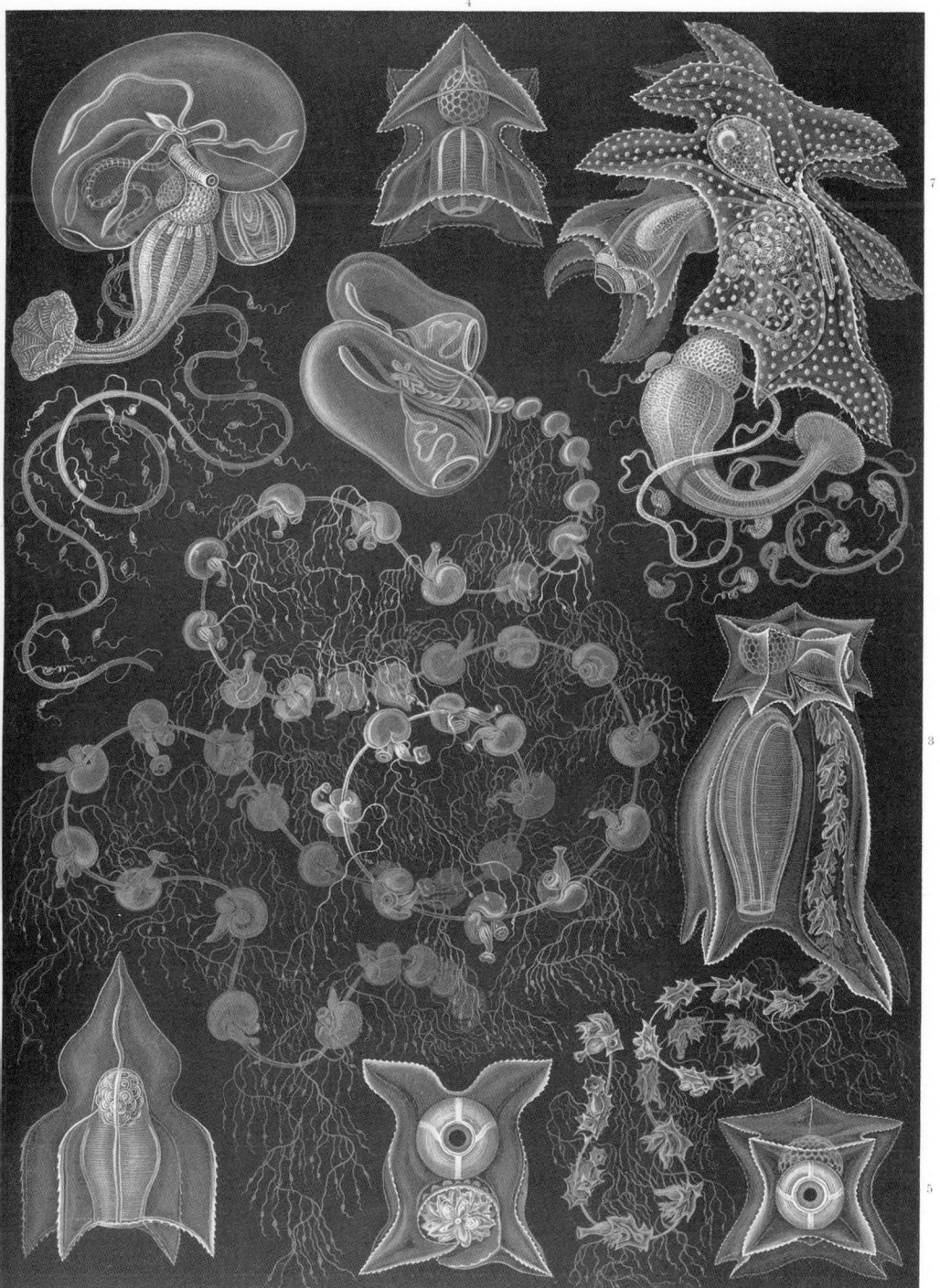

Siphonophorae. — Staatsquallen.

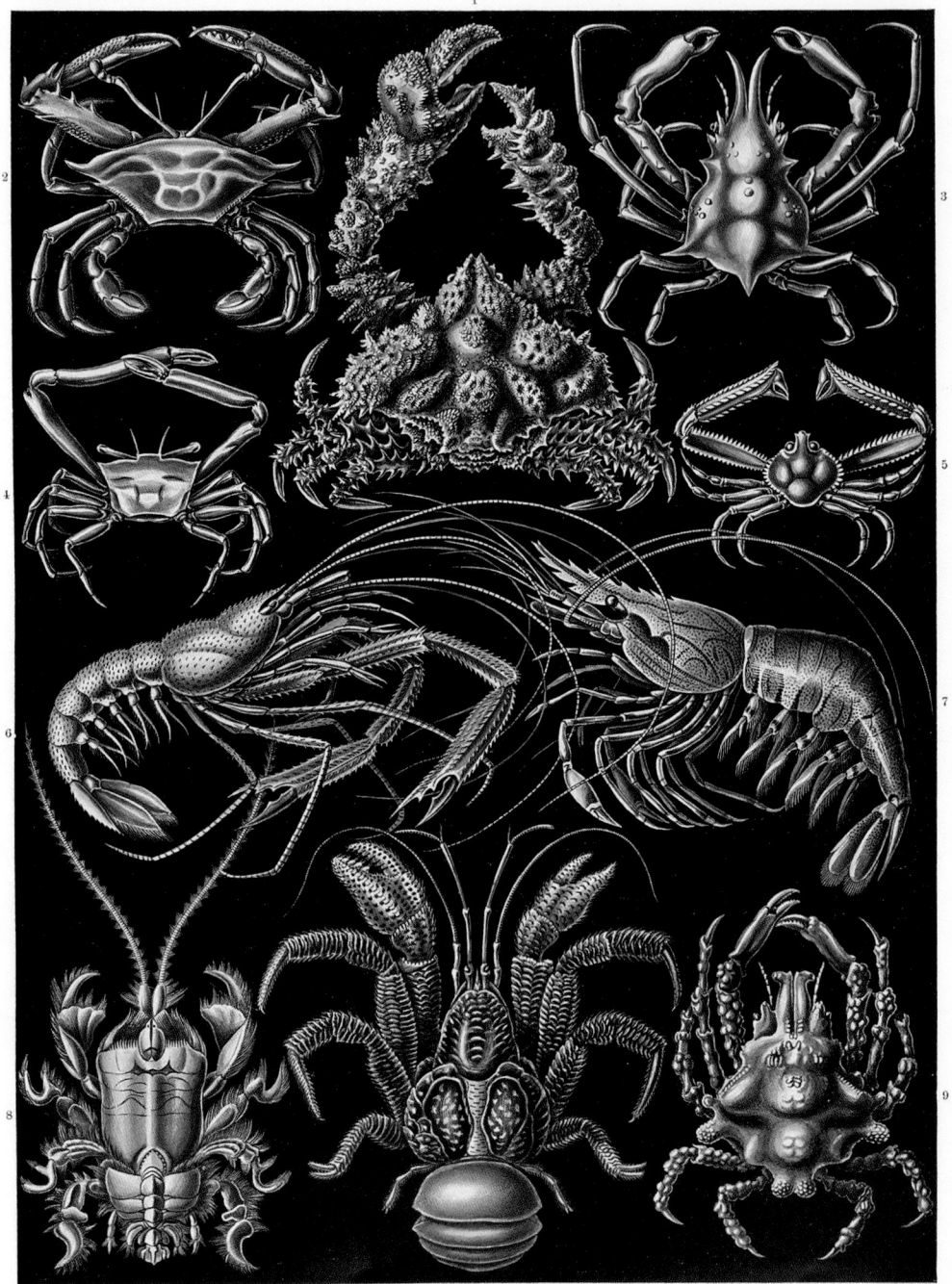

Decapoda. — Zehnfußkrebſe.

PLATE 86

CRUSTACEA

Crustaceans

1 **Parthenope horrida** (FABRICIUS) – *Daldorfia horrida* (LINNAEUS, 1758) Horrid Elbow crab, Horrid crab
2 **Podophthalmus vigil** (LEACH) – *Podophthalmus vigil* (FABRICIUS, 1798) Sentinel crab
3 **Pisa armata** (LEACH) – *Pisa armata* (LATREILLE, 1803) Gibb's sea spider
4 **Gonoplax rhomboides** (DESMAREST) (Gonoplax; sic!) – *Goneplax rhomboides* (LINNAEUS, 1758) Angular crab
5 **Pisolambrus nitidus** (MILNE EDWARDS) – *Leiolambrus nitidus;? Solenolambrus nitidus*
6 **Stenopus hispidus** (LATREILLE) – *Stenopus hispidus* (OLIVIER, 1811)
Spiny shrimp, Redbanded coral shrimp, Banded coral shrimp, Boxer cleaner shrimp
7 **Palaemon serratus** (FABRICIUS) – *Palaemon serratus* (PENNANT, 1777) Common prawn
8 **Albunea symnista** (FABRICIUS) – *Albunea symmysta* (LINNAEUS, 1758) (*symnista*: lapsus in LINNÉ, 1767)
9 **Lissa chiragra** (LEACH) – *Lissa chiragra* (FABRICIUS, 1775)
10 **Birgus latro** (HERBST) – *Birgus latro* (LINNÉ, 1767) Coconut crab, Palm thief, Robber crab, Ganjo crab

PLATE 79
SAUROPSIDA – LEPIDOSAURIA
Sauropsida – Lepidosauria

1 **Chamaeleon montium** (BUCHHOLZ) – *Trioceros montium* (BUCHHOLZ, 1874)
Cameroon sailfin chameleon, Cameroon two-horned mountain chameleon

2 **Lophyrus tigrinus** (DUMÉRIL) – *Gonocephalus chamaeleontinus* LAURENTI, 1768
Chameleon forest dragon, Chameleon anglehead lizard

3 **Draconellus volans** (LINNÉ) – *Draco volans* LINNAEUS, 1758
Common flying dragon, Vietnamese flying dragon

4 **Phrynosoma cornutum** (WIEGMANN) – *Phrynosoma cornutum* (HARLAN, 1825)
Texas horned lizard

5 **Ptychozoon homalocephalum** (KUHL) – *Ptychozoon kuhli* STEJNEGER, 1902
Kuhl's flying gecko, Gliding gecko, Kuhl's parachute gecko

6 **Basiliscus americanus** (DAUDIN) – *Basiliscus basiliscus* (LINNAEUS, 1758)
Common basilisk, Jesus lizard, Basilisk lizard

7 **Chlamydosaurus Kingii** (GRAY) – *Chlamydosaurus kingi* GRAY, 1827 (1825?)
Frilled-neck lizard, Frilled lizard, Frilled dragon

8 **Moloch horridus** (GRAY) – *Moloch horridus* GRAY, 1841
Thorny dragon, Thorny devil, Mountain devil

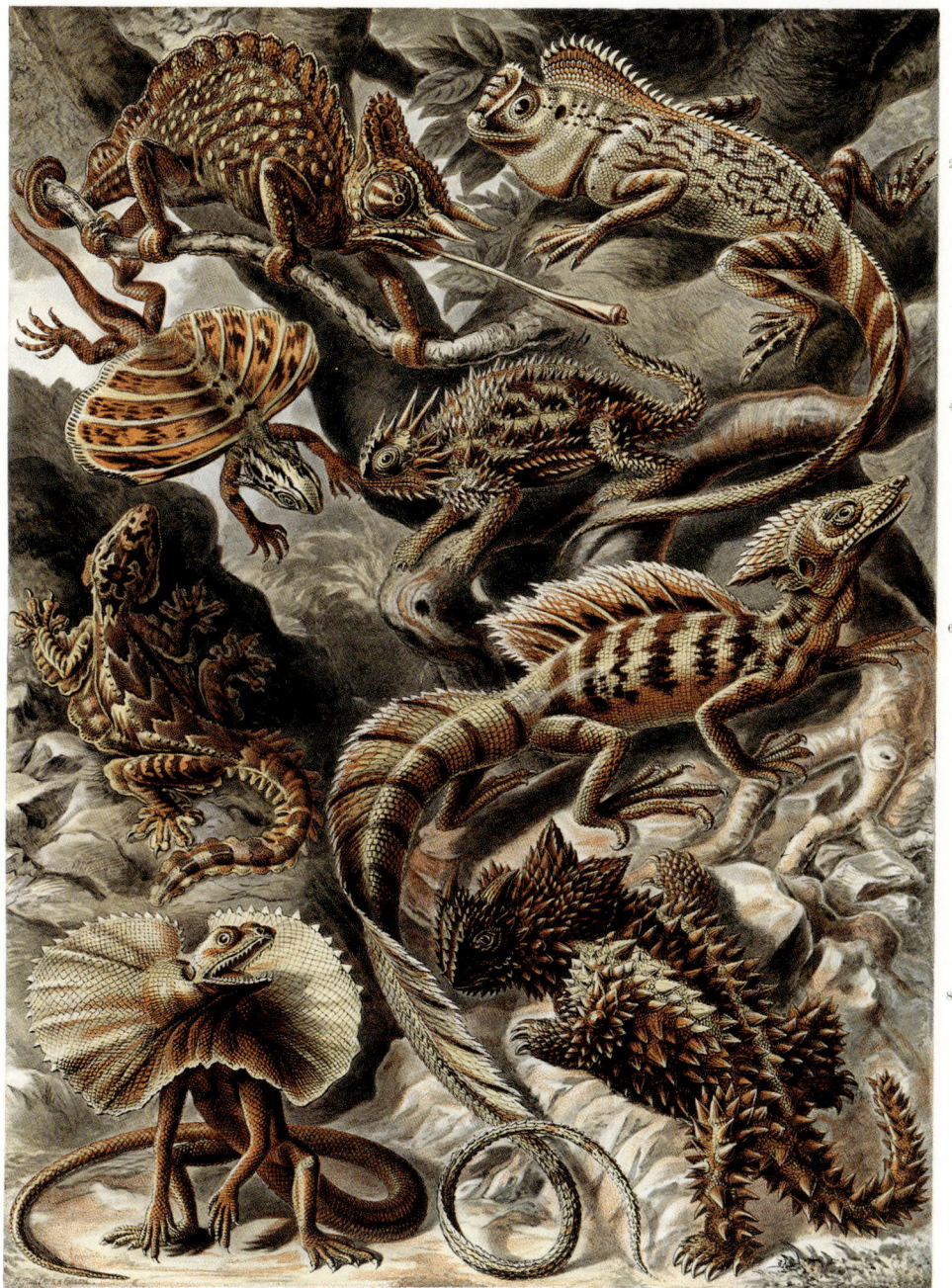

Lacertilia. — Eidechſen.

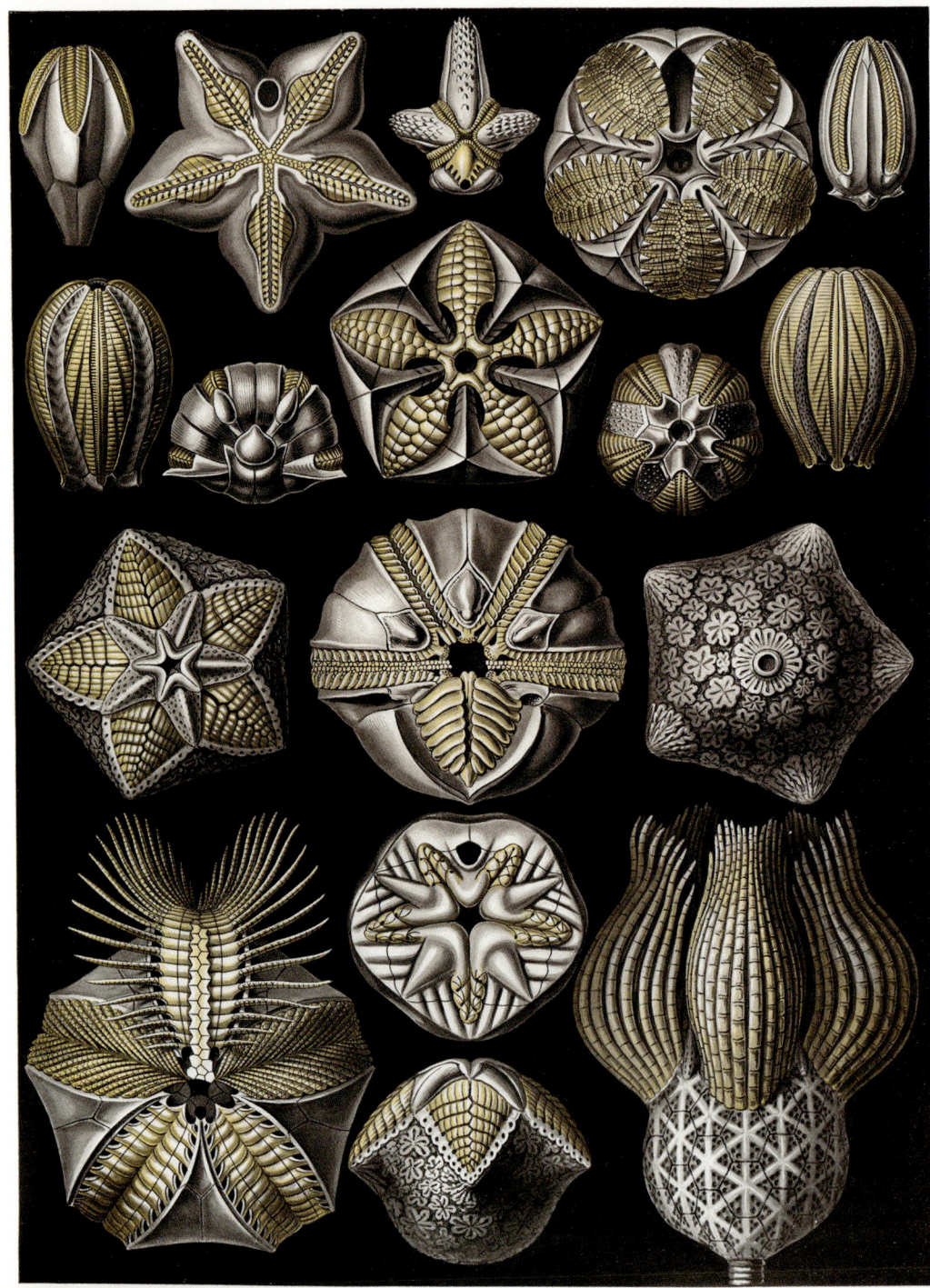

Blastoïdea. — Knospensterne.

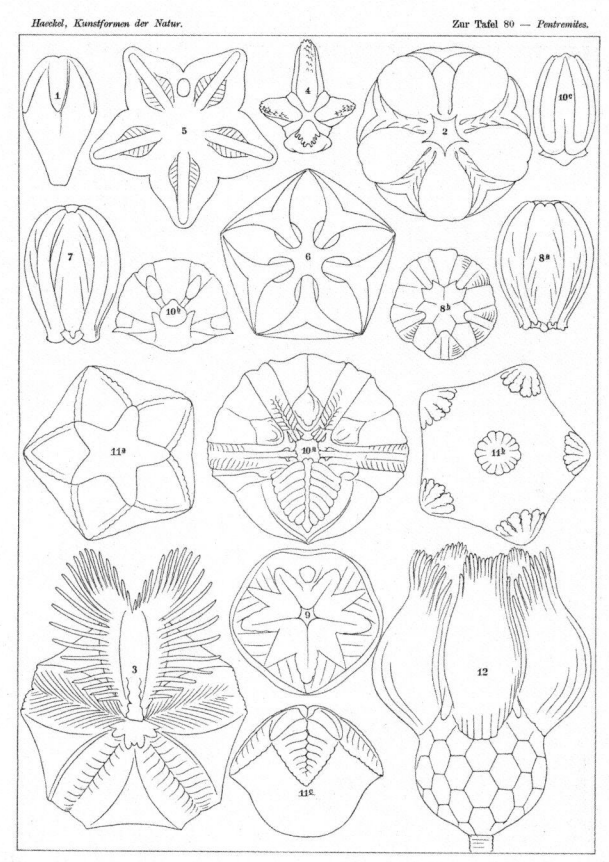

Haeckel, Kunstformen der Natur.   Zur Tafel 80 — Pentremites.

PLATE 80

ECHINODERMATA – BLASTOIDEA

Echinoderms – Blastoids

1 Pentremites pyriformis (SAY) – *Pentremites pyriformis* SAY, 1825
2 Pentremites orbignyanus (KONINCK) – *Orophocrinus orbignyanus* (DE KONINCK, 1842)
3 Pentremites species (ARNOLD LANG) – *Pentremites* sp.
4 Zygocrinus cruciatus (BRONN) – *Astrocrinus cruciatus* (BRONN, 1848)
5 Orophocrinus stelliformis (ETHERIDGE) – *Orophocrinus stelliformis* (OWEN AND SHUMARD, 1850)
6 Phaenoschisma acutum (ETHERIDGE) – *Phaenoschisma acutum* (SOWERBY, 1834)
7 Elaeacrinus olivanites (TROOST) – *Elaeacrinus* sp.
8 Elaeacrinus Verneuili (RÖMER) – *Elaeacrinus verneuili* C. F. ROEMER, 1851
9 Codonaster trilobatus (BATHER) – *Codaster acutus* MCCOY, 1849 (synonym: *C. trilobatus* MCCOY)
10 Eleutherocrinus Cassedayi (SHUMARD) – *Eleutherocrinus cassedayi* SHUMARD & YANDELL, 1856
11 Asteroblastus stellatus (FRIES SCHMIDT) – *Asteroblastus stellatus* EICHWALD, 1862
12 Asteroblastus Volborthi (FRIES SCHMIDT) – *Asteroblastus volborthi* SCHMIDT, 1894

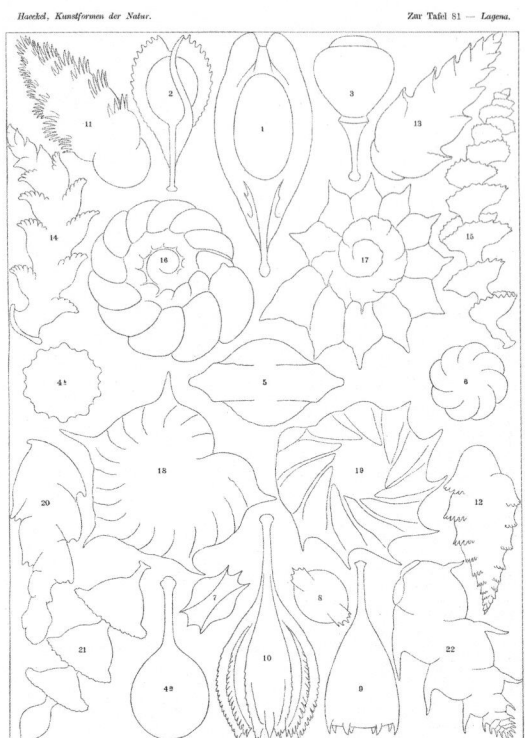

Haeckel, Kunstformen der Natur.   Zur Tafel 81 — Lagena.

PLATE 81
FORAMINIFERA
Foraminiferans, Forams

1 Lagena formosa (SCHWAGER) – *Fissurina formosa* (SCHWAGER, 1866) | 2 Lagena auriculata (BRADY) – *Fissurina auriculata* (BRADY, 1881) | 3 Lagena pannosa (MILLETT) – *Lagena pannosa* MILLETT, 1901 | 4 Lagena torquata (BRADY) – *Cushmanina torquata* (BRADY, 1881) | 5 Lagena squamosa (BRADY) – *Favulina squamosa* (MONTAGU, 1803) (synonym: *Oolina squamosa* (MONTAGU, 1803)) | 6 Lagena Milletti (HAECKEL) – *Walterparria milletti* (CHASTER, 1892) | 7 Lagena Walleriana (JOSEPH WRIGHT) – *Buchnerina walleriana* (WRIGHT, 1886) (synonym: *Fissurina walleriana* (WRIGHT, 1886)) | 8 Lagena castrensis (SCHWAGER) – *Lagena castrensis* SCHWAGER, 1866 | 9 Lagena semistriata (WILLIAMSON) – *Lagena semistriata* WILLIAMSON, 1848 | 10 Lagena plumigera (BRADY) – *Cushmanina plumigera* (BRADY, 1881) | 11 Bulimina spinulosa (WILLIAMSON) – *Bulimina pupoides var. spinulosa* WILLIAMSON, 1858 (synonym: *Protoglobobulimina pupoides* (D'ORBIGNY, 1846)) | 12 Bulimina marginata (D'ORBIGNY) – *Bulimina marginata* D'ORBIGNY, 1826 | 13 Bolivina Durrandii (MILLETT) – *Sagrinella durrandi* (MILLETT, 1900) | 14 Bolivina convallaria (MILLETT) – *Sagrinella convallaria* (MILLETT, 1900) | 15 Uvigerina porrecta (BRADY) – *Siphouvigerina porrecta* (BRADY, 1879) | 16 Truncatulina ungeriana (D'ORBIGNY) – *Truncatulina ungeriana* CUSHMAN, 1921 | 17 Rotalia calcar (D'ORBIGNY) – *Neorotalia calcar* (D'ORBIGNY, 1839) | 18 Polystomella imperatrix (BRADY) – *Parrellina imperatrix* (BRADY, 1881) | 19 Cristellaria calcar (PARKER) – *Lenticulina calcar* (LINNÉ, 1767) | 20 Bifarina Mackinnonii (MILLETT) – *Valvobifarina mackinnoni* (MILLETT, 1900) | 21 Lingulina pagoda (MILLETT) – *Lingulina pagoda* MILLETT, 1902 | 22 Mimosina hystrix (MILLETT) – *Mimosina hystrix* MILLETT, 1900

446

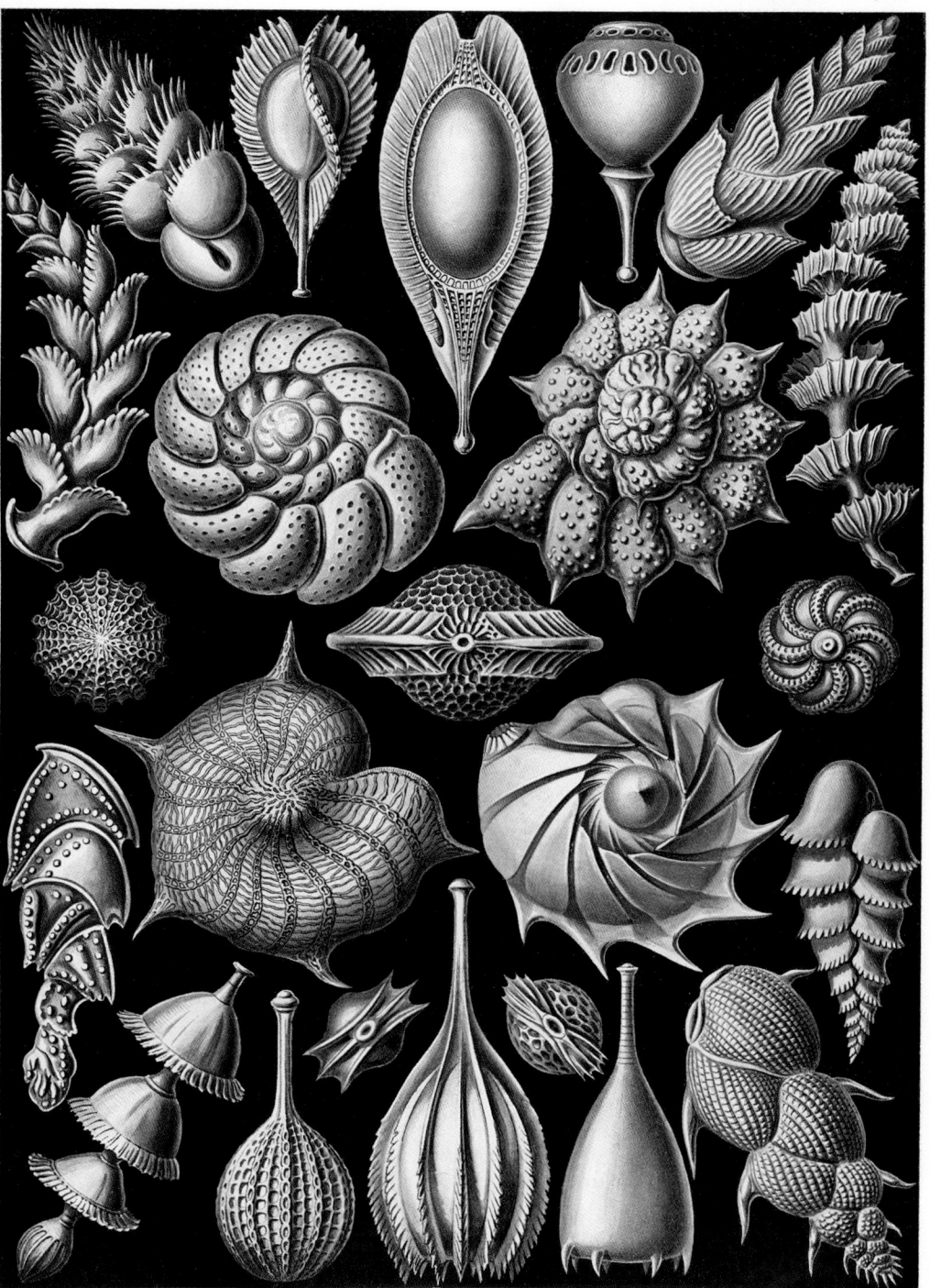

Thalamophora. — Kammerlinge.

PLATE 82

HEPATICAE
Liver worts

1 Marchantia nitida (LEHMANN) – *Marchantia nitida* LEHMANN & LINDENB., 1832
2 Marchantia polymorpha (LINNÉ) – *Marchantia polymorpha* LINNAEUS, 1753
Green-tongue liverwort, Liverwort, Umbrella liverwort
3 Fimbriaria marginata (GOTTSCHE) – *Asterella marginata* (NEES) ARNELL, 1963
4 Fimbriaria venosa (LEHMANN) – *Asterella venosa* (LEHMANN & LINDENBERG) A.EVANS, 1920
5 Fimbriaria cubensis (GOTTSCHE) – *Fimbriaria elegans* (SPRENGEL) LEHMANN var. cubensis GOTTSCHE
6 Fimbriaria sanguinea (LINDENBERG) – *Schisma sanguineum* (MONTAGNE) STEPHANI?
7 Lunularia cruciata (DUMORTIER) – *Lunularia cruciata* (LINNAEUS) DUMORTIER EX LINDENBERG, 1868
Crescent-cup liverwort
8 Jungermannia ventricosa (DICKSON) – *Lophozia ventricosa* (DICKSON) DUMORTIER, 1835 Tumid notchwort
9 Jungermannia conniveus (DICKSON) – *Cephalozia connivens* (DICKSON) LINDENBERG, 1872)
(synonym: *Jungermannia connivens* (DICKSON)) Forcipated pincerwort
10 Lepidozia reptans (NEES) – *Lepidozia reptans* (LINNAEUS) DUMORTIER, 1835 Creeping fingerwort
11 Jubula Hutchinsiae (DUMORTIER) – *Jubula hutchinsiae* (HOOKER) DUMORTIER, 1822
12 Harpalejeunia ancistrodes (SPRUCE) – *Harpalejeunea ancistrodes* (SPRUCE) SCHIFFNER, 1893
13 Scapania undulata (NEES) – *Scapania undulata* (LINNAEUS) DUMORTIER, 1835 Water earwort
14 Scapania subalpina (DUMORTIER) – *Scapania subalpina* (NEES EX LINDENBERG) DUMORTIER, 1835
Northern earwort
15 Scapania umbrosa (NEES) – *Scapania umbrosa* (SCHRADER) DUMORTIER, 1835 Shady earwort
16 Scapania nemorosa (NEES) – *Scapania nemorea* (LINNAEUS) DUMORTIER Grove earwort
17 Scapania aequiloba (NEES) – *Scapania aequiloba* (SCHWÄGRICHEN) DUMORTIER, 1835 Lesser rough earwort

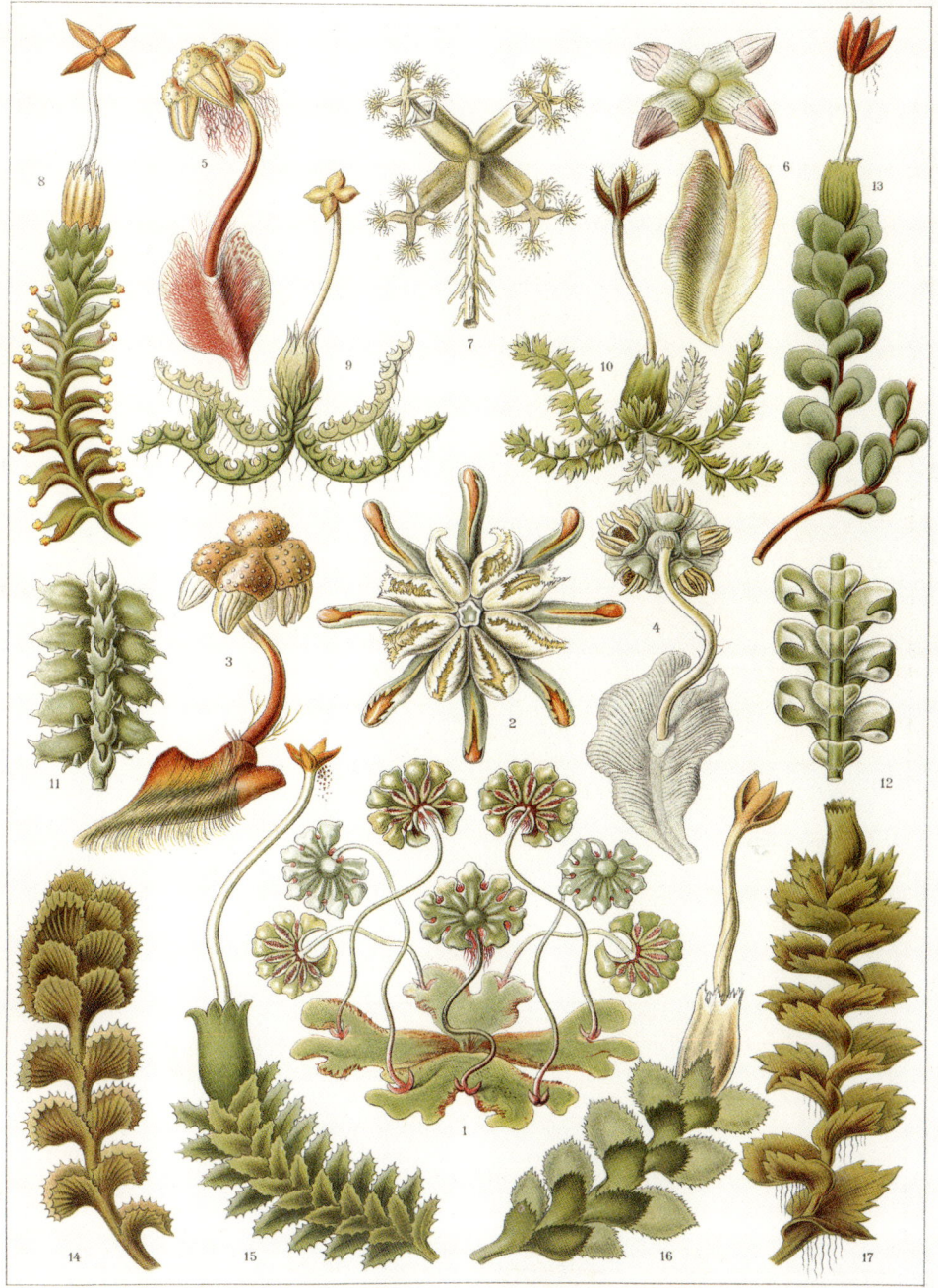

Hepaticae. — Lebermoose.

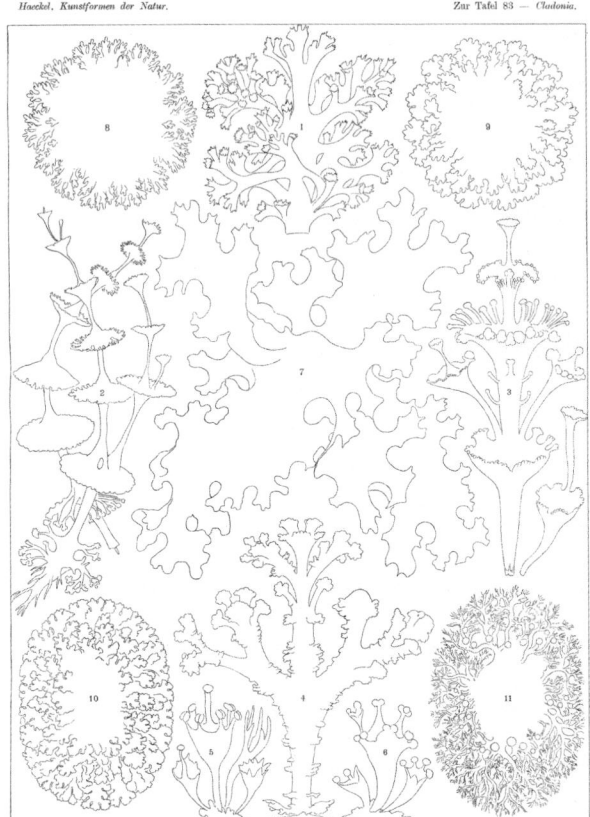

Haeckel, Kunstformen der Natur.   Zur Tafel 83 — *Cladonia.*

PLATE 83

LICHENES

Lichens

1 Cladonia retipora (FLOERKE) – *Cladonia retipora* (LABILLARDIÈRE) FRIES, 1826 Cladonia, Cup lichen

2 Cladonia perfoliata (HOOKER) – *Cladonia perfoliata* FLÖRKE

3 Cladonia verticillata (ACHARD) – *Cladonia verticillata* (G. F. HOFFMANN) SCHAERER, 1823

4 Cladonia squamosa (HOFFMANN) – *Cladonia squamosa* (SCOPOLI) G. F. HOFFMANN, 1796 Dragon cladonia

5 Cladonia fimbriata (FRIES) – *Cladonia fimbriata* (L.) FRIES, 1831 Trumpet lichen

6 Cladonia cornucopiae (FRIES) – *Cladonia coccifera* (LINNAEUS) WILLDENOW, 1787? Cup lichen

7 Sticta pulmonaria (ACHARD) – *Sticta pulmonaria* (LINNAEUS) BIROLI, 1808 (synonym: Lobaria pulmonaria (LINNAEUS) HOFFMANN) Lungwort | 8 Parmelia stellaris (FRIES) – *Physcia stellaris* (LINNAEUS) NYLANDER, 1856 Star rosette lichen, Stellaris rosette lichen | 9 Parmelia olivacea (ACHARD) – *Melanohalea olivacea* (LINNAEUS) BLANCO, CRESPO, DIVAKAR, ESSL., HAWKSW. & LUMBSCH 2004 Spotted camouflage lichen, Spotted brown-shield

10 Parmelia caperata (ACHARD) – *Flavoparmelia caperata* (LINNAEUS) HALE, 1986 (synonym: *Parmelia caperata* (LINNAEUS) ACHARD, 1803) Common greenshield lichen, Flavoparmelia lichen | 11 Hagenia crinalis (SCHLEICHER) – *Anaptychia crinalis* (SCHLEICHER) VEZDA, 1977 Hanging fringe lichen

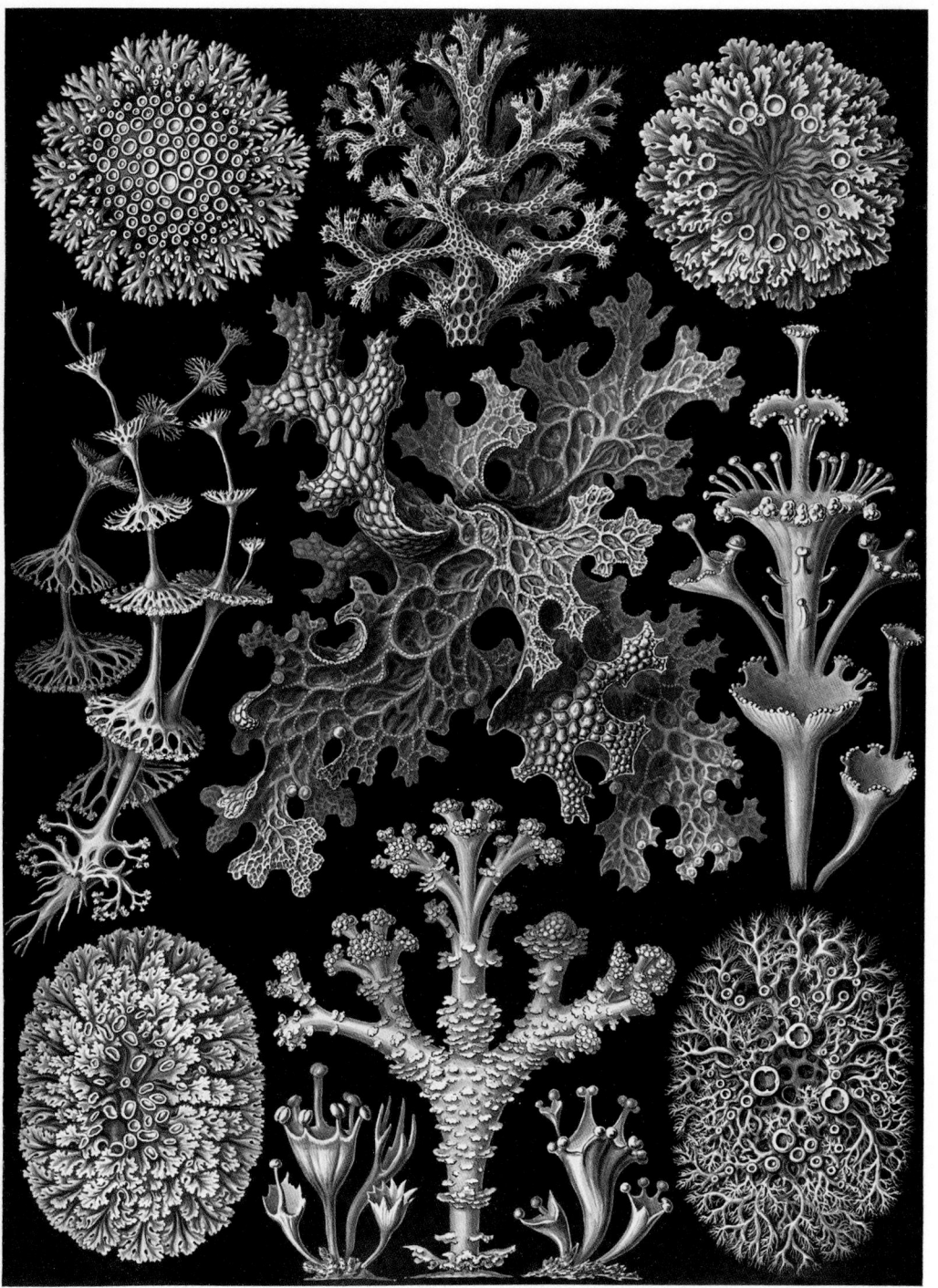

Lichenes. — Flechten.

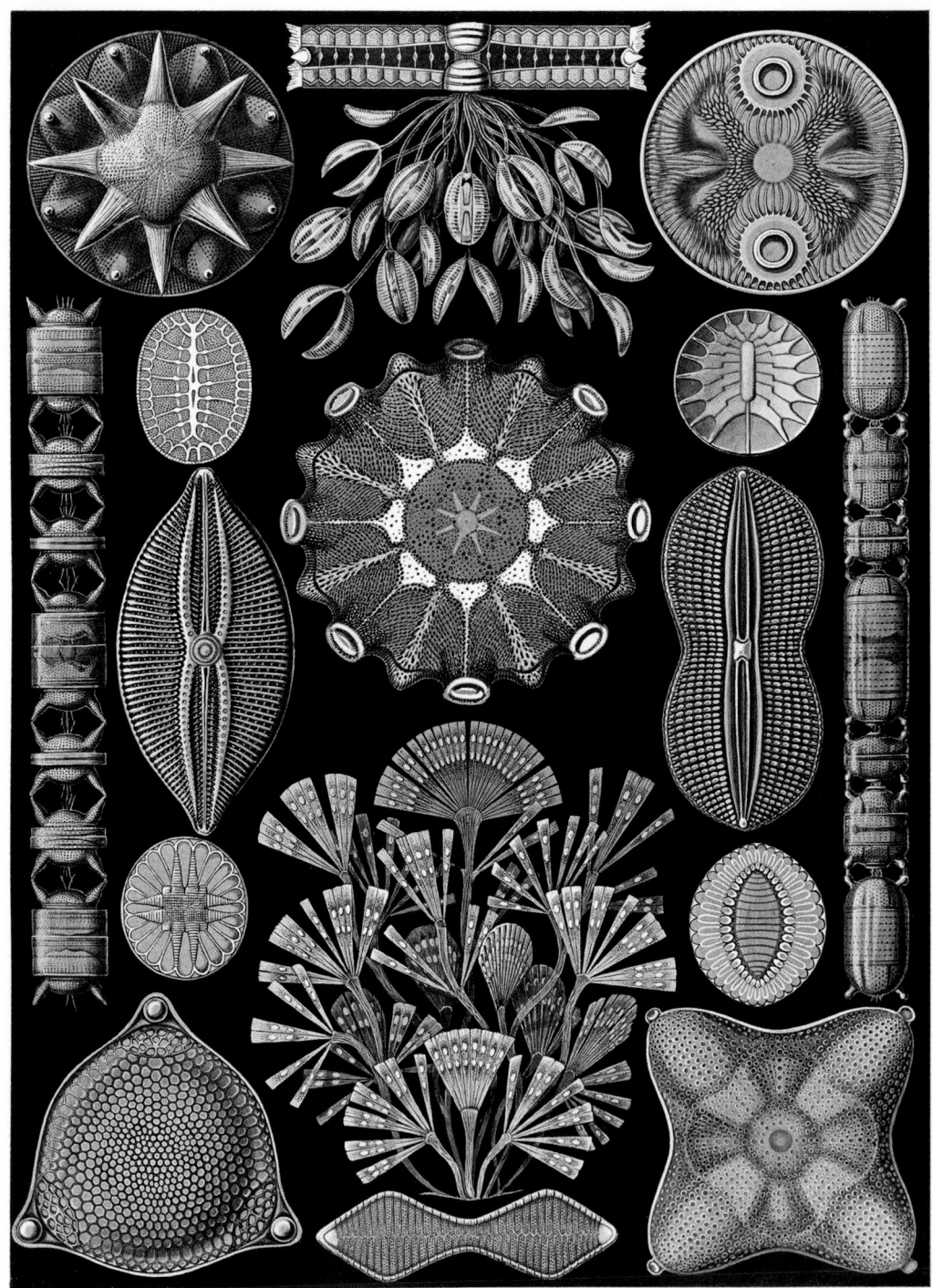

Diatomea. — Schachtellinge.

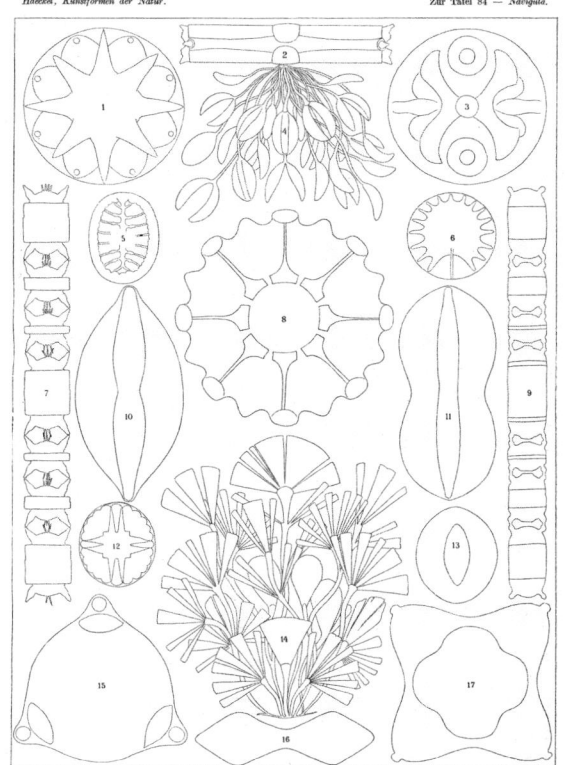

Haeckel, Kunstformen der Natur.   Zur Tafel 84 — Navigula.

PLATE 84
DIATOMEA
Diatoms

1 **Pyrgodiscus armatus** (KITTON) – *Pyrgodiscus armatus* KITTON, 1885 | 2 **Rutilaria monile** (GROVE) – *Rutilaria* GREVILLE, 1863 (synonym: *Pseudorutilaria monile* GROVE & STURT 1886) | 3 **Auliscus elegans** (BAILEY) – *Auliscus elegans* GREVILLE | 4 **Cocconema cistula** (EHRENBERG) – *Cymbella cistula* (EHRENBERG) O. KIRCHNER, 1878 | 5 **Campyloneis grevillei** (W. SMITH) – *Campyloneis grevillei* (W. SMITH) GRUNOW & EULENSTEIN, 1868 | 6 **Asteromphalus imbricatus** (WALLICH) – *Asteromphalus imbricatus* G. C. WALLICH | 7 **Odontella aurita** (LYNGBYE) – *Odontella aurita* (LYNGBYE) C. AGARDH, 1832 | 8 **Grovea pedalis** (GROVE) – *Biddulphia pedalis* E. GROVE & G. STURT | 9 **Biddulphia pulchella** (GRAY) – *Biddulphia biddulphiana* (J. E. SMITH) BOYER, 1900 | 10 **Navicula bullata** (NORMAN) – *Navicula bullata* NORMAN | 11 **Navicula didyma** (GREGORY) – *Diploneis didyma* (EHRENBERG) EHRENBERG, 1839 (1845?) | 12 **Campylodiscus bicruciatus** (GREGORY) – *Campylodiscus bicruciatus* W. GREGORY | 13 **Surirella pulcherrima** (MEARA) – *Surirella pulcherrima* O'MEARA | 14 **Licmophora flabellata** (CARM.) – *Licmophora flabellata* (GREVILLE) C. AGARDH, 1831 | 15 **Triceratium robertsianum** (GREVILLE) – *Triceratium robertsianum* GREVILLE, 1866 | 16 **Gephyria constricta** (GREVILLE) – cf. *Gephyria constricta* GREVILLE, 1866 | 17 **Amphithetras elegans** (GREVILLE) – *Amphitetras elegans* GREVILLE (synonym: *Triceratium elegans* (GREVILLE) GRUNOW IN VAN HEURCK 1883, synonym: *Biddulphia elegans* (R. K. GREVILLE) C. S. BOYER?)

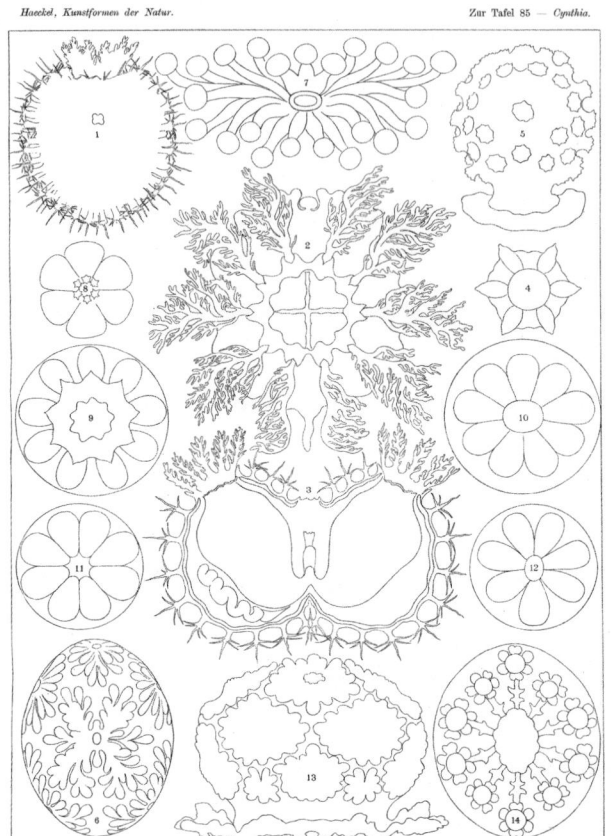

Haeckel, Kunstformen der Natur.　　　　　　　　Zur Tafel 85 — Cynthia.

PLATE 85

TUNICATA

Tunicata

1-3 **Cynthia melocactus** (HAECKEL) – *Boltenia melocactus* HAECKEL, 1904 (HAECKEL: similar *Boltenia echinata* LINNÉ, 1767), *Cynthia* SAVIGNY, 1816 = synonym of *Halocynthia* VERRILL, 1879 (*Cynthia* = Homonym of *Cynthia* FABRICIUS, 1807 [Insecta: Lepidoptera]) Cactus Sea Squirt | 4 **Molgula tubulosa** (FORBES) – *Eugyra arenosa* (ALDER & HANCOCK, 1848) | 5 **Fragarium elegans** (GIARD) – *Aplidium elegans* (GIARD, 1872) 6-7 **Polyclinum constellatum** (SAVIGNY) – *Polyclinum constellatum* SAVIGNY, 1816 | 8 **Synoecum turgens** (PHIPPS) – *Synoicum turgens* PHIPPS, 1774 | 9 **Botryllus polycyclus** (SAVIGNY) – also commons *Botryllus schlosseri* (PALLAS, 1766) Golden star tunicate, Star ascidian, Star squirt | 10 **Botryllus rubigo** (GIARD) – *Botryllus schlosseri* (PALLAS, 1766) (synonym: *B. rubigo* GIARD, 1872) Golden star tunicate, Star ascidian, Star squirt | 11 **Botryllus Marionis** (GIARD) – *Botryllus schlosseri* (PALLAS, 1766) (synonym: *Botryllus marionis* GIARD, 1872) Golden star tunicate, Star ascidian, Star squirt | 12 **Botryllus helleborus** (GIARD) – *? Botryllus schlosseri* (PALLAS, 1766) 13 **Polycyclus cyaneus** (DRASCHE) – *? Botryllus schlosseri* (PALLAS, 1766) | 14 **Botrylloides purpureus** (DRASCHE) – *Botrylloides leachii* (SAVIGNY, 1816) Leach's compound ascidian

454

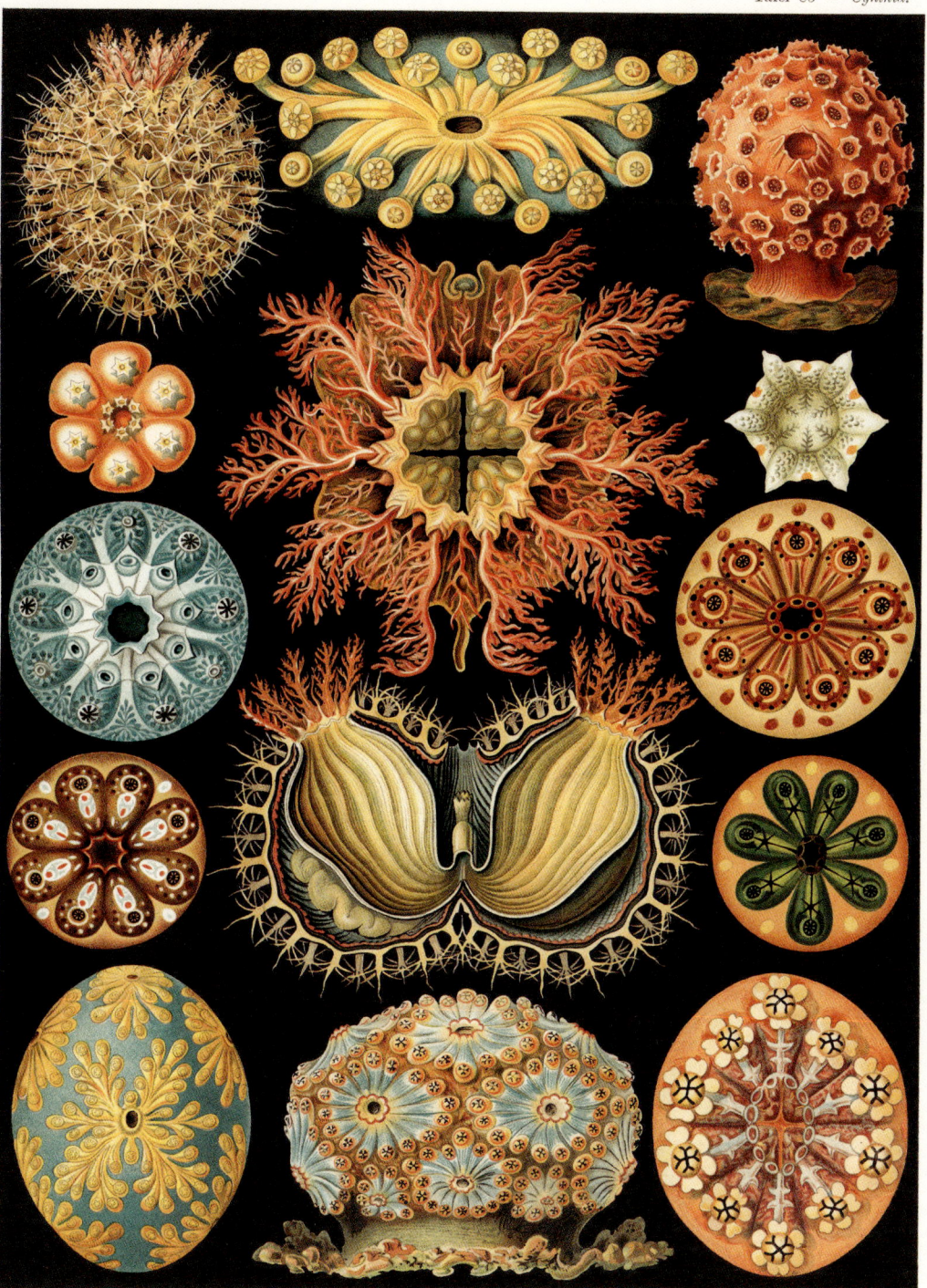

Ascidiae. — Seescheiden.

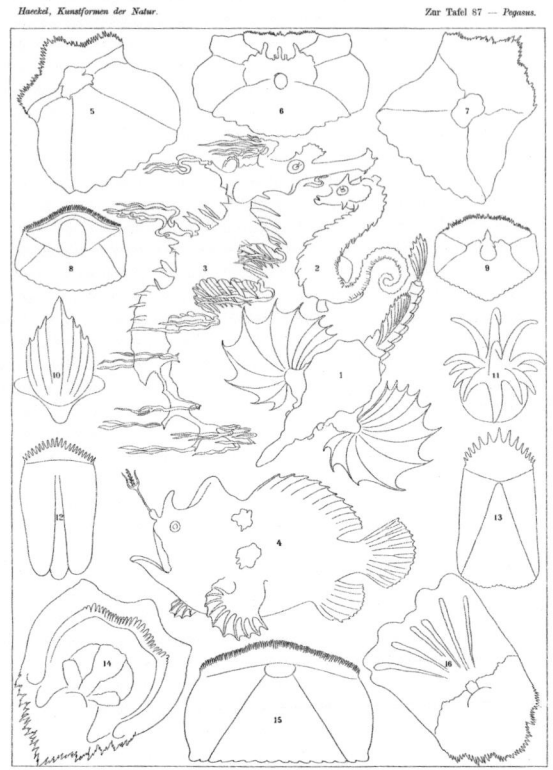

Haeckel, Kunstformen der Natur.   Zur Tafel 87 — Pegasus.

PLATE 87

VERTEBRATA – ACTINOPTERYGII

Vertebrates – Actinopterygii, Ray-finned fishes

1 Pegasus chiropterus (HAECKEL) — *Pegasus laternarius* CUVIER, 1816 Brick seamoth
2 Hippocampus antiquorum (LEACH) — *Hippocampus hippocampus* (LINNAEUS, 1758) Short-snouted seahorse
3 Phyllopteryx eques (GÜNTHER) — *Phycodurus eques* (GÜNTHER, 1865) Glauert's seadragon, Leafy seadragon
4 Antennarius tridens (BLEEKER) — *Antennarius striatus* (SHAW, 1794) Striated frogfish, Splitlure frogfish, Blotched anglerfish
5 Chrysophrys aurata (CUVIER) — *Sparus aurata* LINNAEUS 1758 Gilt-head bream | 6 Pagellus erythrinus (CUVIER) —
Pagellus erythrinus (LINNAEUS, 1758) Spanish sea bream, Common pandorae | 7 Box vulgaris (CUVIER) — *Boops boops*
(LINNAEUS, 1758) Bogue | 8 Anthias sacer (SCHNEIDER) — *Anthias anthias* (LINNAEUS, 1758) Swallowtail seaperch, Barbier,
Sea perch | 9 Apogon imberbis (GÜNTHER) — *Apogon imberbis* (LINNAEUS, 1758) Cardinalfish, Mediterranean cardinalfish
10 Centriscus scolopax (CUVIER) — *Macroramphosus scolopax* (LINNAEUS, 1758) Longspine snipefish, Slender snipefish
11 Hypostomum plecostomum (CUVIER) — *Hypostomus plecostomus* (LINNAEUS, 1758) Suckermouth catfish, Spotted pleco
12 Fistularia chinensis (LACÉPEDE) — *Aulostomus chinensis* (LINNÉ, 1766) Chinese trumpetfish, Pacific trumpetfish,
Painted flutemouth | 13 Solea vulgaris (QUENSEL) — *Solea solea* (LINNAEUS, 1758) Common sole, Black sole, Dover sole
14 Scarus enneacanthus (BLEEKER) — *Chlorurus enneacanthus* (LACEPÈDE, 1802) Captain parrotfish, Parrotfish
15 Haemulon elegans (CUVIER) — *Haemulon sciurus* (SHAW, 1803) Blue striped grunt
16 Cantharus vulgaris (CUVIER) — *Spondyliosoma cantharus* (LINNAEUS, 1758) Black seabream, Black bream

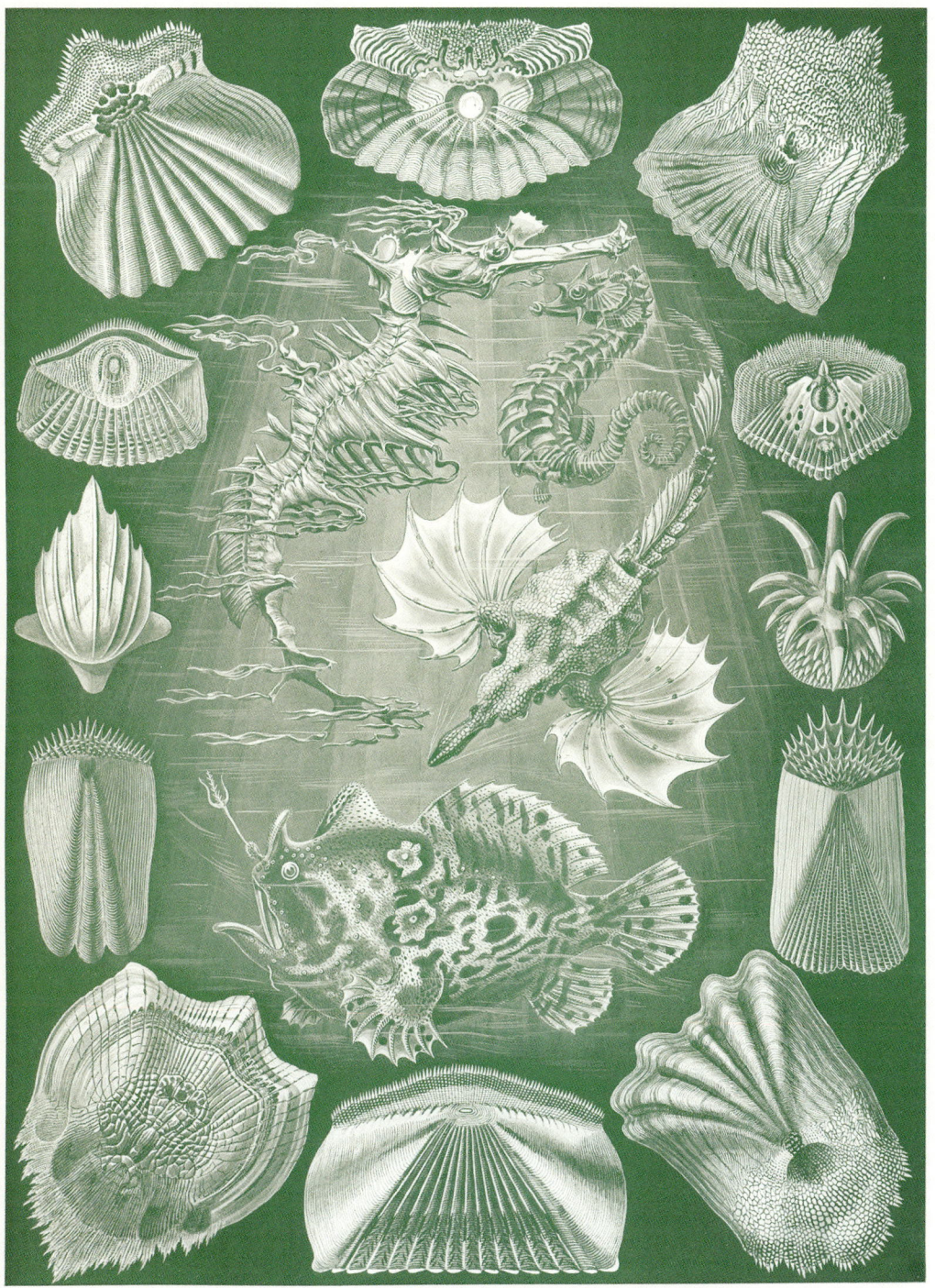

Teleostei. — Knochenfische.

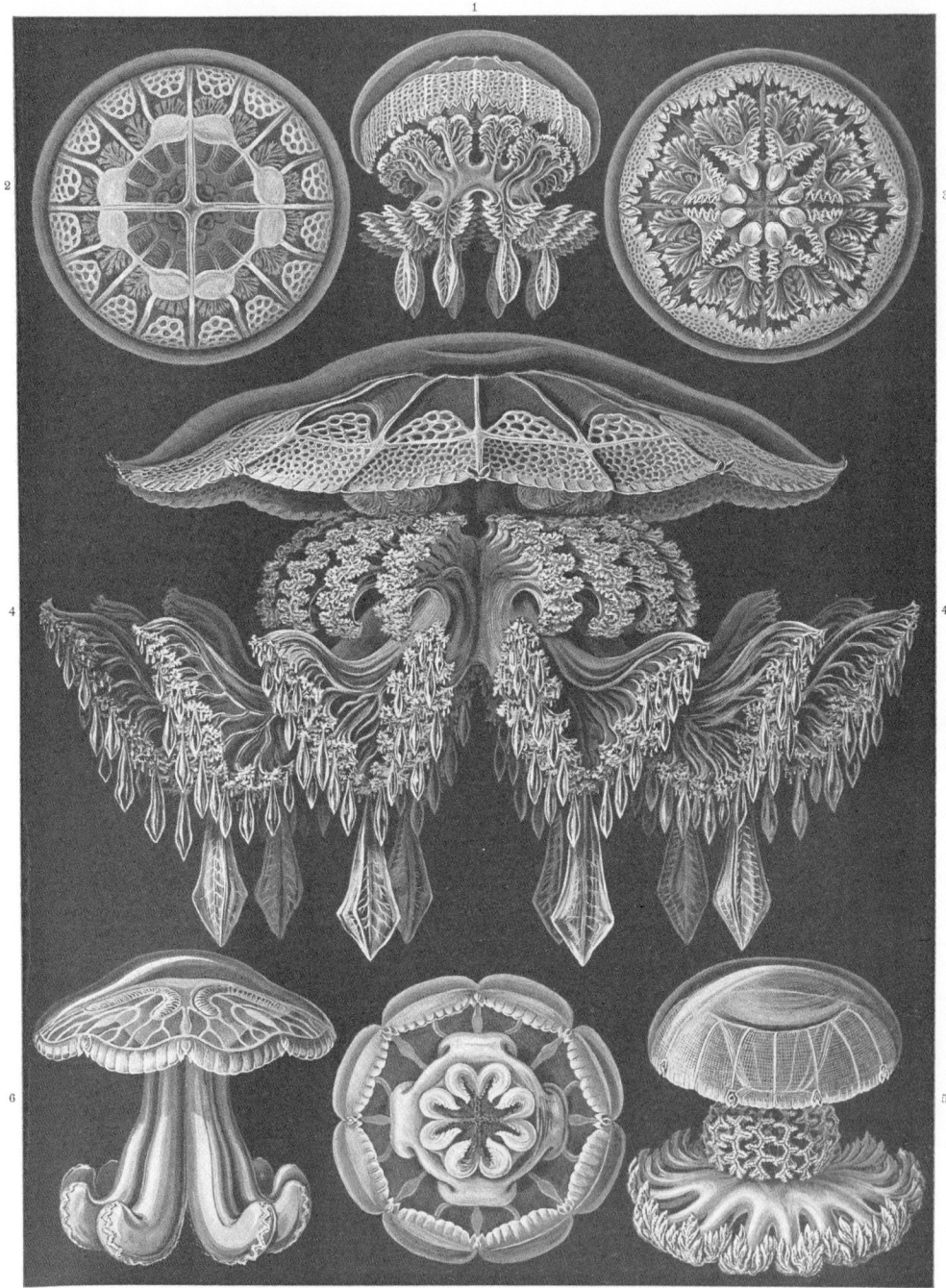

Discomedusae. — Scheibenquallen.

PLATE 88 ❊
CNIDARIA – SCYPHOZOA
Cnidarians – Scyphozoans, True jellyfish

1-3 Pilema Giltschii (HAECKEL) – *Pilema giltschii*
4 Rhopilema Frida (HAECKEL) – *Rhopilema frida*
5 Brachiolophus collaris (HAECKEL) – *Brachiolophius collaris*
Cannonball jellyfish, Cannonball jelly, Cabbagehead
6-7 Cannorrhiza connexa (HAECKEL) – *Cannorrhiza connexa*
❊ *see page 507*

PLATE 89
SAUROPSIDA – CHELONIA
Sauropsida – Tortoises, Turtles

1 Dermatochelys coriacea (BLAINVILLE) – *Dermochelys coriacea* (VANDELLI, 1761)
Leatherback sea turtle, Coffin-back, Leatherback
2 Caretta imbricata (GRAY) – *Eretmochelys imbricata* (LINNÉ, 1766) Hawksbill sea turtle, Hawksbill turtle, Carey
3 Hydromeda tectifera (WAGLER) – *Hydromedusa tectifera* COPE, 1869
South American snake-necked turtle, Argentine snake-necked turtle, South-American snake-headed turtle
4 Chelys fimbriata (DUMÉRIL) – *Chelus fimbriata* (SCHNEIDER, 1783) Matamata turtle, Mata Mata
5 Testudo geometrica (LINNÉ) – *Psammobates geometricus* (LINNAEUS, 1758) Geometric tortoise, Geometric turtle
6 Testudo elephantina (DUMÉRIL) – *Chelonoidis nigra* (QUOY & GAIMARD, 1824) Galapagos giant tortoise
7 Chelydra serpentina (SCHWEIGGER) – *Chelydra serpentina* (LINNAEUS, 1758)
Common snapping turtle, North American snapping turtle

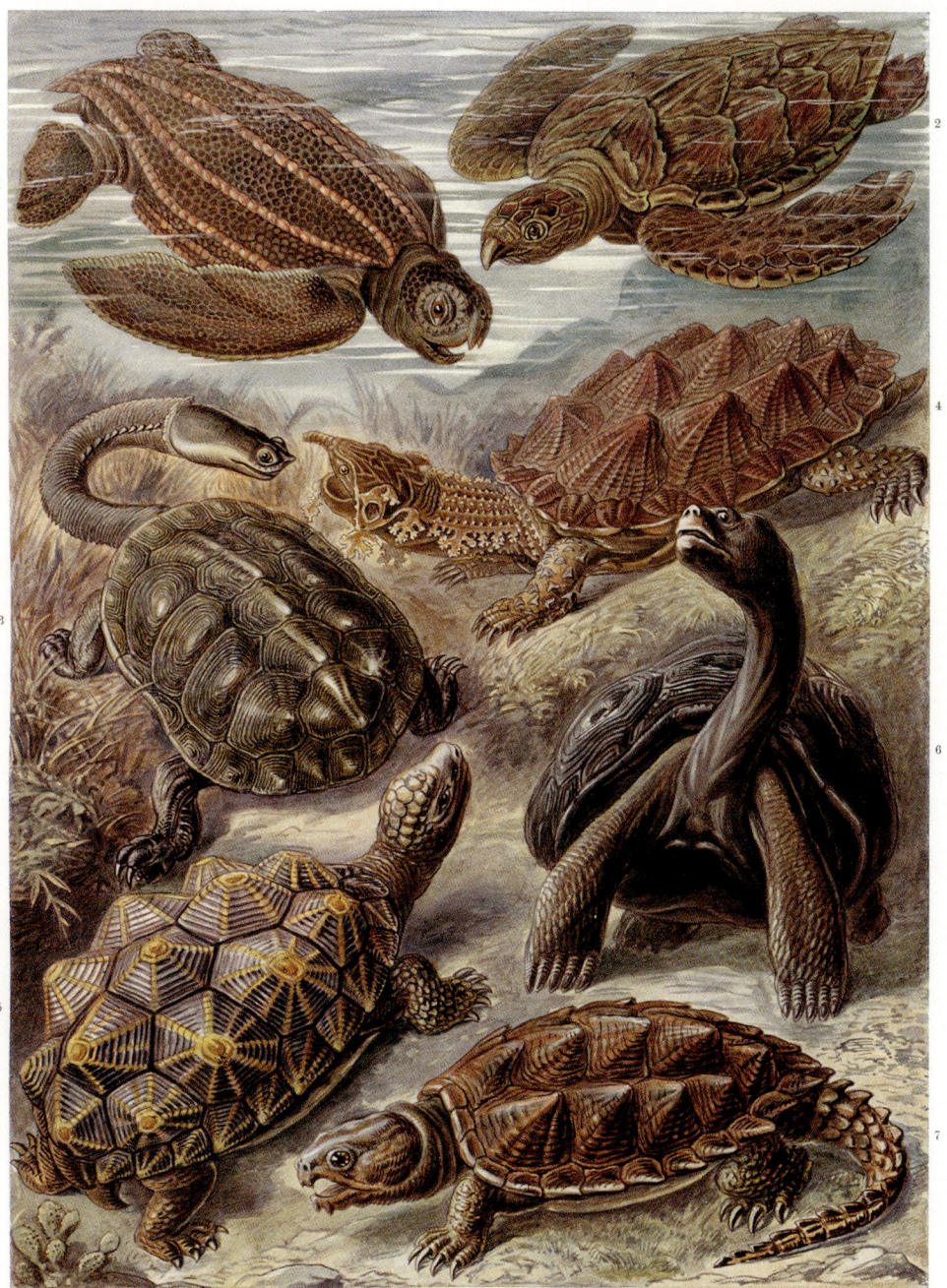

Chelonia. — Schildkröten.

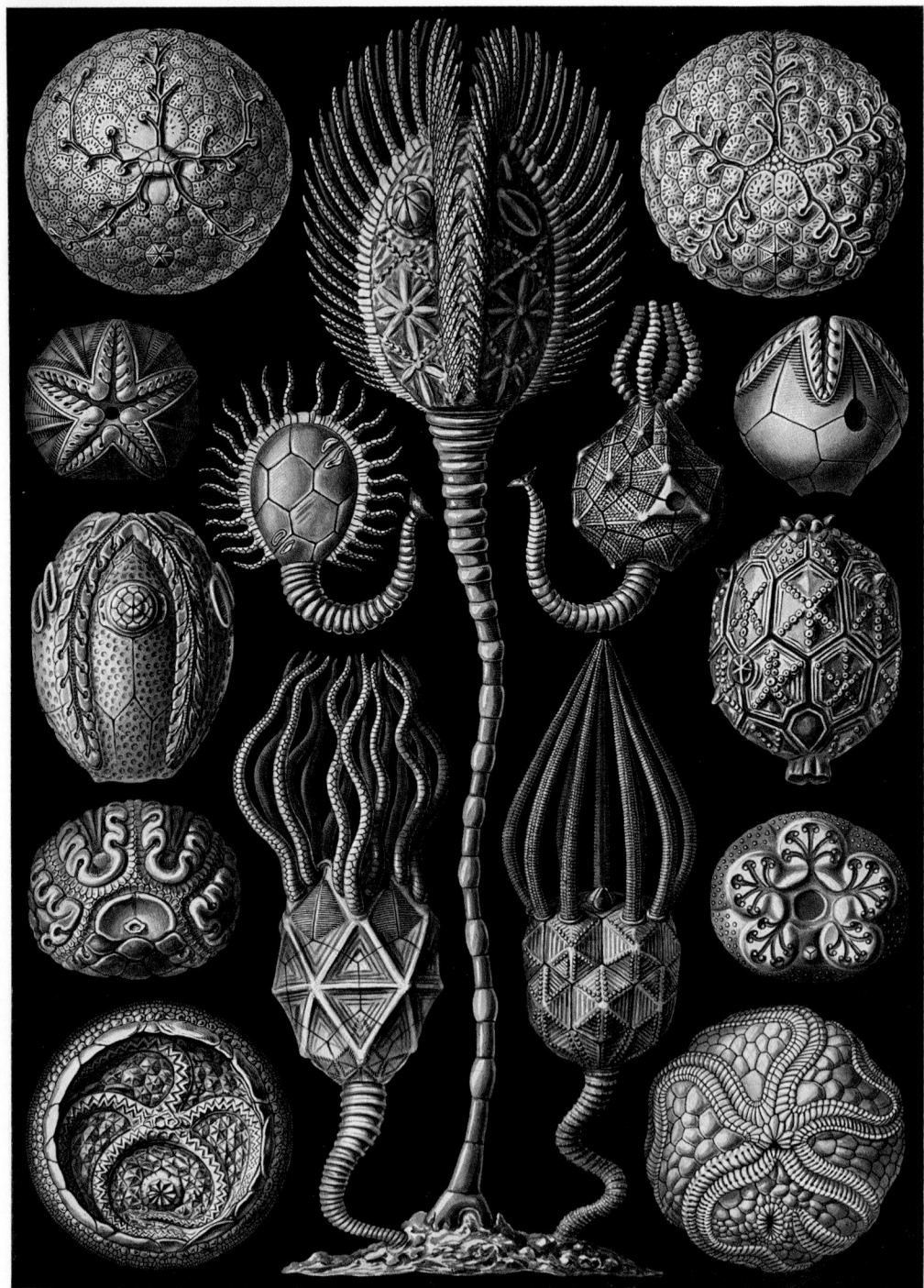

Cystoidea. — Beutelsterne.

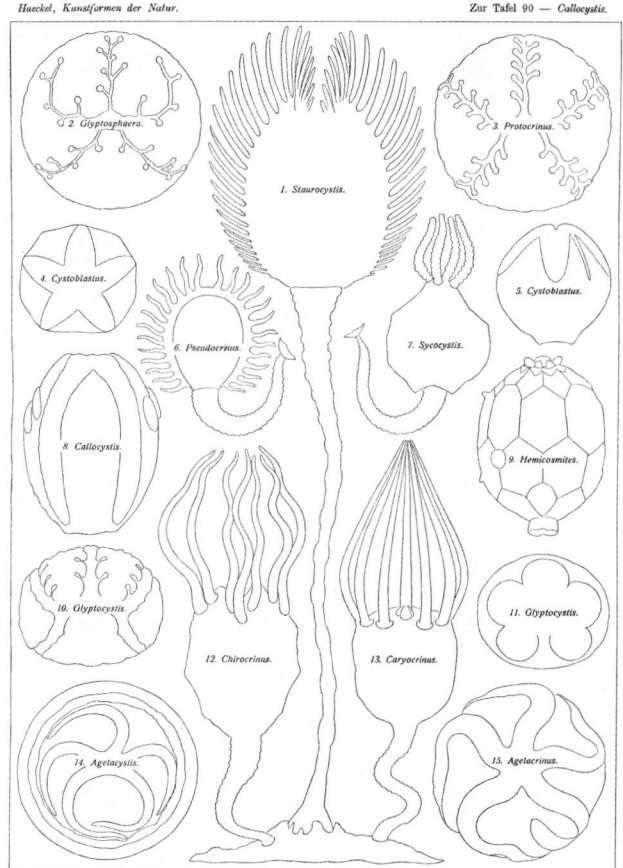

Haeckel, Kunstformen der Natur.　　　　　　　　Zur Tafel 90 — Callocystis.

PLATE 90
ECHINODERMATA – BLASTOIDEA
Echinoderms – Blastoids

1 Staurocystis quadrifasciata (HAECKEL) – *Staurocystis quadrifasciata* (PEARCE, 1843)
2 Glyptosphaera Leuchtenbergii (JOHANNES MÜLLER) – *Glyptosphaerites leuchtenbergi* (VOLBORTH, 1846)
3 Protocrinus fragum (EICHWALD) – *Protocrinites fragum* EICHWALD, 1860 | 4-5 Cystoblastus Leuchtenbergii
(VOLBORTH) – *Cystoblastus leuchtenbergi* VOLBORTH, 1867 | 6 Pseudocrinus bifasciatus (PEARCE) – *Pseudocrinites
bifasciatus* (PEARCE, 1843) | 7 Sycocystis angulosa (LEOPOLD BUCH) – *Echinoencrinites angulosus* (PANDER, 1830)
8 Callocystis Jewetti (HALL) – *Callocystites jewetti* HALL, 1852 | 9 Hemicosmites extraneus (EICHWALD) –
Hemicosmites extraneus EICHWALD, 1840 | 10 Glyptocystis multipora (BILLINGS) – *Glyptocystites multiporus*
BILLINGS, 1854 | 11 Glyptocystis pentapalma (HAECKEL) – *Glyptocystites* sp. | 12 Chirocrinus testudo (HAECKEL) –
Cheirocrinus testudo (nomen nudum) | 13 Caryocrinus ornatus (THOMAS SAY) – *Caryocrinites ornatus* SAY, 1825
14 Agelacystis hamiltonensis (HAECKEL) – *Agelacrinites hamiltonensis* VANUXEM, 1842
15 Agelacrinus vorticellatus (HALL) – *Streptaster vorticellatus* (HALL, 1866)

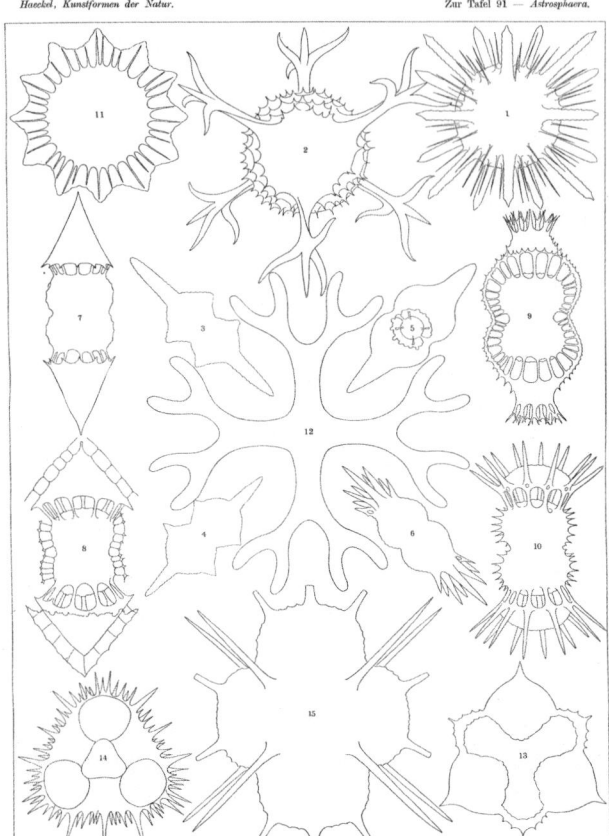

Haeckel, Kunstformen der Natur.   Zur Tafel 91 — Astrosphaera.

PLATE 91
RADIOLARIA – SPUMELLARIA
Radiolarians

1 Astrosphaera stellata (HAECKEL) – *Astrosphaera (Astrosphaeromma) stellata* HAECKEL, 1887 | 2 Hexancistra quadricuspis (HAECKEL) – *Hexancistra quadricuspis* (HAECKEL, 1887) | 3 Cannartidium mammiferum (HAECKEL) – *Cannartidessa mammiferum* HAECKEL, 1887 (synonym: *Didymocyrtis mammifera* (HAECKEL, 1887)) 4 Cannartidium mastophorum – *Cannartidium mastophorum* HAECKEL, 1887 | 5 Cannartiscus amphiconiscus (HAECKEL) – *Cannartiscus amphiconiscus* HAECKEL, 1887 | 6 Cyphinus amphilophus (HAECKEL) – *Cyphinus amphilophus* HAECKEL, 1887 | 7 Panartus diploconus (HAECKEL) – *Panartus diploconus* HAECKEL, 1887 8 Peripanartus amphiconus (HAECKEL) – *Peripanartus amphiconus* HAECKEL, 1887 | 9–10 Panicium coronatum (HAECKEL) – *Panicium coronatum* HAECKEL, 1887 | 11 Trochodiscus stellaris (HAECKEL) – *Trochodiscus stellaris* HAECKEL, 1887 | 12 Dicranastrum bifurcatum (HAECKEL) – *Tetracranastrum bifurcatum* (HAECKEL, 1887) (after ROSS) | 13 Archidiscus pyloniscus (HAECKEL) – *Archidiscus polyniscus* HAECKEL, 1887 14 Pylodiscus triangularis (HAECKEL) – *Polydiscus triangularis* HAECKEL, 1887 15 Tholoma metallasson (HAECKEL) – *Tholoma metallasson* HAECKEL, 1887

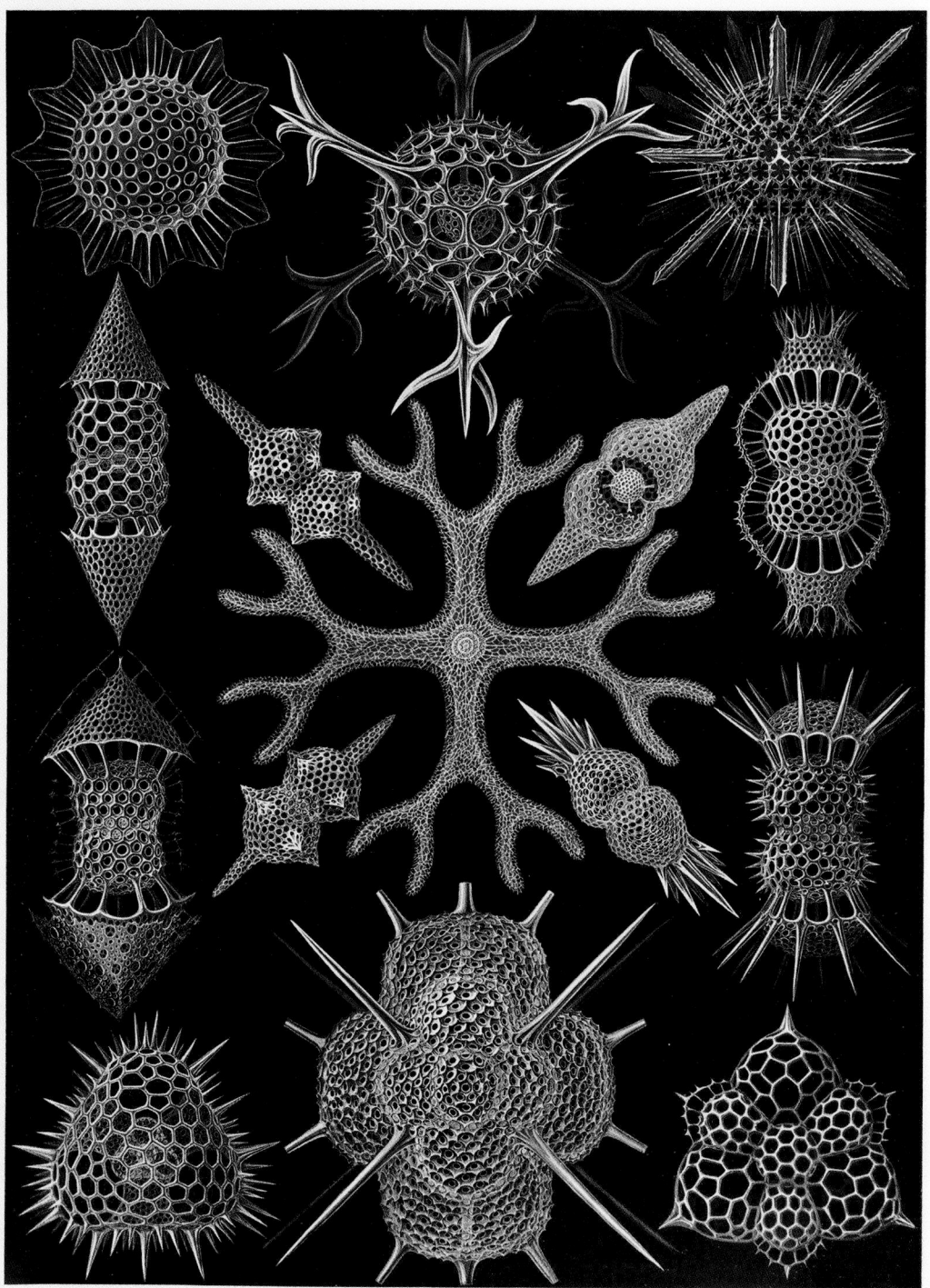

Spumellaria. — Schaumstrahlinge.

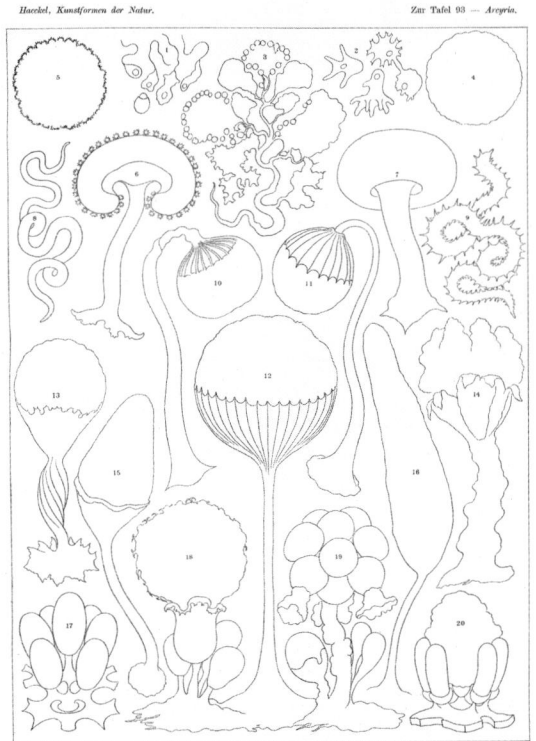

Haeckel, Kunstformen der Natur.   Zur Tafel 93 — Arcyria.

PLATE 93
MYCETOZOA
Slime Molds

1 Arcyria punicea (PERSOON) – *Arcyria denudata* (LINNAEUS) WETTSTEIN, 1886 (synonym: *Arcyria punicea* PERSOON)
2 Trichia varia (PERSOON) – *Trichia varia* (PERSOON EX J. F. GMELIN) | 3 Physarum plumbeum
(MICHELI) – *Badhamia panicea* (FRIES, 1873) | 4 Badhamia panicea (ROSTAFINSKI) – *Badhamia panicea*
(FRIES) ROSTAFINSKI | 5 Didymium nigripes (FRIES) – *Didymium nigripes* (LINK) FRIES 1829
6 Didymium farinaceum (SCHRADER) – *Didymium melanospermum* (PERSOON) T. MACBR., 1899
7 Lepidoderma tigrinum (ROSTAFINSKI) – *Lepidoderma tigrinum* (SCHRADER) ROSTAFINSKI 1873 | 8 Trichia fragilis
(ROSTAFINSKI) – *Trichia botrytis* (J. F. GMELIN) PERSOON, 1794 | 9 Arcyria serpula (MASSEE) – *Hemitrichia serpula*
(SCOPOLI) ROSTAFINSKI, 1873 Pretzel slime mold | 10 Dictydium cernuum (NEES) – *Cribraria cancellata* (BATSCH)
NANN.-BREMEK. 1975 | 11 Cribraria aurantiaca (SCHRADER) – *Cribraria aurantiaca* SCHRADER
12 Cribraria intricata (SCHRADER) – *Cribraria intricata* SCHRADER, 1797 | 13 Cribraria pyriformis (SCHRADER) –
Cribraria piriformis SCHRADER, 1797 | 14 Trichia verrucosa (LISTER) – *Trichia verrucosa* BERKELEY 1859 | 15 Arcyria
cinerea (PERSOON) – *Arcyria cinerea* (BULL.) PERSOON, 1801 | 16 Stemonitis fusca (ROTH) – *Stemonitis fusca*
ROTH, 1787 | 17 Physarum didermoides (ROSTAFINSKI) – *Physarum didermoides* (ACHARIUS EX PERSOON)
ROSTAFINSKI, 1874 (1875?) | 18 Arcyria incarnata (ROSTAFINSKI) – *Arcyria incarnata* (PERSOON EX J. F. GMELIN)
PERSOON, 1796 | 19 Trichia botrytis (PERSOON) – *Trichia botrytis* (J. F. GMELIN) PERSOON, 1794
20 Arcyria adnata (ROSTAFINSKI) – *Arcyria incarnata* (PERSOON EX J. F. GMELIN) PERSOON 1796

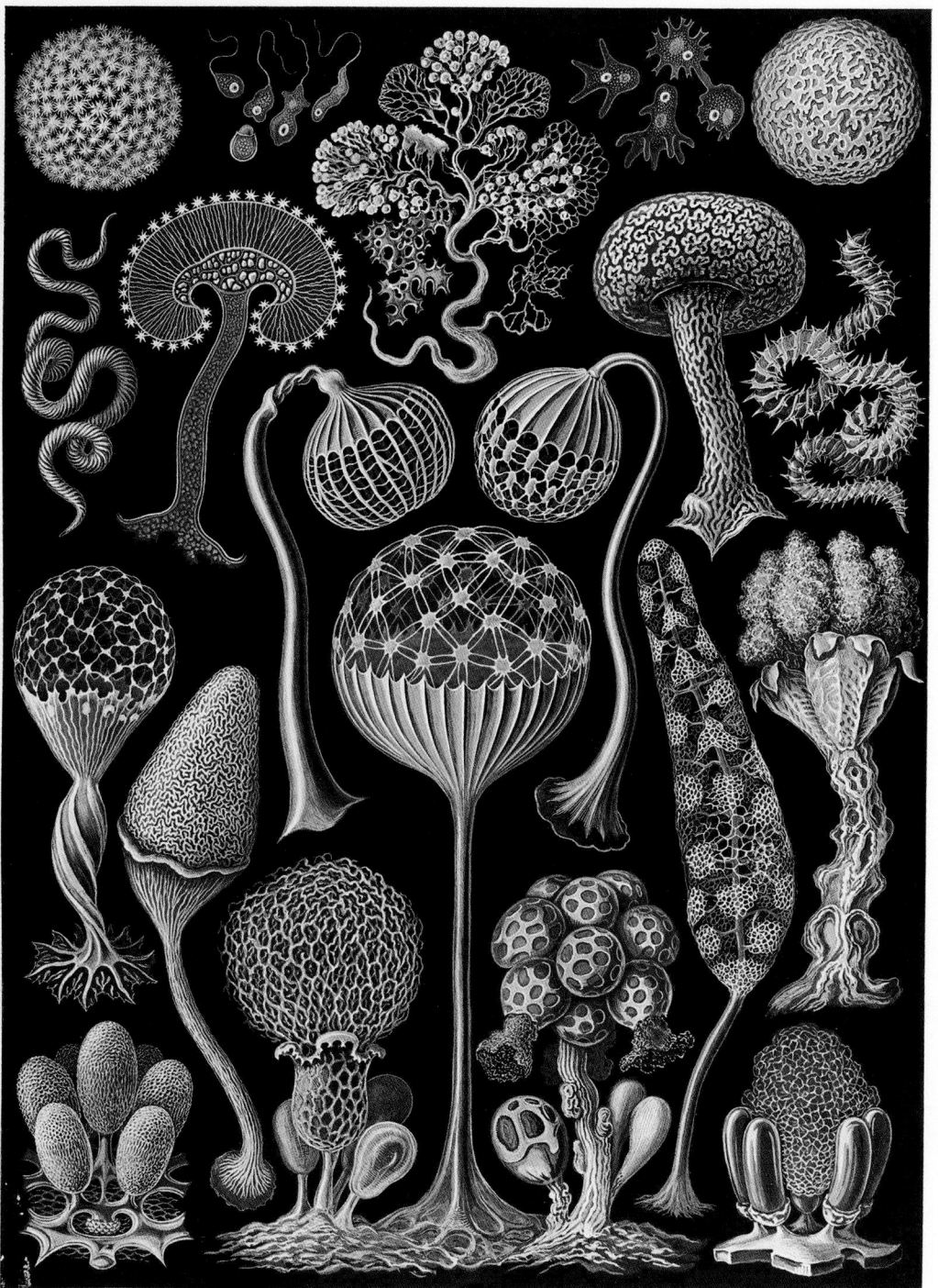

Mycetozoa. — Pilztiere.

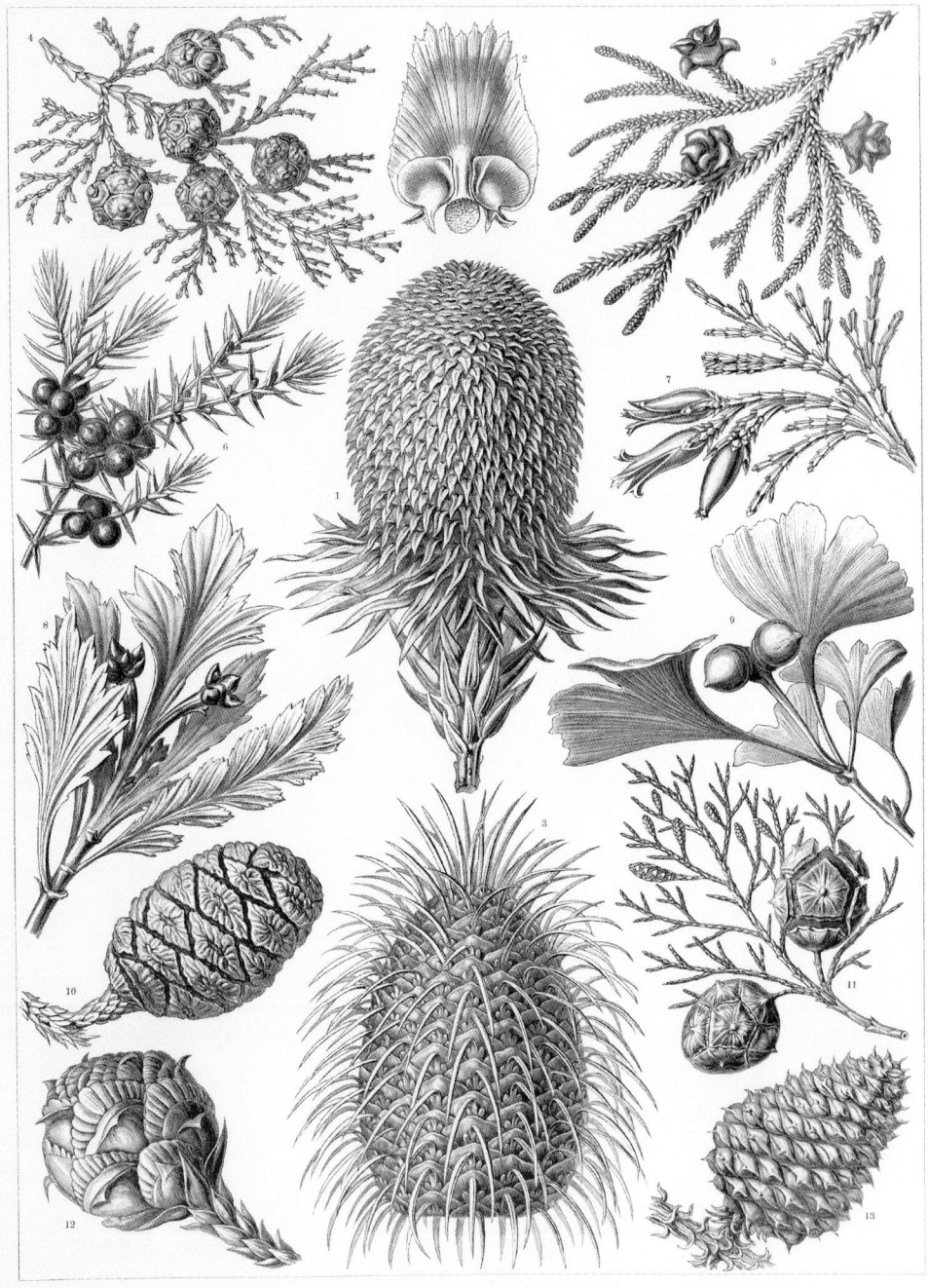

Coniferae. — Zapfenbäume.

PLATE 94
GYMNOSPERMAE
Gymnosperms

1 Araucaria brasiliana (LAMB) – *Araucaria angustifolia* (BERTOLONI) KUNTZE
Candelabra tree, Parana pine

2 Picea excelsa (LINK) – *Picea abies* (LINNAEUS, 1753) H. KARSTEN (synonym: *Picea excelsa* LAMARCK, 1778)
Common spruce, European spruce, Norway spruce

3 Abies bracteata (HOOKER) – *Abies bracteata* (D. DON) POITEAU
Bristlecone fir, Santa Lucia fir, Silver fir

4 Chamaecyparis obtusa (SIEBOLD) – *Chamaecyparis obtusa* (SIEBOLD & ZUCCARINI) ENDLICHER
Japanese cypress, Hinoki cypress

5 Thujopsis dolabrata (SIEBOLD) – *Thujopsis dolabrata* (THUNBERG EX LINNAEUS) SIEBOLD & ZUCCARINI
Hiba, Hiba aborvitae

6 Juniperus communis (LINNÉ) – *Juniperus communis* LINNAEUS, 1753
Common juniper, Ground juniper

7 Libocedrus decurrens (TORR) – *Calocedrus decurrens* (TORREY) FLORIN
Bastard cedar, California incense-cedar, California post cedar, White cedar

8 Phyllocladus rhomboidalis (RICHARD) – *Phyllocladus aspleniifolius* (LABILLARDIÈRE) HOOKER
Celery-top pine, Toatoa

9 Ginkgo biloba (LINNÉ) – *Ginkgo biloba* LINNAEUS, 1753
Ginkgo, Common ginkgo, Maidenhair tree ginkgo

10 Sequoya gigantea (TORR) – *Sequoiadendron giganteum* (LINDLEY) J. BUCHHOLZ
Bigtree, Giant sequoia, Giant redwood

11 Cupressus sempervirens (LINNÉ) – *Cupressus sempervirens* LINNAEUS, 1753
Mediterranean cypress, Uscan cypress, Graveyard cypress, Pencil pine

12 Taxodium distichum (RICHARD) – *Taxodium distichum* (LINNAEUS) RICH.
Bald cypress, Baldcypress, Gulf cypress, Red cypress

13 Pinus serotina (LINNÉ) – *Pinus serotina* MICHAUX
Pond pine, Marsh pine, Pocosin pine, Bay pine

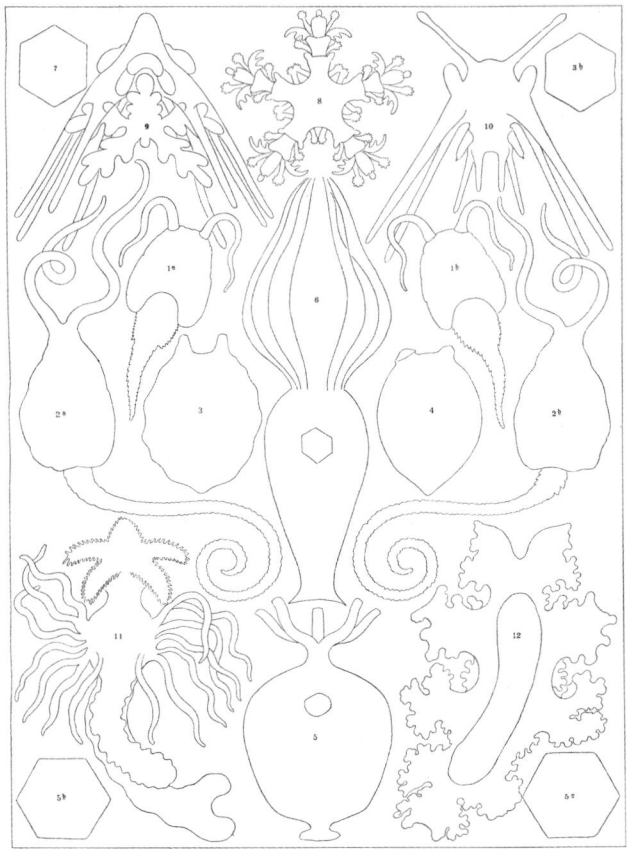

PLATE 95

ECHINODERMATA – AMPHOROIDEA

Echinoderms – Amphoroidea

1 Placocystis crustacea (HAECKEL) – *Enoploura balanoides* (MEEK, 1872) | 2 Pleurocystis filitexta (BILLINGS) – *Pleurocystites filitextus* BILLINGS 1854 | 3 Orocystis Helmhackeri (BARRANDE) – *Orocystites helmhackeri* (BARRANDE, 1887) | 4 Deutocystis modesta (BARRANDE) – *Echinosphaerites* cf. *modestus* (BARRANDE, 1887) 5 Citrocystis citrus (HAECKEL) – *Echinosphaerites citrus* (KLOEDEN, 1834 (non *E. citrus* HISINGER, 1837) (? synonym: *Echinosphaerites kloedeni* JAEKEL 1899) | 6 Acanthocystis briareus (BARRANDE) – *Acanthocystites briareus* BARRANDE, 1887 | 7 Aristocystis bohemicar (BARRANDE) – *Aristocystites bohemicus* BARRANDE, 1887 8 Ophiothrix fragilis (J. MÜLLER) – *Ophiothrix fragilis* (ABILDGAARD, 1789) Common brittle star | 9–12 Larvae 9 Pluteus bimaculatus (J. MÜLLER) – *Ophiura filiformis*, pluteus larva | 10 Plutellus aequituberculatus (J. MÜLLER) – *Arbacia lixula* (LINNAEUS, 1758) (synonym: *Echinocidaris aequituberculata* (BLAINVILLE, 1825), larva) Black sea urchin, Black urchin | 11 Bipinnaria asterigera (J. MÜLLER) – *Luidia sarsi* DÜBEN & KOREN, 1845, larva 12 Auricularia nudibranchiata (CHUN) – *Protankyra brychia* (VERRILL, 1885)

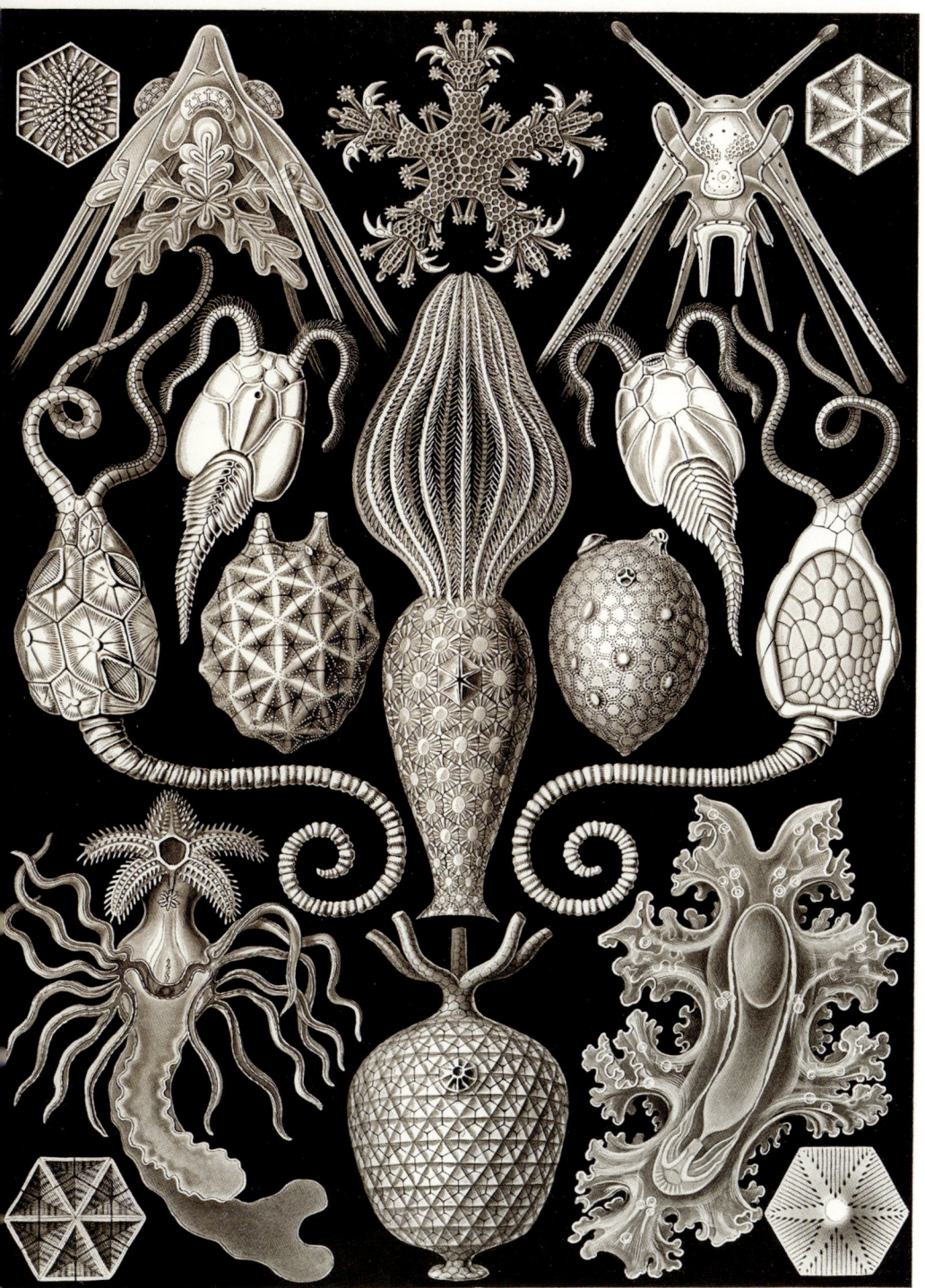

Amphoridea. — Urnensterne.

PLATE 96
ANNELIDA
Segmented worms, Annelids

1 Sabella spectabilis (GRUBE) – *Sabellastarte spectabilis* (GRUBE, 1878)
(Indian) Feather duster worm, Feather duster
2 Serpula contortuplicata (LINNÉ) – *Serpula vermicularis* LINNÉ, 1767
Calcareous tubeworm, Fan worm, Plume worm, Red tube worm
3 Spirographis Spallanzanii (VIVIANI) – *Sabella spallanzanii* (GMELIN, 1791)
Mediterranean fan worm, Feather duster worm, The European fan worm
4 Terebella emmalina (QUATREFAGES) – *Pista cretacea* (GRUBE, 1860)
5 Eunice magnifica (QUATREFAGES) – *Eunice magnifica* GRUBE, 1866
6 Hermione hystricella (QUATREFAGES) – *Hermione hystricella* MILNE-EDWARDS, 1836
7 Chloëia euglochis (EHLERS) – *Chloëia viridis* SCHMARDA, 1861

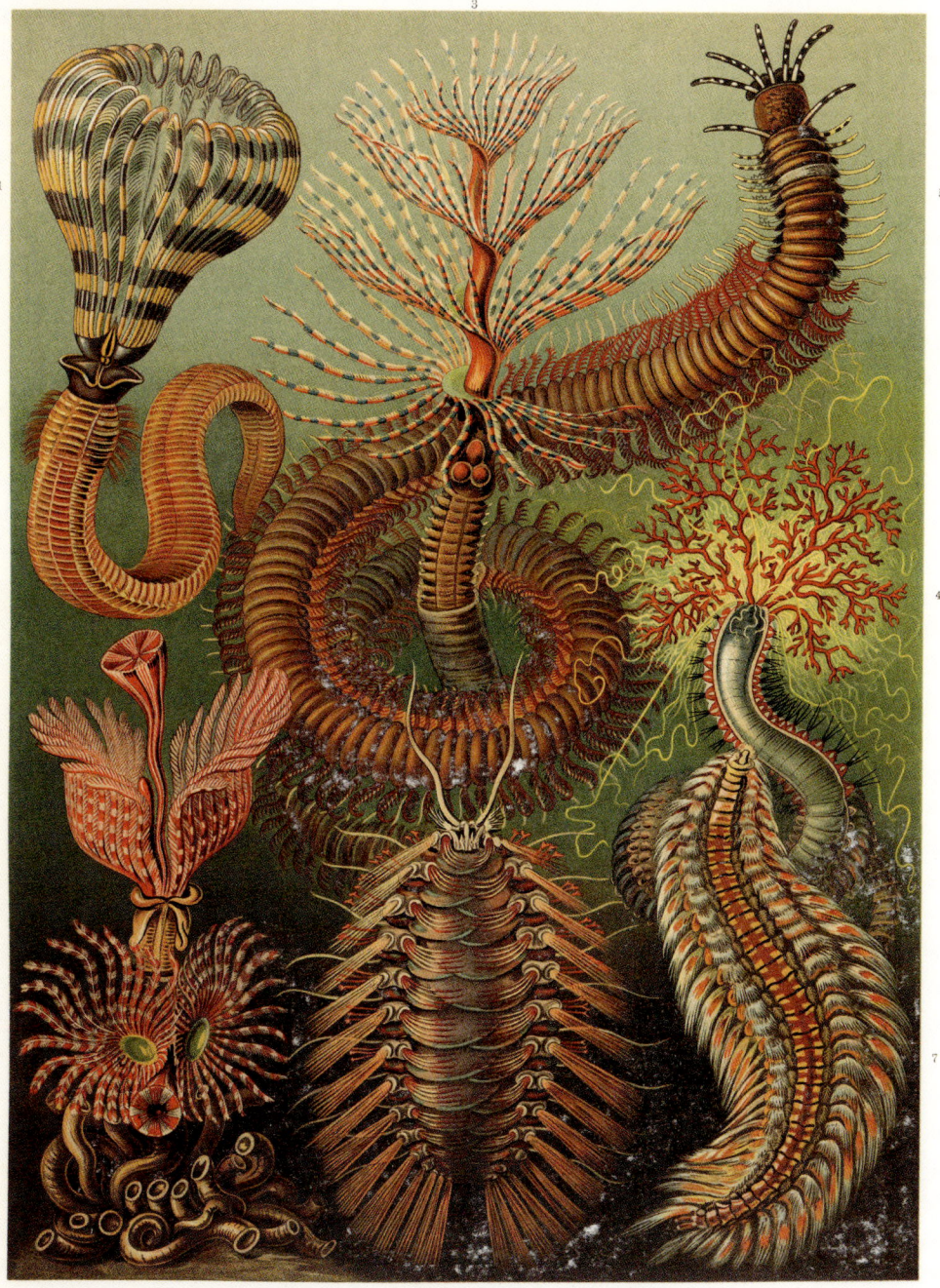

Chaetopoda. — Borstenwürmer.

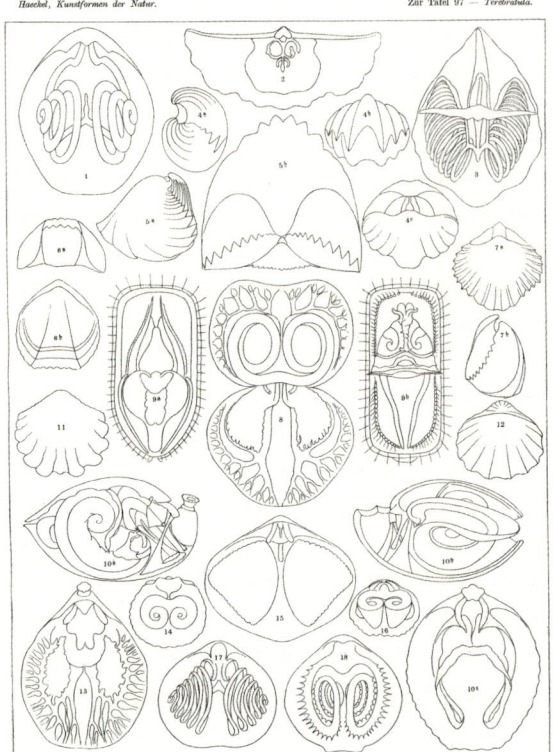

Haeckel, Kunstformen der Natur.   Zur Tafel 97 — Terebratula.

PLATE 97
BRACHIOPODA
Lamp shells, Brachiopods

1 Dayia navicula (SOWERBY) – *Dayia navicula* (J. DE C. SOWERBY, 1837) | 2 Strophonema rhomboidalis (WILCKENS) – *Leptaena rhomboidalis* (WILCKENS, 1769) | 3 Cyrtina heteroclita (SCHLOTHEIM) – *Cyrtina heteroclita* (DEFRANCE, 1824) | 4 Spirifer gibbosus (BARRANDE) –*Ivanothyris gibbosus* (BARRANDE, 1879) (synonym: *Delthyris gibbosus* (BARRANDE, 1879)) | 5 Rhynchonella nympha (BARRANDE) – *Stenorhynchia nympha* (BARRANDE, 1847) | 6 Rhynchonella eucharis (BARRANDE) – *Eucharitina eucharis* (BARRANDE, 1847) | 7 Rhynchonella inaurita (SANDBERGER) – *Rhynchonella inaurita* (SANDBERGER & SANDBERGER, 1856) | 8 Rhynchonella psittacea (DAVIDSON) – *Hemithiris psittacea* (GMELIN, 1790) | 9 Lingula anatina (LAMARCK) – *Lingula anatina* LAMARCK, 1801 | 10 Terebratula flavescens (LAMARCK) = Waldheimia australis (DAVIDSON) –*Magellania flavescens* (LAMARCK, 1819) | 11 Atrypa insolita (BARRANDE) – *Eospinatrypa insolita* (BARRANDE, 1879) | 12 Rhynchonella oblita (BARRANDE) – *Rostricellula ambigena* (BARRANDE, 1847) | 13 Terebratulina serpentis (D'ORBIGNY) – *Terebratulina retusa* (LINNAEUS, 1758) 14 Terebratulina Murrayi (DAVIDSON) – *Eucalathis murrayi* (DAVIDSON, 1878) | 15 Spirigerina concentrica (D'ORBIGNY) –*Athyris concentrica* (VON BUCH, 1834) | 16 Rhynchonella nigricans (FISCHER) – *Notosaria nigricans* (SOWERBY, 1846) (after ROSS) | 17 Nucleospira pisum (SOWERBY) – *Nucleospira pisum* (J. DE C. SOWERBY, 1839) 18 Atrypa marginata (DALMAN) – *Spirigerina marginalis* (DALMAN, 1828)

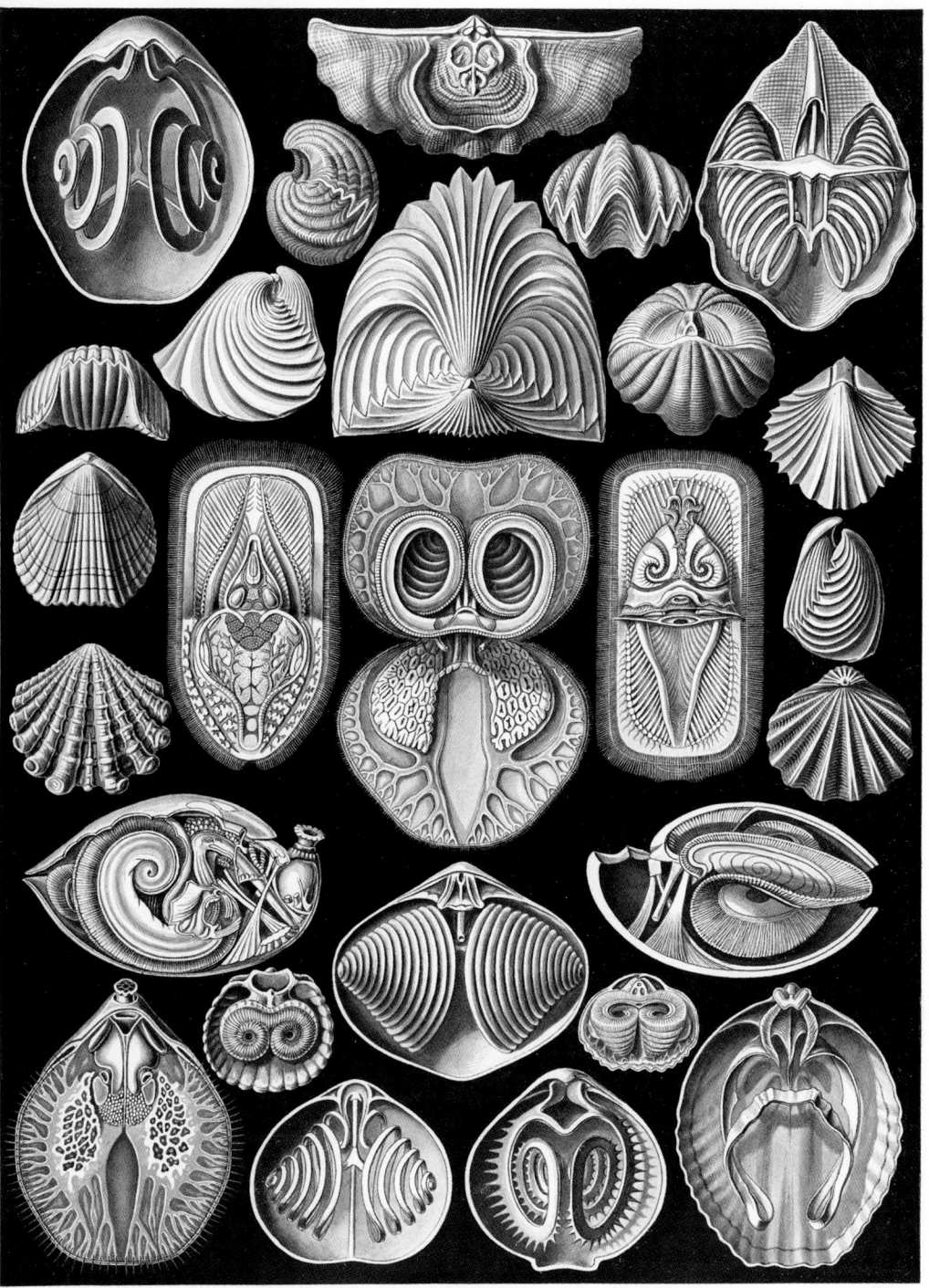

Spirobranchia. — Spiralkiemer.

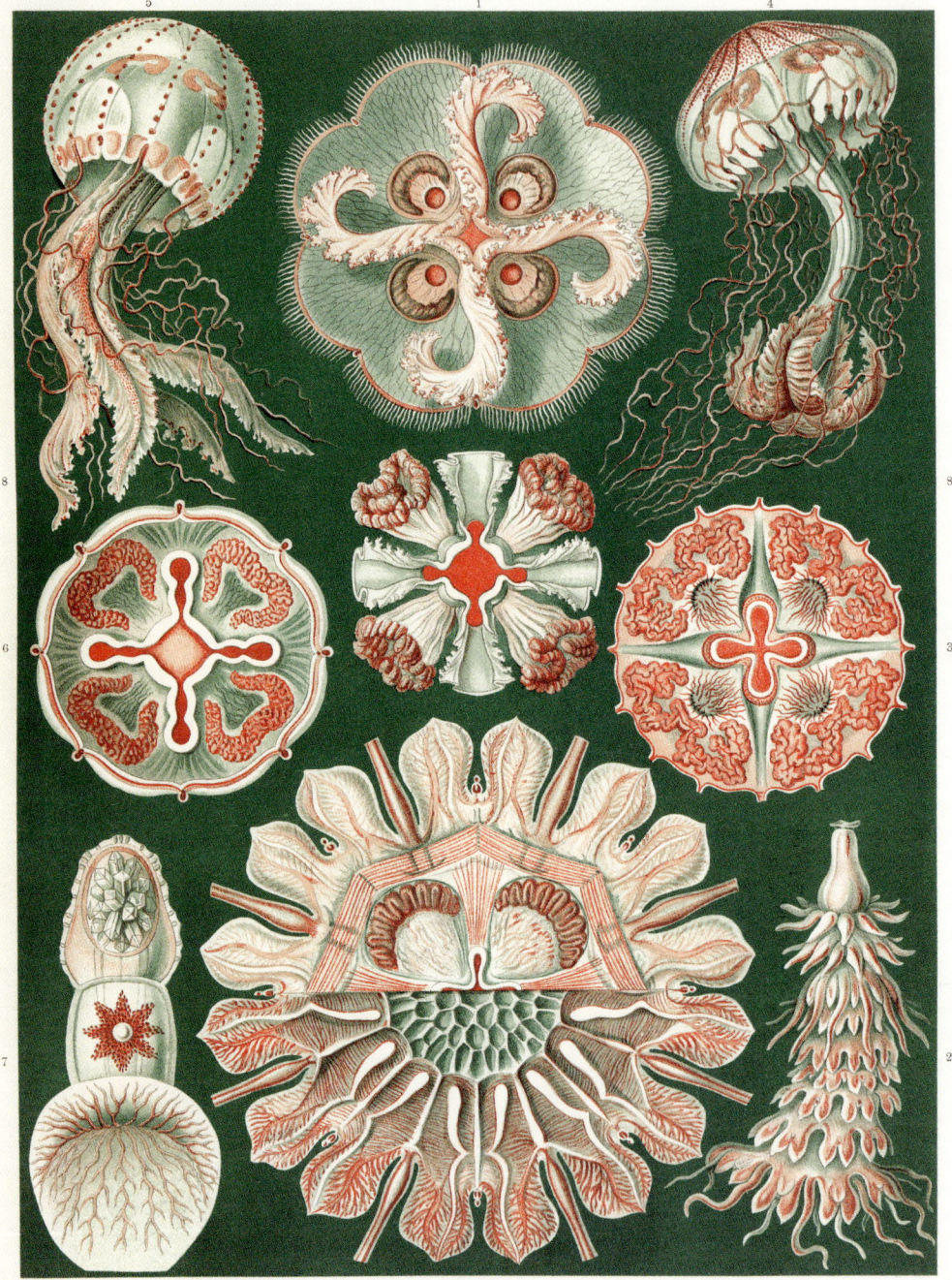

Discomedusae. — Scheibenquallen.

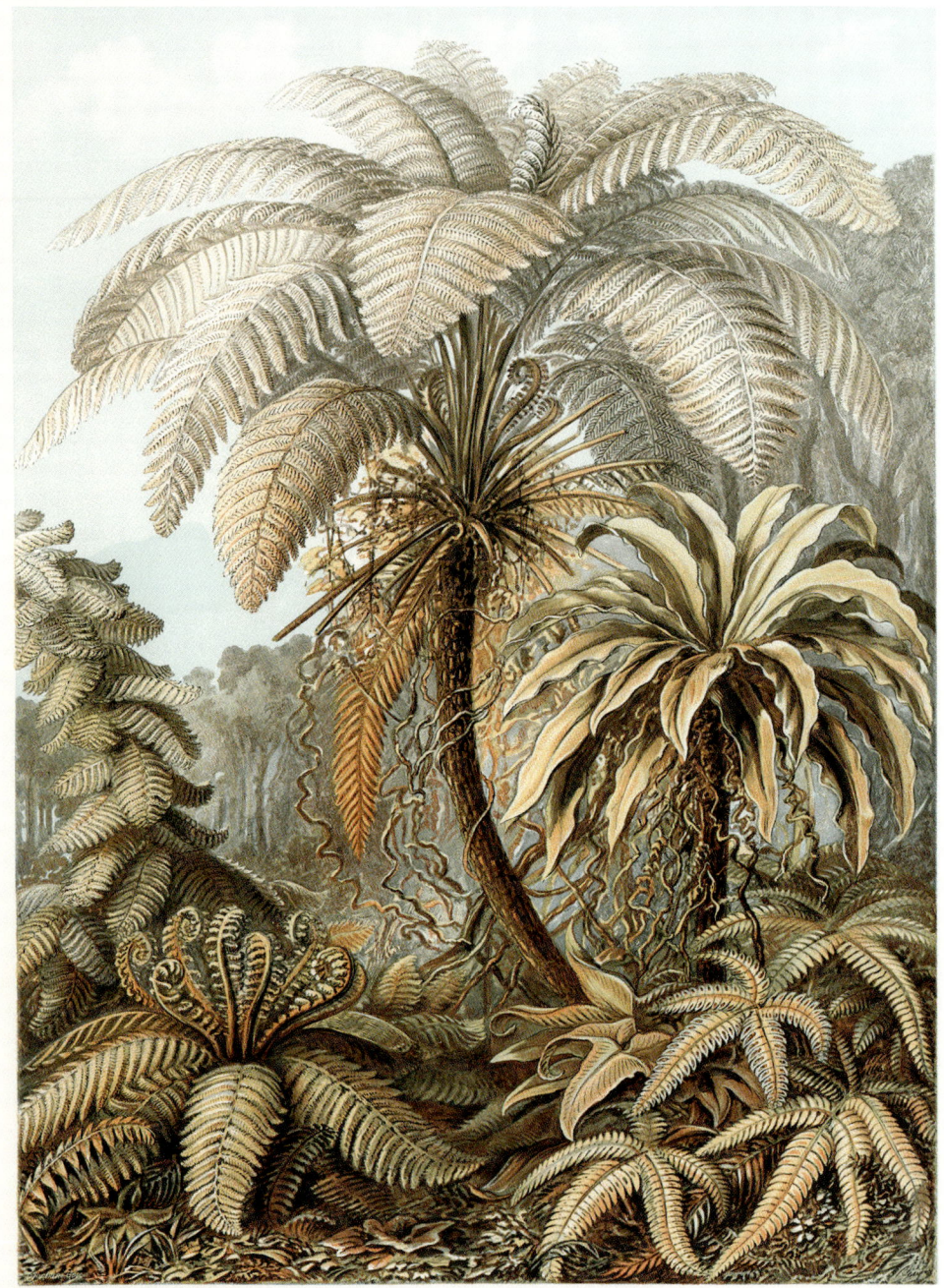

Filicinae. — Laubfarne.

PLATE 92
POLYPODIALES
Polypodiales

1 (centre) **Alsophila** – *Alsophila* sp. Alsophila
2 (centre left) **Polypodium** – *Polypodium* sp. Common ferns, Litorice ferns
3 (centre right) **Asplenium nidus** – *Asplenium nidus* LINNAEUS Bird's nest fern, Hawai'i birdnest fern
4 (bottom left) **Angiopteris** – *Angiopteris* sp.
5 (bottom left, below) **Monogramma** – *Monogramma* sp. Maidenhairs, Shoelace ferns
6 (bottom right) **Pteris quadriaurita** – *Pteris quadriaurita* RETZ.

479

PLATE 100

MAMMALIA – ARTIODACTYLA
Mammals – Artiodactyls

1 Tetraceros quadricornis (BLAINVILLE) – *Tetracerus quadricornis* (BLAINVILLE, 1816)
Four-horned antelope

2 Catoblepas gnu (SUNDEVALL) – *Connochaetes gnou* (ZIMMERMANN, 1780)
Wildebeest, Gnu, Black wildebeest, White-tailed gnu

3 Tragelaphus gratus (SCLATER) – *Tragelaphus spekii gratus* P. L. SCLATER, 1880
Sitatunga, Marshbuck sitatunga

4 Antilocapra americana (OWEN) (= Antilope furcifera (SMITH)) – *Antilocapra americana* ORD, 1815
Pronghorn, Prong buck, Pronghorn antelope

5 Antilope ellipsiprymna (GRAY) = Cervicapra ellipsiprymna (SUNDEVALL) –
Kobus ellipsiprymnus (OGILBY, 1833) Waterbuck

6 Hippotragus niger (HARRIS) – *Hippotragus niger* HARRIS, 1838 Sable antelope

7 Addax nasomacultus (GRAY) – *Addax nasomaculatus* (BLAINVILLE, 1816)
Addax, White antelope, Screwhorn antelope

8 Tragelaphus kudu (GRAY) (= Antilope strepsiceros (PALLAS)) –
Tragelaphus (STREPSICEROS) strepsiceros (PALLAS, 1766) Greater kudu

9 Tragelaphus scriptus (SUNDEVALL) = Antilope maculata (PALLAS) –
Tragelaphus scriptus PALLAS, 1766 Bushbuck

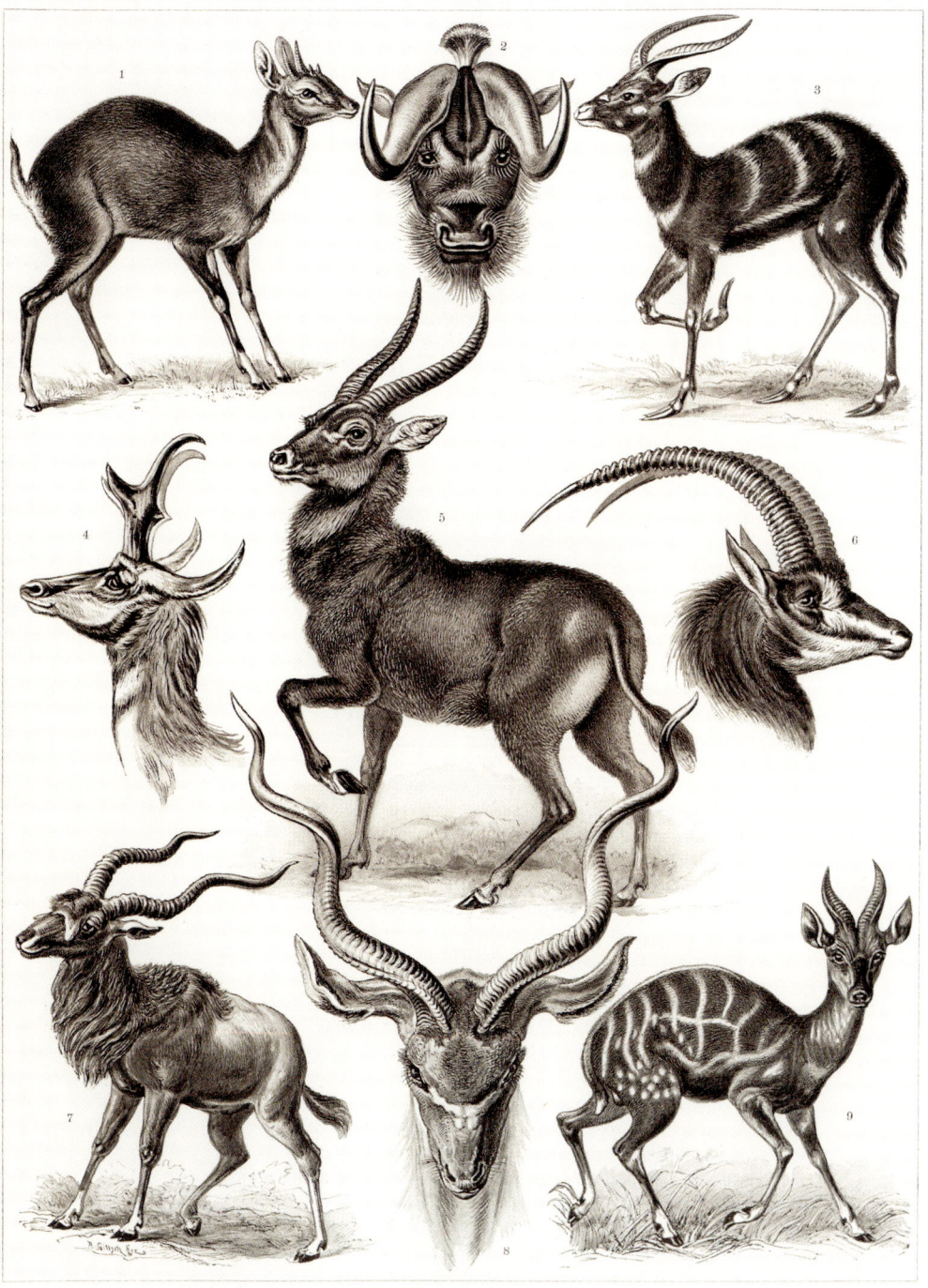

Antilopina. — Antilopen.

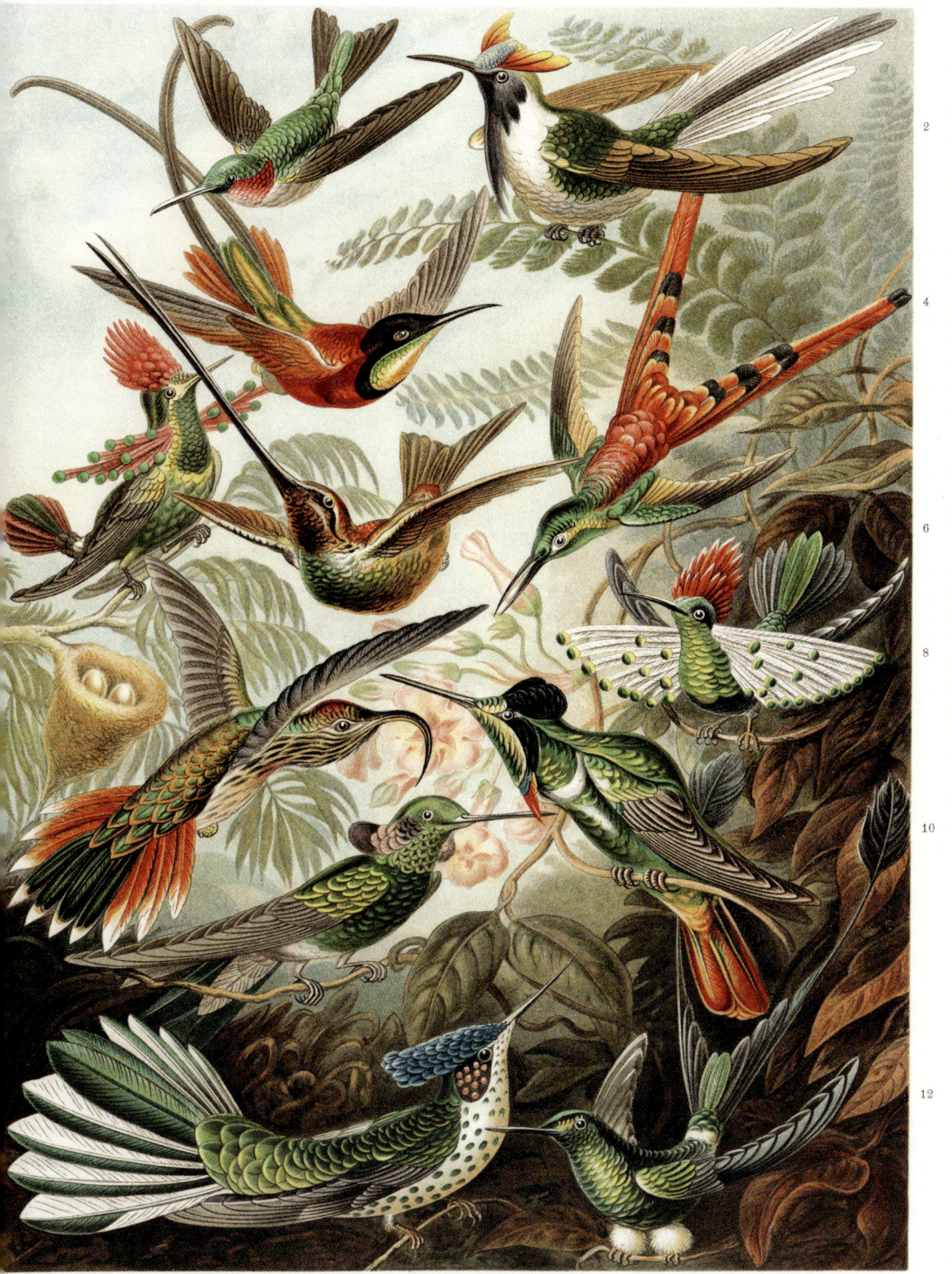

Trochilidae. — Kolibris.

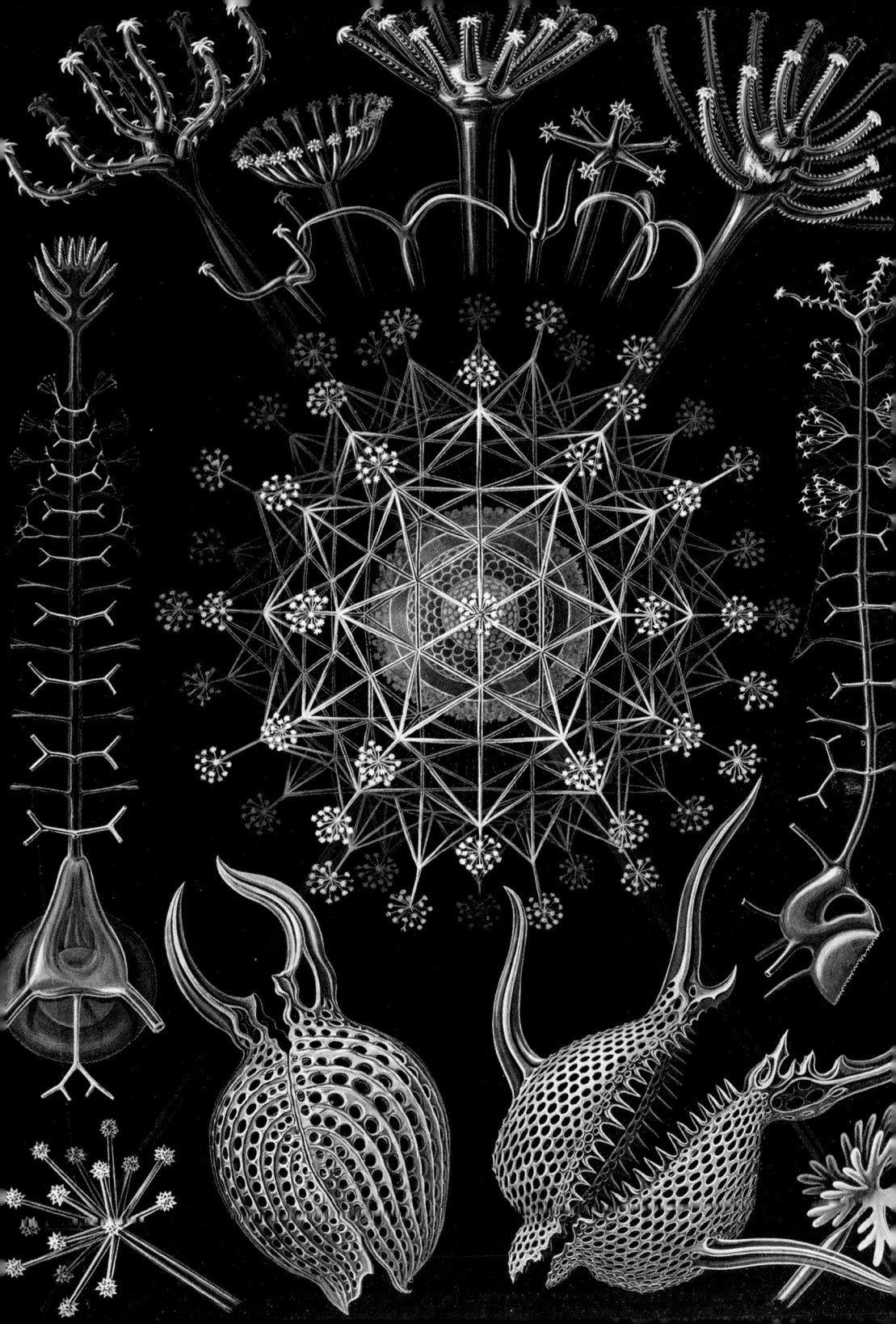

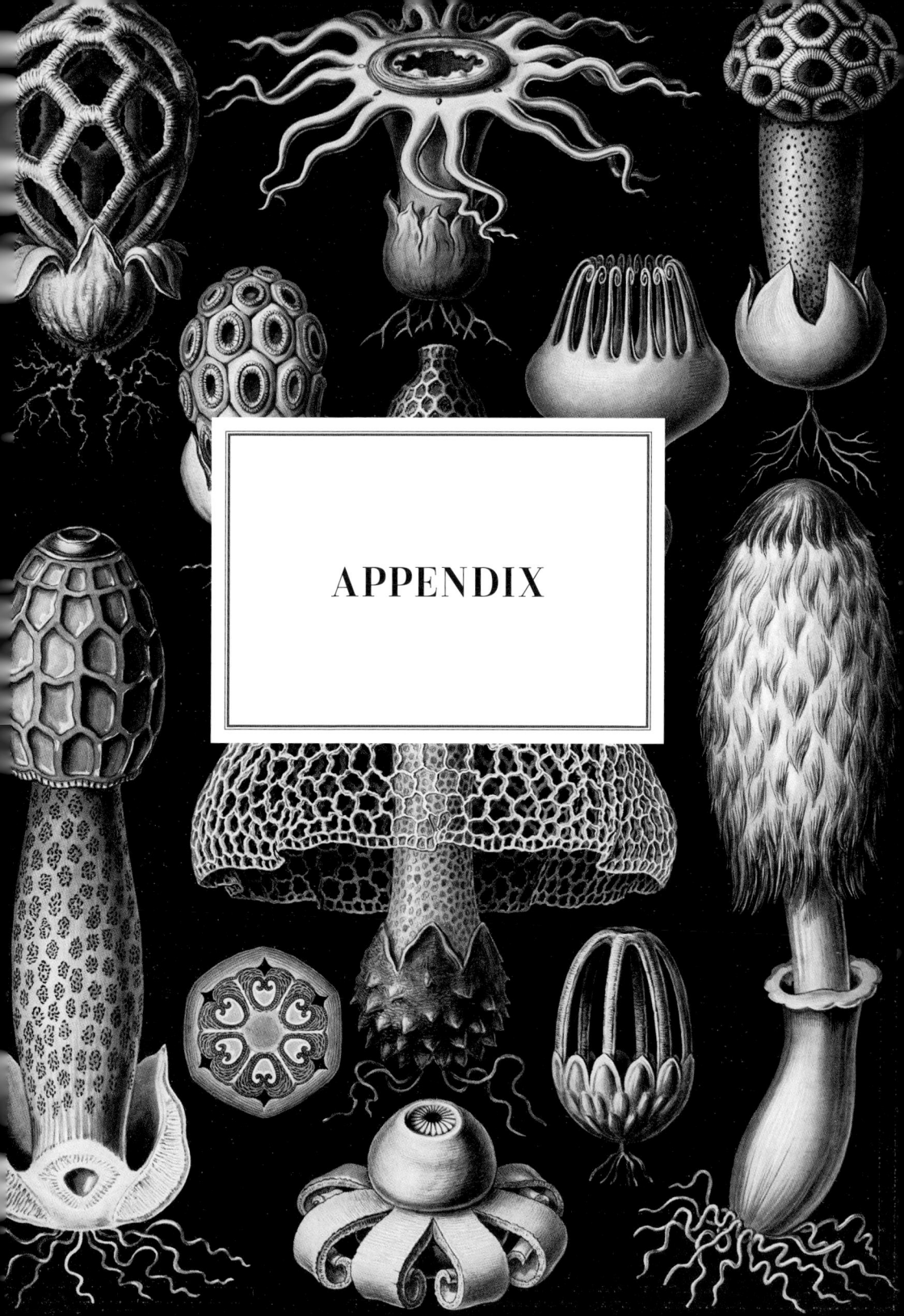

APPENDIX

BIOGRAPHY

1834 Ernst Haeckel is born in Potsdam on 16 February, son of the Prussian government official Carl Gottlob Haeckel and his wife Charlotte (née Sethe).

1835 The Haeckel family moves south to Merseburg, a small town near Halle.

1852 After successfully completing his high school education in Merseburg, Ernst Haeckel embarks on studies of Medicine in Berlin, in his second semester transferring to Würzburg, where he attends lectures given, and takes courses taught by Albert von Kölliker, Rudolf Virchow and Franz von Leydig.

1854 Haeckel continues his studies in Berlin. He becomes a pupil of the highly regarded physiologist Johannes Müller. During a stay on the North Sea island of Heligoland, Haeckel first becomes attracted to marine biology.

1855 Haeckel's first published work appears: *Über die Eier der Scomberesoces* (On the Eggs of the Scomberesocidae), concerning a particular category of bony fish. During the summer semester he returns to Würzburg to study.

1856 Haeckel is appointed assistant to the leading pathologist Rudolf Virchow. In autumn he takes part in a marine biological research trip to Nice, in the South of France, led by Albert von Kölliker.

1857 Haeckel qualifies as a medical doctor at the Medical Faculty of Berlin University, with a dissertation on the histology of the river crab, written in Latin as was then still required: *De telis quibusdam astaci fluviatilis.* Haeckel then spends the summer semester studying in Vienna.

1858 At Berlin University Haeckel passes the Prussian state's own medical examination. He receives formal accreditation permitting him to practise as a physician, specialising in obstetrics and the treatment of wounds. He opens his own medical practice. His teacher Johannes Müller dies on 28 April. On 14 September Haeckel becomes engaged to his cousin Anna Sethe.

1859–1860 Haeckel makes a research trip to Italy in order to study radiolaria (mono-cellular marine organisms) in Messina, Sicily. Travelling through France on his return to Germany, he visits Paris (in particular the Louvre) and Versailles.

Ernst Haeckel with his assistant,
Nicholas Miklouho-Maclay, on Lanzarote 1866/67

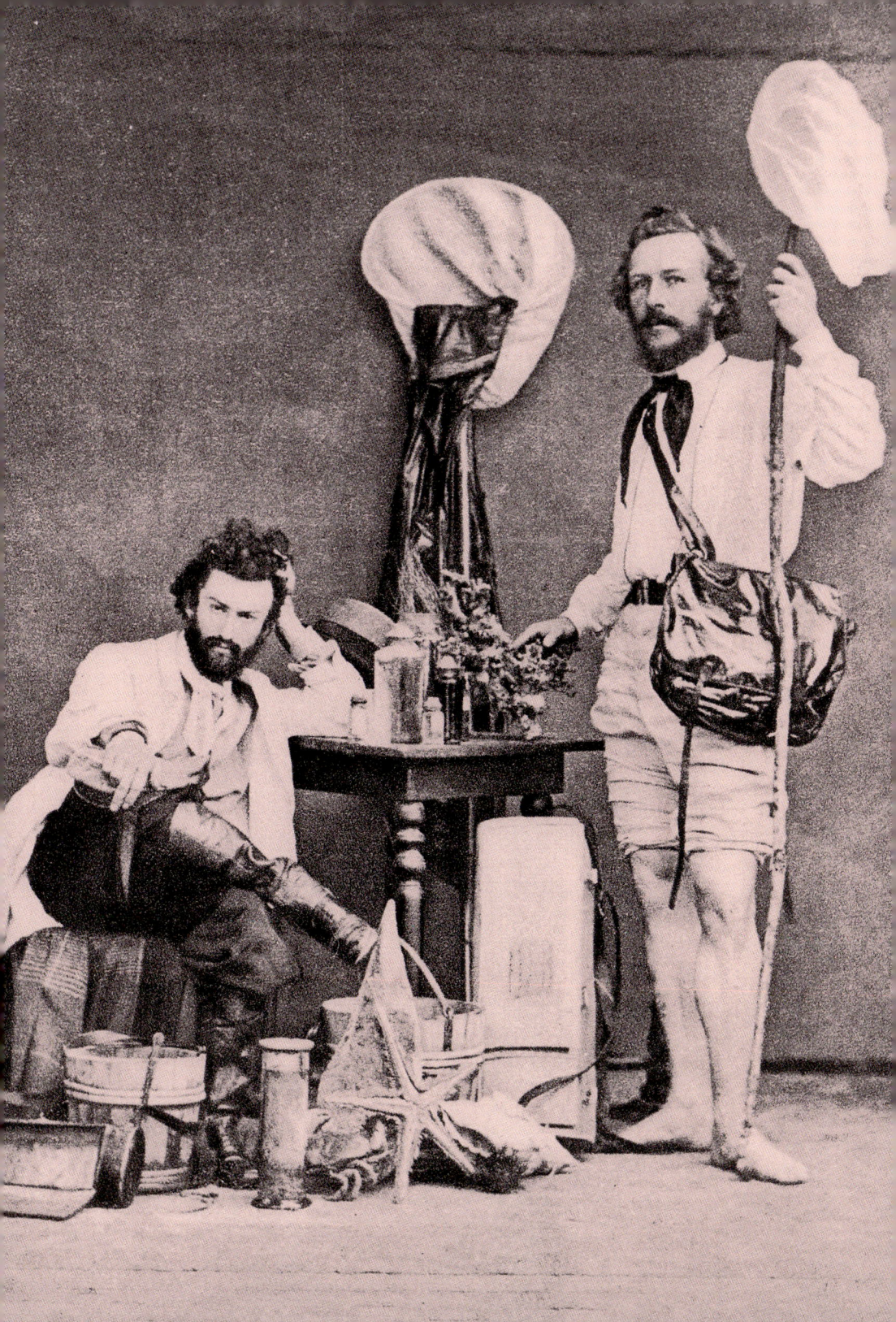

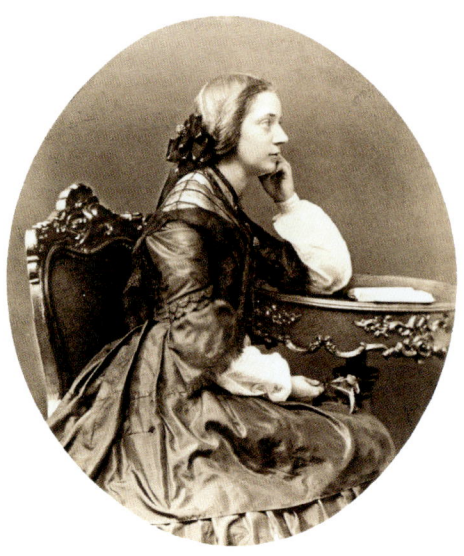

Anna Sethe, Haeckel's first wife, *c.* 1855

Prior to this trip he has, for the first time, entered into negotiations regarding an academic teaching post in Jena. He also toys with the notion of becoming a landscape painter. He reads, with great enthusiasm, the first German translation of Charles Darwin's *On the Origin of Species*.

1861 Haeckel obtains his *Habilitation* at the Medical Faculty at Jena University with a text on the form and taxonomy of marine radiolaria: *De rhizopodum finibus et ordinibus*.

1862 The first volume of Haeckel's study of radiolarian, *Die Radiolarien (Rhizopoda Radiaria)*, is published. (The second volume will follow 25 years later, and the third and fourth in 1888.) Haeckel is appointed Associate Professor in the Medical Faculty at Jena University. On 18 August he marries Anna Sethe in Berlin.

1863 At the Thirty-Eighth Reunion of German Natural Scientists in Stettin [now Szczecin, Poland], Haeckel gives a lecture "On Darwin's Theory of Evolution" ("Über die Entwicklungstheorie Darwins"), in which he unambiguously declares himself a champion of Darwin's ideas.

1864 On 16 February, Haeckel's thirtieth birthday, his wife, Anna, dies. On the very same day he is awarded the Cothenius Medal by the Academia Leopoldina, the German Academy of Sciences, in acknowledgement of his achievements in scientific research.

1865 Haeckel is appointed first Full Professor of Zoology at Jena University.

1866–1867 Haeckel publishes his *Generelle Morphologie der Organismen* (General Morphology of Organisms). This includes the first detailed elaboration of a diagrammatic stem tree of life forms. On a trip to the Canary Islands Haeckel passes through England, where in November he meets Charles Darwin for the first time.

1867 On 20 August Haeckel marries Agnes Huschke, daughter of the former Professor of Anatomy and Physiology at Jena University.

1868 In publishing *Natürliche Schöpfungsgeschichte* (*The History of Creation*, 1876), Haeckel seeks to reach a broader readership for the ideas put forward in his *General Morphology*. In September his son, Walter, is born.

1869 Haeckel travels to Norway, where he undertakes research into calcareous sponges.

1871 In January Haeckel's first daughter, Elisabeth, is born. In order to further pursue his research into calcareous sponges, Haeckel travels to Dalmatia. He is invited to take up the Chair of Zoology at Vienna University, but he declines this offer.

1872 Haeckel publishes a three-volume work on calcareous sponges, in which his notion of a fundamental "biogenetic law" ("*biogenetisches Grundgesetz*") is formulated.

1873 During his first trip to the Middle East, Haeckel undertakes a study of coral reefs in the Red Sea. In October his second daughter, Emma, is born.

1874 Haeckel publishes *Anthropogenie oder Entwickelungsgeschichte des Menschen* (*The Evolution of Man: a Popular Exposition of the Principal Points of Human Ontogeny and Phylogeny*, 1879), in which he applies the methods evolved in his *General Morphology* to humanity as a species. In lectures and in an essay he presents his theory that all multi-cellular life forms ultimately derive from a single organism.

1875 Haeckel undertakes a research trip to Corsica and Sardinia.

1876 Haeckel gives lectures on the Theory of Evolution in numerous German cities. He reports on his recent first trip to the Middle East in the volume *Arabische Korallen* (Arabian Corals). He becomes Vice-Chancellor of Jena University. In September he again visits Darwin in England.

1877 Haeckel makes a research trip to the island of Corfu. A lecture he gives at the Fiftieth Reunion of German Scientists and Physicians in Munich, in which he underlines the fundamental significance of the Theory of Evolution for teaching in schools, gives rise to a bitter dispute with his former teacher Rudolf Virchow.

1878 Haeckel carries out marine biological research off the Atlantic coast of Brittany, France.

1879 Haeckel publishes the first volume of his *Monographie der Medusen* (Monograph on the Medusae). (The second volume will appear two years later.) In September he again visits Darwin in England.

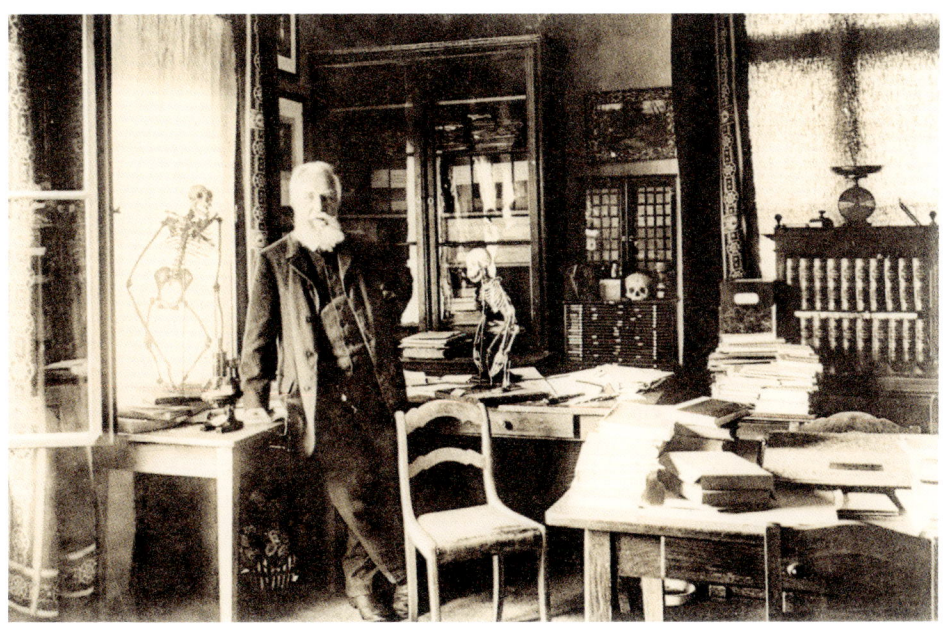

Ernst Haeckel in his working room, 1907

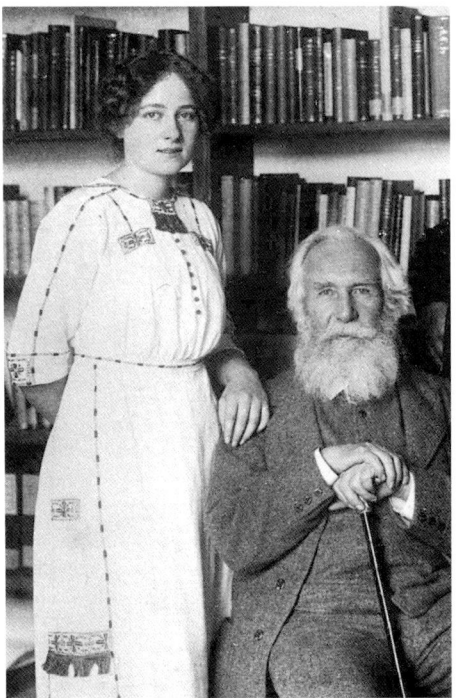

**Ernst Haeckel with his granddaughter,
Else Meyer,** 1916, Jena, Ernst-Haeckel-Haus

1881–1882 Haeckel undertakes his first research trip in the Tropics, visiting India and Ceylon (now Sri Lanka).

1882–1883 Charles Darwin dies on 19 April. In Jena a Zoological Institute is established at the University. Haeckel also has a house for himself built in the city, contributing to its design and decoration. He calls it "Villa Medusa."

1884 In the winter semester Haeckel is again appointed Vice-Chancellor at Jena University. He receives an Honorary Doctorate from Edinburgh University.

1887 Haeckel's English text *Report on the Radiolaria Collected by H.M.S. Challenger* is published.

Haeckel embarks on a research trip to Palestine, Syria, and Asia Minor. A year later he will publish his *Report on the Siphonophorae.*

1889 Haeckel finishes work on his own proposed grouping of the new life forms discovered during the earlier (1872–76) British deep-sea expedition by H.M.S. *Challenger.*

1890 Haeckel travels to Algeria in order to complete his studies on the Mediterranean.

1892 Haeckel gives a lecture on "Monismus als Band zwischen Religion und Wissenschaft" (Monism as the Link between Religion and Science).

1894 Haeckel is awarded the Linné Medal, the highest honour bestowed by the Linnean Society of London.

1894–1896 Haeckel's *Systematische Phylogenie* (Systematic Phylogeny) is published.

1897 Haeckel travels through southern Finland en route to Saint Petersburg, in order to take part in the Seventh International Geologists' Congress. He subsequently travels through Russia. In Moscow he greatly enjoys a visit to the collection of paintings by Russian artists assembled by Pavel Tretyakov (the future Tretyakov Gallery).

1898 Haeckel receives an Honorary Doctorate from Cambridge University, where he gives a lecture: "On our Present Knowledge of the Origin of Man." He meets Frida von Uslar-Gleichen, a woman thirty years his junior, with whom he maintains an amorous friendship for six years. In December 1903 Frida dies all too young – she had overdosed on morphine.

1899 In his volume *Die Welträthsel* (*The Riddle of the Universe*, 1934) Haeckel advances a monist point of view. The book is translated into about 30 languages, the German edition itself selling over 400,000 copies.

1899–1904 Haeckel's *Kunstformen der Natur* (*Art Forms in Nature*, 1974) is published in a series of ten instalments, each comprising ten plates of illustrations.

1900 Haeckel is awarded the Darwin Medal by the Royal Society in London.

1900–1901 Haeckel embarks on his second research trip to the Tropics, visiting Ceylon and Singapore, then travelling on to Java and Sumatra.

1901 Haeckel publishes an account of his travels in Malaya in the volume *Aus Insulinde. Malayische Reisebriefe* (From Insulinde: Letters from a Journey through Malaya).

1904 As a supplement to his earlier volume on *The Riddle of the Universe*, Haeckel publishes *Die Lebenswunder. Gemeinverständliche Studien über Biologische Philosophie* (The Marvel of Life. A Layman's Introduction to Biological Philosophy). In September he attends the International Congress of Free-Thinkers in Rome. According to his own record of this event, he is acclaimed as an "Anti-Pope" by over 2000 participants in the ruins of the Palatine.

1905 Haeckel publishes a volume of his own work as an artist: *Ernst Haeckel: Ernst Haeckels Wanderbilder. Nach eigenen Aquarellen und Ölgemälden* (A Traveller's Pictures. Based on the Author's Watercolours and Paintings in Oils). Haeckel's lectures at the Choral Academy in Berlin, on "Abstammungslehre und Kirchenglaube" (The Theory of Evolution and Religious Belief), "Affenverwandtschaft und Wirbeltierstamm" (Our Kinship with the Apes and the Family of Vertebrate Animals), and on "Unsterblichkeit und Gottesbegriff" (Immortality and the Concept of God) arouse enormous attention in the press.

1906 The Union of German Monists (Deutscher Monistenbund) is formed at the Zoological Institute at Jena University, with Haeckel as Honorary Chairman. Within a year it has 2500 members.

1907 Haeckel travels to Sweden to take part in celebrations marking the tercentenary of the birth of Carl von Linné (Linnaeus). Attending this event as a representative of the Prussian Parliament, the Kiel botanist Johannes Reinke demands that measures against the Union of Monists be instigated under state auspices. In August the foundation stone of a new Phyletic Museum (Museum of the Evolution of Species), an institution financed entirely by individual donations, including that of Haeckel himself, is laid in Jena.

1908 During the festive opening of the Phyletic Museum, this is formally presented to Jena University to mark the 350th anniversary of its own foundation.

1909 Haeckel becomes Professor Emeritus. He receives an Honorary Doctorate from Geneva University.

1910 Haeckel leaves the Evangelical Church.

1911 The first International Monist Congress takes place in Hamburg.

1914 In his volume *Gott-Natur (Theophysis)* (God-Nature [Theophysis]) Haeckel makes public his own understanding of Monism as a means of mediation between religion and science.

1915 On 21 April Haeckel's wife, Agnes, dies.

1917 In what is to prove his last publication, *Kristallseelen* (Crystal Souls), Haeckel explains why he eschews the notion of an immortal soul independent of the body.

1918 The Carl Zeiss Foundation in Jena acquires the "Villa Medusa," which is to be preserved as a memorial to Haeckel's work and achievement.

1919 Haeckel dies at the "Villa Medusa" on 9 August, at the age of 85.

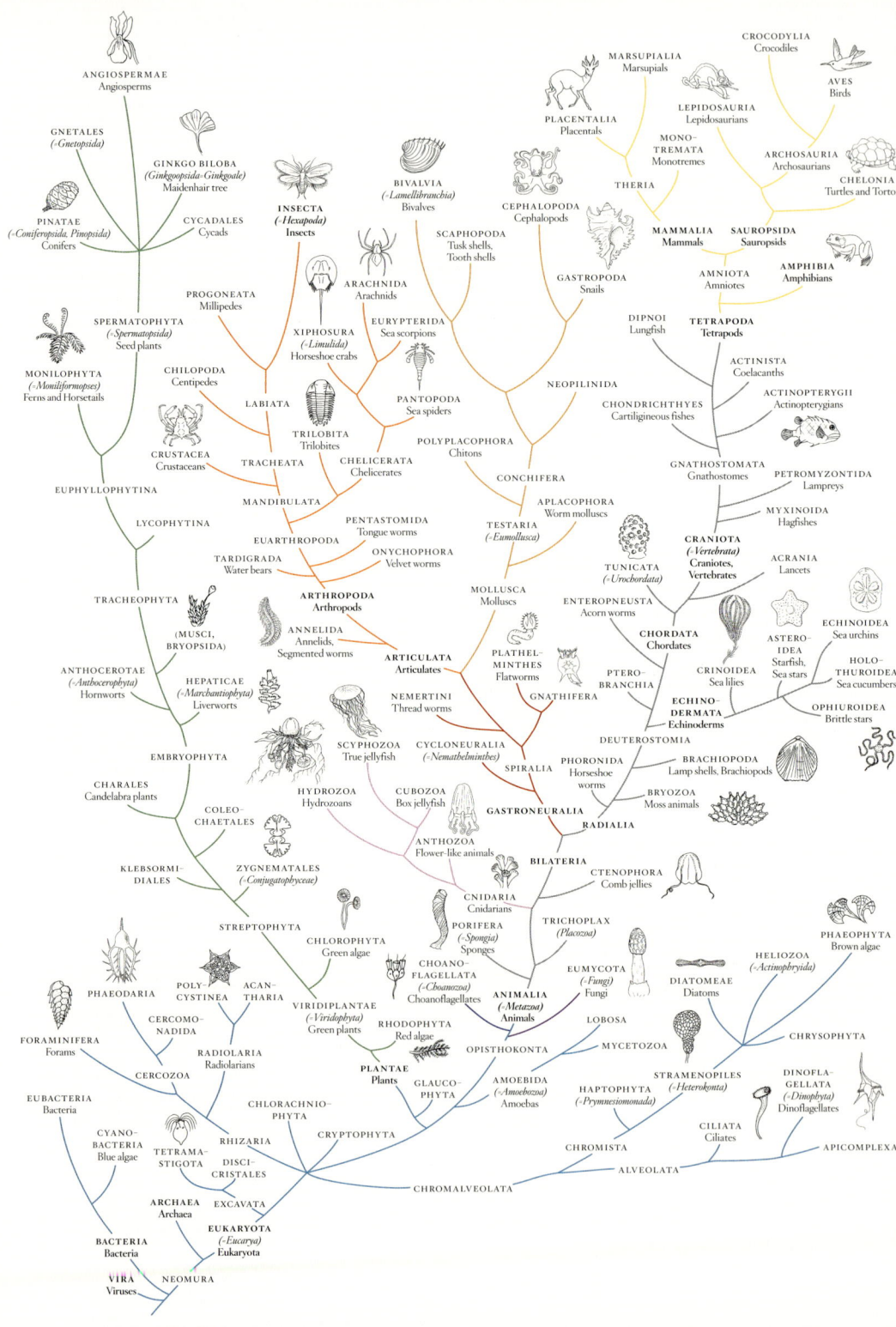

RELATIONSHIPS BETWEEN THE ORGANISMS AND THE BIOLOGICAL SYSTEM

Rainer Willmann

In 1904, Haeckel published a supplementary volume to the ten instalments of his *Kunstformen der Natur* (*Art Forms in Nature*), in which he supplied an overview of the system of the organisms and their relationships[1] – a subject that would pervade all his work, and that he had crested eight years earlier, in 1896, with the third and final volume of his *Systematische Phylogenie* (Systematic Phylogeny).[2] Since Haeckel's time, many of the notions he held have undergone a transformation; and during the second half of the 20th century the language of biosystematics has become considerably more precise as a result of modern phylogenetic systematics. It seems advisable, therefore, and also in the present volume, to supply an overview of the field in the light of the latest research.

By way of introduction it would be well to recall a number of the fundamental rules of biological systematics. Two most closely related species or species groups ("taxa," singular "taxon") are called "sister groups." Together these constitute a group of organisms comprising a stem species – this is hardly ever encountered in nature, and its (earlier) existence has, perforce, to be assumed – and all of its descendants. Such an entity is also termed a "monophyletic group." This is not an arbitrarily assemblage of species, but a group identified as such in relation to the process through which it came about

in nature – through the subdivision of one species into daughter species. In the text that follows, the names for the various species groups in use today will be employed while those terms favoured by Haeckel but are no longer in use will be rarely mentioned.

Haeckel's Approach to Non-natural Groups

As it is documented, Haeckel embarked on his overview of the organisms with his account of the "Protista," a term he introduced in 1866 in the *Generelle Morphologie der Organismen*. He had used this term to refer to unicellular organisms in their entirety. In each of these, all functions are exercised by a single cell; and the underlying structures required for the fulfilment of these functions were not termed "organs" (for these themselves were understood to comprise numerous cells) but "organelles." Haeckel initially distinguished between eight groups of "Protista": Moneres (now termed Bacteria), Protoplasma (including the amoebas), Diatomeae, Flagellata (embracing very diverse groups), Myxomycetes, Noctilucae, Spongiae (although Sponges are, in fact, animals, as Haeckel was only later to learn), and the aquatic Rhizopoda.[3] Protista as such are by no means a "natural" group. However, some are more closely related to plants, others to fungi, and yet others to animals than to each other.

There are also many other groupings that Haeckel believed to be "natural" entities but which, with the progress of biological research, have been shown to be artificial, such as the Rhizopoda. Haeckel believed that this taxon embraced Radiolaria, Foraminifera, and Heliozoa. Their true relationships are revealed here in the phylogenetic tree (ill. p. 492) and the subsequent commentary. In 1866, Haeckel had regarded a further group of unicellular organisms as animals: "Infusoria," comprising Ciliata and Suctoria.

The Earliest Forms of Life

There is no doubt that all organisms derive from a common origin, as attested by the fundamental identity of the hereditary information that they store in encoded form. The most primitive species have a cell with no core or nucleus; they store their hereditary information encoded in a molecular strand lying freely within the cell, as is the case with Bacteria, for instance.

In the case of Bacteria, a key distinction is to be drawn between two groups: Eubacteria and Cyanophyceae, that is to say, between "true" Bacteria and Blue algae. Haeckel saw in these the "common stem group" of all other organisms and he was convinced that Eubacteria evolved from Cyanophyceae. In fact, as was to later become apparent, these are two most closely related taxa (they are sister groups). In 1977, moreover, Archaea were discovered: a further group of organisms similar to Bacteria, in that it featured a cell without a nucleus. Archaea, however, already have the type of cell wall to be found in organisms that possess cells with nuclei (see below).

Even simpler in their structure than Bacteria and Archaea are viruses. As parasitic forms that survive on other living beings it is probable that viruses stem from ancestors that resembled Bacteria but had shed everything they could dispense with in their own way of life, which is almost everything but their genetic information. Viruses therefore profit from the way of life of their host organisms. When devising his first stem trees, Haeckel was not yet aware of viruses. It was not until 1898 that they were securely identified. The fact that viruses are living beings – which was at first doubted – is demonstrated by their genetic programme. This is the fundamental characteristic of life, and it enables the process of evolution through gradual alteration. Viruses are, indeed, among those organisms that evolve very rapidly, as we now know all too well from the evidence of their capacity for adaptation.

Organisms with a Cell Core: the Eukaryota

All the following organisms are characterised by the subdivision of their cell interiors into separate compartments. In the cell core or nucleus are to be found chromosomes that bear genetic information. Mitochondria serve the cell as suppliers of energy. These derive, in evolutionary terms, from Bacteria that had invaded another single cell, merging with this to form an indivisible unit (a symbiosis). Host cells and Mitochondria both profit from this form of community. The forms of life that have a cell core or nucleus are termed Eukaryota. Many of their sub-groups have remained unicellular.

Radiolaria: Haeckel distinguished numerous sub-groups among these unicellular entities, which are to be found in all the world's oceans:

a. Spumellaria (*Art Forms*, plates 11, 51, 91); b. Acantharia (*Art Forms*, plates 21, 41); c. Nasselaria (*Art Forms*, plates 22, 31, 71); d. Phaeodaria (*Art Forms*, plates 1, 61). This combination of groups makes the Radiolaria, however, an assembly of not closely related species: Phaeodaria are not, in fact, one of the Radiolaria, but are closely related to the next entity, the Foraminifera (see stem tree).

Foraminifera (Forams, *Art Forms*, plates 2, 12, 81, where Haeckel calls them Thalamophora): These unicellular organisms – thousands of

Arabische Korallen (Arabian Corals), title page / plate 1

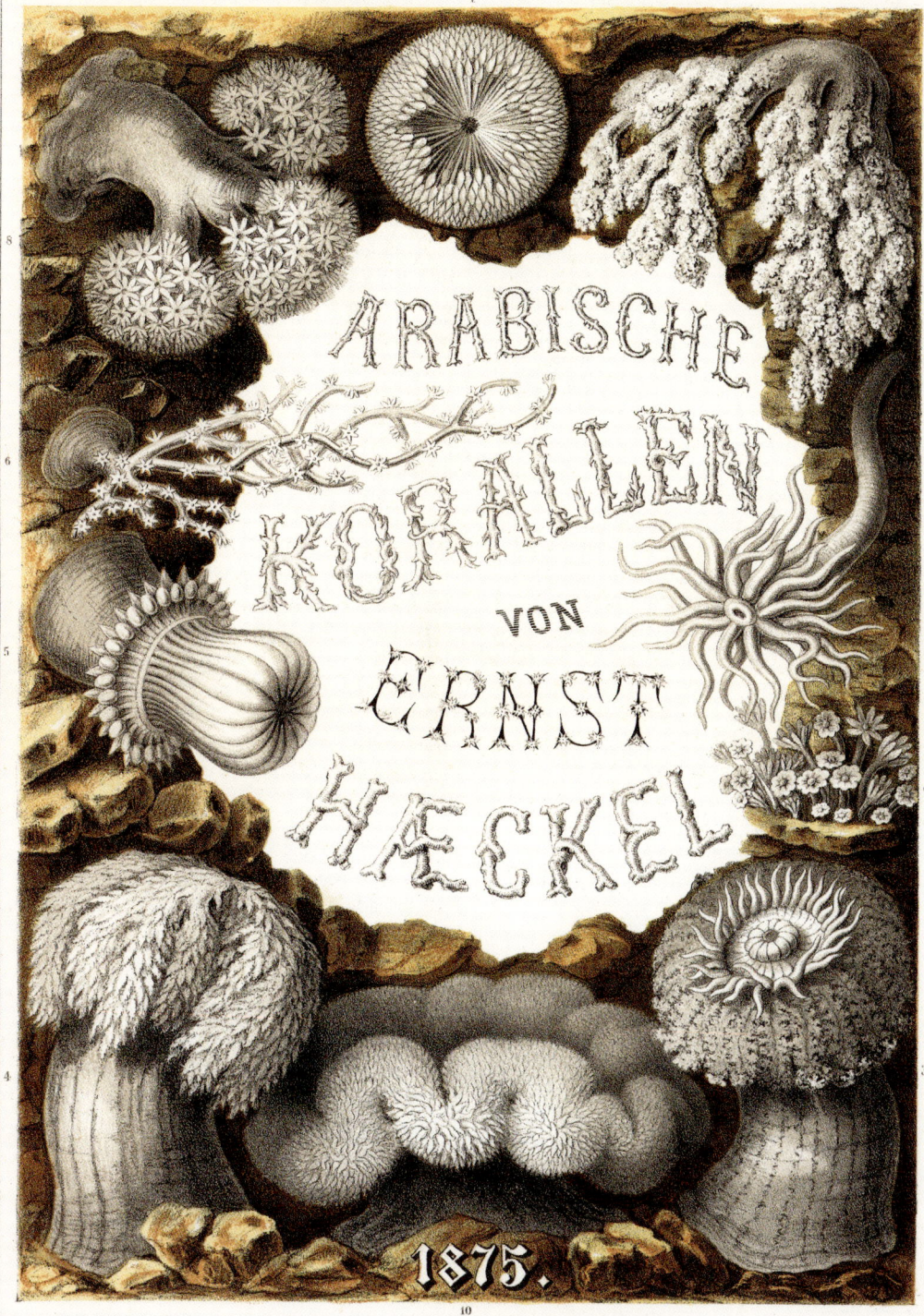

ARABISCHE KORALLEN VON ERNST HAECKEL

1875.

species – have a calcareous shell comprising several chambers, sometimes spiral in form, often arranged along a curving axis. The shells often feature spiny protuberances and diverse appendages that serve for self-defence and as an aid to suspension.

Ciliata (*Art Forms*, plate 3): "Most Ciliata swim about freely in the water, although there are some that may temporarily become attached or that remain perpetually sessile," as Haeckel observed in his *Art Forms in Nature*.[4] These are characterised by the organelles that facilitate movement. In place of just a few long flagellae, these have numerous, shorter hair-shaped projections called cilia.

Peridinea (*Art Forms*, plate 14): Peridinea are a group of Dinoflagellata that may, however, not be a "natural" entity. They are planktonic unicellular organisms found both in the sea and in freshwater. According to Haeckel: "Their cellulose shell is distinguished by a very peculiar and chiefly asymmetrical, form, and it usually features thorny or wing-shaped protuberances that serve as an aid to suspension."[5] Together with Diatomea, most ocean-dwelling Dinoflagellata are the chief primary producers, that is to say, organisms that, by means of photo- or chemosynthesis, generate organic matter and thus constitute the base of the nutritional pyramid.

Closely related to Ciliata and Dinoflagellata are Sporozoa (not illustrated in *Art Forms in Nature*; and, in the stem tree, located among the Apicomplexa), of which Plasmodium is infamous as the cause of malaria.

Choanoflagellata (*Art Forms*, plate 13, figs. 1–3, 6–11): Many species live in isolation without connection to other cells; but some are to be found in colonies. Haeckel illustrates only representatives of the latter. The sack-like structures seen in these plates, from each of which a flagellum protrudes, are effective baskets with "collars" comprising numerous tiny flexible spikes (microvilli), hence the common term "collar flagellates." The Choanoflagellata are close relatives of the animals, among whom altogether similar cells are to be found (choanocytes). Haeckel still

recognised a taxon "Flagellata" (*Art Forms*, plate 13), a notion that was, indeed, to persist long into the 20th century. Flagella are, however, to be found among many unicellular groups not closely related. The form illustrated as fig. 4 on plate 13 of *Art Forms* (Trichonomas), for example, is a representative of Excavata, a large group that branches off at the base of the tree of life (see stem tree), while *Trichomonas* belong to the Tetramastigota.

Diatomea (Diatoms, *Art Forms*, plates 4, 84): Diatomea are distinguished through their bipartite, silicic casing (in fact, consisting of glass-like silicic acid) perforated with very small holes. Haeckel devised the new and unnecessary name Bacillariophyta in 1878 for the term Diatomea that was introduced in 1821 by the Belgian botanist Barthélemy Charles Joseph Dumortier (1797–1878).

Seaweeds or Algae (*Art Forms*, plates 15, 34, 64, 65): Haeckel distinguished four sub-groups: Green seaweeds (Chlorophyceae, plate 64), Red seaweeds (Rhodophyceae, plate 65), Brown seaweeds (Phaeophyceae, plate 15) and Moss seaweeds (Charophyceae). These groups are not closely related; and there is, in fact, no natural "seaweed" or "algae" entity, even though the two terms are still retained within the names of several groups. Brown algae that sometimes resemble large-leafed plants and are to be found throughout the world's oceans, are, in fact, close to diatoms (see stem tree). Red algae (which Haeckel terms Red seaweeds) are the basal lateral branch of plants. Green seaweeds (now called Green algae) are the earliest lateral branch of green plants (Viridiplantae). Moss seaweed (Charophyta, Charales; now commonly known as candelabra plants and not illustrated by Haeckel), on the other hand, are counted as a further, earlier branch of green plants.

The Plants

Among the earliest forms of plant life, we find Green algae and Red algae. Haeckel's Siphoneae (*Art Forms*, plate 64) is one of the Green algae (Chlorophyta). Of these he wrote: "Although the green and many-branched plant body usually resembles one of the higher plant forms [...], it, in fact, consists only of a single cell"[6] – albeit a cell of immense size with numerous nuclei. Green algae are to be found mainly in freshwater. The tall species depicted by Haeckel, however, live in shallower marine coastal waters. The *Pediastrum* species, also a form of Green algae (*Art Forms*, plate 34), are, according to Haeckel in his supplementary volume to *Art Forms*, "freshwater protists that live in communities."[7]

Desmidiales (Conjugata or Cosmaria, *Art Forms*, plate 24):

Desmidiales are a group of Zygnematales and another early branch of green plants; they are almost always to be found in freshwater.

All the following plants derive from ancestors that had settled on the land more than 420 million years ago. Their scientific name is Embryophyta.

Mosses (Bryophyta): Haeckel illustrates Liverworts (Hepaticae, *Art Forms*, plate 82) and Muscinae (*Art Forms*, plate 72). There is also a third group, the Hornworts. These three taxa are, however, distantly related to each other. Muscinae, in fact, constitute a closed group with Tracheophyta while hornworts are the sister group of the two combined. Hepaticae are, on the other hand, as the stem tree reveals, one step removed from these. "Mosses" are therefore not a natural group.

Ferns (Pteridophyta, *Art Forms*, plates 52, 92): Alongside the "true" ferns Haeckel illustrated (Spotted ferns or Polypodiales), he counted among the Pteridophyta "stalk ferns" (Equisetales, Calamariae, horsetails) as well as Scaly ferns (Selagineae, Lycopodales, Club mosses, Lycophytina). Of these, however, the Club mosses (approx. 1,250 species) do not belong in this group (see the stem tree).

Spermatophyta (seed plants) are the overwhelming majority among plants. These embrace two groups: Gymnospermae and Angiospermae.

Gymnospermae (*Art Forms*, plate 94): According to Haeckel, the principal groups of these are "[...] conifers, or Coniferae, [...] to which are to be added several smaller groups, among which palm ferns and Cycadeae are important as phyletically the oldest, while the Ginko [Haeckel's

spelling] (Ginconeae) stands between the last and the first. More recent in date are Meningos (Gnetaceae), which in many respects already anticipate the Angiospermae."[8] The relationships between these groups and their relationship in turn with Angiospermae have, however, still not been elucidated. Presumably, Gymnospermae are not a natural (i. e. monophyletic) group.

Angiospermae (*Art Forms*, plates 62, 74): These include water lilies and their relatives (a very primordial group), and also orchids and cane plants (of which Haeckel illustrates an example); furthermore, Angiospermae include palms, cacti, roses, and beeches (Fagaceae) as well as plants that are close to these, and, among many other groups, grasses. In contrast to Gymnospermae, Angiospermae are a natural (i. e. monophyletic) entity.

Amoebas, Fungi, Choanoflagellata, and the Animals

Amoebas (Amoebida): With amoebas we come to a group that stands at the root of that branch of the tree of life to which animals also belong. Haeckel had, however, not yet applied the name "Amoebas" to them. They consist of numerous sub-groups (each comprising many species), of which Haeckel named two: the Lobosa (which he did not illustrate) and the Mycetozoa (*Art Forms*, plate 93), which were formerly termed slime fungi (Myxomycetes).

Opisthokonta: Haeckel did not yet know this term nor was he aware of a group of this scope. As we now recognise, Fungi, Choanoflagellata, and several species-poor groups of unicellular entities, plus animals (Animalia, Metazoa) all belong to this extensive natural entity. This implies that Fungi are more closely related to animals than to plants. The Greek-derived term Opisthokonta is, indeed, intended to signify this interconnectedness.

Fungi (Mycetes, *Art Forms*, plates 63, 73): The Sponge fungi (Basidiomycetes, *Art Forms*, plate 63), of which we now know of around 31,000 species, is the second-largest taxon among Fungi, a group also embracing the Tube fungi (Ascomycetes, *Art Forms*, plate 73), with its approximately 64,000 species. The term lichens (Lichenes, *Art Forms*, plate 83) is used to designate life forms that are a symbiosis of fungi and a Green algae, or a cyanobacterium.

We have already discussed (see above) the Choanoflagellata, a group which, of all the life forms mentioned so far, is the closest relative to animals.

Animals (Animalia)

Haeckel introduced the term "Metazoa" for application to Animals, having already collectively referred to many unicellular groups as "Protozoa," that is to say, primordial forms of animal life. To the latter he therefore thought of terminologically opposed, multi-cellular animals as organisms composed of complex cellular tissue, that is to say, "Metazoa." But since "Protozoa" are not a natural group, this implicitly undermines the justification for the term "Metazoa" – all the more so since the term "Animalia" had long been in use, having already been introduced in a scientifically valid fashion in 1758 by the pioneering Swedish natural scientist Carl von Linné (1707–1778).

Sponges, or Spongiae were considered by Haeckel in his monograph of the *Kalkschwämme* (Calcareous Sponges, 1872),[9] in the chapter on "Physemarien" in his *Studien zu Gastraea-Theorie* (1877)[10] as well as in *Art Forms* (plates 5, 35). Sponges live in the sea and, in the case of a few species, in freshwater. As organisms chiefly sessile and remaining fixed in one location they filter the water that enters them through their porous surface. The water and all its nutrients are sucked in through numerous pores and pass into a centrally located cavity. From the point of view of evolutionary history, sponges are the most "primitive" of animals in many respects. They have neither a nervous system nor a stomach, digestion occurs instead within cells that cover the surface of their body cavities. There are around 8,000 species of sponges.

In relation to sponges, all animals listed in what follows feature an evolutionary innovation in that digestion proceeds outside individual cells in a hollow space suited for that particular purpose: a digestive tract in which digestive secretions are present (or – as in the case of the simple *Trichoplax* – located at the base of the stem tree of animals – in a temporary swelling on its underside, that serves as a digestive cavity).

Cnidaria: Cnidaria are to be found mainly in the sea, although a few live in freshwater. They may occur in two forms: as polyps and as medusae, the latter more commonly known as jellyfish. In many groups, these two forms are ontogenetically connected. For, as Haeckel observed in 1904: "[...] out of the fertilised egg of the medusa, there evolves the gastrula, which is then sessile and in due course becomes a polyp; and out of this there sprout buds, which then free themselves and develop into medusae, which are capable of swimming about freely."[11] In the case of the best-known of the Cnidaria, the Anthozoa, there are no medusae; and with some of the other groups of Cnidaria there are no polyps. Haeckel devotes a great many plates to the four large groups of Cnidaria:

a. Hydrozoa: in *Art Forms*, plates 6, 16, 25, 26, 36, 45, 46. They are also considered, as Siphonophorae in *Zur Entwicklungsgeschichte der Siphonophorien* (On the Development of the Siphonophorae, 1869), in the *Report on the Siphonophorae Collected by HMS Challenger during the years 1873–76* (1888), and in *Art Forms*, plates 7, 17, 37, 59, 77.

b. Scyphomedusae or Acraspedae, with the following sub-groups: Discomedusae, in *Metagenesis und Hypogenesis von Aurelia aurita* (1881), and in *Art Forms*, plates 8, 18, 28, 88, 98; Peromedusae, in *Art Forms*, plate 38; and the Stauromedusae, in *Art Forms*, plate 48.

c. Cubomedusae, or Box jellyfish in *Art Forms*, plate 78.

d. Corals and Sea anemones (Anthozoa, Flower-like animals) in the *Arabische Korallen* (Arabian Corals, 1876) and in *Art Forms*, plates 9, 19, 29, 39, 49, 69.

Ctenophorae (Comb jellies, *Art Forms*, plate 27): On these Haeckel wrote in 1904: "The tender, gelatinous, extremely watery and ephemeral animals do not, like the Medusae, swim by means

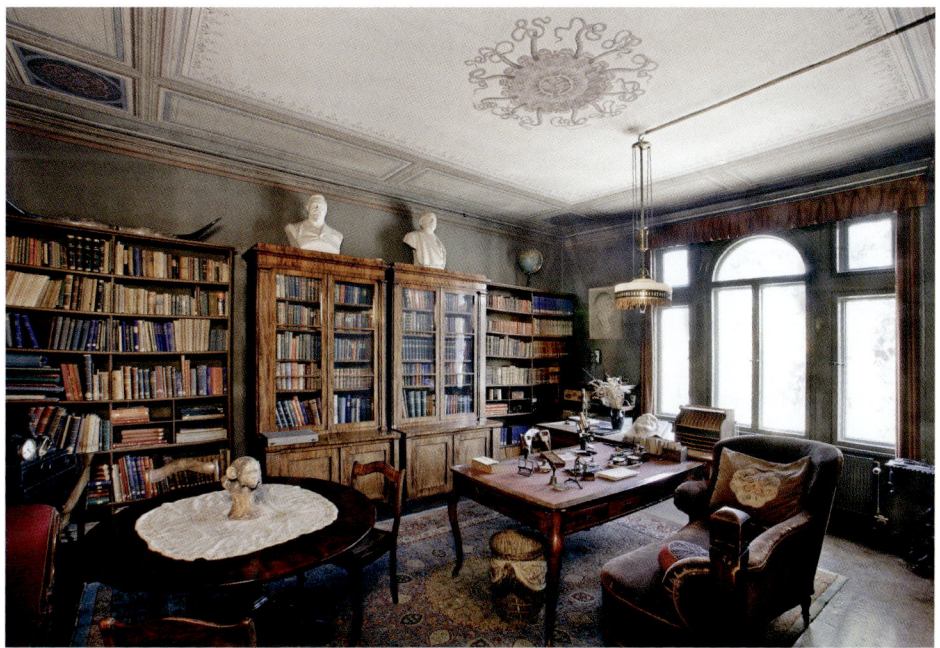

of forcing water out through a hole in their canopy, but by means of intentional, oar-like movements of very numerous cilia."[12] Despite their similarity to jellyfish, Ctenophorae are not Cnidaria, for they lack cells capable of producing a sting. It is possible that they are most closely related to the bilaterally symmetrical animals (Bilatria) as the stem tree indicates. However, it is also conceivable that Cnidaria and Ctenophorae together constitute a monophyletic group, the Coelenterata.

Bilateria (animals of bilaterally symmetrical form): All the following groups of animals are initially distinguished by a bilateral symmetry in relation to the longitudinal axis of their bodies. That is to say their bodies consist of distinct left and right sides in relation to their overall structure. In the fore part is to be found a concentration of nerve cells out of which, in the case of many groups, a well-developed brain has evolved. Bilateria comprise two large sub-groups: Gastroneuralia, in which the chief peripheral nerves pull the body along chiefly on the ventral ("under-") side, and Radialia. This last group embraces, in addition to many other taxa, vertebrates. Among Gastroneuralia are molluscs, Arachnida, and insects.

Flatworms (Plathelminthes or Platyhelminthes, termed by Haeckel "Plattentiere" [flat animals] or "Platodes," *Art Forms*, plate 75): Flatworms originally had a circular cross-section. Only in the case of the more strongly derived forms has the body been flattened. Most of the 25,000 species live in water or in soil; yet many live as parasites in other organisms. Among the latter are to be found the many species of tapeworms which inhabit the alimentary canal of their hosts and live on the latter's own food.

Haeckel's study room
Jena, Ernst-Haeckel-Haus

Rotatoria (*Art Forms*, plate 32): A total of around 1,500 species of Rotatoria live primarily in freshwater, although they are rarely found in the sea. Their ciliate appendages serve to capture food. Rotatoria have a maximum length of 0.5 millimetres. Along with a number of little-known animal groups, most of which have no common names (Cycliophora, Micrognathozoa, Acanthocephala, and *Seison*), Rotatoria constitute the group most closely related to the flatworms, Gnathifera (see stem tree).

Molluscs (Mollusca, *Art Forms*, plates 43, 44, 53, 54, 55): Characteristic of most molluscs is a calcareous shell. The most primitive members of this group, however, are the elongated worm molluscs (Aplacophora). They have delicate calcareous spicules in place of a shelly body covering. All molluscs are distinguished by the presence of a grating apparatus (radula) in their oral cavity, a structure unique to them. The chitons (Polyplacophora), which live only in marine waters, have an eight-part shell; but all other groups have a shell that was originally a single structure and shaped like a cap. The shell has, however, retained this form only in the case of the Neopilinida. Although fossil Neopilinida have long since been known, it was only in 1953 that a living specimen was hauled out of the depths of the ocean. In the case of snails (Gastropoda), the shell is markedly elongated and assumes the form of a spiral; in that of the bivalves (Bivalvia), the shell is divided into two valves; and in that of the Scaphopoda, we encounter a shell in the form of a slightly curved tube. The shells of Cephalopoda, by contrast, are elongated and internally divided into chambers. These chambers can contain gas or liquid in diverse quantities. By this means the shell becomes an organ that allows the animal to regulate its own ascent in the water. Such a shell form is to be found only in the case of the Nautilus and related "living fossils" in the Indo-Pacific region. This is known, above all, through the thousands of species of fossil ammonites. In the case of other Cephalopoda, such as sepia cuttlefish, squids, and octopods, the shell was altogether lost. This is also the case with many further mollusc groups, such as slugs and sea slugs.

In *Art Forms in Nature* Haeckel illustrated representatives of the following groups of molluscs: Snails (Gastropoda, plates 43, 53), bivalves (Bivalvia, plate 55), and Cephalopoda (plates 44, 54). The former of these last two plates shows representatives of the Ammonitida that became extinct during the Cretaceous period.

Articulata

Articulata consists of two sister groups: the Annelida, which include the earthworm, for example, and the Arthropoda. Both groups are distinguished by a great many evolutionary peculiarities, among them a heart that lies above the stomach, an arrangement of the body into several, essentially equal segments, and a correspondingly structured nervous system. On the other hand, molecular research has long since strengthened the hypothesis that Annelida are not closely related to Arthropoda, but to molluscs, Brachiopoda (see below), and other groups (as a whole termed Lophotrochozoa). In addition, Arthropoda, for their part, are related to threadworms, or Nematoda, and their own relatives (termed Ecdysozoa as a whole because they are distinguished by a similar periodic moulting). This widely supported hypothesis would then lead us to the conclusion that there is no such thing as a taxon Articulata.

Annelida (*Art Forms*, plate 96): The 20,000 or so species of Annelida are to be found in every environment, both in the water and on land, the best-known representatives being leeches (Hirudinea) and earthworms (Lumbricidae).

Arthropoda: Among Arthropoda are long and soft-bodied Onychophora (velvet "worms," approx. 180 species in the tropics), tiny Tardigrada (Water bears, approx. 600 species, above all, in bodies of water), Pentastomida (Tongue

Arabische Korallen (Arabian Corals), plate a

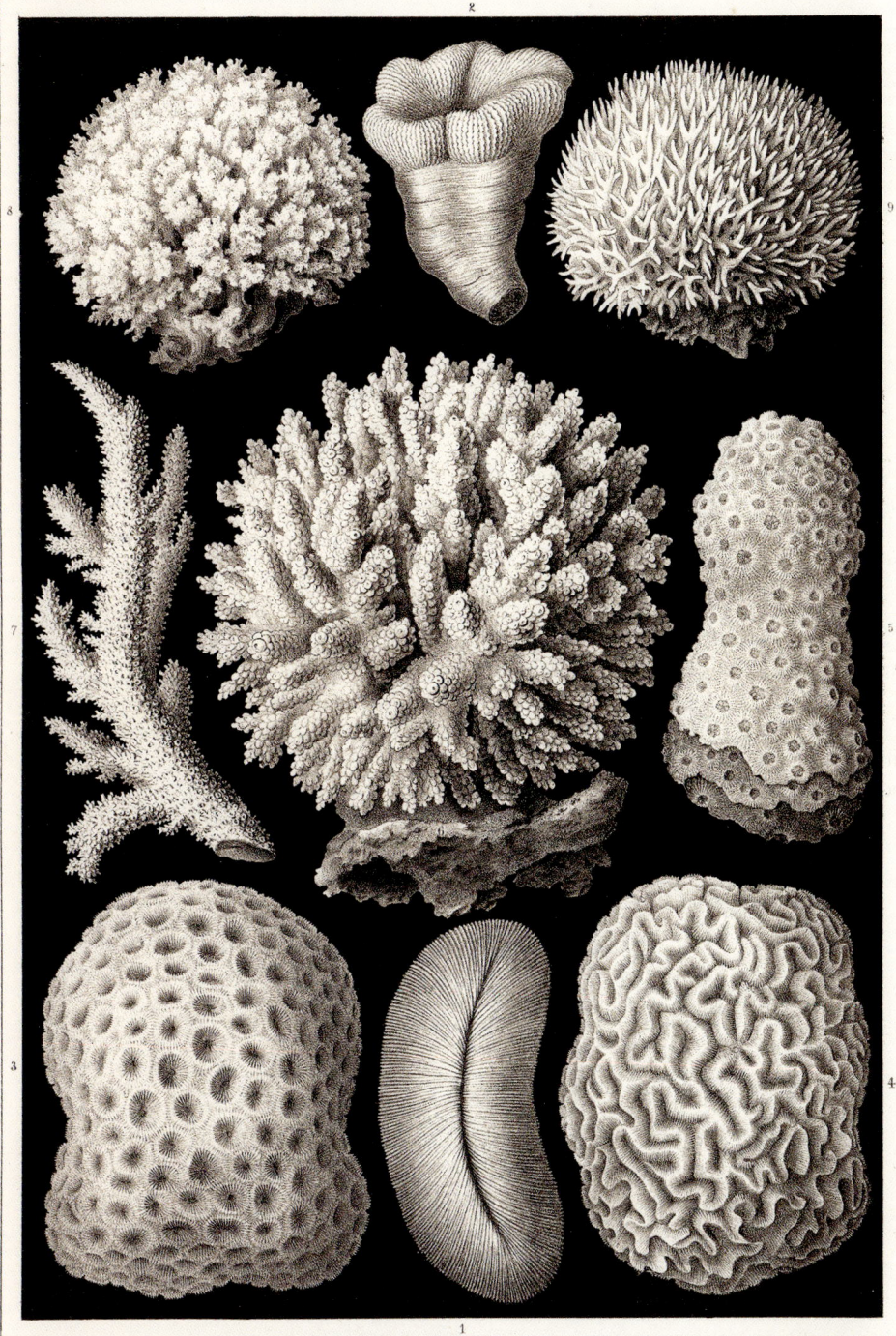

Ernst Haeckel del.   Verlag von G.Reimer in Berlin   Lith.Anst.v.E.Giltsch,Jena

worms, 110 species, which live as parasites within the breathing apparatus of terrestrial vertebrates), and Euarthropoda (see stem tree). Euarthropoda have extremities consisting of several segments and a skeleton made of chitin plates which surrounds the body. This group embraces Chelicerata, crabs, centipedes and millipedes, and insects in addition to a series of now extinct groups such as the trilobites.

Of the insects alone there are more than a million identified species. Yet Haeckel, as is also the case with the spiders and their close relatives (Arachnida), devotes only a single plate to them (see below). There must be several hundred thousand species of Arachnida, many of which have yet to be discovered. The reason is that this group embraces minute mites (Acari) – of which the known species so far number around 50,000, with many still waiting to be discovered and/or properly documented. The crustaceans (Crustacea, approx. 50,000 species, including crabs, lobsters, shrimps, crayfish, and others) are illustrated by Haeckel on four plates in *Art Forms in Nature* (plates 56, 57, 76, 86). On plate 47 Haeckel shows a horseshoe crab (Limulida), several trilobites, which were already extinct during the Palaeozoic era, and a sea scorpion (also extinct), which he united under the term "Aspidonia." Haeckel regarded all of these as crustaceans whereas they actually belonged, as we now know, to the broad arachnata group, of which the spiders are a part.

Arachnata: Horseshoe "crabs" (Limulida or Xiphosura), perhaps also Pantopoda (exclusively marine animals), which Haeckel did not illustrate, along with the aforementioned extinct sea scorpions (Eurypterida, long known also as Gigantostraca, a name introduced by Haeckel), and Arachnida, which are found on dry land, constitute together the group Chelicerata (literally: "scissor-bearers" because of the frontal pair of extremities that serve as scissor-like gripping tongs).

Arachnida (*Art Forms*, plate 66): Arachnida embrace those of the Chelicarata that have become adapted to life on the land. These include scorpions, which still retain features reminiscent of the extinct sea scorpions (*Art Forms*, plate 47),

the tailless whipspiders (Amblypygi), whipscorpions (Uropygi), spiders (Araneae), pseudoscorpions (Pseudoscorpiones), camel spiders (Solifugi), harvestmen (Opiliones, or "daddy longlegs"), Ricinulei, or capuchin spiders, and mites (Acari). Of all these, however, only the Araneae can spin silk. In other words, "Arachnida" are not "spinners" but rather, "spidery" chelicerates.

Insects (Insecta, *Art Forms*, plate 58): It is to be assumed that insects are most closely related to centipedes and millipedes, even if the analysis of molecular sequencing has repeatedly resulted in indications of the contrary. These three groups do have similar tracheae (chitin tubes extending within the body as breathing organs); in their maturity they have a head segment that is suppressed; they have similar excretory organs (Malphigi Vessels), similar mouth parts, and similar antennae. In addition, their legs comprise a single powerful branch (in many other Arthropods there is a second, lateral branch). Haeckel does not illustrate centipedes (Chilopoda, which include the scolopender) or "millipedes" (no such animal has as many as a thousand feet) and their relatives Progoneta in any of his publications.

The Vertebrates and Their Close Relatives

Radialia: All the following animal groups are "Radialia." The most primitive groups of this taxon – horseshoe worms (Phoronida, not illustrated by Haeckel), moss animals (Bryozoa), and Brachiopoda (lampshells and similar kinds) – exhibit a characteristic filtering apparatus made up of tentacles. Pterobranchia, colonial inhabitants of the sea who, in the case of the Graptolithida proved enormously rich in species in the Palaeozoic era, possess similar tentacles.

Moss animals (Bryozoa, *Art Forms*, plates 23, 33): Bryozoa, found both in the sea and in freshwater, live chiefly in colonies and, as Haeckel observed in 1904, their "[...] tender, soft body [...] is surrounded with a protective shell, capsule or chamber (theca). [...] Both the structure of the chambers themselves and the form of the hair, bristles, prickles, scales, etc. that feature on their surfaces are startlingly diverse."[13]

Lampshells (Brachiopoda, also called "Spiro-branchier" by Haeckel; *Art Forms*, plate 97): Haeckel observed in 1904: "[...] this diversely shaped class of animals, found only in the sea, was formerly thought to belong to the molluscs on account of their bivalved calcareous shell, which resembles that of a 'true' mussel."[14] Brachiopoda, like the Bryozoa, are distinguished by their two arms used to catch food. In addition to the only slightly more than 300 species still extant, thousands of fossil species are known.

Echinoderma (Haeckel devised the very apt name "star animals"): Echinoderma, found exclusively in the sea, are distinguished through their pentaradial symmetry. The most important organ systems of the mature individuals are arranged in a corresponding radial form. The earliest larval stages are still bilaterally symmetrical. Echinoderma possess a calcareous skeleton that surrounds the inner organs in the form of a stiff capsule. It comprises numerous individual elements of a characteristic delicacy. This feature is already recognisable in the palaeontologically oldest Echinoderma, which do not yet exhibit a pentaradial symmetry. In the case of many representatives of this group, the radiality has been lost to a large extent, most notably in that of the sea cucumbers, with their markedly elongated body.

In *Art Forms in Nature* Haeckel illustrates three extinct groups that exist only in the form of fossils: Amphoroidea (plate 95, see also *Die Amphoroideen und Cystoideen*),[15] Blastoidea (plate 80), and Cystoidea (plate 90).[16] In addition to these, he depicts representatives of all the extensive taxa known today: Crinoidea (plate 20), Ophiuroidea (brittle fish, plates 10, 70), Asteroidea (starfish and their larval stages, plate 40), Echinoidea (sea urchins, plates 30, 70), and Holothuroidea (sea cucumbers, above all, isolated elements of their skeletons, plate 50).

Relationships of the Echinoderma: These and the sea-dwelling Enteropneusta (approx. 75 species, not illustrated by Haeckel) have larval stages that are similar in shape. It is possible that these two groups, although ostensibly so different, are nonetheless closely related. On the other hand, there is evidence of features shared among vastly different animal groups, for example, a pharynx capable of excreting excess water through openings. Such openings (gill slits) persist in the early developmental stages of the human embryo.

Tunicata (*Art Forms*, plate 85): These marine animals, according to Haeckel in the supplementary volume to *Art Forms in Nature*, were "[...] in earlier times much misunderstood, and were mostly included in molluscs. Later (1866) it was revealed, through study of their ontogenetic development, that they are, rather, most closely related to the vertebrates."[17] It is in particular the common possession of a long, rod-like structure that stabilises the body, chorda dorsalis or notochord that shows this to be so. Among Tunicata there belong both freely swimming and sessile species (the latter includes the Ascidacea), which suck in water to filter out and absorb the nutritional particles it contains.

Vertebrates (Vertebrata): Haeckel designates lancet fishes, or Acrania (approx. 25 species), which he did not illustrate, as the primordial representatives of vertebrates. This is, however, no longer classified so because it does not possess a "true" spine but only a chorda dorsalis or notochord. Lancet fishes are the closest relatives of Craniota, for which only the term "vertebrates" is used as an alternative today. Haeckel did not illustrate what are, in many respects, their earliest representatives: the long, eel-shaped hagfishes (Myxinoidea) and lampreys (Petromyzontida). Both of these are more "primitive" than other vertebrates in that they, among other characters, have neither an upper or lower jaw.

Jaws were first developed in Gnathostomata, a group that extends from cartilaginous fishes to land vertebrates (see stem tree). Within Gnathostomata, cartilaginous fishes (among them sharks, of which rays are a sub-group, and chimaeras) constitute the sister group to all the other species. Haeckel illustrates a cartilaginous fish only once: a somewhat diagrammatic rendering of a shark in the *Arabische Korallen*. In accordance with the custom of the day, he grouped cartilaginous fishes with Actinopterygii

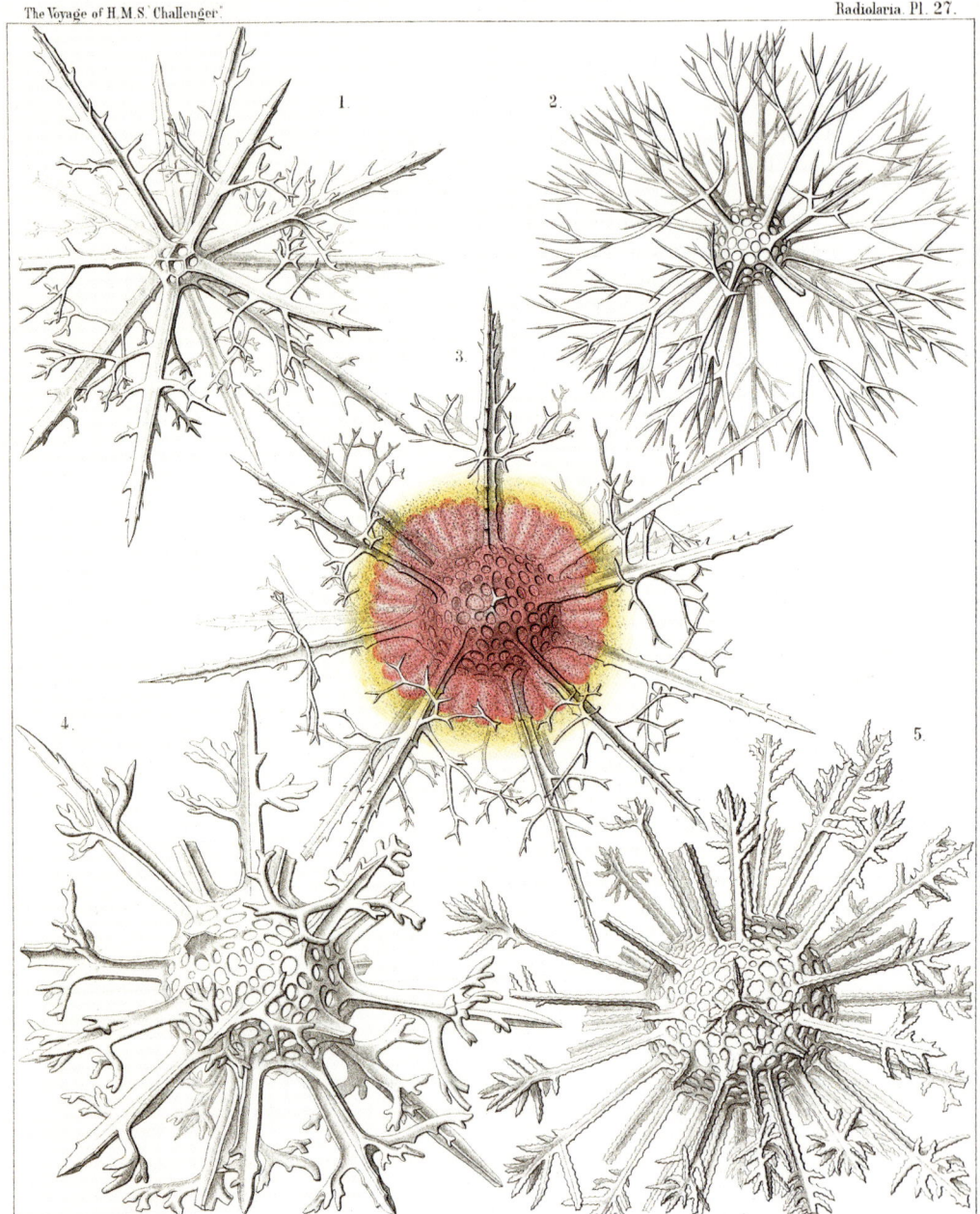

E. Haeckel and A.Giltsch Del.

K.Giltsch, Jena, Lithogr.

CLADOCOCCUS.

as "Pisces," a grouping that corresponds to no phylogenetic, that is to say, monophyletic entity. A small number of Actinopterygii (approx. 30,000 species) are to be found in *Art Forms in Nature* (plates 42, 87).

Lungfishes (Dipnoi, six species in Australia, Africa, and South America), the closest relatives of land vertebrates, were also not illustrated by Haeckel, although he did explain that these already featured a series of characters of land vertebrates.[18] He was, however, mistaken in his assumption that Amphibia derived from Dipnoi, which he also designated "Lurchfische" (amphibious fishes; also see the stem tree). A further and now celebrated group was known to Haeckel only in the form of fossils: coelacanths or Actinistia (lobe-finned fishes). It had been assumed that these had died out in the Cretaceous era until, in 1938, the first living specimen was discovered in the Indian Ocean off the coast of South Africa: *Latimeria*, one of the most spectacular "living fossils."

Land vertebrates (Tetrapoda): Haeckel limited himself to illustrations of a very few forms: Amphibia (*Art Forms*, plate 68), "Reptilia" (*Art Forms*, plates 79, 89), birds, or Aves (*Art Forms*, plate 99), and Mammals (see below). In the supplementary volume to *Art Forms in Nature*, Haeckel wrote: "The anatomical differences between the birds and other classes of reptiles (e.g. the turtles, plate 89, the dragons or dinosaurs, the Pterosauria or "flying lizards," etc.) are not larger than the morphological differences between each of the latter themselves [...] The new phyletic systematics therefore treats even

birds as a sub-class of the legio reptiles, and unites them with the rest in the class Sauropsida."[19] With this observation Haeckel was ahead of his time. As late as around 1980 there was heated discussion on the question as to whether Birds should be treated as a sub-group of reptiles or as a group in their own right existing alongside these. It has since been accepted that birds are the closest relatives of crocodiles, if one takes into account only the animals now in existence. If one includes the fossil record, then birds appear most closely related to a number of the long extinct saurian predators, being in effect feathered dinosaurs. The concept of "Reptilia" has been abandoned in biological systematics: The groups previously distinguished as reptiles and birds are now both united – as Haeckel had himself proposed – as "Sauropsida."

Mammals (Mammalia, *Art Forms*, plates 67, 100): Mammals, including their stem forms (together, known as Synapsida), are the sister group of Sauropsida. Their earliest forms are known from the Carboniferous era and are almost 320 million years old. Today they comprise three large partial taxa: Monotremata, that includes the platypus and the four species of echidnas in the Australian area that still lay eggs like Sauropsida; and the two groups that give birth to their young, namely Marsupialia (280 species, among others the kangaroos) and Placentalia (approx. 4,500 species, among them humankind). Characteristic of all of these are, in addition to many other structures, their hair covering and mammary glands.

Radiolaria, vol. 2, plate 16

NOTES

The sequence numbers refer to the endnotes of the text, in order of appearance within each chapter. The symbols refer to the plate descriptions.

Ernst Haeckel: Art Forms in Life

1   Goldschmidt 1959, p. 33.
2   See Haeckel 1874, p. XIV.
3   See, for example, Haeckel 1874, pp. 12–17.
4   Goldschmidt 1959, p. 33.
5   See Krausse 1987, p. 20.
6   Klemm 1966, p. 9.
7   See Krausse 1987, p. 27.
8   See Aescht 1998, p. 28.
9   See Krausse 1987, p. 37.
10 See Haeckel 1862, vol. 1, p. 232.
11 See Haeckel 1863
12 See Haeckel 1866, vol. 1, p. 71.
13 See ibid., p. 58.
14 See, for example, Haeckel 1870b, p. 177.
15 Quoted from Krausse 1997, p. 57.
16 See Haeckel 1866, vol. 1, p. 104.
17 See ibid., pp. 59–60.
18 Haeckel 1866, vol. 11, p. 286.
19 Haeckel 1868, p. 539.
20 See Haeckel 1906, p. v.
21 See Haeckel 1868, p. 169; and Haeckel 1889a, p. 192.
22 See Haeckel 1870a, p. XXIII.
23 Dobzhansky 1973, p. 125.
24 Society of Systematic Biologists, see https://ncse.com/library-resource/society-systematic-biologists (accessed 23 May 2017).
25 See Haeckel 1895, p. 358.
26 See ibid., p. 400.
27 See Willmann 2016.
28 Quoted from Browne 2002, pp. 270–71.

29 Haeckel 1866, vol. 11, p. 7.
30 See Haeckel 1868, pp. 252–53.
31 See ibid., p. 240.
32 See Haeckel 1877, pp. 68–69.
33 See Richardson and Keuck 2002.
34 See Heberer 1968, p. 524.
35 See ibid.
36 See Zissler 1999.
37 See Haeckel 1866, vol. 1, p. 204.
38 On the biological notion of "species," see Mayr 1942; Hennig 1966; and Wheeler and Meier 2000.
39 See Haeckel 1868, p. 514; and Haeckel 1870a, pp. 570–71.
40 See Haeckel 1868, p. 518; and Haeckel 1870a, p. 612.
41 See Willmann 2010.
42 See Haeckel 1866, vol. 1, p. 288.
43 See Haeckel 1870a, p. 181.
44 See Haeckel 1866, vol. 11, p. CLX.
45 Haeckel 1868, p. 496; see also p. 498; and Haeckel 1870a, p. 577; also Haeckel 1878, p. 34.
46 See Haeckel 1870a, p. 619.
47 See Darwin 1871, p. 199.
48 Haeckel 1915, p. 67.
49 Haeckel 1866, pp. 429–30.
50 See Lötsch 1998, p. 349.
51 See Hopwood 2015, p. 3.
52 See Pennisi 1997; Richardson 1998; and Nüsslein-Volhard and Winnacker 2003.
53 Haeckel 1866, vol. 1, p. 174.
54 See ibid., p. 105.
55 Ibid., p. 67.
56 Haeckel 1893, p. XX.
57 See ibid., p. 21.
58 See ibid., p. 14.
59 See Haeckel 1917.
60 See Di Gregorio 2005.
61 See Haeckel 1899/1918, p. 449.
62 See Haeckel 1915, pp. 42–43.
63 See Haeckel 1904b, pp. 23, 134.

64 See Haeckel 1915, p. 34.
65 Haeckel 1898, p. 740.
66 Ibid., p. 740.
67 See Kutzer 1996, p. 136.
68 See Bibby 1959; and Willmann 2009.
69 Werner 1927.
70 Hemleben 1964, p. 120.
71 Elsner 2000.
72 Loofs 1900, p. 51. Quoted here from the English translation, p. 58.
73 See Schmidt 1900, pp. 18–20.
74 See Haeckel 1904b, pp. 122–23.
75 See Haeckel 1915, pp. 31–32.
76 See ibid., pp. 35–36.
77 See Gasman 1971.
78 See Richards 2008, pp. 446–47.
79 Schaller 1998, p. 12.
80 See Richards 2008, p. 449.
81 Quoted from Heberer 1968, pp. 538–39 (abbreviated).

Ernst Haeckel and the Evolution of Modern Art

1   "*Wer Wissenschaft und Kunst besitzt,/Hat auch Religion*"; from the poem "Paria" (mid- to late 1820s; first published, posthumously, in 1836), in *Goethes Werke*, Hamburg edition, 14 vols., vol. 1, *Gedichte und Epen*, part. 1, ed. Erich Trunz, 2nd ed., Hamburg 1956, p. 367. See also Fischer, Brehm, and Hoßfeld 2008.
2   Plate 1912.
3   Gilbert 1997. See also Hopwood 2015, pp. 286–87.
4   See Richards 2009, pp. 92–102, here p. 92.
5   Ibid., p. 101.
6   Ibid., p. 95.
7   Haeckel 1899–1904, preface (n. p.).

8 Ibid.

9 Breidbach 2006, p. 268.

10 See Kort and Hollein 2009; and Donald and Munro 2009.

11 Morton 2009, pp. 137–38.

12 Harter 2014, p. 183.

13 See ibid., p. 39.

14 See Hopwood 2015, p. 56.

15 See ibid., p. 55.

16 Dossi 2016, pp. 17–24.

17 Haeckel 1984, p. 220.

18 See Harter 2014, pp. 90–91.

19 Haeckel 1878, pp. 73–74. Translated here from the original German; but see also the English version, p. 93.

20 See Voss 2009, pp. 81–82.

21 Haeckel 1868, p. 555.

22 Richards 2008, pp. 224–25.

23 See Hopwood 2015, pp. 68–69.

24 Ibid., p. 6.

25 See ibid., p. 152.

26 See Voss 2016.

27 See Barnett 1994.

28 See Voss and Deines 2015, pp. 35–36.

29 Quoted from Voss 2007, p. 158 (in the English translation p. 120).

30 Schmidt-Burckhardt 2005, p. 296.

31 See Bach 2011.

Haeckel's Volumes of Plates

1 For example in Haeckel 1866, vol. 11, pp. 1x–xx; and Haeckel 1868, p. 318.

2 See Krausse and Nöthlich 1990, p. 71.

3 See Haeckel 1866.

Monograph on the Radiolaria

1 Haeckel 1984, pp. 62–63.

2 Haeckel 1921, pp. 159–60.

3 Haeckel 1862.

4 Quoted from Krausse 1987, p. 49.

5 See Decelle 2012.

6 See Anderson 1983, p. 5; and Zettler 1997.

7 See Müller 1858.

8 See Cavalier-Smith 2003.

9 See Pawlowski and Burki 2009, p. 18.

10 Haeckel 1887b; Haeckel 1888a; Haeckel 1888b.

11 Haeckel 1887a.

12 Haeckel 1887b, p. xiii.

13 Haeckel 1899/1904, commentary on plate 31, fig. 6 in *Art Forms in Nature*.

14 Ibid.

15 See Haeckel 1908.

16 See Haeckel 1984, p. 8.

✳ Haeckel described and determined all organisms on this and the subsequent plates of the first volume in 1860 (resp. 1862): 5, 6, 7, 10, 15, 20, 21, (30, 31).

☙ In the following, Haeckel's specification "n. sp." (*nova species*) was renounced since all the species Haeckel cited here were first determined by him; exceptions are: vol. 2, plate 1, figs. 4–5; plate 30, figs. 1, 4–6; addendum, plate 3, figs. 10–12.

Siphonophorae

1 Quoted from Uschmann 1984, p. 97.

2 Haeckel 1888c, p. 159.

3 See ibid., p. 108.

▣ Haeckel described and determined all organisms on plates 12 and 22 of the *Report on the Siphonophorae* in 1888.

Atlas of Calcareous Sponges

1 Haeckel 1904a, supplementary volume to *Art Forms in Nature*, p. 22. The reference to plates in this quotation relates to that publication.

2 Haeckel 1873, p. xli.

✳ Haeckel described and determined all organisms on this plate in 1870.

Monograph on the Medusae

1 Haeckel 1879, p. xv.

2 Ibid., p. xvi.

3 Haeckel 1881a.

4 Haeckel 1879, p. xx.

5 Ibid., p. 189.

Report on the Deep-sea Keratosa

1 On the systematics of the Demospongiae, see Morrow and Cárdenas 2015.

◉ Haeckel described and determined all organisms on plates 1, 6, and 8 in 1889.

Art Forms in Nature

1 Haeckel 1904a, Postscript, n. p.

2 Ibid., n. p.

3 Haeckel 1913/1924, p. 12.

4 Haeckel 1899/1904, preface, n. p.

5 Haeckel 1904a, postscript, n. p.

6 Richards 2008, pp. 417–19.

7 See Elsner 2000, pp. 902–03.

✿ Haeckel described and determined all organisms on this plate in 1904.

Relationships between the Organisms and the Biological System

1 Haeckel 1904a.

2 Haeckel 1896a.

3 See Haeckel 1866.

4 See Haeckel 1904a, p. 17.

5 Ibid., p. 14.

6 Ibid.

7 Ibid.

8 Ibid., p. 20.

9 Haeckel 1872.

10 Haeckel 1877.

11 Haeckel 1904a, p. 23.

12 Ibid., p. 25.

13 Ibid., p. 29.

14 Ibid.

15 Haeckel 1896b.

16 See also ibid.

17 Haeckel 1904a, p. 30.

18 See ibid., p. 46.

19 Ibid.

BIBLIOGRAPHY

Selected works by Ernst Haeckel

1862: *Die Radiolarien (Rhizopoda Radiaria). Eine Monographie,* 2 vols., Berlin 1862.

1863: "Über die Entwickelungstheorie Darwins," in: *Amtlicher Bericht über die 38. Versammlung Deutscher Naturforscher und Ärzte in Stettin im September 1863,* Stettin 1864.

1866: *Generelle Morphologie der Organismen,* 2 vols., Berlin 1866.

1868: *Natürliche Schöpfungsgeschichte,* Berlin 1868.

1869: *Zur Entwicklungsgeschichte der Siphonophoren,* Utrecht 1869.

1870a: *Natürliche Schöpfungsgeschichte,* 2nd ed., Berlin 1870.

1870b: *Studien über Moneren und andere Protisten nebst einer Rede über Entwickelungsgang und Aufgabe der Zoologie,* Leipzig 1870.

1872: *Die Kalkschwämme,* Berlin 1872.

1873: *Natürliche Schöpfungsgeschichte,* 4th ed., Berlin 1873.

1874: *Anthropogenie oder Entwickelungsgeschichte des Menschen,* 2nd ed., Leipzig 1874.

1875: *Ziele und Wege der heutigen Entwickelungsgeschichte,* Jena 1875.

1876: *Arabische Korallen,* Berlin 1876.

1877: *Studien zur Gastraea-Theorie,* Jena 1877.

1878: *Freie Wissenschaft und freie Lehre,* Stuttgart 1878.

1879: *Das System der Medusen. Erster Theil einer Monographie der Medusen,* Jena 1879.

1881a: *Die Tiefsee-Medusen der Challenger-Reise und der Organismus der Medusen. Zweiter Theil einer Monographie der Medusen,* Jena 1881

1881b: *Metagenesis und Hypogenesis von Aurelia aurita,* Jena 1881.

1887a: *Report on the Radiolaria collected by H.M.S. Challenger during the years 1873–76, Zoology* 18, London, Edingburgh, and Dublin 1887.

1887b: *Die Radiolarien (Rhizopoda radiaria). Eine Monographie. Zweiter Theil,* Berlin 1887.

1888a: *Die Radiolarien (Rhizopoda radiaria). Eine Monographie. Dritter Theil,* Berlin 1888.

1888b: *Die Radiolarien (Rhizopoda radiaria). Eine Monographie. Vierter Theil,* Berlin 1888.

1888c: *Report on the Siphonophorae collected by H.M.S. Challenger during the years 1873–76, Zoology* 28, London, Edingburgh, and Dublin 1888.

1889a: *Natürliche Schöpfungsgeschichte,* 8th ed., Berlin 1889.

1889b: *Report on the Deepsea Keratosa collected by H.M.S. Challenger during the years 1873–76, Zoology* 34, London, Edingburgh, and Dublin 1889.

1893: *Der Monismus als Band zwischen Religion und Wissenschaft,* Bonn 1893.

1894: *Systematische Phylogenie der Protisten und Pflanzen,* Berlin 1894.

1895: *Systematische Phylogenie der Wirbelthiere (Vertebrata),* Berlin 1895.

1896a: *Systematische Phylogenie der Wirbellosen Thiere (Invertebraten),* Berlin 1896.

1896b: *Die Amphorideen und Cystoideen,* Leipzig 1896

1898: *Natürliche Schöpfungs-Geschichte,* 9th ed., Jena 1898.

1899/1904: *Kunstformen der Natur,* Leipzig, Vienna 1899–1904.

1899/1918: *Die Welträthsel,* Bonn 1899.

1904a: *Kunstformen der Natur. Supplement-Heft,* Leipzig and Vienna 1904.

1904b: *Die Lebenswunder,* Stuttgart 1904.

1906: *Prinzipien der Generellen Morphologie der Organismen,* Berlin 1906.

1908: Afterword to the *Welträthsel,* 10th ed., see Haeckel 1899/1918.

1913/1924: *Die Natur als Künstlerin,* Berlin 1924.

1915: *Ewigkeit. Weltkriegsgedanken über Leben und Tod, Religion und Entwicklungslehre,* Berlin 1915.

1917: *Kristallseelen,* Leipzig 1917.

1921: *Italienfahrt. Briefe an die Braut 1859–1860,* Leipzig 1921.

1984: *Ernst Haeckel. Biographie in Briefen,* Gütersloh 1984.

Literature on Ernst Haeckel

Aescht 1998: Aescht, Erna, "Ernst Haeckel – Ein Plädoyer für die wirbellosen Tiere und die biologische Systematik," in: Aescht et al. 1998, pp. 19–83.

Aescht et al. 1998: Aescht, Erna, Gerhard Aubracht, Erika Krausse, Franz Speta (eds.), *Welträtsel und Lebenswunder,* Linz 1998

Breidbach 2006: Breidbach, Olaf: *Ernst Haeckel,* Munich and Berlin 2006.

Di Gregorio 2005: Di Gregorio, Mario A., *From Here to Eternity:*

Ernst Haeckel and Scientific Faith, Göttingen 2005.

Dossi 2016: Dossi, Davide, "Ernst Haeckels 'Kunstformen der Natur' und die Tradition der Ornamentstiche," in: *Verborgene Schönheit. Kunstformen der Natur*, exh. cat., Hessisches Landesmuseum, Darmstadt 2016, pp. 17–24.

Elsner 2000: Elsner, Norbert (ed.), *Das ungelöste Welträtsel. Frida von Uslar-Gleichen und Ernst Haeckel. Briefe und Tagebücher 1898–1903*, Göttingen, 2000.

Fischer, Brehm, and Hoßfeld 2008: Fischer, Martin S., Gunnar Brehm and Uwe Hoßfeld: *Das Phyletische Museum in Jena*, Jena 2008.

Gasman 1971: Gasman, Daniel, *The Scientific Origins of National Socialism*, London and New York 1971.

Goldschmidt 1959: Goldschmidt, Richard, *Erlebnisse und Begegnungen*, Hamburg and Berlin 1959.

Heberer 1968: Heberer, Gerhard, *Der gerechtfertigte Haeckel*, Stuttgart 1968.

Heider 1919: Heider, Karl, "Ernst Haeckel. Ein Wort der Erinnerung, gesprochen zur Eröffnung des Kollegs am 1. Oktober 1919," in: Heberer 1968, pp. 538–39.

Hemleben 1964: Hemleben, Johannes, *Ernst Haeckel in Selbstzeugnissen und Dokumenten*, Reinbek near Hamburg 1964.

Hopwood 2015: Hopwood, Nick, *Haeckel's Embryos*, Chicago and London 2015.

Klemm 1966: Klemm, Peter, *Ernst Haeckel*, Leipzig, Jena, and Berlin 1966.

Krausse 1987: Krausse, Erika, *Ernst Haeckel*, 2nd ed., Leipzig 1987.

Krausse and Nöthlich 1990: Krausse, Erika and Rosemarie Nöthlich, *Das Ernst-Haeckel-Haus der Universität Jena*, Brunswick 1990.

Loofs 1900: Loofs, Friedrich, *Anti-Haeckel. Eine Replik nebst Beilagen*, 3rd ed., Halle/Saale 1900.

Lötsch 1998: Lötsch, Bernd, "Gibt es Kunstformen der Natur? Radiolarien, Haeckels biologische Ästhetik und ihre Überschreitung," in: Aescht et al. 1998, pp. 339–72.

Morton 2009: Morton, Marsha, "Natur und Seele: Österreichs Reaktionen auf Ernst Haeckels evolutionären Monismus," in: Kort and Hollein 2009, pp. 126–41.

Müller 1998: Müller, Irmgard, "Historische Grundlagen des Biogenetischen Grundgesetzes," in: Aescht et al. 1998, pp. 119–30.

Pennisi 1997: Pennisi, Elisabeth, "Haeckel's Embryos: Fraud Rediscovered," in: *Science*, vol. 277, no. 5331 (1997), p. 1435, DOI: 10.1126/science.277.5331.1435a.

Plate 1912: Plate, Ludwig, "Rede zur Einweihung des Erweiterungsbaues des zoologischen Instituts und zur Eröffnung des phyletischen Museums der Universität Jena," held on 21 May 1912, in: *Naturwissenschaftliche Wochenschrift*, vol. 11, no. 30 (1912).

Richards 2008: Richards, Robert J., *The Tragic Sense of Life*, Chicago and London 2008.

Richards 2009: Richards, Robert J., "The Tragic Sense of Ernst Haeckel: His Scientific and Artistic Struggles," in: Kort and Hollein 2009, pp. 92–102.

Richardson 1998: Richardson, Michael K. et al., "Haeckel, Embryos, and Evolution," in: *Science*, vol. 280, no. 5366 (1998), pp. 985–86, DOI: 10.1126/science.280.5366.983c.

Richardson and Keuck 2002: Richardson, Michael K., and Gerhard Keuck, "Haeckel's ABC of Evolution and Development," *Biological Reviews of the Cambridge*

Philosophical Society, vol. 77 (2002), pp. 495–528.

Schaller 1998: Schaller, Friedrich, "Der Zoologe Ernst Haeckel als Sprachschöpfer und Ideenproduzent," in: Aescht et al. 1998, pp. 3–18.

Schmidt 1900: Schmidt, Heinrich, *Der Kampf um die "Welträtsel,"* Bonn 1900.

Werner 1927: Werner, Johannes (ed.), *Franziska von Altenhausen*, Leipzig 1927.

Speta 1998: Speta, Franz, "Vorwort," in: Aescht et al. 1998, pp. v–vii.

Wheeler and Meier 2000: Wheeler, Quentin, and Rudolf Meier (eds.), *Species Concepts and Phylogenetic Theory: A Debate*, New York 2000.

Zettler 1997: Zettler, Linda Amaral et al., "Phylogenetic relationships between the Acantharea and the Polycystinea: A molecular perspective on Haeckel's Radiolaria," in: *Proceedings of the National Academy of Sciences of the United States of America*, vol. 94, no. 21 (1997), pp. 11411–16.

Other literature

Anderson 1983: Anderson, Roger O., *Radiolaria*, New York 1983.

Bach 2011: Bach, Thomas, "Über den wechselseitigen Einfluss von Wissenschaft und Kunst. Gabriel von Max und Ernst Haeckel in Briefen," in: Althaus, Karin, and Helmut Friedel: *Gabriel von Max. Malerstar, Darwinist, Spiritist*, exh. cat., Lenbachhaus, Munich 2011, pp. 282–93.

Barnett 1994: Barnett, Vivian Endicott, "Kandinsky und die Naturwissenschaft: Die Einführung biologischer Motive in der Pariser Periode," in: Gaßner,

Hubertus (ed.), *Elan Vital oder das Auge des Eros. Kandinsky, Klee, Arp, Miró, Calder*, exh. cat., Haus der Kunst, Munich 1994, pp. 39–55.

Bayertz 1998: Bayertz, Kurt, "Darwinismus als Politik. Zur Genese des Sozialdarwinismus in Deutschland 1860–1900," in: Aescht et al. 1998, pp. 229–88.

Bibby 1959: Bibby, Cyril, *T. H. Huxley: Scientist, Humanist and Educator*, London 1959.

Browne 2002: Browne, Janet, *Charles Darwin: The Power of Place. Volume II of a Biography*, Princeton and Oxford 2002.

Cavalier-Smith 2003: Cavalier-Smith, Thomas, "Protist Phylogeny and the High-level Classification of Protozoa," in *European Journal of Protistology*, vol. 39, no. 4 (2003), pp. 338–48.

Darwin 1871: Darwin, Charles, *The Descent of Man, and Selection in Relation to Sex*, New York 1871.

Decelle 2012: Decelle, Johan et al., "An Original Mode of Symbiosis in Open Ocean Plankton," in: *Proceedings of the National Academy of Sciences of the United States of America*, vol. 109, no. 44 (2012), pp. 18000–05.

Dobzhansky 1973: Dobzhansky, Theodosius, "Nothing in Biology Makes Sense Except in the Light of Evolution," in *American Biology Teacher*, no. 25 (1973), pp. 125–29.

Donald and Munro 2009: Donald, Diana, and Jane Munro (eds.): *Endless Forms: Charles Darwin, Natural Science and the Visual Arts*, exh. cat., Yale Center for British Art, New Haven (CT), and The Fitzwilliam Museum, Cambridge 2009, New Haven and London 2009

Gilbert 1997: Gilbert, Scott, *Developmental Biology*, 5th ed., Sunderland (MA) 1997.

Haecker 1908: Haecker, Valentin, *Tiefsee-Radiolarien. Spezieller Teil*, Jena 1908.

Harter 2014: Harter, Ursula: *Aquaria in Kunst, Literatur und Wissenschaft*, Heidelberg and Berlin, 2014.

Hennig 1966: Hennig, Willi, *Phylogenetic Systematics*, Urbana (IL) 1966.

Kort and Hollein 2009: Kort, Pamela, and Max Hollein (eds.): *Darwin: Kunst und die Suche nach den Ursprüngen*, exh. cat., Schirn Kunsthalle, Frankfurt/M. 2009.

Kutzer 1996: Kutzer, Michael: "Gehirnanatomie und 'ein Ausflug in das geistige Land': Anthropologie der Geschlechter im Werk Emil Huschkes," in: Meined, Christoph, and Monika Renneberg (eds.): *Geschlechterverhältnisse in Medizin, Naturwissenschaft und Technik*, Stuttgart 1996, pp. 133–41.

Mayr 1942: Mayr, Ernst, *Systematics and the Origin of Species from the Viewpoint of a Zoologist*, New York 1942.

Morrow and Cárdenas 2015: Morrow, Christine, and Paco Cárdenas, "Proposal for a Revised Classification of the Demospongiae (Porifera)," in: *Frontiers in Zoology*, vol. 12, no. 7 (2015), pp. 1–27.

Müller 1858: Müller, Johannes: *Über die Thalassicollen, Polycystinen und Acanthometren des Mittelmeeres*, Berlin 1858.

Nüsslein-Volhard and Winnacker 2003: "Wir Deutschen sind nicht moralisch höher stehend," Interview with Christiane Nüsslein-Volhard and Ernst Ludwig Winnacker, in: *Die Zeit*, no. 22 (2003).

Pawlowski and Burki 2009: Pawlowski, Jan, and Fabien Burki, "Untangling the Phylogeny of Amoeboid Protists," in: *Journal*

of Eukaryotic Microbiology, vol. 56, no. 1 (2009), pp. 16–25.

Schmidt-Burckhardt 2005: Schmidt-Burckhardt, Astrit, *Stammbäume der Kunst*, Berlin 2005.

Uschmann 1959: Uschmann, Georg, *Geschichte der Zoologie und der zoologischen Anstalten in Jena 1779–1919*, Jena 1959.

Uschmann 1984: Uschmann, Georg, *Ernst Haeckel*, Gütersloh 1984.

Voss 2007: Voss, Julia, *Darwins Bilder*, Frankfurt/M. 2007.

Voss 2009: Voss, Julia, *Darwins Jim Knopf*, Frankfurt/M., 2009.

Voss and Deines 2015: Voss, Julia, and Philipp Deines, *Hinter weißen Wänden / Behind the White Cube*, Berlin 2015.

Voss 2016: Voss, Julia, "Hilma af Klint and the Evolution of Art," in: Peyton-Jones, Julia, and Hans-Ulrich Obrist (eds.), *Hilma af Klint*, exh. cat., Serpentine Gallery, London 2016, pp. 21–35.

Willmann 2009: Willmann, Rainer, *Darwin, Huxley und die Frauen*, Opladen 2009.

Willmann 2010: Willmann, Rainer, "Darwins Artbegriff und heutige Artkonzepte in der Zoologie," in: *Braunschweiger Naturkundliche Schriften*, vol. 9, no. 2 (2010), pp. 95–134.

Willmann 2016: Willmann, Rainer, "The Evolution of Willi Hennig's Phylogenetic Considerations," in: Williams, David, Quentin Wheeler, and Michael Schmitt (eds.), *The Future of Phylogenetic Systematics*, Cambridge 2016.

Zissler 1999: Zissler, Dieter, "Gastraea-Theorie," see www.spektrum.de/lexikon/biologie/gastraeatheorie/26684

PHOTO CREDITS

IMPRINT

Cover: *Art Forms in Nature*, plate 17
Back cover: *Art Forms in Nature*, plate 8
Spine: *Art Forms in Nature*, details of plates 40, 1
and 38 (from top to bottom)
Endpapers: *Art Forms in Nature*, plates 91, 31 and 41
Page 1: *Art Forms in Nature*, plate 17, fig. 2
Pages 2–3: Images for display and prepared specimens
for Haeckel's 1907 lecture at the Volkshaus, Jena,
on "The Problem of Man and the Higher Animals as
Classified by Linnaeus"

Rainer Willmann is Professor of Zoology at the
University of Göttingen. His main scientific interests
are the evolution of animals, the history of life
sciences, and questions of theoretical biology. Until
2019, he was head of the department of systematics
and director of the Museum of Zoology in Göttingen.
In the year 2000 he initiated the Göttingen Center
for Biodiversity and Ecology Research, for which a
separate course of studies was conceived. Willmann
has repeatedly dealt with Ernst Haeckel's biological
works, for instance in his book *Darwin, Huxley und die
Frauen*. He has worked on several editions of historical
works for TASCHEN, starting in 2003 with Albertus
Seba's *Cabinet of Natural Curiosities*.

Julia Voss studied German literature, art history, and
philosophy at the Albert-Ludwigs-Universität in
Freiburg, at the Humboldt-Universität in Berlin, and
at Goldsmiths College in London. Her doctoral dissertation on visual representations of Darwinian evolution theory received the Otto Hahn Medal from the
Max Planck Society. Up until 2017, she was head of the
art department of the *Frankfurter Allgemeine Zeitung*,
and deputy head of the features section. Voss is an
honorary professor at Leuphana Universität Lüneburg
and published the biography *Hilma af Klint – "Die
Menschheit in Erstaunen versetzen"* in 2020. Her
research focusses on the history of abstraction, resti-
tution and provenance, evolution theory, and culture.

EACH AND EVERY TASCHEN BOOK PLANTS A SEED!

Each year, we offset our annual carbon emissions
with carbon credits at the Instituto Terra, a reforest-
ation program in Minas Gerais, Brazil, founded by
Lélia and Sebastião Salgado. To find out more about
this ecological partnership, please check:
www.taschen.com/institutoterra.
Inspiration: unlimited.
Carbon footprint: (almost) zero.

Want to see more? Visit taschen.com to view our
current publications, browse our latest magazine,
and subscribe to our newsletter.

© **2025 TASCHEN GmbH**
Hohenzollernring 53, D–50672 Köln
www.taschen.com

Original edition © 2017 TASCHEN GmbH

Project management: Ute Kieseyer, Cologne
Scientific research: Sophia Willmann and
Julian Leander Willmann
English translation: Elizabeth Clegg, London

Printed in Bosnia-Herzegovina
ISBN 978-3-8365-8428-9